Understanding Saving:

Evidence from the United
States and Japan

Understanding Saving:

Evidence from the United States and Japan

Fumio Hayashi

The MIT Press
Cambridge, Massachusetts
London, England

This book was set in Palatino on the Monotype "Prism Plus" PostScript Imagesetter by Asco Trade Typesetting Ltd., Hong Kong.

Printed and bound in the United States of America.

Library of Congress Cataloging-in-Publication Data

Hayashi, Fumio.
  Understanding saving : evidence from the United States and Japan / Fumio Hayashi.
    p.   cm.
  Includes bibliographical references and index.
  ISBN 0-262-08255-1 (hardcover : alk. paper)
  1. Saving and investment—Japan. 2. Saving and investment—United States. I. Title.
HC465.S3H39   1997
339.4'3'0952—dc21
                                                                96-37681
                                                                CIP

To my late father.

Contents

Preface

This book collects eleven mostly empirical studies on saving written over the last fifteen years. Analysis of consumption and saving decisions by households has always been one of the most active areas of research in economics, for good reason. Private consumption is the most important component of aggregate demand. Explaining consumption is the key element in most macroeconometric forecasting models. Evaluating the effect of government policies invariably requires the knowledge of how they change parameters relevant for household decision making. The renewed and enhanced interest in the empirical analysis of saving almost exactly coincides with my career as an academic. The studies included in this book represent my contribution to this trend.

The book has three parts. Part I, entitled "Liquidity Constraints," contains five studies that test the well-known implication of the Life Cycle–Permanent Income hypothesis that households make saving plans to shield consumption from income fluctuations. Part II ("Risk Sharing and Altruism") contains three chapters examining the interactions between related and unrelated households predicted by the hypothesis. Both the U.S. and Japanese data are used in parts I and II, but the issue at hand is always one that should interest any "mainstream" macroeconomist. Chapter 1, written for this book to review a wide range of topics on household saving, serves as an introduction to parts I and II.

Although studies comprising part III are concerned specifically with Japan, the analytical tools employed there ultimately to explain the high Japanese saving rate are no different from those in the other parts of the book. This reflects the faith of the profession that institutions, not differences in human nature, determine international differences in economic performance. I hope that even those readers not interested in the Japanese economy will take time to read chapter 10, which is an introduction to and summary of part III.

I took this opportunity to update some data and empirical analysis by adding postscripts to chapters 2, 4, and 11. Chapter 10 incorporates the most recent U.S. and Japanese time-series data at the time of this writing.

It was a privilege to collaborate with my former colleagues at the University of Pennsylvania, Albert Ando and Richard Ferris, to produce the work included as chapter 12, and with former classmates Takatoshi Ito and Joel Slemrod for chapter 13. My collaboration with Joseph Altonji of Northwestern University and Laurence Kotlikoff of Boston University has proved to be fruitful and instructive, resulting in two joint chapters included in part II and a few other recent papers. My deepest intellectual debt goes to Dale Jorgenson, my thesis supervisor at Harvard. It took me a few years to realize that my research style exemplified here had been molded during my days as his research assistant.

I

Liquidity Constraints

1

Introduction to Parts I and II: A Review of Empirical Studies of Household Saving

1.1 Introduction

Virtually all modern research on consumption and saving espouses the Life Cycle–Permanent Income hypothesis (hereafter the LC–PIH for short), developed by Modigliani, Brumberg, and Friedman in the 1950s, that the household, wishing to smooth consumption over time, evaluates future income prospects to determine the level of current consumption that it can afford. The formula linking the future to current consumption is called the consumption function, and subsequent empirical research was a quest for the consumption function that has the most explanatory power. This landscape was altered by Hall's (1978) paper, which derived an implication of consumption smoothing, called the Martingale hypothesis, that is valid even if the future is uncertain to the household. The chapters that comprise part I of this book represent my contribution to the empirical research in this new landscape.

In this introduction, I provide a concise but fairly comprehensive review of the literature starting with the consumption function approach. I will emphasize that the Martingale hypothesis is derived from a particular formulation of the LC–PIH that is very specific in two respects. First, it denies households *insurance* opportunities that might in reality be available through markets or through a network of private transfers. That is, it is a model of self insurance. Second, it assumes that the parent and the adult child behave as if they are independent and unrelated households (as in the Life Cycle hypothesis) or else as if they form a single decision unit (as in the Permanent Income hypothesis, alternatively called the Dynasty model). There are other formulations that differ in these two dimensions. Empirically discriminating between the Life Cycle hypothesis and the Dynasty model and examining the extent of income insurance to mitigate the influence of income fluctuations on consumption are the two themes pursued in my work included in part II of this book.

I start out in section 1.2 with a brief account of the consumption function approach. I will point out that this approach left two major issues unresolved. One is whether current income has a liquidity effect on consumption, and the other is whether the consumer's horizon is finite as in the Life Cycle hypothesis or infinite as in the Permanent Income hypothesis. Section 1.3 presents the Martingale hypothesis and derives from it a consumption growth equation that has since become a common vehicle to test the LC–PIH against the liquidity effect of current income. Section 1.4 is a review of this "excess sensitivity" literature. It is deliberately made brief because, as argued at length in section 1.5, contrary to the literature's premise, consumption *should* be excessively sensitive to current income under the Martingale hypothesis.

Sections 1.6 and 1.7 deal with the insurance dimension of the LC–PIH. Section 1.6 surveys empirical studies examining the role of income insurance to shield consumption from income fluctuations, and concludes that in reality income insurance is utilized but not intensively enough to yield complete coverage. Section 1.7 provides a list of recent theoretical models that might be capable of explaining the observed lack of complete insurance.

Section 1.8 deals with the length of the consumer's horizon, the issue the consumption function approach could not settle and the Martingale hypothesis did not address. I argue that the Life Cycle hypothesis, if expanded to allow for the exchange of nonmarket services provided by children for gifts and bequests from parents, becomes very difficult to refute. On the other hand, recent empirical studies I examine in section 1.8 strongly reject the Dynasty model. It is an interesting future research topic to determine whether intergenerational transfers can be explained by the exchange motive alone or some sort of altruism, if not the sort assumed by the Dynasty model, needs to be evoked. This and other concluding remarks are in section 1.9.

A note is added at the end of this chapter to explain the relation of the work included in parts I and II to the literature.

1.2   The Consumption Function

In both the Life Cycle hypothesis of Modigliani and Brumberg and the Permanent Income hypothesis of Friedman, the forward-looking household attempts to smooth consumption over time subject to the intertemporal or long-term budget constraint. The level of smoothed consumption is a function of a measure of total amount of resources available to the household. In the Life Cycle hypothesis, the measure of household resources in the consumption function is the sum of the household's assets and the discounted sum of the stream of (labor) income projected by the household for the rest of its lifetime. In the Permanent Income hypothesis, the horizon is infinite in that the stream of income extends beyond the household's lifetime. This link in the Permanent Income hypothesis between current consumption and income expected for offspring is a logical consequence of the chain of altruistic linkages connecting successive generations, as pointed out by Barro (1974).

Either formulation of the forward-looking consumer, however, involves two difficulties if it is to be put to use to explain actual data. First, the derivation of the consumption function proceeded under the assumption that the household is certain about the future with point expectations about future income. If the future is uncertain, consumption may depend also on some measure of uncertainty about the future. Second, expectations about future income are unobservable to outside observers.

This did not deter empirical researchers from espousing the LC–PIH as the guiding principle. In virtually all specifications of the consumption function, the unobservable expected future income is replaced by a weighted average of current and lagged income, with income coefficients in the weighted average freely chosen by data. Specifications attempting to capture the possible influence of uncertainty on current consumption do so by including variables, such as the unemployment rate, that are thought to capture uncertainty. The consumption function thus derived seemed to explain the fluctuations in aggregate consumption reasonably well, and by the mid 1970s the consumption function of this sort was the central building block of most macroeconometric models. In retrospect, the empirical success of the consumption function should not have been so surprising, given the flexibility afforded by the unrestricted income coefficients and by the lack of discipline in the choice of variables capturing uncertainty.

More important, the practice of proxying expectations about future income by current and lagged income made the consumption function a particularly ill-suited device for discriminating between different versions of the LC–PIH that have widely different policy implications.

It is not possible to discriminate between the Life Cycle hypothesis and the Permanent Income hypothesis on the basis of estimated consumption function, because current and lagged income coefficients cannot determine whether consumption is influenced by expectations about offspring's income. But the distinction is critical for policy analysis. Take, for example, a tax cut financed by a government budget deficit to be eliminated through a tax increase in the future. The Life Cycle hypothesis predicts that the deficit has a stimulative effect on aggregate consumption if the future tax increase is levied on future generations, because consumption by the current generation does not depend on the offspring's income. This is not the case under the Permanent Income hypothesis, which assumes that the current generation and its offspring are essentially the same decision unit; irrespective of whether the future tax increase is paid for by the current or future generations, the tax cut has no effect on consumption. More broadly, the altruistic link between generations renders any social policy such as social security that alters income distribution between generations utterly ineffective, because the income redistribution engineered by the government policy will be offset by compensating private transfers between generations.

Another important issue that the estimated consumption function cannot settle is the liquidity effect of current income. One important qualification to the LC–PIH has always been that at least some households may be *liquidity-constrained*, unable to borrow against future income to finance the level of consumption prescribed by consumption smoothing. If the liquidity constraint is binding, current income has a liquidity effect on consumption over and above its contribution to the household's total resources. Whether current income has the liquidity effect is critical for analyzing the effect of government finance on aggregate consumption. Consider again a deficit-financed tax cut, but this time to be paid for by a future tax levied on the same households that benefit from the tax cut. Under either the Life Cycle hypothesis or the Permanent Income hypothesis, the tax cut has no effect on aggregate consumption, because it does not change household resources. However, for liquidity-constrained households, it provides a means to finance consumption otherwise unavailable to them. Thus, if at least some fraction of the population of households are liquidity-constrained, the tax cut will stimulate aggregate consumption. Unfortunately, the consumption function, with no a priori restriction on the coefficients of current and lagged income, cannot determine whether the current income coefficient includes the liquidity effect.

1.3 The Martingale Hypothesis

Hall's (1978) paper provided a resolution of some, but not all, of the problems of the consumption function approach. Unlike in the original formulation of the LC–PIH, future income is now explicitly treated as uncertain. Nevertheless the household can still borrow and lend at the risk-free interest rate because, as will be emphasized below, the intertemporal budget constraint assumed by Hall requires that the household repays any existing loans without fail.

When future income is uncertain, the consumption function no longer has a closed form solution. Consumption smoothing, however, has a very natural generalization to uncertainty: rather than requiring consumption to be literally constant over time, consumption smoothing now states that *expected* consumption changes are zero—namely, that consumption changes only when the household receives new information about its resources such as an unexpected income change. Furthermore, if the household's expectations are rational, that is, if the household utilizes all the available information efficiently to forecast the future, then the new information should have no relation to what is already known, so the consumption change from the current period to the next should not be correlated with any information currently available, such as current income and expected income changes. This implication about the consumption *change* came to be known as the *Martingale hypothesis*.

To better understand subsequent developments, it is necessary to state formally the hypothesis. Let c_t be the household's consumption in period t and $u(c_t)$ the utility derived from consuming c_t. If β is the discounting factor for the utility one period hence, the marginal rate of substitution between c_t and c_{t+1} is $\beta u'(c_{t+1})/u'(c_t)$ where $u'(c)$ is the marginal utility of consuming c. Without uncertainty, consumption smoothing states that the household should form the consumption plan so that this marginal utility equals $1/(1 + r_{t+1})$: $\beta u'(c_{t+1})/u(c_t) = 1/(1 + r_{t+1})$, where r_{t+1} is the real interest rate from period t to $t + 1$. This condition for consumption smoothing is also called the *Euler equation*. Under uncertainty about future income, it generalizes to the statement that the expected value of the marginal rate of substitution, evaluated on the basis of information available in period t, should equal $1/(1 + r_{t+1})$, or

$$E_t\left[\frac{(1 + r_{t+1})\beta u'(c_{t+1})}{u'(c_t)}\right] = 1, \tag{1}$$

where E_t is the expectation operator conditional on information available in date t. If we assume, as Hall (1978) did, that the utility function is quadratic (so that $u'(c)$ is a linear function of c) and that $(1 + r_{t+1})\beta = 1$ (i.e., the real interest rate is constant and equal to the rate of time preference $1/\beta - 1$), then the Euler equation (1) implies that $E_t(c_{t+1}) = c_t$, namely, the expected consumption change is zero, which is how I stated the Martingale hypothesis above.

Most studies after Hall used a more plausible utility function and did away with the $(1 + r_{t+1})\beta = 1$ assumption. If the utility function $u(c)$ is of the constant-relative-risk-aversion variety $u(c) = c^{(1-1/\sigma)}/(1 - 1/\sigma)$, then, after the approximation to the second order, the Euler equation becomes a statement about the expected consumption growth rather than the expected consumption change:

$$E_t \log(c_{t+1}) - \log(c_t) = \sigma \log(\beta) + \sigma E_t(r_{t+1}) + \sigma \operatorname{Var}_t(\varepsilon_{t+1})/2. \tag{2}$$

where $\varepsilon_{t+1} \equiv (1 + r_{t+1})u'(c_{t+1})/u'(c_t) - E_t[(1 + r_{t+1})u'(c_{t+1})/u'(c_t)]$ and $\operatorname{Var}_t(\varepsilon_{t+1})$ is its variance calculated using information available in period t.[1] This ε_{t+1} represents news that the household receives in date $t + 1$ about the household's remaining lifetime resources, and hence its variance $\operatorname{Var}_t(\varepsilon_{t+1})$ is a measure of uncertainty about the future. Equation (2) says that a higher variance leads to an increase in expected consumption growth. But more uncertainty per se does not make the household wealthier, so the increase in consumption growth has to be achieved by postponing consumption into the future. For this reason the variance term is said to capture the *precautionary motive* for saving.

Provided that the variance $\operatorname{Var}_t(\varepsilon_{t+1})$ is constant over time, the Euler equation can be used to test for liquidity constraints. To see this, first rewrite (2) as

$$\log(c_{t+1}) - \log(c_t) = \sigma \log(\beta) + \sigma r_{t+1} + \sigma \operatorname{Var}_t(\varepsilon_{t+1})/2 + \eta_{t+1}, \tag{2'}$$

where $\eta_{t+1} = \log(c_{t+1}) - E_t[\log(c_{t+1})] - \sigma[r_{t+1} - E_t(r_{t+1})]$. Now consider the following equation which augments (2') by adding income growth to the right-hand-side:

$$\log(c_{t+1}) - \log(c_t) = \alpha + \sigma r_{t+1} + \lambda[\log(y_{t+1}) - \log(y_t)] + \eta_{t+1}, \tag{3}$$

where $\alpha = \sigma \log(\beta) + \sigma \operatorname{Var}_t(\varepsilon_{t+1})/2$, which is assumed constant. Because the error term η_{t+1} represents by definition hitherto unexpected movements in consumption and in the real interest rate in date $t + 1$, it can be correlated with the real rate r_{t+1} and actual income growth $\log(y_{t+1}) - \log(y_t)$. So estimation of equation (3) by Ordinary Least Squares involves biases and will find the income growth coefficient λ to be significantly different from 0 even if the Euler equation (2') is true. But this problem can be dealt with by the use of instrumental variables, variables that are correlated with the right-hand-side variables but not with the error term. Under rational expectations, any variables known in period t affecting the right-hand-side variables are valid instrumental variables, because the error term η_{t+1}, being unexpected changes in period $t + 1$, is uncorrelated with such variables. The estimate of λ by the instrumental variable (IV) technique of (3) involves no biases and hence should not be significantly different from zero, because the IV estimate is essentially the correlation between actual consumption growth and the component of actual income growth predictable on the basis of the instrumental variables. The correlation is zero under (2') if the variance is constant.

How does the IV estimate of λ behave if the household is liquidity constrained? If current income is sufficiently low relative to expected future income, the desired level of current income is likely to be greater than current income, so the household with not enough assets will want to borrow to finance desired consumption. But if borrowing is ruled out, the household will be forced to postpone consumption (thus raising the growth rate of consumption) despite the expectation of higher future income. Therefore, expected income growth is positively correlated with consumption growth and so the IV estimate of λ will be positive and significant. For this reason, the λ coefficient in (3) came to be known as the *excess sensitivity coefficient*.

1.4 Subsequent Work

Most of the subsequent empirical studies on consumption in the 1980s and 1990s (including my own in chapters 2–5 of this book) are concerned about the excess sensitivity coefficient. Surveys of this large literature can be found in Hayashi (1987, included in this book as chapter 6), Deaton (1992, chapter 5), Attanasio (1995), and Browning and Lussardi (1995). For the present purposes, only a very brief review suffices. Initially, equation (3) was estimated on aggregate time-series data with aggregate consumption and income used for the c and y in equation (3). But since the equation is nonlinear in consumption and income, the macro equation cannot be derived from aggregating the micro equations for individual households. Alternatively, the macro equation can be interpreted as describing the fictitious representative consumer, but in order to induce the representative consumer from heterogeneous individual preferences, one needs to assume that markets are complete and the horizon is infinite. As discussed below in section 1.6, a recent string of papers (including Hayashi, Altonji, and Kotlikoff (1996; see chapter 9)) strongly reject complete markets.

Although the aggregation problem can obviously be avoided with panel data that track the same micro units (households) over a number of periods, the use of micro data has its own problem. The number of period covered by available panel data sets is not large; the longest panel is the Panel Study of Income Dynamics (the PSID), which is annual since 1968. For the IV estimation of equation (3) to involve no biases on panels with short time periods but with a large number of households, it is necessary that the *cross-section* correlation between unexpected changes represented by the error term η_{t+1} and variables known in period t is zero. But it is the time-series correlation, not the cross-section correlation, that is guaranteed to be zero under rational expectations (Chamberlain 1984). Most studies using micro data sidestep this problem by assuming that the error term η_{t+1} can be divided into two parts, a macro component common to all households and hence can be treated as a constant in the cross section, and an idiosyncratic component uncorrelated with variables known in period t. The only exception is my own study (Hayashi (1985b); see also chapter 4) which uses a unique panel data set containing information about expectations.

If a series of separate cross-section surveys are available, it is possible to create synthetic panels (or synthetic cohorts) from cell averages to be used in estimation. For the United States, the Consumer Expenditure Survey (CEX), a quarterly survey of households since 1980, now provides synthetic panels of more than fifty quarters. To the extent that that is long enough of a period for the asymptotics in the IV estimation to work, the problem arising from the shortness of available panel data sets is avoided by the use of synthetic panels. The aggregation problem, too, can be avoided since the researcher can calculate desired cohort averages from cross sections.[2]

The evidence about excess sensitivity is mixed to the extreme. The survey of the literature by Browning and Lussardi (1995) lists twenty-five studies that have used genuine and synthetic panels from various developed countries for a variety of preference specifications. About a half of them find a significant and positive λ while the other half find no evidence of excess sensitivity. Most of the twenty-five studies do not allow for the possible nonseparability between consumption and leisure. If leisure affects the marginal utility of consumption, consumption growth has to be adjusted for changes in leisure. In terms of equation (3), the growth rate of leisure enters the right-hand side along with income growth and the interest rate. More recent studies (Attanasio and Weber (1996) using a synthetic panel created from the CEX, and chapter 9 using a genuine panel from the PSID) share the same conclusion that there is no evidence for excess sensitivity, once the nonseparability of consumption and leisure is allowed for.

1.5 Consumption *Should* be Excessively Sensitive

It is curious that the literature has not produced stronger evidence for excess sensitivity, for λ in (3) *should* be positive if Hall's formulation of the LC–PIH is a correct description of reality. There are two issues to consider. One is the point made in chapter 6 that a liquidity constraint is *necessarily* a part of Hall's model, rather than an additional constraint imposed on the model. The other is the role played by the precautionary motive for saving.

A Liquidity Constraint Is Implicit in the Model

To make the point as clearly as possible, consider the two-period version of Hall's model. The budget constraint in the model looks exactly the same as in the case without income uncertainty:

$$A_2 = (1 + r)(A_1 + y_1 - c_1), \qquad (4)$$

$$c_2 = A_2 + y_2. \qquad (5)$$

Here, y_t is the household's labor income in period t $(= 1, 2)$, A_t is assets (or debts if negative) at the beginning of period t, and r is the real interest rate. Consumption in period 2 equals $A_2 + y_2$ because in the second and final period the household consumes all its resources. All this sounds innocuous, but note that A_2, assets to be carried over from period 1, is determined before the household observes y_2. And its value must be such that c_2 is nonnegative even in the worst realization of y_2, which means $A_2 + y_{2,\min} \geq 0$ or $A_2 \geq -y_{2,\min}$, where $y_{2,\min}$ is the lowest possible second period labor income. Substituting (4) into this, we obtain a constraint on current consumption:

$$c_1 \leqslant A_1 + y_1 + \frac{y_{2,\min}}{1 + r}, \qquad (6)$$

which is none other than a liquidity constraint. The nonnegativity constraint on *future* consumption has turned into an upper bound on *current* consumption. This is a consequence of allowing only safe lending and borrowing in the model. If there are T rather than two periods in life, the constraint on current consumption c_t is

$$c_t \leqslant A_t + y_t + \sum_{s=t+1}^{T} \frac{y_{s,\min}}{(1 + r)^{s-t}}. \qquad (6')$$

In particular, if there is a positive probability, however remote, that the household earns no income for the rest of the horizon, the constraint says that the household cannot borrow at all!

That a liquidity constraint is necessarily a part of Hall's model has important implications. First, it logically follows that the test for liquidity constraints described in section 1.3 cannot be a test of the model. Second, the excess sensitivity coefficient λ, which can be positive in the model because of the liquidity constraint, is uninformative about the effectiveness of stabilization policies. Consider, again, a debt-financed tax cut to be paid for by the same household. It raises current (after-tax) income y_t but lowers the future minimum income $y_{s,\min}$ ($s > t$) so that the increase in y_t in (6') is exactly offset by the decrease in the present value of the future minimum income. Consumption remains the same before and after the tax cut. If, instead, the positive λ is due to some other reason such as myopia, then the tax cut will increase consumption.

In chapter 6, I present extensions of Hall's model allowing for personal bankruptcies in the event of poor income realizations. In one model, the household is liquidity constrained in the sense of facing a consumer loan rate higher than the safe interest rate reflecting the default risk. Yet $\lambda = 0$ in equation (3) and a debt-financed tax cut has no effect. In another, the household is liquidity constrained due to asymmetric information in the consumer loan market. The λ parameter is now positive but again the tax cut has no effect. In yet another model, there is a shortage of the supply of consumer loans because of an imperfect enforcement of private debt contracts. The government, with its power to tax and its control over the timing of taxes, is better equipped to arrange loans than banks are. In this case, $\lambda > 0$ and a debt-financed tax cut has an effect. These examples illustrate the point made above that one needs to specify the source of liquidity constraints in order to interpret the excess sensitivity coefficient λ.

Precautionary Saving

Another reason the λ coefficient in equation (3) is not informative has to do with the variance $\text{Var}_t(\varepsilon_{t+1})$ that was included in the intercept term α as part of the constant term. As noted above, this variance captures the precautionary motive for saving.

To see the role it could play in a clearer fashion, consider Hall's model with $u(0) = -\infty$ so that the penalty of zero consumption is prohibitively large. The constant-relative-risk-aversion utility function that was invoked to derive equation (3) has this property. As noted above, the upper bound on current consumption in (6') is a reflection of nonnegativity constraint on future consumption. So if current consumption is driven to the upper limit set by the liquidity constraint (6'), future consumption can be zero, the possibility that the household concerned about the steep penalty of zero consumption wishes to avoid. That is, the consumption plan will be arranged so that the liquidity constraint never binds (Carroll 1992). The excess sensitivity coefficient λ in (3) will be positive because a sufficiently steep decline in current income brings down current consumption along with the upper bound on consumption. Nevertheless the Euler equation (2') (or (2)) remains valid because consumption thus determined never violates the liquidity constraint. Mechanically, the Euler equation accommodates this comovement of consumption and income with an increase in the variance $\text{Var}_t(\varepsilon_{t+1})$. Stated differently, equation (3), assuming a constant variance, is a misspecification of the model. The positive excess sensitivity coefficient λ represents a specification bias reflecting the precautionary motive for saving.[3]

As in the case of binding liquidity constraints, a debt-financed tax cut has no effect on consumption despite the positive λ because it does not change the constraint (6'). In terms of the Euler equation (2'), the tax cut, having no effect on the household's resources, does not affect the variance. Consumption growth remains just the same.

Why Don't We See Excess Sensitivity More Often?

This section's discussion has given two reasons why consumption *should* be excessively sensitive to current income if Hall's model is true: insufficient assets to alleviate the liquidity constraint and uncertain future income that makes it rational not to borrow. We would expect young households early in the life cycle to be particularly vulnerable to those forces. Then why hasn't the literature yielded more definitive evidence for excess sensitivity? There are only two possibilities. One is the low power of the excess sensitivity test, namely that the IV estimate of the excess sensitivity coefficient λ in (3) may often be insignificantly differently zero even if consumption is excessively sensitive to current income. The other possibility is that Hall's model is false.

As already mentioned, the IV estimate of λ on which the excess sensitivity test is based is essentially the correlation between consumption growth and the predictable component of income growth. But if income growth is hard to predict on the basis of the instrumental variables (which is likely to be the case if the instrumental variables are lagged once or twice for a variety of reasons), the IV estimate of becomes insignificantly different from zero. This problem can be illustrated for the panel data set I used in chapter 4, which has information on expectations. If expected income growth $\log(y_{t+1}^e) - \log(y_t)$ (where y_{t+1}^e is the expectation of y_{t+1} as of period t) is used as the instrumental variable for actual income growth in (3), the IV estimate of λ (for $t = 1981{:}Q3$ and $t + 1 = 1981{:}Q4$) is 0.0664 with a t-value of 3.4. If log current income $\log(y_t)$ is used to instrument actual income growth, the IV estimate of λ becomes -0.0838 with a t-value of -1.2.[4]

Another basis for suspecting the low power of the excess sensitivity test is studies documenting the liquidity effect of income without relying on equation (3). Using a single-year cross-section data available from the 1963/64 Survey of Financial Characteristics of Consumers, Hayashi (1985a; see chapter 3) shows that the consumption function estimated from a subsample of households deemed on an a priori basis to be not liquidity-constrained overpredicts consumption by households in the rest of the sample, particularly young households. Wilcox (1989) finds that aggregate consumption reacts to the actual change in Social Security benefits and not to the announcement of the change. According to Jappelli (1990), about 20 percent of those surveyed in the 1983 Survey of Consumer Finances report that they were denied credit or refrained from applying for credit because of fear of denial.

The problem of low power gets exacerbated if the marginal utility of consumption is allowed to be affected by leisure, as noted in section 9.4.2. Consider an extreme case of liquidity constraints of a household with no assets experiencing an income loss whose consumption, therefore, is set equal to current income, and suppose changes in income are due to changes in hours worked. Then consumption growth adjusted for changes in leisure (a fixed time endowment minus hours worked) is a constant and, if consumption or hours worked is measured with error, will equal the measurement error. So even if income growth is well predicted by the instrumental variables, the leisure-adjusted consumption growth will show no significant correlation with the predictable income growth.

The other possibility is that the household in reality has more ways to shift resources between different points in time and different income contingencies than is permitted by just the risk-free borrowing and lending allowed in Hall's model. I will examine this possibility next. To state the conclusion first, those other means to smooth consumption are utilized in reality but not intensively enough to eliminate the comovement of consumption and income.

1.6   An Alternative Formulation of the LC–PIH: Full Insurance

It is a testimony to the influence of Hall's paper that the empirical work in the 1980s and 1990s was not mindful of the fact that Hall's formulation is only one of possible extensions of the LC–PIH to uncertainty, nor was there any conscious attempt to test the assumption of the model that safe lending and borrowing are the only financial securities accessible by households. The model is really a model of *self insurance*, with saving and dissaving in safe assets the only way to shield consumption from income fluctuations.

But there is a substantial body of evidence from data on private transfers pointing to a significant degree of risk sharing between households. Using the President's Commission on Pension Policy survey data, Cox (1990) finds that households experiencing a temporary decline in income are more likely to receive monetary transfers. Using the National Longitudinal Survey, Rosenzweig and Wolpin (1993, 1994) find a similar relationship for transfers between parents and children. Using the 1983 Survey of Consumer Finances, which has a direct measure of whether the household is liquidity constrained, Cox and Jappelli (1990) document that private transfers tend to be targeted toward households facing liquidity constraints, suggesting that interhousehold network of income risk sharing is utilized to supplement self insurance. Using the 1988 wave of the PSID (Panel Study of Income Dynamics), which includes information on living parents and in-laws of the respondents, Ioannides and Kan (1993) and Altonji, Hayashi, and Kotlikoff (1995) find that parental income has a positive effect on the probability and the amount of transfers from parents to children and a negative effect on transfers from children to parents. Hall's model of self insurance is inadequate because it assumes *too little*, not too much, insurance.

An alternative formulation of the LC–PIH under uncertainty that is quite opposite to self insurance, called *full insurance*, is that income risk to each household is spread out evenly to the entire population of households either through a complete set of contingency claims markets or through an informal network of private transfers. The precise formulation has been around in economics since the 1950s in the writings of K. Arrow and others. For the constant-relative-risk-aversion utility function considered in section 1.3, equation (2′) was an implication of self insurance. Under full insurance, (2′) becomes (introducing household subscript "i" to emphasize that here, as in (2′), consumption is for the household in question)

$$\log(c_{i,t+1}) - \log(c_{it}) = \sigma \log(\beta) + p_{t+1}, \tag{7}$$

where p_{t+1} is the (log) price of a so-called Arrow security. The essential difference of (7) from (2') is that, since p_{t+1} is common to all households, consumption growth is a constant in the cross section of households. Different households experience different income realizations. But since income risk is fully covered by insurance, there is no need to adjust consumption to income realizations.

Of course, observed consumption growth will not be literally so predicted, with factors such as preference shifts and measurement error in consumption affecting observed consumption. But if one makes an auxiliary assumption that those other factors are uncorrelated in cross section with income, the prediction of full insurance that consumption growth is the same for all households gets translated into a zero correlation condition: the correlation between the growth rate of consumption and the growth rate of income—be it lagged, concurrent, actual, expected, or future growth—is zero. Because the prediction is about the cross-section, not time-series, correlation, available short panels with a large number of households can be used to test it. This is in sharp contrast to the case of testing for excess sensitivity where what is to be correlated with consumption growth is restricted to variables known in period t such as expected income growth and where the panel has to be sufficiently long for the IV estimate to be free from biases.

I argued above that the excess sensitivity test was not a test of Hall's model. What it is is an (unintended) test of full insurance, because one of the many correlations predicted by full insurance to be zero is between consumption growth and predicted income growth, the correlation the IV estimate of the excess sensitivity coefficient λ is based on. We would expect the power of the test to be higher if the correlation were with actual concurrent income growth rather than with predictable income growth, but it nevertheless is a test. Therefore, studies (such as my own in chapter 4) that have reported significant estimates of λ can be interpreted as rejecting full insurance without knowing it. Also, the independent evidence for liquidity constraints found in Jappelli (1990), Wilcox (1989), and chapter 3 also constitutes evidence against full insurance, under which liquidity constraints cannot arise.

It is only recently that the correlation between consumption growth and *concurrent* income growth was examined using micro data (see, e.g., Cochrane 1991 using the PSID, and Nelson 1994 using the CEX). Those studies find the correlation to be statistically significant. The correlation may, however, be due to a nonseparability of consumption and leisure rather than incomplete insurance; households may reduce consumption in the event of job losses not because they lack income insurance but because they are substituting consumption for leisure. But this possibility is empirically ruled out in chapter 9, which tests full insurance in the PSID allowing for the nonseparability.

1.7   Need for New Formulations

To sum up, contrary to Hall's formulation of the Life Cycle–Permanent Income hypothesis, households in micro data combine self insurance with interhousehold transfers to shield consumption from income fluctuations. Transfers, however, are not intensive enough to eliminate the correlation between consumption and income changes. What is needed is a new formulation of the LC–PIH under uncertainty with which the comovement of consumption and income can be interpreted. Any such formation should acknowledge the incompleteness of insurance markets. It should be explicit about why the markets are incomplete, because policy implication may well depend critically on the source of market incompleteness. For example, the effect of a government policy such as an expansion of unemployment insurance would depend on whether the reason for the incomplete provision of private income insurance is moral hazard or transactions costs.

The economics of information formulates the incomplete provision of insurance as the principal-agent problem with moral hazard and adverse selection. Recent theoretical studies view the household's decision problem as one of an agent in a repeated principal-agent problem (see Green 1987, Taub 1990, Thomas and Worrall 1994, Atkeson and Lucas 1992). Phelan and Townsend (1991) computed information-constrained efficient contracts and examined whether they were consistent with micro data on consumption and income. My view is that these private information models are not suitable for explaining the observed correlation between consumption and income changes. First, it seems unrealistic to assume that income is private information. Most households seem to report income truthfully to the IRS for fear of auditing. If so, the incentive problem of agents telling lies about their income to the principal can be alleviated greatly if transfers from the principal to agents is made contingent on submission of a copy of tax returns. Second, there is a question of who the principal is. Third, for the reason pointed out by Allen (1985), most private information models cannot allow for self insurance, which, as seen above, is empirically an important, albeit incomplete, means of income insurance.

Fourth and more important, the evidence contained in Attanasio and Davis (1994) casts serious doubts on the relevance of moral hazard and adverse selection in general. They show that average consumption for high school graduates in the 1980s declined in tandem with the well-publicized decline in their average real wage rate. If individual households can sign a binding contract or purchase a claim contingent on the realization of average real wage rate, such a decline in consumption should not have taken place. Since the average wage rate is publicly observable and cannot be influenced by low work effort by an individual, neither adverse selection nor moral hazard can be the primary reason for the lack of insurance.

Perhaps a better way to model incomplete insurance is to appeal to time inconsistency. A promise to help each other in times of financial difficulty is easy to make but difficult to keep. A formal model of two households sharing income risk subject to this limited commitment constraint can be found in Coate and Ravillion (1993) and Thomas and Worrall (1994). But the model does not include self insurance either.

It is too early to tell at this stage which formulation will prove more successful in explaining the comovement of consumption and income because none of the formulations mentioned here is rich enough to be confronted with data yet.

1.8 Altruism

The literature reviewed so far has no bearing on the issue of whether the horizon is finite (as in the Life Cycle hypothesis, the LCH for short) or infinite (as in the Permanent Income hypothesis, or PIH, alternatively called the Dynasty model), because the truth of the restrictions on consumption changes examined in the literature do not depend on the horizon. As mentioned in section 1.2, the issue has important implications for government finance and social policies involving redistribution of income between generations. I now turn to a separate and large literature that attempts to discriminate between the LCH and the PIH (i.e., the Dynasty model).

It may first appear that testing the LCH is easy enough. According to the textbook version, the household should start dissaving after retirement so as to exhaust assets at the end of the lifetime. A more sophisticated version recognizing uncertain lifetime predicts that the household will convert all assets into annuities. In either version of the LCH, there should be no unilateral transfers to children in the form of bequests or inter vivos gifts. These are sharp predictions, but one can construct a version of the LCH such that bequests and gifts are not really a unilateral transfer but a *payment* for nonmarket services provided by the child. In Kotlikoff and Spivak (1981), the annuity market is missing and the child acts as an insurance agent. In Bernheim, Shleifer, and Summers (1985) and Cox (1987), the child is the sole supplier of "attention" (e.g., phone calls and visits) desired by the parent.

But once one allows for nonmarket—and hence often unobservable—services being exchanged between the parent and the child, a wide variety of patterns of saving and transfers usually cited as evidence for the Dynasty model and against the LCH becomes consistent with the LCH, making it very difficult to refute the LCH. Consider the following four strands of the literature.[5]

1. There is a literature starting with Shorrocks (1975) and Mirer (1979) that attempts to test the LCH by checking whether wealth declines with age after retirement. Relatively recent evidence from panel data is that the elderly gradually decumulate wealth (Hurd 1990). But the wealth-based studies cannot be a test of the LCH because a wide variety of the age-wealth profile is possible when gifts and bequests are used to pay for the child's service. For example, to make sure the service will be provided in good faith by the child, the parent may ask the child to post a bond to be returned only after the delivery of the service. The parent's wealth could increase until death reflecting the bond deposited by the child in the parent's bank account. A bequest would consist of the bond to be returned to the child and the payment for the service.

2. A number of studies attempt to measure the amount of wealth acquired through intergenerational transfers rather than through saving. The estimate of transfer wealth ranges from less than or about 20 percent of total wealth (Modigliani 1988, Hurd and Mundaca 1989) to at least a half (Gale and Scholz 1994) and to more than 80 percent (Kotlikoff and Summers 1981), depending on the definition of transfer wealth and how it is measured. But the large amount of transfers is consistent with the LCH because it can be interpreted as extra income earned by children by selling nonmarket services desired by parents.

3. If a sample of households includes parents and their adult children forming separate households, it may be possible to test the basic premise

of the LCH that each generation fully consumes its own resources, by checking whether the child's consumption depends on indicators of the parent's resources as well as on the child's permanent income. Such a test is possible with the PSID, which includes split-offs, those households headed by adult children who were dependents in the original households at the start of the survey (in 1968) but who became independent as the survey progressed over time. Those split-offs can be matched with original households in the PSID. Altonji, Hayashi, and Kotlikoff (1992, included in this book as chapter 7) find a significant influence of the parent's resources on the child's consumption, in a variety of specifications about the child's permanent income and the functional form (see tables 7.5–7.7). If the service sold by the child to the parent were also available from the market, having a wealthy parent as a customer would not enhance the child's resources because the price paid by the parent is given by the market. But most likely the parent values the service because it is provided by the child. The significant effect of the parent's resources can be interpreted as a monopoly rent extracted by the child, so the evidence is consistent with the LCH.

4. In the LCH with intergenerational exchange, bequests are intentional. Thus the LCH is consistent with the existence of respondents citing bequests as a primary reason for saving in a household survey (Hurd and Mundaca 1989) and the evidence that households respond to increased annuitization by social security by purchasing life insurance to maintain a desired amount of bequeathable wealth (Bernheim 1991).

Thus, the literature has not produced convincing evidence framed as a statistical rejection of the LCH. In contrast, it is much more straightforward to test the Dynasty model. Under the intergenerational altruism characterizing the Dynasty model, parent and child act as if they form a single decision unit, the family. This produces the following sharp testable implications.

1. If inter vivos transfers are motivated by altruism, the effect of the recipient's income on the amount of transfer receipts should be negative, after controlling for the effect of the donor's income. Using the President's Commission on Pension Policy survey, Cox (1987) finds that for adult children receiving transfers from their parents, the child's income effect is actually positive, which he shows is possible if transfers are motivated by exchange rather than altruism. However, Altonji, Hayashi, and Kotlikoff (1995) argue that Cox's test may be biased against altruism if the degree

of altruism differs across parent-child pairs. Furthermore, in their estimation of the transfer equation using the PSID, the effect of the child's income on the amount of transfers received is negative.

The following other implications of the Dynasty model have been examined in the chapters included in part II of this book.

2. There should be full risk sharing between the parent and the child. The discussion in Section 6 of this chapter has shown that the economywide full risk sharing implies a lack of correlation between consumption growth and income growth. Under full risk sharing between the parent and the child, the difference in the growth rate of consumption between parent and child should not be correlated with the corresponding differential growth rate in income. This prediction is tested and rejected in chapter 9 using the PSID data with split-offs matched with their parent households.

3. Altruism has the neutrality property that the distribution of consumption between the two generations within the family should not be affected by the distribution of resources. If two generations co-reside, the structure of demand for various commodities for the two-generation household as a whole should not depend on the division of resources once the effect of total family resources on demand is taken into account. Since total consumption expenditure is a perfect measure of the family's total resources, Engel curves—which relate expenditures on various commodities to total expenditure—should not be shifted by the parent's share of family income. Hayashi (1995, see chapter 8) carries out this test of neutrality on Japanese cross-section data. The Japanese data provide an attractive setting because a substantial fraction of Japanese households are those two-generation households (which generates a large sample size) and also because there is a sharp intergenerational difference in food tastes (which enhances the power of the test). The results in chapter 8 show that, contrary to the Dynasty model, Engel curves for food items favored by the older generation (such as vegetables and seafood) shift up with the parent's share of family income.

4. Neutrality can be rejected for U.S. households as well. Under some assumptions about preferences, it can be shown that the ratio of the parent's food consumption to the child's is uncorrelated with the corresponding income ratio. If, for example, the child's income is too low to finance the consumption level determined by the desired consumption ratio, there will be a transfer from the parent to achieve the desired ratio. Using the PSID with split-offs, chapter 7 carries out this test with a very

strong rejection. Quite contrary to the prediction of the Dynasty model, the income ratio explains much of the variation in the consumption ratio across parent-child pairs, which suggests that transfers may not be actively used to correct the disparity in consumption between the parent and the child. Altonji, Hayashi, and Kotlikoff (1995) find that, even for the parent-child pairs linked by positive transfers in the PSID, the amount of transfers falls far short of full compensation.

How do we interpret the evidence presented in this section? Although more corroborating empirical work is certainly desirable, I doubt that the strong early rejection of the Dynasty model will be overturned. But bear in mind that the altruism characterizing the model is a very extreme sort involving no disagreement between parent and child as to what the family's objective ought to be. It is also important to remember that the evidence that I have argued is consistent with the LCH with exchange is also consistent with some sort of altruism. The rejection of the Dynasty model means only that, if part or all of the gifts and bequests is motivated by altruism, then that altruism is not the pure altruism of the Dynasty model.

1.9   Conclusion

There are two main conclusions of this review of the literature on household saving.

1. Risk sharing between households exists but is not complete. This follows from the statistically significant correlation between consumption changes and concurrent income changes, the significant excess sensitivity coefficient and other independent evidence of liquidity constraints. What we need now is a theoretical model of incomplete insurance whereby the existing wealth of evidence can be related to parameters characterizing preferences and the environment faced by households. Without such a model, it is not possible to interpret the observed correlation between consumption growth and income growth.

2. Second, a substantial amount of intergenerational transfers is motivated by either the selfish exchange motive or altruism or both, but the altruism is not of the sort assumed in the Dynasty model. Here, a top item on the research agenda is to empirically determine whether the exchange motive alone can account for the observed amount of intergenerational transfers.

Notes on the Relationship of Work in Parts I and II to the Literature

Enough has been said about chapters 4, 6, 7, 8 and 9. Below I briefly describe the other chapters of parts I and II and how they are related to the literature.

Chapter 2 is an attempt to estimate the excess sensitivity coefficient under rational expectations using U.S. time-series data. It is a midway house between the consumption function and the Euler equation approaches in that what is estimated are parameters of a consumption function but the estimation equation is in terms of (quasi) changes. Since there is' no closed-form solution for the household's decision problem under uncertainty, the estimated consumption function is necessarily an approximation to the true solution. It nevertheless captures what came to be understood as the precautionary motive for saving, by letting expected future income be discounted at a rate higher than the interest rate. Because the consumption function is linear, the aggregation problem mentioned in section 1.4 does not arise. The consumption concept is the economically correct one—namely, total consumption with the service flow from the stock of consumer durables. However, the estimate of the excess sensitivity coefficient turned out to be sensitive to how the service flow from consumer durables is measured.

As already mentioned, chapter 3 provides independent evidence for liquidity constraints without using the consumption growth equation. The methodology of doing this without panel data should be of some interest. The basic idea is to split the sample into those households that are likely to be not liquidity constrained and those that are not so likely. The a priori criterion used for the sample splitting is the saving rate. Since the dependent variable (consumption) of the equation to be estimated obviously affects the saving rate, the Tobit technique is used to correct for the selectivity bias. If no households in the whole sample are liquidity constrained, the Ordinary Least Squares provides the most efficient estimate of the equation. Therefore, testing for liquidity constraints amounts to the Hausman test for misspecification.

Chapter 5 is a companion piece to chapter 4. Chapter 4 uses Japanese quarterly interview panel data to estimate the degree of durability of various consumption components by estimating the Euler equation augmented to include the liquidity effect of current income. Chapter 5 uses Japanese monthly diary panel data for the same sample period to estimate the same model. It confirms the conclusions of chapter 4 that consumption components usually labeled as nondurables (such as leisure) are highly durable and that the excess sensitivity coefficient is about 10 percent. It also contains some useful results about measurement erorrs that are a major issue in any study using micro data on households. Comparing the standard deviations of expenditures and disposable income in chapter 4 with those in chapter 5 reveals some useful facts. In particular, disposable income is equally well measured in the interview and diary surveys.

Notes

1. The right-hand side of equation (2) is the expected growth rate of consumption because the change in logs is approximately the growth rate. To derive (2), rewrite (1) as $(1 + r_{t+1})\beta u'(c_{t+1})/u'(c_t) = 1 + \varepsilon_{t+1}$. Taking logs, we obtain

$$\log[u'(c_{t+1})] - \log[u'(c_t)]] = -\log(\beta) - \log(1 + r_{t+1}) + \log(1 + \varepsilon_{t+1}).$$

Using the Taylor approximation to the second order that $\log(1 + x) = x - x^2/2$, we obtain

$$\log[u'(c_{t+1})] - \log[u'(c_t)] = -\log(\beta) - \log(1 + r_{t+1}) - \varepsilon_{t+1}^2/2 + \varepsilon_{t+1}.$$

By construction, $E_t(\varepsilon_{t+1}) = 0$, so $E_t(\varepsilon_{t+1}^2) = \text{Var}_t(\varepsilon_{t+1})$. Taking expectations of both sides, we obtain

$$E_t(\log[u'(c_{t+1})]) - \log[u'(c_t)] = -\log(\beta) - E_t[\log(1 + r_{t+1})] - \text{Var}_t(\varepsilon_{t+1})/2.$$

Equation (2) results from this because $\log(1 + r_{t+1}) \approx r_{t+1}$ and $u'(c)$ under the assumed utility function is $c^{-1/\sigma}$.

2. In terms of equation (3), the equation aggregated to the cohort level involves, for example, the cohort average of $\log(c_t)$ (which should be distinguished from the log of the cohort average of c_t), and such desired cohort averages can be calculated from cross-section data. The use of synthetic cohorts has its own problems, including the error introduced by the discrepancy between the sample and population cell averages. See Deaton (1985) for a discussion of this and other problems and their possible resolutions.

3. The consumption function for Hall's model has a closed-form solution, but the solution can be solved for numerically. Hubbard, Skinner, and Zeldes (1994) simulated data using the numerically solved consumption function for many different income realizations and used the data to estimate equation (3). Their estimate of the excess sensitivity coefficient is 0.5.

4. See addendum to chapter 4 for more details.

5. The discussion here is limited to studies using mostly U.S. data. Those using Japanese data are reviewed in sections 10.4.1 and 10.4.2.

References

Allen, F. 1985. Repeated principal-agent relationships with lending and borrowing. *Economics Letters* 17:27–31.

Altonji, J., F. Hayashi, and L. Kotlikoff. 1992. Is the extended family altruistically linked? Direct tests using micro data. *American Economic Review* 82:1177–98.

———. 1995. Parental altruism and inter vivos transfers: Theory and evidence. National Bureau of Economic Research Working Paper no. 5378.

Atkeson, A., and R. Lucas. 1992. On efficient distribution with private information. *Review of Economic Studies* 59:427–53.

Attanasio, O. 1995. The Intertemporal Allocation of Consumption: Theory and Evidence. *Carnegie-Rochester Conference Series on Public Policy* 42:39–89.

Attanasio, O., and S. Davis. 1994. Relative wage movements and the distribution of consumption. National Bureau of Economic Research Working Paper no. 4771.

Attanasio, O., and G. Weber. 1996. Is consumption growth consistent with intertemporal optimization? Evidence from the Consumer Expenditure Survey. *Journal of Political Economy* 103:1121–57.

Barro, R. 1974. Are government bonds net wealth? *Journal of Political Economy* 82:1095–117.

Bernheim, D. 1991. How strong are bequest motives? Evidence based on estimates of the demand for life insurance and annuities. *Journal of Political Economy* 99:899–927.

Bernheim, D., A. Schleifer, and L. Summers. 1985. The strategic bequest motive. *Journal of Political Economy* 93:45–76.

Browning, M. and A. Lussardi. 1995. Household saving: Micro theories and micro facts. Mimeo., McMaster University and Brown University.

Carroll, C. 1992. Buffer stock saving and the Permanent Income hypothesis. Mimeo., Board of Governors, Washington, DC.

Chamberlain, G. 1984. Panel data. In *Handbook of econometrics, Vol. II*, ed. Z. Griliches and M. Intriligator, 1247–318. Amsterdam: North-Holland.

Coate, S., and M. Ravillion. 1993. Reciprocity without commitment. *Journal of Development Economics* 40:1–24.

Cochrane, J. 1991. A simple test of consumption insurance. *Journal of Political Economy* 99:957–76.

Cox, D. 1987. Motives for private transfers. *Journal of Political Economy* 95:508–46.

———. 1990. Intergenerational transfers and liquidity constraints. *Quarterly Journal of Economics* 105:187–218.

Cox, D., and T. Jappelli. 1990. Credit rationing and private transfers: Evidence from survey data. *Review of Economics and Statistics* 72:445–54.

Deaton, A. 1985. Panel data from time series of cross sections. *Journal of Econometrics* 30:109–26.

Deaton, A. 1992. *Understanding consumption.* Oxford: Oxford University Press.

Gale, W., and J. Scholz. 1994. Intergenerational transfers and the accumulation of wealth. *Journal of Economic Perspectives* 8:145–60.

Green, E. 1987. Lending and the smoothing of uninsurable income. In *Contractual Arrangements for Intertemporal Trade*, ed. E. Prescott and N. Wallace, 3–25. Minneapolis: University of Minnesota Press.

Hall, R. 1978. Stochastic implications of the Life Cycle–Permanent Income hypothesis. *Journal of Political Economy* 96:971–88.

————. 1985a. The effect of liquidity constraints on consumption: A cross-sectional analysis. *The Quarterly Journal of Economics* 100:183–206.

————. 1985b. The Permanent Income hypothesis and consumption durability: Analysis based on Japanese panel data. *The Quarterly Journal of Economics* 100:1083–113.

————. 1987. Tests for liquidity constraints: A critical survey and some new observations. In *Advances in econometrics, Vol. II*, ed. T. Bewley, 91–120. New York: Cambridge University Press.

————. 1995. Is the Japanese extended family altruistically linked? A test based on Engel curves. *Journal of Political Economy* 103:661–74.

Hayashi, F., J. Altonji, and L. Kotlikoff. 1996. Risk-sharing between and within families. *Econometrica* 64:261–94.

Hubbard, R. G., J. Skinner, and S. Zeldes. 1994. The importance of precautionary motives in explaining individual and aggregate saving. *Carnegie-Rochester Conference Series on Public Policy* 40:59–125.

Hurd, M. 1990. Research on the elderly: Economic status, retirement, and consumption and saving. *Journal of Economic Literature* 28:565–637.

Hurd, M., and B. Mundaca. 1989. The importance of gifts and inheritances among the affluent. In *The Measurement of Saving, Investment, and Wealth*, ed. R. Lipsey and H. Tice, 737–58. Chicago: University of Chicago Press.

Ioannides, Y., and K. Kan. 1993. The nature of two-directional intergenerational transfers of money and time: Empirical analysis. Mimeo., Virginia Polytechnic Institute.

Jappelli, T. 1990. Who is credit-constrained in the U.S. economy? *Quarterly Journal of Economics* 105:219–34.

Kotlikoff, L., and A. Spivak. 1981. The family as an incomplete annuity market. *Journal of Political Economy* 89:372–91.

Kotlikoff, L., and L. Summers. 1981. The role of intergenerational transfers in aggregate capital accumulation. *Journal of Political Economy* 89:707–32.

Mirer, T. 1979. The wealth-age relation among the aged. *American Economic Review* 69:435–43.

Modigliani, F. 1988. Measuring the contribution of intergenerational transfers to total wealth: Conceptual issues and empirical findings. In *Modelling the Accumulation and Distribution of Wealth*, ed. D. Kessler and A. Masson, 21–52. Oxford: Clarendon Press.

Nelson, J. 1994. On testing full insurance using consumer expenditure survey data. *Journal of Political Economy* 102:384–94.

Phelan, C., and R. Townsend. 1991. Computing multi-period, information constrained optima. *Review of Economic Studies* 58:853–81.

Rosenzweig, M., and K. Wolpin. 1993. Intergenerational support and the life-cycle incomes of young men and their parents: Human capital investments, co-residence, and interhousehold transfers. *Journal of Labor Economics* 11:84–112.

Rosenzweig, M., and K. Wolpin. 1994. Parental and public transfers to young women and their children. *American Economic Review* 84:1195–212.

Shorrocks, A. 1975. The age-wealth relationship: A cross-section cohort analysis. *Review of Economics and Statistics* 42:155–63.

Taub, B. 1990. The equivalence of lending equilibria and signalling-based insurance under asymmetric information. *RAND Journal of Economics* 21:388–408.

Thomas, J., and T. Worrall. 1988. Self-enforcing wage contracts. *Review of Economic Studies* 55:541–54.

Thomas, J., and T. Worrall. 1994. Informal insurance arrangements in village economies. Mimeo., University of Warwick and University of Liverpool.

Wilcox, D. 1989. Social security benefits, consumption expenditure, and the life cycle hypothesis. *Journal of Political Economy* 97:288–304.

2

The Permanent Income Hypothesis: Estimation and Testing by Instrumental Variables

2.1 Introduction

One of the basic messages of the permanent income hypothesis of consumption is that households look into the future in deciding the amount of current consumption. Yet the conventional practice in the literature has been to proxy permanent income by a fixed distributed lag of current and past disposable income. This has been criticized by Lucas (1976), who argued that there was no theoretical reason for expectations formed by reasonably intelligent economic agents about future variables to be adequately explained by past data in a stable manner. His criticism has to be taken seriously because almost any set of behavioral equations that are derived from the intertemporal optimization considerations depends on expectations about future economic variables.

In recent years, several authors have attempted to empirically implement the forward-looking permanent income hypothesis with rational expectations. Sargent (1978) assumes that consumption and disposable income are generated by a bivariate autoregressive process and tests the restrictions implied by the permanent income hypothesis with rational expectations. He defines permanent income as the present discounted value of current and future disposable income. As Flavin (1981) has shown, the consumption function with this definition of permanent income cannot be derived from the household's intertemporal optimization problem. The reason for this is that future disposable income includes returns from savings which should not affect current consumption decisions.

Unlike Sargent, Hall (1978) avoids an explicit definition of permanent income but derives a testable implication of the permanent income hypothesis with rational expectations. He has shown that the household's

Originally published in *Journal of Political Economy* 90 (October 1982): 895–916. Reprinted with permission. © 1982 by the University of Chicago. All rights reserved.

intertemporal optimization with an additively separable objective function implies that consumption approximately follows a martingale if the utility function is close to quadratic or if the change in marginal utility from one period to the next is small. His main empirical finding is that disposable income has no predictive power in the regression of consumption on its own lagged value and lagged disposable income. Flavin (1981) explicitly defines permanent income as (a constant times) the sum of nonhuman wealth and human wealth which is the present discounted value of current and future labor income. The discount rate for future labor income is constrained to be equal to the rate of return from nonhuman wealth. She shows that the consumption function with this particular definition of permanent income satisfies Hall's martingale equation on consumption. To test the validity of Hall's martingale equation, she estimated the regression equation studied by Hall along with an autoregressive process on disposable income and found that consumption is more sensitive to current income than predicted by Hall's martingale hypothesis.

Our formulation of the permanent income hypothesis is more general than Flavin's in that the discount rate for future labor income is not constrained to be equal to the rate of return from nonhuman wealth. Section 2.2 of this chapter states our formulation of the permanent income hypothesis and indicates the relation of our formulation to Hall's martingale equation and Flavin's formulation. In the same section we introduce and motivate a consumption function which includes the permanent income hypothesis as a special case and which explicitly recognizes the presence of liquidity-constrained households in the population. In Section 2.3 we present our instrumental variables estimation method and discuss several econometric issues associated with it. The basic idea in our estimation method is to exploit the stochastic difference equation on human wealth to eliminate the unobservable human wealth from our estimation equation.[1] The advantage of our method is that we do not have to specify the stochastic process for labor income. Our empirical results are reported in Section 2.4. The main result is that the permanent income can be accepted on the consumption series which includes service flows from consumer durables and can be rejected on the consumption series in the National Income and Product Accounts. Section 2.5 contains an interpretation of our results and briefly discusses its policy implications.

2.2   A Formulation of the Permanent Income Hypothesis

In this paper, we identify the permanent income hypothesis with the following key ingredients: (1) the household's planning horizon is infinite;

(2) the objective function is additively separable and the instantaneous utility function $u(c)$ has a constant relative degree of risk aversion; that is, $u(c) = (1/\beta)c^\beta$ ($\beta < 1$), where c is consumption; (3) the expected real rates of return from assets are constant;[2] and (4) expectations are formed rationally in Muth's (1961) sense. In the deterministic case where the household has point expectations about future labor income and real rates of return, the consumption function, namely, the optimal consumption rule for the household's optimization problem, is written as

$$c_t = \alpha(A_t + H_t), \tag{1}$$

where t represents time period and A_t is real nonhuman wealth. Real *human wealth* H_t is defined as the present discounted value of expected future real labor income:

$$H_t = \sum_{k=0}^{\infty} (1 + \mu)^{-k} {}_t y_{t+k}, \tag{2}$$

where μ is the discount rate and ${}_t y_{t+k}$ represents the household's expectation as of t of real, after-tax labor income at $t + k$. The rational expectations hypothesis implies ${}_t y_{t+k} = E(y_{t+k} | I_t)$, where I_t is the set of information held by the household at t. The propensity to consume out of total wealth $A_t + H_t$ is denoted by α. It is a function of the expected real rates of return from nonhuman wealth and the subjective rate of time preference. If risky assets whose rates of return are stochastic (but whose expected returns are constant) are present along with the safe asset whose real interest rate is nonstochastic, then α depends also on the variance of the stochastic rates of return and the discount rate μ should be equal to the risk-free rate of interest (see Hakansson 1970; Merton 1971).

Now if future labor income is stochastic, the consumption function given by (1) and (2) is no longer the exact solution to the household's optimization problem. In fact, it is in general impossible to derive a closed-form solution for the case of uncertain future labor income. To illustrate the difficulty, consider the simplest case in which the real rate of return ρ is constant and nonstochastic but labor income is subject to a multiplicative shock: $y_t = \bar{y}(1 + \varepsilon_t)$, where ε_t is independently and identically distributed with mean zero. Optimal consumption depends on $\bar{y}$ and initial nonhuman wealth A as well as on the parameters that characterize the distribution of ε_t. The Euler equation for this optimization problem is

$$c(A, \bar{y})^{\beta-1} = \frac{1+\rho}{1+\delta} E(c\{(1+\rho)[A + \bar{y}(1+\varepsilon) - c(A, \bar{y})], \bar{y}\})^{\beta-1}, \tag{3}$$

where δ is the rate of time preference and we have used the budget equation

$$A_t = (1 + \rho)(A_{t-1} + y_{t-1} - c_{t-1}). \tag{4}$$

Optimal consumption $c(A, \bar{y})$ is the solution to this functional equation. If ε is identically zero, then optimal consumption is given by (1) and (2) with $\mu = \rho$ and $_t y_{t+k} = \bar{y}$. Otherwise it is impossible to obtain a closed-form solution since the shock ε enters the right-hand side of (3) in a nonlinear way. However, several qualitative results are available. First, as was shown by Sandmo (1970), Miller (1974), and Schechtman (undated), optimal consumption $c(A, \bar{y})$ is a decreasing function of the variance of ε. Second, it is straightforward to show that $c(A, \bar{y})$ is homogeneous of degree one in A and $\bar{y}$. Thus, the proportionality postulate that consumption is proportional to total wealth carries over to the case of labor income uncertainty.

Any realistic formulation of the household's consumption behavior should take account of the labor income uncertainty; yet no closed-form expression for optimal consumption that is consistent with the constant relative degree of risk aversion is available. Our choice, then, must be a compromise between empirical tractability and consistency with the optimization principle.[3] Our preferred formulation of the permanent income hypothesis is to maintain (1) and (2) but allow the discount rate μ to be different from the risk-free real rate of interest. The basic idea is that, in calculating human wealth, the household discounts the expected value of uncertain future after-tax labor income at a rate somewhat higher than the interest rate by what can be thought of as the risk premium.[4] Although not exactly consistent with the optimization principle, this particular way of taking account of the labor income uncertainty is probably what Friedman (1957, 1963) had in mind and is consistent with the two qualitative properties of optimal consumption mentioned above.

In the empirical implementation of our consumption function we will carry out later in this paper, our definition of nonhuman wealth A_t includes public debt. This does *not* necessarily presume a wealth effect of public debt on consumption and is perfectly consistent with the debt neutrality hypothesis advanced by Barro (1974). Labor income is the sum of several income streams of varying degrees of uncertainty. The discount rate that applies to a sure income stream should be equal to the risk-free rate of interest. The discount rate that applies to a highly uncertain income stream should be much higher than the rate of interest. As Friedman (1963, p. 10) has noted, the overall discount rate μ for future after-tax labor income can be thought of as a weighted average of these specific rates.[5] If the discount rate for future tax liabilities required for servicing public debt is equal to the rate of return on public debt, an increase in the stock of public debt will be exactly offset by a decrease in human wealth (and by a decrease in asset prices, to the extent that profit income bears the increase in future tax liabilities), which leaves total wealth invariant to the stock of public debt outstanding in spite of the fact that public debt is included as part of nonhuman wealth. However, our definition of nonhuman wealth excludes social security wealth. Since our definition of after-tax labor income y_t includes social security benefits and excludes payroll taxes, social security wealth is treated as part of human wealth in our consumption function.

The preceding discussion also suggests that there is no theoretically compelling reason for the overall discount rate μ to be equal to the overall, value-weighted average expected rate of return ρ from nonhuman wealth. But if $\mu = \rho$, our formulation (1) and (2) of the permanent income consumption function implies an equation which embodies Hall's (1978) martingale hypothesis, as we will see in the next section. Furthermore, if $\mu = \rho = \alpha$, it is obvious that our consumption function reduces to Flavin's (1981) formulation of the permanent income hypothesis. The hypothesis that μ is equal to ρ will be tested in Section 2.4, where our consumption function (1) with (3) is estimated.

2.3 Some Econometric Issues

We obtain the "stochastic" version of the permanent income hypothesis by adding the error term to our consumption function:

$$c_t = \alpha(A_t + H_t) + u_t. \tag{5}$$

The error term u_t represents "transitory consumption." This may be regarded as a shock to the instantaneous utility function or as measurement error in c_t and A_t. (Our estimation procedure, to be presented shortly, can handle the case where u_t is identically zero.) Since the equation is linear, aggregation is straightforward and we can think of (5) as the aggregate consumption function.

The problem in estimating (5) is, of course, that we cannot observe human wealth H_t, which is the present discounted value of rational expectations. There are essentially two ways to get around this. The first method, proposed by Hansen and Sargent (1980), seeks to obtain a closed-form expression for H_t in terms of observable variables. They assume that labor income y_t is a part of an n-variate autoregressive process and derive an explicit formula for H_t which is linear in the current and lagged values of the n variables and nonlinear in μ and the coefficients in the autoregression.[6] Estimates of parameters α and μ can be obtained by estimating the consumption function (5) and the n-variate autoregressive process jointly by maximum likelihood. To make the number of parameters finite, it is necessary to assume that the order of autoregression is finite and (somehow) known a priori.

The second method, which is the one we employ in this chapter, avoids the explicit treatment of human wealth.[7] The basic idea is to exploit the following stochastic difference equation for human wealth:[8]

$$H_t = (1 + \mu)(H_{t-1} - y_{t-1}) + e_t, \tag{6}$$

where

$$e_t = \sum_{k=0}^{\infty} (1 + \mu)^{-k} ({}_t y_{t+k} - {}_{t-1} y_{t+k}). \tag{7}$$

This comes directly from the definition (2) of H_t. The term ${}_t y_{t+k} - {}_{t-1} y_{t+k}$ represents the revision of expectations about y_{t+k} that will be made as the household proceeds from period $t - 1$ to period t. Under the assumption that expectations are rational, it is orthogonal to I_{t-1}, the set of information available to the household at $t - 1$. In other words, we have $E({}_t y_{t+k} - {}_{t-1} y_{t+k} | I_{t-1}) = 0$. Thus the term e_t, to be referred to as the *surprise term*, is orthogonal to I_{t-1}—that is, $E(e_t | I_{t-1}) = 0$—and is serially uncorrelated. Now by using (5) we can eliminate H_t and H_{t-1} from (6) to obtain:

$$c_t = (1 + \mu)c_{t-1} + \alpha[A_t - (1 + \mu)(A_{t-1} + y_{t-1})] + v_t, \tag{8}$$

where

$$v_t = u_t - (1 + \mu)u_{t-1} + \alpha e_t. \tag{9}$$

We notice that equation (8) involves a nonlinear constraint: μ appears twice on the right-hand side of (8). The nonlinear least squares (NLS) does not give consistent estimates of μ and α for two reasons. The first is the usual simultaneous equations bias that comes through the correlation between transitory consumption u, measured consumption c, nonhuman wealth A, and labor income y. The second reason is somewhat unconventional: The orthogonality of the surprise term e_t—which is part of the error term v_t in (8)—to the lagged information set I_{t-1} does not exclude a nonzero correlation between e_t and A_t since A_t does not belong to I_{t-1}. To achieve consistent estimation, we need to find a set of instruments Z_{t-1} in I_{t-1} that are uncorrelated with u_{t-1} and u_t. Since Z_{t-1} is in I_{t-1}, the instruments are guaranteed to be uncorrelated with e_t and hence with the error term v_t. We conclude that equation (8) can be estimated by the nonlinear instrumental variables technique (NLIV) of Amemiya (1974) and Jorgenson and Laffont (1974).[9]

This second method has some advantages over the first method we described above. From the computational point of view, the second method involves searching over a much smaller parameter space. The parameter space required by the first method can easily be a huge one if the autoregression involves more than several variables. Another advantage of the second method is that we do not have to explicitly model the stochastic environment the household faces; we do not even have to specify all the variables that influence future after-tax labor income. The main requirement for the consistency (and asymptotic normality) of the NLIV estimator is that the sample covariances between instruments and the right-hand-side variables converge in probability to their population covariances. This requirement certainly is satisfied in the autoregressive environment assumed by the first method. It is satisfied in a more general stochastic environment where the relevant variables in the economy, including the right-hand-side variables, the instruments, and the (political) variables that influence policy rules, are jointly stationary and ergodic. A main advantage of the second method is that the set of instruments does not have to include those political variables which influence after-tax labor income by shifting policy rules.

To indicate the relation of our second method to Hall's (1978) martingale hypothesis and Flavin's (1981) version of the permanent income hypothesis, let ρ stand for the overall, value-weighted expected real rate of return from nonhuman wealth. Then the budget equation can be written as

$$A_t = (1 + \rho)(A_{t-1} + y_{t-1} - c_{t-1}) + \varepsilon_t, \tag{10}$$

where ε_t represents the shock to the budget equation and consists of unanticipated movements in asset prices (which will be orthogonal to the lagged information set I_{t-1}) and measurement errors in A_t, A_{t-1}, y_{t-1}, and c_{t-1}.[10] Now if $\mu = \rho$, equations (8) and (10) imply

$$c_t = (1 + \mu)(1 - \alpha)c_{t-1} + v_t + \alpha\varepsilon_t. \tag{11}$$

If measurement errors and transitory consumption are ignored, the error term $v_t + \alpha \varepsilon_t$ is orthogonal to I_{t-1} under the assumption that ε_t is orthogonal to I_{t-1}. Therefore, (11) represents Hall's martingale hypothesis. It also emphasizes that the identification of μ and α is not possible from equation (8) alone *if* μ equals ρ. If, in addition, ρ is equal to α, then $(1 + \mu)(1 - \alpha)$ is roughly equal to one and we get the equation derived by Flavin (1981): $c_t - c_{t-1} = v_t + \alpha \varepsilon_t$.[11]

In this chapter we wish to test the permanent income hypothesis as well as estimate it. To this end we generalize the consumption function (5) and obtain:

$$c_t = \alpha(A_t + H_t) + \lambda YD_t + u_t, \tag{12}$$

where YD_t is real aggregate disposable income. There are two closely related ways to motivate equation (12). Suppose there are two types of households in the economy: the wealth constrained and the liquidity constrained. The consumption function for the wealth-constrained household is equation (5). The consumption function for the liquidity-constrained household is simply $c =$ disposable income. Aggregate consumption is then a linear function of total wealth of the wealth-constrained households and disposable income of the liquidity-constrained households. If we interpret α as the product of the propensity to consume out of total wealth and the ratio of the wealth-constrained households' total wealth to aggregate total wealth and λ as the liquidity-constrained households' share of disposable income, equation (12) is the consumption function aggregated over the two types of households. Another way to justify (12) is to think of (12) as the result of "artificial nesting" discussed, for example, by Davidson and MacKinnon (1981). Suppose we wish to test the permanent income hypothesis represented by (5) against the alternative hypothesis that aggregate consumption is proportional to aggregate disposable income. The two hypotheses are not nested, but the truth of the permanent income hypothesis can be tested by estimating the consumption function which is a weighted average of the consumption functions implied by the two hypotheses. With this interpretation of (12), α is the propensity to consume out of total wealth multiplied by one minus a weight assigned to the alternative hypothesis and λ is the propensity to consume out of disposable income multiplied by the weight. If the permanent income hypothesis is true, λ is equal to zero.

By using the same argument that led to equation (8), we can derive from (12) the following equation:

$$c_t = (1 + \mu)c_{t-1} + \alpha[A_t - (1 + \mu)(A_{t-1} + y_{t-1})]$$

$$+ \lambda[YD_t - (1 + \mu)YD_{t-1}] + v_t, \tag{13}$$

where v_t is defined by (9). If $\lambda = 0$, equation (13) reduces to (8). We notice that YD_t on the right-hand side of (13) is correlated with the surprise term e_t, which is a part of the error term v_t. The nonlinear restriction is that μ appears three times on the right-hand side of (13).

In sum, we are interested in two restrictions on the two-equation system consisting of (13) and (10). Our version of the permanent income hypothesis requires $\lambda = 0$. Flavin's version of the permanent income hypothesis requires $\mu = \rho$. The two-equation system will be estimated in the next section by NLIV with and without the two restrictions.

We close this section by mentioning another technical issue. The expression for the error term v_t and the definition of the error term ε_t imply that ε_t and v_t are potentially autocorrelated. If u_t is white noise, equation (9) implies that v_t is a first-order moving-average process since e_t is serially uncorrelated. Its first-order autocorrelation coefficient is

$$-(1 + \mu)\frac{x^2 + \alpha rx}{(\mu^2 + 2\mu + 2)x^2 + \alpha rx + \alpha^2}, \tag{14}$$

where r is the correlation coefficient between u_t and e_t and x is the ratio of $\text{var}(u_t)$ to $\text{var}(e_t)$. In order for v_t to be positively autocorrelated, we require that u_t and e_t be negatively correlated and the ratio x be less than $|\alpha r|$, which is possible but not likely. Similarly, we would expect ε_t to be negatively autocorrelated. In our model, the instruments Z_{t-1} can be correlated with v_{t-j} and ε_{t-j} ($j \geqq 1$), because the surprise term e_t and the unanticipated changes in asset prices can be correlated with current *and future* values of the instruments, Z_{t+j} ($j \geqq 0$). In other words, the instruments Z_{t-1} are not econometrically exogenous. In this case the conventional method of transforming the model by the square root of the inverse of the variance-covariance matrix of error terms introduces a bias into the parameter estimates, as Flood and Garber (1980) have shown. However, Hansen (1982) has shown that the instrumental variables estimator which ignores serial correlation is consistent and asymptotically normal under a certain set of regularity conditions.[12] He has also shown how to obtain a correct variance-covariance matrix of the estimator. Our estimation strategy, then, is to first estimate the two-equation system by NLIV disregarding serial correlation; if the residuals indicate a presence of serial correlation, then we can use Hansen's formula for calculating correct standard errors. As will be seen in the next section, the residuals calculated from the NLIV parameter estimates for the two-equation system (13) and (10), without the restriction $\lambda = 0$, do not indicate any significant autocorrelation, and hence we do not have to go through the correction for autocorrelation.

2.4 Empirical Results

This section estimates the parameters α, μ, ρ, and λ of the two-equation system consisting of (13) and (10) on the U.S. annual data for the sample period of 1948–78.[13] Our consumption concept is expenditures on nondurables and services plus service flows from consumer durables. Since c_t is the argument of the household's utility function, this consumption notion is the relevant one for the permanent income hypothesis. We use the real, per capita consumption series carefully constructed by Christensen and Jorgenson (1973 and updates). The six instruments we use for equations (13) and (10) are: the constant; import price index in year $t - 1$ divided by the price index p_{t-1} for consumption in year $t - 1$; per capita government expenditure in year $t - 1$ divided by p_{t-1}; per capita quantity index of exports in year $t - 1$; per capita transfer payments in year $t - 1$ divided by p_{t-1}; and per capita MIB at the beginning of year $t - 1$ divided by p_{t-2}.[14] The price index for consumption is used to convert A_t and y_t into real terms. See the data Appendix for a more complete description of the definitions of c, A, y, and the instruments.

The nonlinear instrumental variables (NLIV) estimator for the two-equation system minimizes

$$S = (\hat{v}', \hat{\varepsilon}')[\hat{\Sigma}^{-1} \otimes Z(Z'Z)^{-1}Z']\begin{pmatrix} \hat{v} \\ \hat{\varepsilon} \end{pmatrix}, \tag{15}$$

where $\hat{v}' = (\hat{v}_1, \ldots, \hat{v}_T), \hat{\varepsilon}' = (\hat{\varepsilon}_1, \ldots, \hat{\varepsilon}_T)$ are residuals, Z is a $T \times 6$ matrix whose tth row is Z_{t-1}, T is the sample size, and $\hat{\Sigma}$ is any consistent estimate of the variance-covariance matrix of (v_t, ε_t). As Hansen (1982) has shown, the NLIV estimator is consistent and asymptotically normal even though the instruments are not econometrically exogenous and (v_t, ε_t) is serially correlated. Strictly speaking, those real, per capita variables must be transformed to become stationary in order for the NLIV estimator to be asymptotically justifiable. For this reason, we transform the two-equation system by dividing both sides of (13) and (10) by $w_{t-1} = \exp[.022(t - 1)]$

to obtain:

$$c_t/w_{t-1} = (1 + \mu)(c_{t-1}/w_{t-1}) + \{\alpha[A_t - (1 + \mu)(A_{t-1} + y_{t-1})]/w_{t-1}\}$$

$$+ \{\lambda[YD_t - (1 + \mu)YD_{t-1}]/w_{t-1}\} + (v_t/w_{t-1}), \tag{13a}$$

$$A_t/w_{t-1} = (1 + \rho)[(A_{t-1} + y_{t-1} - c_{t-1})/w_{t-1}] + (\varepsilon_t/w_{t-1}). \tag{10a}$$

The growth rate 2.2 percent is the average rate of growth of real, per capita consumption during the sample period. The instruments Z_{t-1} are also deflated by w_{t-1}. We assume that c_t/w_t, A_t/w_t, y_t/w_t, YD_t/w_t, and the transformed instruments are jointly stationary and ergodic. Thus, the variables involved in the transformed two-equation system (13a) and (10a) are stationary, and the transformed error terms v_t/w_{t-1} and ε_t/w_{t-1} are homoscedastic. We will report the estimation results for the transformed real, per capita model in table 2.1. The corresponding results for the untransformed real, per capita model (13) and (10) can be found in table 2.3.

To form the quadratic form (15) for the transformed two-equation system, we need a consistent estimate $\hat{\Sigma}$ of the contemporaneous variance-covariance matrix of the transformed error terms v_t/w_{t-1} and ε_t/w_{t-1}. To this end, we estimate the two equations separately by the single-equation (nonlinear) instrumental variables technique with the same set of six instruments and take the sample variance-covariance matrix of the residuals as our estimate $\hat{\Sigma}$.[15] This $\hat{\Sigma}$ is reported in table 2.1. Line 1 of table 2.1 reports the NLIV estimates of α, μ, λ, and ρ that minimize the quadratic form (15) for the transformed two-equation system. The sample first-order autocorrelation coefficient is also calculated for each equation from the residuals given by the NLIV estimates and is reported in line 1.[16] As expected, the error term in each equation shows a mild negative—but not significant—autocorrelation. The reported standard errors are calculated with autocorrelation ignored, but they would not change by much had we taken the trouble of calculating correct standard errors. The point estimate of λ of 17.1 percent suggests a sizable share of the liquidity-constrained households in the population, but its t-statistic of .668 does not constitute a rejection of the permanent income hypothesis $\lambda = 0$.

To obtain another test statistic for the same hypothesis, we estimate the transformed two-equation system under the constraint $\lambda = 0$. The same consistent estimate $\hat{\Sigma}$ is used to form the quadratic form (15). The results are reported in line 2 of table 2.1. As Gallant and Jorgenson (1979) have shown, the difference between the minimized values of the quadratic form (15) with and without a set of restrictions is distributed as

Table 2.1
Parameter Estimates by Nonlinear Instrumental Variables

Line Number	Restriction	α	μ	ρ	λ	First-Order Autocorrelation Coefficient for Eq. (13a)	First-Order Autocorrelation Coefficient for Eq. (10a)	Minimized Value of Eq. (15)	Mean of c_t^*	Mean of A_t^*
1	None	.0674 (.0178)	.173 (.119)	.0340 (.00699)	.171 (.256)	−.132 (.180)	−.269 (.180)	15.77	2.14	10.08
2	$\lambda = 0$	.0687 (.0220)	.132 (.0573)	.0340 (.00699)	0	.127 (.180)	−.269 (.180)	16.27	2.14	10.08
3	$\mu = \rho$	.0165 (.00832)	.0382 (.00678)	.0382 (.00678)	−.0522 (.255)	.415 (.180)	−.257 (.180)	21.81	2.14	10.08
4	$\lambda = 0$ and $\mu = \rho$	.0156 (.00723)	.0381 (.00678)	.0381 (.00678)	0	.421 (.180)	−.257 (.180)	21.85	2.14	10.08
5	None	.0183 (.0184)	−.197 (.138)	...	.892 (.0460)	−.0962 (.180)	...	...	2.06	...

$$\hat{\Sigma} = \begin{pmatrix} .00081548 & -.0055653 \\ & .14411 \end{pmatrix}, \text{ correlation coefficient} = -.513$$

Notes: Numbers in parentheses are standard errors calculated on the assumption that error terms are serially uncorrelated. The consumption measure in line 5 is NIPA's personal consumption expenditures. Line 1–4 use the same consistent estimate $\hat{\Sigma}$ reported above to form the quadratic form (15). For the reason mentioned in the text, equation (10a) is not estimated in line 5.
* $t = 1948, \ldots, 1978$.

chi-squared with the degrees of freedom equal to the number of restrictions. Lines 1 and 2 of table 2.1 also report the minimized value of (15). The difference is only 0.50, and the hypothesis can be accepted at any reasonable level of significance. The estimates of α, μ, and ρ are very plausible from the viewpoint of the permanent income hypothesis, and the sample first-order autocorrelation coefficients for the two equations do not indicate any strong sign of autocorrelation. Our estimate of μ of 13.2 percent is very different from our estimate of ρ of 3.4 percent. To test the restriction $\mu = \rho$, we calculated the t-statistic for $\hat{\mu} - \hat{\rho}$ from the estimated variance-covariance matrix of estimated parameters $\hat{\mu}$ and $\hat{\rho}$. It turned out to be 1.58. On this statistic we cannot reject $\mu = \rho$ at the 10 percent significance level.[17]

Line 3 of table 2.1 reports the parameter estimates under the restriction $\mu = \rho$. The residuals for (13a) now indicate a positive and significant autocorrelation, which suggests that the model with $\mu = \rho$ is a misspecification. The minimized value of the quadratic form is higher than the one in line 1 by 6.04. Since this difference is distributed as chi-squared with one degree of freedom under $\mu = \rho$, the hypothesis $\mu = \rho$ can be rejected at the 2.5 percent level of significance based on this statistic. The parameter estimates under the joint restriction $\mu = \rho$ and $\lambda = 0$ are presented in line 4. Again, the residuals for (13a) show a positive and significant autocorrelation. The difference between the minimized values of the quadratic form with and without the joint restriction $\mu = \rho$ and $\lambda = 0$ is distributed as chi-squared with two degrees of freedom. The difference is equal to 6.08, so we can reject the joint hypothesis $\mu = \rho$ and $\lambda = 0$ at 5 percent. Clearly the restriction $\mu = \rho$ is responsible for the rejection of the joint hypothesis.

To summarize, the permanent income hypothesis $\lambda = 0$ stands quite well on our data, while the hypothesis that the discount rate for future labor income is equal to the real rate of return from human wealth can be rejected rather decisively. However, at this point, we recall that our measure of consumption has been the sum of expenditures on nondurables and services and imputed service flows from consumer durables. It may be argued that the relevant measure of consumption for the liquidity-constrained households is personal consumption expenditures as defined in the National Income and Product Accounts (NIPA), which *excludes* service flows from consumer durables and *includes* expenditures on consumer durables. The foregoing test of the permanent income hypothesis seems to be in some sense unfair to the alternative hypothesis of liquidity constraints. For this reason, we estimate the first equation (13a) of the transformed model using the NIPA's personal consumption expenditures as the measure of consumption. The same six instruments are used, and the implicit price deflator for personal consumption expenditure is used to convert the variables (including the instruments) into real quantities. The relevant notion of consumption in equation (10a) should be the one that includes imputed service flows and excludes expenditures on consumer durables, since our definition of nonhuman wealth includes the stock of consumer durables. This is the reason we estimate α, μ, and λ on equation (13a) by the single-equation instrumental variables technique rather than carry out the joint estimation of the two-equation system. The NLIV estimates of α, μ, and λ which minimize the quadratic form $\hat{v}'Z(Z'Z)^{-1}Z'\hat{v}$ for (13a) are presented in line 5 of table 2.1. They are drastically different from those in line 1: μ picked up the wrong but insignificant sign, α is insignificantly different from 0, and λ is very high, which implies that the bulk of changes in personal consumption expenditure is explained by changes in disposable income. For example, in 1978 personal consumption expenditures was \$1,351 billion and disposable income was \$1,458 billion. Our estimate of λ of 89.2 percent implies that about 96 percent (\$1,301 billion) of personal consumption expenditures is due to the liquidity-constrained households. This can be viewed as a strong confirmation of the presence of the liquidity-constrained households.

To indicate that the above results do not depend on our particular choice of instruments, the same equations are estimated by nonlinear regression, which maximizes the quadratic form (15) with Z replaced by the identity matrix. The results are given in table 2.2. Each line in table 2.2 corresponds to the same line in table 2.1. The same conclusion—that the permanent income hypothesis is supported on one measure of consumption and decisively rejected on the other measure of consumption— emerges from table 2.2. Also, to indicate that our conclusion does not depend on our particular way of transforming the model, the real, per capita model (13) and (10) is estimated by the NLIV technique. The results are reported in table 2.2, whose lines correspond to those in table 2.3. They are very similar to those in table 2.1. The main differences are that the residuals show less serial correlation and that the hypothesis $\mu = \rho$ can also be rejected on the t-statistic for $\hat{\mu} - \hat{\rho}$.

2.5 Concluding Remarks

In this chapter the permanent income hypothesis with rational expectations is restated, estimated, and tested. Our test of the hypothesis

Table 2.2
Parameter Estimates by Nonlinear Regression

Line Number	Restriction	α	μ	ρ	λ	Durbin-Watson Statistic for Eq. (13a)	Durbin-Watson Statistic for Eq. (10a)
1	None	.0325 (.0106)	.0640 (.0154)	.0332 (.00699)	.0456 (.0780)	1.14	2.52
2	$\lambda = 0$	.0355 (.00953)	.0659 (.0148)	.0332 (.00699)	0	1.08	2.52
3	$\mu = \rho$	.00961 (.00516)	.0332 (.0624)	.0332 (.00624)	.0470 (.0748)	1.17	2.52
4	$\lambda = 0$ and $\mu = \rho$	.0105 (.00498)	.0336 (.00610)	.0336 (.00610)	0	1.16	2.52
5	None	.0187 (.0106)	−.364 (.109)	...	.861 (.0307)	2.07	...

Notes: Numbers in parentheses are standard errors calculated on the assumption that error terms are not serially correlated. The consumption measure in line 5 is the NIPA's personal consumption expenditures. The parameter estimates in line 5 minimize the sum of squared residuals for (13a). The parameter estimates in lines 1–4 minimize the quadratic form (15) with Z replaced by the identity matrix. $\hat{\Sigma}$ is estimated from the residuals from single-equation regressions.

Table 2.3
Parameter Estimates for the Untransformed Model by NLIV

Line Number	Restriction	α	μ	ρ	λ	First-Order Autocorrelation Coefficient for Eq. (13)	First-Order Autocorrelation Coefficient for Eq. (10)	Minimized Value of Eq. (15)	Mean of c_t^*	Mean of A_t^*
1	None	.0829 (.0153)	.219 (.119)	.0326 (.00676)	.0998 (.261)	−.0992 (.180)	−.203 (.180)	14.61	2.97	13.99
2	$\lambda = 0$	.0855 (.0162)	.189 (.0600)	.0325 (.00676)	0	−.000224 (.180)	−.203 (.180)	14.76	2.97	13.99
3	$\mu = \rho$	.0206 (.0101)	.0379 (.00647)	.0379 (.00647)	−.466 (.317)	.0482 (.180)	−.182 (.180)	23.61	2.97	13.99
4	$\lambda = 0$ and $\mu = \rho$	.0134 (.00722)	.0377 (.00655)	.0377 (.00655)	0	.337 (.180)	−.184 (.180)	25.85	2.97	13.99
5	None	.0173 (.0179)	−.109 (.181)	...	.943 (.147)	.205 (.180)	...	...	2.86	...

$$\hat{\Sigma} = \begin{pmatrix} .0019300 & -.011634 \\ & .2702 \end{pmatrix}, \text{ correlation coefficient} = -.510$$

*$t = 1948, \ldots, 1978$.

depends very much on the choice of the consumption measure. The fact that we were able to reject the hypothesis on the NIPA's consumption measure may not be really surprising, because it is not the consumption measure that the permanent income hypothesis purports to explain. What is surprising is the high estimate of λ which dwarfs almost all movements in the consumption measure. On the other hand, we should note that the reason we could not reject the hypothesis on the other measure of consumption which includes service flows from consumer durables is the rather high standard error of our estimate of λ. Our point estimate of λ does indicate a sizable fraction of the liquidity-constrained households in the population.

A picture of the consumption behavior that emerges from our empirical results would be the following. Perhaps the majority of the households in the population are the forward-looking consumers envisioned by the permanent income hypothesis trying to shield the flow of consumption from short-run fluctuations in their disposable income. If there were perfect rental markets for consumer durables, the timing of consumer durables purchases would be immaterial for the households. Consumer durables in reality are illiquid, so that each household must derive most of the flow of consumer durables from its own holdings. Furthermore, capital markets are imperfect in that the borrowing rates are substantially higher than the lending rates. Under these circumstances, the best policy for those forward-looking households would be to let lumpy purchases of consumer durables be correlated with the short-run fluctuations in disposable income in order to minimize the borrowing necessary to finance purchases of consumer durables. Since consumption expenditures by the rest of the households are largely determined by their disposable income, aggregate consumption expenditure as defined by the NIPA can be highly correlated with aggregate disposable income. This, however, does not necessarily mean that aggregate flow of consumption is largely a function of disposable income. For each household, changes in the flow of consumer durables services due to lumpy consumer durables purchases can be partially offset by changes in expenditures on nondurables and services. In the aggregate, expenditures on consumer durables are only a fraction of the aggregate stock of consumer durables. Therefore, aggregate flow of consumption, which includes service flows from consumer durables and excludes durables purchases, can behave in a manner quite different from personal consumption expenditures in terms of its relation to disposable income.

This interpretation of our empirical results suggests that the government can control aggregate demand in the short run through its effects on consumption expenditures by the liquidity-constrained and durables expenditures by the wealth-constrained households, which are important components of aggregate demand. Policies which affect credit conditions and/or disposable income would be effective. The important point to notice is that the effectiveness of those policies does not depend on whether they are anticipated or not. For example, a fully anticipated tax cut can influence those components of aggregate demand when it is enacted—even though it has no noticeable effects on permanent income.

Appendix

Description of Data

Nonhuman Wealth
Nonhuman wealth is defined as the sum of the following two items: (1) net financial assets of households at the beginning of the year (source: *Flow of Funds Accounts*); and (2) noncorporate and household capital at replacement cost (source: Christensen and Jorgenson [1973 and updates, table 8]). Item 1 above includes demand deposits and currency, time and savings accounts, public debt, corporate equities, and corporate and foreign bonds. It should be noted that public debt and corporate and foreign bonds are evaluated at face value. Corporate equities are valued at market prices. The computation of item 2 implicitly assumes that there is no substantial discrepancy between the market value and the replacement costs of noncorporate and household capital. Since most of noncorporate and household capital consists of residential structures and consumer durables, this seems to be a reasonable assumption. The data on nonhuman wealth are reproduced in table 2.A1.

Consumption
Consumption is defined as personal consumption expenditures on services and nondurables plus the value of service flows from consumer durables. The consumption series is taken from Christensen and Jorgenson (1973 and updates, table 17) and is reproduced at the end of this Appendix. The National Income and Product Accounts (NIPA) consumption data, called personal consumption expenditures, are taken from table B-2 of *Economic Report of the President* (1980). They are in billions of 1972 dollars. Note

Table 2.A1

Year	A	CON	YL	PC	EX	IMP
1947	709.904	159.796	146.710	.519588	28.2719	.630325
1948	749.610	171.558	161.472	.544995	21.9320	.667549
1949	774.794	174.059	164.422	.538226	21.9657	.633251
1950	827.039	185.757	180.756	.549831	19.5598	.689820
1951	920.268	205.170	196.978	.585142	23.8675	.825251
1952	988.164	221.217	209.236	.606031	22.9719	.794814
1953	1,034.91	228.415	223.925	.607182	21.6309	758736
1954	1,062.91	243.444	227.422	.630681	22.7719	.771752
1955	1,187.46	253.671	242.796	.627833	25.3173	.774037
1956	1,317.70	268.833	259.376	.638227	29.2881	.787940
1957	1,400.39	278.559	272.199	.643046	31.6641	.801365
1958	1,418.51	300.401	278.313	.675624	27.4528	.772226
1959	1,587.77	313.647	296.772	.678481	28.0063	.770122
1960	1,669.96	332.879	308.778	.698678	32.1505	.781740
1961	1,718.78	347.050	319.963	.708394	32.5056	.776148
1962	1,874.76	362.977	337.469	.716886	34.3532	.762781
1963	1,876.74	378.161	351.645	.724486	36.7182	.774355
1964	2,029.19	405.356	380.131	.739038	41.2142	.792174
1965	2,176.29	438.662	406.534	.762510	42.0909	.805602
1966	2,356.02	473.441	438.265	.784118	44.9876	.820923
1967	2,410.54	500.541	469.535	.798221	46.9537	.822164
1968	2,713.98	540.715	511.518	.825612	50.4602	.830516
1969	3,026.67	598.870	553.294	.879323	52.9000	.875729
1970	3,043.46	628.585	603.289	.897942	57.8925	.933581
1971	3,225.43	683.569	656.414	.948880	58.4460	.982109
1972	3,566.91	755.839	708.951	1.00000	63.2460	1.04073
1973	3,981.77	848.907	787.457	1.07245	76.6761	1.22459
1974	4,152.04	916.933	866.915	1.15308	82.8827	1.75560
1975	4,292.45	994.453	959.672	1.21760	81.9049	1.95413
1976	4,868.40	1,122.04	1,052.44	1.30249	85.9343	1.96786
1977	5,494.96	1,266.07	1,159.28	1.40801	87.6909	2.15698
1978	6,019.72	1,414.72	1,288.54	1.50779	96.5916	2.28559

Note: A = nonhuman wealth in billions of current dollars; CON = consumption in billions of current dollars; YL = labor income in billions of current dollars; PC = price index for consumption; EX = quantity index of exports; IMP = imports price index. See the Appendix for the definitions and sources of these variables.

that the NIPA consumption data *include* expenditures on durables and *exclude* service flows from durables.

Labor Income
Labor income after tax is defined as follows:

(1) earnings after income tax (source: Christensen and Jorgenson [1973 and updates, table 4])

+ (2) government transfer payments to persons (source: *Survey of Current Business*, table 3.12, line 1)

− (3) personal transfer payments to foreigners (source: *Survey of Current Business*, table 4.1, line 11)

− (4) personal nontax payments (source: *Survey of Current Business*, table 3.2, line 8, plus table 3.4, line 8)

− (5) contributions to social insurance (source: *Survey of Current Business*, table 3.11, line 1).

The basic assumptions in computing 1 are: (*a*) for each sector of the economy the average labor compensation of proprietors and unpaid family workers is equal to the average labor compensation of full-time equivalent employees in the same sector, and (*b*) personal income tax on earnings is 75 percent of total personal income. Since 2 includes social security benefits, social security wealth is included as part of human wealth. The data on labor income are reproduced in table 2.A1.

Price Index for Consumption
This is defined as the ratio of the value of consumption to the Divisia quantity index of components of consumption. This is taken from Christensen and Jorgenson (1973 and updates, table 4) and is reproduced in table 2.A1. When the NIPA definition of consumption is the relevant notion of consumption, we take the NIPA's implicit price deflator for personal consumption expenditures as the price index for consumption. The implicit deflator is taken from table B-3 of *Economic Report of the President* (1980).

Instruments
The definitions and data sources of our instrments are as follows:

1. MIB at the beginning of the year in billions of current dollars (source: table B-58 of *Eonomic Report of the President* [1980]).

2. Federal purchases of goods and serices (source: *Survey of Current Business*, table 3.2, line 22), plus state and local governments' purchases of goods and services (source: *Survey of Current Business*, table 3.4, line 39).

3. Government transfer payments to persons (*Survey of Current Business*, table 3.12, line 1), minus federal social insurance benefits (*SCB*, table 3.12, line 3), minus stae and local social insurance benefits (*SCB*, table 3.12, line 29), minus personal transfer payments to foreigners (*SCB*, table 4.1, line 7), minus personal nontaxes (*SCB*, table 3.2, line 8 plus table 3.4, line 8).

4. Divisia quantity index of exports of consumption and investment goods (source: Christensen and Jorgenson [1973 and updates]).

5. Divisia price index of import prices of consumption and investment goods (source: Christensen and Jorgenson [1973 and updates]).

Variables 1, 2, 3, and 5 are divided by the relevant price index for consumption to obtain real quantities. Variables 1, 2, 3, and 4, are divided by the population of the United States in milliions (source: table B-26 of *Economic Report of the President* [1980]) to obtain per capita values. The data on 4 and 5 are reproduced in table A1. The constant (one for all years) is added to the list of instruments, so the number of instruments is six in all.

Disposable Income
The data on disposable income are taken from table B-8 of *Economic Report of the President* (1980).

Notes

I am grateful to Dale W. Jorgenson and Olivier J. Blanchard for discussions relating to the present topic. Marjorie Flavin, Craig Hakkio, Robert Hall, Leonard Mirman, Aba Schwartz, Larry Summers, and anonymous referees provided useful comments on earlier drafts. Remaining errors are mine.

1. In contrast, nonhuman wealth is explicitly treated in our estimation equation.

2. We make this assumption because of the lack of reliable data on the expected real rate of interest.

3. The parameters β (the relative degree of risk aversion) and δ (the rate of time preference) can be estimated under the labor income uncertainty by estimating the Euler equation. This has been done by Hasen and Singleton (1982). Their estimation method would require that consumption be measured without error and that aggregate (as opposed to individual) consumption satisfy the Euler equation for the representative household.

4. The idea of adding risk premium to the discount rate can be rigorously justified in the case where the utility funciton shows a constant absolute degree of risk aversion, as shown by Merton (1971). See also Nagatani (1972) for an intuitive justification. An implicit assumption

behind the positive risk premium is that the variance of future income y_{t+k} conditional on information available at t increases as k increases.

5. No attempt is made in this paper to estimate those specific discount rates. An interesting agenda for future research would be to identify two specific discount rates, one for before-tax labor income and the other one for future tax liability.

6. The n variables that constitute the autoregressive process must exhaust all variables that influence future after-tax labor income in order for the Hansen-Sargent maximum likelihood method to be applicable. Receent work by Hansen and Sargent (1982) shows that this requirement can be relaxed.

7. This method was first presented in Hayashi (1979).

8. The same equation for Tobin's q has been derived by Abel (1977, 1980).

9. The two papers assume that the instruments are econometrically exogenous. Hansen (1982) has shown that the NLIV estimator can be applied to a more general case where the instruments are not exogenous but merely predetermined.

10. Anticipated movements in asset prices are absorbed in the expected real rate of return.

11. Flavin (1981) assumes that there are no measurement errors so that $v_t + \alpha \varepsilon_t$ is white noise.

12. The regularity condition is satisfied if the relevant variables are jointly stationary and ergodic and the error term has a moving average structure.

13. Our data do not reflect the December 1980 revision of the National Income and Product Accounts. The statistical package we use if TSP (time-series processor) version 3.5B.

14. Since the value of MIB at the beginning of year $t - 1$ is predetermined for year $t - 1$, the use of p_{t-1} instead of p_{t-2} will make the real money stock endogenous.

15. The estimates given by the single-equation method are similar to those in line 1 of table 1, except that the single-equation estimate of $\lambda = .285$ is somewhat higher.

16. The sample first-order autocorrelation coefficient is asymptotically normal with mean zero and variance T^{-1} (where T is the sample size) under the assumption of no serial correlation.

17. Strictly speaking, ρ is equal to the real rate of return from nonhuman wealth minus the rate of population growth, since the variables are deflated by population.

References

Abel, Andrew B. "Investment and the Value of Capital." Ph.D. dissertation, Massachusetts Inst. Tech., 1977.

————. "Empirical Investment Equations: An Integrative Framework." *Carnegie-Rochester Conference Series on Public Policy*, a supplementary series to the *J. Monetary Econ.* 12 (Spring 1980): 39–91.

Amemiya, Takeshi. "The Nonlinear Two-Stage Least Squares Estimator." *J. Econometrics* 2 (July 1974): 105–10.

Barro, Robert J. "Are Government Bonds Net Wealth?" *J.P.E.* 82, no. 6 (November/December 1974): 1095–1117.

Christensen, Laurits R., and Jorgenson, Dale W. "Measuring Economic Performance in the Private Sector." In *The Measurement of Economic and Social Performance*, edited by Milton Moss. New York: Columbia Univ. Press (for Nat. Bur. Econ. Res.), 1973.

Davidson, Russell, and MacKinnon, James G. "Several Tests for Model Specification in the Presence of Alternative Hypotheses." *Econometrica* 49 (May 1981): 781–93.

Flavin, Marjorie A. "The Adjustment of Consumption to Changing Expectations about Future Income." *J.P.E.* 89, no. 5 (October 1981): 974–1009.

Flood, Robert P., and Garber, Peter M. "A Pitfall in Estimation of Models with Rational Expectations." *J. Monetary Econ.* 6 (July 1980): 433–35.

Friedman, Milton. *A Theory of the Consumption Function*. Princeton, N.J.: Princeton Univ. Press, 1957.

———. "Windfalls, the 'Horizon,' and Related Concepts in the Permanent Income Hypothesis." In *Measurements in Economics: Studies in Mathematical Economics and Econometrics in Memory of Yehuda Grunfeld*, edited by Carl F. Christ. Stanford, Calif.: Stanford Univ. Press, 1963.

Gallant, A. Ronald, and Jorgenson, Dale W. "Statistical Inference for a System of Simultaneous, Non-linear, Implicit Equations in the Context of Instrumental Variable Estimation." *J. Econometrics* 11 (October/December 1979): 275–302.

Hakansson, Nils H. "Optimal Investment and Consumption Strategies under Risk for a Class of Utility Functions." *Econometrica* 38 (September 1970): 587–607.

Hall, Robert E. "Stochastic Implications of the Life Cycle–Permanent Income Hypothesis: Theory and Evidence." *J.P.E.* 86, no. 6 (December 1978): 971–87.

Hansen, Lars P. "Large Sample Properties of Generalized Method of Moments Estimators." *Econometrica* 50 (July 1982): 1029–54.

Hansen, Lars P., and Sargent, Thomas J. "Formulating and Estimating Dynamic Linear Rational Expectations Models." *J. Econ. Dynamics and Control* 2 (February 1980): 7–46.

———. "Instrumental Variables Procedure for Estimating Linear Rational Expectations Models." *J. Monetary Econ.* 9, no. 3 (May 1982): 263–96.

Hansen, Lars P., and Singleton, Kenneth J. "Generalized Instrumental Variables Estimation of Nonlinear Rational Expectations Models." *Econometrica* 50, no. 5 (September 1982): 1269–86.

Hayashi, Fumio. "A New Estimation Procedure under Rational Expectations." *Econ Letters* 4, no. 1 (1979): 41–43.

Jorgenson, Dale W., and Laffont, Jean-Jacques. "Efficient Estimation of Nonlinear Simultaneous Equations with Additive Disturbances." *Annals Econ. and Soc. Measurement* 3 (October 1974): 615–40.

Lucas, Robert E., Jr. "Economic Policy Evaluation: A Critique." In *The Phillips Curve and Labor Markets*, edited by Karl Brunner and Allan H. Meltzer. Amsterdam: North-Holland, 1976.

Merton, Robert C. "Optimum Consumption and Portfolio Rules in a Continuous-Time Model." *J. Econ. Theory* 3 (December 1971): 373–413.

Miller, Bruce L. "Optimal Consumption with a Stochastic Income Stream." *Econometrica* 42 (March 1974): 253–66.

Muth, John F. "Rational Expectations and the Theory of Price Movements." *Econometrica* 29 (July 1961): 315–35.

Nagatani, Keizo. "Life Cycle Saving: Theory and Fact." *A.E.R.* 62 (June 1972): 344–53.

Sandmo, Agnar. "The Effect of Uncertainty on Saving Decisions." *Rev. Econ. Studies* 37 (July 1970): 353–60.

Sargent, Thomas J. "Rational Expectations, Econometric Exogeneity, and Consumption." *J.P.E.* 86, no. 4 (August 1978): 673–700.

Schechtman, Jack. "On the Effect of Uncertainty on the Consumer Behavior." Mimeographed. Rio de Janeiro: Instituto de Matematica Pura e Applicada.

Addendum to Chapter 2:
Estimation Using
Updated Data

After the original publication of this chapter, it was pointed out by Arlie Sterling of Marsoft that the parameter estimates may be imprecise due to an inadvertently loose convergence criterion. Because the model is non-linear in parameters, it requires an iterative method to find the maximum of the objective function (15). A hazardous aspect of the statistical package I used (TSP version 3.5B) that I was not aware of is that the convergence criterion switches from relative to absolute when the parameter in the iteration is below one. For example, if the convergence criterion is 1 percent and the parameter changes from 0.078 to 0.087 during the iteration, the convergence is deemed complete because the change in the parameter is less than 0.01 even though the percentage change of the parameter is much greater than 1 percent.

To correct this potential problem, I reestimated all the parameters shown in chapter 2. This time I write out the equation in the program so that the parameters are stated in percents. I also tighten the convergence criterion and set it at 0.0001 percent. Fortunately, the new estimates are not very different from those shown in the chapter with the first two significant digits generally unchanged.[1] For example, the estimates in the first line of the addendum table are now: $\hat{\alpha} = 0.0655$ (0.0177), $\hat{\mu} = 0.173$ (0.121), $\hat{\rho} = 0.0340$ (0.00711), $\hat{\lambda} = 0.192$ (0.248), with the residual covariance from the first-stage IV estimation of each equation given by

$$\hat{\Sigma} = \begin{bmatrix} 0.00077581 & -0.0052442 \\ -0.0052442 & 0.14891 \end{bmatrix}.$$

With the passage of fourteen years after the publication, it is of some interest to estimate the same model using updated data. As explained in the appendix to the chapter, some of the series for estimation came from the database developed by Lautis Christensen and Dale Jorgenson. The

Addendum Table
Parameter Estimates by Nonlinear Instrumental Variables Updated to 1992

Line no.	Restriction	α	μ	ρ	λ	Minimized value of eq. (15)
1	none	0.0027 (0.0175)	0.0263 (0.0361)	0.0370 (0.00525)	0.479 (0.114)	10.51
2	$\lambda = 0$	0.0471 (0.0225)	0.0812 (0.0410)	0.0370 (0.00525)	0	25.53
3	$\mu = \rho$	0.0077 (0.0033)	0.0368 (0.00521)	0.0368 (0.00521)	0.465 (0.111)	10.59
4	$\mu = 0$ and $\mu = \rho$	0.0183 (0.0044)	0.0388 (0.0052)	0.0388 (0.0052)	0	28.01
5	none	0.0138 (0.0174)	−0.307 (0.123)	—	0.867 (0.0573)	—

$$\hat{\Sigma} = \begin{bmatrix} 0.0029977 & 0.0052756 \\ 0.0052756 & 1.08462 \end{bmatrix}, \text{ correlation coefficient} = 0.093$$

Note: See notes to table 2.1. Here, $t = 1948, \ldots, 1992$. First-order autocorrelations are not shown here because they are small and insignificant.

data on those series updated to 1992 have been kindly made available to me by Dale Jorgenson. Since they are derived from the NIPA before the 1995 Comprehensive Revision, I use the NIPA before the Revision for the other series that are directly available from the NIPA. Data on net financial assets of households are taken from the March 4 edition of the *Balance Sheets for the U.S. Economy 1945–93* compiled by the Board of Governors of the Federal Reserve System.

Besides the longer sample period and minor revisions of the NIPA since the publication of the chapter, the updated data differ from the data used in the chapter in three respects. (1) A weighted average of stock and bond returns is used to value the service flow from consumer durables implicit in the consumption measure in the updated Jorgenson's database; in the original database, the rental rate for commercial office space was used. (2) Since the net financial assets of households in the *Balance Sheets* now includes equity in noncorporate businesses, nonhuman wealth is now defined as the sum of the net financial assets from the *Balance Sheets* and the replacement costs of household capital from the Jorgenson database. (3) The w_{t-1} in (13a) and (10a) is now $\exp[0.020(t-1)]$ rather than $\exp[0.022(t-1)]$ to reflect recent slower growth.

Table 2.A1 updates table 2.1 to 1992. It displays the estimated parameters of the two-equation system (13a) and (10a) for $t = 1948, \ldots, 1992$.

Now the λ parameter is much higher and highly significant. This is reflected in the large increase in the objective function (15) in line 2 when $\lambda = 0$ is imposed. Unlike in table 2.1, the $\mu = \rho$ restriction is easily accepted with only a very slight increase in the objective function in line 3, which means that the risk premium $\mu - \rho$ is hardly significant. On the other hand, the results shown in line 5 for the case where the consumption measure is the NIPA's personal consumption expenditure are very similar to those in table 2.1.

Estimation of the two-equation system using the updated data for the old sample period of 1948–78 produces results similar to those in Table 2A.1. A process of replacing a subset of series in the old data by those from the new data and estimating the system for 1948–78 has revealed that the culprit is the new consumption measure. If the consumption series and the associated price index from the new data replace the consumption series and the price index in the old data with the other series in the old data kept intact, the estimate of λ jumps up from 0.191 to 0.429 with a standard error of 0.166. But perhaps this is not surprising after all, given the result in table 2.1 that the use of the NIPA's personal consumption expenditure raises the estimate of λ from below 0.2 to about 0.9.

Note

1. Contrary to the notes to table 2.2, $\hat{\Sigma}$ was fixed in the iteration to obtain the nonlinear regression estimates in table 2.2, as in table 2.1.

3

The Effect of Liquidity Constraints on Consumption: A Cross-Sectional Analysis

3.1 Introduction

The basic postulate of the life cycle–permanent income hypothesis (here-after to be called the permanent income hypothesis) is that households behave as if they maximize a lifetime utility function subject only to the lifetime budget constraint without being constrained by imperfect capital markets. This postulate, if true, casts serious doubts on the effectiveness of macroeconomic stabilization policies such as temporary tax cuts. If, on the other hand, households are subject to borrowing constraints (or, to use James Tobin's terminology, liquidity constraints), then short-run sta-bilization policies will have some influence on aggregate demand.[1]

Because of the forward-looking nature of the permanent income hy-pothesis, convincing empirical testing of the postulate is impossible, unless the hypothesis is coupled with a sensible assumption about how expec-tations are formed. Recently, Hall (1978), Sargent (1978), Flavin (1981), and Hayashi (1982) have tested the hypothesis on U. S. aggregate time-series data under the assumption of rational expectations. Their test results are mixed, mainly due to the low power of time-series tests.

Subsequently, Hall and Mishkin (1982) turned to panel data to find that food consumption is more sensitive to current disposable income than is predicted by the hypothesis. This work is followed by Bernanke (1984) who examined expenditure on automobiles using a different data set. He found no evidence against the permanent income hypothesis.

The basic testing strategy common to the above-mentioned work is to look at the relationship between current disposable income and *changes* in consumption from current period to the next. The permanent income hy-

Originally published in *The Quarterly Journal of Economics* 100 (February 1985): 183–206. Reprinted with the permission of The MIT Press.

pothesis (cum rational expectations) predicts no correlation between the two; a statistically significant correlation would imply that households are liquidity constrained. It would be highly desirable to extend this analysis to total consumption (as opposed to food consumption or durable goods expenditure), but unfortunately no panel data exist in the United States for total consumption for more than one period. Cross-section data on total consumption do exist, but one needs a different line of approach to test the hypothesis on such data.

A natural approach would be to derive the consumption function (i.e., the optimal consumption rule) for a model, which includes the permanent income hypothesis as a special case and in which borrowing constraints are superimposed, and then to test the restriction implied by the permanent income hypothesis. There are at least two problems with this approach. First, we have the familiar problem that we, as econometricians, cannot observe the household's expectations about future income, so that any variable that helps predict future income can show up in the consumption function, which makes it very difficult to test the restriction implied by the permanent income hypothesis. Second, the permanent income hypothesis does not deliver an explicit optimal consumption rule for the *level* of consumption. Even under the assumption that the lifetime utility function is time-separable with a constant degree of relative risk aversion, no closed-form solution for optimal consumption has been derived when future labor income is uncertain. Moreover, the permanent income hypothesis is not very specific about how the family structure should be incorporated in the consumption function. The problem becomes even less tractable if the additional constraint of imperfect capital markets is superimposed on the permanent income hypothesis.

This chapter is an attempt to test the permanent income hypothesis and evaluate the quantitative importance of liquidity constraints using a single-year cross-section data set complied by the Board of Governors, Federal Reserve System in the early 1960s. As in Kowalewski and Smith (1979), the basic idea is to separate the sample into high-saving households and low-saving households and presume that the high-saving households are not liquidity constrained.[2] A very general reduced form equation for consumption is estimated for such households by the Tobit procedure. We use Tobit because the sample separation is based on the dependent variable (i.e., consumption). The same equation is estimated by OLS (ordinary least squares) on the whole sample. If the two estimates of the same equation for consumption are different, a natural interpretation is that some of the households in the sample are liquidity constrained. A statistical test of this can be carried out using a Hausman (1978)-type specification test. Since the Tobit estimate of the reduced-form equation is consistent even if some of the households in the population (from which the sample was drawn) are subject to liquidity constraints, we can use it to predict desired consumption, namely the level of consumption that would prevail if there were no liquidity constraints in the current period. The advantages of this line of approach are (i) that the test procedure is valid even if measurement error (for consumption) has a nonzero mean or is correlated with the variables on the right-hand side of the reduced-form equation; (ii) that we do not pretend to have a specific form of the optimal consumption rule; and (iii) that, in the event of a (statistical) rejection of the permanent income hypothesis, we can get some quantitative indication as to what extent the permanent income hypothesis deviates from the data.

The plan of this chapter is as follows. Section 3.2 discusses some theoretical issues about the formulation of the permanent income hypothesis and its extension to liquidity constraints. Section 3.3 presents the reduced-form equation and explains how the Tobit procedure can be consistently applied to estimate the reduced-form equation in the presence of liquidity constraints. Section 3.4 is a brief description of the data. In Section 3.5 parameter estimates by OLS and Tobit are presented, and the Hausman test of the permanent income hypothesis is carried out. We then calculate desired consumption predicted by the Tobit estimate of the reduced-form equation and compare it with actual consumption. Also in Section 3.5 a diagnostic test of the normality and homoskedasticity assumptions that are used to justify the Tobit procedure is also undertaken. Section 3.6 contains concluding remarks and qualifications.

3.2 A Theoretical Discussion

In this chapter the permanent income hypothesis is assumed to be the hypothesis that the household maximizes its lifetime utility function (i.e., the expected value of the discounted sum of current and future utilities) subject only to the lifetime budget constraint.[3] The important assumption here is that the household can borrow or lend as much as it desires at a fixed interest rate; i.e., capital markets are perfect. This may be an unrealistic assumption, and we would like to test its validity. A more general hypothesis, which we shall call the hypothesis of liquidity constraints, is that the household maximizes the same lifetime utility function subject to the lifetime budget constraint and to the additional constraint that consumption c cannot exceed some upper bound exogenously given to the household:

$$c_{t+i} \leqslant k_{t+i} \quad (i = 0, 1, 2, \ldots), \tag{1}$$

where the subscript t represents the current year. This hypothesis is more general than the permanent income hypothesis because if the upper bound k is sufficiently large, it reduces to the permanent income hypothesis.[4] Since the permanent income hypothesis is a special case of the alternative hypothesis of liquidity constraints, a natural approach for testing the permanent income hypothesis would be to derive the optimal consumption rule (i.e., the consumption function) for the hypothesis of liquidity constraints and test the restriction implied by the permanent income hypothesis. In particular, one might want to test the well-known restriction that consumption depends only on "permanent income."[5] There are several theoretical and practical problems associated with this approach, especially when we do not have longitudinal data on consumption.[6] First, if the family size affects the lifetime utility, the consumption function will depend on the future family size planned by the household. Such information is not usually available.

Second, neither human wealth nor permanent income is observable. Since they depend on expectations about future income, any variables that help predict future income will show up in the consumption function if neither human wealth nor permanent income is included on the right-hand side. One way to get around this is to specify explicitly a stochastic process for after-tax labor income and find a closed-form representation of human wealth as a distributed lag function of current and past labor income.[7] A practical problem with this is that we need longitudinal information on after-tax labor income extending for more than a few years back in order to obtain a realistic distributed lag representation of human wealth. A theoretical problem is the fact that income tax is a nonlinear function of the household's income. Since nonlabor income is a part of the household's income, the stochastic process for *after-tax* labor income is necessarily affected by the planned time path of saving. It follows from this that human wealth will depend on assets in a nonlinear fashion as well as on current and past labor income.

Third, the permanent income hypothesis (let alone the hypothesis of liquidity constraints) does not deliver a closed-form solution for the optimal consumption if future labor income is uncertain or stochastic. In fact, it seems that no operational definition of permanent income or human wealth is possible except for the tautological one that it is something that is proportional to the optimal consumption.[8] Another source of complication is the presence of risky assets whose rates of return are stochastic. It is true that, as Hakansson (1970) and Merton (1971) have shown, one can still obtain a closed-form solution for the optimal consumption if the stochastic rates of return are independently distributed over time. However, this does not carry over to the case where future labor income is stochastic. The situation becomes even less tractable if borrowing constraints are added to the optimization problem, as Levhari, Mirman, and Zilcha (1980) have shown.

The fourth problem is associated with the error term in the consumption function that summarizes the individual effect or the household-specific component of consumption. The individual effect could be correlated with any of the independent variables on the right-hand side of the consumption function. For example, if the household is more risk averse than the average households, then the error term for that household will be negative; but such risk-averse households will tend to hold a higher fraction of their portfolio in the form of safe assets. So even if the household follows the permanent income hypothesis, the error term will be negatively correlated with, e.g., the amount of demand deposits. Another source of correlation is the budget constraint. The error term in the previous period is likely to be negatively correlated with the amount of assets at the beginning of the current period. So if the error term is positively serially correlated, the current values of the error term and assets will be negatively correlated.

The foregoing argument suggests that any attempt to formulate explicitly the optimal consumption rule as a function of the variables that are typically available in cross-section data is bound to be misspecified and that it is very difficult to give a structural interpretation to a regression of consumption on such variables. For this reason we chose a somewhat unconventional approach that is presented in the next section.

3.3 Methodology

Our aim is to test the permanent income hypothesis against the more general hypothesis of liquidity constraints, without pretending that we can correctly specify the optimal consumption rule. In this section we present our testing strategy. The basic observation is that the optimal consumption c_t can be represented as

$$c_t = \min(c_t^*, k_t). \tag{2}$$

Here, c_t^* solves the *fictitious* intertemporal optimization problem where the *future* borrowing constraints are present, but the *current* borrowing constraint is not.[9] That is, c_t^* solves the intertemporal optimization problem with the budget constraint and the future borrowing constraints:

$$c_{t+i} \leqslant k_{t+i} \quad (i = 1, 2, 3, \ldots). \tag{3}$$

We shall refer to c_t^* as *desired consumption*. Note that c_t^* is not the level of consumption given by the permanent income hypothesis, because in the present optimization problem future borrowing constraints are present. We note, however, that (1) does contain the optimal consumption rule implied by the permanent income hypothesis by letting k_{t+i} $(i = 0, 1, 2, 3, \ldots)$ be sufficiently large. To anticipate, our testing strategy is to compare c_t and c_t^*; if they are different, we can conclude that households are *currently* liquidity constrained, which is sufficient to reject the permanent income hypothesis, which assumes that borrowing constraints are absent for *all* periods.

Let x be a vector of variables (other than consumption) that are available from our cross-section data set. It includes disposable income, assets, and the age of household head. We now make the following assumption. (For the most part, in the rest of this chapter, the time subscripts will be dropped.) The first assumption is that the expectation of desired consumption conditional on x (which is a well-defined concept because we have a random sample of x and which in general is a nonlinear function of x) is a linear function of x; i.e.,

$$E(c^*|x) = x'a, \quad \text{or} \quad c^* = x'a + e, \quad E(e|x) = 0. \tag{A1}$$

In the actual estimation the vector x includes not only disposable income, age, and assets but also their squared terms and interaction terms. Thus, to the extent that the conditional expectation is well approximated by a quadratic function, this assumption is not as restrictive as it might first appear. Because of the problem discussed in the previous section, we place no a priori restriction on the vector of coefficients a. By definition, the error term e includes anything that is not explained by x. For example, e could include individual differences in risk aversion, bequest motives, a stochastic process for income, ability, and so forth. It could also include what is usually referred to as transitory consumption that represents deviations of c^* from the solution to the intertemporal optimization. The equation in A1 will be called the *reduced-form equation* for desired consumption; it is simply a regression c^* on x. Our approach here is similar in spirit to Sims's (1980) vector autoregressive modeling on time-series data. One advantage of our nontheoretical approach is that we do not have to commit ourselves to any particular version of the permanent income hypothesis.

The second assumption is about the upper bound k for current consumption.

$$k \geqslant YD^* + 0.2^*LIQ, \tag{A2}$$

where YD^* is disposable income minus contractual saving (payments on mortgages and installment debts) and LIQ is the amount of liquid assets. Following Tobin and Dolde (1971) and Kowalewski and Smith (1979), we define disposable income as net of contractual saving. The assumption implies that the household can spend (if it wishes) *at least* $YD^* + 0.2^*LIQ$ in the current year. The definition of LIQ in this paper is the sum of demand deposits, saving accounts, bonds, and common stocks. Of course, this assumption does *not* imply that the household cannot sell illiquid assets (e.g., houses) and spend the proceeds for consumption purposes. But the time unit in this chapter is one year, and it may not be possible for the household to sell illiquid assets within a year at a price close to the market value. This is why we do not include assets like houses on the right-hand side of A2. The reason that LIQ is multiplied by a fraction is to guard against the possibility that not all of the reported amount of LIQ may really be cashable on short notice. Our choice of the LIQ coefficient of 0.2 is indeed arbitrary, so we shall report estimation results for different values of the LIQ coefficient. Anyway, there seems to be no doubt that the upper bound k is greater than the right-hand side of A2.

In this chapter consumption (c) is calculated as disposable income (YD^*) plus contractual saving minus saving (net changes in assets). The third assumption is that the only source of measurement error for consumption is disposable income.[10] If we denote the measurement error for disposable income by u, the third assumption can be written as

$$YD = YD^* + u, \quad CON = c + u, \tag{A3}$$

where CON is measured consumption as opposed to true consumption c, and YD is measured disposable income (net of contractual saving). There seems to be no reason that the measurement error u is independent of x. We can allow a fairly general form of correlation between u and x by positing

$E(u|x) = x'd$,   or $u = x'd + v$, $E(v|x) = 0$.   (A4)

This permits, in particular, the measurement error u to have a nonzero mean. This is important because income as reported in our cross-section data is likely to be understated, as most of the sample were taken during the period for filing Form 1040 for tax returns.

Combining A1, A3, and A4, we get

$c^* + u = x'b + (e + v)$,   (4)

where $b = a + d$. This equation, too, will be called the reduced-form equation for desired consumption. This is the equation we shall estimate. It is true that we cannot identify a and d separately, but identifying the "biased" coefficient b is sufficient for our purposes, as we shall see shortly. Now define the *threshold value* U as $U = 0.85^*(YD + 0.2^*LIQ)$.[11] Define the *limited dependent variable* y as

$$Y = \begin{cases} CON & \text{if } CON < U, \\ U & \text{otherwise} \end{cases}$$ (5)

It is just a matter of simple arithmetic to show that (2), (5), and A2 and A3 imply that

$$Y = \begin{cases} x'b + (e + v) & \text{if } x'b + (e + v) < U, \\ U & \text{otherwise.} \end{cases}$$ (6)

For later reference, we shall call the households that satisfy the sample separation rule $CON < U$ is (5), the *nonlimit observations* and the households that do not, the *limit observations*. The parameter b can be estimated by the Tobit procedure if we assume that

Conditional on x and U, the error term $e + v$ has a zero mean and is normal and homoskedastic.   (A5)

Since obviously this assumption cannot be justified on a priori bases, we shall carry out a diagnostic Lagrange multiplier test of normality and homoskedasticity at the end of Section 3.5.

The intuitive idea for using Tobit runs like this: since we are confident that the households with ample liquid assets or with high saving ratios are not currently liquidity constrained, we would like to use their consumption data to estimate the reduced-form equation for desired consumption. But since we suspect that *at least some* of those households that do not have ample liquid assets or whose saving ratio is low are currently liquidity constrained, we do not use their consumption data except for the fact that their consumption is high relative to their liquid assets or to their disposable income.

Thus, two different estimates of the reduced-form equation for desired consumption can be obtained. If the *null hypothesis* that no households in the population (from which the sample was drawn) are *currently* liquidity constrained, then we have $c = c^*$ and

$$CON = x'b + (e + v), \tag{7}$$

from (4) and A3. Thus, an efficient and asymptotically normal estimate of b is given by OLS. The Tobit procedure applied to (6) gives a consistent (and asymptotically normal) estimate of b even if some of the households in the population are currently liquidity constrained. The test procedure that immediately comes to mind is Hausman's (1978) specification test, which is to compare the efficient OLS estimate and the consistent but inefficient Tobit estimate. If the null hypothesis that no households are currently liquidity constrained is true, then the OLS and Tobit estimates should not be statistically different. Thus, a surprisingly large value of the Hausman statistic implies that some households in the population are *currently* liquidity constrained. This is sufficient to reject the permanent income hypothesis which assumes that the *current* and *future* borrowing constraints are irrelevant. A nice thing about this test is that the Tobit estimate of b is consistent in the event of rejection. Since the expectation of e is zero by construction, the gap between c^* and c can be consistently estimated as $\bar{x}'b_{TOBIT} - \overline{CON}$, where $\bar{x}$ and $\overline{CON}$ are the sample means of x and CON, respectively, and b_{TOBIT} is the Tobit estimate of b. Moreover, if the measurement error has a zero mean, then $\bar{x}'b_{TOBIT}$ is a consistent estimate of c^*. Thus, the Tobit estimate of b can provide useful information for assessing the *quantitative* importance of liquidity constraints.

Before turning to empirical analysis, we make several remarks. First, as we mentioned above, for testing purposes we can allow the possibility that the measurement error has a nonzero mean or is correlated with any elements of the right-hand side variables x. Second, the choice of the variables included in x is not crucial for the validity of our testing procedure. In principle, *any* variables that are available in our cross-section data can serve as x. But the power of the test will be affected by the choice of x; a "good" choice of x would be the one that minimizes the variance of $e + v$. However, as we keep including more variables in x, we also have to include squared (and possible cubic) terms of the included variables in order to keep A1 plausible, so that the size of x can easily be huge, making it very expensive to do the Tobit estimation, which requires inverting the

Hessian matrix in each iteration. Therefore, the choice of the variable to be included in x is necessarily a balancing act between the power considerations and the computational considerations. Third, we are *not* assuming that *every* household in the limit observations is liquidity constrained. All that is needed for consistent estimation of b by Tobit is that the sample separation rule $CON < U$ in (5) does not pick up currently constrained households; there may well be nonconstrained households that do not satisfy $CON < U$. For example, young households that follow the permanent income hypothesis and whose desired consumption exceeds current disposable income would not satisfy $CON < U$.

The last remark concerns measurement error for saving. It is true that if measurement error for saving is nonzero so that measurement error for consumption consists of measurement error for disposable income *and* for saving, then A3 becomes $CON = c + u + s$, where s is measurement error for saving. If s is normally distributed, the probability that some liquidity-constrained households satisfy $CON < U$ is not zero, so the Tobit procedure will end up estimating a mixture of the reduced-form equation and $c = k$, the equation for the liquidity-constrained households. This problem of misselection does not appear to be a serious one for the following reasons. First, since the unique feature of the present data set is its exhaustive coverage of various kinds of assets and since income taxes in this chapter will have to be estimated from extraneous information, the variance of measurement error for saving is likely to be small relative to that for disposable income. Second, even though it may not literally be a consistent estimate, the Tobit estimate will be a very close approximation. If the true density function of measurement error for saving does not have long tails like a normal distribution, the probability of liquidity constrained households ending up in the nonlimit observations may well be zero, in view of the high value of the saving ratio (15 percent) used for defining the threshold value U, and the normality assumption will still be a good approximation. Even if the density function does have a long tail, the probability of misselection will be negligibly small. Third and most important, we note that the Tobit estimate is consistent and asymptotically normal under the full hypothesis that no households are currently liquidity constrained. Thus, the Hausman specification test remains valid.

3.4 The Data

The cross-section data for the calculation reported in this chapter came from the 1963–1964 *Survey of Financial Characteristics of Consumers* conducted by the Board of Governors of the Federal Reserve System. A complete description of the survey is in Projector and Weiss (1966). The survey collected detailed information for income, the value of a large number of various categories of assets, as well as for socioeconomic characteristics of the households for two years 1962 and 1963. The quality of data is believed to be very good relative to other available data sets.[12]

The variables used in the analysis are as follows:

CS = contractual saving during 1963 in installment and mortgage debts,

YD = 1963 disposable income excluding capital gains, after estimated federal income and payroll taxes,[13] *minus* CS,

$ASSET$ = total market value of financial and physical assets (including the actuarial value of life insurance, private pensions, annuities, royalties, real estate, and automobiles), at the beginning of 1963,

$SAVING$ = saving during 1963, defined as net changes in assets (including automobiles and houses) after the exclusion of capital gains,

CON = measured consumption during 1963, defined as $YD + CS - SAVING$ (note that $YD + CS$ is disposable income in the conventional sense),

LIQ = amount of liquid assets, defined as demand deposits, plus savings accounts, bonds, and common stocks,

$HOUSE$ = market value of houses and other real estate at the beginning of 1963 ($HOUSE = 0$ for nonhomeowners),

$U = 0.85*(YD + 0.2*LIQ)$, the threshold value for creating the limited dependent variable,

AGE = age of the household head as of December 1962,

FSZ = family size.

The following households are excluded from the initial sample of 2,164 households: (i) households with missing data for the relevant variables (373 cases), (ii) the self-employed and farmers (428 cases), (iii) households whose 1963 disposable income minus contractual saving is less than $1,000 (96 cases), (iv) households whose assets are greater than or equal to one million dollars (38 cases), (v) households with negative consumption (27 cases), (vi) households whose consumption-disposable income ratio is greater than or equal to 5 (5 cases), and (vii) households whose head is 65 or over (166 cases). This reduced the sample size to 1,031 observations.

The self-employed and farmers are eliminated, as their income is least accurately reported and is likely to be understated. In the subsequent analysis we shall deflate the equation to be estimated by YD (disposable income minus contractual saving) to avoid heteroskedasticity. The reason for excluding low- and high-income households is to avoid extreme values when the heteroskedasticity correction is made.[14] Old households are eliminated for the same reason: since their disposable income is likely to be small relative to their consumption, their consumption-income ratio would tend to be high.

The sample mean, standard deviation, and skewness of the variables listed above for the sample of 1,031 observations are reported in Table 3.1. Table 3.2 displays the sample means for four groups broken down by the age of the household.

Table 3.1
Sample Statistics (Sample Size = 1,031)

Variable	Mean	Standard deviation	Skewness
CON	$7,045	7,353	4.93
ASSET	$28,177	83,535	6.82
YD	$7,629	6,912	4.00
LIQ	$12,991	60,220	8.47
HOUSE	$14,349	32,587	15.75
CS	$726	1,288	7.83
FSZ	3.7	1.94	1.17
AGE	42.8	11.7	0.01

Table 3.2
Sample Means for Four Age Groups

Variable	18–33	34–43	44–53	54–64
CON	$4,808	$7,299	$7,617	$8,747
ASSET	$4,970	$16,897	$30,961	$65,820
YD	$5,209	$7,521	$8,373	$9,764
LIQ	$733	$4,845	$13,007	$37,183
HOUSE	$5,239	$14.202	$17,369	$21,705
CS	$570	$869	$870	$574
FSZ	3.6	4.6	3.7	2.6
AGE	27.8	4.6	3.7	2.6
No. of cases	271	261	274	225

3.5 Results

In the subsequent analysis the vector x consists of the following sixteen variables: the constant, AGE-45, $(AGE$-$45)^{**}2$, FSZ, $ASSET$, $ASSET^*(AGE$-45), $ASSET^*((AGE$-$45)^{**}2)$, $ASSET^*$ FSZ, YD, $YD^*(AGE$-45), $YD^*((AGE$-$45)^{**}2)$, YD^*FSZ, LIQ, $ASSET^{**}2$, $YD^{**}2$, and $HOUSE$.[15] To account for possible differences in the consumption behavior by low- and high-income households, squared terms in $ASSET$ and YD are included in the equation. It is possible to calculate disposable income in 1962 from our data set. Disposable income in 1962 was not included in our equation because it was highly correlated with disposable income in 1963 (YD), and a serious multicollinearity problem arose when both variables were included. The reason for including $HOUSE$ is to treat homeowners and nonhomeowners symmetrically; the calculated consumption CON does not include service flows from houses that will be represented by the $HOUSE$ variable in the equation with a negative coefficient. We must include LIQ because A5 assumes that the expectation of $e + v$ conditional on x and U is zero and U is a function of YD and LIQ.

Not surprisingly, inspection of the residuals from a preliminary regression analysis revealed considerable heteroskedasticity across households of different income sizes. Since the Tobit estimation to be carried out shortly assumes that the error term $e + v$ is homoskedastic, a heteroskedasticity correction is necessary. To this end, disposable income YD is used to deflate the equations (6) and (7) to be estimated. In other words, the reduced-form equation we actually estimate has CON/YD as the dependent variable and x/YD as the independent variables. Of course, there is no guarantee that this deflation by YD completely removes heteroskedasticity in the (deflated) error term $e + v$. Later in this section we shall carry out a Lagrange multiplier test for heteroskedasticity and nonnormality. The parameter estimates obtained from applying OLS to the deflated equation,

$$CON/YD = x'b/YD + (e + v), \tag{7'}$$

are reported in Table 3.3. In interpreting the results, it should be kept in mind that the coefficient b in (7) is the sum of a in A1 and d in A4. We note that no variables that involve AGE are significant. We would expect that consumption depends on age to a large extent if the household is trying to isolate consumption from lifetime income movements.

Of the whole sample of 1,031 households, 455 households satisfied the criterion that $CON < U = 0.85^*(YD + 0.2^*LIQ)$. Table 3.4 displays the

Table 3.3
OLS Estimate

	1	AGE-45	(AGE-45)**2	FSZ
1	400	−6.34	−0.376	4.62
	(2.3)	(−0.97)	(−0.74)	(0.13)
ASSET	−0.00805	−0.000606	0.0^5350	0.00843
	(−0.084)	(−1.6)	(0.16)	(5.5)
YD	0.779	0.0^4101	0.0^4669	0.0127
	(12.8)	(0.01)	(0.39)	(1.2)
LIQ	0.00311			
	(0.030)			
ASSET**2	$(−0.0^7179$			
	(−1.9)			
YD**2	$−0.0^5368$			
	(−1.6)			
HOUSE	0.00747			
	(1.0)			
Estimate of var $(e + v) = 0.130$				
	(22.7)			

Note: Numbers in parentheses are t ratios. The point estimate of the coefficient of ASSET, for example, is −0.00805 which is the (2, 1) element of the above matrix. The point estimate of the coefficient of YD* ((AGE-45)**2) is 0.0000669.
$R^2 = 0.936$; mean of the dependent variable $(CON/YD) = 0.950$; sample size = 1,031.

Table 3.4
Sample Statistics of Two Subsamples

	Nonlimit observations $(CON < U)$ 455 cases		Limit observations $(CON \geq U)$ 576 cases	
Variable	Mean	Standard deviation	Mean	Standard deviation
CON	$7,360	7,393	$6,796	7,318
ASSET	$49,888	117,968	$11,026	29,061
YD	$9,709	8,745	$5,987	4,367
LIQ	$26,961	87,653	$1,956	12,383
HOUSE	$19,946	44,644	$9,927	16,844
CS	$739	1,209	$716	1,348
FSZ	3.4	1.7	3.9	2.1
AGE	45.4	11.3	40.7	11.6

Table 3.5
TOBIT Estimate

	1	AGE-45	(AGE-45)**2	FSZ
1	437	−20.3	0.785	−5.19
	(2.2)	(−2.3)	(1.2)	(−0.01)
ASSET	−0.0168	−0.0^{4}867	0.00308	
	(−1.5)	(−0.1)	(1.4)	
YD	0.841	0.00273	−0.000206	0.0302
	(10.9)	(1.2)	−(1.1)	(2.2)
LIQ	0.00760			
	(0.61)			
ASSET**2	0.0^{7}125			
	(1.4)			
YD**2	−0.0^{5}539			
	(−1.5)			
HOUSE	−0.00371			
	(−0.32)			
Estimate of var(e + v) = 0.0921				
(6.4)				

Note: Numbers in parentheses are *t* ratios. The maximum likelihood estimation was carried out by the Newton-Raphson method described in Amemiya [1973]. Log of likelihood function = −391.6; sample size = 1,031.

sample mean and standard deviations of the variables for the nonlimit observations and for the limit observations. Although the sample separation rule $CON < U$ does not necessarily favor high-income households (since it is based on the *ratio* of CON to $YD + 0.2*LIQ$), it ended up selecting relatively rich households into the 455 nonlimit observations. As would be expected, the average age is considerable higher for the nonlimit observations.

The Tobit model (6) (after CON is replaced by CON/YD and x by x/YD) is estimated by maximum likelihood under the assumption (A5) that the (deflated) error term $e + v$ is normal and homoskedastic. The results are reported in Table 3.5. Unlike the OLS case, the $HOUSE$ coefficient picked up the right (negative) sign, but it is not significant. Two of the variables that involve AGE have coefficients whose *t* ratios are over two in absolute value. The negative $ASSET$ coefficient might at first sight seem puzzling. The partial derivative of the estimated equation with respect to $ASSET$ evaluated at $(AGE, FSZ, ASSET) = (45, 3, \$10,000)$, for example is about -0.005. This number, however, does not really represent the effect of an increase in *ASSET* on consumption, because a higher value of *ASSET* with *YD* held constant implies a lower value of labor income.[16]

The two sets of estimates—OLS and Tobit—appear to be different from each other. As Hausman (1978) has shown, the right distance between the two estimates is given by the difference in the variance matrices for the two estimates, as the efficient estimate of b, b_{OLS}, is asymptotically uncorrelated with the difference $b_{TOBIT} - b_{OLS}$, under the null hypothesis. This fact can also be directly verified by looking at the Taylor expansion of the estimates around the true value of b. As Hausman (1978) has shown, the Wald type statistic,

$$(b_{TOBIT} - b_{OLS})'(V_{TOBIT} - V_{OLS})^{-1}(b_{TOBIT} - b_{OLS}),$$

is asymptotically distributed as chi-squared with 16 degrees of freedom under the null hypothesis that no households in the population are currently liquidity constrained. In the above expression, V_{TOBIT} and V_{OLS} are the sample size times consistent estimates of the asymptotic variance matrices of b_{TOBIT} and b_{OLS}, respectively. In the present case the statistic is 745.9, which emphatically rejects the null hypothesis.[17] Technically speaking, the primary reason for such a large statistic appears to be that the standard errors of the Tobit estimate are not much higher than those of the OLS estimate.

A less formal but probably more interesting way to evaluate the importance of liquidity constraints is to compare the sample mean of *predicted desired consumption* $x'b_{TOBIT}$ with the sample mean of measured consumption on the entire sample of 1,031 observations. As was shown in Section 3.3, the gap $c^* - c$ can be consistently estimated by the sample mean of $x'b_{TOBIT} - CON$, if the Tobit estimate is consistent of b. Furthermore, if the (unconditional) expectation of the measurement error u is zero, then the sample mean of $x'b_{TOBIT}$ is a consistent estimate of desired consumption c^*. This is why our interest has been centered around the consistent estimation of b. The (weighted) mean of $x'b_{TOBIT}/YD$ is 1.005, and the (weighted) mean of CON/YD is 0.950. The effect of liquidity constraints is to reduce consumption to about 5.5 percent below the desired level, on average. From the viewpoint of macroeconomic stabilization policies, a more relevant measure is the unweighted mean of consumption. The (unweighted) mean of CON is $7,045, which is about 2.7 percent below the (unweighted) mean of predicted desired consumption, $x'b_{TOBIT}$ of $7,244. Thus, the *quantitative* importance of liquidity constraints does not seem so large as the difference between the Tobit and OLS estimates of the reduced-form equation might suggest.

Table 3.6
Comparison of Averages for Measured and Predicted Desired Consumption for Four Age Groups

	18–33	34–43	44–53	54–64	*ALL*
Measured consumption (weighted)	0.942	0.968	0.937	0.956	0.950
Predicted desired consumption (weighted)	1.069	1.017	0.971	0.957	1.005
Measured consumptions (unweighted)	$4,808	$7,299	$7,617	$8,747	$7,045
Predicted desired consumption (unweighted)	$5,304	$7,373	$7,756	$8,808	$7,244
YD	$5,209	$7,521	$8,373	$9,764	$7,629
No. of cases where $CON < U$ (nonlimit cases)	86	106	132	131	455
No. of cases where $CON < x'b$	52	82	91	82	307
No. of cases	271	261	274	225	1,031

Note: Prediced desired consumption $x'b$ is evaluated at the Tobit estimate of b with $U = 0.85^*(YD + 0.2^*LIQ)$.

Table 3.6 carries out a similar comparison by the age of the household head. As would be expected, the effect of liquidity constraints is most evident for young households. Not only the discrepancy between predicted desired consumption and measured consumption is largest for the young, but also their average ratio of predicted desired consumption to disposable income exceeds one. For only 19 percent (52 cases out of 271) of the households whose heads are 33 or younger, measured consumption is greater than the predicted desired consumption $x'b_{TOBIT}$.

The important assumption in the preceding analysis is that the error term $e + v$ (after deflation by YD) is normal and homoskedastic. We now carry out a Lagrange multiplier test for nonnormality and heteroskedasticity. Following Lee (1981), we assume that the error term, $w = e + v$ (after the deflation by YD), is a member of the general Pearson family of distributions whose density function can be written as

$$f(w) = g(w) \Big/ \left[\int_{-\infty}^{\infty} g(z)dz \right],$$

where

$$g(w) = \exp\left[\int_0^w \frac{c_3 - z}{c_5 - c_3 z + c_4 z^2} \right] dz.$$

The variance under this general Pearson distribution is $c_5/(1 - 3c_4)$. There are several different ways to incorporate heteroskedasticity into this distribution. We assume that the variance is a linear function of $ASSET$ and YD so that c_5 is written as

$$c_5 = c_0 + c_1^* ASSET + c_2^* YD.$$

If, for example, $c_2 > 0$, this expression implies that the variance increase with the household income. The homoskedasticity assumption is that $c_1 = c_2 = 0$, and the normality assumption is that $c_3 = c_4 = 0$. Our null hypothesis, therefore, is that $c_i = 0$ ($i = 1, 2, 3, 4$). The Lagrange multiplier test is based on the fact that the score vector under the null hypothesis has mean zero, and its variance is the elements of the information matrix that correspond to the parameters constrained by the null hypothesis. Its attractive feature is that we do not have to compute the maximum likelihood estimates under the alternative hypothesis. The reader is referred to Engle (1983) for an excellent exposition of the Lagrange multiplier principle. To calculate the Lagrange multiplier statistic, a consistent estimate of the relevant information matrix is necessary; we used the formula given by Lee (1981) to obtain such an estimate. In the present case, the statistic, which is distributed asymptotically as chi-squared with four degrees of freedom under the null hypothesis ($c_i = 0$, $i = 1, 2, 3, 4$), turned out to be 10.7. Thus, we can accept the joint hypothesis of normality and homoskedasticity as a 2.5 percent level of significance.

We conclude this section by examining the robustness of our results with respect to the choice of the LIQ coefficient in the definition of U, the threshold value for the sample separation. Table VII contains the results that correspond to the ones on Table VI for two cases where $U = 0.85^*(YD + 0.5^*LIQ)$ and where $U = 0.85^*YD$. The results with $U = 0.85^*(YD + 0.5^*LIQ)$ are remarkably similar to the case where $U = 0.85^*(YD + 0.2^*LIQ)$. However, when U is simply 0.85^*YD, the estimated reduced-form equation underpredicts consumption for households whose heads are between 54 and 64 years of age. Since by definition c^* should be greater than or equal to c, this is puzzling. However, even in this case with $U = 0.85^*YD$, the weighted average for the whole sample of desired consumption of 0.984 is still higher than the weighted average of measured consumption of 0.950. Also reported in Table 3.7 is the consumption predicted by the OLS estimate of b. It is clear that, unlike any of the Tobit estimates presented so far, the discrepancy between measured consumption and predicted consumption has no relationship to the age of the household.

Table 3.7
Predicted Desired Consumption with Different Threshold Values for Four Age Groups

	18–33	34–43	44–53	54–64	ALL
With $U = 0.85^*(YD + 0.5^*LIQ)$					
Weighted	1.067	1.019	0.981	0.962	1.009
Unweighted	$5,248	$7,391	$7,873	$8,884	$7,282
With $U = 0.85^*YD$					
Weighted	1.041	1.001	0.961	0.924	0.984
Unweighted	$5,189	$7,279	$7,654	$8,204	$7,031
With OLS estimate of b					
Weighted	0.947	0.956	0.949	0.950	0.950
Unweighted	$4,816	$7,076	$7,772	$8,809	$7,045

3.6 Conclusion

The basic message of this chapter can be summarized as follows. The sample was divided into high- and low-saving households. The coefficients in the reduced-form equation for consumption (i.e., the regression of consumption on the variables available in our cross-section data) for the high-saving households appeared to be quite different from those for the rest, even after the selectivity (or sample selection) bias, which arises from a sample separation procedure based on the dependent variable, is removed by the Tobit procedure. When the Tobit estimate of the reduced-form equation for the *high*-saving households was used to predict consumption for the whole sample, it tended to *over*predict actual consumption. Our interpretation of this finding was that some of the low-saving households were unable to consume as much as they want due to borrowing constraints. This is admittedly not the only interpretation, but is the one that seems most natural.

One might want to comment on this by saying that the high- and low-saving households are simply two different types of consumers with respect to their preferences and so it is not really surprising (from the viewpoint of the permanent income hypothesis) to have such a large Hausman statistic. This amounts to questioning the validity of A1, which says that the way desired consumption is related to x is smooth enough to allow a quadratic approximation. Our response to this comment is threefold. First, the error term in our reduced-form equation for desired consumption does include all kinds of individual differences that are not captured by the vector x. The error term for the high-saving households tends to be negative. This is precisely the selectivity bias that can be removed by the Tobit procedure under the normality and homoskedasticity assumption—the assumption that was not strongly rejected by data. Second, if it is in fact the case that two household groups differ in a fundamental way with respect to their consumption behavior, one would like to explain *why* they are different; in particular, one would have to explain why the saving rate is the relevant criterion in dividing households into two totally different types of consumers. Third, the permanent income hypothesis is really an optimization problem with a linear constraint. Unless the objective function is badly behaved, one would expect to see the optimal decision rule to be a smooth function of relevant variables. After all, Milton Friedman's original permanent income hypothesis implies that the expectation of consumption conditional on income is a linear function of income.

Notes

I would like to thank Kim Kowalewski of the Federal Reserve Bank of Cleveland for kindly providing me with the data and for comments in earlier drafts. Earlier versions of this paper were presented at the 1981 Winter Econometric Society Meeting, the Money and Banking Workshop at the University of Chicago, the Macro-Labor Seminar at Northwestern University, and an NBER conference on puzzles in intertemporal macroeconomics organized by Tom Sargent. I would like to thank participants and discussants, particularly Zvi Eckstein, and two referees for helpful comments. Remaining errors are mine.

1. See Tobin (1980) for his latest account of liquidity constraints and their implication to macroeconomic stabilization policies. In this chapter we use the words "liquidity constraints" and "borrowing constraints" interchangeably. We shall not use the word "quantity constraints," because it is usually used to describe the situation where labor supply is exogenously given to the household. This paper assumes that households are quantity constrained; i.e., they are "income takers." Although this is a standard assumption in the literature on the consumption function, it would be preferable to treat both consumption and labor supply as choice variables. Unfortunately, our data set has no information on labor supply or wage rate.

2. Kowalewski and Smith (1979) use the annual Survey of Consumer Finances, conducted by the Survey Research Center at the University of Michigan from the late 1940s until the early 1970s. By an ingenious method they split the sample into liquidity-constrained households and those that are not for each year, and construct time-series data on consumption expenditure and income for the two types of households. They find that the marginal propensity to consume out of income is higher for liquidity-constrained households in the regression of consumption expenditure on income using the time-series data thus constructed.

3. See, e.g., Hall (1978) for a formal statement of the permanent income hypothesis. The assumption that the lifetime utility function is time-separable is not a crucial assumption in this paper.

4. See, e.g., Lucas (1980) for a formal statement of this hypothesis. In Lucas' paper, k is the household's money balance at the beginning of the period. A more general model of liquidity constraints would be to assume that the interest rate is an increasing function of consumption. It seems that a satisfactory treatment of this more general model requires longitudinal information on consumption. The model in the text amounts to assuming that the interest rate becomes infinite as consumption exceeds. k.

5. Permanent income is usually defined as the interest rate times the sum of assets and human wealth. Human wealth is the expectation of the present discounted value of current and future after-tax labor income.

6. If longitudinal data on total consumption were available, we would operate on the Euler equation (the first-order condition for intertemporal optimality), as Hansen and Singleton (1982) did using aggregate time-series data.

7. See Hansen and Sargent (1982) for more details on this approach.

8. There are three cases where permanent income is a well-defined concept. (i) Future labor income is deterministic; (ii) the instantaneous utility function is quadratic; and (iii) the instantaneous utility function has a constant degree of absolute risk aversion, and labor income follows a Poisson process (see Merton (1971)).

9. The representation (2) implicitly assumes that the shadow value of k_t (the derivative of the lifetime utility function with respect to k_t) is a monotone function of k_t. This would be true if the instantaneous utility function is concave.

10. Problems associated with measurement error for saving will be discussed at the end of this section. Note that our definition of disposable income YD^* is net of contractual saving.

11. The reason that $YD + 0.2^*LIQ$ is further multiplied by 0.85 is to reduce the probability that measured consumption by liquidity-constrained households satisfies the sample separation rule $CON < U$ due to measurement error for saving. This point is further discussed in the last paragraph of this section.

12. I also looked at a University of Michigan Survey Research Center panel study entitled *Consumer Durables and Installment Debts, 1967–70*, which has longitudinal information on saving and income. It turned out that calculated consumption (defined as income minus saving) was negative for more than two cases out of ten.

13. The data set contains no information on taxes. Federal income tax was calculated by following the instructions in a handbook entitled *Your Federal Income Tax* (1964 edition, U.S. Internal Revenue Service publication No. 17). The tax deductibility of mortgage payments was incorporated into the calculation. Other taxes were ignored. Property tax could be a substantial omission, but this will be picked up by the variable *HOUSE* in the reduced-form equation. The derivation of the variables used in this paper is in part based on the asset and saving data constructed by Kim Kowalewski of the Federal Reserve Bank of Cleveland, who also used the same data set as Projector and Weiss (1966). The FORTRAN program that I used for deriving the variables is available upon request.

14. It turned out that if households in (iv)–(vii) were not deleted, the normality and homoskedasticity assumption was decisively rejected by the Lagrange multiplier test.

15. Education and the sex of the household head are available from the data set, but they are not included in the equation to maintain the number of the right-hand side variables manageable in our computation of Tobit estimates. If the two variables were to be included, we would also have to include the interaction terms between the two variables, and between

YD and $ASSET$. The choice of the variables included in x has already been discussed in the previous section.

16. The negative $ASSET$ coefficient might be due to transitory consumption that is a part of c^*. As was discussed in Section 3.2, positively serially correlated transitory consumption is likely to be negatively correlated with $ASSET$. This would tend to bias the $ASSET$ coefficient downward in the regression of c^* on x. This point was suggested by a referee.

17. The Hessian matrix of the log of likelihood function evaluated at b_{TOBIT} was used to calculate V_{TOBIT}. A referee has pointed out that $V_{TOBIT} - V_{OLS}$ as calculated in this chapter is guaranteed to be positive definite if the sample moment matrix of x summed over the set of limit observations has full rank. To calculate V_{OLS}, we used the Tobit estimate of var$(e + v)$. If the OLS estimate of var$(e + v)$ is used to evaluate V_{OLS}, some of the diagonal elements of $V_{TOBIT} - V_{OLS}$ become negative. If the hypothesis is that both the coefficients in the reduced-form equation and the variance of the error term $e + v$ are the same, the relevant Hausman statistic is 1,774.

References

Amemiya, Takeshi, "Regression Analysis When the Dependent Variable is Truncated Normal," *Econometrica*, XLI (1973), 997–1016.

Bernanke, Ben, "Permanent Income, Liquidity and Expenditure on Automobiles: Evidence from Panel Data," *The Quarterly Journal of Economics*, XCIX (1984), 587–614.

Engle, Robert, "Wald, Likelihood Ratio, and Lagrange Multiplier Tests in Econometrics," *Handbook of Econometrics*, Zvi Griliches and M. Intriligator, eds. (Amsterdam and New York: North-Holland, 1983).

Flavin, Majorie, "The Adjustment of Consumption to Changing Expectations about Future Income," *Journal of Political Economy*, LXXXIX (1981), 974–1009.

Hakansson, Nils, "Optimal Investment and Consumption Strategies under Risk for a Class of Utility Functions," *Econometrica*, XXXVII (1970), 587–607.

Hall, Robert E., "Stochastic Implications of the Life Cycle-Permanent Income Hypothesis: Theory and Evidence," *Journal of Political Economy*, LXXXVI (1978), 971–87.

————, and Frederic Mishkin, "The Sensitivity of Consumption to Transitory Income: Estimates from Panel Data on Households," *Econometrica*, L (1982), 461–81.

Hansen, Lars P., and Thomas Sargent, "Instrumental Variables Procedures for Estimating Linear Rational Expectations Models," *Journal of Monetary Economics*, IX (1982), 263–96.

————, and Kenneth Singleton, "Generalized Instrumental Variables Estimation of Nonlinear Rational Expectations Models," *Econometrica*, L (1982), 1269–86.

Hausman, Jerry A., "Specification Tests in Econometrics," *Econometrica*, XLVI (1978), 1251–72.

Hayashi, Fumio, "The Permanent Income Hypothesis: Estimation and Testing by Instrumental Variables," *Journal of Political Economy*, XC (1982), 895–916.

Kowalewski, Kim, and Gary Smith, "The Spending Behavior of Wealth- and Liquidity-Constrained Consumers," Cowles Foundation Discussion paper No. 536, September 1979.

Lee, Lung-Fei, "A Specification Test for Normality in the Generalized Regression Models," mimeo, University of Minnesota, May 1981.

Levhari, David, Leonard J. Mirman, and Itzhak Zilcha, "Capital Accumulation under Uncertainty," *International Economic Review*, XXI (1980), 661–71.

Lucas, Robert E., "Asset Prices in a Pure Currency Economy," *Economic Inquiry*, VIII (1980), 203–20.

Merton, Robert C., "Optimum Consumption and Portfolio Rules in a Continuous-Time Model," *Journal of Economic Theory*, III (1971), 373–413.

Projector, Dorothy S., and Gertrude S. Weiss, *Survey of Financial Characteristics of Consumers*, Board of Governors, Federal Reserve System (Washington, D.C.: 1966).

Sargent, Thomas J., "Rational Expectations, Econometric Exogeneity, and Consumption," *Journal of Political Economy*, LXXXVI (1978), 673–700.

Sims, Christopher A., "Macroeconomics and Reality," *Econometrica*, XLVIII (1980), 1–48.

Tobin, James, "Estimation of Relationships for Limited Dependent Variables," *Econometrica*, XXVI (1958), 24–36.

―――, *Asset Accumulation and Economic Activity* (Chicago: University of Chicago Press, 1980).

―――, and Walter Dolde, "Wealth, Liquidity, and Consumption," in *Consumer Spending and Monetary Policy: The Linkages* (Boston: Federal Reserve Bank of Boston, 1971).

4

The Permanent Income Hypothesis and Consumption Durability: Analysis Based on Japanese Panel Data

4.1 Introduction and Summary

The empirical validity of the permanent income hypothesis[1] is a long-standing issue that has been debated for nearly three decades. At the heart of the debate is the question of whether consumption is "too sensitive" to income fluctuations. Its operational meaning was not given until Hall (1978), who has shown that the marginal utility of consumption is a martingale under the permanent income hypothesis with constant real interest rates. Since then, quite a few papers have studied the issue of the excess sensitivity of consumption.[2] Many of them have also tried to estimate the fraction of "liquidity-constrained" (rule-of-thumb) households whose consumption simply tracks disposable income.

As impressive as it is, the literature has failed to pay enough attention to the distinction between consumption and expenditure.[3] As the permanent income hypothesis is a theory about the service flow of consumption, the literature has either looked at perishables (nondurables or services or both) alone or singled out durables for special treatment. But it is not entirely clear that most commodities labeled as nondurables or services are perishable so that consumption and expenditure can be equated. A good example is dental services. People go to a dentist not because they enjoy the treatment but because it is hoped that their teeth will be in good shape for some time to come. So dental services are physically durable. Another example is a pleasure trip. It is physically perishable, but it may have a lasting psychological effect on preferences as people derive utility from the memory of a trip. If so, recreational expenditure should be treated as if it is durable.

Originally published in *The Quarterly Journal of Economics* 100 (November 1985): 1083–113. Reprinted with the permission of The MIT Press.

The present study attempts to address this durability issue as well as to obtain a sharper estimate of the fraction of households in the population for which total expenditure tracks disposable income. It uses a four-quarter panel of Japanese households for several commodity groups. The unique feature of this data set is its inclusion of respondents' expectations about expenditure and income. A surprising fact revealed by the data set is that expenditure changes are negatively correlated over time, a fact that appears to be inconsistent with consumption smoothing. This can, however, be reconciled with the permanent income hypothesis by allowing for "transitory consumption" (measurement error and preference shocks) and the durability of commodities.

The theoretical model in this study takes durability into account by taking consumption to be a distributed lag function of expenditure. If the commodity is perfectly perishable, only current expenditure shows up in the distributed lag. The model also allows for preference shocks by making the utility function depend on a preference shift parameter. The model is standard in other respects: a household's objective function is a time-separable function of consumption, and households can freely borrow and lend at the nominal risk-free interest rate. Under the assumption of static expectations about the real interest rates and for some specific preferences, it is shown that *consumption* follows a martingale (with an intercept term that depends on the real rate), so that a change in *expenditure* on the commodity in question is a univariate autoregression. Thus, the model provides a unified treatment of commodities with differing degrees of durability.

The estimation of the model is carried out with no restrictions on the serial correlation structure of income, preference shocks, and measurement error but with the restriction of geometric decay on the distributed lag function for consumption. The crucial identifying assumption is that neither preference shocks nor measurement error in expenditure is correlated with income and that there is no measurement error in income. Since expectations are directly measured, there is no need to make a specific assumption about expectations of future income and expenditure. The main findings are as follows. Clothes and recreation and education are highly durable. The fraction of the population of wage earners for which total expenditure tracks income is sharply estimated to be around 15 percent. If these "liquidity-constrained" households are allowed for, the model is successful in mimicking the sample covariances between (expected and unexpected) expenditure and income changes. However, only a small fraction of expenditure changes is explained by income.

The plan of the chapter is as follows. Section 4.2 describes the nature of the data set. Section 4.3 examines some summary statistics of the (actual and expected) expenditure and income variables. The theoretical model is presented, and the martingale property of consumption is derived in Section 4.4. The estimation procedure is discussed in Section 4.5. The parameter estimates are presented in Section 4.6.

4.2   The Data and the Variables Used

The data set for the present study is obtained from the 1982 Survey of Family Consumption compiled by the Economic Planning Agency of the Japanese government. This is an interview panel survey in which families reported to visiting interviewers every three months over a four-quarter period (1981:Q2–1982:Q1). More specifically, the respondents were asked at the end of each quarter to provide the following information: (i) expenditures on eleven different and mutually exclusive commodity groups for the quarter,[4] (ii) "normal" income consisting of regular wages and salaries, net of income, social security, and national health insurance taxes, (iii) "temporary" income consisting of (after-tax) bonuses, income from interest, dividends and estates, insurance payments, severance pay, and tax returns at the end of a calendar year, (iv) the respondent's expectations (at the end of each quarter) of all the variables in the above three items for the following quarter and (v) family characteristics (occupation, family size, age of the head, and housing tenure). Since the survey's distinction between "normal" and "temporary" income seems arbitrary, this study uses disposable income (the sum of "normal" and "temporary" income) as the income variable. The survey does not cover one-person households. Although this is not a diary survey, interviewers actually visited the households every quarter and the respondents filled out the questionnaire in the presence of the interviewer. There is practically no attrition: for any quarter at least 99.5 percent of the surveyed 5,837 households responded. Information about food, for example, is elicited by the question: "How much did your family spend on food for the last three months?" and "How much do you expect your family will spend on food for the next three months?"

Our analysis will focus on "workers' households," i.e., households whose head is on a payroll, which are about 58 percent of the original sample. This is because identification of the fraction of the population for which expenditure tracks income rests on the assumption of no measurement error in income. (The results for all households will be mentioned when necessary.) It became necessary to delete the sample from the entire

Tokyo prefecture and some other parts of the country, because a four-quarter panel could not be formed due to some coding problem. At this stage the sample size became 2,707. From this, households with missing values[5] (497 cases), households whose head's age either increases by more than a year or decreases (150 cases), and then households which changed their housing tenure (from a nonhomeowner to a homeowner or from a homeowner to a nonhomeowner)[6] (46 cases) are deleted. This left a sample of 2,014 cases. For this sample the empirical distribution was examined and a decision was made to remove seven cases that reported extreme values.[7] The final sample size for workers' households became 2,007. (The final sample size for all households under a similar sample selection rule became 3,520.)[8]

Although expenditures are classified into eleven groups in the original survey, this study uses a broader classification of seven commodity groups because some of the original commodity groups (e.g., recreation, education, and "cultural" expenses) seem to be close substitutes. The variables used in this study are as follows:

C_1 = food (including liquor and beverages and excluding meals away from home);

C_2 = rents, fuel, and utilities;

C_3 = clothing and household textiles;

C_4 = consumer durables (including furniture, electric appliances, musical instruments, cameras, automobiles, bikes, bicycles, sports equipment, and stainless sinks);

C_5 = recreation and education (including recreational expenditure such as vacation expenses, movies, admission fees, and meals away from home; plus educational expenses such as tuition, books, supplies and equipment for kindergarten, elementary and high schools, colleges and universities; plus "cultural" expenses such as reading materials, tuition for such cultural activities as flower arrangement, cooking, tea ceremony, music and dance; plus "social" expenses such as gifts and contributions);

C_6 = medical expenses not paid by the national health insurance, glasses and medical appliances for personal use;

C_7 = other (including housewares, repairs, personal care services, transportation and communication, telephone charges, private insurance premiums, shoes, umbrellas, and vehicle operation; plus money given to family members other than the head);

YD = disposable income, namely the sum of "normal" income and "temporary" income;

AGE = age of the household head;

FSZ = family size (i.e., the number of people in the family).

We use the second subscript to denote the quarter. For example, C_{11} is food expenditure in the first quarter of the panel (1981:Q1), and C_{14} is food expenditure in the fourth quarter (1982:Q1). Expenditure and income variables are all deflated by the relevant components of the implicit price deflator for personal consumption expenditures in the National Income Accounts. The overall deflator is used to deflate C_7 and YD. Since prices were very stable during the period covered by the panel (the inflation rate during the period was 2.9 percent), the choice of the deflator is immaterial.

The present data set also contains information on expectations held by households. Since the period of the survey is from 1981:Q2 to 1982:Q1, reported expectations refer to the period of 1981:Q3 to 1982:Q2. We shall put superscript "e" to denote expectations. For example, C_{1t}^e denotes the household's expectation, formed at the end of period $t-1$, of C_1 in period t ($t = 2, 3, 4, 5$, or 1981:Q3 through 1982:Q2). As the interview was conducted at the end of each quarter, expectations about variables dated t are based on information available at the end of period $t-1$ that includes actual values of variables dated $t-1$. We assume that relevant components of the implicit price deflator are correctly foreseen by households one quarter in advance, so that actual values of the relevant deflators are used to convert expected values into real terms.

4.3   Some Summary Statistics

The sample means and standard deviations of expenditure and income variables in real terms are shown in Table 4.1. Both expenditure and income exhibit seasonality; they all rise in the fourth quarter of the year. The lumpiness of durables is reflected in the large standard deviation and the high fraction of households that report zero expenditure on durables.

The theory to be presented in the next section is stated in terms of expenditure changes. Table 4.2 shows the sample means and standard deviations of (actual and unexpected) expenditure and income changes. As expected, the most volatile commodity group is durables. Both the level and the change of durables expenditure vary a lot across households. The standard deviation is larger for actual changes than for unexpected changes because part of actual changes is foreseen.

Table 4.1
Means and Standard Deviations of Levels[a]

Variable	1981:Q2	1981:Q3	1981:Q4	1982:Q1
C_1 (food)	213.9	218.0	241.6	216.3
	(84.1)	(84.3)	(96.8)	(86.7)
	[0.0]	[0.0]	[0.0]	[0.0]
C_2 (rents and utilities)	66.7	65.2	74.9	74.7
	(44.8)	(43.4)	(47.9)	(44.3)
	[0.002]	[0.001]	[0.001]	[0.001]
C_3 (clothes)	52.8	50.4	72.9	53.4
	(74.5)	(78.1)	(75.6)	(61.5)
	[0.023]	[0.027]	[0.013]	[0.036]
C_4 (durables)	59.4	61.0	66.0	42.3
	(167.4)	(183.2)	(144.0)	(121.7)
	[0.418]	[0.410]	[0.314]	[0.448]
C_5 (recreation & education)	178.4	186.9	198.8	182.9
	(187.4)	(157.2)	(165.3)	(180.7)
	[0.0]	[0.0]	[0.0]	[0.0]
C_6 (medical)	20.8	21.5	23.8	21.8
	(38.3)	(31.3)	(39.3)	(38.6)
	[0.093]	[0.084]	[0.079]	[0.084]
C_7 (other)	154.6	161.0	180.6	147.7
	(109.5)	(113.3)	(123.4)	(95.6)
	[0.000]	[0.000]	[0.0]	[0.001]
CON (total)	743.5	760.7	857.6	733.2
	(399.1)	(377.8)	(390.4)	(356.0)
	[0.0]	[0.0]	[0.0]	[0.0]
YD (disposable income)	887.6	904.9	1,151.2	745.8
	(493.7)	(422.6)	(559.4)	(326.5)
	[0.0]	[0.000]	[0.0]	[0.000]

a. In thousands of 1980 yen. Sample standard deviations are in parentheses. The numbers in brackets are the fraction of the sample (of 2,007 households) which reported zeros for the variable in question. If no households reported zeros, "0.0" is entered in brackets.

Table 4.3 reports the sample autocorrelation of changes.[9] The first-order autocorrelation coefficients are uniformly negative and large in absolute value. This is surprising, because Hall's (1978) permanent income hypothesis implies that changes in consumption are serially uncorrelated as the level of consumption is changed only when the consumer receives new information. That implication appears to be inconsistent with the data. It is usually suspected that one of the most likely reasons for the failure of the permanent income hypothesis is that it takes time for consumers to adjust to new information (Hall, 1978). But this cannot be the reason for the strong negative autocorrelation, because the lagged responses should

Table 4.2
Means and Standard Deviations of Actual and Unexpected Expenditure and Income Changes[a]

Variable (X)	$X_2 - X_1$	$X_2 - X_2^e$	$X_3 - X_2$	$X_3 - X_3^e$	$X_4 - X_3$	$X_4 - X_4^e$
C_1	4.1	−0.7	23.6	13.6	−25.2	−0.6
	(47.7)	(48.1)	(49.2)	(49.1)	(53.5)	(46.7)
C_2	−1.5	−0.6	9.7	2.3	−0.1	3.3
	(32.5)	(28.7)	(33.1)	(32.2)	(32.3)	(27.0)
C_3	−2.4	6.8	22.4	16.1	−19.5	11.0
	(78.2)	(53.0)	(76.7)	(59.6)	(71.6)	(50.0)
C_4	1.5	27.5	5.0	19.8	−23.7	16.7
	(228.5)	(172.7)	(214.0)	(150.3)	(179.3)	(111.1)
C_5	8.5	16.5	11.9	21.4	16.5	20.8
	(165.2)	(104.4)	(147.5)	(101.7)	(168.9)	(116.7)
C_6	0.7	4.3	2.3	2.8	−2.0	2.1
	(41.9)	(29.6)	(41.8)	(36.8)	(48.1)	(33.2)
C_7	6.4	12.6	19.6	15.7	−32.9	3.6
	(89.7)	(79.2)	(91.1)	(83.9)	(84.0)	(56.0)
CON	17.2	64.9	96.8	90.9	−124.3	55.3
	(322.5)	(233.5)	(290.2)	(226.1)	(292.4)	(196.2)
YD	17.3	29.6	246.4	67.1	−405.5	23.0
	(443.0)	(198.6)	(367.2)	(177.5)	(359.2)	(123.4)

a. Sample standard deviations are in parentheses. In thousands of 1980 yen.

induce *positive* autocorrelation. Another explanation for the negative auto-correlation is the seasonality in expenditure. In particular, the negative correlation between changes from 1981:Q3 to Q4 and from 1981:Q4 to 1982:Q1 must be at least partly due to the general rise in expenditure in 1981:Q4. The right half of Table 4.3 shows the same autocorrelations for seasonally adjusted data.[10] They are not much different from the numbers in the left half of the table.

The negative autocorrelation in expenditure changes can be made consistent with the permanent income hypothesis in several ways. First, survey data on expenditure are subject to measurement error. When expenditure levels are measured with error, changes in measured expenditure will have a moving average term that can induce negative autocorrelation even if ture expenditure changes are not serially correlated. Second, preference shocks that shift the marginal utility will introduce another moving average term. Third and most important, commodities may be durable, so that expenditure and consumption are not the same thing. It is consumption, not expenditure, that should be serially uncorrelated under the permanent income hypothesis. A higher level of expenditure means a larger stock of consumption, which will depress expenditure in the next

Table 4.3
Sample Autocorrelation of Changes

	Seasonally unadjusted		Seasonally adjusted	
	Autocorrelation		Autocorrelation	
Variable	First-order[a]	Second-order	First-order[a]	Second-order
C_1	−0.269***	−0.102***	−0.304***	−0.085***
	−0.496***		−0.421***	
C_2	−0.303***	−0.034	−0.338***	−0.034
	−0.540***		−0.503***	
C_3	−0.408***	−0.128***	−0.504***	−0.102***
	−0.439***		−0.263***	
C_4	−0.555***	0.000	−0.588***	0.020
	−0.469***		−0.355***	
C_5	−0.418***	0.007	−0.409***	0.000
	−0.483***		−0.452***	
C_6	−0.353***	−0.031	−0.349***	−0.028
	−0.500***		−0.448***	
C_7	−0.459***	−0.068**	−0.493***	−0.061**
	−0.541***		−0.460***	
CON	−0.450***	−0.049*	−0.467***	−0.050*
	−0.454***		−0.382***	
YD	−0.563***	0.071**	−0.639***	0.023
	−0.683***		−0.460***	

a. Two first-order autocorrelation coefficients are calculated. The numbers that first appear in the column for first-order autocorrelation are the correlation coefficient between $X_3 - X_2$ and $X_2 - X_1$, and the numbers that appear below them are the correlation coefficient of $X_4 - X_3$ and $X_3 - X_2$ ($X = C_1, C_2, \ldots, C_7, CON, YD$).
* Significant at the 5 percent level.
** Significant at the 1 percent level.
*** Significant at the 0.1 percent level.

period if households behave in a way to smooth out consumption (rather than expenditure) over time. The theoretical model to be presented in the next section will incorporate preference shocks and the durability of commodities, and the estimation of the model will allow for measurement error.

Another useful way to look at the data is to fit a vector autoregression (VAR) consisting of the eight variables (seven commodity groups and income) and examine their dynamic structure. Since the panel is four quarters long and only three successive changes can be calculated, the lag length is two.[11] As is clear from Table 4.4, there is virtually no feedback (particularly from income to expenditures), so that the VAR looks very

Table 4.4
Eight-Variable Vector Autoregression

Equation[a]	Own lags First Second	Significant Feedback from:[b]	SE^c	R^2
C_1 (food)	-0.60^{***} -0.28^{***}	C_6^*	44.3	0.31
C_2 (rents and utilities)	-0.60^{***} -0.21^{***}	$C_6,^*$ YD^*	25.9	0.36
C_3 (clothes)	-0.54^{***} -0.34^{***}	none	58.9	0.32
C_4 (durables)	-0.57^{***} -0.30^{***}	none	147.5	0.33
C_5 (recreation & education)	-0.67^{***} -0.23^{***}	none	142.1	0.29
C_6 (medical)	-0.68^{***} -0.28^{**}	none	39.9	0.31
C_7 (other)	-0.66^{***} -0.38^{***}	$C_2,^*$ C_3^*	63.1	0.43
YD (disposable income)	-0.92^{***} -0.35^{**}	none	219.5	0.63

a. The dependent variable in the C_1 equation, for example, is the change in food expenditure from 1981:Q4 to 1982:Q1, namely $C_{14} - C_{13}$.
b. The presence of feedback is determined by the significance of two lags as a whole. Heteroskedasticity-robust standard errors are used.
c. The sample standard deviation of the residuals.
* Significant at the 5 percent level.
** Significant at the 1 percent level.
*** Significant at the 0.1 percent level.

much like a collection of univariate autoregressions. Own lags are negative and significant, which of course is a reflection of the strong negative autocorrelation of expenditure changes.

The results presented so far are not inconsistent with the permanent income hypothesis with measurement error and preference shocks. But there is also evidence that is not favorable to the hypothesis: the correlation between current expenditure changes and lagged income changes is generally negative and significant. For example, the sample autocorrelation between the change in food expenditure from 1981:Q4 to 1982:Q1 and the lagged change in income is -0.080 and highly significant. If preference shocks and measurement error are uncorrelated with income, then the correlation should be zero, because expenditure changes are forecast errors according to the hypothesis.[12] Using an annual panel data set, Hall

Table 4.5
Correlation Coefficients of Unexpected Changes with Lagged Unexpected and Actual Changes

Variable (X)	Correlation coefficient of $X_4 - X_4^e$ with:			
	$X_3 - X_3^e$	$X_2 - X_2^e$	$X_3 - X_2$	$X_2 - X_1$
C_1	-0.137^{***}	-0.033	-0.145^{***}	-0.067^{***}
C_2	-0.181^{***}	-0.019	-0.134^{***}	-0.033
C_3	-0.010	0.019	-0.035	-0.007
C_4	0.005	0.093^{***}	-0.099^{***}	0.043
C_5	0.022	0.034	-0.054^{*}	0.048^{*}
C_6	-0.004	-0.097^{***}	-0.008	-0.111^{***}
C_7	-0.007	-0.043	-0.035	-0.074^{**}
YD	0.010	0.017	0.102^{***}	-0.093^{***}

* Significant at the 5 percent level.
** Significant at the 1 percent level.
*** Significant at the 0.1 percent level.

and Mishkin (1982) found the same correlation to be -0.055. Their explanation is that some households are "liquidity constrained" in the sense that their consumption tracks income. Consumption by these households will introduce negative autocorrelation because income changes are negatively autocorrelated. There is, however, another explanation, which draws on the durability of commodities. If at least a part of income changes is unexpected, then a rise in income causes expenditure (and hence the stock of consumption to be carried over to the next period) to rise, which tends to depress expenditure next period. Thus, what appears to be the excess sensitivity of consumption to income may be attributable to the durability of commodities and not to liquidity constraints. The estimation procedure in this chapter will distinguish between the two competing explanations of the observed correlation of expenditure with income changes.

Before turning to the theoretical model, we briefly examine the reported expectations data. The sample means and standard deviations of unexpected changes in expenditure and income are already reported in Table 4.2. Table 4.5 shows the sample correlations of changes from 1981:Q4 to 1982:Q1 with lagged unexpected and actual changes. Although they are mostly smaller than 0.1 in absolute value, some of them are statistically significant. This, however, is not a rejection of rational expectations, because the rational expectations hypothesis implies that the correlation between unexpected changes and lagged changes is zero, if the average is taken *over time*, not *across households*.[13] In particular, the mean (across households) of unexpected changes can differ from zero as everyone can be wrong in the same direction at any given point in time. So it is generally incorrect in panel or cross-section contexts to impose the usual rational expectations orthogonality condition that forecast errors are uncorrelated with lagged information.[14] (Our estimation procedure, to be presented in Section 4.5, will *not* use this type of orthogonality condition.) Some of the results in Table 4.2 are favorable to rational expectations, and some are not. Except for food and rents and utilities (C_1 and C_2), the sample standard deviation of the unexpected change from 1981:Q4 to 1982:Q1 in Table 4.2 is smaller than that of the VAR residuals reported in Table 4.4. On the other hand, the sample mean of unexpected changes is generally positive, which suggests consistent underprediction over time.

4.4   The Theoretical Model

This section presents a model of households with preference shocks and the durability of commodities. Consider a household whose intertemporal decision problem is to maximize

$$E_t\left[\sum_{s=0}^{T}\beta^s U(\bar{C}_{t+s};\eta_{t+s})\right], \tag{1}$$

where E_t is the expectations operator associated with the subjective probability distribution (assumed by the household) of future variables that are uncertain to the household, β is a discount factor, T is the length of the remaining life, $\bar{C}$ is a vector of *consumption* of n commodities, $U(.)$ is the instantaneous utility function, and η is a vector of variables (preference shocks) that shift the instantaneous utility function.[15] Preference shocks may exhibit seasonal variations. We shall make no assumptions about the correlation structure of preference shocks (across components and over time). The relationship between the vector of consumption $\bar{C}$ and the associated n-dimensional vector of *expenditure* C is given by

$$\bar{C}_{jt} = \sum_{k=0}^{M}(\rho_{jk}C_{j,t-k}) \equiv \rho_j(L)C_{jt}, \quad j = 1, 2, \ldots, n, \tag{2}$$

where $\rho_j(L) = \sum \rho_{jk}L^k$ is a polynomial in the lag operator L. That is, current consumption is a distributed lag function of current and past expenditure. This is a generalization of the usual formula for durables, where $\bar{C}_{jt}$ is service flow from the stock of durables and the distributed lag coefficients ρ_{jk} ($k = 0, 1, 2, \ldots$) are of the Koyck type.

We assume that the household has access to asset markets including access to a nominal risk-free security whose nominal interest rate is R_t. The maximization of (1) subject to (2) gives the first-order necessary condition for the nominal risk-free security:[16]

$$E_t\left\{\sum_{k=0}^{M'}[\beta^k MU_j(t+k)\rho_{jk}]\right\} = E_t\left\{(1+r_{j,t+1})\beta\sum_{k=0}^{M''}[\beta^k MU_j(t+k+1)\rho_{jk}]\right\},$$

$$j = 1, 2, \ldots, n. \qquad (3)$$

Here, M' is $\min(M, T)$, M'' is $\min(M, T-1)$, $MU_j(t) = \partial U(\bar{C}_t; \eta_t)/\partial \bar{C}_{jt}$ is the marginal utility of commodity j, and $r_{j,t+1}$ is the real rate on commodity j; i.e., $1 + r_{j,t+1} = (1 + R_t)p_{jt}/p_{j,t+1}$, where p_{jt} is the price of commodity j in period t. The left-hand side of this equation is the marginal cost of forgoing one unit of expenditure on the jth commodity. This involves a summation from 0 to M' because a change in current expenditure influences current and future consumption. The right-hand side is the marginal benefit of increasing $1 + r_{j,t+1}$ units of expenditure on commodity j in the next period. This also involves a summation from 0 to M'' for the same reason. In Appendix A it is shown that under (3),

$$E_t[(1 + r_{j,t+1})\beta MU_j(t+1)/MU_j(t)] = 1, \quad j = 1, 2, \ldots, n \qquad (4)$$

holds approximately if M (the length of the distributed lag) is small relative to T (the length of remaining life) and the household has static and point expectations about future real rates, and holds exactly if (as is usually the case for durables) ρ_{jk} is geometrically declining in k and $r_{j,t+1}$ is known in t and $r_{j,t+1} = r_{j,t+2}$. Equation (4) is the usual first-order condition without durability. So, essentially, the price for having the familiar expression like (4) is the assumption of static and point expectations about future real rates.[17]

Equation (4) can be made tractable under two alternative assumptions. First, assume that the instantaneous utility function $U(.)$ takes the following separable form:

$$U(\bar{C}_t; \eta_t) = \sum_{j=1}^{n}\left\{-\mu_j\exp\left[\frac{\eta_j - \bar{C}_{jt}}{\mu_j}\right]\right\}, \quad \mu_j > 0. \qquad (5)$$

Rewrite (4) as

$$(1 + r_{j,t+1})\beta MU_j(t+1)/MU_j(t) = 1 - e'_{j,t+1}, \quad j = 1, 2, \ldots, n, \qquad (6)$$

where $e'_{j,t+1}$ is the difference between the left-hand side of (4) and the left-hand side of (6); that is, $e'_{j,t+1}$ is the forecast error of the left-hand side of (6) and satisfies $E_t(e'_{j,t+1}) = 0$. It therefore consists of new information the household receives in period $t + 1$ about labor income, real rates, and preference shocks. Take the log of both sides of (6) and use the approximation $\ln(1 + x) \simeq x$ to obtain[18]

$$\ln(1 + r_{j,t+1}) + \ln(\beta) + \ln[MU_j(t + 1)] - \ln[MU_j(t)] = -e'_{j,t+1}. \tag{7}$$

Under the assumed utility function (5) this becomes

$$\bar{C}_{j,t+1} - \bar{C}_{jt} = d_{j,t+1} + e_{j,t+1}, \quad j = 1, 2, \ldots, n, \tag{8}$$

where

$$d_{j,t+1} = \mu_j[\ln(1 + r_{j,t+1}) + \ln(\beta)] + \eta_{j,t+1} - \eta_{jt}, \tag{9}$$

and $e_{j,t+1} = \mu_j e'_{j,t+1}$ is the forecast error that is uncorrelated (in the household's judgment) with any information that is known to the household at the end of period t.

Another way to make (4) tractable is to assume that the instantaneous utility function $U(.)$ is quadratic:

$$U(\bar{C}_t; \eta_t) = a'\bar{C}_t - (\tfrac{1}{2})(\bar{C}_t - \eta_t)'B(\bar{C}_t - \eta_t); \tag{10}$$

and that the real rates are constant and the same across commodities:

$$(1 + r_{j,t+1})\beta = 1, \quad j = 1, 2, \ldots, n. \tag{11}$$

It then is easy to show that (4) reduces to (8) with $d_{j,t+1} = \eta_{j,t+1} - \eta_{jt}$. This is the multi-commodity version of Hall's (1978) martingale hypothesis.

Under either assumption about the instantaneous utility function, substitution of (2) into (8) gives equations stated in terms of expenditure changes:

$$\rho_j(L)(C_{j,t+1} - C_{jt}) = d_{j,t+1} + e_{j,t+1}, \quad j = 1, 2, \ldots, n, \tag{12}$$

which shows that, conditional on the intercept $d_{j,t+1}$, expenditure changes are a collection of univariate autoregressions. (Appendix B shows that approximately the same equation can be derived from a continuous-time model where C's in (12) are unit averages over periods of an arbitrary length.) If we can ignore the potential (across households) correlation between the forecast error $e_{j,t+1}$ and lagged expenditure changes mentioned in the last paragraph of Section 4.4, which may be quantitatively unimportant in view of the result in Table 4.5, lagged expenditure changes in other commodities will help explain the current change in expenditure on the commodity in question only when η_t has a contemporaneous correlation across commodities. The result in Table 4.4 that there is no significant feedback among commodities, then, indicates that our maintained assumption about the instantaneous utility function is consistent with the data, since a significant feedback means either that η_t has a contemporaneous correlation (which our model allows for), or that the true instantaneous utility function differs from (5) or (10).

The autoregressive form (12) is not convenient for our purposes because our data set contains only three successive expenditure changes. Our empirical implementation will assume geometric decay for $\rho_j(L)$:

$$\rho_j(L) = 1 + \rho_j L + (\rho_j)^2 L^2 + \cdots = (1 - \rho_j L)^{-1}, \tag{13}$$

so that the autoregressive representation (12) can be inverted to obtain a moving average representation:[19]

$$C_{j,t+1} - C_{jt} = (d_{j,t+1} - \rho_j d_{jt}) + (e_{j,t+1} - \rho_j e_{jt}), \quad j = 1, 2, \ldots, n. \tag{14}$$

This will be utilized in our later estimation.

The *intra*temporal first-order condition for the case of geometric decay can be derived from equation (A.4) in Appendix A as

$$\frac{MU_j(t)}{MU_l(t)} = \frac{(1 + r_{j,t+1} - \rho_j)p_{j,t+1}}{(1 + r_{l,t+1} - \rho_l)p_{l,t+1}}, \quad j, l = 1, 2, \ldots, n,$$

where $p_{j,t+1}$ and $p_{\ell,t+1}$ are assumed to be known in period t. We will not exploit this marginal condition for our four-quarter panel data because there is no way (unless $\rho_j = \rho_\ell$) to transform it into an equation like (14) that involves only a small number of successive expenditure changes.

In the empirical implementation, we wish to test the permanent income hypothesis with durability just presented against the alternative model of "liquidity constraints." A most natural way to incorporate liquidity constraints would be to let the interest rate be endogenous and depend on the household's income and asset position. The present data set has no information on households' assets and liabilities, so that we cannot tell whether the household is borrowing or lending at the margin. Thus, it is impossible to implement the idea of endogenous interest rates in a satisfactory fashion.[20] Our version of liquidity constraints, which is also the one employed in Hall (1978), Hall and Mishkin (1982), and Hayashi (1982), is that the marginal propensity to spend out of current disposable income is unity. If the marginal budget share α_j of commodity j is independent of income, the behavior of liquidity constrained households is described by

$$C_{j,t+1} - C_{jt} = \alpha_j(YD_{t+1} - YD_t), \quad j = 1, 2, \ldots, n, \quad \sum_{i=1}^{n} \alpha_j = 1, \qquad (15)$$

where YD is real disposable income.[21]

We assume that a constant fraction λ of the population is liquidity constrained in the sense just defined, while the remaining households in the population follow the permanent income hypothesis with durability. The model to be estimated is a weighted average of (14) and (15). This model will be referred to as the *augmented model*.

4.5 Econometric Issues

In this section we derive a set of overidentifying restrictions on the covariances of relevant variables implied by the augmented model. These restrictions will serve as a basis for estimation and inference that will be carried out in Section 4.6. Nontechnical readers can skip to the last paragraph of this section without losing continuity.

The discussion can be made clearer if we temporarily drop the commodity subscript j and introduce the household subscript i. To exploit the information on expectations included in our data set, we derive two equations that involve expectations from each of the two equations, (14) and (15). Taking expectations of both sides of (14) and nothing that $E_{it}(e_{i,t+1}) = 0$, we obtain

$$C_{i,t+1}^e - C_{it} = -\rho e_{it} + (d_{i,t+1}^e - \rho d_{it}), \quad i = 1, 2, \ldots, N, \qquad (16a)$$

where $d_{i,t+1}^e = E_{it}(d_{i,t+1})$ is the expectation of $d_{i,t+1}$ held by household i at the end of period t, and N is the number of households in the sample. Equations (14) and (16a) imply that

$$C_{it} - C_{it}^e = e_{it} + (d_{it} - d_{it}^e), \quad i = 1, 2, \ldots, N. \qquad (16b)$$

We note here that d_{it} and d_{it}^e differ across households because they depend on preference shocks η_{it} and on the preference parameters (β, μ) that may differ across households (see (9)). Similarly for (15) we obtain

$$C_{i,t+1}^e - C_{it} = \alpha(YD_{i,t+1}^e - YD_{it}), \qquad (17a)$$

$$C_{it} - C_{it}^e = \alpha(YD_{it} - YD_{it}^e), \quad i = 1, 2, \ldots, N. \qquad (17b)$$

We now allow for measurement error in (actual and expected) expenditure, so that (16) and (17) are rewritten as

$$C^e_{i,t+1} - C_{it} = -\rho e_{it} + u_{1it},$$ (16a')

$$C_{it} - C^e_{it} = e_{it} + u_{2it},$$ (16b')

$$C^e_{i,t+1} - C_{it} = \alpha(YD^e_{i,t+1} - YD_{it}) + v_{1it},$$ (17a')

$$C_{it} - C^e_{it} = \alpha(YD_{it} - YD^e_{it}) + v_{2it}, \quad i = 1, 2, \ldots, N,$$ (17b')

where C_{it} and C^e_{it} now stand for measured (actual and expected) expenditure. The "error terms" (u_{1it}, u_{2it}, v_{1it}, v_{2it}) are composed of preference shocks, individual (household-specific) differences in (β, μ), and measurement for error in expenditure.

Let λ be the fraction of "liquidity-constrained" households in the population (from which our random sample was drawn). For the ith draw from the cross-section joint distribution of (e_{it}, $YD^e_{i,t+1} - YD_{it}$, $YD_{it} - YD^e_{it}$, u_{1it}, u_{2it}, v_{1it}, v_{2it}; $t = 2, 3, 4$), expenditure changes $C^e_{i,t+1} - C_{it}$ and $C_{it} - C^e_{it}$ are generated by (16a', b') with probability $1 - \lambda$ and by (17a', b') with probability λ. So, for example, the population mean of $C^e_{i,t+1} - C_{it}$ is written as

$$E(C^e_{i,t+1} - C_{it}) = (1 - \lambda)[-\rho E(e_{it}) + E(u_{1it})]$$

$$+ \lambda[\alpha E(YD^e_{i,t+1} - YD_{it}) + E(v_{1it})].$$

Here, the expectations operator "E," which denotes the population mean associated with the cross-section joint distribution, should be clearly distinguished from the expectations operation "E_{it}," which is associated with the *subjective* distribution assumed by household i of future variables that are uncertain to the household. In particular, we have that $E_{it}(e_{it}) = 0$ but $E(e_{it})$ is not necessarily zero as explained in the last paragraph of Section 4.3.

Our basic assumption that is required for identification is that preference shocks, measurement error in expenditure, and individual differences in the preference parameter (β, μ_1, μ_2, $\ldots$, μ_n) are all uncorrelated (across households) with disposable income. So u_{1it}, u_{2it}, v_{1it} and v_{2it} are uncorrelated with $YD^e_{i,t+1} - YD_{it}$ and $YD_{it} - YD^e_{it}$. Is this assumption plausible? We have assumed implicitly about the utility function (5) that leisure is separable from commodities. If leisure is nonseparable from commodities, this could be a source of preference shocks η_t, resulting in their correlation with disposable income changes. The same results if leisure is separable (or the utility function is quadratic) but the shock to leisure is correlated with η_t. Either way, it seems that a contemporaneous correlation in the components of η_t is a sign of the importance of the correlation of η_t with disposable income, although it is possible that each component of η_t is correlated with disposable income without a contemporaneous correlation. But, as discussed in the paragraph containing equation (12), the result in Table 4.4 is consistent with the assumption of no strong contemporaneous correlation in η_t. At any rate, the assumption of no correlation between η_t and disposable income is absolutely essential because without it any theory that allows for preference shocks is consistent with any observed correlation between expenditure and income changes.

Under this assumption we can obtain the following expressions for the covariances of expected and unexpected expenditure and income changes (hereafter we drop the household subscript i and reintroduce the commodity subscript j):

$$\text{cov}(C^e_{j,t+1} - C_{jt}, YD^e_{t+1} - YD_t)$$

$$= -(1 - \lambda)\rho_j \, \text{cov}(e_{jt}, YD^e_{t+1} - YD_t) + \lambda \alpha_j \gamma_{1t}, \tag{18a}$$

$$\text{cov}(C^e_{j,t+1} - C_{jt}, YD_t - YD^e_t)$$

$$= -(1 - \lambda)\rho_j \, \text{cov}(e_{jt}, YD_t - YD^e_t) + \lambda \alpha_j \gamma_{2t}, \tag{18b}$$

$$\text{cov}(C_{jt} - C^e_{jt}, YD^e_{t+1} - YD_t)$$

$$= (1 - \lambda) \, \text{cov}(e_{jt}, YD^e_{i,t+1} - YD_t) + \lambda \alpha_j \gamma_{2t}, \tag{18c}$$

$$\text{cov}(C_{jt} - C^e_{jt}, YD_t - YD^e_t)$$

$$= (1 - \lambda) \, \text{cov}(e_{jt}, YD_t - YD^e_t) + \lambda \alpha_j \gamma_{3t}, \quad j = 1, 2, \ldots, n; \, t = 2, 3, 4, \tag{18d}$$

and

$$\text{var}(YD^e_{t+1} - YD_t) = \gamma_{1t}, \tag{19a}$$

$$\text{cov}(YD^e_{t+1} - YD_t, YD_t - YD^e_t) = \gamma_{2t}, \tag{19b}$$

$$\text{var}(YD_t - YD^e_t) = \gamma_{3t}, \quad t = 2, 3, 4. \tag{19c}$$

There are $3 \times 4 = 12$ covariances for each commodity j in (18) and $3 \times 3 = 9$ covariances for income in (19). So in total there are $12n + 9$ covariances. They involve the following $8n + 9$ parameters:

$\lambda; p_1, \ldots, p_n; \alpha_1, \ldots, \alpha_{n-1}$ (note that $\Sigma \alpha_j = 1$);

$$\text{cov}(e_{jt}, YD^e_{t+1} - YD_t), \text{cov}(e_{jt}, YD_t - YD^e_t), \tag{20}$$

$j = 1, \ldots, n$ and $t = 2, 3, 4; \gamma_{1t}, \gamma_{2t}, \gamma_{3t}, \quad t = 2, 3, 4.$

That the $12n + 9$ covariances are functions of the $8n + 9$ parameters is the set of overidentifying restrictions implied by the augmented model.

Let θ be a vector of the $8n + 9$ parameters in (20) and g be a vector of the $12n + 9$ covariances in (18) and (19). The set of overidentifying restrictions can be written compactly as $g = g(\theta)$. It is easy to see that $g(\theta)$ is twice continuously differentiable and that $\partial g(\theta)/\partial(\theta)$ is of full rank unless $\lambda = 0$ or 1. Let θ^* be the true value of θ. It can be shown that $g(\theta) = g(\theta^*)$ implies that $\theta = \theta^*$; namely the model is identifiable. Since our data are a random sample, the $12n + 9$ dimensional vector of sample covariances $\bar{g}$ converges almost surely to $g(\theta^*)$ and the limiting distribution of $N^{\frac{1}{2}}[\bar{g} - g(\theta^*)]$ is normal with mean zero and some variance matrix Δ. If expenditure and income changes have fourth moments, then the sample variance $\bar{V}$ of cross products of expenditure and income changes converges almost surely to Δ.[22] We can then apply Propositions 1 and 2 in Chamberlain (1984) to show that the minimum distance estimator $\hat{\theta}$ of θ, which is obtained from

$$\text{minimize } S(\theta) = N[\bar{g} - g(\theta)]'\bar{V}^{-1}[\bar{g} - g(\theta)], \tag{21}$$

converges almost surely to the true value θ^*, is asymptotically normal, and the asymptotic variance is consistently estimated by $\{[\partial g(\hat{\theta})/\partial\theta]'\bar{V}^{-1} \cdot [\partial g(\hat{\theta})/\partial\theta]\}^{-1}$. Furthermore, the minimized distance $S(\hat{\theta})$ is asymptotically distributed as chi-squared with the degrees of freedom equal to the number of overidentifying restrictions. We can use this statistic to test the overidentifying restrictions.

We now make several remarks on the estimation strategy just presented. (i) A natural question arises as to why we do not look at the covariances between current expenditure changes and lagged income changes like $\text{cov}(C^e_{j,t+1} - C_{jt}, YD^e_t - YD_{t-1})$. As explained in the last paragraph of Section 4.3, even if expectations are rational, such covariances are not necessarily zero and have to be estimated. Adding those to the list of covariances merely increases the number of parameters without increasing the number of restrictions. (ii) We have made no assumptions about the serial correlation of income, preference shocks, and measurement error in expenditure. This is why the set of covariances in (18) does not include autocovariances in expenditure and income changes. (iii) Since expected changes from 1981:Q2 to Q3 are available, (18a) and (19a) could be used not just for $t = 2, 3, 4$ but also for $t = 1$. Doing so would only introduce an unidentifiable parameter $\text{cov}(e_{j1}, YD_2^e - YD_1)$ if $\rho_1 = 0$. (iv) Without the expectations data, it is impossible to identify the parameters $(\lambda, \alpha_1, \ldots, \alpha_n, \rho_1, \ldots, \rho_{n-1})$, unless we impose the orthogonality condition that the correlation between forecast errors and lagged variables across households is zero. Unfortunately, as shown in Table 4.5, the correlation is statistically significant, although its quantitative importance is small. This study is probably the first *not* to impose this type of orthogonality condition. (v) Our minimum distance estimator does not require expenditure and income changes to be normally distributed. As discussed in Chamberlain (1982), the quasi-maximum likelihood estimator—which maximizes the normal likelihood function even though the distribution is not necessarily normal—is consistent, but the true asymptotic variance is not given by the standard information matrix formula.[23] In addition, our minimum distance estimator is more efficient than the quasi-maximum likelihood estimator. (vi) It is necessary to assume that (at least one) income change is measured without error. If income is measured with error, the γ's in (18) and the γ's in (19) are no longer the same, which renders γ unidentifiable, unless we place an arbitrary restriction on one of the γ's in (18). But this model with income measurement error but with one arbitrary restriction on the γ's in (18) did not improve the fit significantly.[24] We therefore assume for the rest of this chapter that there is no income measurement error.

To summarize: under the assumption that preference shocks and expenditure measurement error are uncorrelated with income and that there is no income measurement error, the augmented model (14) and (15) imposes a set of overidentifying restrictions that $12n + 9$ covariances in (18) and (19) are functions of $8n + 9$ parameters listed in (20). Autocovariances in expenditure changes are not included in (18) because we make no assumptions about the serial correlation of preference shocks and measurement error. Our estimation strategy is the minimum distance procedure of choosing parameter values that minimize a suitably defined "distance" between the sample covariances and the corresponding covariances predicted by the model.

4.6 Results

To obtain good starting parameter estimates, the joint minimum distance procedure (of estimating all the parameters simultaneously) is first broken down into seven commodity-wise estimation procedures. In other words, for each commodity j the twelve covariances in (18) are paired with the nine covariances in (19), and a minimum distance procedure is applied to those twenty-one covariances.[25] This gives consistent estimates of ρ_j and $\lambda \alpha_j$ for each commodity j, and an estimate of λ of 0.16 is obtained by summing the commodity-wise estimates of $\lambda \alpha_j$ over j. However, for C_1 (food), the durability parameter ρ_1 fluctuates around zero and does not converge in the minimization iterations, and for C_2 (rents, fuel, and utilities), the estimate of ρ_2 is unreasonably large (about 6.5 and significant). This is not surprising because most expenditures in C_2 cannot actually be changed on a quarterly basis.

In the joint estimation, we therefore drop C_2 and set $\rho_1 = 0$. Fortunately, the commodity-wise estimate of the marginal expenditure share α_2 for C_2 is less than 5 percent, so dropping C_2 will not change our estimate of λ significantly. There are $12 \times 6 + 9 = 81$ covariances to match and $8 \times 6 + 9 - 1 = 56$ parameters to be estimated. The number of overidentifying restrictions (which include $\rho_1 = 0$) is thus 25. The results from the joint estimation are reported in the left half of Table 4.6.[26] The durability parameter ρ exceeds unity for C_3 (clothes) and C_5 (recreation and education), but it is not significantly different from, say, 0.9. On the other hand, C_4 (durables) does not come out to be highly "durable." This may be explained by the lumpiness of durables, an element that is not incorporated in our theoretical model but is present in Table 4.1. The fraction λ of liquidity-constrained households whose total expenditure tracks income is sharply estimated to be 0.16. With C_2 dropped, the augmented model is successful in mimicking the sample covariances: the "distance" between the sample covariances and the fitted covariances implied by our parameter estimates is 34, which is not a surprisingly large value from a $\chi^2(25)$ distribution. Table 4.7 shows the two sets of covariances for food.

Seasonality in our model is represented by preference shocks η, which show up additively in the expenditure equation (14) and hence do not change the covariances in (18) and (19). To see whether this additive specification of seasonality is appropriate, seasonally adjusted sample covariances are calculated using the same multiplicative seasonality factors that we used in the right half of Table 4.3. Since equation (15) for liquidity-constrained households should be in seasonally unadjusted variables, disposable income as well as expenditure on commodity j are multiplied by the *same* seasonality factor specific to commodity j. This means that seasonally adjusted income changes are different across commodities, so the commodity-wise minimum distance estimation is used. The resulting

Table 4.6
Parameter Estimates[a]

Commodity group	Seasonally unadjusted		Seasonally adjusted	
	ρ	α	ρ	α
C_1 (food)	0.0[b]	0.10	−0.10	0.12
		(0.013)	(0.23)	
C_2 (rent & utilities)	—	—	—	—
C_3 (clothes)	1.36	0.17	1.07	0.20
	(0.30)	(0.025)	(0.21)	
C_4 (durables)	0.58	0.22	0.38	0.16
	(0.18)	(0.036)	(0.24)	
C_5 (recreation & education)	1.23	0.21	1.17	0.26
	(0.20)	(0.043)	(0.19)	
C_6 (medical)	0.29	0.02	0.48	0.03
	(0.26)	(0.010)	(0.21)	
C_7 (other)	0.12	0.27	0.23	0.24
	(0.19)	(0.030)	(0.13)	
λ	0.158		0.126	
	(0.020)			

a. Standard errors in parentheses.
b. Constrained to be 0.0 in the minimum distance estimation.

Table 4.7
Sample and Fitted Covariances: Food[a]

	Sample	Fitted
$\mathrm{cov}(C_{13}^e - C_{12}, YD_3^e - YD_2)$	1,282	1,478
$\mathrm{cov}(C_{13}^e - C_{12}, YD_2 - YD_2^e)$	33	−174
$\mathrm{cov}(C_{12} - C_{12}^e, YD_3^e - YD_2)$	−864	−1,080
$\mathrm{cov}(C_{12} - C_{12}^e, YD_2 - YD_2^e)$	611	775
$\mathrm{cov}(C_{14}^e - C_{13}, YD_4^e - YD_3)$	2,463	1,806
$\mathrm{cov}(C_{14}^e - C_{13}, YD_3 - YD_3^e)$	−738	−364
$\mathrm{cov}(C_{13} - C_{13}^e, YD_4^e - YD_3)$	−1,361	−697
$\mathrm{cov}(C_{13} - C_{13}^e, YD_3 - YD_3^e)$	1,159	817
$\mathrm{cov}(C_{15}^e - C_{14}, YD_5^e - YD_4)$	959	763
$\mathrm{cov}(C_{15}^e - C_{14}, YD_4 - YD_4^e)$	−95	−68
$\mathrm{cov}(C_{14} - C_{14}^e, YD_5^e - YD_4)$	−88	−136
$\mathrm{cov}(C_{14} - C_{14}^e, YD_4 - YD_4^e)$	743	621

a. Income and expenditure are stated in thousands of 1980 yen.

Table 4.8
Regression of Change in Food Expenditure on Expected and Unexpected Disposable Income
Changes*

Change in food expenditure $C_{1,t-1} - C_{1t}$	Coefficient of income change		R^2
	Expected $YD_{t-1}^e - YD_t$	Unexpcted $YD_{t-1} - YD_{t-1}^e$	
1981:Q2 to 1981:Q3	0.014	0.022	0.021
	(0.004)	(0.009)	
1981:Q3 to 1981:Q4	0.015	0.035	0.036
	(0.005)	(0.011)	
1981:Q4 to 1982:Q1	0.025	0.035	0.036
	(0.006)	(0.014)	

*Other variables included in the regression are AGE and its square, the change in FSZ, and its square. They contribute only marginally to the R^2. Heteroskedasticity-robust standard errors are in parentheses.

parameter estimates are shown in the right half of Table 4.6. They are not grossly different from the parameter estimates on seasonally unadjusted data. We note that ρ_1 is now estimated and is insignificant.

If $\rho_1 = 0$, less formal but probably more intuitively appealing results can be obtained from a regression of food expenditure changes on expected and unexpected income changes. Apart from the potential bias arising from the correlation between the forecast error $e_{1,t+1}$ and the expected income change $YD_{t+1}^e - YD_t$, the augmented model predicts that the coefficient of the expected income change is $\lambda \alpha_1$. Its OLS estimate reported in Table 4.8 is consistent with that prediction. We also noted in Table 4.8 that income variables explain only a small fraction of expenditure changes. The dominant source of fluctuations of expenditure at the individual level is preference shocks and measurement error.[27]

On the whole, then, the empirical evidence points to a high degree of durability for most of the commodities usually labeled as services or semidurables. Is this consistent with time-series evidence? This is an important question to ask because on the U.S. aggregate time-series data quarterly changes in expenditure on nondurables and services as a whole are very much like white noise (Hall, 1978).[28] The Japanese National Income Accounts have two different classifications (by type of product and type of expenditure) of personal consumption expenditures. Durables in the first classification seem to correspond to C_4 in our data set. The second classification includes six types of expenditure which are listed in Table 4.9 along with durables. They correspond roughly to C_1, C_2, C_3,

Table 4.9
Aggregate Time-Series Estimates[a]

Commodity group in the National Income Accounts	a_{j0}	a_{j1}	a_{j2}	a_{j3}	a_{j4}
1. Food, beverages, and tobacco	0.10 (0.11)	−0.10 (0.18)	−0.32 (0.14)	−0.09 (0.14)	0.025 (0.016)
2. Rents, fuel, and utilities[b]	0.10 (0.08)	−0.17 (0.21)	−0.38 (0.19)	0.04 (0.21)	−0.025 (0.014)
3. Clothes and footware	0.00 (0.10)	−0.31 (0.16)	−0.54 (0.13)	−0.39 (0.15)	−0.005 (0.003)
4. Durables	0.18 (0.06)	0.04 (0.15)	−0.16 (0.14)	0.07 (0.15)	−0.009 (0.008)
5. Recreation and education	0.27 (0.10)	−0.07 (0.17)	−0.49 (0.15)	−0.05 (0.18)	0.002 (0.009)
6. Medical care	0.03 (0.40)	−0.41 (0.23)	−0.24 (0.20)	0.14 (0.34)	−0.008 (0.006)
7. Other[c]	0.16 (0.11)	−0.25 (0.15)	0.06 (0.15)	0.21 (0.16)	−0.006 (0.011)

a. Standard errors are in parentheses. The estimated equation is (23) in the text. The data on expenditure are in real and per capita terms. The interest rate on one-year time deposits is used for the nominal risk-free interest rate. The sample period is 1971:Q1–1983:Q1.
b. Rents here include imputed rents.
c. Communicatin and transportation are not included.

C_5, C_6 and C_7 in our data set. For those commodity groups, we estimate the following equation using the National Income Accounts data:

$$C_{j,t+1} - C_{jt} = \text{const.} + \text{seasonal dummies} + a_{j0}\ln(1 + r_{j,t+1})$$

$$+ a_{j1}(C_{jt} - C_{j,t-1}) + a_{j2}(C_{j,t-1} - C_{j,t-2}) + a_{j3}(C_{j,t-2} - C_{j,t-3})$$

$$+ a_{j4}(YD_{t+1} - YD_t) + \text{error}, \quad j = 1, 2, \ldots, 7. \tag{22}$$

This is a weighted average of (12)—the autoregressive equation for the permanent income hypothesis—and (15). So $a_{j0} = (1 - \lambda)\mu_j$, $a_{jk} = -(1 - \lambda)\rho_{jk}$ ($k = 1, 2, 3$), and $a_{j4} = \lambda\alpha_j$ and the error term includes forecast errors. In (23), $\ln(1 + r_{j,t+1})$ and $YD_{t+1} - YD_t$ are instrumented by $\ln(1 + r_{jt})$ and ($YD_t - YD_{t-1}$) as they can be correlated with forecast errors. The resulting parameter estimates are given in Table 4.9. The coefficients of lagged expenditure changes are mostly negative, which is consistent with the permanent income hypothesis with durability. As in Table 4.6, C_3 (clothes and footware) and C_5 (recreation and education) are most durable, but their estimated durability is not so large.

Appendix A: Proof of (4)

This appendix proves (4) under two alternative assumptions.

Case 1. M is small relative to T and $r_{j,s} = r_j$ for all $s > t$ and j.

Let $_t y_{t+k} = E_t[(1 + r_j)\beta M U_j(t + k + 1) - M U_j(t + k)]$. Then (3) becomes

$$\sum_{k=0}^{M} (_t y_{t+k} \beta^k \rho_{jk}) = 0.$$

This must be true at any future point in the remaining lifetime, so

$$\sum_{k=0}^{K} (_s y_{s+k} \beta^k \rho_{jk}) = 0, \quad s = t, t + 1, \ldots, t + T - 1,$$

where $K = \min(t + T - s, M)$ and $_s y_{t+T} = -E_s[M U_j(t + T)]$. Apply the expectations operator E_t on both sides of this equation to obtain

$$\sum_{k=0}^{K} (x_{s+k-t} \beta^k \rho_{jk}) = 0, \quad s = t, t + 1, \ldots, t + T - 1, \tag{A.1}$$

where $x_\tau = {}_t y_{t+\tau}$. This is an mth-order difference equation in x_τ. If the terminal value x_T is given, (A.1) can determine the remaining value $x_0, x_1, \ldots, x_{T-1}$. (The lifetime budget constraint is necessary to determine the value of x_T.) Since $\beta^k \rho_{jk}$ is declining in k and positive, the difference equation is unstable, so that the initial value x_0 must be small relative to the terminal value. In fact, if T is infinite, then $x_0 = 0$.

Case 2. ρ_{jk} is geometrically declining in k, $p_{j,t+1}$ is known in t, and $r_{j,t+1} = r_{j,t+2}$.

With $\rho_{j,k} = (\rho_j)^k$, (2) implies that $\bar{C}_{jt} = C_{jt} + \rho_j C_{j,t-1}$. Consider the following small deviation from the optimal decision rule: reduce current expenditure on commodity j by one unit and increase the next period's expenditure by ρ_j units. Since this deviation means an additional saving of p_{jt} in period t, the additional income in period $t + 1$ is $(1 + R_t)p_{jt} - \rho_j p_{j,t+1}$. Note that this deviation leaves $\bar{C}_{j,t+1}$ unchanged from its level implied by the optimal decision rule. This small change should neither decrease nor increase the objective function, so that

$$MU_j(t) = \beta E_t\{v_{t+1}[(1 + R_t)p_{jt} - \rho_j p_{j,t+1}]\}, \tag{A.2}$$

where v_{t+1} is the marginal utility of income in $t + 1$, which follows

$$v_t = (1 + R_t)\beta E_t(v_{t+1}). \tag{A.3}$$

If $p_{j,t+1}$ is known at t, (A.2) can be rewritten as

$$MU_j(t) = (1 + r_{j,t+1} - \rho_j)p_{j,t+1}\beta E_t(v_{t+1}). \tag{A.4}$$

The right-hand side of (A.4) has the interpretation of the "user cost of capital" adjusted for the marginal utility of income. Now

$$E_t[(1 + r_{j,t+1})\beta MU_j(t + 1)],$$

$$= E_t[(1 + r_{j,t+1})\beta(1 + r_{j,t+2} - \rho_j), p_{j,t+2}\beta E_{t+1}(v_{t+2})] \qquad \text{(by(A.4))}$$

$$= E_t[(1 + r_{j,t+1})\beta(1 + r_{j,t+2} - \rho_j)(1 + r_{j,t+2})^{-1}p_{j,t+1}v_{t+1}] \qquad \text{(by(A.3))}.$$

If $r_{j,t+1} = r_{j,t+2}$, this is equal to $MU_j(t)$ by (A.4).

Appendix B: Time Aggregation

There is no reason that the length of the unit period for the household's optimization is exactly one quarter. The purpose of this appendix is to show that the quarterly model—equation (12) of the text—can be derived as an approximation to the continuous-time model.

The continuous-time version of (8) is

$$\bar{C}(\tau') - \bar{C}(\tau) = e(\tau, \tau') \quad E_\tau e(\tau, \tau') = 0 \text{ for } \tau' > \tau, \tag{B.1}$$

where the commodity subscript j is dropped and the intercept term $d_{j,t+1}$ is ignored for simplicity. Let $t = 0, 1, 2, \ldots$ be points in continuous calendar time that mark the end of each quarter. Set $\tau = t$ and $\tau' = t + 1$ to obtain

$$\bar{C}(t + 1) - \bar{C}(t) = e(t, t + 1), \quad E_t e(t, t + 1) = 0. \tag{B.2}$$

In the continuous-time model, $\bar{C}$ is related to C by

$$\bar{C}(\tau) = \int_0^\infty \rho(v)C(\tau - v)dv. \tag{B.3}$$

Combine (B.2) and (B.3) to get

$$e(t, t + 1) = \int_0^\infty \rho(v)C(t + 1 - v)dv - \int_0^\infty \rho(v)C(t - v)dv. \tag{B.4}$$

Now, consider the following step function as an approximation to $\rho(v)$:

$$\bar{\rho}(v) = \rho(0) \text{ for } 0 \leqslant v < 1, \quad \bar{\rho}(v) = \rho(1) \text{ for } 1 \leqslant v < 2, \text{ etc.} \qquad (B.5)$$

Then we obtain

$$e(t, t+1) \simeq \int_0^\infty \bar{\rho}(v)C(t+1-v)dv - \int_0^\infty \bar{\rho}(v)C(t-v)dv$$

$$= \rho(0)(C_{t+1} - C_t) + \rho(1)(C_t - C_{t-1}) + \ldots, \qquad (B.6)$$

where C_t is a unit average; i.e.,

$$C_t = \int_{t-1}^t C(\tau)d\tau. \qquad (B.7)$$

Note that $e(t, t+1)$ is orthogonal to information available at the *end* of period t, since $E_t e(t, t \mid 1) = 0$. In (12) e_{t+1} is used for $e(t, t+1)$.

Notes

The author is grateful to participants of workshops at several universities and the 1984 NBER macro conference, particularly Jean Crockett, Paul Evans, Marjorie Flavin, Robert Flood, Robert Gordon, Lars Hansen, Dale Jorgenson, Gregory Mankiw, Stephen Marglin, Robert Pollak, and to anonymous referees for comments and suggestions. All the computations were done at the Economic Planning Agency of the Japanese government where he was a visiting research associate. This is a revised version of his NBER Working Paper No. 1305. Views expressed here are his own and not necessarily those of the Economic Planning Agency or the National Bureau of Economic Research. Errors are his. This chapter was written while the author was at the University of Tsukuba.

1. In this chapter the permanent income hypothesis is taken to mean that households optimize their intertemporal utility function subject to the lifetime budget constraint.

2. See King (1983) for a survey of recent contributions.

3. Most recently, Eichenbaum and Hansen (1984) and Dunn and Singleton (1984) have studied the durability of commodities using U.S. aggregate time-series data.

4. The expenditure data refer to the full cost of purchases even though full payment may not have been made at the date of purchase.

5. Of the 2,707 cases, 331 cases did not report actual values, and 399 cases did not report expected values for all the relevant variables. Thus, we are not deliberately dropping households that cannot form expectations.

6. The reason for doing this is to treat homeowners and nonhomeowners symmetrically. Rents should include imputed rents for homeowners, which will disappear when expenditure changes are taken.

7. One case reported about 3.8 million yen for "other expenses" in period 1. This was a clear outlier. (The next highest value was about 1.2 million yen.) Four cases reported temporary income for period 1 in excess of 10 million yen. If the four cases are included, the sample standard deviation of temporary income in period 1 nearly quadruples. Another case reported temporary income in excess of 10 million yen in period 2. The remaining seventh case reported expected normal income for period 5 of 19.89 million yen. Since its actual normal income in periods 1, 2, 3, and 4 is 1.989 million yen, we concluded that the number was wrong by one decimal.

8. If (i) actual or expected expenditure exceeds 3 million yen in any of the commodity groups excluding durables, or (ii) actual or expected temporary income exceeds 10 million yen, or (iii) expenditure or income variables change by one decimal, then the case is deleted.

9. The summation in the calculation of autocorrelations is over households, not over time. This becomes relevant when we examine the property of unexpected changes. See the last paragraph of this section.

10. *The Annual Report on the Survey of Family Consumption* (the Economic Planning Agency) has quarterly time-series data from 1977:Q2 on average expenditure. We estimate multiplicative seasonality factors using this time-series data and use them to perform seasonal adjustment on the present data set.

11. Four additional variables, AGE, its square, $FSZ_4 - FSZ_3$, and its square, are also included in the autoregressions. Many of them are insignificant.

12. This argument implicitly assumes that the correlation (across households) between forecast errors and lagged information is zero, which is not necessarily true even under rational expectations. See the next paragraph.

13. This is pointed out by Chamberlain (1984). Suppose, to provide our own example, that there is a totally unexpected income tax reform in period t that slashes the tax rates for the rich. The forecast error $YD_t - YD_t^e$ will be positive for the rich and negative for the poor. So the covariance (across households) between the forecast error and YD_{t-1}, which equals

$$\plim_{N \to \infty} N^{-1} \sum_{i=1}^{N} (YD_{it} - YD_{it}^e) YD_{i,t-1}$$

(where N is the sample size and i is the household index), is positive.

14. Examples that use this type of orthogonality condition are Hall and Mishkin (1982); Hotz, Kydland, and Sedlacek (1982); and Bernanke (1984).

15. We omit leisure choices by assuming that utility is separable across leisure and consumption goods. Anyway, these is no information on labor supply in the present data set. This point is further discussed in Section 4.5.

16. A first-order condition similar to (3) has been derived by Dunn and Singleton (1984).

17. Of course, this does not imply that the real rates actually do not change over calendar time.

18. Equation (7) can also be obtained by imposing conditional normality assumption on expenditure levels. See Hansen and Singleton (1983).

19. As long as the household's economic age is greater than one quarter of 1981:Q2, the initial condition problem does not arise here. Equation (14) is a slight generalization of the equation derived by Mankiw (1982).

20. The difficulty is that the relevant interest rate, which may depend on disposable income when the household is borrowing, is exogenous when the household is lending at the margin. The after-tax real rate $r_{j,t+1}$ in $d_{j,t+1}$ also depends on the marginal tax rate on interest income. Since interest income is virtually tax-free in Japan, it is reasonable to assume that the real rates are the same across households. (Interest income for individuals from a principal of up to 3 million yen is tax-free. One can, however, avoid taxes on interest completely by maintaining accounts at several different financial institutions.) Shapiro (1984) exploits the cross-section variation in the after-tax real rates caused by variation in the marginal tax rates among households in the United States. At any rate, on our panel data the model in which the real rate is a time-invariant function of disposable income fails to fit the sample co-variances of expected and unexpected expenditure changes with actual disposable income changes.

21. (i) If the distinction between consumption and expenditure is ignored, (ii) if the household is myopic in the sense that it maximizes the instantaneous utility function subject to the budget constraint that total expenditure equals disposable income, and (iii) if the utility function is given by (5), then (15) with a time-dependent intercept term can be derived with $\alpha_j = \mu_j$ and YD_t = nominal disposable income deflated by $\sum \mu_j p_{jt}$. See Pollak (1971). The intercept term is ignored in (15) because it does not affect the subsequent discussion.

22. See (4.5) in Chamberlain (1982) for the formula for $\bar{V}$.

23. Hall and Mishkin (1982) and Bernanke (1984) use the quasi-maximum likelihood procedure.

24. The model with income measurement error and with one arbitrary restriction has eight additional parameters. The reduction in the distance (21) due to the increased number of parameters is 7.8, which is not surprisingly large for a variable from $\chi^2(8)$ distribution. In this minimum distance estimation with income measurement error, data on C_2 are not used and $\rho_1 = 0$ is imposed for reasons explained in the next section. The estimates of ρ and α are similar to those in the left half of Table 4.6. If the sample includes all households, the reduction in the distance (21) is about 19, which is significant at close to the 1 percent level. The estimate of λ if the sample includes all households is about 0.22 with a standard error of 0.036 when the identifying restriction with income measurement error is that the γ_{33} in (18) equals the γ_{33} in (19c).

25. The minimization algorithm that we use first transforms the distance into the sum of squares and then applies a locally available subroutine for minimizing a sum of squares by a modified Levenberg-Marquardt-Morrison method. The convergence criterion is that iterations continue until no parameter changes by more than 0.01 percent. In the commodity-wise estimation, two starting values, 0.01 and 0.99, are tried for ρ_j.

26. As the reader may have noticed, our estimation ignores the role of family size and age. If we use as our basic income and expenditure changes the residuals from regressions of raw changes on AGE, AGE^2, change in FSZ, and its square, it makes little difference to the results. In fact, we have $\lambda = 0.165$ (0.021), $\rho_3 = 1.47$ (0.37), $\rho_4 = 0.72$ (0.19), $\rho_5 = 1.26$ (0.20), $\rho_6 = 0.32$ (0.26), and $\rho_7 = 0.13$ (0.19).

27. In a study that uses diary panel data (Hayashi, 1985), it is also found that income explains only a small fraction of expenditure changes. Thus, it is preference shocks that are the dominant source of fluctuations in expenditure.

28. However, using updated data for the United States, Christiano (1984) finds that expenditure on nondurables and services has a positive serial correlation.

References

Bernanke, Ben, "Permanent Income, Liquidity, and Expenditure on Automobiles: Evidence from Panel Data," this *Journal*, XCIX (1984), 587–614.

Chamberlain, Gary, "Panel Data," in *Handbook of Economics*, Zvi Griliches and Michael Intriligator, eds., (Amsterdam and New York: North Holland, 1984).

Christiano, Laurence J., "A Critique of Conventional Treatments of the Model Timing Interval in Applied Econometrics," manuscript, University of Chicago, 1984.

Dunn, Kenneth B., and Kenneth J. Singleton, "Modelling the Term Structure of Interest Rates Under Nonseparable Utility and Durability of Goods," National Bureau of Economic Research Working Paper No. 1415, 1984.

Eichenbaum, Martin S., and Lars P. Hansen, "Uncertainty, Aggregation, and the Dynamic Demand for Consumption Goods," manuscript, Carnegie-Mellon University, 1984.

Hall, Robert E., "Stochastic Implications of the Life Cycle-Permanent Income Hypothesis: Theory and Evidence," *Journal of Political Economy*, LXXXVI (1978), 971–87.

Hall, Robert E., and Frederic S. Mishkin, "The Sensitivity of Consumption to Transitory Income: Estimates from Panel Data on Households," *Econometrica*, L (1982), 461–81.

Hansen, Lars P., and Kenneth J. Singleton, "Stochastic Consumption, Risk Aversion, and the Temporal Behavior of Asset Returns," *Journal of Political Economy*, LXCI (1983), 1269–86.

Hayashi, Fumio, "The Permanent Income Hypothesis: Estimation and Testing by Instrumental Variables," *Journal of Political Economy*, XC (1982), 895–918.

————, "An Extension of the Permanent Income Hypothesis and Its Test on Diary Panel" (in Japanese), *Economic Analysis* (a publication of the Economic Planning Agency), 1985.

Hotz, V. Joseph, Finn E. Kydland, and Guilherme L. Sedlacek, "Intertemporal Preferences and Labor Supply," manuscript, Carnegie-Mellon University, 1982.

King, Mervyn A., "The Economics of Saving," National Bureau of Economic Research Working Paper No. 1247, 1983.

Pollak, Robert A., "Additive Utility Functions and Linear Engel Curves," *Review of Economic Studies*, XXXVIII (1971), 401–14.

Mankiw, N. Gregory, "Hall's Consumption Hypothesis and Durable Goods," *Journal of Monetary Economics*, X (1982), 417–25.

Shapiro, Matthew, "The Permanent Income Hypothesis and the Real Interest Rate," *Economics Letter*, XIV (1984), 93–100.

Addendum to Chapter 4:
Consumption Growth Equation
for Food

Under the constant-absolute-risk-Aversion utility function assumed in the text, the Euler equation becomes an equation in changes, rather than growth rates, in consumption. The specification more popular in the literature is the constant-relative-risk-aversion utility function, which produces the Euler equation in growth rates, as shown in, e.g., chapter 1. For the sake of comparison with other studies in the literature, I estimate here the standard consumption growth equation for food using the present panel data on Japanese households. The Euler equation augmented to include demographics and income growth is

$$E_t[\log(c_{t+1})] - \log(c_t) = \text{constant} + \beta_1 \cdot \text{(change in the family size from}$$
$$\text{period } t \text{ to } t+1) + \beta_2 \cdot \text{(head's age in period } t)$$
$$+ \lambda \cdot (E_t[\log(YD_{t+1})] - \log(YD_t)) + \text{error}, \qquad (1)$$

where c_t is food consumption by the household in question in quarter t and YD_t is disposable income. Since the interest rate is common to all households, the interest rate term in the consumption growth equation has been submerged in the constant. Rows 1 through 4 of the addendum table estimate (1) by OLS with $\log(c_{t+1}^e)$ and $\log(YD_{t+1}^e)$ used for $E_t[\log(c_{t+1})]$ and $E_t[\log(YD_{t+1})]$, respectively, where $c_{t+1}^e (YDC_{t+1}^e)$ is the expectation of $c_{t+1} (YD_{t+1})$ as of quarter t.

This ignores the difference between the expected value of the log of a variable and the log of the expected value of the variable. Therefore, in rows 5 through 10, I estimate the growth equation with actual growth rates:

$$\log(c_{t+1}) - \log(c_t) = \text{constant} + \beta_1 \cdot \text{(change in the family size from}$$
$$\text{period } t \text{ to } t+1) + \beta_2 \cdot \text{(head's age in period } t)$$
$$+ \lambda \cdot (\log(YD_{t+1}) - \log(YD_t)) + \text{error}. \qquad (2)$$

Addendum Table
Consumption Growth Equation for Food

Row no.	Consumption growth	Period	Mean & std. dev. of cons. growth	OLS or IV?	Change in family size	Age × 10⁻³	Actual income growth	Expected income growth	Standard error of equation	R²	R² in first stage regression
1	expected	81:Q2–81:Q3	0.0234 0.0902	OLS	−0.00763 (0.00949)	0.449 (0.189)	—	0.0353 (0.00494)	0.089	0.027	—
2	expected	81:Q3–81:Q4	0.0414 0.126	OLS	−0.0268 (0.0165)	−0.786 (0.265)	—	0.0561 (0.0104)	0.125	0.019	—
3	expected	81:Q4–82:Q1	−0.102 0.144	OLS	0.0212 (0.0174)	−0.580 (0.304)	—	0.0887 (0.0128)	0.142	0.025	—
4	expected	82:Q1–82:Q2	0.00347 0.116	OLS	—	0.0728 (0.243)	—	0.0611 (0.0108)	0.115	0.016	—
5	actual	81:Q2–81:Q3	0.0238 0.235	IV[a]	−0.0179 (0.0248)	−0.466 (0.493)	0.0746 (0.0150)	—	0.233	—	0.763
6	actual	81:Q3–81:Q4	0.0985 0.207	IV[a]	−0.0374 (0.0273)	0.384 (0.437)	0.0664 (0.0195)	—	0.206	—	0.704
7	actual	81:Q4–82:Q1	−0.111 0.241	IV[a]	0.0681 (0.0291)	−0.780 (0.509)	0.140 (0.0269)	—	0.237	—	0.643
8	actual	81:Q2–81:Q3	0.0238 0.235	IV[b]	−0.0183 (0.0248)	−0.442 (0.494)	0.103 (0.0260)	—	0.233	—	0.256
9	actual	81:Q3–81:Q4	0.0985 0.207	IV[b]	0.00709 (0.0285)	0.148 (0.462)	−0.0838 (0.0698)	—	0.212	—	0.063
10	actual	81:Q4–82:Q1	−0.111 0.241	IV[b]	0.0659 (0.0291)	−0.987 (0.518)	0.217 (0.0439)	—	0.237	—	0.250

Notes: The sample size is 2,005. For rows 5–10, the last column reports the R^2 for the regression of actual income growth on the constant, change in the family size, age, and the instrument for actual income growth.

a. In rows 5–7, the instrument for actual income growth $\log(YD_{t+1}) - \log(YD_t)$ is expected income growth $\log(YD^e_{t+1}) - \log(YD_t)$.

b. In rows 8–10, the instrument for actual income growth is current income $\log(YD_t)$.

Because the actual income growth $\log(YD_{t+1}) - \log(YD_t)$ is correlated with the error term, it is instrumented by a set of instrumental variables. This is the specification most widely estimated in the literature. In rows 5 through 7, the instrument for actual income growth is expected income growth $\log(YD_{t+1}^e) - \log(YD_t)$, while in rows 8 through 10, the instrument is log current income $\log(YD_t)$.

Because of the need to take logs, I eliminate from the sample of 2,007 households those whose disposable income is zero for at least one quarter. This reduces the sample size to 2,005.

As is clear from the table, the excess sensitivity coefficient λ is highly significant. In most other studies estimating the consumption growth equation (2), the coefficient λ is difficult to estimate because of the lack of instruments predicting income growth well. Here, the expected income growth is an excellent predictor of actual income growth. In the first-stage regressions associated with the IV estimation in rows 5–7, where actual income growth is regressed on the constant, the change in the family size, age, and expected income growth, the R^2 ranges from two-thirds to three quarters, as shown in the last column of the table. The importance of having a good instrument can be seen from rows 8 through 10. The standard error of the excess sensitivity coefficient is now much higher and, at least for the 1981:Q3–1981:Q4 change, the IV estimate is no longer significantly different from zero.

5

Testing the Life Cycle–
Permanent Income
Hypothesis on Japanese
Monthly Panel Data

5.1 Introduction and Summary

This is a companion chapter to be read after or in conjunction with Hayashi (1985, included in this book as chapter 4). Both chapters examine the connection between the negative serial correlation in expenditure changes—the tendency of a change in expenditure to be followed in time by a change in the opposite direction—and the durability of commodities. The econometric technique for identifying the λ parameter, the fraction in the population of households for which expenditure tracks income, is also used in this chapter. The difference is that this chapter uses a different data set on Japanese households. The data used in the previous chapter (chapter 4) are a quarterly interview survey, whereas the data of this chapter are two monthly panels constructed from diaries kept by respondents participating in a different household survey.

The use of monthly diary data has obvious advantages. The information collected through diaries should be more accurate than through recollections at the interview time. The basic premise that the household's decision interval is the same as the sampling interval is probably more tenable with monthly data. On the other hand, the quarterly interview survey used in the previous chapter is unique in that it contains the respondent's expectation about expenditure and income, so that expected and unexpected changes can be calculated. This information was used to identify the durability of commodities as well as the λ parameter, even in the case where the connection between the negative correlation in expenditure changes and durability of commodities is made less transparent by measurement errors in expenditure and shifts in tastes. The monthly diary survey used in this chapter contains no information about expectations. As a result, this chapter's estimation can identify only one model parame-

Originally published in *Keizai Kenkyu*, no. 101 (1986): 1–23. Reprinted with permission.

ter—the λ parameter—in the general case with measurement errors and taste shifters. Another disadvantage of this monthly survey is that it is a "rolling" survey where one-sixth of the sample is replenished every month so that each respondent stays in the survey for only six months.

Our finding from the monthly diary survey is similar to that from the quarterly interview survey in some respects. If the commodity is durable, the utility from the commodity is proportional to a weighted average of the stream of current and past expenditures. For durable commodities, the weighted average is more like the simple average, so the sampling interval (quarterly versus monthly) matters less. Therefore, if most commodities (not just those labeled as durables) are highly durable, which is what we found in the previous chapter (chapter 4), the estimated model parameters will not depend on the sampling interval. In fact, we find that the estimates of λ obtained in this chapter from the monthly data are very close to those obtained in the previous chapter from the quarterly data. The degree of durability parameters would be similar on the monthly data, but we cannot tell this because the durability parameters are not identified in the present data set that has no information on expectations.

We also find that the different nature of the data affects the statistics that are not specific to the model parameters in predictable ways. The negative serial correlation in expenditure changes is stronger in monthly than in quarterly changes. The fraction of expenditure changes explained by income changes is much smaller for monthly changes. These are consistent with the view that the level of measured expenditure is subject to serially uncorrelated monthly shifts in preference and measurement errors. When quarterly data are constructed from the present monthly diary survey, the standard deviation of the level of quarterly expenditure is about 20 percent smaller than that calculated from the quarterly interview survey. This is consistent with our earlier presumption that diary surveys are more accurate than interview surveys. For disposable income, there is no comparable reduction in the standard deviation, which is consistent with the identifying assumption we used in the previous chapter and will use in this chapter that income has no measurement error.

The organization of this chapter is as follows. Section 5.2 describes the Japanese household survey and explains how the monthly panel used in this study is constructed. Section 5.3 briefly describes the equation for expenditure changes derived from the model of chapter 4. In section 5.4, we present estimates of univariate and vector autoregressions in expenditure changes and interpret the results in terms of the durability of commodities. Finally in section 5.5, we estimate λ, the fraction in the population of households for which expenditure equals income.

5.2 Characteristics of the Family Income and Expenditure Survey

The Family Income and Expenditure Survey (henceforth the FIES), conducted every month by the Management and Coordination Agency of the Japanese government, provides detailed micro information on consumption for individual households. The survey covers about eight thousand households, one-sixth of which is replaced by new households every month. Therefore, each household stays in the survey for six months. The FIES is a diary survey: each household is given a diary, to be collected twice a month, for recording expenditures on hundreds of items and income. Because the information is collected not through recollections by the respondent, its reliability should be very high.

This study uses the data from the FIES for the Japanese fiscal year 1981 (April 1981 through March 1982). We aggregate those hundreds of expenditure items into five commodity groups as follows (figures in parentheses are the FIES classification code).

i. food = "food" (1) − "eating out" (1.12) + "cigarettes and cigars" (10.1.4)

ii. nondurables other than food = "heating and water" (3) + "household nondurables" (4.5) + "drugs" (6.1) + "books and other printed matters" (9.3) + "other miscellaneous goods" (10.1.5)

iii. semi-durables = "repairs and maintenance" (2.2) + "household miscellaneous utensils" (4.4) + "clothing and footwear" (5) − "services related to clothing" (5.8) | "automobile maintenance" (7.2.3) + "recreational equipments" (9.2) + "beauty aids" (10.1.2) + "miscellaneous goods" (10.1.3)

iv. durables = "footwear" (4.1) + "room ornaments" (4.2) + "beds" (4.3) + "medical equipments" (6.2) + "automobiles" (7.2.1) + "bicycles" (7.2.2) + "recreational durables" (9.1)

v. services = "eating out" (1.12.1) + "rent" (2.1) + "household services" (4.6) + "services related to clothing" (5.8) + "medical services" (6.3) + "transportation" (7.1) + "communication" (7.3) + "education" (8) + "recreational services" (9.4) + "services related to beauty" (10.1.1) + "social expenses" (10.3)

This grouping parallels that of the National Income Accounts. See the *Report on the Family Income and Expenditure Survey* (various months) for more details on the FIES classification codes. The definition of food here, including alcoholic beverages and cigarettes, is the same as that in chapter 4.

The FIES survey excludes singles and the occupation excludes agriculture and fishery. This study utilizes the subsample consisting of the so-called worker households, households whose head is on a payroll, thus excluding the self-employed and the retired. We focus on worker households, because information on income taxes and disposable income is available only for such households, and because the monthly pattern of income is very different between worker and nonworker households thanks to bonuses. Two panels over a six-month period can be created from the data: panel A is from April 1981 through September 1981 and panel B from October 1981 through March 1982.

The process of creating the two panels is as follows. First, for each month, we select worker households with no missing values for relevant variables. This leaves us with about 5,200 to 5,300 households out of about 8,000. There are very few records with missing data, which corroborates the reliability of the FIES. We then select from this sample those households that stayed in the survey continuously from April to September 1981 for panel A and from October 1981 to March 1982 for panel B. Records from different monthly files are deemed to be for the same household if the following five items are the same for six months: (i) the city/town/village code, (ii) the area block code, (iii) the household ID within the area block, (iv) the "serial household ID," and (v) the previous year's annual income. That is, six-month panels were created from six monthly files through match-merging by those five items. Therefore, those households that moved or changed the previous year's annual income were removed. This produced a panel of 775 households for panel A and 722 households for panel B.

We further delete households if (a) the age of the household head decreases or increases by two years during the six-month period (one household from panel A and four from B), (b) the housing tenure changes from renter to owner or from owner to renter (four from A and one from B), (c) total expenditure or disposable income increases or decreases by tenfold (no such households in either panel), and (d) for each of the four expenditure groups excluding durables, the amount exceeds one million yen (two from A and three from B). This reduces the sample size to 768 for panel A and 714 for panel B.

Table 5.1 displays the mean and the standard deviation of real consumption expenditure and disposable income in thousands of 1980 yen. The relevant component of the CPI was used to convert nominal expenditure into real terms. For disposable income, the overall CPI was used. Since the inflation rate was low (2.8% per year) in the fiscal year 1981, how one converts nominal into real values is immaterial.

The following are noteworthy from table 5.1. For food, nondurables other than food, and services, average monthly expenditure is stable over time. In contrast, semidurables and durables are fairly volatile. This contrast between food and durables is also evident in the ratio of the mean to the standard deviation. For each month, this ratio, which measures the interhousehold variability in expenditure, is greater for durables than for food, which is due to the lumpiness of durables expenditure. The lumpiness can also be seen from the fact that the ratio of the mean to the standard deviation for durables declines sharply when monthly expenditure is aggregated to a quarter for each household. The last row of the table shows the mean and the standard deviation of the growth rate for each household of expenditures and disposable income from the first quarter to the second quarter of the sample period. (The growth rate is not calculated for durables because expenditure is zero even over a quarter for some households in the sample.) In terms of the standard deviation of the quarterly growth rate, food remains the most stable commodity.

It is useful to compare those simple statistics for quarterly values derived from the present monthly diary survey with those presented in the previous chapter that uses a quarterly interview survey. The samples used in the two chapters are for the same period and the same segment of the population (worker households excluding singles). Table 5.2 collects statistics from table 5.1 and tables 4.1 and 4.2 for easy comparison. The definition of food and disposable income is the same for both chapters, but total consumption expenditure of this chapter differs from that of the previous chapter in that it excludes expenditure on unspecified items and remittance to members outside the household. This explains why the mean of total expenditure is substantially lower in the monthly diary survey. The standard deviations of the level of food and total expenditure are generally 20 to 25 percent lower with the monthly diary survey, which is attributable to the more accurate measurement in the diary survey than in the interview survey. When the measurement error is serially uncorrelated but the variable being measured has some positive serial correlation, the signal-to-noise ratio decreases when the first difference is taken. This explains why the proportionate reduction in the standard deviation is somewhat more pronounced for changes in expenditure than for levels. In contrast, the standard deviations of the level and the change of disposable income are about the same between the two surveys.

Table 5.1
Means and Standard Deviations

Panel A: April 1981–September 1981 (768 Households)

	Food	Nondurables other than food	Semidurables	Durables	Services	Total	Disposable income
April	65.2 (23.2)	25.3 (33.6)	40.2 (50.9)	15.7 (74.4)	72.8 (71.0)	218.9 (140.2)	234.9 (121.2)
May	65.0 (22.8)	23.4 (27.5)	36.0 (42.1)	14.4 (85.2)	67.0 (53.3)	205.7 (133.6)	249.7 (122.6)
June	63.2 (22.7)	23.7 (22.6)	43.5 (66.4)	15.2 (57.4)	62.7 (47.1)	208.3 (128.0)	437.5 (332.5)
July	68.3 (26.7)	22.0 (19.5)	43.6 (46.7)	17.1 (55.7)	76.1 (66.2)	226.8 (123.7)	353.6 (258.6)
August	68.8 (25.9)	23.8 (37.6)	38.7 (48.6)	13.1 (55.8)	76.1 (60.0)	219.7 (126.5)	282.8 (140.8)
September	62.8 (23.0)	22.6 (21.8)	35.8 (58.5)	10.1 (45.1)	60.4 (48.2)	191.8 (109.5)	249.4 (122.0)
April–June	193.4 (63.4)	72.4 (56.6)	119.7 (109.4)	45.3 (129.8)	202.5 (125.2)	632.9 (306.2)	922.1 (468.3)
July–September	199.9 (67.8)	68.5 (52.4)	118.1 (108.4)	40.3 (93.4)	212.5 (134.1)	638.2 (279.8)	885.8 (394.9)
Change over the two quarters	6.5 (33.7)	−3.9 (63.3)	−1.6 (113.3)	−5.0 (155.7)	10.0 (118.8)	5.4 (263.0)	−36.3 (439.7)
Growth rate over the two quarters	0.028 (0.179)	−0.034 (0.439)	−0.028 (0.724)	—	0.024 (0.463)	0.014 (0.309)	−0.009 (0.440)

Note: Standard errors in parentheses. In thousands of 1980 yen.

Panel B: October 1981–March 1982 (714 Households)

	Food	Nondurables other than food	Semidurables	Durables	Services	Total	Disposable income
October	68.6 (23.7)	22.1 (23.0)	37.3 (42.6)	13.1 (70.2)	67.6 (53.1)	208.8 (123.9)	241.0 (108.8)
November	65.5 (23.0)	23.4 (29.7)	37.2 (40.8)	14.0 (62.8)	66.0 (47.2)	206.0 (113.1)	259.5 (139.9)
December	100.1 (46.6)	33.4 (30.2)	70.0 (82.2)	31.1 (105.0)	96.7 (74.2)	331.0 (198.8)	707.8 (409.1)
January	54.6 (20.6)	25.7 (18.7)	35.7 (41.4)	10.6 (55.5)	76.3 (50.8)	202.7 (102.4)	248.1 (122.2)
February	56.5 (20.3)	27.6 (31.3)	33.0 (56.3)	14.7 (85.4)	64.1 (73.5)	195.5 (142.5)	243.7 (108.8)
March	63.5 (23.8)	29.3 (45.3)	46.0 (58.0)	12.1 (59.0)	87.5 (93.5)	237.8 (165.9)	287.3 (173.3)
October–December	234.1 (83.9)	78.9 (53.5)	144.5 (127.2)	58.2 (164.1)	230.2 (135.3)	745.8 (353.6)	1,208.4 (568.4)
January–March	174.6 (58.5)	82.6 (62.7)	114.7 (104.5)	37.4 (120.1)	227.9 (165.3)	636.1 (306.2)	779.0 (341.9)
Change over the two quarters	n.a.	n.a.	n.a.	—	n.a.	n.a.	n.a.
Growth rate over the two quarters	−0.288 (0.209)	0.039 (0.422)	−0.284 (0.732)	—	−0.044 (0.491)	−0.164 (0.311)	−0.421 (0.303)

Note: Standard errors in parentheses. In thousands of 1980 yen. Means and standard deviations of changes over two quarters for panel B cannot be reported because records are no longer available to the author.

Table 5.2
Comparison to Qaurterly Panel

A. Quarterly Panel (Source: Tables 4.1 and 4.2)

Variable	1981:Q2	1981:Q3	1981:Q4	1982:Q1
Food	213.9 (84.1)	218.0 (84.3)	241.6 (96.8)	216.3 (86.7)
Change in food	4.1 (47.7)	23.6 (49.2)	−25.2 (53.5)	
Total consumption	743.5 (399.1)	760.7 (377.8)	857.6 (390.4)	733.2 (356.0)
Change in total consumption	17.2 (322.5)	96.8 (290.2)	−124.3 (292.4)	
Disposable income	887.6 (493.7)	904.9 (422.6)	1,151.2 (559.4)	745.8 (326.5)
Change in disposable income	17.3 (443.0)	246.4 (367.2)	−405.5 (359.2)	

B. Quarterly Values Created from the FIES Monthly Panel

Variable	1981:Q2	1981:Q3	1981:Q4	1982:Q1
Food	193.4	199.9	234.1	174.6
	(63.4)	(67.8)	(83.9)	(58.5)
Change in food	6.5		n.a.	
	(33.7)			
Total consumption	632.9	638.2	745.8	636.1
	(306.2)	(279.8)	(353.6)	(306.2)
Change in total consumption	5.4		n.a.	
	(263.0)			
Disposable income	922.1	885.8	1,208.4	779.0
	(468.3)	(394.9)	(568.4)	(341.9)
Change in disposable income	−36.3		n.a.	
	(439.7)			

Note: In thousands of 1980 yen. For part B, statistics for 1981:Q2 and 1981:Q3 are from panel A and those for 1981:Q4 and 1982:Q1 are from panel B.

It appears that disposable income is accurately measured even in the interview survey.

Coming back to table 5.1, disposable income rises temporarily in June/ July and December due to bonuses. In particular in December, expenditure rises sharply for all commodities. Whether this is due to the temporary rise in disposable income or to the seasonality in expenditure, is an important question. If the former is true, it is consistent with the view that disposable income has a liquidity effect, as in the Keynesian consumption function.

We will come back to this issue of whether income has the liquidity effect, but here we estimate the Keynesian consumption function and see how much explanatory power disposable income has for consumption. Table 5.3 reports the results from regressing total expenditure on disposable income for each month or quarter. As is clear from the table, the R^2 is low, especially in monthly regressions. The marginal propensity to consume (the income coefficient) fluctuates from month to month. However, for consumption and disposable income aggregated to a quarter,

Table 5.3
Keynsian Consumption Function

| Period | Intercept | | Slope | | |
	Point estimate	Standard error	Point estimate	Standard error	R^2
April 1981	144.9	10.6	0.31	0.04	0.07
May	142.0	10.6	0.26	0.04	0.05
June	123.0	6.6	0.19	0.01	0.26
July	161.6	7.0	0.18	0.02	0.15
August	157.4	9.9	0.22	0.03	0.06
September	103.4	8.3	0.35	0.03	0.16
October	123.3	10.7	0.35	0.04	0.10
November	125.5	8.3	0.31	0.03	0.15
December	165.1	13.0	0.23	0.02	0.23
January 1982	129.2	8.1	0.30	0.03	0.13
February	75.0	12.1	0.49	0.05	0.14
March	91.7	10.2	0.51	0.03	0.28
April 1981–June 1981	328.5	21.1	0.33	0.02	0.26
July 1981–September 1981	352.9	22.1	0.32	0.02	0.21
October 1981–December 1981	353.4	26.6	0.32	0.02	0.27
January 1982–March 1982	221.6	23.0	0.53	0.03	0.35

Note: Estimates for April 1981–September 1981 are from panel A, and those for October 1981–March 1982 are from panel B.

both the intercept and the coefficient are stable over time, except for the first quarter of 1982. That the marginal propensity is lower in the monthly regressions than in the quarterly regressions would mean that expenditure is more stable over time than disposable income.

In the empirical analysis below, we will utilize monthly changes in expenditure and income. To remove seasonal factors evident in table 5.1, monthly expenditure and disposable income were divided by their respective monthly means before calculating monthly changes. That is, if X_{it} is the value of variable X for household i in month t, the seasonally adjusted monthly change from month t to $t + 1$ is calculated as

$$D_{it} = X_{i,t+1}/\overline{X}_{t+1} - X_{it}/\overline{X}_t, \tag{2.1}$$

where $\overline{X}_t$ is the mean over households of variable X for month t. The problem with this procedure is that $\overline{X}_t$ includes macro fluctuations as well as seasonal fluctuations in X. However, somehow identifying the macro component and removing it from $\overline{X}_t$ would not make much difference in our results because most of the fluctuations over time in $\overline{X}_t$ are due to seasonal factors.

The correlations in changes to be reported shortly were not affected when the effect of household characteristics (the head's age and sex, household size in persons, housing tenure, region, occupation, industry, and degree of urbanization) was removed by regressing expenditure and income on those characteristics and using the residual from the regressions in calculating correlations. In all the regressions, the R^2 was about 5 percent and the t-values for those household characteristics were mostly less than two in absolute value. For this reason, the analysis below uses expenditure and income seasonally adjusted as described above but not adjusted for household characteristics.

Table 5.3 reports the standard deviation and the autocorrelation coefficients for expenditure and disposable income thus obtained. The autocorrelations reported there are between monthly changes for each variable in question. For example, if D_{it} is the change in (seasonally adjusted) disposable income from month t to $t + 1$ for household i, the autocorrelation between month t and month s for disposable income is

$$\frac{\displaystyle\sum_{i=1}^{N} (D_{it} - \overline{D}_t)(D_{is} - \overline{D}_s)}{\sqrt{\displaystyle\sum_{i=1}^{N} (D_{it} - \overline{D}_t)^2}\sqrt{\displaystyle\sum_{i=1}^{N} (D_{is} - \overline{D}_s)^2}},$$

where $\bar{D}_t$ is the mean over households of D_{it} and N is the sample size. (Since $\bar{D}_{it}$ is calculated as in (2.1), $\bar{D}_t$ is actually zero by construction.) As evident from table 5.4, the first-order autocorrelation (the correlation between two successive monthly changes) is negative and highly significant for all commodity groups and disposable income.[1] The second and higher order autocorrelations, in contrast, are generally not significantly different from zero. Those results are similar to those reported in table 4.3 for a quarterly interview survey, except that the negative first-order autocorrelation is somewhat stronger here. A negative first-order autocorrelation means that an increase from one month to the next tends to be followed by a decrease. This appears inconsistent with the stochastic implication of the Life Cycle–Permanent Income Hypothesis derived in Hall (1978) that consumption is a martingale (and hence serially uncorrelated).[2]

One explanation for the negative first-order autocorrelation is that consumption expenditure is measured with error. If measured expenditure is the sum of true expenditure and a measurement error, the change in measured expenditure can have negative autocorrelation even if true expenditure is not serially correlated. Let C_{it} be expenditure on the commodity in question in month t and m_{it} be the measurement error. Measured expenditure is $C_{it} + m_{it}$. If there is no serial correlation in true changes (i.e., $\text{Cov}(C_{i,t+1} - C_{it}, C_{it} - C_{i,t-1}) = 0$) as in Hall's (1978) martingale hypothesis and also no serial correlation in the measurement error (i.e., $\text{Cov}(m_{i,t+1}, m_{it}) = 0$), then the first-order autocovariance in $C_{it} + m_{it}$ is $-\text{Var}(m_{it})$ which is negative. However, it is hard to imagine that measurement errors in a diary survey such as the FIES are so large that they alone are responsible for the negative correlation as large as in table 5.4.

If measurement errors alone do not account for the magnitude of the serial correlation, the martingale hypothesis is inconsistent with data. To reconcile the negative serial correlation with the Life Cycle–Permanent Income Hypothesis, we follow chapter 4 and allow for the possibility that all commodities, not just commodities conventionally classified as durables, are durable. As will be made clear in the next section, expenditure changes have negative serial correlation under durability.

5.3 Expenditure Changes under Consumption Durability

This section presents the equation for expenditure changes derived from the extension in chapter 4 of the Life Cycle–Permanent Income Hypothesis with consumption durability. The reader is referred to chapter 4 for the

Table 5.4
Standard Deviations and Correlation Coefficients Seasonally Adjusted Expenditures and Income

Panel A: April 1981–September 1981
1. Food

	Standard deviation	Correlation coefficient			
		May–June	June–July	July–August	August–September
April–May	0.22	−0.37***	0.01	0.00	−0.02
May–June	0.24		−0.46***	−0.01	0.06
June–July	0.29			−0.53***	−0.51
July–August	0.31				−0.52***
August–September	0.28				

2. Nondurables Other than Food

	Standard deviation	Correlation coefficient			
		May–June	June–July	July–August	August–September
April–May	1.58	−0.50***	0.05	0.03	−0.03
May–June	1.40		−0.47***	−0.05	0.04
June–July	1.13			−0.32***	0.03
July–August	1.74				−0.79***
August–September	1.77				

3. Semidurables

	Standard deviation	Correlation coefficient			
		May–June	June–July	July–August	August–September
April–May	1.60	−0.50***	0.15***	−0.10**	0.01
May–June	1.79		−0.72***	0.21***	−0.10**
June–July	1.39			−0.49***	0.10**
July–August	1.39				−0.44***
August–September	1.83				

4. Durables

	Standard deviation	Correlation coefficient			
		May–June	June–July	July–August	August–September
April–May	7.61	−0.70***	0.50	−0.01	−0.01
May–June	7.05		−0.40***	−0.00	0.01
June–July	4.91			−0.39***	−0.03
July–August	5.18				−0.54***
August–September	6.16				

Table 5.4 (cont.)

5. Services

	Standard deviation	Correlation coefficient			
		May–June	June–July	July–August	August–September
April–May	1.07	−0.39***	−0.09*	0.08*	−0.07
May–June	0.87		−0.39***	−0.05	0.01
June–July	0.93			−0.54***	−0.12***
July–August	0.91				−0.43***
August–September	0.88				

6. Total Expenditure

	Standard deviation	Correlation coefficient			
		May–June	June–July	July–August	August–September
April–May	0.76	−0.66***	0.12***	−0.03	0.04
May–June	0.75		−0.51***	0.03	−0.04
June–July	0.64			−0.43***	−0.03
July–August	0.60				−0.50***
August–September	0.63				

7. Disposable Income

	Standard deviation	Correlation coefficient			
		May–June	June–July	July–August	August–September
April–May	0.55	−0.41***	0.11**	−0.10**	0.06
May–June	0.73		−0.74***	0.24***	0.11**
June–July	1.04			−0.70***	−0.01
July–August	0.79				−0.46***
August–September	0.52				

*** = significant at 0.1%, ** = significant at 1%, * = significant at 5%.

Panel B: October 1981–March 1982
1. Food

	Standard deviation	Correlation coefficient			
		May–June	June–July	July–August	August–September
April–May	0.23	−0.22***	−0.12**	0.06	0.06
May–June	0.33		−0.73***	0.12**	0.15***
June–July	0.43			−0.53***	−0.16***
July–August	0.29				−0.35***
August–September	0.24				

Table 5.4 (cont.)

2. Nondurables Other than Food

	Standard deviation	Correlation coefficient			
		May–June	June–July	July–August	August–September
April–May	1.56	−0.65***	−0.01	0.00	−0.01
May–June	1.48		−0.44***	0.04	−0.02
June–July	1.00			−0.34***	0.04
July–August	1.27				−0.54***
August–September	1.88				

3. Semidurables

	Standard deviation	Correlation coefficient			
		May–June	June–July	July–August	August–September
April–May	1.24	−0.44***	−0.00	−0.06	0.03
May–June	1.30		−0.49***	0.05	−0.07
June–July	1.52			−0.44***	0.03
July–August	1.99				−0.65***
August–September	1.84				

4. Durables

	Standard deviation	Correlation coefficient			
		May–June	June–July	July–August	August–September
April–May	6.91	−0.73***	0.22***	−0.04	0.01
May–June	5.66		−0.34***	0.02	0.01
June–July	6.26			−0.57***	−0.03
July–August	7.63				−0.56***
August–September	7.56				

5. Services

	Standard deviation	Correlation coefficient			
		May–June	June–July	July–August	August–September
April–May	0.82	−0.44***	0.06	0.03	−0.08*
May–June	0.81		−0.56***	−0.02	0.05
June–July	0.77			−0.27***	0.02
July–August	1.09				−0.65***
August–September	1.31				

Table 5.4 (cont.)

6. Total Expenditure

	Standard deviation	Correlation coefficient			
		May–June	June–July	July–August	August–September
April–May	0.60	−0.57***	0.16***	−0.03	−0.03
May–June	0.63		−0.54***	0.02	0.01
June–July	0.63			−0.39***	0.02
July–August	0.77				−0.62***
August–September	0.83				

7. Disposable Income

	Standard deviation	Correlation coefficient			
		May–June	June–July	July–August	August–September
April–May	0.47	−0.64***	0.16***	0.02	−0.07
May–June	0.59		−0.63***	−0.05	0.22***
June–July	0.49			−0.46***	−0.15***
July–August	0.40				−0.37***
August–September	0.53				

*** = significant at 0.1%, ** = significant at 1%, * = significant at 5%.

model itself and the derivation more detailed than given here. Let $\overline{C}_{jt}$ be the household's *consumption* of commodity j in month t.[3] It is a distributed lag function of current and past *expenditures* on commodity j:

$$\overline{C}_{jt} = \sum_{k=0}^{M} \rho_{jk} C_{j,t-k},$$ (3.1)

where C_{jt} is the household's expenditure on commodity j and $\{\rho_{jk}\}$ ($k = 0, 1, \ldots, M$) is the decay pattern with ρ_{j0} normalized to unity. Usually, the decay pattern is assumed geometric, so $\rho_{jk} = (\rho_j)^k$ and $M = +\infty$ where ρ_j is one minus the depreciation rate. It is shown in section 4.4 that if (a) the real interest rate is constant and (b) the utility function is additively separable across commodities and is of the constant absolute risk aversion variety or else not necessarily additively separable but quadratic, then the expenditure change follows the univariate autoregression

$$C_{j,t+1} - C_{jt} = d_{jt} - \rho_{j1} \cdot (C_{jt} - C_{j,t-1}) - \rho_{j2} \cdot (C_{j,t-1} - C_{j,t-2}) - \cdots$$
$$- \rho_{jM} \cdot (C_{j,t-M+1} - C_{j,t-M}) + e_{j,t+1}.$$ (3.2)

In this autoregression, $e_{j,t+1}$ is the *forecast error* for $C_{j,t+1}$, which is the difference between the actual expenditure change from month t to $t+1$ and the planned change. The term d_{jt} in (3.2) is defined as

$$d_{jt} = \mu_j[\log(1+r_j) + \log(\beta)] + \eta_{j,t+1} - \eta_{jt}, \tag{3.3}$$

where μ_j is the absolute degree of risk aversion for commodity j, r_j is the commodity-specific real interest rate assumed constant over time,[4] β is the discounting factor, and η_{jt} is an unobservable taste shifter that affects the utility from $\overline{C}_{jt}$. If expenditures are measured with error, then the term η_{jt} also includes the measurement error in C_{jt}. For the case of a quadratic utility function, μ_j in (3.3) is zero.

If the commodity is durable, p_{jk}'s are positive and so the lagged expenditure changes in (3.2) are inversely related to the current expenditure change. Thus the model has two sources for the negative correlation in expenditure changes: consumption durability and the change in the taste shifter/measurement error η_{jt}.

5.4 Analysis by Autoregressions

In this section we proceed under the assumption that the taste shifter/ measurement error η_{jt} is zero and ask whether the negative correlation in expenditure changes can be explained by durability alone. So the intercept term d_{jt} is constant across households as well as over time. Also, if the forecast error for consumption, $e_{j,t+1}$, which under rational expectations is uncorrelated over time with any information available in period t, is idiosyncratic to the household, then there should be no cross-section correlation between $e_{j,t+1}$ and the right-hand-side variables that are lagged expenditure changes. Therefore, the decay coefficients p_{jk} can be estimated by Ordinary Least Squares (OLS). Also, neither lagged changes in expenditures on other commodities nor lagged disposable income changes affect the current expenditure change for the commodity in question, provided that its own lagged changes are included in the regression. That is, neither other expenditure nor disposable income changes Granger cause the expenditure change on the commodity. We estimate the decay pattern by estimating univariate autoregressions for each commodity and test for Granger causality by estimating a six-variable autoregression for the five commodities and disposable income.

The caveat, of course, is that only five successive monthly changes in expenditure are available from the data and any further lagged changes have to be truncated and included in the error term as the truncation remainder. Thus the equation to be estimated for commodity j is the following autoregression:

$$C_{j,t+1} - C_{jt} = -\rho_{j1} \cdot (C_{jt} - C_{j,t-1}) - \cdots - \rho_{j4} \cdot (C_{j,t-3} - C_{j,t-4}) + v_{j,t+1}, \quad (4.1)$$

with the *truncation remainder*, $\sum_{k=5}^{M} \rho_{jk} \cdot (C_{j,t-k+1} - C_{j,t-k})$, included in the error term $v_{j,t+1}$:

$$v_{j,t+1} = e_{j,t+1} - \sum_{k=5}^{M} \rho_{jk} \cdot (C_{j,t-k+1} - C_{j,t-k}). \quad (4.2)$$

Here, the intercept term d_{jt} has been dropped since, as noted in section 5.2, seasonally adjusted expenditure changes have zero mean by construction. If M (the length of the decay) is less than 5, then $v_{j,t+1} = e_{j,t+1}$ and the OLS estimators of the coefficients of lagged expenditure changes are consistent.

Table 5.4 reports the results from the OLS estimation of the autoregression (4.1) for the five commodities ($j = 1, 2, \ldots, 5$). The dependent variable for panel A, which covers April 1981–September 1981, is the expenditure change from August to September 1981. That for panel B is the expenditure change from February to March 1982. The table also reports similar autoregressions for disposable income. If the commodity is perfectly perishable, then $M = 0$ and the OLS coefficient estimates of lagged expenditure changes should not be significantly different from zero. The coefficient estimates reported in the table indicate that even food and other nondurables are not really perishable.[5]

If the commodity is durable, then ρ_{jk} remains positive even for large k and the truncation remainder included in the error term (4.2) is not negligible. Since monthly expenditure changes have negative serial correlation, the error term would be positively correlated with the first four lagged changes, which are the regressors in the autoregression (4.1). Therefore, the OLS estimates of $\rho_{j1}, \ldots, \rho_{j4}$ would be biased toward zero, making the commodity look less durable than it really is. This probably is the reason why the estimated coefficients are substantially below one for durables. What may be surprising about table 5.5 is that the coefficients for services are as high as those for durables. But it should not be so surprising in view of the fact that expenditure on services include items (such as dental services) that are really durable.

Turning to the six-variable vector autoregression, table 5.6 reports our results. For each commodity, lagged changes in other commodities are hardly significant. The lagged change in disposable income is significant

Table 5.5
Univariate Regression in Changes

Panel A: April 1981–September 1981

Variable	ρ_{j1}	ρ_{j2}	ρ_{j3}	ρ_{j4}	R^2
Food	0.78	0.63	0.35	0.14	0.47
	(0.03)	(0.04)	(0.04)	(0.04)	
Nondurables other than food	0.93	0.57	0.28	0.11	0.70
	(0.02)	(0.04)	(0.03)	(0.03)	
Semidurables	0.78	0.46	0.37	0.20	0.25
	(0.05)	(0.06)	(0.06)	(0.05)	
Durables	0.84	0.53	0.27	0.17	0.39
	(0.04)	(0.05)	(0.04)	(0.03)	
Services	0.81	0.71	0.42	0.19	0.46
	(0.03)	(0.04)	(0.04)	(0.03)	
Disposable income	0.86	0.70	0.50	0.20	0.52
	(0.03)	(0.04)	(0.04)	(0.03)	

Panel B: October 1981–March 1982

Variable	ρ_{j1}	ρ_{j2}	ρ_{j3}	ρ_{j4}	R^2
Food	0.65	0.49	0.31	0.10	0.34
	(0.04)	(0.04)	(0.04)	(0.04)	
Nondurables other than food	0.92	0.50	0.27	0.18	0.33
	(0.05)	(0.08)	(0.07)	(0.05)	
Semidurables	0.82	0.66	0.53	0.28	0.58
	(0.03)	(0.04)	(0.05)	(0.04)	
Durables	0.89	0.73	0.28	0.05	0.52
	(0.03)	(0.04)	(0.05)	(0.04)	
Services	0.86	0.43	0.24	0.17	0.46
	(0.04)	(0.06)	(0.06)	(0.05)	
Disposable income	0.86	0.66	0.25	0.15	0.28
	(0.06)	(0.07)	(0.06)	(0.06)	

Note: Standard errors in parentheses.

only for food, and even for food its significance is at most marginal. (This result also holds for non–seasonally adjusted data.) The apparent significance of lagged expenditure changes on other commodities may be due to a possible erroneous classification of expenditure items into the five commodity groups. For example, if items that should have been included in food are included in some other commodity group, then the lagged change on that commodity group will affect current food changes.

One explanation for the (marginally) significant lagged disposable income changes in the equation for food is that lagged income changes enter the equation through their correlation with the truncation remainder,

Table 5.6
Vector Autoregression in Changes

Panel A: April 1981–September 1981

Dependent variable	Lag	Own lag coefficients	Lagged income coefficients	Other significant commodity	R^2
Food	1	−0.78***	0.038*	none	0.49
	2	−0.63***	0.026		
	3	−0.36***	0.025		
	4	−0.15***	−0.009		
Nondurables other than food	1	−0.93***	−0.039	durables (2nd lag*)	0.71
	2	−0.56***	−0.067	services (4th lag*)	
	3	−0.28***	−0.168		
	4	−0.09**	−0.139		
Semidurables	1	−0.76***	0.189	none	0.27
	2	−0.45***	0.093		
	3	−0.35***	0.114		
	4	−0.19***	0.151		
Durables	1	−0.85***	0.452	none	0.40
	2	−0.53***	0.272		
	3	−0.27**	0.193		
	4	−0.16***	0.124		
Services	1	−0.79***	0.004	other nondurables	0.50
	2	−0.69***	−0.007	(1st lag**, 4th lag**)	
	3	−0.42***	0.004	durables	
	4	−0.20***	−0.006	(1st lag***, 2nd lag*)	
Disposable income	1	−0.86***		other nondurables	0.56
	2	−0.69***		(4th lag*)	
	3	−0.50***		durables (4th lag*)	
	4	−0.19***			

which is part of the error term (see (4.2)). However, it is hard to imagine that the durability of food is so high that the truncation remainder is important for current changes. A more plausible explanation is that disposable income has a liquidity effect.

Finally, table 5.7 displays the standard deviations and correlations of the residuals from the vector autoregression. For either panel, the residual correlation between disposable income and the five commodities is generally positive and significant. This is consistent with the model in section 5.3. Recall that the error term in the expenditure change equation is the forecast error $e_{j,t+1}$. One important reason for an expenditure plan made in month t to be changed is new information about income that the

Table 5.6 (cont.)

Panel B: October 1981–March 1982

Dependent variable	Lag	Own lag coefficients	Lagged income coefficients	Other significant commodity	R^2
Food	1	−0.66***	0.016	semidurables	0.37
	2	−0.50***	0.079**	(3rd lag*, 4th lag*)	
	3	−0.32***	0.053		
	4	−0.10**	0.036		
Nondurables	1	−0.92***	0.138	none	0.34
other than food	2	−0.51***	0.166		
	3	−0.29***	0.238		
	4	−0.19**	0.065		
Semidurables	1	−0.78***	−0.094	other nondurables	0.61
	2	−0.61***	−0.079	(3rd lag***, 4th lag***)	
	3	−0.49***	0.012		
	4	−0.25***	−0.146		
Durables	1	−0.89***	0.015	services (1st lag***)	0.54
	2	−0.73***	−0.328		
	3	−0.27***	0.094		
	4	−0.05	−0.543		
Services	1	−0.86***	−0.094	food (1st lag*, 2nd lag*)	0.48
	2	−0.41***	−0.014	other semidurables	
	3	−0.24***	0.011	(2nd lag*)	
	4	−0.14**	−0.075		
Disposable income	1	−0.86***		none	0.29
	2	−0.65***			
	3	−0.24***			
	4	−0.14*			

*** = significant at 0.1%, ** = significant at 1%, * = significant at 5%.

household receives in month $t + 1$. Such information is included in the error term of the equation for disposable income changes.

5.5 Reintroducing the Taste Shifter/Measurement Error

One problem in the above empirical analysis is the high durability of food shown in table 5.5. We would expect ρ_{jk}'s for food to be zero. Another problem is the weak residual correlation between income and expenditures reported in table 5.7. If new information about income is the only factor that prompts the household to deviate from the planned change in expenditure and if the residual from the income autoregression represents

Table 5.7
Correlation of Residuals from Vector Autoregression

Panel A: April 1981–September 1981

Equation for	Standard deviation	Correlation coefficient				
		Other nondurables	Semidurables	Durables	Services	Disposable income
Food	0.20	0.13***	0.08*	0.02	−0.03	0.08*
Other nondurables	0.95		−0.03	0.03	0.13***	0.03
Semidurables	1.57			0.04	0.04	0.07
Durables	4.76				0.01	0.03
Services	0.63					0.11**
Disposable income	0.35					

Panel B: October 1981–March 1982

Equation for	Standard deviation	Correlation coefficient				
		Other nondurables	Semidurables	Durables	Services	Disposable income
Food	0.19	−0.03	−0.00	0.02	−0.03	0.08*
Other nondurables	1.52		0.14***	0.02	0.25***	0.43***
Semidurables	1.15			0.08*	0.00	0.18***
Durables	5.14				0.07	−0.00
Services	0.95					0.11**
Disposable income	0.44					

*** = significant at 0.1%, ** = significant at 1%, * = significant at 5%.

the new information about income, the correlation should be one. Further evidence of the weak link between income and expenditure changes is shown in table 5.8, where expenditure changes are regressed on current and lagged income changes. The explanatory power of income is very low, and for panel A, no income changes are significant at 5 percent. It thus seems that expenditure changes are mostly due to factors other than income and that those factors contribute to the negative correlation in changes. In this section, we reintroduce the taste shifter/measurement error η_{jt}, which is the factor other than income that affects expenditure changes.

With a moving average of η_{jt} in the error term (see (3.3)), it is no longer possible to measure durability of the commodity from the autoregressive coefficients. However, as long as η_{jt} is uncorrelated with income, the model still predicts that lagged changes in disposable income should not be significant if included in the autoregressions for expenditure changes. If

Table 5.8
Regression of Expenditure Changes on Income Changes

Panel A: April 1981–September 1981

Expenditure change (August 1981– September 1981)	Income changes					
	August– September	July– August	June–July	May–June	April– May	R^2
Food	0.04	0.05	0.03	0.02	−0.03	0.009
Other durables	−0.02	−0.30	−0.30	−0.27	−0.14	0.005
Semidurables	0.19	0.28	0.28	0.32	0.37	0.007
Durables	0.18	0.44	−0.08	0.36	0.20	0.007
Services	0.13	−0.01	−0.01	0.03	−0.01	0.008
Total expenditure	0.10	0.05	0.01	0.05	0.04	0.009

Panel B: October 1981–March 1982

Expenditure change (Feburary 1982– March 1982)	Income changes					
	February– March	January– February	December– January	November– December	October– November	R^2
Food	0.04*	0.01	0.05	0.04	0.03	0.012
Other durables	1.50***	1.13***	1.25***	0.76**	−0.25	0.167
Semidurables	0.39*	−0.04	−0.17	0.07	−0.09	0.016
Durables	0.34	0.57	0.48	0.90	−0.42	0.006
Services	0.20	−0.35	−0.46*	−0.36	−0.31	0.022
Total expenditure	0.37***	0.06	0.09	0.06	−0.18	0.070

*** = significant at 0.1%, ** = significant at 1%, * = significant at 5%.

lagged income changes are significant, that is a sign of the liquidity effect of income.

A standard way to incorporate the liquidity effect into the model is to suppose that the population of households consists of two groups, with the first group of households following (3.2) and the second group following the Keynesian consumption function. Let λ be the fraction of the second type in the population and $1 - \lambda$ the fraction for the first type. Thus for the second group, the expenditure change for each commodity is given by

$$C_{j,t+1} - C_{jt} = \alpha_j \cdot (YD_{j,t+1} - YD_{jt}) \qquad (j = 1, 2, \ldots, 5), \qquad (5.1)$$

where α_j is the marginal propensity to spend on commodity j and YD_{jt} is disposable income.[6] We assume that the total marginal propensity to consume, $\sum_{j=1}^{5} \alpha_j$, is unity. This is an identifying assumption: as seen below, we can identify the product $\lambda \sum_{j=1}^{5} \alpha_j$, but not λ and $\sum_{j=1}^{5} \alpha_j$ separately. For the first group following (3.2), we assume that the decay pattern $\{\rho_{jk}\}$ is geometric: $\rho_{jk} = (\rho_j)^k$. So the autoregression (3.2) can be written in the moving average form

$$C_{j,t+1} - C_{jt} = (\eta_{j,t+1} - \eta_{jt}) - \rho_j \cdot (\eta_{jt} - \eta_{j,t-1}) + (e_{j,t+1} - \rho_j e_{jt}), \qquad (5.2)$$

which does not involve the truncation remainder. Because the variables have been seasonally adjusted, the constant term can be ignored.

If expenditure changes follow (5.1),

$$\mathrm{Cov}(C_{j,t+1} - C_{jt}, YD_{jt} - YD_{j,t-1}) = \alpha_j \mathrm{Cov}(YD_{j,t+1} - YD_{jt}, YD_{jt} - YD_{j,t-1}), \qquad (5.3)$$

provided that there is no correlation between η_{jt} and YD_{js}. Similarly, under (5.2),

$$\mathrm{Cov}(C_{j,t+1} - C_{jt}, YD_{jt} - YD_{j,t-1}) = -\rho_j \mathrm{Cov}(e_{jt}, YD_{jt} - YD_{j,t-1}). \qquad (5.4)$$

Since (5.3) holds for fraction λ of the population and (5.4) for fraction $1 - \lambda$, the covariance for income and expenditure drawn from this population is a weighted average of the two:

$$\mathrm{Cov}(C_{j,t+1} - C_{jt}, YD_{jt} - YD_{j,t-1})$$
$$= \lambda \alpha_j \gamma_{j1t} - (1 - \lambda)\rho_j \mathrm{Cov}(e_{jt}, YD_{jt} - YD_{j,t-1}), \qquad (5.5a)$$

where

$$\mathrm{Cov}(YD_{j,t+1} - YD_{jt}, YD_{jt} - YD_{j,t-1}) = \gamma_{j1t}. \qquad (5.5b)$$

Similarly, the covariance between $C_{j,t+1} - C_{jt}$ and $YD_{j,t-1} - YD_{j,t-2}$ can be expressed as

$$\mathrm{Cov}(C_{j,t+1} - C_{jt}, YD_{j,t-1} - YD_{j,t-2}) = \lambda \alpha_j \gamma_{j2t}, \qquad (5.5c)$$

where

$$\mathrm{Cov}(YD_{j,t+1} - YD_{jt}, YD_{j,t-1} - YD_{j,t-2}) = \gamma_{j2t}. \qquad (5.5d)$$

The length of the panel is six, so t ranges from 1 to 6. The four covariances on the left hand sides of (5.5a)–(5.5d) can be calculated for $t = 3$, 4, and 5, for each of the five commodities. Therefore, there are $4 \times 3 \times 5 = 60$ covariances, and they are functions of the following 50 parameters:

$\lambda, \alpha_1, \alpha_2, \ldots, \alpha_4$ (note that $\Sigma_j \alpha_j = 1$), $\rho_j \, \text{Cov}(e_{jt}, YD_{jt} - YD_{j,t-1})$

(for $t = 3, 4, 5$ and $j = 1, \ldots, 5$), $\gamma_{j1t}, \gamma_{j2t}$ (for $t = 3, 4, 5$ and $j = 1, \ldots, 5$).

Those fifty parameters can be estimated by the minimum distance method presented in, for example, Chamberlain (1984). Since ρ_j and $\text{Cov}(e_{jt}, YD_{jt} - YD_{j,t-1})$ enter the expression for covariances as a product, it is not possible to identify ρ_j and $\text{Cov}(e_{jt}, YD_{jt} - YD_{j,t-1})$ separately. Applying the minimum distance method to the two panels, we obtain the following estimate of λ:

Panel A: $\lambda = 0.074$ (standard error $= 0.062$),

Panel B: $\lambda = 0.15$ (standard error $= 0.14$).

In either panel, λ is not sharply estimated. As a result, one cannot reject the hypothesis that $\lambda = 0$. However, the point estimate of λ is similar to the estimate of $\lambda = 0.126$ obtained in chapter 4 using different data.

Notes

This is an English translation by the author of Hayashi (1986). In the process of translation, several paragraphs and one table (table 5.2) have been added to make the relation to the previous chapter more transparent.

1. The first-order autocorrelations when monthly changes are not seasonally adjusted, too, are negative, but their values change from month to month. For example, the first-order autocorrelations for disposable income over October 1981 through March 1982 are: $-0.30, -0.95, -0.11, -0.33$. When seasonally adjusted, they change to $-0.64, -0.63, -0.46, -0.37$, as can be seen from the table.

2. The autocorrelation and autocovariance discussed here are averages over households, not over time. For example, the autocovariance between D_{it} and D_{is}, $\text{Cov}(D_{it}, D_{is})$, equals

$$\text{plim}_{N \to \infty} N^{-1} \sum_{i=1}^{N} (D_{it} - \bar{D}_t)(D_{is} - \bar{D}_s).$$

But this does not necessarily equal

$$\text{plim}_{T \to \infty} T^{-1} \sum_{i=1}^{N} (D_{it} - \bar{D}_i)(D_{is} - \bar{D}_i),$$

where i is the mean of D_{it} over $t = 1, \ldots, T$. Hall's martingale hypothesis is that the covariance in the latter sense is zero. However, if the change in consumption for each household is brought about by factors specific to the household, then the covariance in the former sense is also zero under the martingale hypothesis. For more details, see chapter 4.

3. For notational simplicity, we henceforth drop the household subscript i.

4. If i_{t+1} is the nominal interest rate from period t to $t+1$ and p_{jt} is the price of commodity j, then $1 + r_{j,t+1} = (1 + i_{t+1})(p_{jt}/p_{j,t+1})$.

5. However, this conclusion will be altered when we reintroduce the taste shifter/measurement error (the η_{jt} in (3.3)).

6. Here, YD has subscript j because the seasonal adjustment for disposable income involves the mean over households of C_{jt}. If starred variables are seasonally unadjusted, seasonally adjusted disposable income YD_{ijt} is calculated as

$$YD_{ijt} = YD_{it}^* / \bar{C}_{jt}^* \qquad (i = 1, 2, \ldots, N),$$

where N is the sample size, i is the household subscript (in the text, the household subscript i has been dropped), and $\bar{C}_{jt}^*$ is the mean of C_{ijt}^* over i. Equation (5.1) can be derived from

$$C_{ijt}^* = a_j YD_{it}^*.$$

References

Chamberlain, G. 1984. Panel data. In *Handbook of econometrics*, Vol. II, ed. Z. Griliches and M. Intriligator, 1247–318. Amsterdam: North-Holland.

Hall, R. 1978. Stochastic implications of the Life Cycle–Permanent Income Hypothesis: Theory and evidence. *Journal of Political Economy* 86:971–87.

Hayashi, F. 1985. The Permanent Income Hypothesis and consumption durability: Analysis based on Japanese panel data. *Quarterly Journal of Economics* 100:1083–113.

Hayashi, F. 1986. *Koujoushotoku Kasetsu No Kenshouto Sono Kakuchou* (A test of the Permanent Income Hypothesis and its extension). *Keizai Bunseki* 101:1–23.

6

Tests for Liquidity Constraints: A Critical Survey and Some New Observations

6.1 Introduction

The issue of liquidity constraints comes up in several areas of economics. The main ingredient in modern theories of business cycles is the consumer who executes intertemporal optimization through trading in perfectly competitive asset markets. Traditionally, the life cycle–permanent income hypothesis has been the label for such consumer behavior. Some authors have argued that the observed comovements of consumption and income (or the lack thereof) can best be explained by examining the role of liquidity constraints as the additional constraint in the consumers' decision problem.[1] The notion that consumers are unable to borrow as they desire is also used to argue against the Ricardian doctrine of the equivalence of taxes and deficits. In the literature on implicit labor contracts, the assumption is often made that workers are unable to borrow against future earnings. Liquidity constraints have even been used in some instances as an excuse to focus on static single-period analyses.

Despite its popularity, the term *liquidity constraints* has not yet gained a precise and unique definition. To some the term might be associated with agents facing the cash-in-advance constraint. The most widely accepted definition, however, is that consumers are liquidity constrained if they face quantity constraints on the amount of borrowing (credit rationing) or if the loan rates available to them are higher than the rate at which they could lend (differential interest rates). In this survey, we will employ this definition of liquidity constraints, thereby abstracting from the interesting and important issue of why people hold money.

The survey is selective in other ways too. We will ignore the possible connection between consumption and income arising from the

Originally published in *Advances in Econometrics, Vol. II.*, ed. T. Bewley (Cambridge University Press, 1987), 91–120. Reprinted with the permission of Cambridge University Press.

consumption–leisure choice. This is justified if consumption and leisure are separable in the utility function. We will also ignore the large literature on econometric studies of the consumption function. Our focus, therefore, is on what has come to be called the *Euler equation approach*, which has been the rapidly growing segment of the literature on consumer behavior. Our choice of being selective is motivated by the recent exhaustive survey ably done by Mervyn King (1985).

The questions we would hope to answer by the available empirical evidence may be divided into three groups. First, can the life cycle–pe˙ manent income hypothesis be rejected in favor of the hypothesis of liquidity constraints? Although there exist many studies rejecting the hypothesis, another careful scrutiny may be warranted. Second, if liquidity constraints are shown to exist, how do we proceed to identify the preference parameters under liquidity constraints? The identification of the structural parameters is a necessary prelude to the construction of macro-models that would allow us to study business cycles and analyze policy interventions. Third, which of the standard conclusions derived under no liquidity constraints will survive and which will not? More specifically, under liquidity constraints how does consumption respond to temporary income changes? Does the Ricardian equivalence theorem cease to hold? The available empirical work will be examined critically on these three scores.

The organization of the chapter is as follows. Section 6.2 outlines the test for liquidity constraints based on the Euler equation and contrasts it with the approach based on the consumption function. Problems associated with the Euler equation approach are also discussed. Section 6.3 examines the available empirical evidence from aggregate data and microdata. The discussion of technical issues is contained in this section. In Section 6.4, which contains original material, we will consider three specific models of liquidity constraints and argue that the economic implication of the available evidence cannot be determined unless the cause of liquidity constraints is identified. Section 6.5 is a brief conclusion.

6.2 Intertemporal Optimization with and without Liquidity Constraints

Throughout this section and Section 6.4, we will focus for expositional ease on the conventional two-period model of intertemporal optimization, although most of the discussion can be readily extended to the many-period case. The objective function of the consumer is the expectation of lifetime utility that is time separable:

$$u(c_1) + \beta E_1 u(c_2) \tag{2.1}$$

Where c_t is consumption in period t $(t = 1, 2)$, $u(\cdot)$ is the instantaneous utility function, β is the discount factor, and E_1 is the expectations operator conditional on information available to the consumer in period 1. Let A_t and w_t be nonhuman wealth and after-tax labor income in period t. Then A_t follows:

$$A_2 = (1 + r)(A_1 + w_1 - c_1) \tag{2.2}$$

where r is the market risk-free real rate. The constraint to the consumer is that debt be eventually paid back, which means under no bequests that, for any realization of (possibly stochastic) future labor income w_2,

$$c_2 = A_2 + w_2 \tag{2.3}$$

Combining (2.2) and (2.3), we obtain the *lifetime budget constraint*:

$$c_1 + c_2/(1 + r) = A_1 + w_1 + w_2/(1 + r) \tag{2.4}$$

The important observation to be made here is that the consumer is constrained only by the lifetime budget constraint, so that consumption can be shielded from period-to-period fluctuations in income through borrowing and lending. Any changes in the configuration of (w_1, w_2) lead to revisions in the optimal consumption plan (c_1^*, c_2^*) only insofar as they change the distribution of $w_1 + w_2/(1 + r)$. Thus, the MPC (marginal propensity to consume) out of a temporary increase in w_1 (which leaves unaltered the distribution of w_2) will be much smaller than the MPC out of a permanent increase in w_1 (which shifts the distribution of w_2 by the amount of increase in w_1).[2]

However, as recent research to be surveyed in the next section indicates, consumption appears to be more sensitive to current income than is implied by intertemporal optimization. One explanation that has often been mentioned is the existence of *liquidity constraints* or *imperfect loan markets*. It means either that consumers are credit rationed (so that there is a lower bound on nonhuman wealth) or that the loan rates available to consumers are higher than the lending rate (the market interest rate). The consequence of liquidity constraints can be seen most easily for the deterministic case in which the consumer has a point expectation w_2^e about future labor income w_2. Figure 6.1(a) is the familiar diagram showing that

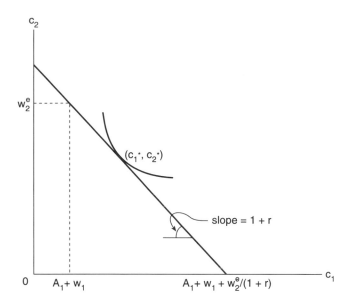

Figure 6.1(a)

the optimal consumption plan (c_1^*, c_2^*) in the absence of liquidity constraints is the point where the marginal rate of substitution $u'(c_1)/[\beta u'(c_2)]$ is equated to the marginal rate of transformation $1 + r$. As long as *total wealth* (the sum of nonhuman wealth A_1 and human wealth $w_1 + w_2^e/(1 + r)$) is held constant, changes in the configuration of (w_1, w_2^e) have no influence whatsoever on current consumption. Panels (b) and (c) of Figure 6.1 illustrate the two versions of liquidity constraints: In Figure 6.1(b) the consumer is credit rationed, with the amount of rationing being $c_1^* - A_1 - w_1$, whereas in Figure 6.1(c) the consumer faces a schedule of loan rates as an increasing function of the loan quantity. Under liquidity constraints consumption is *excessively sensitive* to income in the following sense. If the consumer is credit rationed and if the amount of rationing is constant, the optimal consumption plan moves from point A to B in Figure 6.1(b) as current income increases from w_1 to w_1'. So the MPC out of a temporary current income increase is unity. It is less than but still close to unity when the consumer faces an upward-sloping borrowing rate schedule. It is also clear that under liquidity constraints current consumption is not invariant to changes in the configuration of (w_1, w_2^e) that hold total wealth constant.

Following the lead of Hall (1978), recent tests for liquidity constraints have utilized the "Euler equations" (first-order conditions characterizing

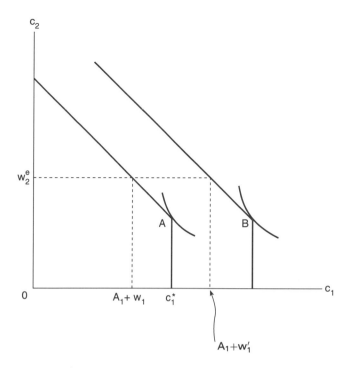

Figure 6.1(b)

the optimal consumption plan) rather than the consumption function (optimal contingency rule that relates optimal current consumption to the set of information currently available to the consumer). As seen above, the implication of the lifetime budget constraint is that consumption is invariant to changes in income if total wealth is controlled for. The test for liquidity constraints based on the consumption function exploits this by regressing consumption on total wealth and current income and by examining the significance of the income coefficient. There are several reasons against this consumption function approach. We mention two of them.[3] First, when future income is uncertain, a closed-form optimal contingency rule cannot in general be derived, which renders the notion of "total wealth" unoperational. Even if a closed-form solution is available, the definition of total wealth is not preference free. For instance, if the instantaneous utility function is quadratic, the consumption function is

$$c_1^* = a_0 + a_1[A_1 + w_1 + E(w_2)/(1 + r)] \tag{2.5}$$

where a_0 and a_1 depend on r and the parameters characterizing the

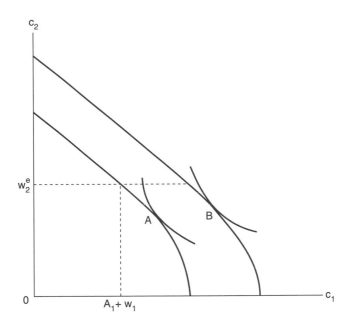

Figure 6.1(c)

instantaneous utility function. If the instantaneous utility function exhibits a constant absolute risk aversion, the consumption function is

$$c_1^* = b_0 + b_1[A_1 + w_1 + (\ln[E_1[\exp(-\mu w_2)]])^{-\mu/(1+r)}] \qquad (2.6)$$

where μ is the constant degree of absolute risk aversion. The definition of total wealth, which is the expression in the outer braces, depends on the utility function. This example also highlights the second difficulty with the consumption function approach: Total wealth (if it is well defined) cannot be calculated without data on the distribution of future income. Such data are not typically available.

The Euler equation approach exploits another implication of inter-temporal optimization subject to the lifetime budget constraint, namely, that at optimum the marginal rate of substitution between current and future consumption is set equal to the marginal rate of transformation [see Figure 6.1(a)]. The beauty of this approach is that it can easily accommodate stochastic real rates as well as stochastic labor income:

$$u'(c_1) = \beta E_1[(1 + r)u'(c_2)] \qquad (2.7a)$$

or

$$E_1[(1 + r)\beta u'(c_2)/u'(c_1)] = 1 \qquad (2.7b)$$

or

$$E_1(e_2) = 0 \qquad (2.7c)$$

where $e_2 = 1 - (1 + r)\beta u'(c_2; \theta)/u'(c_1; \theta)$, where θ is a parameter vector characterizing the utility function. The interpretation of the Euler equation is familiar: The left-hand side of (2.7a) is the marginal utility benefit of increasing c_1 by one unit, whereas the right-hand side is the marginal utility cost of a reduction in c_2 arising from the reduced current saving. Equation (2.7b) indicates that, ex ante, the marginal rate of substitution and the marginal rate of transformation are equated. Ex post, the two rates can differ because the realization of future income and real rates are not perfectly foreseen. The discrepancy is represented by the consumption innovation e_2. The most attractive feature of the Euler equation approach is that it allows a direct estimation of preference parameters (θ, β) as done by Hansen and Singleton (1982). If x_1 is a vector of variables in the period 1 information set, (2.7c) implies that the conditional expectation $E(e_2|x_1)$ is zero, which in turn means $E(e_2 x_1) = 0$. Under rational expectations, the consumer's subjective distribution about future stochastic variables agrees with the objective distribution, so that the *orthogonality condition* $E(e_2 x_1) = 0$ (and hence $\mathrm{Cov}(e_2, x_1) = 0$) must hold on data. This is precisely the situation for which Hansen's (1982) GMM (generalized methods of moments) estimation is designed to estimate the unknown preference parameters under the orthogonality condition.

The Euler equation does not hold in the presence of liquidity constraints because consumers who would like to borrow at the market rate but who are prevented from doing so consume relatively less in period 1 and more in period 2 than in the absence of liquidity constraints. Thus, under liquidity constraints, there should be a negative correlation between the marginal rate of substitution and $A_1 + w_1$ or any variable that reduces the severity of liquidity constraints [see Figures 6.1(b) and (c)]. This is the basic strategy of testing for liquidity constraints by the Euler equation. In its most sophisticated form, the procedure is Hansen's (1982) test of overidentifying restrictions: Estimate the preference parameters (θ, β) from the nonlinear Euler equation (2.7c) by the GMM where the set of instruments x_1 in the period 1 information set excludes variables (like A_1 and w_1) pertinent to the consumer's liquidity; estimate by the GMM where x_1 is expanded to include liquidity variables and compare the two estimates. If they significantly differ, liquidity constraints must be binding. This test takes a familiar form for some commonly used utility functions because the Euler equation can be made linear. In the case of quadratic utility $[u(c) = -(\alpha - c)^2]$ with a deterministic interest rate r, the Euler equation is

$$c_2 = [1 - \beta^{-1}(1 + r)^{-1}]\alpha + \beta^{-1}(1 + r)^{-1}c_1 + \varepsilon_2 \qquad \varepsilon_2 = c_2 - E_1(c_2) \quad (2.8)$$

In the case of a constant absolute risk aversion $[u(c) = -\exp(-\mu c), \mu > 0]$, it is

$$c_2 - c_1 = \mu^{-1}\ln(\beta) + \mu^{-1}\ln(1 + r) + \mu^{-1}e_2 \qquad (2.9)$$

where e_2 is defined in (2.7c).[4] In the case of a constant relative risk aversion $[u(c) = c^{1-1/\sigma}, \sigma > 0]$, it is

$$\ln(c_2) - \ln(c_1) = \sigma\ln(\beta) + \sigma\ln(1 + r) + \sigma e_2 \qquad (2.10)$$

This σ is called the elasticity of intertemporal substitution. We can test for liquidity constraints by adding a set of variables in the period 1 information set that represent the consumer's liquidity to the Euler equation. Since the consumption innovation e_2 and ε_2 is uncorrelated with any variable in the period 1 information set, the regression estimate of the liquidity variable coefficients should be insignificant if the consumer is not liquidity constrained.[5]

Before turning to a survey of recent empirical work, we point out three nontechnical problems with the Euler equation approach; technical problems will be discussed in the next section. The last two are also shared by the consumption function approach. The first problem, which is completely obscured by our focus on the two-period model, is that the Euler equation does not exhaust all the implications of intertemporal optimization subject only to the lifetime budget constraint. Although it captures the important implication that under rational expectations the change in the marginal utility of consumption (the consumption innovation) is uncorrelated with any variable (like anticipated income changes, permanent or temporary) in the period 1 information set, the Euler equation does not by itself place any restrictions on the relation between the consumption innovation and unanticipated income changes. The Euler equation will be satisfied even if the consumer is myopic in that he or she cares only about the first two periods of the multiperiod life. Even though the consumer's planning horizon is infinite, the likelihood of future liquidity constraints effectively shortens the horizon.[6] For example, if the consumer expects that he or she will face a binding constraint of a ban on borrowing n

periods from now, the optimal consumption plan will be such that non-human wealth in that period is zero. So the consumer will act as if the horizon is only n periods. From the Euler equation alone we cannot tell how the consumer would react to an unanticipated temporary income change. This problem can be alleviated by the use of the Euler equation between c_1 and c_{t+n} : $u'(c_1) = \beta^n E_1[(1 + r_n)^n u'(c_{1+n})]$, where r_n is the n-period real rate. If the Euler equation is satisfied for all n, $1 \leqslant n \leqslant T$, then the effective horizon is longer than T periods. However, the horizon length to be tested is limited if the data are a short panel. Another solution is to make an auxiliary assumption about the stochastic process generating labor income and derive a theoretical relationship involving the horizon length between the consumption innovation e_2 and innovations in labor income.[7] This forms the basis of what we will call the excess sensitivity test.

Second, the derivation of the Euler equation and the consumption function has ignored the nonnegativity constraint $c_t \geqslant 0$. This is justified if disutility of zero consumption is prohibitive [i.e., $u'(0) = +\infty$] *and* if the consumer has to go through zero consumption in the event of default. No plan allowing defaults can be chosen. Otherwise, the consumer may plan to default when the second-period labor income turns out to be insufficient to repay the loan, which will either put a premium in the loan rate or limit the quantity of the loan available to the consumer. For example, if the loan market can provide only risk-free loans, the constraint that $c_2 = A_2 + w_2 \geqslant 0$ [see (2.3)] for any realization of the stochastic variable w_2 implies that the loan repayment $(-A_2)$ must be less than or equal to the sure part of w_2. This certainly blurs the distinction between intertemporal optimization with and without liquidity constraints. This important issue will be discussed later at some length in a separate section (Section 6.4).

The third problem is closely related to the second. In the test for liquidity constraints described, no intertemporal optimization problem under liquidity constraints is explicitly spelled out. The maintained hypothesis is that the utility function is correctly specified. The null hypothesis is intertemporal optimization without liquidity constraints (the life cycle–permanent income hypothesis). Rejection of the null hypothesis is often taken to be a confirmation of the existence of liquidity constraints, even though the alternative hypothesis is kept vague. One possible specification of the alternative hypothesis is that the loan rate available to the consumer is an increasing function of the loan quantity $c_1 - A_1 - w_1$. This delivers a Euler equation under liquidity constraints that the ex ante marginal rate of substitution equals 1 plus the loan rate on marginal loans. Since the marginal loan rate is a function of the loan quantity under liquidity constraints, we can test for liquidity constraints by examining the relationship between the marginal rate of substitution and the loan quantity. This is essentially the test for liquidity constraints already discussed. One could further proceed to estimate under this specification of liquidity constraints both preference parameters and the loan rate schedule using this Euler equation. But it leaves unanswered the question of *why* there exists a gap between the loan rate and the risk-free rate. If the gap is a premium that compensates for possible defaults, the rate of return on a loan is no longer exogenous to the consumer in that its ex post value depends on the loan quantity: It equals the contracted loan rate if the consumer repays the loan in full and -1 if the consumer defaults on the loan. Then the Euler equation under liquidity constraints will take a different form because the level of the second-period consumption in the event of default is unaffected by marginal changes in the loan quantity. Thus, the estimate of preference parameters under liquidity constraints is sensitive to the nature of the loan market underlying the loan rate schedule. An example in which this is the case will be provided in Section 6.4.

6.3   Recent Empirical Work

6.3.1   Tests for Liquidity Constraints Using Aggregate Time Series Data

Two types of tests can be distinguished in the literature. The first test, which may be called the *orthogonality test*, checks whether the consumption innovation e_t [defined in (2.7) for $t = 2$] is orthogonal to any variables in the information set Ω_{t-1} available to the consumer in period $t - 1$. Recent studies (see, e.g., Dunn and Singleton 1984) have extended the Hansen and Singleton (1982) paper by including durables or by examining several asset returns simultaneously. Typically, the overidentifying restrictions are strongly rejected.[8] This, however, cannot be taken as evidence in favor of liquidity constraints because, the estimation of preference parameters being their primary concern, these studies did not specifically include liquidity variables in the set of additional variables used for the test of overidentifying restrictions. Most time series tests for liquidity constraints assume constant real rates.[9]

The second test may be called the *excess sensitivity test*. Since under constant real rates labor income is the only source of uncertainty, the consumption innovation must be proportional to the labor income innovation. Now make the auxiliary assumption that labor income follows a univariate autoregressive process:

$$w_t = \mu + \rho_1 w_{t-1} + \rho_2 w_{t-2} + \cdots + \rho_{t-n} w_{t-n} + u_t \qquad E_{t-1}(u_t) = 0 \qquad (3.1)$$

Then, as shown by Flavin (1981) for the case of quadratic utility with $\beta(1+r) = 1$, we obtain the following relation between the consumption and labor income innovations when the horizon length is infinite: $\Delta c_t = k u_t$, where

$$k = \frac{r/(1+r)}{1 - \rho_1(1+r)^{-1} - \rho_2(1+r)^{-2} - \cdots - \rho_n(1+r)^{-n}}$$

If an estimate of k is greater than this expression, consumption is more sensitive to current labor income than is justified by intertemporal optimization without liquidity constraints. The failure of the orthogonality test is sufficient, but not necessary, for the excess sensitivity test to fail because myopic consumers whose horizon is short but longer than two periods will also satisfy the Euler equation.

In Flavin's (1981) testing procedure the lagged income coefficients in the regression of the consumption innovation on Ω_{t-1} have a certain structural interpretation, as the following example shows. Suppose, as Hall (1978) suggested, that there are two types of consumers. Consumers in the first group (the "rule-of-thumb" consumers) simply consume all of their disposable income, either because they face a binding constraint of a ban on debt or because they are myopic. If these consumers earn a fraction λ of aggregate disposable income y, the change in their consumption is $\lambda(y_t - y_{t-1})$. Consumers in the second group follow the Euler equation (2.8) with $\beta(1+r) = 1$. Namely, consumption by the second group is a *random walk*. Then aggregate consumption is described by

$$\Delta c_t \equiv c_t - c_{t-1} = \lambda \Delta y_t + \varepsilon_t \qquad (3.2)$$

It is incorrect to estimate λ in (3.2) by regressing Δc_t on Δy_t because Δy_t, not necessarily in Ω_{t-1}, can be correlated with ε_t. To extract (part of) the disposable income change that is forecastable on the basis of Ω_{t-1}, the least-squares projection of y_t is written on lagged disposable income as

$$y_t = \mu + \rho y_{t-1} + v_t \qquad (3.3)$$

By construction, v_t is uncorrelated with lagged disposable income. Since there may be other variables in Ω_{t-1} that help predict y_t, this v_t is not necessarily the true innovation to disposable income [i.e., $E_{t-1}(e_t)$ may not be equal to zero]. The consumption equation (3.2) can be rewritten as

$$\Delta c_t = \lambda\mu + \lambda(\rho - 1)y_{t-1} + (\varepsilon_t + \lambda v_t) \tag{3.4}$$

Now the error term $\varepsilon_t + \lambda v_t$ is uncorrelated with lagged disposable income. The parameters (λ, μ, ρ) can be estimated from (3.3) and (3.4) by the multivariate regression with the cross-equations restriction that the same autoregression coefficient ρ appear in both equations. This estimate of λ is numerically identical to the estimate obtained from (3.2) by the instrumental variables technique with y_{t-1} as the instrument for Δy_t. The test statistic for the hypothesis $\lambda = 0$ is numerically identical to the t statistic in the regression of Δc_t on y_{t-1}. Flavin's estimate of λ based on detrended quarterly U.S. data on nondurables and disposable income was so large that almost all of aggregate consumption was attributable to the rule-of-thumb consumers.

One technical and potentially serious problem can be pointed out at this junction: The use of detrended data biases the test toward rejection of the hypothesis that $\lambda = 0$ if disposable income is a random walk.[10] As noted by Hall (1978), the model consisting of (3.3) and (3.4) becomes unidentifiable if disposable income is a random walk (so that $\rho = 1$) because the lagged income coefficient $\lambda(\rho - 1)$ is zero no matter what the value of λ is. Now consider what happens when λ is zero and detrended data are used. Since the consumption innovation ε_t is proportional to the labor income innovation, the consumption and disposable income series will be highly correlated random walks. Furthermore, detrended series from random walks exhibit spurious cycles. Thus, detrended consumption and disposable income will move up and down together in a cyclical fashion. Mankiw and Shapiro (1985) have shown that if such series are used to estimate (3.4), the lagged income coefficient is likely to be significant.

Other empirical studies that assume constant real rates include Bilson (1980), Hayashi (1982), and Flavin (1985). Bilson uses data from the United States, the United Kingdom, and West Germany. Because of data limitations, his consumption concept is total consumption expenditure (which includes durables expenditure), whereas Hayashi, using U.S. annual data, excludes durables expenditure and includes service flows from durables. Hayashi estimates λ, the fraction of the rule-of-thumb consumers, by the instrumental variables technique. Flavin (1985) finds that the change in the unemployment rate is highly significant if it is included in the consumption equation (3.2). Her interpretation is that the rule-of-thumb consumers are liquidity constrained rather than myopic. Overall, the studies surveyed so far point to rejection of the hypothesis of intertemporal optimization without liquidity constraints.

These studies use different consumption concepts. Although inclusion of durables expenditure in the consumption concept is unwarranted because it is service flows from durables that yield utility, the focus on a particular consumption category can be justified if the instantaneous utility function is separable across commodities. That is, if

$$u(c_t) = u_1(c_{1t}) + u_2(c_{2t}) + \cdots + u_n(c_{nt})$$

(where n here is the dimension of the consumption c_t), the Euler equation holds for each consumption component. The rejections reported in the empirical studies may be attributable to nonseparability across commodities. Bernanke (1985) studied a simultaneous determination of nondurables and durables purchases. The quadratic instantaneous utility function he estimated is

$$u = -\tfrac{1}{2}(\bar{c} - c_t)^2 - \tfrac{1}{2}a(\bar{K} - K_t)^2 - m(\bar{c} - c_t)(\bar{K} - K_t) - \tfrac{1}{2}d(K_{t+1} - K_t)^2$$

$$(3.5)$$

where c_t is nondurables (plus services) and K_t is the stock of consumer durables. The third term captures the interaction between nondurables and durables. Adjustment costs in changing the stock of durables are also introduced by the fourth term. If $m = 0$, the Euler equation for nondurables is (2.8) and does not involve K_t. If $m = a$ and $d = 0$, then nondurables and durables are perfect substitutes, so the correct consumption concept must include service flows from the stock of durables. Bernanke rejected the hypothesis of intertemporal optimization without liquidity constraints because consumption is too sensitive to labor income innovations. His estimates of a, m, and d are too imprecise to determine what the relevant consumption concept should be. His rejection of the hypothesis, however, may be due to his use of detrended data.

As mentioned above, under constant real rates the consumption innovation should be proportional to the labor income innovation. Results in Kotlikoff and Pakes (1984) for the United States and Weissenberger (1986) for the United Kingdom and West Germany show that the labor income innovations estimated from univariate time series models explain only a very small fraction of the consumption innovation. This suggests that changes in real rates and *"transitory"* consumption (i.e., shocks to the utility function and measurement errors in consumption) are important determinants of consumption changes. Even if real rates are constant, simultaneity bias caused by transitory consumption is sufficient to invalidate the orthogonality tests. Suppose, for example, that there is a whitenoise taste shock η_t to the quadratic utility function: $u(c_t) = -(\alpha + \eta_t - c_t)^2$. As shown by Flavin (1981), the Euler equation with $\beta(1 + r) = 1$ is

$$\Delta c_t = \varepsilon_t + \eta_t/(1 + r) - \eta_{t-1} \tag{3.6}$$

So consumption is no longer a random walk. If η_{t-1} is correlated with y_{t-1} through general equilibrium interactions, lagged income will be significant in the regression of Δc_t on y_{t-1}. Even if there is no transitory consumption, the neglect of changes in real rates may lead econometricians to erroneously conclude that the excess sensitivity test fails. Consider, for example, Lucas's (1978) model of asset prices where agents intertemporally optimize without liquidity constraints. Assume that endowments are white noise, so that all endowment changes are temporary. Since there is no saving in equilibrium, observed consumption perfectly tracks income!

Another reason for the random-walk hypothesis to appear to fail is time aggregation. There is no reason that the decision interval coincides with the data-sampling interval. Christiano (1984) shows using quarterly U.S. data on nondurables plus services and disposable income that the random-walk hypothesis (in levels and in logs), although it can be rejected if the decision interval is taken to be the sampling interval, is consistent will the quarterly data if the decision interval is semiquarterly.

And then there is the question of aggregation across consumers. Unless the utility function takes a specific form like a quadratic form, the Euler equation does not aggregate across consumers. What then is it that we have been estimating on aggregate data? As Constantinides (1982) has shown, at least in Arrow-Debreu economies, there exists a fictitious representative consumer who maximizes a utility function defined over the aggregate of individual consumptions generated by consumers with heterogeneous preferences. But since, in general, that representative consumer's utility function depends on income distribution, the preference parameters estimated on aggregate data are not invariant to changes in policy rules that induce redistribution of income.[11]

This list of caveats suggests that the time series evidence is far from conclusive. Furthermore, key parameters (preference parameters and the λ parameter) have not been sharply estimated. Our interest, therefore, naturally turns to the wealth of information contained in microdata. By using microdata, we may be able to avoid problems associated with simultaneity, aggregation, and nonstationarity that are inherent in aggregate time series data. However, as we will see, microdata have their own problems.

6.3.2 Tests Using Microdata

To implement the Euler equation approach at a microlevel, we need panel data because the Euler equation involves consumption at two points in time. A typical panel data set has information for a large number (N) of households, but the number of periods covered (T) is small. If x_{it} is the value of x for household i at time t and if the population of households from which the sample is drawn is represented by a uniform distribution over the unit interval, the (population) mean of x_{it} is $\int_0^1 x_t(\omega)d\omega$, which can be consistently estimated by the cross-sectional average $N^{-1}\sum_{i=1}^{N} x_{it}$. The variance and the covariance are defined accordingly. A very useful discussion of the econometrics of panel data can be found in Chamberlain (1984).

Hall and Mishkin (1982) were the first implementation of the Euler equation approach on panel data. They examined the relation between consumption innovations and income innovations. The data come from the University of Michigan's Panel Study of Income dynamics (PSID), which contains information on food consumption (including expenditure in restaurants) in an average week of the year and income over several years. The following is a simplified version of the model. Make the auxiliary assumption that labor income w_t is described by

$$\Delta w_t \equiv w_t - w_{t-1} = u_t + \Delta v_t \tag{3.7}$$

where u and v are serially and mutually uncorrelated shocks to labor income. Thus, u and v are permanent and temporary shocks. Under the assumption of quadratic utility and $\beta(1 + r) = 1$, the change in consumption under no liquidity constraints is directly tied to these shocks as

$$\Delta c_t = \alpha u_t + \alpha k v_t + \Delta \xi_t \tag{3.8}$$

where ξ is an additive measurement error in consumption and α is the marginal expenditure share of food.[12] The temporary-income coefficient k should be close to zero. Under an infinite horizon, it equals $r/(1 + r)$ [see the expression for k right below (3.1)]. This model, however, turned out to be inconsistent with the data because it failed the orthogonality test: The lagged income change was negative and significant in the regression of Δc_t on Δy_{t-1}. So the model is augmented to encompass the rule-of-thumb consumers (whose consumption simply tracks income) as

$$\Delta c_t = (1 - \lambda)(\alpha u_t + \alpha k v_t) + \lambda(\alpha u_t + \alpha \Delta v_t) + \Delta \xi_t \tag{3.9}$$

Equations (3.7) and (3.9) imply that each element of the covariance matrix of the vector $(\Delta c_1, \ldots, \Delta c_T, \Delta w_1, \ldots, \Delta w_T)$ is a function of the parameters of the model (which include α, k, λ, and the variance of u, v, and ξ). Hall and Mishkin (1982) use the maximum-likelihood procedure assuming normality. The normality assumption is unwarranted if a constant fraction λ of the population (rather than of consumption) is assumed to follow the rule of thumb because then Δc_t will have a binomial element. If the distribution is not normal, their point estimate is consistent, but standard errors are biased probably downward (see Chamberlain 1984). They use disposable income for w, presumably because under constant real rates there should be no shocks to property income. Their estimates indicate that more than 90 percent of the variance in Δc is accounted for by the consumption measurement error. Their estimate of k of 0.17 is somewhat larger than the theoretical prediction. Also, λ is estimated to be 0.20 with a t value of about 3. Bernanke (1984) applied this methodology to data on automobile expenditure (University of Michigan's Survey of Consumer Finances). His estimate of λ does not indicate the presence of rule-of-thumb expenditure. This may be explained by the fact that automobile expenditure can easily be financed.

Probably, the most serious criticism of the methodology just described is its neglect of income measurement error. Since the autocorrelation of income changes gets garbled by (possibly serially correlated) income measurement errors, it is difficult to model the true income process with confidence. Also, even under a given specification of the income process, the model becomes very difficult to identify. A small correlation between consumption and income changes is consistent with intertemporally optimizing consumers partially responding to mostly transitory income changes. But it is also consistent with rule-of-thumb consumers weakly responding to noisy measure of income changes. The excess sensitivity test in microdata with income measurement error is practically impossible. The issue of income measurement error in the PSID data is taken up by Altonji and Siow (1986), who use the log-linear version (2.10) of the

Euler equation. By allowing for a taste shock η in the constant relative risk aversion utility function $u(c) = \exp(\eta/\sigma)c^{1-1/\sigma}$ and a multiplicative measurement error ξ in consumption, the error term in (2.10) becomes $\sigma e_2 + \Delta\eta_2 + \Delta\xi_2$. Treating the real rate r as constant across consumers, the relation of the forecast error e_2 with the current income change $\Delta \ln y_2 \equiv \ln(y_2) - \ln(y_1)$ can be estimated by regressing $\Delta \ln c_2 \equiv \ln(c_2) - \ln(c_1)$ on $\Delta \ln y_2$ (provided, of course, that η and ξ are uncorrelated with $\Delta \ln y_t$). But if y_t contains measurement error, we have the classical errors-in-variables problem that the regression estimate of the $\Delta \ln y_2$ coefficient is biased toward zero. This can be avoided by the use of instrumental variables that are uncorrelated with the income measurement error. Altonji and Siow's regression estimate of the coefficient is 0.08 (see column 6 of their Table 2). If such variables as the change in wage rates, hours of unemployed, past quits, and layoffs are used as instruments, the estimate jumps to somewhere between 0.3 and 0.4 with a t value of above 4. Another indication of the importance of income measurement error is the low explanatory power of $\Delta \ln y_2$ evidenced by a meager R^2 of below 0.5 percent.

Altonji and Siow also conducted the orthogonality test by regressing $\Delta \ln c_2$ on variables dated 1. Contrary to Hall and Mishkin (1982), they found that no variables (not even lagged income changes) were significant as a group or individually. They note that the difference is attributable to their sample selection rule of eliminating both high-income and low-income families due to the requirement that valid data be available on the variables used as instruments. This is an example in which treatment of extreme cases in microdata could influence results in an important way.

Exactly the type of orthogonality test for liquidity constraints described in the previous section is carried out by Runkle (1983) using the Denver Income Maintenance Experiment and by Zeldes (1986) using the PSID data. Both use the log-linear version (2.10). Zeldes found that, in coordance with the hypothesis of liquidity constraints, the coefficient of lagged income y_1 (to use the notation in the previous section) is negative and significant for low-wealth families (which are likely to be liquidity constrained). Because of the cross-sectional difference in the marginal income tax rate, the after-tax real rate r in (2.10) differs across households in the sample. Since high-wealth households are not likely to be liquidity constrained, their consumption should follow (2.10) if the assumed utility function is the correct utility function. This permits the estimation of the intertemporal substitution elasticity σ. Estimates by Runkle and Zeldes, however, are imprecise and insignificantly different from zero.

The last three studies cited do not fully exploit the panel nature of the data. Instead of estimating T equations as a system where the tth equation has $\Delta \ln c_t$ as the dependent variable, they pooled the equations into one. Because the error term—which consists of the consumption innovation (forecast error) e_t, the change in consumption measurement error $\Delta \xi_t$, and the change in taste shock $\Delta \eta_t$—is likely to be negatively serially correlated, the standard errors computed by those studies are likely to be biased upward. Another technical problem, which applies to all the models that have the forecast error term as part of the error term, has been pointed out by Chamberlain (1984). The empirical studies have used the orthogonality condition that e_t is uncorrelated with x_{t-1} in the lagged information set Q_{t-1}, which justifies the use of the regression technique in the time series context. Although it guarantees that a time average of $e_t x_{t-1}$ converges to zero as $T \to \infty$, the rational expectations orthogonality condition does not necessarily mean that a cross-sectional average converge to zero as $N \to \infty$. Namely, it does not guarantee that $\int_0^1 e_t(\omega) x_{t-1}(\omega) d\omega = 0$ (to use the notation introduced at the start of this section). Therefore, all the significant coefficients of lagged variables discovered in the literature using panel data can in principle be explained away by the (cross-sectional) correlation between e_t and x_{t-1}. The practical importance of this problem, however, is hard to evaluate.[13] It is somewhat reassuring to note that this problem does not arise if the structure of the economy is such that the forecast error e_t is the sum of an economywide common shock (which can be separated from e_t as a constant across agents and an idiosyncratic shock. The economywide shock, however, renders the original intercept term [e.g., $\sigma \ln(\beta)$ in (2.10)] unidentifiable.

The failure of the orthogonality test can also be explained by the often neglected distinction between consumption and expenditure, which is important when the commodity is durable. The unanticipated part of an increase in income calls for an upward revision in the level of consumption and hence an increase in expenditure. But if the commodity is durable, the increased expenditure means a higher level of the stock of consumption to be carried over to the next period, which will depress expenditure in the next period. This explains the negative correlation of the change in expenditure with the lagged income level and change. This also shows that expenditure on durables cannot be a random walk (Mankiw 1982). The issue of durability of a wide range of commodities was investigated by Hayashi (1985b), who used a Japanese panel data set on expenditure on several commodities (the 1982 Survey of Family Consumption, conducted by the Economic Planning Agency). He found that nondurables and services excluding food are highly durable. His estimate of λ, the fraction of the rule-of-thumb consumers in the population consisting of wage earners, is about 0.15 with a t value of about 8. He was able to avoid the problem mentioned in the previous paragraph because in his data set expectations are directly measured. The low estimate of λ is also evidenced in his regression, where food expenditure responds to unanticipated income changes much more strongly than to anticipated income changes. The R^2 of the regression, however, is less than 0.04.

Besides income measurement errors, there are a couple of explanations for the low explanatory power of current income changes in the equation for consumption changes reported in the literature. Changes in income, if either perfectly foreseen or fully ensured, do not lead to revisions in consumption. But this is at variance with the result in Altonji and Siow (1986) and Hayashi (1985b) that the income change coefficient is statistically significant. The other explanation is that consumption changes are dominated by changes in transitory consumption (consumption measurement errors and taste shocks). The standard deviation of the growth rate (measured as the change in logs) of consumption is 0.36 in Zeldes's (1986) data where the consumption concept is food expenditure and 0.33 in Runkle's (1983) data where the consumption concept is nondurables plus services. In the data set used by Hayashi (1985b) (where data are collected by interviewers actually visiting households in the survey), the ratio of the standard deviation of the change in food expenditure to the mean of the level is about 0.2. Using a Japanese monthly diary, data set on hundreds of expenditure items (the Family Income and Expenditure Survey compiled by the Prime Minister's Office) where diaries are colected twice a month, Hayashi (1986) calculated the standard deviation of the growth rate of quarterly food expenditure (including expenditure in restaurants) to be about 0.2. Since the measurement error in this monthly diary survey is likely to be small, we may conclude that close to half of the food expenditure growth in the PSID data set (where at least some data in later waves are collected over the phone) is attributable to measurement error. As for the division of the remaining part of food expenditure changes into the forecast error and the taste shock, Hayashi (1986) reports that the first-order serial correlation coefficient of monthly food expenditure changes is roughly -0.5 on average. Because there is no durability in food, the change in food expenditure net of measurement errors is the sum of the forecast error (the random-walk component) and a moving average of a taste shock [see (3.6)]. It seems that the change in food expenditure is dominated by a taste shock that is close to a white noise. Even with an ideal microdata set, we would never be able to explain more than, say, 10 percent of changes in food-expenditure by income changes.

Finally, there are two studies based on cross-sectional data that specifically address the issue of liquidity constraints. Both use the 1963–4 Survey of Financial Characteristics of Consumers compiled by the Board of Governors of the Federal Reserve System. Mariger (1986) uses the implication of deterministic intertemporal optimization that the growth rate of consumption after adjustment for family size is constant over an interval between two successive occurrences of binding credit rationing. Given the age profile of income, this is sufficient to estimate from the level of current consumption and wealth the length of the horizon for each household in the sample. He estimates that 7 percent of the sample (which oversampled wealthy families) has a one-year horizon. His estimation procedure seems to depend critically on the assumption that the instantaneous utility is independent of age. Hayashi (1985a) splits the sample into high- and low-saving families and finds that the correlation structure between consumption and other variables, including income, significantly differ between the two subsets of the sample even after a removal of the possible bias arising from the sample splitting. He interprets the difference as evidence for the presence of liquidity constraints on the ground that high-saving families are not likely to be liquidity constrained.

The conclusions we may draw from microstudies are the following. First, at least a small fraction of the population appears to be liquidity constrained in that the Euler equation fails in a way predicted by the hypothesis of liquidity constraints. Second, because most tests on microdata are the orthogonality tests, we still do not know with confidence the average horizon of those that satisfy the Euler equation. That information is necessary to calculate the response of consumption to a temporary income change and, more generally, to a change in the stochastic process for income. Third, the change in consumption is dominated by the transitory consumption component. Only a small fraction of the change is explainable by income changes. This suggests the fourth (and somewhat pessimistic) conclusion: The observed correlation of the change in consumption with lagged income is also attributable to a correlation between consumption measurement error and income measurement error or between consumption taste shock and leisure taste shock. The latter correlation can occur despite our basic maintained assumption that consumption and leisure are separable in the utility function. To identify the model, we need variables that are uncorrelated with transitory consumption. Such variables are hard to find.

6.4   In What Sense is the Loan Market "Imperfect"?

It is not entirely clear what we do with the hard-won evidence that some consumers are liquidity constrained. Does a consensus estimate of λ (the share of rule-of-thumb consumers in the population) of (say) 0.15 imply that a debt-financed tax cut of $100 for everyone increase per capita consumption by $15? How is the size of the lagged income coefficient related to aggregate fluctuations? The problem stems from the vagueness of the terms *liquidity constraints or imperfect loan markets* that we noted in Section 2. We will argue by three examples that unless the exact nature of the imperfection of the loan market is identified, the economic implication of the available evidence cannot be determined. In all three examples the Euler equation fails, and so consumption shows excess sensitivity. The MPC out of a temporary income increase varies across the examples. Only in the last example the Ricardian equivalence theorem fails to hold.

Consider a consumer in the two-period model whose second-period labor income w_2 is a random variable that takes with probability p a low value of w_2^L and with probability $1 - p$ a high value of w_2^H. We assume that $u'(0) < +\infty$, so that the consumer may choose a consumption plan that allows default with zero consumption. If an actuarially fair insurance is available, the risk-averse consumer will engage in an insurance scheme that eliminates the income risk entirely. So the intertemporal optimization problem is exactly as in Figure 6.1(a) with the w_2^e in the figure replaced by $pw_2^L + (1 - p)w_2^H$. The relevant marginal loan rate is the riskfree rate r. If we had data on the consumption and income changes for consumers whose utility function may differ in a way unrelated to the difference across consumers in the distribution of w_2, there should be no significant correlation between the two variables. This is a test proposed by Scheinkman (1984) of the Arrow-Debreu complete-markets paradigm. Note that this restriction is stronger than the Euler equation, which by itself places no restrictions on the contemporaneous correlation of actual consumption changes with actual income changes.

In the following three examples we assume that, for reasons to be discussed later, such income risk sharing is not available to the consumer. In the first example lenders have the same opinion about the distribution of w_2. Let Z and R be the loan principal and the contracted repayment. Since

w_2 is at least w_2^l with probability 1, the loan rate (the borrowing rate available to the consumer) must equal the market rate r under perfect competition among lenders where $Z \leqslant w_2^l/(1+r)$. However, when $Z > w_2^l/(1+r)$, the consumer will default with probability p on a marginal loan above $w_2^l/(1+r)$. The loan rate r^* on such a marginal loan satisfies

$$1 + r^* = (1+r)/(1-p) \tag{4.1}$$

if lenders are risk neutral or if there are many consumers of the same characteristic. Thus, the marginal loan rate schedule jumps up from r to r^* at $Z = w_2^l/(1+r)$. If the consumer defaults, the second-period consumption is zero. So the expected lifetime utility under a loan contract (Z, R) is

$$u(w_1 + Z) + p\beta u[\max(0, w_2^l - R)] + (1-p)\beta u[\max(0, w_2^H - R)] \tag{4.2}$$

Since the focus of this chapter is on liquidity constraints, we suppose that the value of (w_1, w_2^l, w_2^H) is such that the consumer facing this marginal loan rate schedule plans to default in the low-income state. Thus, the consumer behaves as if the middle term in (4.2) is absent. It is easy to show that the Euler equation is

$$u'(c_1) = \beta(1+r^*)(1-p)u'(c_2^H) \tag{4.3}$$

where $c_1 = w_1 + Z$ and $c_2^H = w_2^H - R$. This is a violation of the Euler equation without liquidity constraints because the latter requires

$$u'(c_1) = \beta(1+r)[pu'(0) + (1-p)u'(c_2^H)] \tag{4.4}$$

It also is different from the Euler equation that would result if (as we will assume for the third example below) the gap between the loan rate and the risk-free rates were exogenously given and unrelated to defaults:

$$u'(c_1) = \beta(1+r')[pu'(c_2^l) + (1-p)u'(c_2^H)] \tag{4.5}$$

where $1 + r' = dA_2/d(A_1 + w_1 - c_1)$ and c_2^l is the second-period consumption in the low-income state. Despite the existence in this first example of the loan rate schedule as an increasing function of the loan quantity, the preference parameters cannot be estimated by (4.5).

Because the Euler equation without liquidity constraints (4.4) fails, consumption shows excess sensitivity.[14] However, the Ricardian equivalence theorem still holds. To see this, suppose the government cuts taxes in real terms by x in exchange for a second-period tax increase of $(1+r)x$. This increases w_1 by x but reduces both w_2^l and w_2^H by $(1+r)x$. Thus, the marginal loan rate schedule shifts to the left by exactly x. But the demand for private loans is also reduced by x because of the newly acquired government loan. The net result of a debt-financed tax cut, therefore, is that the government loan thus provided crowds out the private loan market on a dollar-for-dollar basis and leaves the optimal consumption plan unaltered.

It is not at all clear why income insurance markets are not present in this example where both borrowers and lenders have common knowledge about the distribution of future income. The equilibrium loan contract (Z, R) is really a combination of two things: (i) an actuarially fair insurance whose payoff inclusive of the premium is $(1 + r)Z - w_2^L$ when $w_2 = w_2^L$ and $-[p/(1 - p)][(1 + r)Z - w_2^L]$ when $w_2 = w_2^H$ and (ii) a risk-free loan of principal Z. The insurance implicit in the loan is constrained so that $c_2 = 0$ when $w_2 = w_2^L$. So the loan market cannot be a perfect substitute for insurance markets, although one would not call this loan market "imperfect."

The next example we consider is somewhat similar to the model considered by Jaffee and Russel (1976). For each class of consumers indexed by the first-period income w_1, there are two types (type L and type H) of consumers. Labor income in periods 1 and 2 is (w_1, w_2^L) for type L and (w_1, w_2^H) for type H consumers. That is, p is unity for type L and zero for type H consumers. The type is *private information*: No one knows the type of other consumers but oneself. This eliminates private income insurance markets. But the loan market will still exist. In Figure 6.2 the horizontal and vertical axes represent consumption and income in the two periods. The origin for type L consumers is the point 0^L on the vertical axis, reflecting the difference in the second-period income between the two types. The same point E represents the initial endowments both for type L with (w_1, w_2^L) and for type H with (w_1, w_2^H). The slope of the line ED is $1 + r$ because if the loan principal in less than $FD[= w_2^L/(1 + r)]$, no defaults will occur. Let π be the share of type L consumers in the population consisting of consumers with the same first-period income w_1. If the loan principal is greater than FD and if both types apply for the loan, only a fraction $(1 - \pi)$ of a marginal loan above $w_2^L/(1 + r)$ will be repaid, so that the marginal loan rate that is consistent with the zeroprofits condition for lenders is r^* and satisfies the condition analogous to (4.1): $1 + r^* = (1 + r)/(1 - \pi)$. Thus, the line DC with a slope of $1 + r^*$ along with the line ED with a slope of $1 + r$ represents the set of (c_1, c_2) available to type H consumers when both types apply for the same loan.

As we know from Rothchild and Stiglitz (1976) and Wilson (1977), there are two types of equilibrium in this *informationally imperfect* loan

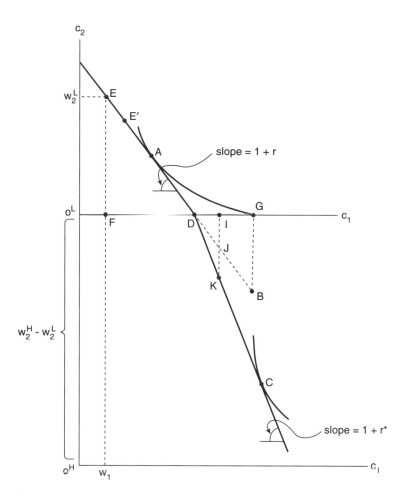

Figure 6.2

market. In a separating equilibrium, type L consumers choose the point A, whereas the consumption plan for type H is the point B. Since type L consumers are indifferent between A and B (which translates into the point G as type L consumers will not repay the loan in full), they have no incentive to switch from A to B by claiming that they are of type H. Type H consumers are *credit rationed* in the sense that they would like to borrow more at the stated loan rate of r. No defaults occur. In a pooling equilibrium both types choose the loan contract represented by the point C where an indifference curve for type H is tangent to the line DC. If type H prefers B to C, then a pair of loan contracts (A, B) is the separating equilibrium [Wilson's (1977) E1 equilibrium]. Otherwise, the point C is the equilibrium loan contract (Wilson's E2 equilibrium). Since type L consumers prefer C to A, they also apply for the loan contract represented by the point C knowing that they will default. Clearly, the Euler equation fails to hold for both types in the pooling equilibrium and for type H in the separating equilibrium. In particular, for type H the MPC out of a temporary increase in current income should be about unity in the separating equilibrium. We can think of type H consumers as ones experiencing a temporary drop in income. Because they are mixed up with low-income people in the loan market, their consumption is forced to be temporarily low. Thus, their consumption appears to be tracking income.

It is now easy to see that, whichever equilibrium obtains, a debt-financed tax cut of quantity x in exchange for a tax increase in the second period of $(1 + r)x$ will have no real effects. The tax cut will move the initial endowment from E to E'. Now lenders realize that the fraction π of a marginal loan above $w_2^L/(1 + r) - x$ will be defaulted if both types apply for the loan. In the separating equilibrium, the amount of credit available is cut back by exactly x. In the pooling equilibrium, the loan principal at which the loan rate jumps up from r to r^* is also reduced by x. The equilibrium consumption plan is left unaltered.

This irrelevance result remains valid even if type L consumers fail to pay the second-period tax in full in the event of default, as long as the unpaid tax is borne by type H consumers of the same first-period income. Although income redistribution between the two types occurs, the following argument for irrelevance does not assume homothetic preferences. Suppose the size of a debt-financed tax cut is FI in Figure 6.2. The second-period tax to be paid by type L exceeds w_2^L. If the unpaid tax bill when type L defaults is to be picked up by type H consumers, the second-period tax on type H is precisely EF plus IJ, where the point J is the vertical projection of I on DB.[15] Thus, the feasible set of (c_1, c_2) for type H when both types apply for the same loan is unchanged, which leaves the initial pooling equilibrium C undisturbed. If the initial equilibrium is the separating equilibrium (A, B), it, too, is undisturbed by the tax cut. What type L would do is purchase the public debt of amount FI (which is just sufficient to "undo" the tax cut) and then borrow from private lenders the amount that equals the horizontal distance between points E and A, or, equivalently, lend the amount that equals the horizontal distance between points I and A.

The intuition behind this irrelevance result is simple enough. In the present example of the informationally imperfect loan market, type L is exercising a negative externality over type H; if there were no type L consumers, the budget line for type H would be the straight line EDB, which dominates the kinked budget line EDC. Because this externality, which manifests itself as liquidity constraints, is caused by imperfect information, it cannot be removed by the government unless the government has some superior information about the type of consumers. In particular, the tax cut of size FI has no real effect because it merely replaces part of the negative externality in the form of the collection by the tax authority of the unpaid tax from type H consumers. Unlike Wilson's (1977) model of insurance markets where government actions can make Pareto improvements by compelling purchase of some insurance policy, the present model of loan markets does not seem to allow any Pareto-improving government actions. This is because type L's indifference curves are vertical (like GB) below the type L horizontal axis.

This informationally imperfect loan market can be readily embedded into a general equilibrium model. The simplest way to do this is to assume another type of consumers, distinguishable from type L and type H, whose first-period income is higher than the second-period income and who are therefore willing to lend for the second-period consumption. The equilibrium interest rate r (and hence r^*) can be determined by the loan market equilibrium where the loan supply comes from this third type. This two-period model of general equilibrium can be easily converted to an overlapping generations model. It seems clear that the irrelevance result carries over to such a model.

In the preceding two examples, the excess sensitivity of consumption is not exploitable for stabilization purposes through substitution of taxes for the public debt. We now turn to the last example, where the excess sensitivity *is* exploitable. Here the basic premise is that the government is more efficient than the private loan market in arranging loans. This may arise if transactions costs for collecting private loans are higher than for collecting taxes or if the court does not honor at least some private loan contracts. As shown by Barro (1984), a debt-financed tax cut will increase aggregate consumption because the government's increased share of lending activity raises the overall efficiency. In the extreme case where the private loan market is nonexistent because the legal system does not honor any private loan contracts, the MPC out of an increase in income induced by a debt-financed tax cut is exactly 1, not zero. A model in which the Ricardian equivalence theorem does not hold but in which the gap between the loan rate and the risk-free rate is based on imperfect information is also constructed by King (1986). Unlike our second example, King assumes that lenders cannot observe the total loan quantity a consumer borrows from various lenders.

6.5   Concluding Remarks

By way of concluding, let us see what answers have been provided by recent empirical work to the three questions raised at the beginning of this chapter. The answer to the first question is positive. Some consumers are liquidity constrained in the sense of credit rationing or differential interest rates. But the same conclusion can be obtained from the following simple observation: According to the *Federal Reserve Bulletin*, the average rate on 24-month personal loans in 1982 was 18.65 percent, whereas the yield on two-year U.S. Treasury notes in 1982 was 12.80 percent. This is a piece of evidence for liquidity constraints with a standard error of zero. Put differently, the existence of liquidity constraints is a nonissue. What has been done in the literature is like testing whether the mean stock returns are higher than the risk-free interest rate. IOUs issued by the government and IOUs issued by a consumer are simply different securities.

The estimation of the preference parameters under liquidity constraints is probably meaningless if done on aggregate data because it would be impossible for economies with imperfect loan markets to induce the utility function of the representative consumer from heterogeneous consumers. If microdata are to be used, consumers who are likely to be liquidity constrained should be excluded from the sample because their first-order optimality condition depends on the specification of the loan market. The estimation of the preference parameters using a short panel is possible only when we can get cross-sectional variations in after-tax interest rates.

The available evidence gives only a partial answer to the third question. The finding that the Euler equation fails for a fraction of the population does imply that consumption is excessively sensitive to temporary income changes. But that does not allow us to calculate quantitatively (even abstracting from the general equilibrium interaction running from consumption to income) the response of consumption to a hypothetical temporary increase in labor income. This is partly because the horizon of those who satisfy the Euler equation is unknown and partly because the concomitant changes in the loan rate schedule depend on the specification of the loan market. For the Ricardian equivalence theorem, the available evidence has no implication.

Notes

Presented at a symposium on consumer behavior in the Fifth World Congress of the Econometric Society, Cambridge, Massachusetts, August 18–24, 1985. The author is grateful to Ken Judd, Tom MaCurdy, and Larry Summers for comments and discussions. The research reported here was supported by Japan's Ministry of Education Science and Culture grant in aids No. 60301081 and the Yoshida international Education Fund.

1. Dornbusch and Fischer (1984, pp. 186–87) cite liquidity constraints as the candidate to explain the excess sensitivity of consumption to income. Delong and Summers (1984) credits the increased availability of consumer loans with the reduced variability of aggregate demand in the postwar United States. Scheinkman and Weiss (1986) shows in an equilibrium model of business cycles inhabited by optimizing agents that borrowing constraints fundamentally alter the time series properties of the model. In Walsh's (1984) general equilibrium model anticipated money has real effects as it changes the probability of people being short of cash and lines of credit.

2. The statements in this paragraph about the MPCs remain valid if risky assets are introduced.

3. See Hayashi (1985a) for other reasons against the consumption function approach.

4. The derivation of (2.9) and (2.10) uses the approximation that $\ln(1 + x) \simeq x$.

5. If the realization of r is not known in period 1, the consumption innovation is correlated with r. Thus, r must be instrumented by some variable (e.g., lagged value of r) in the period 1 information set.

6. See Muellbauer (1983), Mariger (1986), and Zeldes (1986). Rotemberg (1984) shows that expected future liquidity constraints can explain why people hold financial assets and liabilities simultaneously.

7. If the utility function is quadratic and if $\beta(1 + r) = 1$, the consumption innovation is simply the change in consumption. Kotlikoff and Pakes (1984) show how to calculate the consumption innovation for general nonlinear utility functions.

8. However, Miron (1986) reports that when the seasonal fluctuations in consumption are explicitly included in the utility function, the overidentifying restrictions cannot be rejected.

9. One exception is Summers (1982), who puts $c - \lambda w$ (consumption minus a fraction of labor income) in place of c in the Euler equation and estimates λ. Here λw is the part of aggregate consumption by liquidity-constrained agents. His estimate of λ is too imprecise to draw any conclusions. See text for the definition of λ.

10. Delong and Summers (1984) and Mankiw and Shapiro (1985) show that disposable income in postwar United States is a random walk.

11. See, however, Eichenbaum and Hansen (1984), who show that a restriction on individual heterogeneity makes the representative agent's utility function free from income distribution. They also incorporate durability of commodities into the model.

12. The term ξ can also be interpreted as a preference shock. See (3.6).

13. Hayashi (1985b) gives a somewhat contrived example in which an unanticipated income tax reform causes a cross-sectional correlation between e_2 and y_1.

14. A simple calculation under the assumption that $\beta(1 + r) = 1$ shows that the MPC out of a temporary income increase is $(1 + r^*)/(2 + r^*)$. Under a complete income risk pooling the MPC is $(1 + r)/(2 + r)$.

15. If type L consumers default, the additional tax to be levied on a type H consumer is $DI \times (1 + r)\pi/(1 - \pi)$. This equals KJ in Figure 6.2 Because IJ equals $DI \times (1 + r^*) = DI \times (1 + r)/(1 - \pi)$ and IK equals $DI \times (1 + r)$.

References

Altonji, J. G., and A. Siow (1986), "Testing the Response of Consumption to Income Changes with (Noisy) Panel Data," NBER Working Paper No. 2012.

Barro, R. J. (1984), *Macroeconomics*, Wiley, New York.

Bernanke, B. S. (1984), "Permanent Income, Liquidity, and Expenditure on Automobiles: Evidence from Panel Data," *Quarterly Journal of Economics* **98**, 587–614.

(1985), "Adjustment Costs, Durables and Aggregate Consumption," *Journal of Monetary Economics* **15**, 41–68.

Bilson, J. F. O. (1980), "The Rational Expectations Approach to the Consumption Function: A Multi-Country Study," *European Economic Review* **13**, 273–99.

Chamberlain, G. (1984), "Panel Data," in *Handbook of Econometrics*, Z. Griliches and M. Intriligator, eds., North-Holland, New York.

Christiano, L. J. (1984), "A Critique of Conventional Treatments of the Model Timing Interval in Applied Econometrics," University of Chicago, mimeo.

Constantinides, G. M. (1982), "Intertemporal Asset Pricing with Heterogeneous Consumers and without Demand Aggregation," *Journal of Business* **55**, 253–67.

Delong, J. B., and L. H. Summers (1984), "The Changing Cyclical Variability of Economic Activity in the United States," NBER Working Paper No. 1450.

Dornbusch, R., and S. Fischer (1984), *Macroeconomics*, 3rd ed., McGraw-Hill, New York.

Dunn, K. B., and K. J. Singleton (1984), "Modelling the Term Structure of Interest Rates under Nonseparable Utility and Durability of Goods," NBER Working Paper No. 1415.

Eichenbaum, M. S., and L. P. Hansen (1984), "Uncertainty, Aggregation, and the Dynamic Demand for Consumption Goods," Carnegie-Mellon University, mimeo.

Flavin, M. A. (1981), "The Adjustment of Consumption to Changing Expectations about Future Income," *Journal of Political Economy* **89**, 974–1009.

(1985), "Excess Sensitivity of Consumption to Current Income: Liquidity Constraints or Myopia?" *Canadian Journal of Economics* **18**, 117–36.

Hall, R. E. (1978), "Stochastic Implications of the Life Cycle–Permanent Income Hypothesis: Theory and Evidence," *Journal of Political Economy* **86**, 971–87.

Hall, R. E., and F. S. Mishkin (1982), "The Sensitivity of Consumption to Transitory Income: Estimates from Panel Data on Households," *Econometrica* **50**, 461–81.

Hansen, L. P. (1982), "Large Sample Properties of Generalized Method of Moments Estimators," *Econometrica* **50**, 1029–54.

Hansen, L. P., and K. J. Singleton (1982), "Generalized Instrumental Variables Estimation of Nonlinear Rational Expectations Models," *Econometrica* **50**, 1269–86.

Hayashi, F. (1982), "The Permanent Income Hypothesis: Estimation and Testing by Instrumental Variables," *Journal of Political Economy* **90**, 895–918.

(1985a), "The Effect of Liquidity Constraints on Consumption: A Cross-Sectional Analysis," *Quarterly Journal of Economics* **100**, 183–206.

(1985b), "The Permanent Income Hypothesis and Consumption Durability: Analysis Based on Japanese Panel Data," *Quarterly Journal of Economics* **100**, 1083–1113.

(1986), "An Extension of the Permanent Income Hypothesis and Its Test" (in Japanese) *Keizai Bunseki* (Economic Analysis) No. 101, Institute of Economic Research, Economic Planning Agency of the Japanese Government.

Jaffee, D. M., and T. Russel (1976), "Imperfect Information, Uncertainty and Credit Rationing," *Quarterly Journal of Economics* **90**, 651–66.

King, M. A. (1985), "The Economics of Saving," in *Frontiers in Economics*, K. J. Arrow and S. Honkapohja, eds., Black well, New York.

(1986), "Capital Market 'Imperfections' and the Consumption Function," *Scandinavian Journal of Economics* **88**, 59–80.

Kotlikoff, L. J., and A. Pakes (1984), "Looking for the News in the Noise—Additional Stochastic Implications of Optimal Consumption Choice," NBER Working Paper No. 1492.

Lucas, R. E., Jr. (1978), "Asset Prices in an Exchange Economy," *Econometrica* **86**, 1429–46.

Mankiw, N. G. (1982), "The Permanent Income Hypothesis and the Real Interest Rate," *Economics Letters* **7**, 307–11.

Mankiw, N. G., and M. D. Shapiro (1985), "Trends, Random Walks, and Tests of the Permanent Income Hypothesis," *Journal of Monetary Economics* **16**, 165–74.

Mariger, R. P. (1986), *Consumption Behavior and the Effects of Government Fiscal Policies*, Harvard University Press, Cambridge.

Miron, J. A. (1986), "Seasonal Fluctuations and the Life Cycle–Permanent Income Model of Consumption," *Journal of Political Economy* **94**, 1258–79.

Muellbauer, J. (1983), "Surprises in the Consumption Function," *Economic Journal* (Suppl.), 34–50.

Rotemberg, J. (1984), "Consumption and Liquidity Constraints," Sloan School, Massachusetts Institute of Technology, mimeo.

Rothchild, M., and J. E. Stiglitz (1976), "Equilibrium in Competitive Insurance Markets: An Essay on the Economics of Imperfect Information," *Quarterly Journal of Economics* **90**, 629–50.

Runkle, D. (1983), "Liquidity Constraints and the Permanent Income Hypothesis: Evidence from Panel Data," Brown University, mimeo.

Scheinkman, J. A. (1984), "General Equilibrium Models of Economic Fluctuations: A Survey of Theory," University of Chicago, mimeo.

Scheinkman, J. A., and L. Weiss (1986), "Borrowing Constraints and Aggregate Economic Activity," *Econometrica* **54**, 23—46.

Summers, L. H. (1982), "Tax Policy, the Rate of Return, and Savings," NBER Working Paper No. 995.

Walsh, C. E. (1984), "A Model of Liquidity Constraints, Credit and the Real Effects of Monetary and Fiscal Policy," Princeton University, mimeo.

Weissenberger, E. (1986), "Consumption Innovations and Income Innovations: The Case of the United Kingdom and Germany," *Review of Economics and Statistics* **68**, 1—8.

Wilson, C. (1977), "A Model of Insurance Markets with Incomplete Information," *Journal of Economic Theory* **16**, 167—207.

Zeldes, S. (1986), "Consumption and Liquidity Constraints: An Empirical Investigation," Wharton School, University of Pennsylvania, mimeo.

II

Risk Sharing and Altruism

7

Is the Extended Family Altruistically Linked? Direct Tests Using Micro Data

What is the basic economic decision-making unit? Is the household or the extended family? For questions of public policy, knowing the size and scope of economic decision-making units is of great importance. As Robert Barro (1974) and Gary Becker (1974, 1981) stressed, nondistortionary government redistribution among members of an altruistically linked economic unit will not alter the collective budget constraint and, therefore, will not alter any of the unit's economic choices. If large altruistically linked economic units exist, this line of argument implies that private behavior will neutralize most, if not all, of the government's intergenerational and intragenerational redistribution.

In this paper we use extended-family data from the Panel Study of Income Dynamics (PSID) to test directly the assumption of operative altruistic linkages between parents and children against the alternative of zero linkage.[1] On an ongoing basis, the PSID surveys child "split-offs." These are children of the original 1968 respondents who subsequently became heads or spouses in their own households. By combining data on food consumption, income, assets, transfers, and household characteristics for these split-off adult children with the same data for their parents (the original survey respondents who have also been continually reinterviewed), one can use the PSID to form a unique and rich data set covering at least a portion of the extended family.[2]

The intuition behind our tests is quite simple. If parents and children are altruistically linked, their consumption will be based on a collective budget constraint, and the distribution of consumption between parents and children will be independent of the distribution of their incomes. In contrast to the altruism model, the nonaltruistic pure life-cycle model

Originally published in *The American Economic Review* 82 (December 1992): 1177–98, with J. Altonji and L. Kotlikoff. Reprinted with the permission of the American Economic Association.

predicts that the distribution of incomes is a critical determinant of the distribution of consumption between parent and children.

While this simple idea underlies our tests, the actual form of our tests involves specifications of food demand functions. Under both the altruism and life-cycle models, one can express the consumption and leisure choices of parents (children) as functions of the parents' (children's) marginal utility of income and of prices.[3] An implication of the altruism model's single-collective-budget constraint is that parents and children have the same marginal utility of income. In contrast, under the life-cycle model, parents and children maximize their own preferences subject to their own budget constraints and have different marginal utilities of income.

The marginal utility of income is captured by a fixed effect in our food demand regressions. Given that we control for this fixed effect, according to the altruism model, the exogenous incomes and asset positions of parents (children) should not enter into our estimated demand functions for the parent's (children's) food consumption. Under the life-cycle hypothesis, in contrast, knowing the parent's fixed effect will not control perfectly for the child's fixed effect, and vice versa; hence, the exogenous incomes and asset positions of parents and children should enter into our estimated demand functions.

After estimating demands at a point in time, we combine the data over time and estimate the first differences of the demand functions. We find strong evidence against the altruism model both in the levels and first-differenced estimates of the food demand functions.[4] At a point in time, the distribution of consumption between parents and children is highly dependent on the distribution of their incomes; and over time, the distribution of consumption changes between parents and children is highly dependent on the distribution of their income changes. As we discuss below, the first-difference results rule out the possibility that the correlation we find in the levels reflects a correlation between parental preferences for particular children and the permanent incomes of those children.

In addition to showing that the distribution of extended-family resources matters for extended-family consumption, we test the life-cycle model by asking whether only own resources matter (i.e., whether the resources of extended-family members have no effect on a household's consumption). Our results indicate that extended-family member resources have at most a modest effect on household consumption after one has controlled for the fact that extended-family resources help predict a household's own permanent income.

The paper proceeds in Section 7.1 by developing our empirical tests of altruism. Section 7.2 describes the linked PSID data. Sections 7.3 and 7.4 contain, respectively, our findings from static and dynamic tests of altruism. Section 7.5 presents results of tests that take the life-cycle model, rather than the altruism model, as the null hypothesis. Section 7.6 summarizes and concludes the chapter.

7.1 Testable Implications of the Altruism Model

A Static Illustration

To see in the simplest possible terms the force of altruism, consider the case of a parent who is altruistic toward a child, but the child is not altruistic toward the parent. Suppose the parent's utility function is given by $U_p = \theta_p U(C_p) + \theta_k U(C_k)$, where C_p stands for the parent's consumption, C_k stands for the child's consumption, and θ_p and θ_k are the respective weights the parent attaches to his own utility from consumption, $U(C_p)$, and to the child's utility, $U(C_k)$. The child's consumption, C_k, will equal the child's resources, R_k, plus T, the transfer made to the child (i.e., $C_k = R_k + T$). The parent's consumption will equal the parent's resources less the transfers to the child (i.e., $C_p = R_p - T$). These two constraints imply the combined budget constraint: $C_k + C_p = R_k + R_p$.

Suppose that the child takes the parent's transfer as given. Then the parent's choice of his own consumption and transfer (assuming it is positive) leads the parent to set $\theta_p U'(C_p) = \theta_k U'(C_k) = \lambda$, where λ is the marginal utility of income. This first-order condition and the collective-budget constraint can be used to solve for C_p and C_k. Hence, as first shown by Becker (1974) and Barro (1974), the parent and child act as if they are maximizing the parent's utility function subject to the combined-budget constraint. This type of outcome is generic in one-sided, two-sided, or, indeed, many-sided altruistic models assuming that recipients of transfers take such transfers as given [i.e., the game between the donor and recipient is noncooperative Nash and there are positive (operative) transfers].[5]

Next assume that the utility function is of the isoelastic form, $U(C) = C^{1-\gamma}/(1-\gamma)$. From the first-order conditions, we have $\log C_p = -(1/\gamma)\log \lambda + (1/\gamma)\log \theta_p$ and $\log C_k = -(1/\gamma)\log \gamma + (1/\lambda)\log \theta_k$. Obviously, C_p will exceed C_k if θ_p is greater than θ_k. If the true values of C_p and C_k differ from the measured values, C_p^m and C_k^m, by multiplicative errors, whose logarithms we denote u_p and u_k, respectively, we have the following statistical representation of the demand system:

$$\log(C_{ip}^m) = -\left(\frac{1}{\gamma_i}\right)\log\lambda_i + \left(\frac{1}{\gamma_i}\right)\log\theta_{ip} + u_{ip} \tag{1}$$

$$\log(C_{ik}^m) = -\left(\frac{1}{\gamma_i}\right)\log\lambda_i + \left(\frac{1}{\gamma_i}\right)\log\theta_{ik} + u_{ik}. \tag{2}$$

In equations (1) and (2) the subscript i refers to parent-child pair i. With data on a sample of parent-child pairs one can estimate (1) and (2) jointly treating the terms $\log\lambda_i$ for each parent-child pair as a fixed effect.[6] Since controlling for the fixed effect fully controls for the combined resources of the parent and child, one can test the model by asking whether the parent's resources, R_{pi}, enter into the parent's consumption equation and whether the child's resources, R_{ki}, enter into the child's consumption equation.[7] The altruism model predicts zero coefficients on own resources, controlling for combined resources. In contrast, the life-cycle and Keynesian models predict that own resources are significant determinants of own consumption. As we show below, this basic test procedure carries over to more realistic dynamic models with multiple consumption goods, uncertainty, and endogenous labor supply.

Two-Sided Altruism

Before turning to those issues we need to remark on how the results of the proposed test should be interpreted if altruism is two-sided. By two-sided altruism we mean that the child cares about the parent's utility and vice versa. It is easy to show that with two-sided altruism there will be different transfer regimes (three in the case of a single parent and a single child) determined by the division of resources between the parent and child. As the share of joint resources owned by the parent increases from zero to unity, the regime shifts from one in which the child transfers to the parent to one in which there are no transfers and then to one in which the parent transfers to the child. Changes in the resource distribution between the parent and child that are large enough to shift the transfer regime will be associated with changes in the ratio of the parent's consumption to the child's consumption.

Hence, one response to a finding of a significant own-resource coefficient in the fixed-effect test discussed above is that extended families are indeed altruistic but that the test is simply capturing the fact that transfer regimes change as the distribution of resources changes between parent and child.

While this may be true, its implication with respect to Barro's neutrality proposition, at least for large government redistributions between parents and children, is the same as if there is no altruism, namely, that such government redistribution is not neutral. One way to test whether the Barro proposition holds for small government redistributions—those that are not likely to alter the transfer regime—is to focus on the subset of parent-child pairs in which the parent's resource share is much larger than that of the child. For this subset of observations one would expect no correlation between consumption and resource shares. While we do not know precisely the resource shares of our parent-child pairs, we can conduct this more refined test of altruism by running our fixed-effects test for parent-child pairs in which the parent has high income and the child has low income.

A Dynamic Formulation

Given that within a transfer regime the standard altruism model can be summarized by the maximization of a single objective function subject to a single collective budget constraint, we proceed by referring to the extended family as the dynasty and by expressing the general problem of the dynasty as

$$\max E_t \left\{ \sum_{s=t}^{\infty} b^s U(Z_s, \mathbf{p}_s; \mathbf{x}_s) \right\} \tag{3}$$

subject to

$$A_{t+1} = (1 + r_t)A_t + Y_t - Z_t$$

where

$$Y_t = \sum_{k=1}^{m_t} Y_{kt}$$

and where

E_t = expectation operator,

m_t = number of households in the dynasty at time t,

Y_{kt} = labor earnings of the kth household of the dynasty at time t,

Z_t = total nominal consumption expenditure by the dynasty at t,

A_t = the dynasty's wealth at time t,

r_t = nominal interest rate at time t,

$\mathbf{x}_{kt}$ = vector of demographics for the kth household at time t,

$\mathbf{x}_t$ = vector consisting of $\mathbf{x}_{kt}$ ($k = 1, \ldots, m_t$),

$\mathbf{p}_t$ = vector of commodity prices, and

b = discount factor.

In (3) we assume that labor supply is exogenous. The dynasty's indirect intertemporal utility function $U(Z_t, \mathbf{p}_t; \mathbf{x}_t)$ is defined as the maximized value of the following static optimization problem:

$$\max_{\{\mathbf{C}_{kt}\}} \sum_{k=0}^{m_t} u(\mathbf{C}_{kt}; \mathbf{x}_{kt}) \tag{4}$$

subject to

$$\mathbf{p}_t' \sum_{k=0}^{m_t} \mathbf{C}_{kt} \leqslant Z_t$$

where $u(\mathbf{C}_{kt}; \mathbf{x}_{kt})$ is the dynasty's time-t utility from the vector of consumption of household k, $\mathbf{C}_{kt}$, with demographic characteristics $\mathbf{x}_{kt}$. The term $\mathbf{p}_t$ stands for the time-t price vector.

The key prediction of this more general model—namely, that resources are shared by altruistically linked individuals within the dynasty and, therefore, by households within the dynasty—can be formalized as follows. Let λ_t be the scalar shadow price for the budget constraint in (3). Then the first-order conditions from the maximization in (4) imply the demand functions:

$$\mathbf{C}_{kt} = f(\lambda_t, \mathbf{p}_t; \mathbf{x}_{kt}) \qquad k = 0, 1, \ldots, m_t. \tag{5}$$

As suggested above, the important point here is that the scalar shadow price λ_t, which is a "sufficient statistic" for dynasty resources at time t, is common across dynasty members, while in the life-cycle hypothesis it depends on the household identifier k. For a wide range of utility functions the shadow price λ_t can be treated as a component of a fixed effect. In the case of exogenous labor supply, since the price vector $\mathbf{p}_t$ is also common across dynasty members, the fixed effect can also depend on prices. Since the only consumption component available in our data is food consumption, we now focus on the food component of (5) and require that the demand function for food be of the form:

$$f_{kt} = h(\mathbf{x}_{kt}, \mathbf{p}_t) + \alpha(\mathbf{p}_t, \lambda_t) \tag{6}$$

where f_{kt} is either the level or the logarithm of food consumption. Since the $\alpha(\cdot, \cdot)$ function does not depend on k, we treat it as a fixed effect. As described in Altonji et al. (1989), a large class of utility functions satisfy the demand specification given in (6). The class includes the familiar constant-elasticity-of-substitution (CES) functions and constant-absolute-risk-aversion functions.[8]

Testing the Dynasty Model

With (6) as our starting point, our statistical representation is given by

$$f_{kt} = \beta_t' x_{kt} + \alpha_t + u_{kt} \qquad k = 0, 1, \ldots, m_t \tag{7}$$

where α_t is the fixed effect. The error term u_{kt} accommodates measurement error for food consumption and unobserved household characteristics that are unrelated to x_{kt} and α_t.

To implement tests of the dynasty model, we have to resolve a few problems. First, we do not observe all the dynasty member households. Let $\{0, 1, 2, \ldots, n\}$ stand for the set of dynasty members we can observe in the PSID, with $k = 0$ being the parent household and $k = 1, 2, \ldots, n$ representing split-offs. The second problem is that this n varies across dynasties and over time. Third, we do not have a specific model of how the marginal utility of dynasty income, λ_t, is related to observable variables.

To see how these problems can be resolved, we suppress the time subscript in (7), but add the dynasty index i to obtain

$$f_{ik} = \beta' x_{ik} + \alpha_i + u_{ik} \qquad k = 0, 1, \ldots, n_i \quad i = 1, 2, \ldots, N \tag{7'}$$

where N is the number of dynasties with at least one split-off in the sample and n_i is the number of split-offs of dynasty i. This is exactly the fixed-effect model for panel data. Because the fixed effect controls for household preferences/characteristics and measurement errors that are common across all members of the dynasty, the error term u_{ik} consists of household deviations in preferences and measurement error from the dynasty mean.

We can nest this model with the life-cycle alternative by augmenting (7') to include an earnings term:

$$f_{ik} = \beta' x_{ik} + \psi Y_{ik} + \alpha_i + u_{ik} \qquad k = 0, 1, \ldots, n_i \quad i = 1, 2, \ldots, N \tag{8}$$

where Y_{ik} stands for earnings of member-household k of dynasty i. This additional variable Y need not be restricted to earnings. Under the life-cycle hypothesis, variables like nonlabor income, assets, and the history of earnings should matter even when the fixed effect is controlled for. As discussed below, if we allow for variable labor supply, then nonlabor income, assets, possibly current wage rates, and lagged wage rates can be used to test the altruism model.

We now make the basic identifying assumption that the error term u (which consists of consumption measurement error and unobservable household characteristics unrelated to the observable characteristics $\mathbf{x}$) is uncorrelated with earnings (or our other controls for household k's resources). According to the dynasty model the fixed effect α_i (which is time-specific) should be correlated with earnings Y_{ik} (or our other controls for household k's resources), but the earnings coefficient ψ is, nonetheless, identified to be zero under the null hypothesis of the dynasty model. This is because the fixed effect is removed in the estimation. Note that if some (or all) of the dynasties in the sample are linked, the fixed effect α_i will be numerically the same for each of these dynasties. Hence, our fixed-effect test is robust to altruistic linkages across dynasties.

In contrast to the dynasty model, which predicts a value of ψ equal to zero, under the life-cycle and Keynesian alternatives, ψ should be positive. The reason is that under these alternatives to the dynasty model consumption depends not on the collective resources of one's extended family, but rather simply on one's own resources. Hence, under the alternative models controlling for extended-family resources by controlling for the marginal utility of income of the extended family will not control for the resources used in making consumption decisions. Indeed, under the life-cycle or Keynesian alternatives the fixed effect α_i has the interpretation of common environmental and genetic components of the unobservable characteristics common to the family, rather than the interpretation of a transform of the extended family's marginal utility of income.

Does Variable Labor Supply Alter the Test Procedure?

If labor supply is variable, the price vector $\mathbf{p}_t$ in (6) includes the wage rates of different household members, which could differ across member households within the dynasty as well as across members within particular dynasty households. Thus, the $\alpha(\cdot, \cdot)$ function in (6) cannot, in general, be treated as a fixed effect, and we have to restrict preferences further to ensure that the $\alpha(\cdot, \cdot)$ function is independent of wage rates, which may differ across households. One can show (see Richard Blundell, 1986) that for the demands to take this form the utility function must be either homogeneous or additively separable as in (7′).

For the case in which f_{kt} stands for the level of food expenditure, Martin Browning et al. (1985) provide a complete characterization of preferences in which demand functions can be written as the sum of an $\alpha(\cdot, \cdot)$ function that does not depend on wage rates plus an $h(\cdot, \cdot)$ function that may include wage rates. Constant absolute risk aversion, expanded to include leisure, is one example of such a preference structure. For this particular preference structure crossprice effects do not arise in the demands; hence the demand function is of the form given by (6), but $h(\cdot, \cdot)$ depends only on demographics and the price of food (and not wage rates), and $\alpha(\cdot, \cdot)$ depends only on λ_t. For other preferences described by Browning et al. the $h(\cdot, \cdot)$ function, but not $\alpha(\cdot, \cdot)$ may depend on wage rates. For this latter set of preferences in which $h(\cdot, \cdot)$ may include wage rates, the significance of own wage rates in the food demand does not constitute evidence against altruism. However, for these preferences, one can test altruism by including own nonlabor income and own assets in addition to wage rates.

Since nonlabor income and assets may reflect idiosyncratic tastes that are not fully captured by our demographic controls and, therefore, enter the error term u_{ik} in (8), we also estimate specifications that include both current and lagged wage rates. If preferences are time-separable, past wage rates will not enter $h(\cdot, \cdot)$, and they will affect consumption only through the marginal utility of income. Consequently, we can test the altruism model by determining whether the lagged wage rate is significantly greater than zero.

Dynamic Tests

A dynamic version of the static fixed-effect equation is derived from the time-differencing of equation (8), which yields

$$\Delta f_{ikt} = \beta' \Delta x_{ikt} + \theta \Delta Y_{ikt} + \Delta \alpha_{it} + \Delta u_{ikt} \tag{9}$$

where $\Delta f_{ikt} = f_{ikt} - f_{ikt-1}$ in the case of one-year differences and $\Delta f_{ikt} = f_{ikt} - f_{ikt-2}$ in the case of two-year differences. The term $\Delta \alpha_{it}$ equals the corresponding difference over time in dynasty i's logarithm of its marginal utility of income (i.e., it equals $\alpha_{it} - \alpha_{it-1}$ in the case of first differences and $\alpha_{it} - \alpha_{it-2}$ in the case of second differences).[9] Since $\Delta \alpha_{it}$ does not depend on the household identifier k, it is the same across all dynasty households (although its value differs in the case of one-year and two-year differences). Assuming exogenous labor supply, one can test the dynamic version of the altruism model by including the change in current earnings, ΔY_{ikt}, where $\Delta Y_{ikt} = Y_{ikt} - Y_{ik,t-1}$ in the case of one-year differences and $\Delta Y_{ikt} = Y_{ikt} - Y_{ik,t-2}$ in the case of two-year difference. If the altruism model holds, the coefficient on this variable will be zero. This is true despite the fact that the income-change term is correlated over time with changes in the marginal utility of income. The reason is that the fixed-effect technique fully controls for changes in the marginal utility of income. Thus, the proposed dynamic test of the dynasty model is simply the fixed-effect first-differenced version of the static fixed-effect test.[10]

The dynamic test, however, does have one advantage over the static test. It controls for the remote possibility that the dynasty's preferences toward its member households are correlated with their earnings capacity. Such a correlation could arise if parents invested more in the human-capital accumulation of favorite children. Such preferences could be represented by a household-specific constant in equation (8). However, these constants would drop out in the time-difference results; that is, favorite children may get to consume more and, as a result of past investments, earn more, but their change in consumption should depend on the dynasty's total change in income, not on the particular income change they experience.

The dynamic test also raises the issue of risk sharing. The dynamic test can distinguish the altruism model from the life-cycle model with no risk sharing, but it does not have power against the life-cycle model with selfish risk sharing among extended-family members. To see why not, take the case of a selfish parent and selfish child who overlap for, in the simplest case, two periods, time t and $t + 1$. Suppose the parent's and child's incomes at time s ($s = t$, $t + 1$) are Y_{ps} and Y_{ks}, respectively. The parent and child must make consumption decisions at time t knowing Y_{pt} and Y_{kt}, but not knowing Y_{pt+1} and Y_{kt+1}. Let V_p and V_k stand, respectively, for the expected utilities of the parent and child, where

$$V_p = C_{pt}^{1-\gamma}/(1 - \gamma) + bE_t C_{pt+1}^{1-\gamma}/(1 - \gamma)$$

$$V_k = C_{kt}^{1-\gamma}/(1 - \gamma) + bE_t C_{kt+1}^{1-\gamma}/(1 - \gamma)$$

and where E_t is the expectation operator at time t conditional on information at time t and C_{ps} (C_{ks}) stands for the parent's (child's) consumption at time s. Suppose the selfish parent and child choose to pool their income risk and that they reach an efficient bargain. In this case their behavior can be described as a decision to maximize $\theta_p V_p + (1 - \theta_p) V_k$, where the bargaining weight θ_p agreed to by the parent and child will depend on the known values of Y_{pt} and Y_{kt} and the distributions of Y_{pt+1} and Y_{kt+1}. At time s ($s = t, t + 1$) this maximization will lead to

$$\log C_{ps} = \left(\frac{1}{\gamma}\right)\log \theta_p - \left(\frac{1}{\gamma}\right)\log \lambda_s$$

and

$$\log C_{ks} = \left(\frac{1}{\gamma}\right)\log (1 - \theta_p) - \left(\frac{1}{\gamma}\right)\log \lambda_s$$

where λ_s is the Lagrangian multiplier for the time-t parent-child combined-budget constraint. From these relations we have

$$\log C_{pt+1} - \log C_{pt} = -\left(\frac{1}{\gamma}\right)(\log \lambda_{t+1} - \log \lambda_t)$$

and

$$\log C_{kt+1} - \log C_{kt} = -\left(\frac{1}{\gamma}\right)(\log \lambda_{t+1} - \log \lambda_t).$$

With the addition of measurement error and taste variations, this is the dynamic fixed-effect model specified in (11). Hence, selfish risk sharing, like altruism, can lead to identical changes in the logarithm of the marginal utility of income for extended-family members. The dynamic test must, therefore, be viewed as a test of the altruism/life-cycle models with risk sharing against the Keynesian/life-cycle models with no risk sharing.[11]

Using Extended-Family Data to Test the Life-Cycle Model

The discussion thus far has centered on tests that can lead to the rejection of the altruism model; but the altruism model is not the only interesting null hypothesis. For example, one would also like to test the pure life-cycle model against its alternatives. By pure life-cycle model we mean that households neither fully nor partially share resources with their extended-family members. This rules out selfish risk sharing as well as altruism. The new data on extended family provide an opportunity for testing the pure life-cycle model's prediction that the household's resources and only the household's resources affect its consumption.

The test is simply to determine whether extended-family resources affect a household's consumption after one has controlled for the fact that extended-family resources help predict the household's permanent income.

Consider again equation (7), but modified in accordance with the life-cycle model's prediction to permit the marginal utility of income to be household-specific:

$$f_{kt} = \boldsymbol{\beta}'_t \mathbf{x}_{kt} + \alpha_{kt} + u_{kt} \qquad k = 0, 1, \ldots, m_t. \tag{10}$$

According to the life-cycle model α_{kt} in equation (10) will depend on household-specific resources, although in general this dependence will not be simple. We proxy this relationship by considering the projection of α_{kt} on the household's current wealth, A_{kt}, its current nonasset income, e_{kt}, and z lags of past nonasset income, $e_{kt-1}, \ldots, e_{kt-z}$. Hence, we can write $\alpha_{kt} = \alpha_{kt}(A_{kt}, e_{kt}, \ldots, e_{kt-z})$. Assuming that the elements of the α_{kt} projection fully capture the household's marginal utility of income and assuming that the life-cycle model is true, the corresponding dynasty-average values of wealth and current and past nonasset income should not enter significantly in the regression equation given in (11):

$$f_{kt} = \boldsymbol{\beta}'_t \mathbf{x}_{kt} + \ell_1 A_{kt} + \ell_2 e_{kt-1} + \ldots + \ell_{z+1} e_{kt-z} + \bar{\ell}_1 \bar{A}_{kt}$$

$$+ \bar{\ell}_2 \bar{e}_{kt-1} + \ldots + \bar{\ell}_{z+1} \bar{e}_{kt-z} + \varepsilon_{kt}. \tag{11}$$

In addition to incorporating the substitution of the α_{kt} projection into equation (10), equation (11) permits household food consumption to depend on the dynasty-average values of $A_{kt}, e_{kt}, \ldots, e_{kt-z}$, where the dynasty averages (denoted with overbars, "$-$") at time t are taken over all time-t members of the dynasty in the data including the own household. We test the life-cycle model by considering whether the $\bar{\ell}_i$'s ($i = 1, \ldots, z + 1$) are zero.

With additional assumptions one can refine the testing strategy underlying equation (11). Assume that utility is quadratic and that households face only earnings uncertainty. Then α_{kt} can be written as the sum of the present expected value of human wealth plus nonhuman wealth, where f_{kt} now stands for the level of food consumption. Let us further assume that the household's labor earnings e_{kt} equal the sum of a permanent component, e_{kt}^{P}, which evolves as a random walk, and an independent and identically distributed transitory component, $\tilde{e}_{kt}$; that is,

$$e_{kt} = e_{kt}^{\mathrm{P}} + \tilde{e}_{kt}. \tag{12}$$

Assume that the present expected value of human wealth may be approximated by e_{kt}^P divided by the interest rate plus $\tilde{e}_{kt}$. Together these assumptions imply the following specification of (10):

$$f_{kt} = \boldsymbol{\beta}_t'\mathbf{x}_{kt} + \delta_1 A_{kt} + \delta_2 e_{kt}^P + \delta_1 \tilde{e}_{kt} + \varepsilon_{kt}. \tag{13}$$

The econometric problem in estimating (13) is that we do not have independent measures of the permanent and transitory components of e_{kt}. Substituting into (13) for e_{kt}^P from (12) and allowing for the possibility that the dynasty-average values of A_{kt} and e_{kt}, $\bar{A}_{kt}$ and $\bar{e}_{kt}$, enter the equation yields

$$f_{kt} = \boldsymbol{\beta}_t'\mathbf{x}_{kt} + \delta_1 A_{kt} + \delta_2 e_{kt} + \bar{\delta}_1 \bar{A}_{kt} + \bar{\delta}_2 \bar{e}_{kt} + \varepsilon_{kt}'. \tag{13'}$$

where, under the life-cycle hypothesis, the error term $\varepsilon_{kt}' = \varepsilon_{kt} + (\delta_1 - \delta_2)\tilde{e}_{kt}$. Since e_{kt} is correlated with ε_{kt}', we estimate (13') using instrumental variables. Our test of the life-cycle model is that $\bar{\delta}_1$ and $\bar{\delta}_2$ equal zero.

Unfortunately, the PSID has data on assets and liabilities only for 1984. Hence, we conduct the test in equation (11) and the test in equation (13') for 1984. In order to use data from the other years, we again estimate (11) but use, instead of the nonasset income and wealth variables, the following variables: current and lagged values of own and dynasty-average total income and current values of own and dynasty-average home equity. Equation (13') can also be estimated in the absence of wealth data by using own and dynasty-average current total income in the place of current own and dynasty-average nonasset income and current wealth and by instrumenting own and dynasty-average current total income. This formulation is simply Friedman's permanent-income hypothesis augmented to allow the average permanent income of the dynasty to affect household consumption. In conducting our tests of (11) and (13') we measure food consumption both in the levels and in the logs.

A final test that we conduct of the life-cycle model is to regress the change in the logarithm of food consumption against changes in the log of household's total income (head's wage rate) and changes in the average value of dynasty total income (heads' wage rates). Considering whether changes in relatives' resources affect a household's consumption may more sharply test the life-cycle model than tests based on the level of relatives' resources. The reason is that even if the life-cycle model is true, dynasty resource variables, which are correlated with household resource variables, will enter into equation (11) if we have not controlled properly for the household's marginal utility of income. In contrast, while dynasty resources may help predict the level of a household's resources, changes in dynasty resources are less likely to help predict changes in a household's resource position.

7.2   Data and Sample Selection

The PSID

The PSID began in 1968 with a sample of over 5,000 households. The PSID has reinterviewed the heads and spouses of the initial sample each year since 1968. In the case of divorce or separation, the PSID has followed both the head and spouse into their new households. Such new households that are added to the PSID are referred to as "split-offs." In addition to split-offs from divorce or separation, there are child split-offs that arise whenever one of the children of the 1968 respondents, who was not living independently of the respondents in 1968, leaves the respondents' household to form (or become a spouse in) his or her own household.[12] The same set of information that has been collected for the parent households has also been collected for all split-offs. Hence, the PSID provides a matched data set of parents together with at least a subset of their independent children.

Our data come from the 1985 PSID, specifically the families and individuals tape that does not include households who dropped out of the PSID prior to 1985. The 1985 tape contains date collected for 1984 as well as for all previous years. We first identify all individuals in the 1985 PSID who are listed, in 1968, as children. We then identify the 1968 parents of these children. These parents are referred to as the "earliest parents," since they may or may not be the natural parents. Our second step is to follow, starting in 1968, each identified child and determine whether and when he or she formed an independent household, by which we mean became a head or spouse in a household different from that of the child's earliest parents. The third step involves collecting data on consumption, labor supply, income, and so forth for such independent children in each year that they are independent together with contemporaneous date for the households that include their earliest parents. If there is only one earliest parent or if both earliest parents are still living together, we collect data on the single households containing such earliest parents. If there are two earliest parents but they are no longer living together, we collect contemporaneous data on the two households containing each of the two earliest parents, including data on possible step-parents. Hence, in a given year there will be data for one or two earliest-parent households for each independent child. We are able to link the data on each of the independent-children households to the data for their independent siblings as well as to the data for their earliest parents. In order to run the fixed-effect model, we need at least two observations on extended-family members in a given year. Hence, if data are available on an independent child who has no independent siblings and who has no parents (because of death, missing data, or attrition from the sample), we exclude the observation from the analysis. We also require that each dynasty in the regression samples contain at least one parent and one child.

Since there are new split-offs every year, the number of independent-child household observations in the data increases over time. The number of earliest-parent household observations also changes through time because of divorce, remarriage, death, and sample attrition. Table 7.1 reports for each year the number of earliest-parent households as well as the number of independent-child households used in our analysis after we have applied the sample selection rules described below. The table also distinguishes the number of independent-children observations according to whether they are associated with one or two earliest-parent households. Finally, it distinguishes the number of earliest-parent households by the number of associated independent-child households. The table, as well as our empirical work, begins with the 1976 data; prior to 1976 there are relatively few observations on independent children, and information needed to construct our income measure is missing.

The number of independent children increases from 713 in 1976 to 2,178 in 1985. The corresponding figures for earliest parents are 544 in 1976 and 1,171 in 1985. To understand the table, take 1985 as an example. In that year 764 of the 2,178 independent children have only one earliest parent, while the rest (1,293 + 121) have two earliest parents. Of those children with two earliest parents in the 1985 PSID, 121 have two earliest parents who are living in separate households in 1985. Next consider the 1,171 earliest parents listed in the table for 1985. A total of 531 of these parents have only one independent child in the data set; 344 have two children in the data set, and the rest (296) have three or more children in the data set.

As mentioned, the PSID so far has included a complete list of assets and liabilities only for the 1984 wave. Our 1984 wealth measure uses the 1984 PSID data on holdings of stocks, bonds, real estate, vehicles, business and farm assets, checking and saving accounts, house value, and the value of outstanding mortgages. For years other than 1984, when relatively

Table 7.1
Enumeration of Independent-Child and Earliest-Parent Household Observations

| | Independent children | | | | Earliest parents | | | |
| | | | Two parents | | | | | |
Year	Total	1 Parent	Married	Divorced/ separated	Total	One child	Two children	Three or more children
1976	713	314	386	13	544	396	121	27
1977	775	315	447	13	576	411	129	36
1978	971	387	563	21	692	462	173	57
1979	1,201	481	685	35	792	484	211	97
1980	1,384	524	816	44	883	508	258	117
1981	1,550	591	900	59	945	515	280	150
1982	1,731	635	1,017	79	1,019	522	307	190
1983	1,892	699	1,114	79	1,068	512	332	224
1984	2,043	725	1,219	99	1,129	530	341	258
1985	2,178	764	1,293	121	1,171	531	344	296
Total	14,438	5,435	8,440	563	8,819	4,871	2,496	1,452

Table 7.2
A Description of the Data

Variable	Child households		Parent households		Total	
	Mean	SD	Mean	SD	Mean	SD
Household income	8,608	5,599	9,297	9,740	8,869	7,452
Dynasty income	7,871	3,965	9,103	7,752	8,336	4,227
Total food	1,234	691	1,326	751	1,269	716
Food away from home	259	279	214	307	242	291
Food at home	975	610	1,112	633	1,027	622
Black	0.310	0.463	0.315	0.464	0.312	0.463
Asian	0.002	0.049	0.002	0.042	0.002	0.047
American Indian	0.002	0.053	0.003	0.057	0.003	0.054
Other nonwhite	0.005	0.070	0.004	0.065	0.005	0.068
Married	0.699	0.458	0.683	0.465	0.693	0.461
Divorced	0.074	0.262	0.106	0.307	0.086	0.280
Female	0.503	0.500	0.362	0.480	0.449	0.497
Age of head	29.1	3.96	56.7	7.71	39.5	14.5

complete asset data are not available, we can use information on the house value less the remaining mortgage. We also use data on nonlabor income, which includes income from assets and income from exogenous sources (e.g., social security benefits).

Additional Sample Selection Criteria

The PSID's survey questions about income and consumption for a particular year refer to income earned in the previous year and consumption expenditures at the time of the survey (typically March or April). Since children who are first recorded as independent in year t are asked about income and consumption during year $t - 1$, some or all of which time may have been spent with their earliest parent(s), we exclude from the analysis data from the year in which a child is first reported as independent. For the same reason, data are excludes on parents who split off by divorcing or separating in the first year the parents are reported as split-offs. Parents and children must also be either a head or a spouse. In addition, we exclude household observations in which either reported annual income is less than $500 or annual consumption is less than $250, where both numbers refer to 1967 dollars. Finally, we require that the age of parent is greater than 38 and the age of each child is greater than 24. Table 7.2

reports, for both child and parent households, means and standard deviations of many of the variables used in this analysis.

7.3 Results of Static Tests of Altruism

Static Tests Based on Current Income

The first row of Table 7.3 reports the income coefficients from the static fixed-effect test for both logarithm and level specifications. These are the results of fitting equation (8) to the data polled across years. As described in Altonji et al. (1989), disaggregating by year has no material effect on the results. Income is defined here as total family income less transfers received by the household head from family members living outside the household. Hence, the income variable consists of labor income plus non-

Table 7.3
Regression Estimates of the Effect of Income on Food Consumption

Test	Fixed effect Log	Level	No fixed effect Log	Level	Sample size Log	Level
Static Tests of Altruism:						
Food	0.240	0.201	0.286	0.028	23,257	23,257
	(23.289)	(4.163)	(33.067)	(5.083)		
Food at home	0.165	0.010	0.201	0.014	23,148	23,257
	(14.940)	(3.732)	(22.868)	(4.573)		
Food away from home	0.383	0.010	0.497	0.013	19,723	23,257
	(17.545)	(4.085)	(24.156)	(5.268)		
Food lagged one year	0.242	0.020	0.279	0.026	20,565	20,565
	(22.802)	(4.016)	(31.231)	(4.954)		
Rich parent, poor child	0.228	0.057	0.246	0.062	7,036	7,036
	(12.567)	(10.888)	(17.457)	(14.885)		
Nonlabor income	0.028	0.014	0.041	0.019	12,534	12,534
	(5.144)	(1.944)	(7.865)	(2.068)		
Instrumental variable for income with Education/ Occupation	0.306 (9.510)	0.042 (7.972)	0.340 (13.500)	0.046 (10.016)	15,687	15,687
Dynamic Tests of Altruism:						
One-year difference in food	0.063 (5.013)	0.002 (1.518)	0.074 (7.108)	0.002 (1.295)	18,189	18,189
Two-year difference in food	0.137 (10.425)	0.003 (1.005)	0.144 (13.352)	0.005 (1.191)	15,439	15,439

Note: Numbers in parentheses are *t* statistics testing the null hypothesis that the coefficient is zero.

labor income, where the latter variable includes asset income plus government transfers but excluded private transfers. The demographic controls in these and subsequent static regressions are the number of males and females in the household in 11 age brackets,[13] dummies for the household's race, dummies for the household's marital status, a fourth-order polynomial in the age of the head, a dummy for the sex of the head, a dummy for whether the household is a child or parent household,[14] the square of the number of children, the number of adults squared, and the square of the household's size. The standard errors in this and subsequent regressions are White standard errors (see Halbert White, 1984). Specifically, they allow for an arbitrary covariance pattern of errors across years and households for each extended family.

In contrast to the altruism model's prediction of zero income coefficients when one controls for the fixed effects, both the log and level income coefficients are positive and highly significant. From the double logarithmic specification it is immediate that the income elasticities are economically large and reasonable. These income coefficients are also quite large when compared with the income coefficients that arise if one omits the fixed effects. In the case of the log specification the fixed-effect coefficient is 84 percent as large as the non-fixed-effect coefficient; in the level specification the fixed-effect coefficient is 75 percent as large.

While the income coefficients are larger when the fixed effects are omitted, one would expect such an outcome if the life-cycle model were true and current income were not a perfect measure of permanent income. To see this, suppose each dynasty member had an identical permanent income. In this case the fixed effects would control perfectly for the household's permanent income and, given that one has controlled for permanent income, the coefficient on current income should be zero. Now clearly, the permanent income of different dynasty members will differ; but if they are correlated, which is surely the case, the force of the argument should go through.[15]

The strong rejection of the altruism model found in the first row of Table 7.3 is robust to the definition of food consumption. Rows 2 and 3 of the table report the income coefficients for food at home and food away from home. All four of these coefficients are statistically significant and economically significant when compared with the size of the coefficients when fixed effects are omitted.

The rejection of altruism is also robust to the temporal pairing of the consumption and income data. In the base case we pair year t's response to the consumption question with year t's response to the income question. However, the year-t income question refers to income in the previous year, while the year-t consumption question refers to the respondent's household's usual weekly consumption expenditure (although the data are reported on an annual basis). It may be that the response to the consumption question refers to consumption in the current year. In row 4 of Table 7.3 we regress year $t-1$'s consumption against year t's income. The results are quite similar to those in the first row of Table 7.3.

One response to these findings is that, while the altruism model may not hold for all parent and child pairs, it may hold for a subset of households such as those that engage in transfers with one another. Unfortunately, there are relatively few observations across all the years in which the household head reports receiving transfers from other family members. A larger sample that might be likely to satisfy the predictions of altruism and also avoid the problem discussed in Section 7.2 of switches in transfer regimes is the sample of parents with incomes above the median for parents together with that subset of their children whose incomes are below the median for children. Row 5 of Table 7.3 reports the results for this sample of rich parents and poor children. The results also very strongly reject the altruism model.

Static Tests Based on Nonlabor Income, Wage Rates, and Assets

Row 6 of Table 7.3 repeats the fixed-effect tests but uses nonlabor income rather than total income when estimating equation (8). We restrict the sample to households with $50 or more of nonlabor income. The results again reject the altruism model. Table 4A reports a regression that replaces income with the wages of the head and spouse plus the household's nonlabor income. For the level regression, wage rates and nonlabor income are entered in their levels, while in the logarithmic regression these variables are entered in their logs. An additional sample selection rule imposed here is that wage rates exceed $0.50 per hour in 1967 dollars. The regression sample in this case includes wives with reported wages less than $0.50. To control for such wives, many of whom simply do not work, we included a dummy.

The findings in Table 7.4A add to the case against the altruism model. In the fixed-effects regressions the coefficients on annual wage rate are significant statistically and economically, which, depending on the form of preferences, may itself constitute evidence against the altruism model. The

Table 7.4
Regression Estimates Including Wage Rates and Dummy for Nonworking Wife

A. Current Wage Rates and Nonlabor Income:

	Fixed effect			No fixed effect			
Regression	Head's wage	Spouse's wage	Nonlabor income	Head's wage	Spouse's wage	Nonlabor income	Sample size
Levels	0.379	0.180	0.012	0.549	0.339	0.012	8,237
	(5.540)	(1.871)	(1.683)	(7.491)	(3.669)	(1.419)	
Logs	0.136	0.071	0.030	0.178	0.107	0.047	8,237
	(10.255)	(3.838)	(5.252)	(14.183)	(6.867)	(8.967)	

B. Current and Lagged Wage Rates:

	Fixed effect			No fixed effect			
Regression	Head's wage	Spouse's wage	Lagged wage	Head's wage	Spouse's wage	Lagged wage	Sample size
Levels	0.354	0.257	0.293	0.412	0.406	0.401	14,421
	(6.469)	(3.126)	(4.653)	(7.683)	(5.070)	(6.299)	
Logs	0.114	0.065	0.069	0.134	0.097	0.099	14,421
	(9.588)	(4.466)	(5.752)	(13.063)	(7.705)	(9.793)	

Note: Numbers in parentheses are t statistics testing the null hypothesis that the coefficient is zero.

nonlabor-income coefficient in the log regression is highly significant. In addition, the nonlabor-income coefficients are close in magnitude (the level coefficients are identical to three digits) for the fixed-effects and non-fixed-effects regressions. We also estimated the models of Table 7.4A but excluded nonworking wives. The regression results are quite similar.

Next we estimated pooled regressions for a sample defined like that of Table 7.4A (including wives with wages less than $0.50), except that home equity rather than nonlabor income was used to test the altruism model. In these regressions (not reported), we required that households have $1,000 or more of home equity to be included in the sample. In the fixed-effects regressions (sample size = 6,257) the levels coefficient on home equity is 0.004 ($t = 1.97$), and the log coefficient is 0.042 ($t = 3.39$). The corresponding non-fixed-effects coefficients are 0.008 ($t = 5.15$) and 0.075 ($t = 7.43$). Again, contrary to the altruism model's prediction, the fixed-effects coefficients are nontrivial compared with the non-fixed-effects coefficients.

Finally, in Table 7.4B we use the lagged wage of the household head to test the altruism model. The regressions also include current wages of the household head and spouse. Recall that if the dynasty's utility function is time-separable, current wages may enter the demand functions, but lagged wages will not. The advantage of testing altruism with lagged wages is that, compared with nonlabor income, they are less likely to be correlated with that component of the error term that reflects household preferences not captured by our demographic controls. The lagged wage coefficients are highly significant in both rows. While the lagged wage coefficients are larger if one excludes the fixed effects, the lagged wage coefficients in the fixed-effects regressions are, nevertheless, quite substantial.

Static Tests of Altruism under Asymmetric Information

One response to these results is that they only reject the symmetric-information altruism model. If dynasty members are imperfectly informed about each other's income, then the component of dynasty members' income that is unobservable may affect the members' consumption. If parents are altruistic toward children and wealthier than them and if children are less altruistic toward parents, then the component of a child's household income that is unobservable to parents will affect the child's consumption relative to other members of the extended family. Income components that parents know about will not be related to the distribution of consumption in the dynasty. In this case, parents may act to neutralize intergenerational government transfers (which they can observe), even though our results show that they do not neutralize all within-dynasty differences in income.

We allow for this possibility in the seventh row of Table 7.3 by instrumenting income with education and two-digit occupation dummies of the household head under the assumption that these are observable to all dynasty members. The sample consists of 15,687 household-year observations with valid data on the occupation and education variables and excludes persons who left the survey in 1986 or 1987, but the departure from our basic sample does not affect the results. The coefficient on the instrumented log of income is 0.306 with a t statistic of 9.51 when fixed effects are included, which compares to 0.340 ($t = 13.5$) when fixed effects are excluded. In the linear case, the instrumented regression coefficient is 0.042 with a t statistic of 7.92 when fixed effects are included and 0.046 when they are excluded. Evidently, the dynasty does not neutralize income differences that are easily observable.

7.4 Dynamic Tests

The results from estimating the basic model in one-year and two-year differences are given in the last two rows of Table 7.3. These are the results of fitting equation (9) to the pooled data. As the table indicates, the magnitudes of the income-change coefficients are very similar whether one includes or excludes the fixed effects. The effect of changes in own income on household consumption appears to be equally large whether or not one controls for changes in the resource positions of the household's relatives. For example, the coefficient on the second difference in the log of income is 0.137 ($t = 10.425$) in the fixed-effect regression and 0.144 ($t = 13.352$) in the non-fixed-effect regression. The low t statistics in the linear regressions may reflect the problem of greater noise relative to signal associated with first-differencing (see Zvi Griliches and Jerry Hausman, 1986).

These dynamic results reject the standard altruism model and a modified altruism model in which favorite children receive more human capital and, as a result, end up with higher earnings. The results also reject the hypothesis selfish risk sharing among extended-family members.

7.5 Can One Reject the Life-Cycle Model?

Table 7.5 reports the ordinary least-squares (OLS) results of estimating equation (11). Recall that this equation relates food consumption to current and two lagged values of own and dynasty nonasset income and current own and dynasty values of wealth. The results in both the logs and the levels (columns 1 and 2) seem, on balance, to suggest a role for dynasty resources in influencing household consumption. In the case of the logs, the sum of the dynasty nonasset income coefficients is about two-fifths the corresponding sum for household nonasset income. The dynasty asset coefficient, although insignificant, in 38 percent of the household asset coefficient.

Table 7.5 also contains the results for 1984 from estimating equation (13') by instrumental variables (IV). Recall that (13') arises from assuming that utility is quadratic and that nonasset income consists of a random walk plus a transitory component. In this structural model, consumption is determined by current wealth and the instrumented value of current income. The instrumental variables we use for current (1984) nonasset incomes of the household and dynasty are the demographic controls, household and dynasty wealth, and the separate means (across years) of

Table 7.5
The Effects of Household and Dynasty Nonasset Income and Wealth on the Log of Food
Consumption, 1984

Variable	OLS		IV on current nonasset income	
	Logs	Levels	Logs	Levels
Household nonasset income	0.124	0.013	0.281	0.040
in 1984	(4.08)	(1.96)	(10.63)	(5.02)
Household nonasset income	0.049	0.007		
in 1983	(1.46)	(0.906)		
Household nonasset income	0.041	0.014		
in 1982	(1.35)	(2.23)		
Household wealth in 1984[a]	0.00142	2.27	0.0011	1.823
	(2.96)	(2.46)	(2.60)	(1.347)
Dynasty nonasset income in	0.113	0.021	0.057	0.0069
1984	(2.44)	(2.31)	(1.71)	(2.15)
Dynasty nonasset income in	−0.058	−0.020		
1983	(1.22)	(2.01)		
Dynasty nonasset income in	0.035	0.013		
1982	(0.825)	(1.61)		
Dynasty wealth in 1984[a]	0.00054	1.397	0.0007	1.523
	(0.671)	(2.46)	(1.09)	(1.22)
Sum of household income	0.214	0.034		
coefficients	(9.43)	(7.66)		
Sum of dynasty income	0.090	0.015		
coefficients	(2.80)	(2.31)		
Number of households:	2,045	2,045	2,507	2,507
X^2 statistic[b] on dynasty	15.10	18.84	6.70	6.98
income and wealth [P value]:	[0.005]	[0.001]	[0.035]	[0.030]

Notes: Numbers in parentheses are t statistics testing the null hypothesis that the coefficient
is zero.
a. Wealth is measured is thousands of 1967 dollars.
b. The chi-square test statistics in columns 1 and 2 (3 and 4) have 4 (2) degrees of freedom.

nonasset income for the household and for all dynasty households. In forming these means we exclude data for 1984.

The IV results suggest a smaller role of dynasty resources than the previous reduced-form results. In the log regression, the point estimate of the coefficient on dynasty current nonasset income is only one-fifth that of the household; in addition, the dynasty wealth coefficient, though numerically large, is insignificant. Even these results may overstate the true size of the dynasty coefficients since modeling income as a random walk plus a white-noise component may be inappropriate, and the dynasty variables may be correlated with the misspecification error.

The findings of Table 7.5 are reinforced by those in Table 7.6. Table 7.6 is another reduced-form version of (11), but one that uses data for all past years. Since data on wealth are not available, the regressions of Table 7.6 include home equity as well as current and two lags of nonasset income. In the pooled log results the sum of the dynasty income coefficients are almost 30 percent of the corresponding sum of household income coefficients. The dynasty home-equity coefficient is three-quarters the size of the household's home-equity coefficient and is significant.

Table 7.7 returns to the structural permanent-income formulation [equation (13')] but uses the data for all the years. Since wealth data is available only for 1984, we used total income and instrumented total income with the mean (over past and future years) of total income. The IV coefficients on dynasty income are much smaller than the IV coefficient on own income. In the case of the pooled log IV regression the coefficient on dynasty income is not statistically significant, and it is one-eighteenth of the coefficient on household total income.[16] Note that, as predicted, the difference between the own-income and dynasty coefficients is larger for the IV estimates than for the OLS estimates.

Table 7.8 considers how changes in household and dynasty total income and wage rates (of heads) influence changes in household consumption. The results here are slightly more supportive of the life-cycle model. Consider first one-year changes in consumption. Here, the change in dynasty income has an insignificant influence on the change in consumption, although the magnitude of the point estimate is not trivial. In the case of two-year changes, the two-year change in dynasty income has zero (to three decimal places) effect on the two-year change in household consumption. The wage-rate changes of the dynasty are uniformaly insignificant, even after we instrument the wage measure with an alternative wage measure to reduce bias from measurement error.

Table 7.6
The Effects of Current and Lagged Household and Dynasty Nonasset Income and Home Equity on Food Consumption

	Pooled regression	
Variable	Logs	Levels
Household income in year:		
t	0.151	0.013
	(10.42)	(3.39)
$t-1$	0.030	0.006
	(2.27)	(2.07)
$t-2$	0.027	0.011
	(2.34)	(3.32)
Dynasty income in year:		
t	0.061	0.016
	(3.20)	(2.14)
$t-1$	-0.0066	0.001
	(0.34)	(0.22)
$t-2$	0.008	-0.002
	(0.42)	(0.48)
Home equity:		
Household	0.0027	4.57
	(3.69)	(3.06)
Dynasty	0.0020	2.40
	(1.44)	(1.02)
Sum of income coefficients:		
Household	0.208	0.031
	(13.97)	(8.43)
Dynasty	0.062	0.015
	(3.04)	(3.68)
Number of households:	11,905	11,905
X^2 [P value]:	19.58	19.10
	[0.0006]	[0.0007]

Notes: Numbers in parentheses are t statistics testing the null hypothesis that the coefficient is zero. X^2 statistics and associated P values are for the joint test that dynasty income and wealth variables are all zero.

Table 7.7
Tests of the Life-Cycle Model

Pooled regression	Number of households	OLS estimates		IV estimates	
		Household total income	Dynasty total income	Household total income	Dynasty total income
Logs	21,711	0.261 (25.3)	0.048 (3.29)	0.337 (21.4)	0.023 (1.12)
Levels	21,711	0.0219 (4.11)	0.0142 (5.52)	0.040 (7.01)	0.010 (3.02)

Note: Numbers in parentheses are *t* statistics testing the null hypothesis that the coefficient is zero.

7.6 Summary and Conclusion

In recent years the infinite-horizon altruism model has played an important role in theoretical analysis and policy debate. This is surprising, given the lack of direct micro empirical support for the model. The long delay in testing the model with micro data reflects the paucity of data on the extended family. Fortunately, the ongoing PSID now provides sufficient extended-family data to test the operative altruism model. The key prediction of the altruism model is that altruistically linked family members fully share resources in the sense that the division of their total consumption should be independent of the division of their collective resources.

This paper directly tests whether the distribution of resources affects the distribution of consumption among parents and children. We find overwhelming evidence that it does. Our test procedure is attractive because it does not require solving the extended family's dynamic programming problem or knowing either the precise level of extended-family resources or the boundaries of the altruistically linked extended family. According to the altruism model, all members of the extended family will have the same marginal utility of income, and their consumption demands can be written as functions of this variable and relative prices. Once one controls (through the fixed-effect technique) for the extended family's marginal utility of income, the resource position of particular extended family members should not influence the consumption of those members.

In our tests we use total income, nonlabor income, home equity, and wage rates as proxies for the resource position of particular extended-family members. We find that each of these proxies is a significant variable in explaining the consumption of extended-family members even

Table 7.8
Dynamic Tests of the Life-Cycle Model: The Effects of Household and Dynasty Income and Wage-Rate Changes on Changes in Food Consumption

Variable	One-year changes			Two-year changes		
	OLS	OLS	IV	OLS	OLS	IV
Household variables:						
Change in log of household income	0.065 (5.39)			0.138 (13.2)		
Change in log of wage of household head		0.035 (2.67)	0.455 (2.86)		0.061 (5.05)	0.280 (3.77)
Dynasty variables:						
Change in log of average dynasty income	0.022 (1.16)			0.000 (0.013)		
Change in log of wage of average dynasty head		−0.014 (0.728)	−0.228 (1.31)		−0.026 (1.37)	0.086 (0.80)
Number of observations:	18,200[a]	12,203	6,621	14,284	9,747	5,038

Notes: All equations include year dummies and controls for changes in demographics. The equations that include wage rates also include dummy variables for year t and $t - j$ $(j = 1, 2)$ that equal 1 if a wife was present in the given year and worked a positive number of hours in the previous year at an hourly wage rate greater than $0.50.

The wage rate in the consumption equation is annual labor earnings of the head divided by annual hours. It refers to the calendar year before the survey. The samples for columns 2 and 3 (columns 5 and 6) exclude households in which the household head did not work or had an average wage rate of less than $0.50 in either year t or year $t - 1$ (t and $t - 2$). The principal instrument for the change in the average hourly wage in columns 3 and 6 is the change in a second wage measure that refers to the job held at the time of the survey. This second wage measure is based on a direct question about the hourly wage in the case of hourly workers and is imputed from a question about earnings per week, per month, and so forth in the case of salaried workers. The other instruments are the mean of this alternative wage-change measure taken across households in the dynasty and all the control variables that appear in the consumption-change equation. The sample in column 3 (6) is further restricted to households for which both wage measures are available in years t and $t - 1$ (t and $t - 2$). However, the difference in the samples has little to do with the increase in the absolute value of the coefficients that arises when instruments are used. Altonji (1986) discusses the properties of this instrumental-variables estimator. The large increase in the coefficient estimates when instruments are used is due to the correction for measurement error and the fact that the second wage measure and the consumption data both refer to the time of the survey.

[a] Due to a minor discrepancy in the computation of lagged values, the sample for column 1 exceeds the sample for the dynamic fixed-effects tests of the life-cycle model by 11 observations. This has no effect on the results.

after one has controlled for the extended family's marginal utility of income. The strong rejection of the altruism model holds up for the subset of the sample consisting of rich parents and poor children. It also holds up whether or not labor supply is viewed as endogenous and whether or not the tests are run in levels or first differences.

In addition to showing that own resources matter given extended-family resources, we test the life-cycle model by asking whether only own resources matter (i.e., whether the resources of extended-family members have no effect on a household's consumption). Our results suggest that extended-family member resources have at most a modest effect on marginal household consumption decisions after one has controlled for the fact that extended-family resources help predict a household's own permanent income.

Despite our findings, we do believe that significant altruistically motivated transfers occur in the United States, particularly among the wealthy, who are underrepresented in the PSID. Our findings suggest, however, that very few U.S. households are altruistically linked at the margin in the sense that redistribution between the donor and recipient will be neutralized. The altruistically motivated transfers that one observes in the United States may come in the form of less than fully efficient educational support to liquidity-constrained children (as described by Becker [1974] and Allan Drazen [1978]), in-kind transfers by paternalistic altruists (as described by Robert A. Pollak [1988]), incentive-oriented transfers by altruistic parents concerned about freeriding children (as described by Kotlikoff and Assaf Razin [1988]), and end-of-life transfers by parents concerned that children will squander what they receive at an early age and ask for more (as described by Kotlikoff [1987], Lindbeck and Weibull [1988], and Bruce and Waldman [1989, 1991]).

While liquidity-constrained, paternalistic, and strategically constrained altruism may abound, our findings nevertheless indicate that changing the distribution of resources within the extended family significantly changes its distribution of consumption. Given this finding, the notion that an extended family, let alone an entire country, can be modeled as a single representative consumer with an infinite horizon seems highly questionable.

Notes

We are very grateful to Paul Taubman for assisting our acquisition of data. We thank Robert Barro, Gary Becker, Fisher Black, Richard Blundell, Steve Davis, Gary Chamberlain, V. Chari,

Bill English, Zvi Griliches, Dale Jorgenson, Kevin Lang, Bruce Lehrman, Robert Lucas, Greg Mankiw, Jeff Miron, Kevin Murphy, Michael Riordan, Sherwin Rosen, Mark Rosenzweig, Robert Townsend, Paul Taubman, Laurence Weiss, Stephen Zeldes, and seminar participants at a number of universities for very helpful comments. Patricio Arrau, Jinyong Cai, Jagadeesh Gokhale, and Christian Stadlinger provided outstanding research assistance. We are grateful to the National Institute of Aging (grant no. 1RO1AG8655-01) and to the Center for Urban Affairs and Policy Research, Northwestern University, for research support. The 1985 Panel Study of Income Dynamics used in this study is available through the University of Michigan Survey Research Center.

1. One might think that directly studying transfers (see Donald Cox [1987] for a survey of the literture) would be a more appropriate way to test altruism than studying consumption. However, in the absence of liquidity constraints (see Becker, 1974; Allan Drazen, 1978; David Altig and Steven Davis, 1989) or strategic considerations (see Assar Lindbeck and Jörgen Weibull, 1988; Neil Bruce and Michael Waldman, 1989, 1991), the timing of transfers is arbitrary in altruistic models. Secondly, transfers are difficult to measure since they may be in kind or in forms whose prices are not available (e.g., partnership shares). Third, transfers may arise for nonaltruistic reasons, and the mere occurrence of transfers is not, in itself, evidence of altruism.

2. Other studies that have used the PSID child split-offs include Altonji (1988), Jere Behrman et al. (1989), Gary Solon et al. (1987), and Solon (1992). While food expenditures comprise the only consumption data in the PSID (other than expenditures on utilities and information on housing and automobiles, for which rental services would need to be imputed), food is a nondurable and is a major component of nondurable consumption expenditure. Food expenditures should respond to altruistic transfers unless those transfers are in kind and the amount of such in-kind transfers exceeds what the household would voluntarily purchase if the transfer had instead been made in cash.

3. These are Frisch demand functions.

4. Our first-difference results accord with those in the revised version of Andrew Abel and Kotlikoff (1988) and John Cochrane (1991). Other studies in this literature are Mark R. Rosenzweig (1988), Robert M. Townsend (1989), and Barbara Mace (1991).

5. See Kotlikoff et al. (1990) for a model in which transfers are not taken as given.

6. See James Heckman and Thomas MaCurdy (1980) and MaCurdy (1981) for an early use of fixed-effects methods in estimating Frisch demand functions from panel data on individuals.

7. The fixed-effect estimation in this case of only one child and one parent is equivalent to taking the difference between the logarithm of C_{pi} and the logarithm of C_{ki} as the dependent variable. Clearly, the fixed effect drops out of this regression, and the log difference of the parent's and child's consumption should depend only on the weights θ_p and θ_k and not on the difference between the parent's and child's incomes.

8. As described in note 8 of our working paper (Altonji et al., 1989) a CES function leading to (6) can be viewed as an indirect utility function that incorporates optimal within-household allocation of the total household consumption of each good.

9. If the dynasty is not liquidity-constrained, this difference plus a term involving the time-t interest rate equals the logarithm of the multiplicative Euler error. Note that our dynamic tests, as well as our static tests, are valid even if the dynasty is liquidity-constrained.

10. In contrast to the Euler-equation approach to testing intertemporal consumption choice (see Hayashi [1987] for a survey), our test of the altruism model against the life-cycle/

Keynesian alternatives controls for the Euler error through the fixed-effect estimation and, as such, does not require any assumption about the correlation (or lack thereof) across households of the time-t Euler error with information available at time $t-1$.

11. Note that the static fixed-effects test of altruism verses the Keynesian/life-cycle models remains valid even if there is selfish life-cycle risk sharing. At a point in time s, life-cycle risk sharing leads to the fixed-effect model: $\log C_{ps} = (1/\gamma)\log\theta_p - (1/\gamma)\log\lambda_s$ and $\log C_{ks} = (1/\gamma)\log\theta_k - (1/\gamma)\log\lambda_s$. If one regresses the log of consumption against the fixed effect $-(1/\gamma)\log\lambda_s$, demographics, and household income, household income will enter significantly because the bargaining weights, θ_p and θ_k, will depend on the initial resource position of the parent and child. This is not the case in the altruism model, in which utility weights reflect preferences, not bargaining power.

12. We include divorced parents in the dynasty because their altruism for their children will lead to altruistic linkages between them (see Kotlikoff, 1983; B. Douglas Bernheim and Kyle Bagwell, 1988).

13. We constructed the age-sex variables by counting the number of persons who were in a particular household and in a particular age-sex category in a given year. See Altonji et al. (1989 note 16) for a description of the construction of these variables.

14. In terms of the simple model described in equations (1) and (2), the child dummy captures the terms involving θ_{ip} and θ_{ik}.

15. For evidence on this correlation found in the PSID data see Solon et al. (1987) and Solon (1992).

16. The R^2 values for the first stage of the pooled IV estimation underlying Table 7 are 0.714 for Y_{ikt} and 0.764 for Y_{it}. The R^2 of the pooled OLS consumption regression is 0.381.

References

Abel, Andrew and Kotlikoff, Laurence J., "Does the Consumption of Different Age Groups Move Together? A new Nonparametric Test of Intergenerational Altruism," National Bureau of Economic Research (Cambridge, MA) Working Paper No. 2490, 1988.

Altig, David and Davis, Steven J., "Altruism, Borrowing Constraints, and Social Security," mimeo, Hoover Institution, May 1989.

Altonji, Joseph G., "Intertemporal Substitution in Labor Supply: Evidence from Micro Data," *Journal of Political Economy*, June 1986, 94 S176–S215.

————, "The Effects of Family Background and School Characteristics on Education and Labor Market Outcomes," mimeo, Northwestern University, December 1988.

Altonji, Joseph G., Hayashi, Fumio and Kotlikoff, Laurence J., "Is the Extended Family Altruistically Linked? Direct Tests Using Micro Data," National Bureau of Economic Research (Cambridge, MA) Working Paper No. 3046, July 1989.

Barro, Robert, "Are Government Bonds Net Wealth?" *Journal of Political Economy*, November–December 1974, 82, 1095–1117.

Becker, Gary, "A Theory of Social Interactions," *Journal of Political Economy*, November–December 1974, 82, 1063–93.

————, *A Treatise on the Family*, Cambridge, MA: Harvard University Press, 1981.

Behrman, Jere, Pollak, Robert and Taubman, Paul, "The Wealth Model: Efficiency in Education and Equity in the Family," mimeo, Department of Economics, University of Pennsylvania, 1989.

Bernheim, B. Douglas and Bagwell, Kyle, "Is Everything Neutral?" *Journal of Political Economy*, April 1988, *96*, 308–38.

Blundell, Richard, "Econometric Approaches to the Specification of Life Cycle Labour Supply and Commodity Demand Behavior," *Econometric Reviews*, 1986, *5*(1), 89–146.

Browning, Martin, Deaton, Angus and Irish, Margaret, "A Profitable Approach to Labor Supply and Commodity Demand over the Life-Cycle," *Econometrica*, May 1985, *53*, 503–44.

Bruce, Neil and Waldman, Michael, "The Rotten-Kid Theorem Meets the Samaritan's Dilemma," *Quarterly Journal of Economics*, February 1989, *105*, 155–65.

————, "Transfers in Kind: Why They Can Be Efficient and Nonpaternalistic," *American Economic Review*, December 1991, *81*, 1345–51.

Cochrane, John, "A Simple Test of Consumption Insurance," *Journal of Political Economy*, October 1991, *99*, 957–76.

Cox, Donald, "Motives for Private Income Transfers," *Journal of Political Economy*, June 1987, *95*, 508–46.

Drazen, Allan, "Government Debt, Human Capital, and Bequests in a Life Cycle Model," *Journal of Political Economy*, June 1978, *86*, 505–16.

Griliches, Zvi and Hausman, Jerry, "Measurement Error in Panel Data," *Journal of Econometrics*, February 1986, *31*, 93–110.

Hayashi, Fumio, "Tests for Liquidity Constraints: A Survey and Some New Observations," in T. Bewley, ed., *Advances in Econometrics II, Fifth World Congress*, Cambridge: Cambridge University Press, 1987, pp. 91–120.

Heckman, James J. and MaCurdy, Thomas E., "A Life-Cycle Model of Female Labour Supply," *Review of Economic Studies*, January 1980, *47*, 47–74.

Kotlikoff, Laurence J., "Altruistic Linkages Within the Extended Family, A Note," Sloan Foundation Proposal, 1983: reprinted in Laurence J. Kotlikoff, *What Determines Savings?*, Cambridge, MA: MIT Press, 1989.

————, "Justifying Public Provision of Social Security," *Journal of Policy Analysis and Management*, Spring 1987, *6*, 674–89.

Kotlikoff, Laurence J., and Razin, Assaf, "Making Bequests without Spoiling Children," National Bureau of Economic Research (Cambridge, MA) Working Paper, October 1988.

Kotlikoff, Laurence J., Razin, Assaf, and Rosenthal, Robert, "A Strategic Altruism Model in which Ricardian Equivalence Does Not Hold," *Economic Journal*, December 1990, *100*, 1261–8.

Lindbeck, Assar and Weibull, Jörgen W., "Altruism and Time Consistency: The Economics of Fait Accompli," *Journal of Political Economy*, December 1988, *96*, 1165–82.

Mace, Barbara, "Full Insurance in the Presence of Aggregate Uncertainty," *Journal of Political Economy*, October 1991, *99*, 928–56.

MaCurdy, Thomas E., "An Empirical Model of Labor Supply in a Life Cycle Setting," *Journal of Political Economy*, December 1981, *89*, 1059–85.

Pollak, Robert A., "Tied Transfers and Paternalistic Preferences," *American Economic Review*, May 1988 *(Papers and Proceedings)*, *78*, 240–4.

Rosenzweig, Mark R., "Risk, Implicit Contracts, and the Family in Rural Areas of Low Income Countries," *Economic Journal*, December 1988, *98*, 1148–70.

Solon, Gary, "Intergenerational Income Mobility in the United States," *American Economic Review*, June 1992, *82*, 393–408.

Solon, Gary, Corcoran, May, Gordon, Roger and Laren, Debra, "The Effect of Family Background on Economic Status: A Longitudinal Analysis of Sibling Correlations," National Bureau of Economic Research (Cambridge, MA) Working Paper No. 2282, June 1987.

Townsend, Robert M., "Risk and Insurance in Village India," mimeo, University of Chicago, February 1989.

White, Halbert, *Asymptotic Theory for Econometricians*, Orlando, FL: Academic Press, 1984.

8

Is the Japanese Extended Family Altruistically Linked? A Test Based on Engel Curves

8.1 Introduction

In the standard model of the family, all members of the family jointly maximize a common objective function. This is because members are altruistic to each other, or because of the Rotten Kid Theorem of Becker (1981), that selfish members find it in their best interest to conform to the altruist's objective. The model has a strong neutrality implication that consumption is invariant to how resources are divided within the family as long as total family resources are controlled for. For the United States, neutrality does not seem an adequate description of household behavior. Using data on individual households linked by parent-child relation, Altonji, Hayashi, and Kotlikoff (1992) have shown that the allocation of consumption across households forming a single family is closely related to division of income within the family. It would be interesting to see if neutrality fares better in other cultures that appear to value family ties. The purpose of this chapter is to test neutrality for Japan.

Although there is no Japanese data on households linked by relation, a substantial fraction of a cross section of Japanese households are extended families or two-generation households in which two adult generations co-reside.[1] Since consumption data are for the household as a whole, it is not possible to study the allocation of total household consumption within two-generation households. Still, neutrality has an implication that, for each commodity, the household's total demand is invariant to division of resources between co-residing generations. We test this demand neutrality by checking whether a demand system, which in a cross section of households is a collection of Engel curves, is affected by intergenerational

Originally published, in slightly shorter form, in *Journal of Political Economy* 103 (June 1995): 661–74. Reprinted with permission.

division of resources. Demand would also be neutral if co-residing generations had identical tastes. However, it can be documented from data on Japanese nuclear households that food taste is very much generational.

If co-residence is a result of a residence status choice made by parent and child who could have lived separately as two separate nuclear households, the sample of two-generation households is a choice-based sample. Correcting the sample selection bias is very difficult, because nuclear households contained in our data set are not linked by relation, providing no information on the characteristics of parent-child pairs that chose living apart over co-residence. Consequently, we ignore the sample selection bias in our estimation of Engel curves. This is probably innocuous, because the Engel curves we estimate are for a subset of commodities (food). We will provide in section 8.4 an example in which the endogeneity of the residence status does not bias parameter estimates of Engel curves.

The idea of testing whether demand is neutral is not new. There is a literature on the invariance of demand to division of resources between spouses.[2] However, a typical testing procedure is to see if nonearned income of a husband and wife has the identical effect on demand, with no attempt to control for total resources. If, for example, a husband's income is more permanent than his wife's, then under neutrality the husband's income should have more weight for demand because it is more closely related to total resources. Our Engel curve-based test does not have this problem because total consumption expenditure in Engel curves serves as a perfect control for the household's total resources. Also, to our knowledge this chapter is a first attempt to test neutrality of household demand to intergenerational distribution, which, from the viewpoint of macroeconomics, would be more interesting than testing neutrality within generations.

The content of the chapter is as follows. In the next section, section 8.2, we briefly describe the Japanese cross-section data set of about fifty thousand households, more than one-fifth of which are two-generation households. Section 8.3 documents some stylized facts about determinants of co-residence and the generational difference in food tastes. In section 8.4 we examine altruistic models of the residence status and make precise the sense neutrality entails on two-generation households in these models. We also provide a parametric example that is capable of explaining the stylized facts about co-residence and in which the sample selection bias for Engel curves does not exist. Section 8.5 presents our Engel curve-based test of demand neutrality. Section 8.6 contains a few concluding remarks.

8.2   The Data

The data we utilize is the 1979 and 1984 surveys of the *National Survey of Family Income and Expenditure* (NSFIE), conducted by the Japanese government every five years since 1959. In the text, we focus on the results from the 1984 survey. The results from the 1979 survey will be presented in appendix 8.2. We briefly describe the aspects of the data relevant to the present study; a detailed description and evaluation of the data can be found in Hayashi, Ando, and Ferris (1988). The survey consists of two cross-section data sets: about four thousand singles and about fifty thousand nonsingles households. The sampling ratio differs between singles and nonsingles as well as between geographical regions. On average, singles are underrepresented by a factor of three. Respondents are required to keep a diary on hundreds of expenditure and receipt items throughout the three-month period of the survey from September to November (for singles in 1984, the survey is for September only). In the last month of the survey, the respondent reports information on the household's financial assets, consumer durables, and annual income for the latest twelve-month period. Each income component (e.g., employment income, interest and dividend income) is broken down by household member, but the breakdown is rather coarse: "head," "spouse," and "all other household members," where "head" is defined to be the main income earner.

A very important fact about Japanese households, which is well reflected in the data, is the prevalence of two-generation households (extended families). For reasons to be made clear in the next paragraph, we take a rather narrow definition of a two-generation household. Define an *adult* to be an individual who is either working, 25 years or older, married, or the head of a singles household, and a *generation* to be either a married couple or an unmarried adult. If the generation is a couple, its age is the average age of the couple. We define a *two-generation household* to be a household of two generations sharing the same budget, one of which is the father, mother, or both, of the other generation, such that (1) the older generation be 55 or older while the younger generation be less than 55 years of age, (2) there be no other adults, and (3) the older generation have no nonadult co-residing children. Accordingly, a *nuclear household* is a generation with or without nonadult co-residing children. Thus singles are a nuclear household. A nuclear household is either a *young nuclear household* whose generation is younger than 55, or an *old nuclear household* 55 or older. We require, in line with the definition of two-generation households, that old nuclear households have no nonadult co-residing children.

We adopt the age requirement (requirement (1) above) so that we can compare generations living with their offspring with those living alone; any generation 55 or older is either in the pool of old nuclear households or the older generation of a two-generation household. Similarly, any generation younger than 55 is either in the pool of young nuclear households or the younger generation of a two-generation household. We will exploit this facet of the data to study the choice of *residence status* (live alone or co-reside) for the old and the young. Requirement (2) is dictated by the coarse breakdown of household income by member mentioned above. We will equate the income of the non-head generation with that of "all other household members." If there were other adults in the two-generation household, the nonhead generation's income thus identified would include their income as well. Requirement (3) is adopted for convenience and simplicity. There are very few old generations that have nonadult co-residing children in the data. For the same reason we ignore three-adult generation households.

Figure 8.1 should make it clear how we create *three* samples—two-generation households, young nuclear households, and old nuclears—from two raw data sets (one on singles and the other on nonsingles). Elimination of cases with officially designated missing values for relevant variables reduces the data set size to 3,924 for singles and 47,393 for non-singles. These 51,317 (= 3,924 + 47,393) records are directed to 32,266 nuclear, 12,265 two-generation, and 6,786 other households. After the application of the age requirement and the requirement that the older generation have no nonadult children, there are 26,498 young nuclear, 5,538 old nuclear, and 10,068 two-generation households. Using the survey's definition of the head (the main income earner), we can further divide the sample of two-generation households into two parts: those whose head is the older generation (3,386 households) and those whose head is the younger generation (remaining 6,682 households).

8.3 Stylized Facts

Sample means of selected variables for the three samples are displayed in table 8.1. For two-generation households, household income can be divided between the two generations, while expenditures are for the household as a whole. Income and expenditures are as in the raw data, with no modifications and imputations to make them conformable to

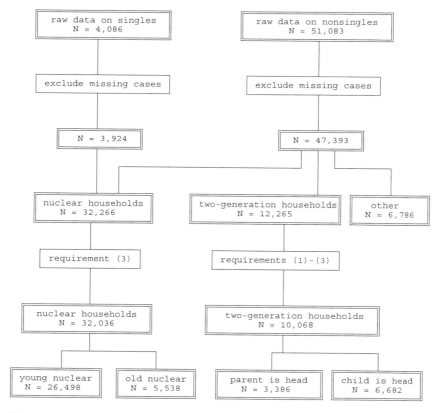

Figure 8.1
Derivation of samples, 1984.

national income accounts definitions.[3] The sample means in the table are weighted by the sampling weights provided by the survey (see notes to table 8.1 for more details).

The following are the noteworthy points about the table.

1. Comparison of the sample size and the estimated population size for old nuclear and two-generation households confirms that the majority of old individuals live with their children.

2. The old generation's marital status does not depend heavily on the residence status, although widows are somewhat more likely to be in two-generation households.

3. On the other hand, the old generation's income depends on the residence status: it is less for those co-residing with offspring. This is partly

Table 8.1
Simple Statistics by Household Type

	Household type			
			Two-generation	
	Young nuclear	Old nuclear	Younger generation	Older generation
1. Sample size	26,498	5,538	10,068	
2. Population estimate (millions)	20.5	5.0	6.2	
3. Age of the generation	36.3	64.3	37.0	67.1
4. # adults	1.7	1.6	1.8	1.5
5. # nonadults	1.3	0	1.5	0
6. % couples	73.6	55.5	76.8	51.3
7. % single male	15.9	8.1	12.9	6.8
8. % single female	10.5	36.3	10.4	42.0
9. Annual income	443.6	299.0	403.4	190.6
10. % annual income = 0	0.3%	0.8%	10.6%	29.2%
11. Annual transfer receipts if > 0	83.7	39.8	158.1	63.5
12. % annual transfer receipts > 0	5.2%	12.2%	1.7%	2.5%
13. Total consumption expenditure	277.2	194.7	334.3	
14. Food	79.5	46.5	91.8	
15. % share, cereal	10.6%	13.9%	12.5%	
16. % share, seafood	11.3%	18.7%	17.3%	
17. % share, meat and dairy	14.5%	12.3%	17.5%	
18. % share, vegetables	15.8%	24.4%	19.0%	
19. % share, eating out	34.2%	16.9%	17.9%	
20. % share, other	13.5%	13.8%	15.7%	

Note: Weighted means are calculated as follows. Let w_i be the sampling weight from the survey. Because our sample excludes missing cases, the weight must be inflated so that the sample mean is unbiased for the population mean. The inflation factor is given by $x/(y \times z)$, where $x =$ the number of families in the population, $y =$ sample size after elimination of missing cases, and $z =$ sample average of w_i. For singles, $x = 7.243$ million, $y = 3,924$. For nonsingles, $x = 30.095$ million, $y = 47,393$. So, for example, the sum of the inflated w_i over the sample is the estimate of the number of families in the population.

Annual income, annual transfer receipts, and expenditures in ten thousand yen. Transfer receipts are private monetary transfers from relatives and others. Income does *not* include transfers. Both income and transfers are for the twelve-month period ending November 1984, while total consumption expenditure and food expenditure are over the three-month period (September–November) at annual rates. A generation's income is the sum of husband's and wife's income if the generation is a couple. If the generation is an individual, its income is the individual's income. The definition of food components is as follows: cereal = rice, bread, noodles, flour, and other cereals; seafood = fish and shellfish; meat and dairy = meat, dairy products, and eggs; vegetables = vegetables and fruits, eatingout = cooked food, restaurants; other = oil, sweets, beverages, and excludes tobacco and alcohol.

due to the high fraction of the old in two-generation households reporting zero income (see line 10). As discussed in the appendix, there is reason to believe that some of them are false zeros—that is, missing cases with positive income miscoded as zeros. However, also as discussed in the appendix, the extent of possible miscoding is probably not enough to alter the conclusion. The same is true for the young, albeit to a much less degree.

4. The incidence of annual private monetary transfer receipts (see line 12) for two-generation households is low because transfers between parents and children are internal and hence not recorded. For young nuclear households, the annual transfer incidence of 5 percent (see line 13) is much less than the annual incidence reported for the United States of about 20 percent.[4] On the other hand, the average transfer amount among those who received transfers is a much larger fraction of their income for Japan than for the United States.

5. There is a substantial difference in the pattern of food expenditure between young and old nuclear households.[5] The young prefer "western" staples such as meat and dairy products while the old spend a higher fraction of their food budget on cereal, fish, and vegetables. Somewhere in the middle lies the food expenditure pattern of two-generation households. Whether this food pattern is influenced by division of resources within two-generation households is the main question to be addressed in the chapter.

Another noteworthy fact about two-generation households is that the older generation's income is *negatively* correlated with the younger generation's; the correlation for pairs reporting positive values is -0.12. If false zeros were identified and taken into the calculation, the negative correlation would have been stronger.

To explore factors determining the residence status, we estimated a Probit co-residence equation. Since we have no information for nuclear families on variables pertaining to the parents or adult children of the head, we have to deviate from the more desirable specification of including both parents' and offsprings' labor incomes. We instead estimate the co-residence equation separately for the young and the old. The dependent variable takes a value of 0 (living apart) if the observation is from nuclear households and 1 (co-residence) if from two-generation households. Thus the sample size is 36,566 (= 26,498 + 10,068) for the young and 15,606 (= 5,538 + 10,068) for the old. To control for the possible

Table 8.2
Probit Estimates: Determinants of Co-residence

Independent variable	1 Young		2 Old		3 Old	
No. of observations	36,566		15,606			
% co-residence	27.5%		64.5%			
Number of children	0.094	(11)	—		—	
Single male	0.69	(21)	0.19	(3.5)	0.17	(3.1)
Single female	−0.056	(0.8)	0.42	(12)	0.39	(12)
Husband works	−0.39	(5.6)	0.002	(0.0)	0.033	(1.0)
Wife works	0.37	(23)	−0.10	(3.8)	−0.10	(3.7)
Age of the generation	9.9×10^{-4}	(1.0)	0.037	(19)	0.037	(19)
Labor income	−0.018	(5.2)	−0.032	(6.4)	−0.023	(4.6)
Labor income = 0	1.6	(29)	0.47	(8.8)	0.53	(9.5)
Pension income	—		−0.29	(17)	−0.24	(14)
Pension income = 0	—		0.44	(13)	0.44	(13)
Capital income	—		—		−0.032	(2.1)
Capital income = 0	—		—		0.36	(13)
Mean log likelihood	−0.5322		−0.5330		−0.5260	

Note: Income in ten thousand yen. Absolute values of *t*-values in parentheses. Capital income is the sum of dividends, interests, and rents. Since old nuclear households have no nonadult children, the equation for the old does not include the number of children on the right-hand side. Other independent variables included are eight regional and four citysize dummies.

miscoding that produced many zero incomes, we include a zero income dummy for the relevant income component as an independent variable.

Column 1 of table 8.2 reports the co-residence equation for the young. The base for the marital dummy variables is couples, so that, for example, the positive coefficient on the dummy for single males imply that single males are more likely to co-reside with parents than with couples. The number of nonadult children of the younger generation and the working wife dummy have positive coefficients, most likely due to the child care services provided by co-residing parents. Even after the effect of zero income is controlled for, income has a negative effect on co-residence.[6] The corresponding co-residence equation for the old is in column 2 of the table. The negative effect of income on co-residence is highly significant for the old, particularly for pension income, which is consistent with the view that the development of social security has contributed to the decline of extended families.[7] The negative coefficient on capital income reported in column 3 of the table means that those with high bequeathable wealth tend to live apart from children.[8]

Table 8.3
Tobit Estimates: Determinants of Monetary Transfer Receipts

Independent variable	Young		Old	
No. of observations	26,498		5,538	
% transfer > 0	4.7%		9.2%	
Mean transfer if > 0	100.4		41.5	
Constant	−255	(11.4)	−148	(6.6)
Number of children	30	(6.7)	—	
Head is single male	−68	(3.5)	5.5	(0.5)
Head is single female	−13	(0.9)	7.8	(1.4)
Age of generation	0.23	(0.4)	1.5	(4.4)
Labor income	−0.68	(45.8)	−0.23	(15.2)
Pension income	—		−0.31	(12.5)
Error variance	274		81	
Mean log likelihood	−0.2259		−0.2742	

Note: Annual income, annual monetary transfer receipts, and net financial assets in ten thousand yen. Absolute values of *t*-values in parentheses. The standard errors are calculated from the cross product of the score. The percent of the sample receiving monetary transfers and the mean transfer are different from those reported in table 8.1 because here observations are not weighted. Regional and citysize dummies are not included in the equation because they turned out insignificant when included.

We also estimated a monetary transfer receipts equation by Tobit. Unlike the co-residence equation, the sample excludes two-generation households because most monetary transfers are internal for two-generation households. As in the co-residence equation, variables pertaining to the other generation are not included. Capital income is excluded to avoid endogeneity bias. The Tobit estimates reported in table 8.3 show that labor income has a negative and highly significant effect on transfer receipts. Its magnitude is much larger for the young, perhaps because transfer from parents is timed to alleviate liquidity constraints.[9] The coefficient on the number of nonadult children implies that an additional child increases transfer receipts by 300,000 yen per year.[10]

8.4   Altruistic Models of Co-Residence

In this section we will examine models of co-residence in which an altruistic family, consisting of a parent generation (P) and its offspring (K), chooses between living apart to form two separate nuclear households and co-residence in a two-generation household, and show that demand neutrality—invariance of consumption demand to division of resources within families—holds for families choosing co-residence. We will also argue that neutrality is unlikely to hold if the two generations are not altruistic.

8.4.1 Housing as a Public Good

The family wishes to maximize

$$\theta u_P(c_P, h_P, \varepsilon_P; r) + (1 - \theta)u_K(c_K, h_K, \varepsilon_K; r) \qquad 0 < \theta < 1, \tag{4.1}$$

where u_i is generation i's own utility function ($i = P, K$), h_i is housing services, ε_i an unobservable taste shifter, c_i a nonhousing consumption vector, and r is the residence status (live apart or co-reside) that affects the utility functions. When the two generations live apart, the budget constraints for two separate nuclear households are combined through monetary transfers into a single constraint

$$p'(c_P + c_K) + q(h_P + h_K) = y_P + y_K, \tag{4.2}$$

where y_i is generation i's income, p is the nonhousing consumption price vector, and q is the price of housing services. When they live together to form a single two-generation household, housing is a public good. The budget constraint is

$$p'(c_P + c_K) + qh = y_P + y_K, \tag{4.3}$$

where h is the common housing consumption. The family chooses the residence status that yields higher family utility.

For later use, we note that the family's problem in the case of co-residence can be expressed as follows. The family's *induced preferences* over total consumption are given by

$$u(c, h, \theta, \varepsilon_P, \varepsilon_K; r) = \max (4.1) \text{ subject to } c_P + c_K = c \text{ and } h_P = h_K = h. \tag{4.4}$$

So the family's problem is to maximize the induced family utility subject to the budget constraint $p'c + qh = y_P + y_h$. This way of looking at the problem is useful because we do not observe individual consumption vector (c_P, c_K)—all we observe is total consumption c—for two-generation households.

The model has a *neutrality* property: given total family resources (in this static model represented by $y \equiv y_P + y_K$), consumption demand does not depend on how total family resources are divided within the family. To be more precise, neutrality for two-generation households has two parts. The first is *demand neutrality*. As clear from the discussion of the induced utility (4.4), the arguments of household demand function include prices, total consumption expenditure (which in this static model coincides with y by the budget constraint), and taste shifters, but not division of total resources. The second is the neutrality of residence status choice: the choice is a function of taste shifters and total resources $(\theta, \varepsilon_P, \varepsilon_K, y)$ but not of division of total resources. Since the residence status choice is endogenous, there is a *sample selection bias* in that the distribution of taste shifters entering the demand function for two-generation households is already conditional on co-residence. An implication of the neutrality of residence status choice is that the conditional distribution does not depend on individual resources as long as it is conditional on total resources.

8.4.2 An Example

To illustrate these points, consider the following log-linear example, which also can explain the stylized facts about the relationship between co-residence and income documented in the previous section. The utility function is

$$u_i(c_i, h_i, \varepsilon_i; r) = v_i(c_i) + \lambda(r)\log(h_i) \qquad i = P, K, \tag{4.5}$$

where $\lambda(\text{live apart}) = 1$ while $\lambda(\text{co-residence}) \equiv \lambda < 1$, to reflect the disutility of co-residence arising from the loss of privacy. Let $v_i(.)$ be such that its indirect utility function takes the following Gorman polar form:[11]

$$[\log(x_i) - \log(a(p, \eta_i))]/b(p) \qquad i = P, K, \tag{4.6}$$

where x_i is nominal expenditure on nonhousing consumption; this x_i should replace the $p'c_i$ in the budget constraints (4.2) and (4.3). The taste shifter, ε_i, has two elements (η_i, λ). It is easy to show that the family chooses co-residence if and only if $y \leq y^*$, where the threshold income level y^* is given by[12]

$$\log(y^*) = \phi(\theta, \lambda) + \log(q). \tag{4.7}$$

Note that the taste shock η_i does not affect the residence status because its effect on family utility does not depend on the residence status.

The induced family utility (4.4) in terms of nonhousing expenditure and housing consumption for two-generation households becomes

$[\log(x) - \log(a(p, \eta_P, \eta_K))]/b(p) + \lambda \log(h),$ (4.8)

where $x = x_P + x_K$ is total nonhousing expenditure and $\log(a(p, \eta_P, \eta_K)) = \theta \log(a(p, \eta_P)) + (1 - \theta) \log(a_K(p, \eta_K))$. Thus the strong separability between housing and non-housing consumptions that we assumed for individual utility functions is preserved.

The share of housing expenditure, $qh/(x + qh)$, equals $\lambda b(p)$, which does not involve division of resources, verifying demand neutrality. The taste shifter entering the share equation is λ. Its mean conditional on co-residence, y, and any indicator, say d, of division of y does not depend on d because $E(\lambda|\text{co-residence}, y, d) = E(\lambda|y \leqslant y^*, y, d) = E[\lambda|\log(y) \leqslant \phi(0, \lambda) + \log(q), y, d] = E[\lambda|\log(y) \leqslant \phi(\theta, \lambda) + \log(q), y]$.

Clearly, this example can explain why income is lower for generations who co-reside (see stylized fact (3) in the previous section), and why either generation's income has the negative effect in the Probit co-residence equation of table 8.2: unless y_P and y_K are strongly negatively correlated, $Pr(y \leqslant y^*|y_i)$ decreases with y_i. It also explains the negative correlation noted in the previous section, because the correlation between y_P and y_K conditional on co-residence (i.e., conditional on $y_P + y_K \leqslant y^*$) can be negative even if the unconditional correlation is positive. Finally, that the threshold income y^* increases with housing costs (q) is consistent with the prevalence of co-residence in a high housing price country like Japan.

8.4.3 Time Transfers

We have supposed that the benefit from co-residence is returns to scale in housing. Is neutrality specific to how we model the costs and benefits of co-residence? Another plausible reason for co-residence is the ease of time transfers. To focus on time transfers, consider the following altruistic model:

$$\max \theta u_P(c_P, t_K, l_P; r) + (1 - \theta) u_K(c_K, t_P, l_K; r)$$

$$\text{subject to: } p'(c_P + c_K) = w_P[T - \delta(r)t_P - l_P] + w_K[T - \delta(r)t_K - l_K],$$

(4.9)

where T is time endowment, t_i ($i = P, K$) is time spent by generation i with the other generation, l_i is leisure, w_i is the wage rate, and $\delta(r)$ is an (inverse) efficiency index of time transfer that equals 1 if $r = $ co-residence and δ (>1) if $r = $ live apart.

The induced family utility given the residence status r is given by

$$u(c, n_P, n_K, \varepsilon_P, \varepsilon_K; r) = \max (4.9)$$

$$\text{subject to: } c_P + c_K = c, \delta(r)t_P + l_P = T - n_P, \delta(r)t_K + l_K = T - n_K,$$

(4.10)

where n_i $(i = P, K)$ is labor supply or hours worked. The family's problem conditional on co-residence is to maximize (4.10) subject to $p'c = w_P n_P + w_K n_K$, which makes it clear that demand neutrality is conditional on hours worked: household demand c is invariant to individual wages, given prices, taste shifters, total consumption expenditure $p'c$, and hours worked.[13] However, the residence status choice now depends on individual wages, thanks to the price effects of wages on hours worked.

8.4.4 Nonaltruistic Models of Co-Residence

Is neutrality a hallmark of altruism? To be sure, altruism is not a prerequisite for co-residence; models of co-residence for two selfish agents wishing to share benefits from co-residence can readily be found from the literature on marriage. In the Nash cooperative bargaining models of marriage,[14] the equilibrium is assumed to be Pareto efficient. So consumption maximizes the weighted utility (4.1) for some θ. The difference from the altruistic model is that the weight θ depends on division of total resources because so does the threat point. Therefore, neutrality would not hold for nonaltruistic models of co-residence that assume Pareto efficiency.

One can view the model of noncooperative provision of a public good as a noncooperative model of co-residence with housing being the public good. Warr (1983) and Bergstrom, Blume, and Varian (1986) have shown that consumption is invariant to division of resources if both agents make strictly positive donations to the public good. However, their result should be interpreted with care. First, the pairs of agents who play the public goods game may be self-selected and the selection may depend on individual incomes. Second, as Lundberg and Pollak (1993a) note, corner solutions are plausible in the case of multiple public goods. Third, one can question whether the one-shot noncooperative approach is appropriate for modeling the parent-child relationship.[15]

8.5 Testing Neutrality

8.5.1 Specification of Engel Curves

As seen in the previous section, neutrality implies that the system of demand functions for two-generation households does not involve any indicator of how total resources are divided between two generations. In cross-section data with common prices to all households, demand functions are *Engel curves*. We test neutrality by including intrahousehold

division indicators in Engel curves and checking for their significance in
these augmented Engel curves. In order to implement the test, we have to
address four issues.

The first issue is treatment of durables. The total consumption expenditure in Engel curves includes service flows from durables. But there is evidence from a separate Japanese micro data that all commodities except
food are (psychologically) durable.[16] For such commodities it is impossible to calculate service flows because there is no information on cumu-
lative expenditures. We avoid this difficulty by assuming that food is
weakly separable from other commodities in the induced family utility
and focus on the allocation of food expenditure among food components.
Weak separability will be tested below.

The second issue is treatment of hours worked. Lacking information on
hours worked and wage rates, we are too constrained to provide a completely satisfactory treatment here. Available evidence (see Browning and
Meghir (1991) for the U.K.) is that hours worked and food are not weakly
separable, and indeed in our data when employment status is included in
Engel curves it is statistically significant. Thus food demand must be con-
ditioned on hours worked, as in section 8.4.3, but we do not have valid
instruments such as wage rates for hours worked in our data. Thus, *we
are forced to make an untestable assumption that hours worked are exogenous*.
Furthermore, hours worked will be proxied by two dummy variables for
work and part-time work.

Third, food expenditure, being a function of taste shifters, is an endogenous variable that we instrument by the household's (current) income,
its square, capital income, its square, and net financial assets. Under the
assumption that hours worked are exogenous, both capital income and
labor income (which is part of current income) are valid instruments.

Fourth and most important, we have to deal with the possible sample
selection bias. Since the distribution of unobservable taste shifters entering Engel curves as the error term for two-generation households is
already conditional on co-residence, the error term may be correlated with
instruments (e.g., income) that affect the residence status choice. Correcting the bias is very difficult. The standard Heckit procedure is infeasible
here because our sample of nuclear households is not linked by relation,
providing no information on the characteristics of families having chosen
living apart.[17] Thus *we are forced to ignore the sample selection bias*. This is
less onerous than it sounds, since the Engel curves we estimate are only a
subsystem of demand functions. In fact, in the example given in section
8.4.2, the taste shifters entering nonhousing demand, η_P and η_K, do not

enter the residence status choice, so there exists no sample selection bias, provided that η_P and η_K are independent of the taste shifters that do enter the residence status choice. Also, if the error term in Engel curves is dominated by measurement error, no bias arises.

8.5.2 Engel Curves for Nuclear Households

Before proceeding to test the hypothesis, we document that there is a substantial intergenerational difference in tastes for food by estimating Engel curves for nuclear households, which may also be of independent interest. The form of Engel curves we entertain permits some functional flexibility:

$$s_j = z'\alpha_j + \beta_j x^{\{\gamma\}} + \eta_j \quad \text{with } x^{\{\gamma\}} \equiv (x^\gamma - 1)/\gamma, \tag{5.1}$$

where $x^{\{\gamma\}}$ is the Box-Cox transform, x is nominal food expenditure for the household in question, z is a vector of demographics (including age) and employment status for the household, s_j is the share (in percents) of the j-th food component in food budget, and η_j is the error term. Following Blundell, Browning, and Meghir (1989), we try three values for γ: $\gamma = 1, 0, -1$. If p is the price vector, the Engel curves (5.1) can be derived from the indirect utility function $[x/a(p)]^{\{-\gamma\}}/b(p)$, which reduces to the indirect (sub)utility function in section 8.4.2 when $\gamma = 0$, quasi-homothetic preferences when $\gamma = -1$, and quadratic Engel curves when $\gamma = 1$.[18] As in table 8.1, we divide food into six food components: cereal, fish, meat and dairy, vegetables, eating out, and other food.

We assume that the error term is conditionally homoskedastic because parameter estimates under the more general case of conditional heteroskedasticity are very similar. Then, since both the instruments and the right-hand-side variables are the same across equations, the three-stage least squares reduces to the two-stage least squares. Table 8.4 reports the two-stage least squares estimation of the five equation system for the sample of 32,036 nuclear households (26,498 young nuclear plus 5,538 old nuclear households). The Engel curve for the sixth food component, other food, is dropped because it is a linear combination of the first five Engel curves.

Panel A of the table shows parameter estimates for the log case ($\gamma = 0$); those for $\gamma = 1$ or -1 are similar and not reported here. The results accord very well with our a priori expectations. Cereal is more important for households with children perhaps because of their higher calorie needs.

Table 8.4
Share Equations, Nuclear Households (32,036 households)

Panel A: Two-Stage Least Squares Estimates for $\gamma = 0$

Right-hand-side variables	Cereal		Fish		Meat and dairy		Vegetables		Eating out	
# children, $0 \leqslant$ age < 5	1.6	(19)	0.1	(1)	2.4	(33)	0.1	(1)	−6.5	(43)
# children, $5 \leqslant$ age < 10	2.5	(30)	−0.2	(3)	0.5	(7)	−0.1	(2)	−4.4	(29)
# children, $10 \leqslant$ age < 15	3.6	(38)	−0.3	(3)	1.1	(13)	−0.4	(5)	−5.3	(31)
# children, $15 \leqslant$ age < 20	4.2	(36)	−0.1	(1)	2.1	(21)	−0.6	(6)	−6.9	(33)
# children, $20 \leqslant$ age < 25	3.1	(14)	−0.5	(3)	1.6	(8)	−0.6	(3)	−4.5	(11)
Marital status: head is single male	−8.0	(42)	−8.8	(51)	−12.8	(77)	−13.1	(77)	52.6	(151)
Marital status: head is single female	−7.5	(28)	−2.0	(8)	−4.0	(17)	0.0	(0)	18.2	(37)
Emp. status: husband works	−1.4	(7)	2.2	(13)	1.0	(6)	0.3	(2)	−1.4	(4)
Emp. status: husband works part-time	1.3	(2)	−1.5	(2)	−1.0	(1)	−0.3	(0)	0.6	(0)
Emp. status: wife works	−0.9	(10)	0.4	(5)	−1.0	(12)	−1.2	(15)	3.0	(18)
Emp. status: wife works part-time	−1.1	(8)	−0.4	(3)	0.2	(2)	0.5	(4)	−1.0	(4)
Age	0.12	(28)	0.25	(65)	−0.00	(0)	0.23	(63)	−0.56	(73)
$x^{(y)} = \log(\text{food})$	−9.0	(29)	−1.9	(7)	0.5	(2)	−0.8	(3)	16.9	(30)
Mean of dependent variable (%)	12.2		13.8		16.0		18.3		24.9	
Standard deviation (%)	7.3		7.4		7.5		7.7		20.5	
Residual standard deviation (%)	6.8		6.1		5.9		6.0		12.3	

Panel B: Diagnostics

Sargan's test of overidentifying restrictions	$\gamma = +1$:	$\chi^2(20) = 136.6$	(p-value $= 3.2 \times 10^{-19}$)	[equivalent t-value $= 9.0$]
	$\gamma = 0$:	$\chi^2(20) = 126.7$	(p-value $= 1.6 \times 10^{-17}$)	[equivalent t-value $= 8.5$]
	$\gamma = -1$:	$\chi^2(20) = 129.0$	(p-value $= 6.0 \times 10^{-18}$)	[equivalent t-value $= 8.6$]
Wald test of absence of medical expenditure in the share equations	$\gamma = +1$:	$\chi^2(5) = 48.2$	(p-value $= 3.3 \times 10^{-9}$)	[equivalent t-value $= 5.9$]
	$\gamma = 0$:	$\chi^2(5) = 34.7$	(p-value $= 1.7 \times 10^{-6}$)	[equivalent t-value $= 4.8$]
	$\gamma = -1$:	$\chi^2(5) = 13.0$	(p-value $= 2.4 \times 10^{-2}$)	[equivalent t-value $= 2.3$]

Note: Food is treated as endogenous, instrumented by household income, its square, capital income, its square, and net financial assets. Other right-hand variables included are eight regional and four citysize dummies.

The share of eating out depends heavily on the wife's employment status and increases with food expenditure. The substantial reduction in the residual variation for eating out is mostly due to the sample's inclusion of singles who tend to eat out much more frequently. More important, the household's age very strongly affects budget shares. The old spend more on cereal, fish, and vegetables, and less on eating out.

We computed several diagnostics statistics, some of which are reported in panel B.[19] The Sargan statistic for the five-equation system is highly significant.[20] This may not be totally surprising given the very large sample size. To test weak separability, we added the same Box-Cox transform of medical expenditure to the share equations, treating it as endogenous.[21] The Wald statistic for joint significance in the five equations is fairly large, but not overwhelmingly so.

In sum, despite some evidence of misspecification, our estimation of Engel curves for nuclear households has served our purpose: it unambiguously confirms the very strong effect of age on the structure of food demand.

8.5.3 Engel Curves for Two-Generation Households

We now turn to the sample of two-generation households to test neutrality. We use the same form of Engel curves (5.1), with the z vector now including demographics and employment statuses of two generations. We use two indicators of intrahousehold division of resources: parents' share of household income, $y_P/(y_P + y_K)$ (where y_P and y_K are parents' and children's current incomes) and the dummy that parents are the head of household.[22] Under the maintained hypothesis that labor supply is exogenous, parents' income share can be treated as exogenous. The household head dummy is also exogenous because the head is defined as the main income earner. Thus the complete set of instruments is demographics and employment statuses for two generations, household income, its square, household capital income, its square, net financial assets, and the two resource division indicators.

Table 8.5 presents results from our estimation of augmented Engel curves. Again, the parameter estimates are not very sensitive to the value of γ in the Box-Cox transform, so in panel A we present relevant coefficients for the log case (where $\gamma = 0$). In four of the five equations, either indicator comes out strongly. The Wald statistic for the hypothesis that the coefficients of the two indicators are zero in all five equations, also reported in panel A of the table, implies that demand neutrality can be

Table 8.5
Test of Altruism (10,068 Households)

Panel A: Two-Stage Least Squares Estimates for $\gamma = 0$

Right-hand-side variables	Cereal	Fish	Meat and dairy	Vegetables	Eating out
$x^{(\gamma)} = \log(\text{food})$	-4.5 (7.6)	-3.3 (6.2)	-0.9 (1.9)	0.4 (0.9)	14.8 (17.8)
Parent's share of income	2.4 (5.2)	0.5 (1.2)	-0.7 (2.0)	0.7 (2.0)	-2.8 (4.6)
Parents are the head	0.1 (0.4)	0.8 (2.9)	0.2 (0.8)	1.0 (4.3)	-1.9 (4.3)
Mean of dependent variable (%)	12.4	17.5	17.7	18.8	17.8
Standard deviation (%)	7.8	7.5	6.5	6.3	10.8
Residual standard deviation (%)	7.7	6.9	5.8	5.8	10.6

Joint significance of parents' income share	$\chi^2(5) = 41.2$ (p-value $= 8.6 \times 10^{-8}$)	[equivalent t-value = 5.4]
Joint significance of parent head dummy	$\chi^2(5) = 31.6$ (p-value $= 7.3 \times 10^{-6}$)	[equivalent t-value = 4.5]
Joint significance of both indicators	$\chi^2(10) = 139.4$ (p-value $= 5.5 \times 10^{-25}$)	[equivalent t-value = 10.3]

Panel B: Diagnostics

Sargan's test of overidentifying restrictions	$\gamma = +1$:	$\chi^2(20) = 79.8$	[equivalent t-value = 5.9]
	$\gamma = 0$:	$\chi^2(20) = 69.8$	[equivalent t-value = 5.2]
	$\gamma = -1$:	$\chi^2(20) = 65.2$	[equivalent t-value = 4.9]
Wald test of absence of medical expenditure in the share equations	$\gamma = +1$:	$\chi^2(5) = 12.7$	[equivalent t-value = 2.2]
	$\gamma = 0$:	$\chi^2(5) = 9.3$	[equivalent t-value = 1.6]
	$\gamma = -1$:	$\chi^2(5) = 4.3$	[equivalent t-value = 0.7]

Note: The two indicators (parent's income share and the household head dummy) are treated as endogenous, instrumented by household income, its square, capital income, its square, net financial assets, *and* the two indicators. Other right-hand variables included are eight regional and four citysize dummies, age distribution of children, and the marital status, employment status, and age of the two generations.

rejected rather decisively. Furthermore, the coefficients' sign pattern accords with the age effect shown in table 8.4 for nuclear households: the expenditure share rises with parents' share of household resources precisely for food components favored by the old.

The Sargan statistic, reported in panel B of the table, is fairly significant, possibly because the effect of intrahousehold division of resources is not fully captured by the two indicators that are here assumed to affect food demand additively. To check whether the significance of the indicators is due to the failure of weak separability, we add to each equation the corresponding Box-Cox transform of medical expenditure and treat it as endogenous. As the Wald statistic for its joint significance in the system attests, weak separability cannot be rejected. The two indicators of parents' share of resources remain highly significant even when medical expenditure is included.

8.6 Concluding Remarks

A hallmark of altruism is the neutrality property that consumption is invariant to division of resources within the family. When applied to two-generation households, it implies that the demand system should not be affected by intergenerational division of resources. We were able to reject this neutrality implication since expenditure on precisely the food items favored by old generation is found to be sensitive to the older generation's share of household income.

The rejection of neutrality, however, does not necessarily mean a complete lack of altruism between parents and children. What it does mean is that there is a conflict between parents and children as to what the family's objective ought to be. There seems to be no question that children are altruistic toward parents albeit imperfectly; otherwise we would not see children co-residing with parents with very low income, as observed in our data. One could argue that co-residence is a manifestation of income risk sharing. However, a parent may have been poor before a child is born. Even if parent and child can agree to a contract before observing income, it is difficult to explain why a child provides help when a parent is poor, despite the absence of enforcement.[23]

Evidence against neutrality presented in this chapter for Japan and in Altonji, Hayashi, and Kotlikoff (1992) for the United States casts serious doubts on the empirical basis for the view that generations act as if they form a single immortal dynasty.

Appendix

Possible Miscoding of Missing Cases

For two-generation households, there is clear evidence that genuine missing values are sometimes miscoded as zeros. It is known that about 90 percent of two-generation households (with nonadult children) in which at least one individual 60 years or older is present received public pension in 1984.[24] Table 8.A1 reports the old generation's pension income for old nuclear households (panel A), heads in two-generation households (panel B), and nonheads in two-generation households (panel C). Thus the income of the old in panel C is that of "all other household members." The fraction receiving positive pension income is somewhat lower in panel B than in panel A most likely because the old in panel B are active people, still maintaining the household head status despite the presence of

Table 8.A1
Pension Income by Type

Panel A: Old Nuclear

| | Age | | | |
	55–<65	65–<75	75–	Total
Cell size	3,416	1,787	335	5,538
% pension income > 0	63.6%	94.2%	96.7%	75.5%
Mean pension income if > 0	167.5	158.1	121.2	160.0

Panel B: Heads in Two-Generation Households

| | Age | | | |
	55–<65	65–<75	75–	Total
Cell size	2,460	835	91	3,386
% pension income > 0	48.7%	78.3%	82.4%	56.9%
Mean pension income if > 0	142.8	123.7	111.3	94.3

Panel C: Nonheads in Two-Generation Households

| | Age | | | |
	55–<65	65–<75	75–	Total
Cell size	1,831	3,146	1,705	6,682
% pension income > 0	43.1%	51.8%	46.1%	48.0%
Mean pension income if > 0	103.4	84.1	70.6	85.6

Note: Pension income in ten thousand yen.

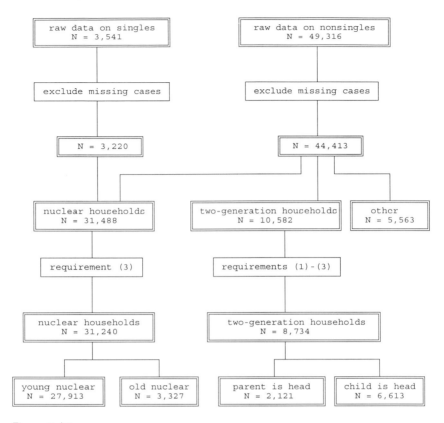

Figure 8.A1
Derivation of samples, 1979.

adult children co-residing in the same household. On the other hand, the old in panel C are no longer head and are likely to be retired. That the fraction of them receiving positive pension income is much less can only be explained by a confusion of missing cases with zeros. Perhaps in many instances the respondent (usually the spouse of the head), unaware of the existence of the parents' pension income, left the relevant box in the questionnaire blank, which was officially coded as a zero. Many of these official zeros are undoubtedly genuine zeros, and true pension income for the rest of the official zeros is likely to be low. Furthermore, as reported in the table, the mean pension income for those reporting a positive value is lower for the old in two-generation households, particularly for nonheads. Therefore, it is highly likely that the true mean of pension income is sub-

Table 8.A2
Simple Statistics by Household Type, 1979

			Household type	
			Two-generation	
	Young nuclear	Old nuclear	Younger generation	Older generation
1. Sample size	27,913	3,327	8,734	
2. Population estimate (millions)	21.7	3.1	5.2	
3. Age of the generation	35.7	63.9	36.9	67.5
4. # adults	1.8	1.5	1.8	1.4
5. # nonadults	1.3	0	1.5	0
6. % couples	75.8	53.5	80.6	43.3
7. % single male	13.1	8.3	10.0	7.6
8. % single female	11.2	38.2	9.4	49.1
9. Annual income	354.6	227.9	357.6	111.1
10. % annual income = 0	0.2%	1.4%	7.9%	48.9%
11. Annual transfer receipts if > 0	—	—	—	—
12. % annual transfer receipts > 0	—	—	—	—
13. Total consumption expenditure	229.3	152.7	281.9	
14. Food	68.8	38.9	82.4	
15. % share, cereal	10.5%	14.7%	12.8%	
16. % share, seafood	12.5%	18.5%	17.7%	
17. % share, meat and dairy	15.9%	13.6%	18.3%	
18. % share, vegetables	17.1%	25.4%	19.7%	
19. % share, eating out	29.9%	14.1%	16.1%	
20. % share, other	14.0%	13.6%	15.3%	

Note: Weighted means are calculated as follows. Let w_i be the sampling weight from the survey. Because our sample excludes missing cases, the weight must be inflated so that the sample mean is unbiased for the population mean. The inflation factor is given by $x/(y \times z)$, where x = the number of families in the population, y = sample size after elimination of missing cases, and z = sample average of w_i. For singles, x = 6.376 million, y = 3,220. For non-singles, x = 28.493 million, y = 44,413. So, for example, the sum of the inflated w_i over the sample is the estimate of the number of families in the population.

Annual income, annual transfer receipts, and expenditures in ten thousand yen. Transfer receipts are private monetary transfers from relatives and others. Income does *not* include transfers. Both income and transfers are for the twelve-month period ending November 1984, while total consumption expenditure and food expenditure are over the three-month period (September–November) at annual rates. A generation's income is the sum of husband's and wife's income if the generation is a couple. If the generation is an individual, its income is the individual's income. The definition of food components is as follows: cereal = rice, bread, noodles, flour and other cereals; seafood = fish and shellfish, meat and dairies = meat, dairy products and eggs, vegetables = vegetables and fruits, eatingout = cooked food, restaurants, other = oil, sweets, beverages, excludes tobacco and alcohol.

Table 8.A3
Probit Estimates, Determinants of Co-residence, 1979

Independent variable	1 Young		2 Old	
No. of observations	36,647		12,061	
% co-residence	23.8%		72.4%	
Number of children	0.10	(12)	—	
Single male	0.70	(20)	0.28	(4.1)
Single female	−0.086	(1.1)	0.51	(13)
Husband works	−0.43	(5.9)	0.27	(7.1)
Wife works	0.33	(21)	0.033	(0.9)
Age of the generation	0.0029	(2.7)	0.026	(10)
Labor income	0.013	(3.2)	—	
Labor income = 0	1.6	(27)	—	
Total income	—		0.043	(5.9)
Total income = 0	—		2.1	(28)
Mean log likelihood	−0.5063		−0.4208	

Note: Income in ten thousand yen. Absolute values of t-values in parentheses. Capital income is the sum of dividends, interests, and rents. Other independent variables included are eight regional and four citysize dummies.

stantially lower for the old in two-generation households than for old nuclear households.

Results from the 1979 Survey of the NSFIE

Figure 8.A1 shows the process of constructing samples from raw data sets for 1979. Since transfer receipts are not separated out from annual income in the 1979 survey, it is not possible to estimate the Tobit equation of table 8.3. Below we display the tables for 1979 that correspond to tables 8.1, 8.2, 8.4. and 8.5 of the text. As seen from table 8.A2, there are relatively fewer old individuals in the 1979 survey and the share of eating out in the food budget is less than in 1984. The parameter estimates for the Probit equation and the demand equations are very similar to those for 1984 and require no further comments. That the neutrality hypothesis is rejected on this separate sample makes the results in the text even more persuasive.

Table 8.A4
Share Equations, Nuclear Households, 1979 (31,240 households)

Panel A: Two-Stage Least Squares Estimates for $\gamma = 0$

Right-hand-side variables	Cereal		Fish		Meat and dairy		Vegetables		Eating out	
# children, $0 \leqslant$ age < 5	1.7	(20)	-0.2	(2)	2.4	(32)	-0.0	(1)	-6.3	(44)
# children, $5 \leqslant$ age < 10	2.8	(32)	-0.3	(4)	0.0	(0)	-0.2	(2)	-4.2	(27)
# children, $10 \leqslant$ age < 15	4.0	(36)	-0.4	(4)	0.1	(1)	-0.6	(6)	-4.7	(24)
# children, $15 \leqslant$ age < 20	4.1	(32)	-0.2	(2)	1.2	(11)	-0.8	(7)	-6.1	(27)
# children, $20 \leqslant$ age < 25	2.3	(10)	-0.1	(0)	1.0	(5)	-0.7	(4)	-3.8	(10)
Marital status: head is single male	-7.7	(37)	-10.7	(57)	-13.3	(69)	-13.3	(74)	55.3	(150)
Marital status: head is single female	-7.6	(25)	-3.4	(12)	-3.5	(12)	0.6	(2)	19.0	(35)
Emp. status: husband works	0.4	(2)	2.0	(10)	0.0	(0)	1.2	(6)	-3.0	(8)
Emp. status: husband works part-time	1.4	(1)	-2.0	(2)	-1.3	(1)	-0.5	(1)	2.1	(1)
Emp. status: wife works	-0.4	(5)	0.2	(2)	-1.6	(19)	-0.7	(9)	3.1	(19)
Emp. status: wife works part-time	0.8	(5)	-0.2	(2)	0.5	(3)	0.3	(2)	-1.4	(5)
Age	0.14	(31)	0.21	(50)	-0.01	(2)	0.20	(52)	-0.50	(62)
$x^{(y)} = \log(\text{food})$	-11.2	(29)	-2.2	(6)	3.0	(8)	-1.9	(6)	18.7	(28)
Mean of dependent variable (%)	11.9		14.6		17.5		19.0		21.9	
Standard deviation (%)	6.8		7.1		7.6		7.0		18.7	
Residual standard deviation (%)	6.7		6.0		6.2		5.8		11.8	

Table 8.A4 (cont.)

Panel B: Diagnostics

Sargan's test of overidentifying restrictions	$\gamma = +1$:	$\chi^2(20) = 112.9$	(p-value $= 5.7 \times 10^{-15}$) [equivalent t-value $= 7.8$]
	$\gamma = 0$:	$\chi^2(20) = 102.2$	(p-value $= 5.0 \times 10^{-13}$) [equivalent t-value $= 7.2$]
	$\gamma = -1$:	$\chi^2(20) = 129.2$	(p-value $= 5.4 \times 10^{-18}$) [equivalent t-value $= 8.6$]
Wald test of absence of medical expenditure in the share equations	$\gamma = +1$:	$\chi^2(5) = 10.3$	(p-value $= 6.6 \times 10^{-2}$) [equivalent t-value $= 1.8$]
	$\gamma = 0$:	$\chi^2(5) = 17.9$	(p-value $= 3.1 \times 10^{-3}$) [equivalent t-value $= 3.0$]
	$\gamma = -1$:	$\chi^2(5) = 9.6$	(p-value $= 8.6 \times 10^{-2}$) [equivalent t-value $= 1.7$]

Note: Food is treated as endogenous, instrumented by household income, its square, capital income, its square, and net financial assets. Other right-hand variables included are eight regional and four citysize dummies.

Table 8.A5
Test of Altruism, 1979 (8,734 Households)

Panel A: Two-Stage Least Squares Estimates for $\gamma = 0$

Right-hand-side variables	Cereal	Fish	Meat and dairy	Vegetables	Eating out
$x^{(y)} = \log(\text{food})$	−7.6 (8.9)	−3.0 (4.3)	2.3 (3.6)	−1.2 (2.1)	14.4 (14.4)
Parents' share of income	1.1 (2.0)	0.7 (1.5)	−0.6 (1.4)	1.3 (3.4)	−2.4 (3.5)
Parents are the head	2.0 (4.6)	0.4 (1.2)	−0.3 (0.8)	1.2 (4.2)	−3.4 (6.6)
Mean of dependent variable (%)	12.6	18.1	18.4	19.5	15.8
Standard deviation (%)	7.9	7.1	6.7	6.0	9.7
Residual standard deviation (%)	8.3	6.7	6.2	5.6	9.7
Joint significance of parents' income share	$\chi^2(5) = 21.9$	(p-value $= 5.4 \times 10^{-4}$)		[equivalent t-value $= 5.4$]	
Joint significance of parent head dummy	$\chi^2(5) = 56.1$	(p-value $= 7.8 \times 10^{-11}$)		[equivalent t-value $= 6.5$]	
Joint significance of both indicators	$\chi^2(10) = 187.8$	(p-value $= 5.7 \times 10^{-35}$)		[equivalent t-value $= 12.3$]	

Panel B: Diagnostics

Sargan's test of overidentifying restrictions	$\gamma = +1$:	$\chi^2(20) = 76.4$	[equivalent t-value $= 5.7$]	
	$\gamma = 0$:	$\chi^2(20) = 67.2$	[equivalent t-value $= 5.0$]	
	$\gamma = -1$:	$\chi^2(20) = 62.7$	[equivalent t-value $= 4.7$]	
Wald test of absence of medical expenditure in the share equations	$\gamma = +1$:	$\chi^2(5) = 16.2$	[equivalent t-value $= 2.7$]	
	$\gamma = 0$:	$\chi^2(5) = 14.8$	[equivalent t-value $= 2.5$]	
	$\gamma = -1$:	$\chi^2(5) = 12.9$	[equivalent t-value $= 2.3$]	

Note: The two indicators (parents' income share and the household head dummy) are treated as endogenous, instrumented by household income, its square, capital income, its square, net financial assets, *and* the two indicators. Other right-hand variables included are eight regional and four citysize dummies, age distribution of children, and the marital status, employment status, and age of the two generations.

Notes

The author is grateful to Robert Pollak and Mark Rosenzweig for useful discussions. The research reported here was supported by grants from National Science Foundation and National Institute of Aging. All the computations using Japanese data were done while I was affiliated with Osaka University.

1. According to the *1984 Basic Survey of Welfare Administration* (Ministry of Health and Welfare Government of Japan), p. 92, about 63 percent of all individuals 60 years or older in Japan live with their children.

2. See, for example, Cai (1989), Schultz (1990), and Thomas (1990).

3. A detailed discussion of how the raw data should be adjusted to national income accounts definitions and for underreporting can be found in Hayashi, Ando, and Ferris (1989).

4. See Rosenzweig and Wolpin (1992, 1993) (which uses the NLS (National Longitudinal Survey), and Altonji, Hayashi, and Kotlikoff (1993) and Ioannides and Kan (1993) (which use the Panel Study of Income Dynamics).

5. Of course this could be due to differences in demographics and income. We will show that the strong age effect remains even after controlling for those factors by estimating Engel curves on the sample of nuclear families in section 8.5.

6. This is consistent with the studies by Kotlikoff and Morris (1990) and by Rosenzweig and Wolpin (1993) for the United States. Because they were able to match parents with children in their data sets, their co-residence equation has both the parent's and child's income. Both incomes have negative coefficients.

7. See, for example, Soldo and Lauriat (1976).

8. These results are in sharp contrast to those in Ohtake (1991), which reports for a different sample of Japanese households that bequeathable wealth has a positive effect on co-residence while the effect of pension income is insignificant. Due to data limitations, the form of co-residence Ohtake considered is the so-called quasi-residence, which means that the two generations live under the same roof but do not share a common budget. Our result about the effect of bequeathable wealth is consistent with Ando and Kennickell (1987) using the 1974 and 1979 survey of the NSFIE.

9. Cox and Jappelli (1990) shows for the United States that private transfers are targeted to those that are liquidity constrained.

10. This is consistent with the results from the NLS that the number of children increases the incidence of transfer receipts. See Rosenzweig and Wolpin (1992).

11. Particular parameterizations of this Gorman polar form include the Translog model of Christensen, Jorgenson, and Lau (1975) and the Almost Identical Demand System of Deaton and Muelbauer (1980). The $b(p)$ in (4.6) can depend on the generation but it complicates the calculation without affecting the points to be made.

12. The ϕ function in (4.7) is

$$-[\theta\log(\theta) + (1 - \theta)\log(1 - \theta)]/(1 - \lambda) - \log(b) + \lambda\log(\lambda)/\lambda$$
$$-[(1 + b\lambda)\log(1 + b\lambda) - (1 + b)\log(1 + b)]/(\beta(1 - \lambda)).$$

13. If consumption c is weakly separable from hours worked in the induced utility function, or if hours worked are the same across households, as in the model of section 4.1, then demand neutrality is unconditional on hours worked.

14. See the literature cited in Behrman (1992).

15. Lundberg and Pollak (1993b) show that neutrality does not hold in a repeated game context.

16. See Hayashi (1985). His estimate of the depreciation rate for recreational expenditure is 5 percent per year.

17. For example, if the explanatory variable in the Probit selection equation is income, we need for limit observations (families whose residence status choice is live apart) the sum of parents' income and children's income.

18. For $\gamma = -1$, the shape of (5.1) depends on how x is scaled. We deflate food expenditure x by its sample mean.

19. The Hausman exogeneity test is not reported here because the test statistic was extremely large or (less frequently) negative. In particular, the OLS estimate of the coefficient of $x^{\{\gamma\}}$ is very different from the two-stage least squares estimate; the log food coefficient in the share equation for cereal, for example, is -3.2.

20. The Sargan statistic for the system is calculated as $e'(S^{-1} \times X(X'X)^{-1}X)e$ where $e' = (e'_1, \ldots, e'_5)$, e_j is the residual vector from the j-th equation, X is the matrix of instruments, and S is the 5×5 residual covariance matrix. The degrees of freedom are 20 because the number of instruments exceeds that of the right-hand-side variables by 4 in each equation.

21. We also tried total nondurables expenditure (total expenditure less durables) instead of medical expenditure to test weak separability, but because of a serious multicollinearity between food and nondurables the parameter estimates were imprecise and the test was inconclusive.

22. Parent's share of household capital income is also tried, but because of numerous cases with zeros, it was not significant. Hayashi, Ando, and Ferris (1988) argues that capital income in the NSFIE is severely underreported.

23. A caveat: it is possible that children living with apparently very poor parents are doing so because the parent was able to offer a house to live.

24. Ministry of Health and Welfare, *1984 Basic Survey of Welfare Administration*, p. 102.

References

Altonji, J., F. Hayashi, and L. Kotlikoff. 1992. Is the extended family altruistically linked? Direct tests using micro data. *American Economic Review* 82(5):1177–98.

———. 1993. The effects of income and wealth on time and money transfers between parents and children. Mimeo., Northwestern University.

Ando, A., and Kennickell. 1987. How much (or little) life cycle is there in micro data? In *Macroeconomics and finance, Essays in honor of Franco Modigliani*, ed. R, Dornbusch, S. Fischer, and J. Bossons, 159–223. Cambridge, MA: MIT Press.

Becker, G. 1981. *A treatise on the family*. Cambridge, MA: Harvard University Press.

Behrman, J. 1992. Intrahousehold distribution and the family. Mimeo., University of Pennsylvania.

Bergstrom, T., L. Blume, and H. Varian. 1986. On the private provision of public goods. *Journal of Public Economics* 29:25–49.

Blundell, R., M. Browning, and C. Meghir. 1989. A microeconomic model of intertemporal substitution and consumer demand. Mimeo., University College, London.

Browning, M., and C. Meghir. 1991. The effects of male and female labor supply on commodity demands. *Econometrica* 59:925–52.

Cai, J. 1989. Are husbands and wives altruistically linked? Evidence from the micro data. Mimeo., Boston University.

Christensen, L., D. Jorgenson, and L. Lau. 1975. Transcendental logarithmic utility functions. *American Economic Review* 65:367–83.

Cox, D., and T. Jappelli. 1990. Credit rationing and private transfers: Evidence from survey data. *Review of Economics and Statistics* 72:445–54.

Deaton, A., and J. Muelbauer. 1980. *Economics and consumer behavior*. New York: Cambridge University Press.

Hayashi, F. 1985. Permanent income hypothesis and consumption durability: Analysis based on Japanese panel data. *Quarterly Journal of Economics* 90:895–916.

———, A. Ando, and R. Ferris. 1988. Life cycle and bequest savings: A study of Japanese and U.S. households based on data from the 1984 NSFIE and the 1983 Survey of Consumer Finances. *Journal of the Japanese and International Economies* 2:450–91.

———. 1989. Life cycle and bequest savings. *NIRA Research Output* 2:38–86.

Ioannides, Y., and K. Kan. 1993. The nature of two-directional intergenerational transfers of money and time: An empirical analysis. Mimeo., VPI.

Kotlikoff, L., and J. Morris. 1990. Why don't the elderly live with their children? A new look. In *Issues in the Economics of Aging*, ed. D. Wise, 149–69 Chicago: University of Chicago Press.

Ohtake, F. 1991. Bequest motives of aged households in Japan. *Recerche Economiche* 45:283–306.

Lundberg, S., and R. Pollak. 1993a. Separate Spheres Bargaining and the Marriage Market. *Journal of Political Economy* 101, no. 6:988–1010.

———. 1993b. Distribution within marriage: Noncooperative bargaining models. Mimeo., University of Washington.

Rosenzweig, M., and K. Wolpin. 1992. Inequality among young adult siblings, public assistance programs, and intergenerational living arrangements. Mimeo., University of Pennsylvania.

———. 1993. Intergenerational support and the life-cycle incomes of young men and their parents: Human capital investments, co-residence and intergenerational financial transfers. *Journal of Labor Economics* 11:84–112.

Schultz, T. 1990. Testing neoclassical model of family labor supply and fertility. *Journal of Human Resources* 15:599−634.

Soldo, B., and P. Lauriat. 1976. Living arrangements among the elderly in the Unites States. *Journal of Comparative Family Studies* 7:351−66.

Thomas, D. 1990. Intra-household resource allocation: An inferential approach. *Journal of Human Resources* 15:635−64.

Warr, P. 1983. The private provision of a public good is independent of the distribution of income. *Economics Letters* 13:207−11.

9

Risk Sharing between and within Families

9.1 Introduction

This chapter uses data from the Panel Study of Income Dynamics (PSID) to test full risk-sharing across and within American families. Understanding the extent of risk sharing is important for assessing the performance of private insurance markets as well as the efficacy of government social insurance policies. It is also important to the proper modeling of the economy. Absent strong evidence to the contrary, many macroeconomic analyses proceed on the assumption of full risk sharing.

Household data provide ideal ground for testing full risk sharing. Controlling for tastes and leisure, changes over time in the consumption of households who are fully sharing risk depend on changes in their collective resources, but not on changes in the distribution among them of those resources. Testing full risk sharing across a set of households simply requires examining the cross-section correlation between their changes in consumption and their changes in resources.

The PSID permits testing full risk sharing among related as well as unrelated households. This is because the PSID surveys, on an ongoing basis, not only those original households included in its initial 1968 survey, but also those households, called *split-offs*, that were formed after 1968 by members of the original households. The PSID is, thus, a random sample of *families*, each consisting of an original household and its split-offs observed over a number of years. Being able to test family risk sharing among related households is important. Related households are likely to have much better information about each other's resources than are unrelated households and, thus, be in a better position to insure one

Originally published in *Econometrica* 64 (March 1996): 261–94, with J. Altonji and L. Kotlikoff. Reprinted with the permission of the Econometric Society.

another. But testing family risk sharing with the PSID requires addressing two imbalances in its data. First, the number of households differs across families, and second, the number of times a household is observed differs across households. Thus the PSID includes a wide variety of family types differing in the pattern of missing household-years. One of the contributions of this chapter is developing a method to deal with the unbalanced nature of these data.

There is a growing literature testing full risk sharing. The earliest test appears to be in Leme (1984), who examined aggregate consumption growth rates for a cross section of countries.[1] Two more recent tests, both of which are based on the PSID, are those of Altug and Miller (1990) and Cochrane (1991). Cochrane finds that changes in the log of food consumption (the only consumption item, besides rent, recorded in the PSID) are significantly related to changes in employment status and other indicators of household resources. He suggests that this may reflect non-separability of the utility function in food consumption and leisure, rather than a rejection of full risk sharing. Altug and Miller (1990) take account of such nonseparability, permitting, in the process, leisure to be endogenous. They fail to reject full risk sharing.

However, the test of Altug and Miller has no power against a particular alternative. Intuitively, they are testing the proposition that, at any given moment in time, risk-sharing households will experience the same food consumption change (adjusted for changes in leisure) regardless of their past economic circumstances, as proxied by their past wages. But consider Hall's (1978) martingale hypothesis: households have no access to income insurance and the only way to prepare against income uncertainty is *self-insurance*, that is, through saving and dissaving in assets whose return is not perfectly correlated with the household's income. As is well known, households engaged in self-insurance change their consumption only when they receive unanticipated shocks to household resources, so the time-series correlation between consumption changes and past wage changes is zero.[2] If we further assume that the unanticipated shocks to household resources consists of a macro component common to all households and an idiosyncratic component, then the cross-section correlation between consumption change and past wage changes, too, is zero. This is why Altug and Miller's test has no power against this particular version of self-insurance.[3] As described below, our test overcome this difficulty by using current and future wage changes to proxy current shocks to household resources. The consumption change will be uncorrelated with these proxies if households share risk, but will be correlated with these proxies if they merely self-insure.

Altonji, Hayashi, and Kotlikoff (1992) also use the PSID, but to study altruism. However, their dynamic test of altruism also represents a test of family risk sharing. This test regresses households' changes in food consumption on their income changes as well as a fixed effect for the family. If family members share risk fully, the change in a particular member's consumption associated with income changes will be fully captured by the family fixed effect. Therefore, the highly significant income coefficient found by Altonji, Hayashi, and Kotlikoff can be interpreted as a rejection of family risk sharing. However, there are two shortcomings to their approach, both of which are addressed here. First, they assume that food is additively separable from leisure. Second, they ignore the possible endogeneity of leisure.

This chapter makes several contributions. First, it entertains possible nonseparability in food consumption and leisure by using the 1985–87 waves of the PSID to match the timing of food and leisure.[4] Second, it exploits the implication of full risk sharing that one-year consumption changes are uncorrelated with the wage rate at all leads as well as lags. It does so by examining the correlation of long changes (changes over extended periods of time) as well as one-year changes in consumption and the wage rate. As emphasized above, exploiting this restriction is essential for discriminating between risk sharing and self-insurance. Third, our methodology for studying long as well as one-year changes also allows us to include in the sample *all* those family types for which full risk sharing produces testable restrictions.[5]

Our methodology can be summarized as follows. The PSID provides for each family a vector specifying the consumption of each available household-year. If preferences are iso-elastic, the logarithm of consumption adjusted for demographics and leisure is equal to the marginal utility of consumption. Hypotheses such as full inter- or intrafamily risk sharing imply that the marginal utility has a particular factor structure. For each factor structure, a linear transformation of short and long time-differences can be used to eliminate the factors from the consumption vector. If the null hypothesis is true, the transformed consumption will be uncorrelated with the wage rate that is a determinant of the marginal utility. If it is false, transformed consumption will still involve the marginal utilities, and so will be correlated with the wage rate. Since the transformation can be tailored to any family type, this test is applicable to all families in the sample; we do not need to restrict our test to families with the same number of split-offs or to families whose households are continuously observed over the same time period.

Our results rely on two different PSID panels. One is the panel of original households used by Altug and Miller (1990). It contains all those original households who were continuously in the survey from 1968 through 1981. In using this panel, we first attempt to replicate Altug and Miller's test statistic for full interfamily risk sharing. This is important because their study is notable for its failure to reject full risk-sharing, with a p-value of 80 percent. The p-value we produce is 12 percent, far lower than theirs but still a very weak evidence against full risk sharing. Including the 1971–74 consumption change not used by Altug and Miller and aggregating the zero correlation conditions over time brings the p-value down to 0 percent, whereas controlling the consumption change for age brings it back up to above 5 percent. If we add current and future wage changes to the list of instruments, the p-value again drops to 0 percent. That is, we fail to reject self-insurance at 5 percent but strongly reject full interfamily risk sharing. The second panel is drawn from the 1985–87 PSID, but it includes split-offs. We use this panel to test intra- as well as interfamily risk sharing. Full interfamily risk sharing, again, is strongly rejected. We also reject intrafamily risk sharing, which reflects the basic fact that there is very little covariation in consumption changes within families.

The chapter proceeds in section 9.2 by presenting our method of testing these factor structures. Section 9.3 briefly describes the data, relegating a fuller account to an appendix. Section 9.4 reports our results. Section 9.5 summarizes our principal findings and draws conclusions.

9.2 Methodology

9.2.1 Risk Sharing and the Factor Structure of the Marginal Utility of Consumption

We begin by deriving the factor structure of the marginal utility of consumption for two models of risk sharing, full interfamily risk sharing, which we refer to simply as full risk sharing and full intrafamily risk sharing, which we call family risk sharing. The derivation of the factor structure under full risk sharing is well known (see, e.g., Townsend (1987)). We include it here for the sake of completeness.

Under full risk sharing, households have access to a full menu of contingency claims. Let e_t be the state of the world in period t (or the date-event pair, to use Kreps's (1990) terminology) and let $C_{ik}(e_t)$ and $L_{ik}(e_t)$ be consumption and leisure, respectively, for household k from family i in e_t.[6] The household's objective is to maximize the time-separable expected discounted utility

$$\sum_{e_t} \text{Prob}(e_t)\beta^t u_{ik}(C_{ik}(e_t), L_{ik}(e_t); e_t), \tag{2.1}$$

where the summation is over all possible date-event pairs. If $q(e_t)$ is the price of a unit of consumption good in e_t as of the current period, the household's lifetime budget constraint is

$$\sum_{e_t} q(e_t)C_{ik}(e_t) = A_{ik} + \sum_{e_t} q(e_t)w_{ik}(e_t)[1 - L_{ik}(e_t)], \tag{2.2}$$

where A_{ik} is initial assets in the current period, $w_{ik}(e_t)$ is the real wage for the head of household ik in date-event pair e_t, and $1 - L_{ik}(e_t)$ is labor supply with the time endowment normalized to one.

The first-order condition for optimality with respect to consumption in e_t, $C_{ik}(e_t)$, is

$$\text{Prob}(e_t)\beta^t \frac{\partial u_{ik}(C_{ik}(e_t), L_{ik}(e_t); e_t)}{\partial C_{ik}(e_t)} = \Lambda_{ik} \cdot q(e_t), \tag{2.3}$$

where Λ_{ik} is the Lagrange multiplier for the single lifetime budget constraint (2.2) for household ik. Taking logs of both sides of (2.3), we obtain

$$\theta_{ik}(e_t) = \lambda_{ik} + p(e_t), \tag{2.4}$$

where

$$\theta_{ik}(e_t) = \log\left(\frac{\partial u_{ik}(C_{ik}(e_t), L_{ik}(e_t); e_t)}{\partial C_{ik}(e_t)}\right) \tag{2.5}$$

is the log marginal utility in e_t and

$$\lambda_{ik} = \log(\Lambda_{ik}), p(e_t) = \log(q(e_t)) - \log(\text{Prob}(e_t)) - t \cdot \log(\beta). \tag{2.6}$$

That is, full risk sharing implies that the log marginal utility for household ik has a simple factor structure, consisting of two factors, one, λ_{ik}, representing household ik's lifetime resources and the other, $p(e_t)$, an undiversifiable aggregate shock. We note here that the factor structure for the marginal utility of consumption is derived assuming that households have the common discounting factor β and common probability assessment Prob(e_t) about future states of nature. On the other hand, as is clear from the derivation, the factor structure holds irrespective of whether leisure is a choice variable.

In the other model, *family risk sharing*, efficient risk sharing is not necessarily possible between families. This is equivalent to a situation in which contingency claims are traded within but not necessarily between families. The security prices can differ across families, so the first-order condition under family risk sharing is

$$\theta_{ik}(e_t) = \lambda_{ik} + p_i(e_t). \tag{2.7}$$

Note the difference from (2.4)—the "p" factor can differ across i. This form of risk sharing is efficient in that the marginal utility is equalized within families.

For the rest of the chapter, we take as given a particular history of the state of the world, so that the dependence on the state can be represented by subscript t. Then the first-order conditions implied by the two models of risk sharing can be written as

$$\theta_{ikt} = \lambda_{ik} + p_t \quad \text{(full risk sharing)}, \tag{2.8a}$$

$$\theta_{ikt} = \lambda_{ik} + p_{it} \quad \text{(family risk sharing)}. \tag{2.8b}$$

For each factor structure, the unobservable marginal utility can be eliminated with a suitable linear transformation, giving rise to sets of testable orthogonality (zero correlation) conditions. The rest of this section derives these conditions, showing how the form of the conditions depends on the presence of split-offs in the data.

9.2.2 The Maintained Hypothesis

Consumption Equation
To establish the link between the marginal utility and consumption, we assume that the instantaneous utility function is the sum of two sub-utilities, the first of which is

$$(1 - \rho_0)^{-1}(C_{ikt})^{1-\rho_0}(L_{h,ikt})^{\rho_h\rho_0}(L_{w,ikt})^{\rho_w\rho_0} \exp(\rho_0\eta_{ikt}) \quad (\rho_0 > 0), \tag{2.9}$$

where C_{ikt} is food consumption by household k in family i at date t, $L_{h,ikt}$ is husband's leisure, $L_{w,ikt}$ is wife's leisure, and η_{ikt} is a taste shifter. The second subutility is a function of all goods except food, but can include leisures $L_{h,ikt}$ and $L_{w,ikt}$. Therefore, the marginal utility of food consumption is the derivative of (2.9) with respect to C_{ikt}. The first subutility (2.9) does not have to satisfy the concavity restrictions with respect to the husband's and wife's leisures; that is, ρ_h or ρ_w may be negative. This slight generalization of the utility function considered in Altug and Miller (1990) permits both the husband's and wife's leisures to interact with food consumption. The taste shifter η_{ikt} consists of a vector of observable household characteristics (b_{ikt}) and an unobservable component (ε_{ikt}):

$$\eta_{ikt} = b'_{ikt}\beta + \varepsilon_{ikt}. \tag{2.10}$$

Redefining θ_{ikt} to be the log marginal utility of food divided by $-\rho_0$ and using (2.9) and (2.10), yields the *consumption equation*

$$c_{ikt} = b'_{ikt}\beta + l_{h,ikt}\rho_h + l_{w,ikt}\rho_w + \theta_{ikt} + \varepsilon_{ikt}$$

$$\equiv z'_{ikt}\delta + \theta_{ikt} + \varepsilon_{ikt}, \tag{2.11}$$

where lower case letters c and l are in logs, and

$$z'_{ikt} = (b'_{ikt}, l_{h,ikt}, l_{w,ikt}), \delta' = (\beta', \rho_h, \rho_w). \tag{2.12}$$

In (2.11) c and l stand for measured consumption and leisure, respectively. So, if consumption and leisure are measured with error, the error term ε_{ikt} also includes measurement errors in these variables.

Both the first-order condition (2.8) and the consumption equation (2.11) are valid irrespective of whether leisure is freely chosen or is constrained to equal zero or some other amount. Of course, if leisure is freely chosen or is measured with error, then leisure is a variable whose endogeneity must be considered in the estimation.

Exogenous Variables

As noted in the introduction, the PSID is a random sample of *families*, each of which consists of an original household and its split-offs. Let $K - 1$ be the maximum number of split-offs (so that families can have up to K member households), and let T be the length of the panel. For any particular family, household-year (k, t) may be missing either because household k does not exist or because the household did not participate in the survey in year t.

To use the unbalanced panel of families, we need to specify the mechanism by which these household-years are selected. Before doing so, however, we make some assumptions about the error term. Specifically, we assume that the error term ε_{ikt} has mean zero and is independent of a vector of exogenous variables x_{ihs} (to be specified below) for household h in year s:

$$E(\varepsilon_{ikt}) = 0 \qquad (k = 1, 2, \ldots, K; t = 1, 2, \ldots, T), \qquad\qquad (2.13a)$$

$$\varepsilon_{ikt} \text{ is independent of } x_{iks} \qquad (k = 1, 2, \ldots, K; t, s = 1, 2, \ldots, T), \qquad (2.13b)$$

$$\varepsilon_{ikt} \text{ is independent of } x_{ihs} \qquad (k, h = 1, 2, \ldots, K, k \neq h; t, s = 1, 2, \ldots, T),$$
$$(2.13c)$$

where expectations are taken here and elsewhere over the population of families. Equation (2.13b) states that, for each household k, the exogenous variables and the error term are independent *at all leads and lags*, whereas (2.13c) assumes the same, but for two different households k and h in the same family. We require (2.13c) because our orthogonality conditions for family risk sharing involve linear transformations of the consumption equations of different households belonging to the same family.

Our exogenous variables, apart from the constant, are demographics (b_{ikt}), a vector of two variables for instrumenting the two leisures in the consumption equation (denoted by g_{ikt}), and a variable (w_{ikt}) that proxies for the household's initial resources or wealth (i.e., the household's initial assets plus the present value of pretransfer wages). Thus,

$$x'_{ikt} = (b'_{ikt}, g'_{ikt}, w_{ikt}). \qquad\qquad (2.14)$$

We will use the wage rate for the resource indicator w_{ikt}. In some specifications, the g_{ikt} is lagged leisure, in which case (2.13b) and (2.13c) are not satisfied for at least some s greater than t.[7] In these specifications, we will not utilize those conditions. With respect to the other exogenous variables, demographics (b_{ikt}), and the indicator of the household's resources (w_{ikt}), we do exploit the implication of (2.13b) and (2.13c) that the error term ε_{ikt} is uncorrelated with current, lagged, and *future* values of the instrument.[8]

Sample Selection Mechanism

Turning to our assumed sample selection mechanism, let v_{ik} be the permanent component (if any) of the error term ε_{ikt} distributed independently of the remaining component of ε_{ikt}, and let $x_{ik} = (x_{ik1}, \ldots, x_{ikT})'$. Assume that there is a function $\phi_t(v_{ik}, x_{ik})$ such that[9]

household-year (k, t) is observed iff $\phi_t(v_{ik}, x_{ik}) \geqslant 0$. $\qquad\qquad (2.15)$

(If the instruments g_{ikt} for leisure are lagged leisures, the x_{ik} in (2.15) is understood to exclude g_{ikt}.) We will refer to the set of available household-years as the *family type*. Since the expectation of the time-difference $\Delta_1 \varepsilon_{ikt} \equiv \varepsilon_{i,k,t+1} - \varepsilon_{ikt}$ conditional on $(v_{i1}, \ldots, v_{iK}, x_{i1}, \ldots, x_{iK})$ is zero by (2.13) and since the family type is a function of $(v_{i1}, \ldots, v_{iK}, x_{i1}, \ldots, x_{iK})$, we have, for any given family type,

$$E(\Delta_1 \varepsilon_{ikt}) = 0 \text{ and } E(x_{ihs} \cdot \Delta_1 \varepsilon_{ikt}) = 0$$

$$(t = 1, 2, \ldots, T - 1; s = 1, \ldots, T; k, h = 1, 2, \ldots, K), \tag{2.16}$$

where it is implicit (as for all the expectations in sections 9.2.3–9.2.6) that the expectation is conditional on the given family type. We use this implication of (2.13) and (2.15) repeatedly.[10]

We emphasize that this assumption—that the sample selection is based on the exogenous variables and the permanent component of the error term but not on the remaining component of the error term—is made, often implicitly, in virtually all panel data studies on consumption. For example, this assumption is required to rule out sample selection bias in balanced panels. Panel data studies that use cross-section variation in levels of variables make the stronger assumption that sample selection is independent of the permanent components.

Our methodology developed below builds on the first-order condition (2.8), the consumption equation (2.11), and the orthogonality conditions (2.16). These, in turn, have been derived from the following list of assumptions: (1) agents have the same discounting factor and probability assessments about the states of nature, (2) the utility function is time-separable with the instantaneous utility function that is separable between food and other goods except leisure, (3) the error term is independent of exogenous variables such as the wage rate, and (4) the probability of a household-year being included in the sample depends only on the exogenous variables and the permanent component of the error term.

9.2.3 Testing Full Risk Sharing on a Balanced Panel

To describe our procedure for testing the factor structure, we begin with the familiar case of testing full risk sharing on a balanced panel of length T that excludes split-offs. Thus families included in the sample are of the same family type: each family has exactly one household (so the index k is set to 1 in this and subsequent subsections), and the household is observed for all T periods.

Combining the factor structure (2.8a) for full risk sharing and the consumption equation (2.11) and taking first time-differences, we can eliminate the household-specific component of the marginal utility λ_{ik}:

$$\Delta_1 c_{i1t} = \Delta_1 z'_{i1t}\delta + (p_{t+1} - p_t) + \Delta_1 \varepsilon_{i1t}$$

$$\equiv \Delta_1 z'_{i1t}\delta + d'_t\pi + \Delta_1 \varepsilon_{i1t} \qquad (t = 1, \ldots, T-1), \qquad (2.17)$$

where $\Delta_1 c_{i1t} \equiv c_{i,1,t+1} - c_{i1t}$, $\pi = (\pi_1, \ldots, \pi_{T-1})'$, $\pi_t = \Delta_1 p_t$ is a time-dependent intercept capturing the change in the macro factor from t to $t+1$, and $d_t = (0, 0, \ldots, 0, 1, 0, \ldots, 0)'$ is a $T-1$ dimensional vector of time dummies whose elements are all zero except for the t-th element, which is one.

Since the *adjusted consumption change*, $\Delta_1 c_{i1t} - \Delta_1 z'_{i1t}\delta - d'_t\pi$, equals the change in the error term, $\Delta_1 \varepsilon_{i1t}$, by (2.17), we can combine (2.16) for the family type in question and (2.17) to generate a large number of ortho-gonality conditions. If M is the number of exogenous variables (i.e., the dimension of x_{ikt}), these conditions are $(T-1) + T \cdot (T-1) \cdot M$ in number. As in most panel studies, however, our sample size is too small to exploit all of them.[11] Even if the sample size were greater than the number of available orthogonality conditions, the chi-square test statistic uti-lizing this many orthogonality conditions might have a very poor small sample distribution.[12] For this reason we consider a much smaller number of linear combinations of the available orthogonality conditions.

The set of orthogonality conditions we use is the following:

$$E(\Delta_1 c_{i1t} - \Delta_1 z'_{i1t}\delta - d'_t\pi) = 0 \qquad (t = 1, 2, \ldots, T-1), \text{ or equivalently,}$$

$$E\left[\sum_{t=1}^{T-1} d_t \cdot (\Delta_1 c_{i1t} - \Delta_1 z'_{i1t}\delta - d'_t\pi)\right] = 0; \qquad (2.18a)$$

$$E[\Delta_1 x_{i1t} \cdot (\Delta_1 c_{i1t} - \Delta_1 z'_{i1t}\delta - d'_t\pi)] = 0 \qquad (t = 1, 2, \ldots, T-1), \qquad (2.18b)$$

where $\Delta_1 x_{i1t}$ ($= x_{i,1,t+1} - x_{i1t}$) is the first time-difference in the exogenous variables x_{i1t} given in (2.14).[13] These are $(T-1)(M+1)$ linear combina-tions of the available orthogonality conditions, $T-1$ from (2.18a) and $(T-1)M$ from (2.18b), where M is the dimension of x_{i1t}. They are more numerous than the parameters (δ, π). We use GMM (generalized methods of moments) to estimate the parameters and test the null of full risk sharing using the chi-square statistic for overidentifying restrictions.[14] This is equivalent to estimating the system of $T-1$ transformed con-sumption equations (2.17) with $\Delta_1 x_{i1t}$ as instruments for $\Delta_1 z_{i1t}$ in the t-th equation. We use the time-difference, rather than the level, of w_{i1t} (the indicator of the household's resources) as an instrument, because, under most plausible alternatives to the null, including self-insurance, we would expect consumption changes to be correlated with the resource indicator mainly through its changes.

If the null is false, then (2.17) is no longer valid because taking time-differences does not eliminate the household-specific component of marginal utility from the consumption equation. In this case, the adjusted consumption change, $\Delta_1 c_{i1t} - \Delta_1 z'_{i1t}\delta - d'_t \pi$, involves the change in the marginal utility as well as the change in the error term $\Delta_1 \varepsilon_{i1t}$. Therefore, our orthogonality conditions will fail under at least some alternatives. This is the basis of our test.

If the panel covers many time periods or if there are many instruments, then the number of orthogonality conditions, $(T - 1)(M + 1)$, may still be too large relative to the sample size. So we consolidate orthogonality conditions by aggregating over time the $(T - 1)M$ conditions (2.18b) to obtain the following M conditions:

$$E\left[\sum_{t=1}^{T-1} \Delta_1 x_{i1t} \cdot (\Delta_1 c_{i1t} - \Delta_1 z'_{i1t}\delta - d'_t \pi)\right] = 0. \tag{2.19}$$

This need not entail a loss of information. In fact, under stationarity where the expectations in (2.18b) are independent of t, this simple averaging is the optimal way to combine temporal orthogonality conditions.

9.2.4 The Orthogonality Conditions Used by Altug and Miller (1990)

The orthogonality conditions used by Altug and Miller (1990) in their test of full risk sharing utilizing the consumption equation can be written as (2.18a) and (2.18b), where the instruments are not the changes in the exogenous variables, $\Delta_1 x_{i1t}$, but a set of variables that includes lagged wage rates, $w_{i,1,t-1}$ and $w_{i,1,t-2}$, but not future wage rates. As shown in Hall (1978), under self-insurance, the adjusted change in consumption from time t to $t + 1$ is unforcastable on the basis of information available at time t, which implies that the time-series correlation between the adjusted consumption change and any variable known in date t is zero. Although, as first pointed out by Chamberlain (1984) and subsequently emphasized by a number of authors, a zero time-series correlation does not necessarily imply a zero cross-section correlation, the cross-section correlation will also be zero if the stochastic environment faced by the household is such that the unforcastable consumption change can be represented by the sum of a macro component common to all households and an idiosyncratic component. Therefore, under the joint hypothesis of self-insurance and this assumed structure of the unforcastable consumption change, the orthogonality conditions for the wage rate used by Altug and Miller (1990) hold, and the test of full risk sharing based on those conditions has no power against this particular alternative hypothesis. In what follows we will refer to this joint hypothesis simply as *self-insurance*.

9.2.5 Use of Long Time Differences

Even when the instruments include the contemporaneous change in the wage rate, the orthogonality conditions for the wage rate, $E[\Delta_1 w_{i1t} \cdot (\Delta_1 c_{i1t} - \Delta_1 z'_{i1t}\delta - d'_t \pi)] = 0$, may have low power under the alternative of self-insurance if the wage change is known one period in advance or if the short-term changes in wages are dominated by transitory measurement error or transitory wage changes. To avoid this possibility of low power of the test, we also utilize time-differences over two periods or longer. Since long time-differences are the sum of consecutive first differences, the τ-th time difference in the error term, $\Delta_\tau \varepsilon_{i1t} \equiv \varepsilon_{i,1,t+\tau} - \varepsilon_{i1t}$, can be derived from (2.17) as

$$\Delta_\tau \varepsilon_{i1t} = \Delta_\tau c_{i1t} - \Delta_\tau z'_{i1t}\delta - (d_t + \cdots + d_{t+\tau-1})'\pi,$$

where d_t is the $T-1$ dimensional vector of time dummies whose t-th element is one. With orthogonality conditions of longer time-differences stacked on those of one-year differences, (2.19) becomes

$$E\left[\sum_{t-1}^{T\tau} \Delta_\tau x_{i1t} \cdot \{\Delta_\tau c_{i1t} - \Delta_\tau z'_{i1t}\delta - (d_t + \cdots + d_{t+\tau-1})'\pi\} \right] = 0$$

$$(\tau = 1, 2, \ldots, T-1). \qquad (2.20b)$$

For example, for $\tau = 2$, this is the expected value of the sum of $T-2$ cross products of overlapping two-year changes. The expected value is zero because it is a linear combination of the zero moments in (2.16) for the family type in question.

By including long time-differences, we are utilizing the orthogonality conditions that will fail if the adjusted one-year change in consumption is correlated with either current or *future* one-year changes in the exogenous variables. For example for $\tau = 2$, the cross product of two-year changes, $\Delta_2 x_{i1t} \cdot \Delta_2 \varepsilon_{i1t}$ (where $\Delta_2 \varepsilon_{i1t} = \Delta_2 c_{i1t} - \Delta_2 z'_{i1t}\delta - (d_t + d_{t+1})'\pi$), equals

$\Delta_1 x_{i1t} \cdot \Delta_1 \varepsilon_{i,1,t+1} + \Delta_1 x_{i1t} \cdot \Delta_1 \varepsilon_{i1t} + \Delta_1 x_{i,1,t+1} \cdot \Delta_1 \varepsilon_{i,1,t+1} + \Delta_1 x_{i,1,t+1} \cdot \Delta_1 \varepsilon_{i1t}$.
Under self-insurance, the expectation of the first term is zero. The expectations of the second and the third terms are zero under self-insurance if concurrent changes in x are anticipated by the household. The expectation of the last term, however, will not be zero unless the household can anticipate one-period-ahead changes in x. Thus our orthogonality conditions will fail under the alternative of self-insurance.

Regarding the other orthogonality conditions (2.18a), no new restrictions are gained by considering orthogonality conditions of long changes associated with time dummies, because they are linear combinations of (2.18a). However, to anticipate our treatment of unbalanced data, we modify (2.18a) by adding long differences to the sum:

$$E\left[\sum_{\tau=1}^{T-1} \sum_{t=1}^{T-\tau} (d_t + \cdots + d_{t+\tau-1}) \cdot \{ \Delta_\tau c_{i1t} - \Delta_\tau z'_{i1t} \delta - (d_t + \cdots + d_{t+\tau-1})' \pi \} \right] = 0.$$

$$(2.20a)$$

Since long time-differences are the sum of one-year differences, these $T - 1$ restrictions are linear combinations of the $T - 1$ restrictions in (2.18a). Thus (2.18a) and (2.20a) represent the same restrictions.

9.2.6 Testing Full Risk Sharing with Split-Offs

Next we consider the case in which the common family type in the panel has the same number, K, of member households *and* each household is observed for all T periods. Rather than stacking the orthogonality conditions (2.20) across different member households, which would lead to a proliferation of orthogonality conditions, we aggregate them over households belonging to the same family to obtain the following $(T - 1)(M + 1)$ conditions:

$$E\left[\sum_{k=1}^{K} \sum_{\tau=1}^{T-1} \sum_{t=1}^{T-\tau} (d_t + \cdots + d_{t+\tau-1}) \cdot \{ \Delta_\tau c_{ikt} - \Delta_\tau z'_{ikt} \delta - (d_t + \cdots + d_{t+\tau-1})' \pi \} \right]$$
$$= 0,$$

$$(2.21a)$$

$$E\left[\sum_{k=1}^{K} \sum_{t=1}^{T-\tau} \Delta_\tau x_{ikt} \cdot \{ \Delta_\tau c_{ikt} - \Delta_\tau z'_{ikt} \delta - (d_t + \cdots + d_{t+\tau-1})' \pi \} \right] = 0$$

$$(\tau = 1, 2, \ldots, T-1). \quad (2.21b)$$

The sum in (2.21) is commutative in k, which makes our test robust to a possible erroneous identification of the birth order of split-offs.

9.2.7 Family Risk Sharing

We now turn to the test of family risk sharing whose factor structure is given by (2.8b). As before, the time-invariant factor λ_{ik} of the marginal utility θ_{ikt} can be eliminated by time-differencing. In addition, the family-specific factor p_{it} common to all member households can be eliminated by subtracting its family average from θ_{ikt}. Let $\tilde{\Delta}_\tau$ stand for this time-difference/family fixed-effect operator:

$$\tilde{\Delta}_\tau \xi_{ikt} = \Delta_\tau \xi_{ikt} - (\Delta_\tau \xi_{i1t} + \cdots + \Delta_\tau \xi_{iKt})/K \text{ for any variable } \xi.$$

Then $\tilde{\Delta}_\tau \theta_{ikt} = 0$ under the factor structure (2.8b). Applying this operator to the consumption equation (2.11) yields

$$\tilde{\Delta}_\tau \varepsilon_{ikt} = \tilde{\Delta}_\tau c_{ikt} - \tilde{\Delta}_\tau z'_{ikt} \delta, \tag{2.22}$$

which no longer involves the time-dependent intercepts.

The following $(T-1)M$ orthogonality conditions

$$E\left[\sum_{k=1}^{K} \sum_{t=1}^{T-\tau} \tilde{\Delta}_\tau x_{ikt} \cdot (\tilde{\Delta}_\tau c_{ikt} - \tilde{\Delta}_\tau z'_{ikt} \delta) \right] = 0 \quad (\tau = 1, 2, \ldots, T-1), \tag{2.23}$$

which are obtained from (2.21b) by replacing the operator Δ_τ by $\tilde{\Delta}_\tau$ and eliminating time dummies, hold because they are linear combinations of the zero moments in (2.16). We test the null hypothesis of family risk sharing by forming the GMM chi-square statistic for the overidentifying restrictions implied by (2.23).

9.2.8 Treatment of Unbalanced Panel

It is now easy to show how to adapt our orthogonality conditions—(2.21) under full risk sharing and (2.23) under family risk sharing—to an unbalanced panel of different family types. We first describe the procedure and then make some remarks.

If household-year (k, t) is missing, we cannot calculate the changes that use this household-year, $\Delta_\tau \xi_{ikt}$ and $\Delta_\tau \xi_{i,k,t-\tau}$ $(\tau = 1, \ldots, T-1)$, for any variable ξ. We replace those incalculable changes by zeros, so that the sum in (2.21) is defined for any family type. Then, under this redefinition of the sum, (2.21) holds for any given family type, because it is a linear

Table 9.1
Examples of Family Types

	Panel A			Panel B		
	$k = 1$	$k = 2$	$k = 3$	$k = 1$	$k = 2$	$k = 3$
$t = 1$	✓	✓	n.a.	✓	✓	n.a.
$t = 2$	✓	✓	✓	n.a.	✓	✓
$t = 3$	✓	n.a.	✓	✓	n.a.	✓

combination of the zero moments in (2.16).[15] Therefore, the expectation, *un*conditional on the particular family type, of the sum in (2.21) is zero, so that orthogonality conditions (2.21) hold for all families in the unbalanced panel.

Similarly for (2.23), if we redefine the time-difference/fixed-effect operator $\tilde{\Delta}_\tau$ to be the deviation from the average over member households for which the time-difference can be calculated (see below for an example), the transformed consumption equation (2.22) still holds. With this redefinition of the transformation $\tilde{\Delta}_\tau$, orthogonality conditions (2.23) hold under family risk sharing for all families in the unbalanced panel.

To illustrate the formation of the sum in (2.23), consider the family type whose pattern of available household-years is as in panel A of table 9.1. For one-year changes ($\tau = 1$), (2.23) is the expectation of the sum of the following four cross products: $\zeta_{i,1,85}$, $\zeta_{i,2,85}$, $\zeta_{i,1,86}$, and $\zeta_{i,3,86}$, where $\zeta_{ikt} \equiv \tilde{\Delta}_1 x_{ikt} \cdot (\tilde{\Delta}_1 c_{ikt} - \tilde{\Delta}_1 z'_{ikt}\delta)$, and for $\xi = x, c$, and z

$$\tilde{\Delta}_1\xi_{i,1,85} = \Delta_1\xi_{i,1,85} - (\Delta_1\xi_{i,1,85} + \Delta_1\xi_{i,2,85})/2,$$

$$\tilde{\Delta}_1\xi_{i,2,85} = \Delta_1\xi_{i,2,85} - (\Delta_1\xi_{i,1,85} + \Delta_1\xi_{i,2,85})/2,$$

$$\tilde{\Delta}_1\xi_{i,1,86} = \Delta_1\xi_{i,1,86} - (\Delta_1\xi_{i,1,86} + \Delta_1\xi_{i,3,86})/2,$$

$$\tilde{\Delta}_1\xi_{i,3,86} = \Delta_1\xi_{i,3,86} - (\Delta_1\xi_{i,1,86} + \Delta_1\xi_{i,3,86})/2.$$

For two-year changes in (2.23), the sum is set to zero because there is no household pair for which two-year changes are observed over the same period.

Note that if we used only first differences to form orthogonality conditions, we would be unable to exploit information available from households which, for example, are observed every other year. In fact, any family that includes at least one household observed at least two points in time is *informative* in testing full risk sharing, because two observations of the same household are enough to eliminate the time-invariant household-specific factor λ_{ik}. Our test of full risk sharing utilizes *all* such families because the sum in (2.21) is not zero for at least one τ. This is the second benefit from the use of long time-differences, the first being that the orthogonality conditions will fail under the alternative of self-insurance.[16]

Strictly speaking, for family risk sharing, the first benefit is not fully realized in our test. We provide in appendix 9.2 a method to determine, for a general class of linear factor structures including (2.8), which families are informative for testing the factor structure and derive all the available orthogonality conditions for those families. There are certain types of families our test of family risk sharing would miss. For example, consider the family type in panel B of table 1. This family is informative because the following transformation eliminates the marginal utilities under (2.8b): $(\theta_{i,1,87} - \theta_{i,1,85}) - (\theta_{i,2,86} - \theta_{i,2,85}) - (\theta_{i,3,87} - \theta_{i,3,86}) = (p_{i,87} - p_{i,85}) - (p_{i,86} - p_{i,85}) - (p_{i,87} - p_{i,86}) = 0$. But such families are missed by our test because the sum in (2.23) for this family type is zero.[17] However, in practice, our test misses no informative families because our particular sample of 1,300 families includes no families for which the sum is set to zero.

9.3   The Data

The original 1968 PSID sample contained 2,930 households representative of the U.S. population.[18] This PSID wave as well as all subsequent waves through 1989 are available in the 1989 PSID CD-ROM. Using this CD-ROM, we created two panels. The first panel covers the three wave years 1985–87. This choice of years maximizes the number of split-offs and also provides us with data on hours worked concurrent with food, data that are available only in those wave years.[19] The other panel is one that closely matches the panel of original households used by Altug and Miller (1990, henceforth AM) and covers the wave years 1968–81. We examine this panel to reproduce, as closely as possible, the findings by AM and to highlight the difference our methodology makes. We briefly describe each sample in turn.

9.3.1   The 1985–87 Panel

The sample selection procedure detailed in appendix 9.1, when applied to the three waves of the PSID, yields 2,253 continuously married house-

Table 9.2
Enumeration of Families by Type, 1985–87 Panel

	# parent households			
	0	1	2	Total
# child split-offs = 0	0	554	15	569
# child split-offs = 1	166	255	7	428
# child split-offs = 2	56	137	2	195
# child split-offs ⩾ 3	33	74	1	108
Total	255	1,020	25	1,300

holds whose husband or wife (or both) was in one of 1,300 original households as a head, a spouse, or a child. Those households, some of which are observed for less than three years during 1985–87, represent 5,863 household-years, and can be divided between original households headed during 1986–87 by the original head and split-offs. A split-off is either a household whose head or spouse is an initial child (to be referred to as a *child split-off*) or a household of a divorced wife. We refer to the latter type of split-offs and original households collectively as *parent households*. Table 9.2 divides these 1,300 families by the number of parent households and child split-offs, and figure 9.1 presents the frequency distribution of household-years. The most frequently observed family type is families with three household-years, virtually all of which are families of just one household observed for all three years.

Panel A of table 9.3 lists and describes our key variables, and reports their sample statistics. The important features of these variables, which are described in more detail in appendix 9.1, are the following. (1) Judging from the PSID questionnaire, the period over which food consumption (FOOD) is reported appears to be the month before the interview, which took place in March, April, or May for most households. Hours worked per week (HRSH, HRSW), which is available only for wave years 85, 86, and 87, is defined as the average hours worked per week during the year of the wave up through the date of the interview. It is thus reasonable to suppose that data on food and leisure (calculated as 168 hours less hours worked per week) available from wave year t are *concurrent*, covering roughly the same period of a few months within calendar year t. For this reason the leisure in this panel will be called *current leisure*. (2) We use a measure of the husband's potential wage rate (WAGEH) to serve as an indicator of the household's resources. In the majority of cases (56% of

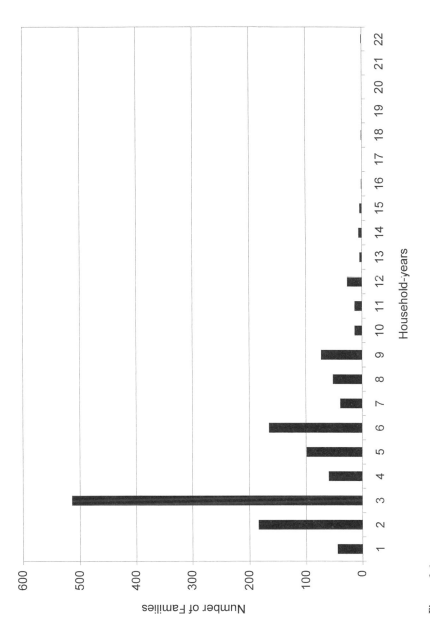

Figure 9.1
Frequency of household-years.

household-years for parents and 84% for children), the husband's hourly wage rate from either the current or the last job is directly measured at the time of the interview, and we use it as WAGEH. Otherwise WAGEH is the hourly rate calculated from the *previous* year's annual labor income (or pension income if the husband is retired) and annual hours worked (set to 2,000 if the husband is retired), also available from wave year t. This still leaves a substantial fraction of household-years (about 15%) without WAGEH. Virtually all of them are from retired households. If WAGEH is missing for the year for the household, we set it to the average of available wage rates for the household.[20]

Since the PSID is a sample of families, not households, there can be a correlation between households within families. Comparison of the total and within-family variances of consumption and the wage rate in Panel B of table 9.3 indicates the extent of commonality within families. For both consumption and the wage rate, the within-family variance is considerably smaller for levels than for changes. A common factor that is present in levels disappears in changes.

9.3.2   The 1968–81 Panel

This second panel was chosen to include original households whose head was no older than 46 in the initial year, continuously in the survey, continuously married, and worked every year. The excellent data appendix of AM allowed us to follow their sample selection procedure and variable construction. However, we were not able to reproduce their sample exactly: we produced a panel of 469 original households, whereas the panel used by AM has 434. Appendix 9.1 records the discrepancy in each of the steps of the sample selection procedure. The sample statistics for this panel is not reported here because they are similar to those reported in table 9.1 of AM.

Notable features of AM's variable construction for the 1968–81 panel, which we followed, are the following. Leisure and the wage rate are calculated differently from the procedures we used in the 1985–87 panel and are based on *annual* hours worked and labor income in the previous year, which are available in all waves. That is, annual hours worked in year t (available from wave year $t + 1$) are used for calculating leisure (as 8,760 hours less annual hours worked) for year t, and the ratio of annual labor income to annual hours worked in year t (available from wave year $t + 1$) is the wage rate for year t. Thus, the same variable (annual hours worked) is used for constructing annual leisure and the wage rate for the same

Table 9.3
Descriptive Statistics, 1985–87 Panel

Panel A: List of Key Variables and their Simple Statistics

		1,300 Families			
		Parents (1,070 households)		Children (1,183 households)	
		2,828		3,035	
		Mean	Std. dev.	Mean	Std. dev.
Variable	Description				
	Sample size (number of household-years)				
AGE	age of household husband	57.1	12.5	32.4	6.1
HSZ	# persons in household	2.9	1.2	3.6	1.2
NADLT	# persons older than 17 years of age	2.3	0.65	2.0	0.24
NKID5	# persons aged 5 or less	0.06	0.28	0.75	0.84
NKID13	# persons aged 6–13	0.22	0.57	0.72	0.92
NKID17	# persons aged 14–17	0.25	0.53	0.14	0.43
FOOD	current food expenditure at annual rate, in 1987 dollars	$4,980	$2,469	$4,813	$2,056
INCOME	annual income in previous year, in 1987 dollars	$43,492	$37,815	$38,720	$26,236
WAGEH	current hourly wage rate, husband (excludes missing household-years)	$13.8	$10.3	$11.8	$8.4
HRSH	current hours worked per week, husband	28.4	23.6	42.0	15.1
HRSW	current hours worked per week, wife	15.9	18.7	23.1	18.6
WKSUH	fraction of weeks unemployed in current year to interview date, husband	0.022	0.13	0.039	0.16
WKSUW	fraction of weeks unemployed in current year to interview date, wife	0.014	0.10	0.028	0.14
HLTH	1 if husband's health is "excellent" or "very good," 0 otherwise	0.50	0.50	0.77	0.42
HLTW	1 if wife's health is "excellent" or "very good," 0 otherwise	0.48	0.50	0.70	0.46

Panel B: Total and Within-Family Variances of Consumption and Wage[a]

	# families with at least two households with relevant level or change	# households with relevant level or change	log FOOD		log WAGEH	
			Total	Within	Total	Within
Level, 1985	484	1,237	0.189	0.162	0.318	0.249
Level, 1986	491	1,251	0.179	0.154	0.309	0.244
Level, 1987	486	1,243	0.190	0.158	0.320	0.237
Change, 1985–86	418	1,044	0.103	0.098	0.071	0.071
Change, 1986–87	420	1,044	0.097	0.099	0.076	0.076
Change, 1985–87	400	994	0.117	0.115	0.093	0.101

a. For any variable, if ξ_{ikt} is its value for household k from family i for year t, its within-family variance for year t is $\Sigma_i \Sigma_k (\xi_{ikt} - \bar{\xi}_i t)^2 / (\Sigma_i K_{it} - N_t)$ where $\bar{\xi}_{it}$ is the mean of ξ_{ikt} over k, K_{it} is the number of households available in year t in family i, and N_t is the number of families with $K_{it} \geq 2$. Since the families included in the calculation are those with at least two member households, the number of families and households differ across rows. For the level of consumption and the wage rate in 1985, for example, $N_t = 484$ and $\Sigma_i K_{it} = 1,237$. The within-family variance can be greater than the total variance due to sampling error. Estimated wage rate is used for household-years with missing wage rates.

year. Since the error term ε_{ikt} in the consumption equation (2.11) includes measurement error in annual hours worked when annual leisure thus constructed is used for the leisure variable in the consumption equation, the wage rate is correlated with the error term. This is taken into account in forming orthogonality conditions. To align consumption with leisure derived from annual hours worked, AM calculates annual food consumption for year t as 25 percent of FOOD from wave year t plus 75 percent of FOOD from wave year $t + 1$.[21] Therefore, in order to calculate all relevant variables for a year, one needs two successive PSID waves. This, by itself, does not lead to a loss of sample size because the panel is balanced in the first place. In contrast, in the 1985–87 panel, values of food and other variables for the same year are available from a single wave.

9.4   Results

We now report results from our tests of full risk sharing using the 1968–81 panel of original households and the 1985–87 panel of original and split-off households. After rejecting full risk sharing in both data sets, we use the 1985–87 panel to test the weaker hypothesis of family risk sharing.

9.4.1   Testing Full Risk Sharing Using the 1968–81 Panel of 469 Original Households

Most of the results reported in table 9.2 of AM pertain to the orthogonality conditions derived from three equations—the consumption equation, which is similar to ours, a wage equation, and an equation of the equality of the marginal rate of substitution between food consumption and leisure with the wage rate. However, AM (see p. 560 of AM) also reports the chi-square statistic for the orthogonality conditions of the form (2.18a) and (2.18b) derived from the consumption equation alone. It uses eight first-differences in log annual food consumption, 69–70, 70–71, 74–75, ..., 79–80.[22] We start by reproducing, as closely as possible, AM's findings. We then depart from AM's specification by including the 71–74 consumption change, consolidating orthogonality conditions, specifying demographics in more detail, and using orthogonality conditions that have more power against self-insurance.

In AM's specification, household size (HSZ) is the only demographic variable and husband's leisure is excluded in the consumption equation, so the $\Delta_1 z_{i1t}$ in the equation (2.17) of the (log) consumption change from t to $t + 1$ is the change in HSZ and the change in the wife's log annual leisure.

The instruments are the 13 variables specified as set A in the note to table 9.4. This set includes the (log) wage rate for $t - 1$ and $t - 2$ but not for t or $t + 1$ because of the correlation between the wage rate and the error term ε_{ikt} mentioned in section 9.3.2. The orthogonality conditions can be written as (2.18a) and (2.18b) where the "$\Delta_1 x_{i1t}$" is understood to be the level of the 13 variables. With 8 consumption changes and 13 instruments, there are 112 orthogonality conditions, 8 from (2.18a) and 8 × 13 from (2.18b). The number of parameters are the eight time-dependent intercepts (the π in (2.18)) and the two coefficients δ of $\Delta_1 z_{i1t}$. So the degrees of freedom total 102.

Column 1 of table 9.4 reports our estimate of δ along with the chi-square statistic.[23] The wife's leisure coefficient, which is the ρ_w in the subutility function (2.9), is estimated to be -0.41. A negative value for the parameter ρ_w is consistent with the concavity of the instantaneous utility function, but it is at odds with the interpretation of the subutility as the household production function of a meal with the wife's leisure as an input. Since our sample consists only of married couples with or without children, changes in the household size are mostly due to changes in the number of (adult or nonadult) children in the household. Thus our estimate of the ΔHSZ coefficient of 0.051 in column 1 implies that an additional child increases household food consumption by 5.1 percent. The chi-square statistic of 118.7 with a p-value of 12.3 percent, although not representing a strong rejection, is substantially greater than the value of 90 (whose p-value is 80%) reported in AM, partially (but not entirely) due to the fact that our sample size is 469, while that of AM is 434.

This rather weak evidence against full risk sharing, however, is not robust to the departures we examined. The specification in column 2 adds the 71–74 change, increasing the number of consumption changes (and hence the number of time-dependent intercepts) by one and the number of orthogonality conditions by 14. This reduces the p-value from 12.3 percent to 0.044 percent. The small sample property of the test statistic with this many orthogonality conditions may, however, be poor. Column 3 uses the consolidated orthogonality conditions (2.19) (where the $\Delta_1 x_{i1t}$ is still the level of 13 instruments) to reduce the number of orthogonality conditions to 22 (9 from (2.18a) and 13 from (2.19)). This consolidation of orthogonality conditions produces an even lower p-value. Consolidation without the 71–74 change (whose results are not reported in the table) also produced a fairly strong rejection with a p-value of 0.506 percent, which should be compared to the p-value in column 1.

The rejection might be due to possible endogeneity of some instruments. To check this, we omit house value in t and $t + 1$ and rent in t and

Table 9.4
Test of Full Risk Sharing Using Original Households, 1968–81 Panel

	1	2	3	4	5	6	7	8	9
Orthogonality conditions	(2.18a,b)	(2.18a,b)	(2.18a,19)	(2.18a,19)	(2.18a,19)	(2.18a,19)	(2.18a,19)	(2.20a,b)	(2.20a,b)[a]
Long changes used?	no	no	no	no	no	no	no	yes	yes
Consolidation of orth. conditions	none	none	over t	over t	over t	over t	over t	over t	over t, τ
71–74 change used?	no	yes	yes	yes	yes	yes	yes	yes	yes
Instruments (Δx_{ilt})[b]	set A	set A	set A	set B	set C	set D	set E	set E	set E
Estimated coefficient of:[c]									
ΔHSZ [# persons in household]	0.051 (0.0059)	0.057 (0.0053)	0.065 (0.0072)	0.071 (0.0074)	0.050 (0.0078)	—	—	—	—
ΔNADLT [# adults]	—	—	—	—	—	0.048 (0.0086)	0.047 (0.0086)	0.055 (0.0073)	0.084 (0.010)
ΔNKID5 [# persons aged 0–5]	—	—	—	—	—	0.043 (0.014)	0.041 (0.014)	0.049 (0.012)	0.054 (0.018)
ΔNKID13 [# persons aged 6–13]	—	—	—	—	—	0.044 (0.012)	0.047 (0.012)	0.053 (0.0087)	0.067 (0.011)
ΔNKID17 [# persons aged 14–17]	—	—	—	—	—	0.064 (0.0094)	0.067 (0.0095)	0.074 (0.0075)	0.096 (0.0092)
ΔAGE^2/100	—	—	—	—	−0.095 (0.015)	−0.092 (0.016)	−0.086 (0.016)	−0.055 (0.0098)	−0.060 (0.012)
Δlog husband's annual leisure	—	—	—	—	—	0.15 (0.25)	0.033 (0.26)	−0.24 (0.17)	0.29 (0.24)
Δlog wife's annual leisure	−0.41 (0.14)	−0.36 (0.11)	−0.77 (0.17)	−0.72 (0.16)	−0.48 (0.17)	−0.47 (0.18)	−0.49 (0.18)	−0.38 (0.13)	−0.26 (0.20)

# orthogonality conditions	112	126	22	15	14	18	17	81	17
χ^2	118.7	172.2	61.4	44.5	5.9	6.1	9.5	93.7	22.9
Degrees of freedom	102	115	11	4	2	2	1	65	1
p-value (%)	12.322%	0.044%	0.000%	0.000%	5.320%	4.798%	0.211%	1.136%	0.000%

a. The orthogonality conditions in (2.20b) are aggregated over τ.

b. The set of instruments (besides time dummies) is

Set A: HSZ_{t-1t}, $HSZ_{t-1,t,t+1}$, husband's experience in year $t+1$, its square, log husband's wage in years $t-1$ and $t-2$, log wife's wage in year $t-1$ (set to 0 if the wife does not work), log wife's annual leisure in years $t-1$ and $t-2$, log value of homeowner's house in years t and $t+1$ (set to 0 if not a homeowner), log rent in years t and $t+1$ (set to 0 if not a renter) (13 instruments).

Set B: ΔHSZ from year t to $t+1$, husband's experience in year $t+1$, its square, log wife's annual leisure in year $t+1$, log husband's wage in years $t-1$ and $t-2$ (6 instruments).

Set C: ΔHSZ from year t to $t+1$, ΔAGE^2 from year t to $t+1$, log wife's annual leisure in year $t-1$, log husband's annual leisure in years $t-1$ and $t-2$ (5 instruments).

Set D: $\Delta NADLT$, $\Delta NKID5$, $\Delta NKID13$, $\Delta NKID17$, ΔAGE^2, all from year t to $t+1$, log husband's annual leisure in year $t-1$, log wife's annual leisure in year $t-1$, log husband's wage in year $t-1$ and $t-2$ (9 instruments).

Set E: $\Delta NADLT$, $\Delta NKID5$, $\Delta NKID13$, $\Delta NKID17$, ΔAGE^2, all from year t to $t+\tau$, log husband's annual leisure in year $t-1$, log wife's annual leisure in year $t-1$, log husband's wage in year $t-1$ (8 instruments) $\tau=1$ for column 7. τ ranges from 1 to 9 in columns 8 and 9. For this panel, following AM, we take the value of all variables except annual food for year t from wave year $t+1$. As explained in the text, annual food for year t is derived from wave years t and $t+1$.

c. Standard errors in parentheses. Estimated time-dependent intercepts are not reported.

$t + 1$ from the list of instruments for the equation of the (log) consumption change from t to $t + 1$. We also omit the wife's wage in $t - 1$ and the wife's annual leisure in $t - 2$ because their correlation with changes in the wife's annual leisure is very weak. We also combine HSZ in t and $t + 1$ into a single variable Δ_1HSZ. This rather drastic realignment, which reduces the number of instruments from 13 to 6, makes no difference to the test results, as shown in column 4.

The strong rejection, however, gets overturned when we include the change in AGE^2 in the consumption equation, as reported in column 5.[24] The coefficient of $\Delta_1 AGE^2$ is highly significant, and full risk sharing cannot be rejected even at a significance level of 5 percent. Column 6 shows that including the change in the (log) husband's annual leisure and expanding demographics by replacing household size with the number of adults (NADLT which, as mentioned above, is essentially the number of children over 17) and the age distribution of nonadult children (NKID5, NKID13, NKID17) produce similar results. It is interesting and reassuring to note that the impact of children on household food is largest for teenagers. The husband leisure coefficient is not precisely estimated.

Thus, there is not much evidence against full risk sharing when appropriate demographic controls are included. This is true even after the orthogonality conditions are consolidated and the 71–74 consumption change is incorporated. However, this is not surprising because the consumption change is paired with lagged wage rates, but not with *future* wage rates. As we remarked in section 9.2.4, the test of full risk sharing using lagged wages, as formulated in column 6, has no power because the same orthogonality conditions hold under the alternative hypothesis of self-insurance.[25] In fact, the model in column 6 *is* a test of self-insurance insofar as it tests that the change in consumption, adjusted for demographics and leisure, is uncorrelated with current and lagged values. Its chi-square statistic shows that we fail to reject self-insurance.

Our next specification, then, replaces lagged wage rates in $t - 1$ and $t - 2$ with the "bracketing" wage change from $t - 1$ to $t + 2$. We do not use the wage change concurrent with the adjusted consumption change because of the correlation with the error term mentioned earlier for this panel. As reported in column 7, this change of instruments makes an important difference. Now full risk sharing is rejected with a p-value of 0.211 percent. The specification in column 8 forces the orthogonality conditions to further depend on the correlation of the current consumption change with future wage rate changes by including long differences.[26] With the same 8 instruments as in column 7, there are 81 orthogonality conditions, 9 from (2.20a) and 9×8 from (2.20b). The p-value rises to

1.136 percent. Again, its small sample distribution may be poor. If we further consolidate orthogonality conditions by aggregating (2.20b) over τ (the length of changes), the rejection gets very strong, as shown in column 9. The effect of demographics is larger than in other columns. This can be explained as follows. By aggregating over τ, we assign greater weights to orthogonality conditions corresponding to long changes than in column 8 and certainly columns 1–7 (where the weight is zero). The garbling effect on consumption changes of the moving-average operation in calculating the level of annual food mentioned in section 9.3.2 is less severe for long changes.

We conclude that when we use orthogonality conditions that have power against the alternative of self-insurance, there is strong evidence against full risk sharing.

9.4.2 Testing Full Risk Sharing Using the 1985–87 Panel

We now turn to the 1985–87 panel of original and split-off households and apply our technique for unbalanced panels to test full risk sharing. Our choice of the right-hand-side variables and instruments for this panel is different in several respects from that for the previous panel and exploits the greater availability of variables. First, we use for leisure the *current* leisure derived from HRSH and HRSW (see table 9.3 for definition), and accordingly use FOOD itself, rather than the moving average of it, for food consumption. Thus food and leisure are directly measured and concurrent. As in the previous specification, the change in (log) leisure from year t to $t + \tau$ is instrumented by the level of annual leisure in year $t - 1$. Second, WAGEH is the measure of the wage rate. It is directly measured for the majority of household-years and may be a better indicator of household resources. Third, we are able to control for health by including indicators of health as part of demographics. Our test would be invalid absent the inclusion of consumption taste shifters that are correlated with instruments. The prime candidate for such variables is health, and indeed our health dummies (HLTH, HLTW) are very strongly related to the wage rate. Fourth, for this panel with no age restriction, we add ΔAGE^3 to account for possible nonlinear effects of age on consumption changes.

To make clear the connection to the previous specifications and also to highlight the effect of including the unbalanced data later on, we first test, in column 1 of table 9.5, the same orthogonality conditions (2.20) as in column 8 of table 9.4, using the subsample that includes only original households continuously observed for all three years. The instruments are the set E' specified in the note to table 9.5. In this set, the change in the

Table 9.5
Full Risk Sharing, Self-Insurance, and Family Risk Sharing, 1985–87 Panel

	1	2	3	4	5
Orthogonality conditions	(2.20)	(2.21)	(2.21)	(2.21)	(2.23)
Null hypothesis tested	full risk sharing	full risk sharing	full risk sharing	self-insurance	fam. risk sharing
Subsample used	original households	original and households	original and split-offs	original and split-offs	original and split-offs
Time-balanced?	yes	no	no	no	no
# families	697	1,251	1,251	1,251	500
# households	697	2,066	2,066	2,066	1,298
# one-year changes	1,394	3,473	3,473	3,473	—
# two-year changes	697	1,681	1,681	1,681	—
Instruments (Δz_{ikt})[a]	set E′	set E′	set F	set F	set E′
Estimated coefficient of:[b]					
ΔNADLT	0.093	0.097	0.095	0.10	0.066
[# adults]	(0.019)	(0.016)	(0.016)	(0.016)	(0.034)
ΔNKID5	0.099	0.071	0.062	0.072	0.039
[# persons aged 0–5]	(0.055)	(0.021)	(0.023)	(0.021)	(0.031)
ΔNKID13	0.065	0.093	0.087	0.097	0.064
[# persons aged 6–13]	(0.033)	(0.018)	(0.019)	(0.019)	(0.030)
ΔNKID17	0.13	0.12	0.12	0.12	0.070
[# persons aged 14–17]	(0.027)	(0.019)	(0.019)	(0.019)	(0.035)
ΔAGE^2/100	−0.035	0.006	0.001	0.009	−0.002
	(0.049)	(0.030)	(0.026)	(0.028)	(0.033)
ΔAGE^3/1000	0.025	−0.016	−0.011	−0.018	−0.038
	(0.037)	(0.024)	(0.022)	(0.022)	(0.034)

ΔHLTH [husband in good health]	0.051 (0.018)	0.031 (0.011)	0.025 (0.011)	0.028 (0.011)	0.001 (0.019)
ΔHLTW [wife in good health]	0.037 (0.017)	0.020 (0.011)	0.020 (0.011)	0.022 (0.011)	0.014 (0.017)
Δlog husband's current leisure	0.04 (0.35)	−0.04 (0.19)	−0.47 (0.13)	−0.19 (0.20)	−0.31 (0.25)
Δlog wife's current leisure	−0.38 (0.45)	−0.40 (0.22)	−0.24 (0.29)	−0.32 (0.22)	−0.16 (0.26)
# orthogonality conditions	24	24	24	24	22
χ^2	20.0	30.4	31.6	20.2	28.9
Degrees of freedom	12	12	12	12	12
P-value (%)	6.724%	0.242%	0.157%	6.374%	0.412%

a. The set of instruments (besides time dummies) is
Set E': ΔNADLT, ΔNKID5, ΔNKID13, ΔNKID17, ΔAGE^2, ΔAGE^3, ΔHLTH, ΔHLTW, previous year's log annual leisure for husband and wife, Δlog(WAGEH) (11 instruments).
Set F: ΔNADLT, ΔNKID5, ΔNKID13, ΔNKID17, ΔAGE^2, ΔAGE^3, ΔHLTH, ΔHLTW, ΔWKSUH, ΔWKSUW, Δlog(WAGEH) (11 instruments).
Set G: ΔNADLT, ΔNKID5, ΔNKID13, ΔNKID17, ΔAGE^2, ΔAGE^3, ΔHLTH, ΔHLTW, previous year's log annual leisure for husband and wife, log(WAGEH) for year t (11 instruments).
b. Estimated time-dependent intercepts are not reported for columns 1–4. Standard errors in parentheses.

(log) wage rate is now concurrent with the change in current leisure, rather than the "bracketing" change in the previous specifications, because variables used for constructing current leisure in this panel are not used for constructing the wage measure. With 11 instruments and three time-periods, the number of orthogonality conditions is 24 (2 from (2.20a) and 2×11 from (2.20b)). With two time-dependent intercepts and 10 right-hand-side variables, the degrees of freedom are 12. Parameters are less precisely estimated here than in table 9.4, reflecting the shortness of the current panel. Household composition (NADLT, NKID5–NKID17) has larger effects, most likely due to the fact that the food variable here is not a moving average. The health dummies are significant and have the right sign. The small chi-square statistic illustrates the difficulty of rejecting full risk sharing based only on original households.

If we expand the sample of original households by including 216 additional original households observed two, but not three, points in time, the parameter estimates in this time-unbalanced panel of original households are very similar and are hence not reported in the table. The p-value falls to 4.815 percent.

In the next specification in column 2, split-offs are included, so the relevant orthogonality conditions are those in (2.21). This is the largest possible sample available from the 1985–87 PSID: 2,066 households from 1,251 families who were observed at two or more points in time. Because the sample now includes split-offs whose heads are much younger, the age coefficients change their signs, reflecting the nonlinear effect of age on consumption changes. We can now reject full risk sharing fairly decisively. Here is a benefit of including all possible family types in the sample.

We have used the previous year's annual leisure to instrument the change in current leisure for husband and wife. To check robustness with respect to the choice of instruments, we also tried the concurrent changes in the number of weeks unemployed (WKSUH, WKSUW, see table 9.3 for definition) as instruments. There is evidence in the literature that unemployment is exogenous (see Ham (1986)). This, however, does not mean that WKSUH and WKSUW are valid instruments, because they also depend on participation that may well be correlated with unobservable preference shifters. But this problem is mitigated by our use of changes rather than levels as instruments. With these caveats, the chi-square statistic in column 3 represents an equally strong rejection. The leisure coefficients are still imprecisely estimated. If leisure is treated as exogenous, the leisure coefficients for husband and wife are -0.29 and -0.11

with much lower standard errors of 0.054 and 0.052, respectively. Estimates of other coefficients are very similar, and the p-value of the chi-square statistic is 0.036 percent. Apparently the choice of instruments for changes in current leisure does not affect the test of full risk sharing.[27]

The next specification in column 4 differs from that in column 2 in that the change in the wage rate from t to $t + \tau$ ($\tau = 1, 2$) in the instrument set is replaced by the level in t. Since the current wage rate is known in date t, the orthogonality condition (2.21) holds under self-insurance.[28] The chi-square statistic shows that we fail to reject self-insurance in this panel also. However, the estimated subutility function with negative leisure coefficients, although meeting the usual concavity requirement, is hard to rationalize. As already mentioned, it does not admit the interpretation of the subutility as a household production function of a meal. A more natural interpretation of the negative leisure coefficient may be that the sample includes households prevented from self-insurance due to liquidity constraints: households who have exhausted assets to serve as a cushion would respond to exogenously reduced hours (hence an increase in leisure) by decreasing consumption. For these households, the leisure-adjusted consumption change may be uncorrelated with the wage rate before the onset of the liquidity constraint. In this case, the test of self-insurance has no power against liquidity constraints.

9.4.3 Family Risk Sharing

We turn to the test of family risk sharing using the orthogonality conditions (2.23). In this sample of 1,300 families, there are only 500 families that are informative in testing the factor structure implied by family risk sharing. The reduction of the sample size is mainly due to exclusion of original households without split-offs, which also explains why the average age of head in this smaller sample is considerably lower (by about 5 years). Our test misses no informative families because for each informative family in the sample the sum in (2.23) is nonzero for some τ ($= 1, 2$). With no time-dependent intercepts to be estimated, the number of parameters is 10, and the degrees of freedom equal 12. Parameter estimates as well as the chi-square statistic are not sensitive to the choice of instruments for leisure changes, so we report in column 5 of table 9.5 the results with lagged annual leisure serving as instruments.

Family risk sharing differs from full risk sharing in allowing for the family-specific component (p_{it} in (2.8b)) in consumption changes. However, the comparison between total and within-family variances in panel B

of table 9.3 has revealed the unimportance of the family-specific component. It is not surprising, then, that family risk-sharing is rejected in column 5 almost as strongly as full risk sharing is in column 2, despite the
considerably smaller sample size. This corroborates the result in Altonji,
Hayashi, and Kotlikoff (1992, table 3), which use the 1976–85 waves of
the PSID, that the effect of income changes is significant in the regression
of consumption changes on contemporaneous changes in income allowing
for the family fixed effect. Our results show that family risk sharing can be
rejected even after allowing for nonseparability of consumption and leisure and the endogeneity of leisure. This is true even though restricting
the sample to the 1985–87 period in which consistent data on wages,
hours, and consumption are available results in a much smaller sample
than that used in Altonji, Hayashi, and Kotlikoff (1992). Our method
permits us to make up for the loss of sample size by exploiting additional
orthogonality conditions implied by the null.

9.4.4 Additional Tests of Risk Sharing

Our results constitute strong evidence against full or family risk sharing.
But the chi-squared statistic does not tell us how much (or little) risk
sharing there is. Previous authors used the "variable addition" method to
test full risk sharing by appending income changes in the consumption
equation. In Nelson (1994), for example, the (log) income change has a coefficient of 0.04 with a standard error of 0.02 in the regression of the (log)
food consumption change. However, if leisure is endogenous or if food
consumption and leisure are nonseparable, the income change can be significant even under full risk sharing. For the 1985–87 panel, the change in
(log) wage rate does not have this problem. If we append $\Delta \log(\text{WAGEH})$
to the right-hand side of the consumption equation in the specification in
column 2 of table 9.5, it picks up a coefficient of 0.076 with a standard
error of 0.023. The p-value rises from 0.242 percent without the addition
of $\Delta \log(\text{WAGEH})$ to 4.192 percent, which suggests that the concurrent
wage change does not explain all the change in the marginal utility. The
wage change coefficient rises to 0.136 with a standard error of 0.038
when $\Delta \log(\text{WAGEH})$ is added to the specification for family risk sharing
in column 5 of table 9.5. This can be explained by the fact that the sample
for column 5 is considerably younger; the wage rate is probably a better
measure of household resources for young households than for older
households.

9.5   Conclusion

We have tested whether households fully share risk across or within families using the Panel Study of Income Dynamics. Our test accommodates nonseparability of food consumption and leisure as well as endogenous leisure. Our findings can be summarized as follows. First, contrary to AM's results, we reject full interfamily risk sharing using data from early waves of the PSID, provided we include in the test the restrictions that may fail under the alternative of self-insurance. Second, if we require that consistent data on food, hours, and wages be used for testing, the sample from the PSID is restricted to a short period of 1985–87. Nevertheless, our method, using all the informative families of the sample, produced a fairly strong rejection of both inter- and intrafamily risk sharing. Third, we cannot reject the hypothesis of self-insurance. However, the estimated interaction of consumption and leisure may be more naturally explained by the existence of liquidity-constrained households in the sample.

Our result that there is no full insurance even among related households should serve as a final blow to the complete market paradigm. Rejecting full insurance, however, does not necessarily mean that there is no risk sharing at all between households. Future research should be directed to estimating the extent of consumption insurance over and above self-insurance. The result in section 9.4.4 that the correlation between the leisure-adjusted consumption change and the wage change is larger for younger households is consistent with the view that the bulk of consumption insurance is due to self-insurance. Our finding that a common factor within families that is present in the level of household consumption cannot be found in consumption changes reinforces this view.

Appendix 9.1: Data Description

The 1985–87 Panel

Households and Families
The 1989 PSID CD-ROM has separate single-year household files (referred to as family files in the PSID) and a cross-year individual file. The single-year household files contain household-level variables collected in each wave, and the single cross-year individual file contains individual-level variables collected from 1968 to 1989 for all individuals who were

ever in the survey. Using the cross-year individual file, we select from the single-year household file households whose head or spouse (1) is in the household in the survey year, (2) was either a head, spouse, or a child in the initial survey, and (3) was in a household in the nonpoverty sample of the initial 1968 survey. We do this for each of the sample survey years 1985–87 to create a file of 11,039 household-years. By construction we can associate each household-year in the file with a unique initial member, an individual who was in an initial household. (If both head and spouse of a household-year are initial members, we pick the initial member associated with the head.) A *household* is defined as a set of household-years associated with the same initial member, and a *family* is a set of households whose associated members are from the same initial household. The 1985–87 waves of the PSID yield 3,917 households from 1,819 families. We define an *original household* to be a household associated with an initial head, whereas a *split-off* is a household that is not an original household. A split-off can either be a household associated with a divorced wife or a *child split-off* associated with an initial child. A *parent household* is either an original household or a household of a divorced wife.

Sample Selection
From the file of 11,039 cases (household-years) we drop the following cases.

Female-headed Married Couples
In the PSID the husband is defined as the head. There are 19 cases in which the wife is the head, with no information about the husband.

Singles
We deleted singles and couples with changes in marital status during 1985–87 and kept only married couples without marital status changes, resulting in a loss of 4,251 cases and leaving us with a sample of 6,769 cases (household-years).

Cases with Missing Values
We delete 16 cases for which the husband's age or the date of interview is missing. We then delete 102 cases with either missing values or data inaccuracy flags for food components, and 609 cases with missing values for relevant variables needed to construct hours worked (HRSH and HRSW defined below).

Extreme Cases

We delete 9 cases for which either annual food expenditure (food at home and away from home, plus the value of food stamps) ⩽ $52, or weekly hours worked ⩾ 120 for husband or wife. (There are 3 clear outliers whose food expenditure at home equals $52,000. Inspection of their records led us to conclude that their food values are off by one digit, so we decided to divide their food expenditure at home by 10.) We then delete 63 households accounting for 170 cases such that for either FOOD or WAGEH (see below for definition) its one- or two-year change is greater than 300 percent or less than −75 percent. (This exclusion from the sample of households with extreme changes in FOOD or WAGEH did not affect results. For example, when these households are included, the *p*-values in columns of table 9.5 become: 6.704 percent, 0.289 percent, 0.118 percent, 6.598 percent, and 2.085 percent.)

This leaves us with a sample of 5,863 household-years, 2,253 households from 1,300 families.

Key Variables for Analysis

Age Distribution of Persons 17 Years or Younger (NKID5, NKID13, NKID17)   This information is created from the cross-year individual file. The single-year household files contain similar variables, but they are about children of the head or spouse and exclude unrelated individuals.

Current Food Expenditure (FOOD)   This is the sum of food at home, food away from home, and food stamps, stated at an annual rate. The value of food stamps refers to the value in the month before the interview, which on average is in April but ranges from late February to late November. Food at home and away from home are for an "average week." Since questions on food at home and away from home follow right after those on food stamps in the questionnaire, it is natural to assume that the "average week" is taken by respondents to be one in the month or possibly recent months preceding the interview.

Health Dummies, Husband and Wife (HLTH, HLTW)   The PSID since 1984 contains categorical data on husband's and wife's health ranging from "excellent" to "poor." For husband and wife, a dummy variable is created corresponding to the answers "excellent" and "very good."

Current Hours Worked per Week, Husband and Wife (HRSH, HRSW) For the wave years 1985, 1986, and 1987 only, the PSID collected data on hours worked in the current year of the survey, so that the timing of food and leisure can be roughly matched. From data on the number of weeks worked to the date of the interview and the average hours worked per week conditional on working, we calculate total hours worked up to the interview date. We divide this by the number of weeks to the interview date to obtain average hours worked per week (unconditional on working).

Fraction of Weeks to Date Unemployed or Laid Off, Husband and Wife (WKSUH, WKSUW) There is information available on the number of weeks in the current year up to the date of interview during which the person was unemployed and looking for work or temporarily laid off. This is divided by the number of weeks up to the interview date. For a very few cases in which the number of unemployed weeks is not available (5 cases for the husband and 8 cases for the wife), it is set to 0.

Husband's Current Wage Rate (WAGEH) For most cases, it is the wage rate directly available from the questionnaire. It is the average hourly wage rate in the current year of the survey if the husband is salaried or paid by the hour on the main job, or the hourly wage rate from the last job if the husband is not working but this wage is available. This information is available for 56 percent of household-years for parents and 84 percent for children. Otherwise WAGEH is the hourly wage rate implied by wage income and total hours worked for the previous year (if greater than 10 hours) reported in the current year's survey, or else the previous year's household pension income reported in the current year's survey (divided by total annual work hours of 2,000) for the husband. It is still missing for 30 percent of household-years of parents and 2 percent of children. For most of them, the husband is retired with no reported pension income. The remaining few cases are either that both the current hours worked and the previous year's annual hours worked are zero or that the husband is in family business. For each household with missing WAGEH, we estimate it as follows. For years for which WAGEH is missing, we set it to the average of available wage rates for the household. For example, if the household is observed for 85 and 87 and WAGEH is missing for 85, then it is set to WAGEH for 87. If it is missing for *all* years for which the household is observed (716 cases), we set WAGEH to $12.60 which is the sample mean of WAGEH. The number we assign does not affect parameter estimates and test statistics for those specifications in table 9.5 that use changes in WAGEH. The number we assign does matter for the specification in column 4, which uses the level of WAGEH as an instrument. When we assigned $3 rather than $12.60, the results did not change substantially. The p-value in column 4 of table 9.5 changed from 6.374 percent to 5.658 percent.

The 1968–81 Panel

Altug and Miller (1990) (hereafter AM) created their sample from the 1968–83 cross-year household (family)-individual file available from the 1983 PSID data tapes for current respondents. We used the cross-year individual file and the single-year household files from the 1989 PSID CD-ROM, which is a superset of the 1983 tape, to create our sample. (We produced the same sample we created from the 1989 PSID CD-ROM when we used the 1968–87 cross-year household-individual file available from the 1987 PSID data tapes.) As in AM, we were able to create a file of 6,852 households who responded in the 1983 wave. From there we were able to duplicate AM's sample selection process only up to a point. The following table records discrepancies between AM and our procedure in the losses of households associated with each criterion applied consecutively to the sample of 6,852 households.

The age distribution of persons 17 years or younger was created from the cross-year individual file. This information, though not necessary for replicating AM's results in column 1 of table 9.4, is used for other specifications in the table. For constructing annual food and the husband's age, which are necessary for replicating AM's results, the following features might differ from AM's construction. As mentioned in section 9.3.2, AM defines annual food consumption as an average of food expenditures available from two successive waves. We converted food expenditure for each year into real terms *before* averaging, using the deflator reported in AM. Since the interview date is not fixed across years, the change in husband's age from one year to the next is not necessarily equal to one. We forced the husband's age to increase by one year from one year to the next to be consistent with the fact that consumption and leisure are annual.

There are twenty household-years whose annual food value is missing due to top-coding of food variables in the PSID. Consumption changes that use those household-years are set to zero, as explained in section 9.2.8.

Criterion for Deletion	Losses	
	AM	This chapter
Households in which there occurred a change in either the head or wife during the sixteen-year survey period from 1968 to 1983	4,912	4,912
Households that had been surveyed as part of the poverty sample	765	765
Households that had husbands older than 46 in the 1968 survey year	526	489
Households with missing data for the education of the husband	1	3
Unmarried households	68	73
Households with missing data on the age of youngest child	34	0
Households failing to satisfy the following condition: husband had positive annual hours for every year of the sample period (1968–83), and wife had positive annual hours for at least one year		98
Annual hours were positive but average hourly earnings were zero, or vice versa for some years	112	41
Annual hours exceeded 8760 for some years		0
Average hourly earnings for husband or wife were coded as 9s in 1968, or average hourly earnings coded as 9999 for other years		2
Number of households left	434	469

Appendix 9.2: Derivation of Available Orthogonality Conditions

Derivation for a General Class of Factor Structures

Consider a panel of N observations of length n. For any variable ξ, let an n-dimensional vector ξ_i be the i-th observation from the sample and assume that the following relationship holds:

$$c_i = Z_i\delta + \theta_i + \varepsilon_i \qquad (i = 1, 2, \ldots, N), \tag{A1}$$

where N is the sample size, Z_i is an $n \times q$ matrix of observations of q variables from i. Here θ_i and ε_i are unobservables, but θ_i has a factor structure given by

$$\theta_i = \Gamma\phi_i + G_i\pi, \tag{A2}$$

where ϕ_i is a vector of unobservable factors of dimension smaller than n, Γ a conformable matrix of known constants, G_i a matrix of observables with n rows, and π a conformable vector of constants. Substituting (A2) into (A1), we obtain

$$c_i = \Gamma\phi_i + Z_i\delta + G_i\pi + \varepsilon_i. \tag{A3}$$

We allow the panel to be unbalanced and assume that some rows of $(c_i \, Z_i \, G_i)$ may not be available. Let σ_i be an n-dimensional vector whose j-th element is 1 if the j-th row of $(c_i \, Z_i \, G_i)$ is observable and is 0 otherwise. This σ_i represents the pattern of missing cases. If n_i ($\leqslant n$) is the number of available rows, we define an $n_i \times n$ selection matrix S_i by deleting rows of zeros from an $n \times n$ diagonal matrix whose diagonal is σ_i. So $S_i'S_i = \operatorname{diag}(\sigma_i)$, and, for any variable ξ, $S_i'S_i\xi_i$ is an n-dimensional vector whose elements that are not observable are filled with zeros and $S_i\xi_i$ is an n_i-dimensional vector collecting observable elements of ξ_i.

Let $R(\sigma_i)$ be the matrix of orthonormal vectors spanning the null space of $S_i\Gamma$. That is, if $\operatorname{rank}(S_i\Gamma) \neq n_i$, $R(\sigma_i)$ is an $n_i \times (n_i - \operatorname{rank}(S_i\Gamma))$ matrix such that

$$R(\sigma_i)'R(\sigma_i) = I \text{ and } R(\sigma_i)'S_i\Gamma = 0. \tag{A4}$$

If $\operatorname{rank}(S_i\Gamma) = n_i$, then $R(\sigma_i)$ is an n_i-dimensional vector of zeros. Let $L = n - \operatorname{rank}(\Gamma)$. Then $R(\iota_n)$ is $n \times L$ where ι_n is the n-dimensional vector of ones. We define an $n \times L$ matrix Q_i by

$$Q_i' \equiv R(\iota_n)'S_i'R(\sigma_i)R(\sigma_i)'S_i. \tag{A5}$$

It can be shown that the rank of Q_i is $n_i - \text{rank}(S_i\Gamma)$. Multiplying (A3) from the left by Q_i' and using (A4), we can eliminate the unobservable factors ϕ_i and obtain the following L transformed equations:

$$Q_i'c_i = Q_i'Z_i\delta + Q_i'G_i\pi + Q_i'\varepsilon_i. \tag{A6}$$

Note that, since the last matrix of Q_i' in (A5) is the selection matrix S_i, $(Q_i'c_i, Q_i'Z_i, Q_i'G_i)$ can be calculated from the unbalanced panel.

To generate orthogonality conditions, assume that there exist m exogenous variables, whose observations from i are an $n \times m$ matrix X_i, such that

$$F(X_i \otimes \varepsilon_i | \sigma_i) = 0. \tag{A7}$$

Let $\zeta_i \equiv S_i'S_iX_i \otimes (Q_i'c_i - Q_i'Z_i\delta - Q_i'G_i\pi)$, which is calculable from the unbalanced panel. We show that (A7) implies the following $L \cdot m \cdot n$ available orthogonality conditions:

$$E[\text{vec}(\zeta_i)|\sigma_i] = 0, \text{ and hence } E[\text{vec}(\zeta_i)] = 0. \tag{A8}$$

To show this, note that $\zeta_i = (S_i'S_i \otimes Q_i')(X_i \otimes \varepsilon_i)$ by (A6). Since S_i and Q_i are functions of σ_i, $E(\zeta_i|\sigma_i) = E[(S_i'S_i \otimes Q_i')E(X_i \otimes \varepsilon_i|\sigma_i)] = 0$.

Remark

If the pattern of missing cases σ_i is such that $n_i = \text{rank}(S_i\Gamma)$, then Q_i is a matrix of zeros and ζ_i is 0 for all i with this σ_i. We call such σ_i *uninformative*. If the panel is balanced so that $\sigma_i = \iota_n$ and $S_i = I_n$, then $Q_i = R$ and $\zeta_i = X_i \otimes R'\varepsilon_i$. Since the $n \times L$ matrix R is of full column rank, $E(\mu_i\mu_i'|\sigma_i)$ is nonsingular where $\mu_i = \text{vec}(\zeta_i)$. Therefore, if the probability that $\sigma_i = \iota_n$ is positive, then $E(\mu_i\mu_i')$ is nonsingular.

Special Case of (2.8a) or (2.8b)

In the case considered in the text, elements of ζ_i are household-years (k, t)'s with $n = KT$. Thus σ_i can be interpreted as the *family type*. We order household-years first by $k \ (= 1, \ldots, K)$ and then by $t \ (= 1, \ldots, T)$. So $\xi_i = (\xi_{i11}, \xi_{i12}, \ldots, \xi_{i1T}, \ldots, \xi_{iK1}, \ldots, \xi_{iKT})'$. For full risk sharing (2.8a), $\Gamma = A$ with $\text{rank}(\Gamma) = K$, $G_i = \iota_K \otimes I_T$, where $A = I_K \otimes \iota_T$. For family risk sharing (2.8b), $\Gamma = (\iota_K \otimes I_T A)$ with $\text{rank}(\Gamma) = K + T - 1$, and $G_i = 0$.

We show below that under either factor structure (2.8a) or (2.8b) the available orthogonality conditions (A8) can be derived from (2.13) and

(2.15) of the text without the aid of (A7). We do so by showing that: (1) (2.13) and (2.15) imply (2.16), as claimed in the text; (2) Q_i is a transformation of first differences; and (3) (2.16) implies (A8). Before proceeding, we introduce additional notation. Let v_{ik} be the permanent component of ε_{ikt} and $\eta_{ikt} = \varepsilon_{ikt} - v_{ik}$. Then $\varepsilon_i = Av_i + \eta_i$, where $v_i = (v_{i1}, \ldots, v_{iK})'$, and η_i is a KT-dimensional vector whose element corresponding to (k, t) is η_{ikt}. The first difference operator is a $KT \times (K(T - 1))$ matrix $D = F \otimes I_T$ where F is a $T \times (T - 1)$ matrix given by

$$
F = \begin{pmatrix}
-1 & 0 & 0 & . & 0 \\
1 & -1 & 0 & . & 0 \\
0 & 1 & -1 & . & 0 \\
. & . & . & . & . \\
0 & . & 0 & 1 & -1 \\
0 & . & . & 0 & 1
\end{pmatrix}. \tag{A9}
$$

(1) Since $D'\varepsilon_i = D'Av_i + D'\eta_i = D'\eta_i$, $X_i \otimes D'\varepsilon_i = (X_i \otimes D')(I \otimes \eta_i)$. Since by (2.15) σ_i is a function of (v_i, X_i), $E(X_i \otimes D'\varepsilon_i | \sigma_i) = E[(X_i \otimes D')(I \otimes \eta_i) | \sigma_i] = E\{E[(X_i \otimes D')(I \otimes \eta_i) | v_i, X_i] | \sigma_i\} = E[(X_i \otimes D')E(I \otimes \eta_i | v_i, X_i) | \sigma_i]$. But $E(I \otimes \eta_i | v_i, X_i) = 0$ by (2.13). Thus,

$$
E(X_i \otimes D'\varepsilon_i | \sigma_i) = 0, \tag{A10}
$$

which is a restatement of (2.16).

(2) Since under either factor structure (2.8a) or (2.8b) Γ includes A ($= I_K \otimes \iota_T$), we have $Q_i'A = 0$. But $D'A = 0$, rank$(A) = K$, and rank$(D) = KT - K$, so $(D \vdots A)$ spans the entire KT-dimensional space. Thus columns of Q_i are linear combinations of columns of D and so there exists an $(KT - K) \times L$ matrix B_i such that $Q_i' = B_i'D'$.

(3) By (A6) and (2), $Q_i'c_i - Q_i'Z_i\delta - Q_i'G_i\pi = Q_i'\varepsilon_i = B_i'D'\varepsilon_i$. Thus $\zeta_i \equiv S_i'S_iX_i \otimes (Q_i'c_i - Q_i'Z_i\delta - Q_i'G_i\pi) = (S_i'S_i \otimes B_i')(X_i \otimes D'\varepsilon_i)$. So $E(\zeta_i | \sigma_i) = E[(S_i'S_i \otimes B_i')(X_i \otimes D'\varepsilon_i) | \sigma_i] = (S_i'S_i \otimes B_i')E(X_i \otimes D'\varepsilon_i | \sigma_i) = 0$ by (A10).

Remark 1

Because of (2), the ζ_i in the $L \cdot m \cdot KT$ available orthogonality conditions (A8) just derived from (2.13) and (2.15) can be written as

$$
\zeta_i = (S_i'S_i \otimes B_i')[X_i \otimes (D'c_i - D'Z_i\delta - D'G_i\pi)], \tag{A11}
$$

which makes it clear that the orthogonality conditions (2.21) or (2.23) of the text are linear combinations of (A8).

Remark 2

In the case of full risk sharing (2.8a), $L = KT - K$. If $\sigma_i = \iota_{KT}$, that is, if the family has no missing household-years, then $S_i = I_{KT}$, $Q_i = R$, so that D and Q_i span the same subspace of the KT-dimensional space. Thus the B_i for this case is a $(KT - K) \times (KT - K)$ nonsingular matrix, so that $\zeta_i = (I \otimes B_i)(X_i \otimes D'\varepsilon_i)$ is a nonsingular transformation of $X_i \otimes D'\varepsilon_i$. Thus the available orthogonality conditions (A8) are equivalent to (A10) or (2.16).

Notes

The authors are grateful to V. V. Chari, F. Diebold, M. Rosenzweig, and anonymous referees for useful comments or discussions. The research reported here was supported by grants from the National Institute for Aging, the National Science Foundation, and the Center for Urban Studies and Policy Research, Northwestern University. The former title of the chapter is "Risk-sharing, Altruism, and the Factor Structure of Consumption" (National Bureau of Economic Research Working Paper no. 3834).

1. Recent tests of full risk sharing using various micro data sets include Abel and Kotlikoff (1988), Mace (1991), Nelson (1994), and Townsend (1994). As noted in Hayashi (1987), all papers that have regressed consumption changes on current or lagged income or lagged income changes using micro data have tested full risk sharing implicitly.

2. As pointed out by Hayashi (1987, p. 100 and Section 4), this assumes that the household can repay the debt by negative consumption. If the nonnegativity constraint on consumption is imposed, the solvency condition (that the terminal net wealth be nonnegative) becomes the liquidity constraint that the household can borrow only up to the present value of the worst possible draw of the stream of future labor income. However, if the disutility of zero consumption is large enough, the household will arrange its consumption plan so that the liquidity constraint is never binding and Hall's martingale hypothesis remains valid.

3. The instruments used in their test include not only lagged wages but also current housing consumption whose changes may be correlated with unanticipated shocks to household resources. But housing consumption is likely to be endogenous. If so, the inclusion of housing consumption renders the test inconsistent. Besides the inclusion of current housing consumption, the instruments used by Altug and Miller (1990) are essentially the variables used by many other studies on liquidity constraints.

4. In all the PSID waves, the period over which food expenditure is reported is in an early part of the wave year. Consistent data on leisure concurrent with food are available only from the 1985–87 PSID waves.

5. In addition, we relax assumptions about exogeneity of instruments such as lagged leisure. These issues are addressed in detail in Ham and Jacobs (1994).

6. Here, $C_{ik}(e_t)$ is a scalar. Generalization to a multiconsumption good case is immediate.

7. For example, if $g_{ikt} = l_{h,k,t-1}$, then (2.13b) and (2.13c) do not hold for $s = t + 1$.

8. As noted in section 9.3.2, in one of the two data sets we use, the wage rate is calculated as the ratio of annual labor income to annual hours worked. If hours worked, which is also used to calculate leisure, is measured with error, the calculated wage rate will be correlated with the leisure measurement error that forms part of the error term ε_{ikt}. In this case, (2.13b) does

not hold for $t = s$ for the wage rate and hence is not used in the estimation In our other data set, the wage rate does not depend on the variables used for calculating the leisure in the consumption equation, so this complication does not arise.

9. An example of (2.15) is that (k, t) is in the survey if the wage rate in the year is above some threshold value.

10. For more formal proof that (2.13) and (2.15) implies (2.16), see part (1) of appendix 9.2.

11. In one of our two data sets, $T = 10$, $M = 13$ for some specifications, and the sample size is 469.

12. The Monte Carlo simulation by Tauchen (1986) in a time-series context shows that the number of orthogonality conditions should be kept small relative to the sample size.

13. If the instruments for leisure, g_{ikt}, are lagged leisures, the level in date $t - 1$ rather than the first difference from t to $t - 1$ of leisure will be used, in which case the $\Delta_1 x_{ikt}$ should be understood to represent $(\Delta_1 b'_{i1t}, g'_{i1t}, \Delta_1 w_{i1t})'$ where g_{i1t} is leisure in date $t - 1$.

14. Let the $(T - 1)(M + 1)$ orthogonality conditions be written as $E[h_i(\partial, \pi)] = 0$ where h_i is a $(T - 1)(M + 1)$ dimensional vector for family i whose first element, for example, is $\Delta_1 c_{i11} - \Delta_{12} z'_{i11} \partial - d'_i \pi$. Given the GMM estimator, say $(\hat{\partial}, \hat{\pi})$, the chi-square statistic is $N \cdot \bar{h}' V^{-1} \bar{h}$ where $\bar{h}$ is the sample mean over families of $h_i(\hat{\partial}, \hat{\pi})$, V is a consistent estimate of the variance of $h_i(\partial, \pi)$, and N is the number of families.

15. This follows straightforwardly from the law of iterated expectations. See part (3) of appendix 9.2 for a more formal proof.

16. Although not evident from their text, the method of replacing incalculable changes by zeros was used by Altug and Miller (1990), as confirmed by a phone conversation with one of the authors. Despite the requirement that only original households continuously in the survey be included, their panel is not strictly balanced because food expenditure is missing for a dozen household-years due to top-coding. Apart from the treatment of split-offs and the choice of instruments, an important difference between our methodology and that of Altug and Miller is that they used only first time-differences to form orthogonality conditions.

17. The rather arcane algebra in appendix 9.2 obscures the intuitive link between the null hypotheses and the restrictions on consumption changes we are testing. It did not seem worthwhile to present this algebra in the text.

18. There is also a supplemental sample of 1,872 low-income households. Following Altug and Miller (1990) and other studies, we do not use this low-income supplement.

19. We do not use the 1988 and 1989 waves of the PSID because they do not have data on food and current hours worked.

20. See appendix 9.1 for more details on how the missing wages are estimated. The assignment of WAGEH for missing cases introduces measurement error in WAGEH. However, note that measurement error that is uncorrelated with measurement error in consumption and current leisure will not lead to bias in the parameter estimates or the tests against the null. Measurement error will reduce the precision of the parameter estimates and the power of the tests.

21. This is a dubious procedure because the period over which FOOD is measured is in an early part of the wave year. In fact, results in table 9.6 suggest that taking moving averages only obscures changes in food consumption from one year to the next.

22. There are only eight first time-differences because (1) the instruments for the adjusted consumption change from t to $t + 1$ include variables for years $t - 1$ and $t - 2$, (2) AM calculate annual food for year t as $0.25 \times \text{FOOD}_t + 0.75 \times \text{FOOD}_{t+1}$ where FOOD_t is the value of food available from wave year t, and (3) the PSID has no food data for wave year 1973 so that annual food cannot be calculated for 1972 and 1973.

23. To calculate the weighting matrix in GMM, some initial estimates of the coefficients (∂, π) are needed. Our initial estimates were obtained by GMM with the weighing matrix set at the sample moment matrix of the cross products of the instruments and the *un*adjusted changes in consumption. When we instead used the identity matrix for the weighing matrix, the chi-square statistic was 116.5.

24. The change in AGE is constant across households and is subsumed in the time-dependent intercept.

25. The problem is made more serious by the predating effect of the moving average in calculating annual food. The orthogonality condition for the wage rate for $t - 1$ pertains to the correlation of the wage rate in year $t - 1$ with the change in annual food from year t to year $t + 1$, but this annual change equals $0.25 \times (\text{FOOD}_{t+1} - \text{FOOD}_t) + 0.75 \times (\text{FOOD}_{t+2} \times \text{FOOD}_{t+1})$, where FOOD_t, available from wave year t, is food expenditure over a few months in an early part of year t.

26. With this panel, for which annual food in 72 and 73 are not available, the time-differences involved for $t = 2$, for example, are 69–71, 70–74, 71–75, 74–76, ..., 78–80. The wage rate change for the 71–75 consumption change, for example, is from 70 to 76.

27. Since the early drafts of our chapter were circulated, an independent study by Ham and Jacobs (1994) has conducted a detailed investigation of full risk sharing using the PSID. They provide further evidence on whether correlation of the wage, lagged leisure, and the employment status with the error term (unobserved preference components and measurement error in consumption or leisure) may be responsible for our rejection of full risk sharing and our rejection of family risk sharing in the next subsection. They use orthogonality conditions that involve unemployment rates in the household head's industry or occupation, which are unlikely to be correlated with the error term. They strongly reject full risk sharing. In view of their findings, it seems unlikely that our rejection is due to the use of invalid instruments.

28. The change in health dummies is not instrumented because our attempt to instrument it by its level produced very imprecise parameter estimates and a very low test statistic. In the 1968–81 panel, we did not use the current wage for year t in column 6 of table 9.6 in testing self-insurance, because it is correlated with the error term through the measurement error in annual hours worked.

References

Abel, A., and L. Kotlikoff. 1988. Intergenerational altruism and the effectiveness of fiscal policy—New Tests Based on Cohort Data. Mimeo., University of Pennsylvania and Boston University.

Altonji, J., F. Hayashi, and L. Kotlikoff. 1992. Is the extended family altruistically linked? Direct tests using micro data. *American Economic Review* 82:1177–1198.

Altug, S., and R. Miller. 1990. Household choices in equilibrium. *Econometrica* 58:543–70.

Chamberlain, G. 1984. Panel data. In *Handbook of Econometrics, Volume 2*, ed. Z. Griliches and M. Intriligator, 1247–318. Amsterdam: North-Holland.

Cochrane, J. 1991. A simple test of consumption insurance. *Journal of Political Economy* 99:957–76.

Hall, R. 1978. Stochastic implications of the life cycle–permanent income hypothesis: Theory and evidence. *Journal of Political Economy* 96:971–87.

Ham, J. 1986. Testing whether unemployment represents intertemporal labor supply behavior. *Review of Economic Studies* 53:559–78.

Ham, J., and K. Jacobs. 1994. Using exogenous information on sector specific and idiosyncratic shocks to test for full insurance. Mimeo., Department of Economics, University of Pittsburgh.

Hayashi, F. 1987. Tests for liquidity constraints: A critical survey and some new observations. In *Advances in econometrics II, Fifth World Congress*, ed. T. Bewley, 91–120. New York and London: Cambridge University Press.

Kreps, D. 1990. *A course in microeconomic theory*. Princeton: Princeton University Press.

Leme, Paulo. 1984. Integration of international capital markets. Mimeo., University of Chicago.

Mace, B. 1991. Full insurance in the presence of aggregate uncertainty. *Journal of Political Economy* 99:928–56.

Nelson, J. 1994. On testing for full insurance using consumer expenditure survey data. *Journal of Political Economy* 102:384–94.

Tauchen, G. 1986. Statistical properties of generalized method-of-moments estimators of structural parameters obtained from financial market data. *Journal of Business and Economic Statistics* 4:397–416.

Townsend, R. 1987. Arrow-Debreu programs as microfoundations of macroeconomics. In *Advances in Economic Theory: Fifth World Congress*, ed. T. Bewley, 379–428. New York and London: Cambridge University Press.

Townsend, R. 1994. Risk and insurance in village india. *Econometrica* 62:539–92.

III Japanese Saving Behavior

10

Introduction to Part III:
A Review of Recent
Literature on Japanese
Saving

10.1 Introduction

Given that the United States is the largest economy in the world as well as the center for modern research in economics, it was inevitable that the theory of saving was developed with United States data in mind. Indeed, the desire to explain the surprisingly stable U.S. aggregate saving rate prompted the birth of the modern theories of household saving. Are theories tailored for the United States universally applicable? In this respect, the Japanese economy represents an intellectual challenge because of its many idiosyncracies. Particularly striking when compared to the United States is its high saving rate. Understanding the Japanese saving behavior is not just an academic exercise; from the viewpoint of policymakers, reducing Japan's saving rate—and raising the U.S. saving rate—is a key to eliminating the persistent bilateral trade imbalance.

This chapter is an introduction to part III of this book, which includes my work on saving in Japan. By relating my work to research done by others on the same subject, the chapter also serves as a review of the recent literature. What is curious about the literature is that stylized facts about Japanese saving have not been elucidated until very recently. The key stylized facts to be identified in this review include the following. Japan's national saving rate is not as high as commonly thought, though it was indeed quite high during the high growth era. The accumulation of wealth by Japanese households starts very early and lasts until very late in life, with unconsumed wealth transferred to the next generation in the form of bequests. In this review, I will focus on studies that are directly relevant to documenting and explaining those and other stylized facts. For an encyclopedic catalog of the recent literature on saving in Japan, the reader is referred to Horioka (1993).

This chapter is organized as follows. In section 10.2, I will state macro stylized facts about Japan's aggregate saving rates before and after World War II, with special emphasis on the accounting of depreciation, which is one reason why Japan's saving rates appear so high relative to the U.S. rates. Section 10.3 starts out with a discussion of how micro data about individual households should be organized to be informative about the saving behavior of a typical Japanese household. In the same section I will present micro facts. Section 10.4 examines models of saving that are capable of explaining the macro and micro stylized facts identified in this review. Section 10.5 contains concluding comments and an agenda for future research.

10.2 Macro Stylized Facts

10.2.1 Postwar Period

At first glance, Japan's postwar saving rate is extraordinary. As shown in Table 10.1, which is taken directly from the *1996 Annual Report on (Japanese) National Accounts*, Japan's national saving rate as a fraction of GDP is far higher than those of most other countries. This comparison is very misleading, however. As I argued in Hayashi (1986, included in this book as chapter 11), much of the apparent gap between the United States and Japan is a statistical illusion. Two of the most important differences in the way Japan and the United States compile their national income statistics are (1) depreciation accounting, and (2) treatment of government capital.

The Japanese National Income Accounts (hereafter the NIA) compiled by the Economic Planning Agency of the Japanese government (hereafter the EPA) is a complete accounting frame in that both income/expenditure accounts and capital accounts are included. But it has one major short-

Table 10.1
National Saving and Depreciation as Percent of GDP for 1993

	Japan	Canada	France	Germany	Italy	Sweden	U.K.	U.S.
National saving	17.0	0.9	n.a.	7.1	6.0	−1.7	2.4	2.7
Depreciation	15.6	12.3	13.3	13.3	12.0	14.1	10.4	12.2

Source: Table 39 of *1996 Annual Report on (Japanese) National Accounts*. The original source for countries other than Japan is the OECD National Accounts (1995).

coming: the depreciation in the income/expenditure accounts is at historical costs. In an inflationary environment such as the postwar Japanese economy, depreciation at historical costs is less than at replacement costs. This can lead to a significant upward bias in net saving. It is possible, however, to remove the bias by combining published NIA tables, because the capital stock in the stock section of the NIA is valued at replacement costs. My work included in this book as chapter 11 was the first to back out replacement cost depreciation from the NIA tables and calculate net saving based on replacement cost depreciation. My original procedure is in chapter 11, and its improved procedure taking into account the suggestion of Iwamoto (1995) is in the addendum to the chapter. As the discussion in the addendum makes clear, the improved procedure can recover from the published NIA tables the EPA's estimate of replacement cost depreciation almost exactly, at least for the years since 1970 for which the deflator for the capital stock is available from the NIA tables. The gap between the replacement cost depreciation thus estimated and the historical cost depreciation published in the NIA is very substantial, higher than 4 percent of NNP for many years.

The second important difference is about net government capital formation (gross government investment less depreciation on government capital). Until the end of 1995, the national income accounts for the United States (the National Income and Product Accounts, the NIPA for short) complied by the U.S. Bureau of Economic Analysis (BEA) did not credit the government sector for its capital formation. All of government expenditures (including govenment investment) were treated as consumption, so government saving in the NIPA equaled a government budget surplus. This has been changed in the 1995 Comprehensive Revision of the NIPA, first released in January 1996. The NIPA now recognizes government investment and consequently government saving includes net government capital formation.[1] However, the net capital formation in the (Japanese) NIA does not seem comparable to this newly available estimate of net capital formation for the United States. In the NIA, government depreciable assets except for buildings are not depreciated, which means that the stock of government capital in the stock section of the NIA is essentially a gross stock and that depreciation in the flow section is only for buildings (and at historical costs). Thus net government capital formation in the NIA, about 6 percent of GDP in 1994, is very severely overstated.[2] Furthermore, much of government investment is "pork," used to please agricultural constituents. It is not difficult in these days to find well-paved but very lightly traveled roads separating rice paddies wide enough to be used as airplane runways.

To make the saving rates from the two countries comparable, chapter 11 calculates Japan's saving rates according to the old definition of the NIPA. This means that both government capital formation and the gap between replacement and historical cost depreciation are taken out from Japanese saving. The result of the calculation is summarized in Figure 10.1, which graphs the adjusted and unadjusted national saving rate along with the U.S. national saving rate. As is clear from the figure, the adjustment makes a big difference.[3] In 1979 the U.S. national saving rate almost equaled Japan's. The stylized facts emerging from figure 10.1 are the following:

Macro Fact #1: Japan's national saving rate is not as high as commonly thought, but it is still substantially higher than the U.S. rate.

Macro Fact #2: Japan's national saving rate peaked around 1970 and thereafter declined quickly until 1983.

Figure 10.2 gives the decomposition of Japan's national saving into household, corporate, and government saving for Japan. Here, too, government capital formation is not included, so government saving equals a government budget surplus. Unlike the national saving rate, the household saving rate continued to rise until 1976. Nevertheless the national saving rate declined thanks to the steep decline in corporate saving. Why there was such a large-scale reallocation of saving from the corporate to household sector in the early seventies may be an interesting research topic, but a more interesting fact is

Macro Fact #3: The movement in the national saving rate in the 1980s and the 1990s mirrors that in the government saving rate.

While the private saving rate (the sum of the household and corporate saving rates) has been declining steadily since 1970, there was a dramatic improvement in the government budget balance since 1978 followed by an equally dramatic deterioration since 1991. The figure shows that the hump in the national saving rate from 1983 to the present coincides with this large swing in government saving. A natural interpretation is that the large shift in government finance caused national saving to rise. This runs counter to the Ricardian doctrine that the allocation of national saving between sectors is arbitrary.

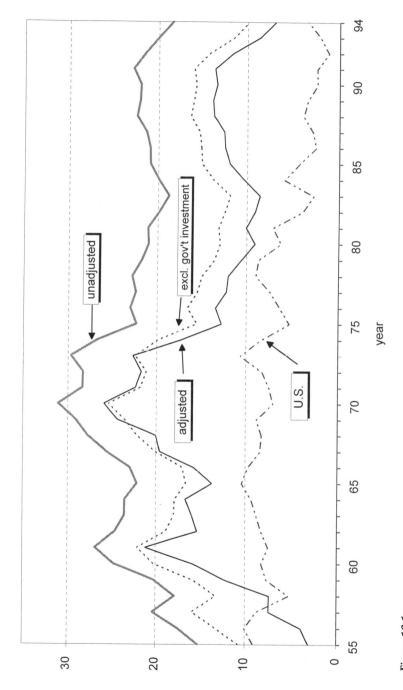

Figure 10.1
National saving rates, 1955–94 (percent of NIP).

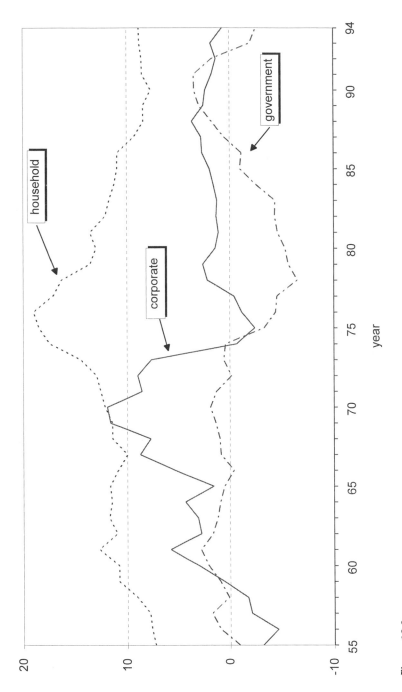

Figure 10.2
Breakdown of national saving (percent of NIP).

10.2.2   Is Depreciation Too Large?

The large discrepancy between replacement cost and historical cost depreciation shown in figure 10.1 has prompted some to wonder whether my adjustment of depreciation has gone too far.[4] To address this issue, table 10.2 reports replacement cost depreciation relative to both GNP and the capital stock. As is well-known and can be seen from the table, the ratio of depreciation to GNP for the United States is about 10 percent. The same ratio for Japan is over 15 percent for most years. The implicit depreciation rate, namely the ratio of depreciation to the capital stock, is nearly twice as large for Japan than for the United States.

The difference in the (overall) implicit depreciation rate can be due to the different asset composition between the two countries. Table 10.3, which updates table 10.2, displays asset-specific depreciation rates for three broad asset categories (residential structures, nonresidential structures, and producer durable equipments) along with the asset composition for the United States and Japan.[5] That the Japanese housing depreciation rate is higher than the U.S. rate is not surprising, given that a large portion of Japanese housing is made of paper and wood. It would be puzzling if the Japanese housing depreciation were as low as that of the United States. That the most durable asset (residential structures) occupy nearly half of the nation's capital stock contributes to the low overall depreciation rate for the United States. What is puzzling is the high Japanese depreciation rate for equipments, which is 1.8 times as large as the U.S. rate. Equipments are internationally tradable and its depreciation rate should not depend on the location. In fact, in the hedonic price equation estimated by Kuninori (1988) using data on prices of used equipments, the depreciation rates are about 25 percent for power shovels and 20 percent for bulldozers, which are similar to the depreciation rates estimated by Hulten and Wykoff (1981) for the same equipment types using U.S. data. Why does the same piece of equipment depreciate faster in the Japanese national accounts?

The question of a high depreciation rate in the NIA is an old one. There is a direct estimate of the capital stock of the nation in the *National Wealth Survey* (NWS). The two most extensive surveys are for 1955 and 1970. According to the EPA (1978, p. 231), the Japanese NIA takes the 1970 NWS estimate of the (net) capital stock to be the capital stock for 1970 and uses the same depreciation rates used in the NWS to generate capital stock for other years. However, it has been recognized by practitioners of the perpetual inventory method that it requires implausibly

Table 10.2
Depreciation, Capital Stock, and GNP for the United States and Japan

				United States		
Year	Depreciation	Capital stock	GNP	Depr./cap. stock (%)	Depr./GNP (%)	Capital stock/GNP
70	88.8	1,548.3	1,017.1	5.7	8.7	1.52
71	97.6	1,673.8	1,104.9	5.8	8.8	1.51
72	109.9	1,854.6	1,215.7	5.9	9.0	1.53
73	120.4	2,110.5	1,362.3	5.7	8.8	1.55
74	140.2	2,408.3	1,474.3	5.8	9.5	1.63
75	165.2	2,794.3	1,599.1	5.9	10.3	1.75
76	182.8	3,101.5	1,785.5	5.9	10.2	1.74
77	205.2	3,415.4	1,994.6	6.0	10.3	1.71
78	234.8	3,872.6	2,254.5	6.1	10.4	1.72
79	272.4	4,462.0	2,520.8	6.1	10.8	1.77
80	311.9	5,132.7	2,742.1	6.1	11.4	1.87
81	362.4	5,814.2	3,063.8	6.2	11.8	1.90
82	399.1	6,412.9	3,179.8	6.2	12.6	2.02
83	418.4	6,737.3	3,434.4	6.2	12.2	1.96
84	433.2	6,987.0	3,801.5	6.2	11.4	1.84
85	454.5	7,348.0	4,053.6	6.2	11.2	1.81
86	478.6	7,715.8	4,277.7	6.2	11.2	1.80
87	502.2	8,224.3	4,544.5	6.1	11.1	1.81
88	534.0	8,729.1	4,908.2	6.1	10.9	1.78
89	580.4	9,108.3	5,266.8	6.4	11.0	1.73
90	602.7	9,650.3	5,567.8	6.2	10.8	1.73
91	626.5	10,116.5	5,740.8	6.2	10.9	1.76
92	658.5	10,384.8	6,025.8	6.3	10.9	1.72
93	669.1	10,751.2	6,347.8	6.2	10.5	1.69
94	709.2	11,290.9	6,726.9	6.3	10.6	1.68

Note: Excludes government capital. Capital stock at the beginning of year. See the appendix for data sources. U.S. depreciation and capital stock in billions of dollars. Japanese depreciation and capital stock in trillion yen.

Table 10.2 (cont.)

			Japan			
Year	Depreciation	Capital stock	GNP	Depr./cap. stock (%)	Depr./GNP (%)	Capital stock/GNP
70	9.21	59.54	72.86	15.5	12.6	0.82
71	10.32	76.12	80.22	13.6	12.9	0.95
72	12.04	90.79	91.99	13.3	13.1	0.99
73	14.87	116.58	112.05	12.8	13.3	1.04
74	21.42	162.94	133.44	13.1	16.1	1.22
75	22.99	203.02	147.50	11.3	15.6	1.38
76	25.66	222.31	165.63	11.5	15.5	1.34
77	28.61	255.06	184.63	11.2	15.5	1.38
78	30.88	277.29	203.42	11.1	15.2	1.36
79	34.14	303.75	220.63	11.2	15.5	1.38
80	39.44	351.65	238.71	11.2	16.5	1.47
81	41.27	390.94	255.82	10.6	16.1	1.53
82	43.82	416.04	268.92	10.5	16.3	1.55
83	45.76	438.48	280.19	10.4	16.3	1.56
84	48.85	453.70	299.04	10.8	16.3	1.52
85	51.73	478.35	319.48	10.8	16.2	1.50
86	52.93	500.44	334.54	10.6	15.8	1.50
87	55.58	517.07	349.57	10.7	15.9	1.48
88	58.82	548.52	373.95	10.7	15.7	1.47
89	63.43	585.49	400.39	10.8	15.8	1.46
90	69.32	648.13	430.46	10.7	16.1	1.51
91	76.23	711.22	459.64	10.7	16.6	1.55
92	81.50	765.76	473.44	10.6	17.2	1.62
93	84.27	800.22	477.05	10.5	17.7	1.68
94	85.61	821.45	480.04	10.4	17.8	1.71

high depreciation rates for the EPA's investment series between 1955 and 1970 to be consistent with the NWS capital stock for the two years. For example, Dean, Darrough and Neef (1990) report that the depreciation rate has to be about 10 percent for structures and 30–50 percent for equipments. This has prompted some prominent students of productivity growth to take the position that the depreciation rates in the National Wealth Survey are too high and that the NWS *gross* capital stock should be used as the capital stock (Kuroda (1990, p. 266)). The detailed examination of the Japan–U.S. productivity comparison in Jorgenson, Kuroda and Nishimizu (1987) is based on this premise.

Table 10.3
Depreciation Rates by Assets

Year		Residential structures		Nonresidential structures		Equipments		Total	
		Value share	Depr. rate	Value share	Depr. rate	Value share	Depr. rate	Value share	Depr. rate
1970	U.S.	48.6	2.8	28.1	5.1	23.3	13.0	100.0	5.7
	Japan	20.6	9.5	54.7	9.9	24.7	28.7	100.0	11.5
1975	U.S.	47.8	2.9	29.5	5.1	22.7	13.5	100.0	5.9
	Japan	23.5	8.8	52.6	3.5	23.9	22.6	100.0	8.5
1980	U.S.	49.6	2.9	27.4	5.7	23.0	13.7	100.0	6.1
	Japan	26.1	9.0	56.5	5.4	17.4	23.8	100.0	8.5
1985	U.S.	46.9	2.9	29.0	5.6	24.0	13.6	100.0	6.2
	Japan	23.6	8.5	59.4	3.7	17.0	22.8	100.0	7.7
1990	U.S.	47.3	2.9	28.9	5.4	23.8	14.0	100.0	6.2
	Japan	22.5	8.6	59.6	4.5	17.9	23.2	100.0	8.0
1994	U.S.	48.9	3.0	27.8	5.4	23.3	14.3	100.0	6.3
	Japan	20.8	10.1	60.6	5.0	18.6	19.9	100.0	8.6

Note: See the appendix for data sources. It is not possible to calculate from the Japanese NIA the asset-specific depreciation rates by sector. The depreciation rates shown here for Japan are for the nation's capital stock, 20–30 percent of which is government capital. This is the reason why the overall depreciation rate for the nation is lower because government capital is mainly in the form of nonresidential structures. The overall depreciation rate here does not agree with that in table 10.2 for Japan.

The high equipment depreciation rate in the NIA does not necessarily imply that my (and the EPA's) estimate of replacement cost depreciation is overstated. First, the level of depreciation for a given asset is the product of the depreciation rate and the capital stock. The effect of too high a depreciation rate should be more or less offset by the low capital stock that results from the high depreciation rate. Second, for the other asset categories (residential and nonresidential structures), which are more than three-quarters to five-sixth of the Japanese capital stock, there is no obvious reason to suspect the Japanese depreciation rate is too high.

10.2.3 Prewar Period

My conclusion that the phenomenon of extremely high Japanese saving rates is limited to the period 1965–1975 is reinforced in a longer time span. Figure 10.3 includes the gross and net national saving rates as percent of GNP since 1885. The data for the prewar period are from the *Long Term Economic Statistics* (Ohkawa and Shinohara (1974),[6] hereafter the LTES), painstakingly put together by a group of economists at Hitotsubashi University. The data for the postwar period from 1955 are from the NIA, as in figures 10.1 and 10.2. Gross national saving is defined as GNP minus private consumption minus government consumption including military expenditure but excluding government capital formation. Thus, unlike in figure 10.1, national saving *includes* net government capital formation. Figure 10.3 also displays the current account as percent of GNP. That the most volatile component of national saving for the prewar period was the current account (the other component being net increase in domestic tangible assets) can be clearly seen. The large deficit in trade balance in 1905 indicates that much of the Russo-Japanese war was financed by external debt, while the huge surplus during World War I is due to the capital outflow to finance the war effort by the Allies. A stylized fact about saving evident from the figure is

Macro Fact #4: The prewar saving rate is not high by international standards. Thus the phenomenon of an extremely high Japanese saving rate is limited to the ten to fifteen years surrounding 1970.

10.2.4 Capital Stock since 1885

This fact is reflected in the history of Japan's real capital stock (tangible depreciable assets including housing and nonmilitary government capital

300

Chapter 10

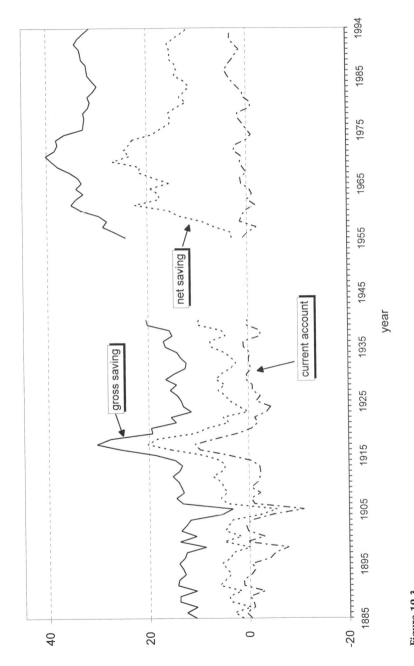

Figure 10.3
Saving and current account (percent of GNP).

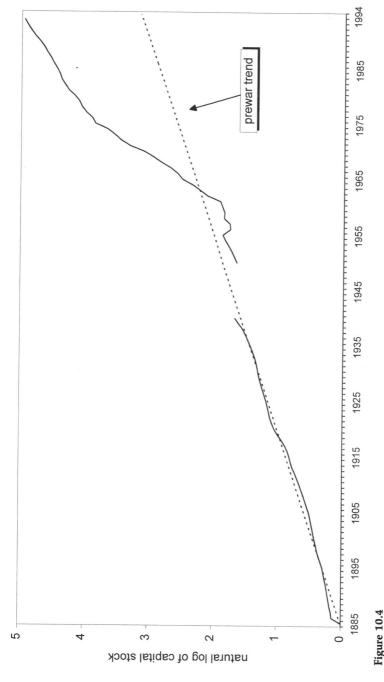

Figure 10.4
Real capital stock (log of capital stock set to 0 for 1885).

but excluding inventories). Figure 10.4 displays in log scale the real value of the capital stock in 1934–36 yen. There are no reliable records for constructing consistent net capital stock series between 1940 and 1955. See the appendix to this chapter for my procedure of splicing the prewar and the postwar capital stock series. The capital stock series since 1955 is from the stock section of the NIA.[7] To convert the nominal capital stock into real for the years from 1955 on, I used the flow deflator for gross fixed capital formation because the stock deflator in the NIA is available only since 1970. One curious feature of the early postwar capital stock is the slight decline in the late 1950s. The use of the flow deflator may be partly responsible for this; the nominal capital stock in the NIA for this period is monotonically increasing.

The capital stock series linking the pre- and postwar periods is consistent with whatever scant evidence there is about the wartime destruction of the Japan's capital stock by Americans. Okita (1949) reports that about a quarter of the capital stock was destroyed during World War II. If one extrapolates the prewar trend to obtain a capital stock value for 1945 and compares it with another value for 1945 that one obtains by "backcasting" using the 1950–55 trend, the gap is about half the 1945 value implied by the prewar trend. This leaves a quarter to be accounted for, but that may be attributable to the slowdown in nonmilitary capital accumulation that must surely have taken place during the war. No matter what the extent of wartime destruction, there is no question that the rapid capital accumulation associated with the extraordinarily high national saving between 1965 and 1975 has put Japan's capital stock well above the prewar trend.

10.2.5 GNP since 1885

Another noteworthy feature of the postwar capital accumulation in figure 10.4 is that it appears to be tapering off; it appears as though the time path of wealth is converging to a new time trend, which I think is significant because it is happening precisely when Japan's per capita GNP is catching up with that of the United States. The United States has had at least a hundred years of uninterrupted capital accumulation (with a relatively minor disruption during the Great Depression), so it is reasonable to suppose that the U.S. economy has been on a steady state growth path for over a century. The view that Japan has been converging to the steady state path represented by the United States from a lower level is

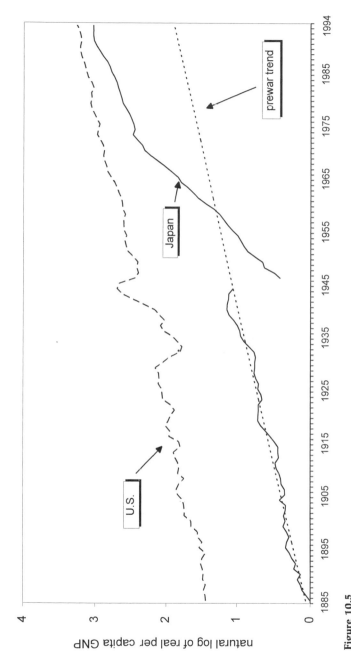

Figure 10.5
Real per capita GNP (log of Japanese GNP set to 0 for 1885).

born out in figure 10.5 where real GNP per capita since 1885 is graphed for the two countries. Note, however, that the process of convergence did not start until after World War II; the Japanese prewar trend is almost parallel to the U.S. trend.

The stylized fact emerging from figures 10.4 and 10.5 may be summarized as

Macro Fact #5: The prewar saving rate is not just lower than the postwar rate. It was too low to initiate a convergence to the steady state path.

To anticipate, the standard neoclassical growth theory can explain the convergence in the postwar period and the hump in the saving rate. To the best of my knowledge, there is no well-articulated explanation of why Japan waited until after the self-destructive war to start the process of convergence.

10.3 Evidence from Data on Age Cohorts

To study the saving behavior of a typical household over the life cycle, the ideal source of information is panel data tracking the same set of households over a number of years. But Japanese panel data sets, with their shortness of the period covered, do not suit the purpose, so available studies resort to cross-section age profiles to infer the life cycle of a typical household. The average wealth held by the cohort aged 25–29 in 1979, for example, is in the 25–29 age bracket of an 1979 age profile of wealth, and the wealth held by the same cohort five years later when its members turn 30–34 is in the 30–34 bracket of a 1984 age profile, and so forth. Longitudinal, as opposed to cross-section, profiles created this way are called *synthetic cohorts*. It is also possible to infer a longitudinal profile from a single cross-section age profile, but some assumption is needed to control for the *cohort effect* that the multiple cohorts forming a cross-section profile differ in their lifetime resources. For example, wealth declines with age in a cross-section age profile even if each household maintains its wealth, because older cohorts are less wealthy thanks to secular productivity growth. In this section, I summarize as micro stylized facts the results from my work included in this book as chapter 12 (Hayashi, Ito, and Slemrod (1988)) and recent studies by others about longitudinal age profiles. Evidence from econometric studies using data on individual households will be reviewed in the next section.

10.3.1 Issues in the Definition of Saving

Before turning to evidence, however, it is necessary to address a number of issues related to the measurement of saving at the household and the cohort level.

Compliance with the National Accounts
Conceptually, creating a cross-section age profile of saving from a random sample drawn from the population of households is a straightforward task: for each household in the sample, define saving as the difference between disposable income and consumption, and then calculate average saving for each age bracket. The implied aggregate, calculated as average saving for all age brackets multiplied by the number of households in the population, should equal aggregate saving in the national accounts. In practice, the task is not so trivial. The disposable income in household surveys, defined as cash income less taxes and social security contributions, differs from the disposable income in the national accounts in several respects. Appendix 12.2 lists the required steps to calculate from household surveys disposable income, consumption, and saving in accordance with the national accounts definition. Those steps include, for example, inclusion in disposable income and consumption of imputed rent on owner-occupied housing and government transfers in kind. Other reasons why the implied aggregate may not match the national accounts value include underreporting of income and consumption in household surveys, and the possibility that the sample is not representative of the population. This issue is addressed at length in chapter 12.

With its large sample (of more than fifty thousand households) and detailed information on income, expenditure, and assets/liabilities, the household survey most suitable for studying the saving behavior is the National Survey of Family Income and Expenditures (hereafter the NSFIE), which has been conducted by the government every five years since 1959. The work included in chapter 12 calculates income, consumption, and saving for each household in the 1984 wave of the NSFIE, incorporating most of the required steps to be consistent with the national accounts definition.[8]

Imputation of Corporate Saving
If one takes the view that the distinction between the household sector and the corporate sector is arbitrary, household saving calculated as disposable income less consumption misses the saving done on the house-

hold's behalf in the form of corporate retained earnings. The calculation of saving in chapter 12 (and for that matter any existing micro studies on saving to my knowledge) does not incorporate this.[9] However, at least for the years since the mid 1970s, corporate saving is not large (see figure 10.2). To the extent that this component of saving is important, household saving defined as disposable income less consumption understates saving by households that have already accumulated wealth such as old households.

Imputation of Government Saving
One does not have to subscribe to the Ricardian doctrine of government finance to believe that households would view one component of government saving—social security contribution—as part of saving and social security benefits as part of dissaving. Household saving calculated in accordance with the national accounts definition does not include this important component of saving. This omission, which results in an understatement of saving by younger cohorts, should be kept in mind in the discussion below.

Interhousehold Transfers
Private transfers between households are a key to understanding Japanese saving. A transfer given to someone outside the household may be a unilateral transfer, in which case it should be either excluded from the donor's income or included in the donor's expenditure so that it is not included as part of saving. Accordingly, the transfer receipt should be included in the recipient's income. Or a transfer may be an informal contractual payment, representing new lending, a repayment of past informally arranged loans, or insurance payments as part of an informal risk-sharing arrangement. In this latter case a transfer payment is an increase in net (invisible) claims on others, so it should be included in saving. Or the transfer may be a combination of both. Since the outside observer does not know what fraction of a transfer is an increase in claims, there is no single correct way of dealing with private transfers, but one should always be clear about how transfers are treated in the definition of saving. In what follows, unless otherwise noted, I take the invisible claim view and define saving as disposable income (excluding transfer receipts) less consumption (excluding transfer payments). Thus, for example, if the excess of consumption over income is entirely financed by a transfer receipt, saving is negative under our definition; it would be zero if the transfer were treated as unilateral.

It should also be kept in mind that in Japanese household surveys only "regular" transfers are recorded, so bequests and one-time gifts, which can be an important source of wealth accumulation for recipients, are not included in our definition of saving. Transfer receipts, recorded in the household survey or not, are not included in our definition of saving.

10.3.2 Do the Elderly Dissave?

For the case of Japanese household surveys, there are other caveats one should be aware of. To illustrate, consider the cross-section age profile of the saving rate created by a simple tabulation by age of the household head. Figure 10.6 displays such profiles from official tabulations of the past waves of the NSFIE.[10] It is not possible from the published tabulations to incorporate the required adjustments mentioned above. So there is no reason for the cross-section average of the saving rates to agree with the NIA household saving rate for the same years, which is also displayed in the figure as the "macro" saving rate. Also, contrary to our definition, the published tabulations include transfer receipts in income and transfer payments in expenditure. One striking feature of the figure is that the saving rate is highest for the 65+ age bracket.

One needs to exercise extra caution with Japanese cohort data, for several reasons. First, no government household survey reports taxes paid by households other than the so-called worker households (households whose head is on a payroll), which means that one can never observe from published reports the saving rate for the retired. The saving rate displayed in figure 10.6 is for the worker households only; the saving rate for the 65+ age bracket is really for those who are still working after turning 65, a group hardly representative of the 65+ age cohort.

Second, *extended (multigenerational) households*, which make up about a quarter of Japanese households, coexist with nuclear households in published tabulations by age. That is, a subset of households included in the 25–29 age bracket, say, are extended households in which a 25 to 29-year-old child is living with his or her parents. This has profound consequences. Not only does the 25–29 age bracket not include all individuals of that age bracket, but it also includes individuals from other age brackets. Furthermore, this cohort mixing is not random for two reasons. First, the head of a household in household surveys is defined to be the main income earner. For those aged 25–29 in the 25–29 age bracket, for example, there are two types: those in nuclear households and those

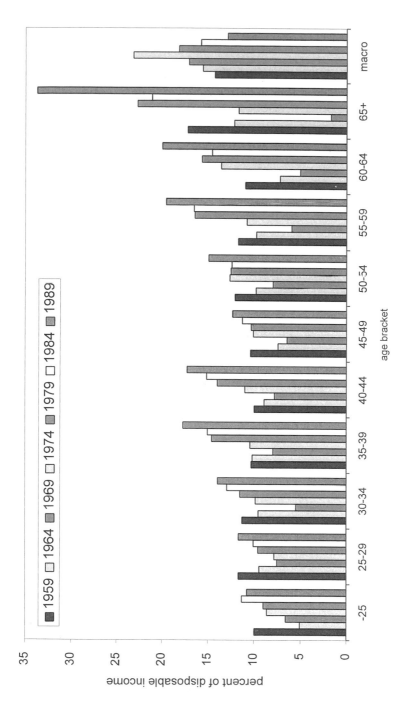

Figure 10.6
Cross-section age profile of saving rate.

in extended households qualifying as a household head. The latter type of individuals, already earning more than their co-residing parents, are wealthier than a typical individual aged 25–29. Second, as documented in table 12.3c and more formally in the probit equation for co-residence in table 8.2, old individuals who choose to live with their children tend to be poor, so the old nuclear households are overrepresented by wealthier old individuals. I record this as

Micro Fact # 1:   About a quarter of Japanese households are extended households. The independent aged (who maintain an independent house-hold) are on average wealthier than the dependent aged (who live with their children).

One needs to have access to micro data to deal with those problems. The work included in chapter 12, using the 1984 NSFIE data tapes, is the first and only study to produce age tabulations free from those problems. Income tax and hence saving for all households (not just for worker households) are imputed, so that the retired can be brought into the age tabulations. To deal with the distortion due to the prevalence of extended households, tabulations by age are for nuclear and extended households separately, and for extended households the household head is *redefined* to be the younger generation who may or may not earn more than the co-residing older generation. Figure 10.7, derived from table 12.3a, displays the age profile of the saving rate for the two household types for 1984. Now the saving rate is much more dependent on age than is indicated in figure 10.6, which underlies the seriousness of the distortion in published age tabulations. The saving rate of the independent aged declines with age and becomes negative starting with the 80–84 age group. The saving behavior of the rest of the older cohorts, who are in extended households, can be inferred from comparing the age profile for nuclear households with that for extended households. Note that for younger age groups, the saving rate for nuclear households is *lower* than the saving rate for extended households whose younger generation are similarly aged. That is, the effect of the presence of the dependent aged is to raise the saving rate. This remains true until the 45–49 age bracket for which the dependent aged are about 80–84 years old (see the age of parents in panel B of table 12.3a). Thus, the second stylized fact is

Micro Fact # 2:   Both the independent and dependent aged save until they get very old (about eighty to eighty-five).

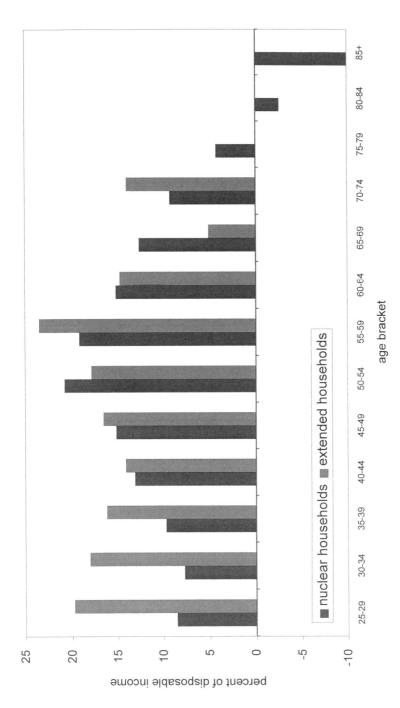

Figure 10.7
Cross-section age profile of saving rate, 1984.

Since interhousehold transfer receipts are excluded from income, the negative saving in micro fact #2 means that the very aged finance the excess of their consumption over their own income (which includes public and company pension benefits) by decumulating either conventional wealth (such as stocks and bonds) or collecting as private transfers (invisible) debts from others (most likely their children) or both.

10.3.3 Intergenerational Transfers

Another interesting fact about wealth accumulation in Japan can be obtained from the age profile of wealth for nuclear and extended households shown in figure 10.8, which is also derived from table 12.3a. Two features are noteworthy. (1) The cross-section age profile of wealth (net financial assets plus real assets) is much steeper for younger nuclear households—whose saving rate is lower by micro fact #2—than for extended households. This seemingly paradoxical fact can be explained by intergenerational transfers. For nuclear households, intergenerational transfers from parents are an interhousehold transfer leading to wealth accumulation over and above saving (recall that saving here does not include transfer receipts), whereas for extended households, intergenerational transfers are internal and do not contribute to increased wealth of the household. Furthermore, extended households by definition do not receive bequests from outside: upon death of the older generation, the extended household becomes nuclear. Section 12.3.4 shows that the longitudinal wealth profile for younger nuclear households that can be inferred from the cross-section age-wealth profile after adjusting for the cohort effect is in fact too steep to be accounted for by the household's own saving. (2) The cross-section age profile for old nuclear households is declining. A detailed discussion in section 12.3.7 shows that the implied longitudinal wealth profile is slightly *declining*.[11] This is despite the fact that the aged continue to save until very late in life. This must be due to inter vivos transfers: transfers from the aged to their children is financed by saving *and* a slight running down of wealth. It is argued in chapter 12 that this source of intergenerational transfers accounts for only a small part of the rapid wealth accumulation by younger nuclear households. This means that the bulk of the flow of intergenerational transfers is in the form of bequests.

One can imagine from the preceding discussion that it must be possible to estimate the flow of transfers from age profiles of saving and wealth.

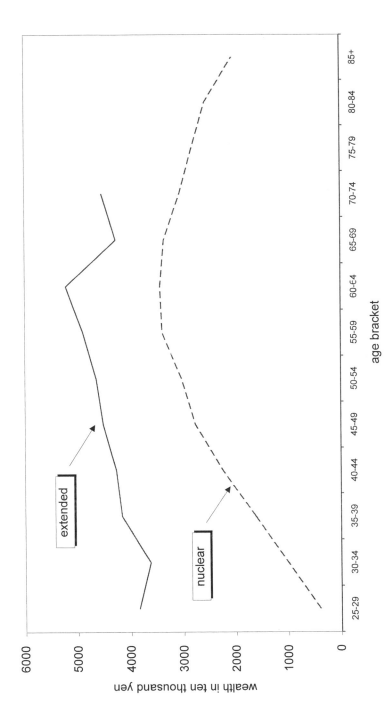

Figure 10.8
Cross-section age profile of wealth, 1984.

The flow of intergenerational transfers can be identified as the change in wealth less saving less capital gains. In chapter 11, I estimate the flow of intergenerational transfers over the period 1979–84 using synthetic cohorts created from published age profiles for 1979 and 1984. As I acknowledge in chapter 11, however, the calculation, based on the distorted age profiles from published tabulations, is only a very loose lower-bound estimate of the flow of intergenerational transfers. Takayama, Arita, and Kitamura (1994), who had access to the NSFIE data tapes for 1979, 1984, and 1989, find that for cohorts aged 40 or under, transfer receipts are the most important component of changes in wealth.

There are other studies using different methodologies that point to the prevalence of intergenerational transfers. Barthold and Ito (1991) find that taxable transfers available from tax records are a substantial portion of existing wealth. Tachibanaki and Shimono (1991) note a high variability of wealth-income ratio for relatively low income households in a micro data set different from the NSFIE and interpret this as a result of bequests and gifts. Ohtake and Horioka (1996) document from a public opinion survey that about one in two respondents plans to leave bequests. This discussion about wealth can be summarized as

Micro Fact #3: A substantial fraction of wealth held by the aged is eventually transferred to their children mainly through bequests.

10.3.4 Age Profile of Consumption

Another noteworthy feature of figure 10.7 is that the saving rate is positive for young cohorts under age 30. Since saving there does not include saving through transfer receipts and social security contributions, it is certain that their saving in any definition is positive. This is part of a larger fact about the age profile of consumption. Figure 10.9 displays the cross-section age profile of consumption taken from official tabulations for the past waves of the NSFIE. As in figure 10.6, being derived from published tabulations, nuclear and extended households are mixed up, so the hump in the true age profiles must be more pronounced than in the figure. This will reinforce the point I am about to make. Also, no adjustments necessary to be compatible with the national accounts are performed, due to data limitations. This, too, reinforces the point because imputed rent and government transfers in kind fall mostly on older cohorts. From this series of cross-section profiles, one can create synthetic cohorts by tra-

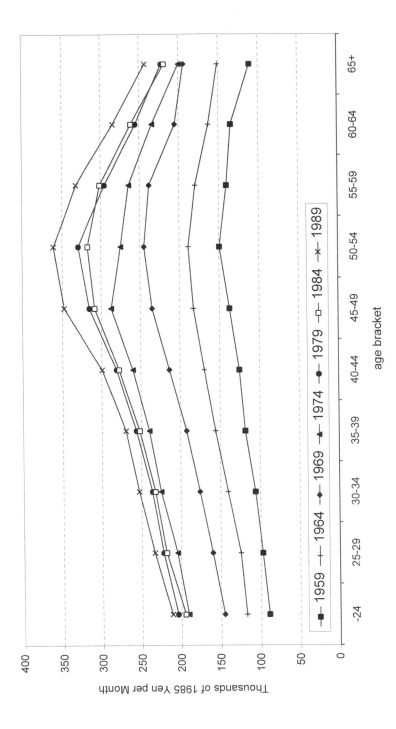

Figure 10.9
Cross-section age profile of consumption.

versing across the cross-section profiles. For example, the longitudinal profile for the cohort aged 25–29 in 1959 is the curve connecting the 25–29 node for 1959, the 30–34 node for 1964, and so forth. The point is that

Micro Fact #4: The longitudinal profile of consumption is very steep. Consumption by young cohorts is so low that the young save over and above their accumulation of social security wealth.

Comparison with the U.S. data shows that the Japanese profile is much steeper than the longitudinal consumption profile for the United States (see Carroll and Summers (1991)).

This micro fact in and of itself does not account for the high aggregate saving rate in Japan, because increased saving due to low consumption when young can finance a higher level of consumption later in the life cycle. It is the combination of micro facts #2, #3, and #4 that accounts for Japan's high saving rate: a substantial fraction of wealth steadily accumulated from very early until very late in life is not consumed and left to subsequent generations. Why the Japanese household saving has these characteristics is the subject of the next section.

10.4 Theoretical Explanations

The two fully articulated models of household saving in economics are the Life Cycle hypothesis (the LCH for short) and the Dynasty model (i.e., the Permanent Income hypothesis). In the LCH, households are selfish in that they are not concerned about the welfare of their offspring. In its textbook version, wealth accumulated during working years finances consumption after retirement. So the saving rate for the aged should be negative and wealth should be exhausted at the time of death. In a more sophisticated version, taking into account the longevity risk (that the timing of death cannot be foreseen) and the risk of illness, wealth consists exclusively of annuities and insurance policies covering medical expenditures. In the Dynasty model, generations are linked by altruism and act as if they form a single immortal dynasty. If one generation's resources are not enough to finance its consumption dictated by the dynastic preferences, there will be transfers to the generation from other generations of the dynasty. Therefore, consumption by a generation is *neutral* to the distribution of resources within the dynasty, given total dynasty resources. It is not necessary that intergenerational altruism be mutual for generations to be so linked. In the case of one-way altruism where the parent cares about the child but not vice versa, the promise of bequests and inter vivos gifts induces the adult child to submit to the parent's preferences (Becker's (1981) Rotten Kid theorem).

10.4.1 Consistency with Micro Facts

The Dynasty model is consistent with the micro stylized facts #2 and #3 that households continue to save until very late in life in order to transfer wealth to the next generation mainly in the form of bequests. The model can be extended to incorporate the choice between co-residence and living apart. In the altruistic model of co-residence in Rosenzweig and Wolpin (1993) and Hayashi (1995, included in this book as chapter 8), for example, whether two generations choose to live together or not is determined by a tradeoff between the benefit of shared living arising from the public good nature of housing and the loss of privacy. The parameters of the model can be chosen so that generations with low joint income tend to live together, as in micro fact #1. Regarding micro fact #4 that the longitudinal consumption profile is skewed toward old ages, it is inconsistent with the Dynasty model where altrusim is mutual, because the excessively low consumption when young could be avoided if the parent transferred wealth earlier in the form of inter vivos gifts than in bequests later in life. In the case of one-way altruism, however, there is a reason for the altruistic parent not to transfer wealth too early: if the parent experiences income losses after transferring most of its wealth to the child, the child cannot be relied upon to provide financial help. Thus, even a remote possibility of future financial difficulties could make the parent reluctant to transfer wealth early.[12] The combination of this, the rapid income growth, and the assumption of liquidity constraints that the young cannot mortgage their own future income to finance current consumption can explain micro fact #4. Note, however, that a redistribution of wealth from the parent to the child enforced by a third party, such as an abolition of the social security system, will increase the child's consumption. Thus, the neutrality of consumption with respect to the distribution of resources within the dynasty, which is the hallmark of the Dynasty model, fails under one-way altruism.

   The LCH as stated above is clearly at odds with micro stylized facts #2 and #3 about the aged. The failure of the pure LCH has long been recognized, and in response to that the model has been extended to include various factors. These extensions are based on the assumption that some services (including insurance) are not available from markets. They include:

1. *self insurance.* For whatever reason, reasonably priced insurance policies (including annuity contracts) are not supplied by the market. The household is forced to use conventional wealth to deal with the longevity and other risks. Since wealth must be available to finance consumption in the event of exceptional longevity, most households leave some wealth at death. This unspent wealth is called an accidental bequest.

2. *children as a provider of insurance.* When the parent lives "too long" or becomes ill, the child provides financial help. The child must be compensated for doing this. A transfer from parent to child is an insurance premium in disguise.

3. *children as a provider of attention otherwise unavailable to parents.* The child is the sole supplier to the parent of attention (such as phone calls and visits), which is the service desired by parents. The price of the service charged by the child is a transfer from the parent.

Factor (1) can explain the existence of bequests (although it is not clear why children are the beneficiaries) but not the existence of inter vivos gifts. It can partially explain micro fact #2 (positive saving until very old), although an extremely high degree of risk aversion would be needed to explain the lack of negative saving until as late in life as age 80.

Factors (2) and (3) can explain the prevalence of extended families (micro fact #1) because co-residence is a vehicle whereby the service is provided to parents. They also explain the prevalence of transfers (micro fact #3) because transfers are informal contractual payments for the service delivered by children. The payment by the parent would not be before the child delivers the service, because the child may renege on the promise after collecting the payment. This limited commitment consideration explains why the predominant form of intergenerational transfers is bequests. To convince the parent that the service will be rendered in good faith, the child may even have to post a bond with the parent, in which case the parent would continue accumulating wealth to be returned to child upon death. Thus, both (2) and (3) can explain a wide variety of age-wealth profiles for the aged. Yet wealth broadly defined to include (implicit) debts issued by parents when they received financial help or attention from children is fully exhausted at death, preserving the basic tenet of the LCH. The LCH thus extended to include transfers as payments for services provided by children is sometimes called the *exchange model*.

Micro fact #2 that the aged finance consumption by their own income can be explained by (3) but not by (2). Under (3), consumption is mismeasured because household surveys do not measure the attention consumed by the parent. Since the deferred payment for attention is bequests, their measured saving is positive.[13] Factor (2) cannot be an explanation of micro fact #2 for the independent aged because, as noted in the previous section, they are on average providers, not recipients, of financial help.

As in the Dynasty model, micro fact #4 about the young can be explained by liquidity constraints and the high income growth. Without altruistic parents providing informal income insurance, fear of low future income realizations may be enough to make the young abstain from borrowing from the market even if it is feasible. That is, under the LCH, the low consumption by the young can also be explained by precautionary saving.

10.4.2 Evidence from Econometric Studies Using Micro Data

Thus, the exchange model is consistent with micro facts, whereas the Dynasty model, at least the version maintaining neutrality, is not. This is also the conclusion from the small number of available econometric studies. Hayashi (1995) provides a strong statistical rejection of the neutrality property of the Dynasty model using data on Japanese extended households. There is no study for Japan comparable to Cox's (1987) test for the exchange model based on the transfer equation relating transfer receipts to the recipient s and the donor's incomes. In Cox's test, a significantly positive coefficient of the recipient's income is taken as evidence against the Dynasty model. Such test is not feasible for Japan because available data sets miss either the donor's or the recipient's income. For example, in the transfer equation I estimate using the NSFIE micro data reported in table 8.3, the donor's income cannot be included. The inverse relationship I find there between transfer receipts and the recipient's income can be interpreted as a result of income risk sharing between parents and children, which is consistent with the exchange model as well as the Dynasty model.

Section 11.7 contains an econometric test to discriminate between the Dynasty model and the LCH. The test exploits the large expansion of the Japanese social security system that took place in 1973. Since the expansion entails a transfer of wealth from young to old cohorts, it should increase consumption by old cohorts under the LCH whereas under the Dynasty model the effect should be zero. In table 11.11, I estimate the Euler equation (an equation for consumption growth) using the synthetic cohorts created from the past waves of the NSFIE and find that the social security dummy in the equation gets a negative coefficient. But the coefficient is not very sharply estimated.[14]

Thus, the econometric literature has not provided convincing evidence against the exchange model. But this should *not* be interpreted as a rejection of any type of altruism. Being altruistic to children does not prevent parents from employing children as a provider of insurance or attention otherwise unavailable from markets. In fact, the original statements of the exchange model (Bernheim, Shleifer, and Summers (1985) and Cox (1987)) assume a one-way altruism by expressing the parent's utility as a function of the parent's own consumption, the child's attention, and the child's utility. The difference from the standard Dynasty model with neutrality is that the desire for attention creates disagreements between altruistic parent and child over the distribution of consumption and the amount of attention to be supplied. Furthermore, the exchange motives alone may not be enough to explain the size of aggregate flow of intergenerational transfers. The exchange model without any sort of altruism implies that the value of attention supplied by children and sold to parents equals the flow of intergenerational transfers. I doubt that the child's attention is worth that much, but this issue cannot be settled now because there is as yet no reliable estimate of the size of intergenerational transfers.

Illuminating in this context is the public opinion survey result reported in Ohtake and Horioka (1996). In 1989, for example, 32 percent of households expressed an altruistic motive by agreeing to the proposition "We want to leave as large a bequest as possible to our children, etc., regardless of whether or not they look after us in our old age." Another 20 percent expressed what can be interpreted as the exchange motive "We want to leave as large a bequest as possible to our children, etc., provided they look after us in our old age." It seems clear to me that both the exchange and altruistic motives are important for explaining saving.

10.4.3 Consistency with Macro Facts

So far I have argued that some combination of the pure LCH and the pure Dynasty model can explain the available micro evidence on individual households and age cohorts. Now I argue that both of the two polar models can explain the high postwar Japanese aggregate saving rate.

The available explanation by the Dynasty model uses the logic of the standard neoclassical growth model, a growth model inhabited by the representative immortal dynastic family that has access to the diminishing returns-to-scale neoclassical production function. When the capital stock is low, as in Japan immediately after the war, the return from saving is unusually high because of diminishing returns to scale. This immediately sparks rapid capital accumulation that lasts until the capital-labor ratio gets close to the steady state value. This feature of an immediate investment boom is inconsistent with the postwar Japanese experience where the phenomenon of high saving did not occur until the mid 1960s. However, Christiano (1989) shows that the standard growth model can be made consistent with the hump-shaped Japanese saving rate. Suppose that there is some subsistence level of consumption at which the marginal utility of consumption is very high, and suppose Japan after the war was at that subsistence level. Then the dynastic family would choose to consume rather than save even though the return from saving is high. But eventually, as the standard of living gradually improves, the high return from saving wins out and the family starts accumulating wealth. Christiano (1989) simulated the neoclassical growth model that has this subsistence feature to generate a hump in the saving rate around 1970.[15] In his simulation, the increase in the growth rate precedes the increase in the saving rate, an important feature of postwar Japanese economic growth noted by Romer (1986).

Simulations under the LCH can be found in section 11.4 and a more elaborate study by Hayashi, Ito, and Slemrod (1988, included in this book as chapter 13). It is known from Tobin's (1967) original steady-state simulation taking into account the age-earnings profile for the United States that the life-cycle economy cannot generate very high saving rates. This conclusion may be altered if the U.S. age-earnings profile is replaced by the much steeper Japanese age-earnings profile and if the constant steady-state growth rate is raised to match the Japanese growth rate. The simulation study in chapter 11 shows that those changes of model parameters to match the Japanese features actually reduce the aggregate saving rate. It is true that a higher growth rate, by reducing the economic weight of old cohorts relative to younger cohorts, diminishes the negative contribution by old cohorts to aggregate saving. But this effect is offset by increased consumption by younger cohorts who postpone saving in anticipation of higher future income.

Another Japanese feature that differs from its U.S. equivalent, and that might affect the aggregate saving rate, is the low consumption by young cohorts (micro fact #4). In the simulation study of chapter 13, this distortion of the age profile of consumption is a result of the household's decision to purchase a house. A combination of very high housing prices, a high downpayment ratio, and liquidity constraints forces young cohorts to save. The study shows, however, that this serious distortion of the consumption profile hardly affects the aggregate saving rate. After examining such factors as the tax rate on capital income and the bequest motive, the study finds that the steady-state assumption is the culprit. That is, if the steady-state assumption is dropped and households are assumed to have foreseen the actual path of the (nonconstant) postwar growth rate, the simulation starts to generate aggregate saving rates that resemble Japan's saving rate. For example, the simulated saving rate for 1980 is 16.12 percent whereas the actual rate is 18.29 percent (see table 13.3). The reason is that, in addition to diminishing the economic weight of the aged, the high growth rate in the 1960s, which under the assumption of perfect foresight was seen as temporary, increases saving by middle-aged cohorts who benefited from it much more than it increases consumption by younger cohorts. This non-steady state simulation predicts that the Japanese private saving rate will decline gradually, to 15.03 percent in year 2000, 12.96 percent in 2010, and 5.27 percent in 2030.

It is easy to find faults with these simulations. Christiano's simulation under the Dynasty model, while successful in duplicating the saving rate hump, underpredicts the saving rate for more recent years because the model predicts that the economy will converge quickly to the steady state after the saving/investment boom. The simulations performed in chapters 11 and 13 under the LCH take the growth rate and the interest rate as exogenously given. But this can be remedied by including the production function in the model. A more serious problem is that older cohorts in the model dissave, contrary to the micro stylized facts. On the other hand, these simulation studies do suggest that some hybrid model combining the exchange model with some type of altruism, which I have argued is consistent with micro facts, can be made consistent with macro stylized facts also.

10.5   Concluding Comments

I hope this chapter has convinced the reader that much has been learned about the Japanese saving behavior. The research reviewed here has unearthed important stylized facts about the macro and micro aspects, which ten years ago were unknown or only poorly understood. We can now profitably contemplate what sort of model is best suited for explaining those stylized facts. It has become clear that intergenerational linkages through the exchange of nonmarket services and through altruism will be an essential ingredient.

The agenda for future research that emerged from this review is the following.

1. A sharper estimate of the aggregate flow of intergenerational transfers is needed to determine the importance or unimportance of the altruistic bequest motive.

2. More difficult is to construct an operational model of intergenerational interactions, operational in the sense that one can simulate the model to generate aggregate saving, as has been done for the LCH and the Dynasty model.

3. The intergenerational linkages include the exchange of attention through coresidence. A typical Japanese individual forms an independent nuclear household upon marriage years before merging with the parent's household. The saving behavior in the period of a nuclear household will depend on whether and when to live with parents to form a two-generation household and how much assets parents can bring. To my knowledge, no theory of saving treating as endogenous the formation and resolution of two-generation households has been developed.

4. The point that a high saving rate necessarily follows from the convergence to the steady state from a low capital stock needs to be verified for other Asian newly developed countries. The question of the high Japanese saving rate is really a question of economic development. The research reviewed here does not answer why the process of convergence did not start until after the war. Ultimately, research on saving should be directed to understanding institutional and other factors that served as a catalyst for postwar Japanese economic growth.

Appendix: Data Sources

Figures 10.1, 10.2

The unadjusted national saving rate with or without government capital formation is from the National Income Accounts (NIA). National saving is from table 1-[2]-I-2, government capital formation from 1-[2]-III-3, and NNP from table 1-[2]-I-1 of the NIA. The adjusted series are from table U3 of chapter 11. For the United States, national saving, depreciation, and NNP are from the NIPA before the 1995 Comprehensive Revision mentioned in section 2.1 of the text.

Figure 10.3

For the prewar period, the data are from Ohkawa and Shinohara (1979). Gross saving is defined as

$$Y - CP - CG - (I - MNIL),$$

where $Y =$ "gross national expenditure at market prices" (table A1 of Ohkawa (1979)), $CP =$ "personal consumption expenditure" (table A1), $CG =$ "general government consumption expenditure" (table A1), $I =$ "gross domestic fixed-capital formation" (table A1, A38), $NMLI =$ "gross domestic fixed capital formation excluding military" (table A38).

Net saving is gross saving less replacement cost depreciation. Depreciation is "Provisions for the consumption of fixed capital" (table A7). The current account is calculated as $Y - CP - CG - I$.

For the postwar period, gross saving and GNP are from the NIA (table 1-[2]-I-1, 2). Depreciation (including depreciation on government capital) is from table U2 of chapter 11.

Figure 10.4

The capital stock for the prewar period is from table 1, vol. 3 of the Long Term Economic Statistics (LTES) (Ohkawa and Shinohara (1974)). For the postwar period, data splicing is needed. The 1950 value of the real capital stock is assumed to be 1.1 times the 1938 value. This factor of 1.1 was taken from chapter 4 of the LTES. There, the *gross* capital stock in the LTES for 1938 was converted in 1960 prices using price indexes for various assets for 1938 and 1960, and then it was compared to the 1950 value in 1960 prices of a gross capital stock series (the H series reported in table 4-1 of chapter 4 of the LTES). It turned out that the latter was 1.1 times the former. I assume that the same factor of 1.1 applies to (net) capital stock. For 1950–55, I assume that the growth rate of the net capital stock is the same as that of the gross capital stock series from the H-series. The nominal net capital stock and the deflator for gross capital formation (referred to in the text as the flow deflator) since 1955 are taken from the NIA (table 2-I-1 and Table 1-[2]-IV-1). The real capital stock since 1955 is the ratio of the nominal stock to the deflator.

Figure 10.5

Japanese prewar real GNP is taken from table A3 of Ohkawa and Shinohara (1979). Table A4 of Ohkawa and Shinohara reports two additional real GNP series: Y1 = "gross national expenditure in millions of 1934–36 prices for 1940–51 (excluding 1945), and Y2 = gross national expenditure in billions of 1965 yen for 1952–75. The prewar real GNP series and Y1 can be used to cover the period 1885–1951 (excluding 1945). The Y1 and Y2 series do not overlap, so I assume that the growth rate of real GNP from 1951 to 1952 is the same as the real GNP growth rate from 1952 to 1953 given by Y2. The Y2 series and the GNP in the NIA since 1955 are spliced at year 1955.

For the United States real GNP for 1885–1929 is taken from Balke and Gordon (1989). Real GNP since 1929 is taken from the NIPA before the Comprehensive Revision.

The population for 1885–1940 and 1950–1970 is taken from table A53 of Ohkawa and Shinohara (1979). The 1940–50 gap is filled by linear interpolation. Japan's population since 1970 and the U.S. population are from the census data.

The position of U.S. per capita GNP relative to that of Japan assumes that the latter for 1994 is 20 percent less than the former. This is consistent with most available estimates of the purchasing power parity value of the yen.

Figure 10.6

The data for "worker households" (excluding singles) on after-tax income and consumption are from the *Reports on National Survey on Family Income and Expenditures* (various years, hereafter the NS). After-tax income is pretax income less income tax less social security contributions. The following published tables from the NS are used: table 12, vol. 1 for 1956; table 7, vol. 1 for 1964; table 17, vol. 1 for 1969; table 6, vol. 1 for 1974; table 6, no. 1, vol. 1 for 1979; table 9, no. 1, vol. 1 for 1984; and table 6, no. 1, vol. 1 for 1989.

Figures 10.7, 10.8

Table 3a of chapter 12.

Figure 10.9

For 1964, 1974, 1979, 1984, and 1989, the data are from published tables for all households excluding singles. The following tables from the NS are used: table 6, vol. 1 for 1964; table 6, vol. 1 for 1974; table 6, no. 1, vol. 1 for 1979; table 9, no. 1, vol. 1 for 1984; and table 6, no. 1, vol. 1 for 1989. For 1959 and 1969, the tables for "worker households" listed above for figure 10.6 are used.

Table 10.1

Illustrative table 39, *1996 Annual Report on National Accounts* (Economic Planning Agency of the Japanese government).

Table 10.2

For the United States, replacement cost depreciation and the capital stock are from *Fixed Reproducible Tangible Wealth in the United States, 1925–89* (Bureau of Economic Analysis, 1993) and updates, and GNP is from the NIPA before the 1995 Comprehensive Revision. For Japan, replacement cost depreciation is calculated as explained in the addendum to chapter 11. The private capital stock at year beginning (i.e., at the end of the previous year) is the sum of line 2 of table 2-II-1, line 1 of table 2-II-2, line 1 of table 2-II-4, and line 2 of table 2-II-5. To be consistent with the definition of GNP in the NIPA before the Comprehensive Revision, historical cost depreciation for the government sector in the NIA must be deducted from the GNP in the NIA; see section 11.A.5.

Table 10.3

The depreciation rate is the ratio of depreciation for the asset to the stock of the asset at the beginning of the year. For the United States, depreciation and the capital stock are for the private sector and are from *Fixed Reproducible Tangible Wealth in the United States, 1925–89* (Bureau of Economic Analysis, 1993) and updates. For Japan, depreciation and the capital stock are for the nation as a whole (including the government sector), because only for the nation as a whole data on depreciation and capital by asset are available from the NIA. The procedure for calculating replacement cost depreciation by asset for the nation as a whole is similar to the procedure for replacement cost depreciation by sector explained in the addendum to chapter 11. Let $I(t)$ = gross investment in the asset in question, $KD(t)$ = capital stock at the beginning of year t, $PKD(t)$ = its deflator, $UKD(t)$ = Okinawa's capital stock for $t = 1972$ and 0 otherwise, $APKD(t)$ = average deflator value = $[PKD(t + 1) + PKD(t)]/2$. Then $DEPR(t)$, replacement cost depreciation in year t for the asset in question, is calculated as

$$DEPR(t) = I(t) - APKD(t) \cdot \left[\frac{KD(t + 1)}{PKD(t + 1)} - \frac{KD(t) + UKD(t)}{PKD(t)} \right]$$

For each asset, $I(t)$ is available from table 1-[3]-15, $KD(t)$ and $PKD(t)$ are from table 2-IV-1, and $UKD(1972)$ is assumed to be 0.0691215 percent of $KD(1972)$. Since government capital is not depreciated except for buildings in the NIA, this procedure, although producing a much higher value of depreciation than is reported in the NIA, merely captures discards at replacement costs for government capital. For this reason, $DEPR(t)$ is likely to be an underestimate, particularly for structures.

Notes

Much of the material of this chapter draws on Hayashi (1989, 1991, 1992).

1. See the September 1995 issue of *Survey of Current Business* for a review of the Comprehensive Revision focusing on government investment.

2. According to a February 1996 release of the revised NIPA, net government capital formation in 1994 is about 1 percent of GDP for the United States.

3. The big adjustment for the 1950s may be due to my use of the flow deflator for the price index of the capital stock, which is needed for carrying out the adjustment for the years before 1970. This is closely related to the decline in the capital stock, converted into real terms by the flow deflator, in the 1950s shown in figure 10.4 below.

4. See Dekle and Summers (1991).

5. The numbers for Japan are for the nation as a whole, because depreciation and capital stock by asset is available only for the nation as a whole in the NIA. Since the government capital in the NIA is more like a gross stock, as mentioned in section 10.2.1, and since most of the government capital is structures, the value share of structures in the table for Japan is overstated. This explains why the implicit depreciation rate for structures is lower for Japan.

6. The English summary is Ohkawa and Shinohara (1979).

7. As noted above, the level of the postwar capital stock in the NIA might be underestimated. This, however, is not a serious problem here because the splicing adjusts the postwar level so that the 1955 value is in a certain proportion to the prewar value.

8. The only missing step in the calculation is the allocation of government transfers between households. Inclusion of government transfers, raising income and consumption by the same amount, does not change the level of household saving, however.

9. To allocate corporate saving between households and between age cohorts, one needs a household survey with information on earnings per share for all shares owned by the household. Failing that, blowing up the household's dividend income by the reciprocal of the average retention ratio may be a good approximation.

10. *Report on National Survey of Family Income and Expenditures* (1959, and every five years thereafter).

11. My conclusion that the aged decumulate wealth agrees with the finding of the Horioka et al. (1995) finding from a different data set that has a direct measure of the change in wealth for each household in the sample. For other studies looking at the longitudinal wealth profile, which in my view either are unreliable due to small sample sizes or improperly adjust for the cohort effect, see the literature cited in Horioka (1993).

12. See Becker (1981, 188). For a further formalization, see the theoretical model in Altonji, Hayashi, and Kotlikoff (1996).

13. This point is most easily understood by considering the following extreme case. The only consumption desired by parents is children's attention, to be paid for by bequests. Measured consumption is zero. Measured income is interest income from wealth. Thus the saving rate is 100 percent until death!

14. The t value is 2.4, but it is based on the assumption that consumption changes are uncorrelated across cohorts. Allowance for possible correlations would reduce the t value.

15. The saving rate in Christiano's simulation and in the simulations discussed below should be interpreted as the private saving rate, because the model does not include the government sector.

References

Altonji, J., F. Hayashi, and L. Kotlikoff. 1996. Parental altruism and inter vivos transfers: Theory and evidence. National Bureau of Economic Research Working Paper no. 5378.

Balke, N., and R. Gordon. 1989. The estimation of prewar Gross National Product: Methodology and new evidence. *Journal of Political Economy* 97:38–92.

Barthold, T., and T. Ito. 1991. Bequest taxes and accumulation of household wealth: U.S.–Japan Comparison. In *The political economy of tax reform*, ed. T. Ito and A. Krueger, 235–90. Chicago: University of Chicago Press.

Becker, G. 1981. *A treatise on the family*, Cambridge, MA: Harvard University Press.

Bernheim, B., A. Shleifer, and L. Summers. 1985. The strategic bequest motive, *Journal of Political Economy* 93:1045–76.

Carroll, C., and L. Summers. 1991. Consumption growth parallels income growth: Some new evidence. In *National saving and economic performance*, ed. B. Bernheim and J. Shoven, 305–43. Chicago: University of Chicago Press.

Christiano, L. 1989. Understanding Japan's saving rate: The reconstruction hypothesis, *Federal Reserve Bank of Minneapolis Quarterly Review* (spring): 10–25.

Cox, D. 1987. Motives for private income transfers. *Journal of Political Economy* 95:508–46.

Dean, E., M. Darrough, and A. Neef. 1990. Alternative measures of capital inputs in Japanese manufacturing. In *Productivity growth in Japan and the United States*, ed. C. Hulton, 229–65. Chicago: University of Chicago Press.

Dekle, R., and L. Summers, 1991. Japan's high saving rate reaffirmed. *Bank of Japan Monetary and Economic Studies* 9:63–78.

EPA. 1978. *Kokumin Keizai Keisan no Mikata Tsukaikata* (Guide to the new national economic accounts). Government Printing Office, Ministry of Finance. Tokyo, Japan.

Hayashi, F. 1986. Why is Japan's saving rate so apparently high? *NBER Macroeconomics Annual 1986*, ed. Stanley Fischer, 147–210. Cambridge: MIT Press.

Hayashi, F. 1989. Japan's saving rate: New data and reflactions. National Bureau of Economic Research Working Paper no. 3205.

Hayashi, F. 1991. Reply to Dekle and Summers. *Bank of Japan Monetary and Economic Studies* 9:79–89.

Hayashi, F. 1992. Explaining Japan's saving: A review of recent literature. *Bank of Japan Monetary and Economic Studies* 10:63–78.

Hayashi, F. 1995. Is the Japanese extended family attruistically linked? A test based on Engel curves. *Journal of Political Economy* 103 (June): 661–74.

Hayashi, F., A. Ando, and R. Ferris. 1988. Life cycle and bequest savings: A study of Japanese and U.S. households based on data from the 1984 NSFIE and the 1983 Survey of Consumer Finances. *Journal of the Japanese and International Economies* 2 (December): 450–91.

Hayashi, F., T. Ito, and J. Slemrod. 1988. Housing finance imperfections, taxation, and private saving: A comparative simulation analysis of the United States and Japan. *Journal of the Japanese and International Economies* 2 (September): 215–38.

Horioka, C. 1993. Saving in Japan. In *World savings: An international survey*, ed. A. Heertje, 238–78. Oxford, UK: Blackwell Publishers.

Horioka, C., N. Kasuga, K. Yamazaki, and W. Watanabe. 1995. Do the aged dissave in Japan? Evidence from micro data. Mimeo., Osaka University.

Hulten, C., and F. Wykoff. 1981. The measurement of economic depreciation. In *Depreciation, inflation and the taxation of income from capital*, ed. C. Hulten, 81–125. Washington, DC: Urban Institute.

Iwamoto, Y. 1995. Japan's saving rate is indeed lower than Professor Hayashi revealed. *Japan and the World Economy* 187:1–7.

Jorgenson, D., M. Kuroda, and M. Nishimizu. 1987. Japan-U.S. Industry-Level Productivity Comparisons, 1960–1979. *Journal of the Japanese and International Economies* 1:1–30.

Kuninori, M. 1988. *Setsubi No Shoukyakuritsu Ni Tsuite* (On the depreciation rate of equipments). *Keiei Keizai Kenkyu* 9-3, 47 pages.

Kuroda, M. 1990. Comment. In *Productivity growth in Japan and the United States*, ed. C. Hulton, 265–66. Chicago: University of Chicago Press.

Ohkawa, K., and M. Shinohara. 1974. *1868 Nen Irai No Nihonkeizai no Chouki Toukei* (Estimates of long-term economic statistics of Japan since 1868). Tokyo: Toyo Keizai Shinposha.

Ohkawa, K., and M. Shinohara, eds. 1979. *Patterns of Japanese economic development: A quantitative appraisal.* New Haven, CT: Yale University Press.

Ohtake, F., and C. Horioka. 1996. Saving motives in Japan. In *The Distribution of Income and Wealth in Japan*, ed. T. Ishikawa. Oxford, UK: Oxford University Press.

Okita, S. 1949. *Taiheiyo Sensou niyoru Wagakuni no Higai Sogo Hokokusho* (Comprehensive report on the damage in Japan during the Pacific War). Domestic Document no. 8, Economic Stabilization Agency, April.

Romer, P. 1986. Comment on Hayashi. *NBER Macroeconomics Annual* 1:220–32.

Rosenzweig, M., and K. Wolpin. 1993. Intergenerational support and the life-cycle incomes of young men and their parents: Human capital investments, co-residence and intergenerational financial transfers. *Journal of Labor Economics* 11:84–112.

Tachibanaki, T., and K. Shimono. 1991. Wealth accumulation processby income class. *Journal of the Japanese and International Economies* 5:239–60.

Takayama, N., F. Arita, and Y. Kitamura. 1994. *Kakei Chochiku no Zouka to Sono Youin* (Increases in household assets and their causes). *Keizai Kenkyu* 45:16–30.

Tobin, J. 1967. Life cycle saving and balanced growth. In *Ten Economic studies in the tradition of Irving Fisher*, ed. W. Fellner, 231–56. Now York: Wiley.

11   Why Is Japan's Saving
Rate So Apparently High?

11.1   Introduction

The huge U.S. trade deficit with Japan, which totaled $50 billion in 1985 and accounts for a thumping one-third of the total U.S. trade deficit, has worried policy makers and economists alike for some time. The widening trade gap has cost jobs in the United States, particularly in the manufacturing sector, providing ample ammunition for protectionists. The identity in the national income accounts states that the excess of saving over investment equals the trade surplus. The blame for Japan's large trade surplus with the United States must therefore fall on Japan's high saving or her slumping investment. The widespread sentiment that the Japanese save too much was even echoed in a 1985 speech by the U.S. Secretary of State.[1] The sentiment has some empirical grounds. In 1984 the most widely mentioned saving rate—the rate of personal saving— was 16 percent for Japan, a full 10 percentage points higher than that in the United States.

The purpose of this article is to explore possible factors that contribute to Japan's high saving rate. That Japan's saving rate is high by international standards has been recognized in Japan for more than two decades, yet the reason for it is poorly understood: I quote the last sentence of a recent survey in the Japanese literature. "In any event ... Japan's high personal saving rate remains a mystery to be resolved."[2] It is not that empirical investigations have been hampered by a scarcity of data. Although consistent time series in the Japanese national income accounts do not start until 1965, a large amount of micro data on households is available from various surveys that have been conducted regularly by the

Originally published in *NBER Macroeconomics Annual 1986* (MIT Press, 1986), 147–210. Reprinted with permission.

Japanese government. Perhaps the issue of Japan's high saving rate has not attracted enough of the empirical attention it deserves.

I will begin with very down-to-earth facts about aggregate saving in Japan and the United States. Those are contained in section 11.2, which tries to see if the perception of high savings in Japan has any empirical basis. It will be argued that some conceptual differences between U.S. and Japanese national accounting explain a substantial portion of the observed differences in the saving rates. Section 11.3 summarizes the explanations that have been offered in the literature. (I will examine them further in later sections.) The first theory of saving, to be taken up in section 11.4, is the life-cycle hypothesis. After rejecting the life-cycle explanations, I turn in section 11.5 to micro data on households analyzed by age group to locate possible deviations from the life-cycle hypothesis of the actual Japanese saving behavior. It turns out that the cross-section age profile of saving in Japan appears to defy any simple life-cycle explanation, including an explanation based on the high housing-related saving by younger generations. Continuing the theme at the end of section 11.5 that bequests might be an important factor, section 11.6 digresses somewhat to calculate the aggregate flow of intergenerational transfers that can be inferred from the cross-section saving profiles. Other aspects of household behavior, including the impact of social security, relevant to assessing the importance of bequests will be analyzed in section 11.7. Section 11.8 then takes up a separate issue, tax incentives for saving. The Japanese tax system does seem to be geared to promote saving. Taxes, however, are probably not the main factor behind the high saving rate, I argue, because saving does not appear to be responsive to interest rates.

11.2 Facts about Japan's Aggregate Saving Rates

11.2.1 Which Saving Rate?

When comparing saving behavior between the two countries, we must first decide which saving rate to use. The choice of the saving rate has several dimensions. The first is the boundary of the relevant sector. Should we look at the household sector, the private sector, or the nation as a whole? The focus on *personal* (household) saving is unwarranted if undistributed profits (corporate saving) are fully reflected in the capital gains in stock prices that are recognized by households as part of income, or if corporations are just an accounting device for individuals to receive corporate tax treatment on their income.[3] We should then look at *private* saving (the sum of personal and corporate saving). But even private saving is inappropriate if the private sector can see through the government veil and internalize the government budget constraint. The Ricardian Equivalence Thorem states that a government budget deficit is recognized by the private sector as a tax of the same amount because the public debt is just a signal of future increased taxes. The relevant notion of saving then is *national* saving (the sum of private and government saving). The question of the relevant boundary is one of the basic issues in economics yet to be resolved, and in this article we will not commit ourselves to any one particular saving rate. We should, however, bear in mind that the substance of the corporate sector in the Japanese National Accounts is somewhat different from corporate business in the U.S. National Income and Product Accounts. At one end of the corporate sector in the Japanese national accounts there are numerous token corporations that are essentially a disguised form of the household sector. At the other end lie most government enterprises (including the central bank as well as institutions that are not corporations in the legal sense).[4]

The second dimension in the choice of the saving rate is the definition of income. Should we include in income, and hence in saving, revaluation (capital gains/losses) of assets? Perhaps fully anticipated revaluation should be included, but that is difficult to identify. If revaluation is recognized as part of income, private saving is a more meaningful saving concept than personal saving.

The third dimension is the scope of assets, which is where the treatment of consumer durables is relevant. In principle, any commodity that is durable should be regarded as an object of saving. But measurement of the durability of commodities in general is a difficult task.[5] The importance of consumer durables will be touched upon when we compare the personal saving rate between the two countries in figure 11.2. Depending on the stand one takes in each of the three dimensions, there can be multitudes of saving rates. Only a subset of the possible saving rates will be discussed in the text. The data appendix to this chapter provides information necessary for calculating not only the saving rates discussed in the text but also several others that the reader might care to entertain.

11.2.2 Data Comparability

Even after the choice of the saving rate is made, there is a measurement problem that makes international comparison tricky. There are (at least) four major conceptual differences between the United States and Japan in the compilation of national accounts.

1. A very surprising fact about the Japanese national income accounts is that depreciation is valued at *historical costs*.[6] This means that personal saving is overstated during and after the inflationary period of the 1970s.[7] Remember that personal disposable income is a *net* concept—it excludes depreciation of household assets. Since personal saving is defined as personal disposable income minus consumption, it is net of depreciation. Corporate saving is severely overstated for the same reason. There must, however, be an official estimate of replacement-cost depreciation floating around within the Economic Planning Agency, the statistical mill of the Japanese national accounts data, since the stock of assets is valued at replacement costs in the capital accounts (balance sheets and stock-flow reconciliations) of the Japanese national accounts. Although the official estimate is neither published nor released, we can recover it fairly accurately from the numbers published in the *Annual Reports on National Accounts*. Detailed descriptions of our calculation procedure and our estimate of capital consumption adjustments (the excess of depreciation at replacement costs over depreciation at historical costs) are given in the data appendix. The basic idea is to separate out the revaluation component from the reconciliation accounts and identify the residual as capital consumption adjustments. The calculation can be done only for the post-1969 period because the capital accounts start in 1970. Since investment goods prices were more or less stable until the first oil crisis of 1973–74, the capital consumption adjustment is not significant for that period. However, the size of the adjustment to private depreciable assets has increased rapidly since then, reaching as much as 30 percent of reported private saving in several recent years. (See table 11.A2.)

2. Unlike most other countries (including Japan), the U.S. National Income and Product Accounts compiled by the Bureau of Economic Analysis (BEA) treat all types of government expenditure as consumption and fail to credit the government for the value of its tangible assets. The BEA definition of government saving is therefore the government's budget surplus, while government saving in the Japanese national accounts includes in addition the net increase in government tangible assets. This conceptual difference also means that even GNP and NNP are not directly comparable because the BEA definition does not include output service flows from government tangible assets.

To make matters even more complicated, the Japanese national accounts do not depreciate government depreciable assets except buildings.

Thus reported depreciation of government assets is very substantially understated: it is valued at historical costs and it covers only buildings. In the data appendix we constructed time series on the stock of government depreciable assets by the perpetual inventory method and the associated depreciation at replacement costs, so that the saving rate series for which government assets are included as components of assets can be constructed for Japan. We decided not to construct such saving rate series for the United States. When we compare the Japanese to the U.S. data, we will recalculate the Japanese saving rates according to the BEA convention.

Readily available data sources on U.S. government capital accounts are Ruggles and Ruggles (1982) and Eisner (1985).[8] The definition of government assets in Ruggles and Ruggles appears comparable to that in the Japanese national accounts, but the data do not extend beyond 1980. The ratio to NNP of net government capital formation for the United States was roughly around 1 percent in the 1970s. Eisner's data encompass a much broader spectrum of assets and are thus not directly comparable. According to our estimate of government assets, the ratio to NNP of net government capital formation is about 3–5 percent (see table 11.A5). Thus the exclusion of government capital alone makes a 2–4 percent difference to the BEA definition of the national saving rate. However, it is not clear that all government capital formation should be counted as saving. Government investment projects in Japan, often politically motivated and not necessarily justifiable on economic grounds, may be viewed by the private sector as wasteful and incapable of yielding any useful service flows. It could even be argued that government capital is inherently unobservable, in which case it would be difficult to estimate the useful (as viewed by the private sector) asset lives for municipal buildings, highways, dams, and tunnels.

3. The Japanese national accounts do not adjust after-tax income for "capital transfers" (wealth taxes and lump-sum transfers), so in the capital transactions (saving/investment) accounts the sum of saving, depreciation, and capital transfers equals the sum of investment in tangible and financial assets plus a statistical discrepancy. In what follows we include transfers as part of saving, which is consistent with the U.S. practice. For the household sector, capital transfers are negative because they are mainly bequest and gift taxes. In 1984 these are about 5 percent of reported personal saving. Almost all of the reduction of personal saving is transferred to corporate saving, making little difference to national saving.

4. (very minor) In the U.S. national accounts personal consumption and saving do not add up to personal disposable income because interest paid

by households to business and to foreigners is included in personal disposable income. In what follows that interest component will be subtracted from U.S. personal disposable income.[9]

All the saving rates to be presented are adjusted as described above. The data source for Japan is the *1986 Annual Report on National Accounts* (which incorporates the latest benchmark revision). For the U.S. National Income and Product Accounts data we use the *1985 Economic Report of the President* (which does not incorporate the January 1986 benchmark revision). It is supplemented by the *Balance Sheets for the U.S. Economy, 1945–84* (compiled by the Board of Governors of the Federal Reserve System) for balance sheet information, without addressing the question of compatibility between the two sets of U.S. data.

11.2.3 A Look at Aggregate Saving Rates

The most widely cited evidence in support of the notion that the Japanese like to save far more than Americans do is Japan's exceptionally high personal saving rate (the ratio of personal saving to personal disposable income). Is it still higher than the U.S. personal saving rate after the needed adjustments? Figure 11.1 shows the adjusted personal saving rate for

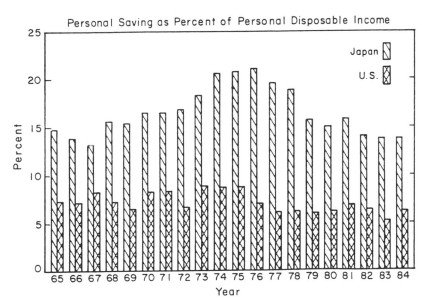

Figure 11.1
Personal saving as percent of personal disposable income.

Japan and the United States. Japan's personal saving rate in 1984 was 13.7 percent, about 2.5 percent lower than the personal saving rate reported in the national accounts and about 7 percent higher than the U.S. rate. The difference between the adjusted and the reported rate is mainly due to the capital consumption adjustments. The adjusted personal saving rate still exhibits the same basic pattern: it surges after the first oil crisis of 1973–74 to a peak in 1976 of 21.1 percent. The U.S. personal saving rate is stationary and has been fluctuating around 6 percent. It is clear that even after the needed adjustments Japan's personal saving rate is substantially higher.

Figure 11.2 shows the effect of including consumer durables as assets. Personal consumption thus excludes expenditures on durables but includes gross service flows from consumer durables. Personal disposable income now includes net service flows from consumer durables. A depreciation rate for consumer durables of 19 percent and a constant real rate of 4 percent are used for imputation. (See the data appendix for a detailed description of the imputation process.) It is well known in the United States that inclusion of consumer durables raises the personal saving rate by a few percent. That is not the case for Japan—the personal saving rate is little

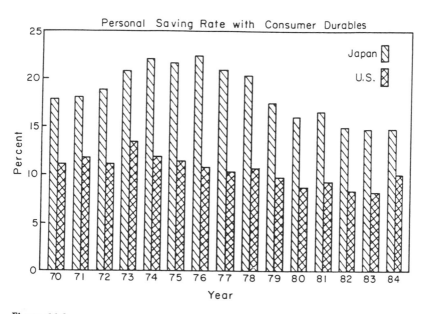

Figure 11.2
Personal saving rate with consumer durables.

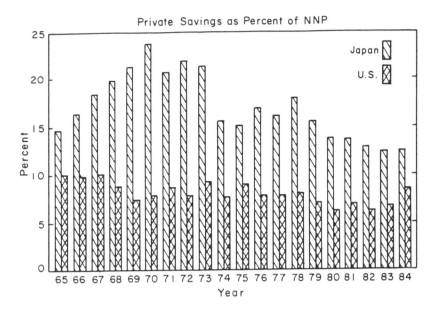

Figure 11.3
Private saving as percent of NNP.

affected, thus narrowing the gap between the two countries for 1984 to about 4 percent.

Figure 11.3 (and column (1) of table 11.1) displays the private saving rate (the ratio of private saving to NNP, where Japan's NNP is calculated according to the BEA convention of not including net service flows from government assets). It does not include consumer durables. The U.S. rate is more or less stationary. For Japan the behavior of the private saving rate is very different from that of the personal rate. It *declines* during and after the first oil crisis and has a declining trend since 1970. This is brought about by the sharp drop in corporate saving depicted in figure 11.4 which shows the ratios of personal, corporate, and government saving to NNP for Japan. (The NNP here includes service flows from government capital.) The corporate saving rate declined by 9 percent points from 1973 to 1974 in the face to stagnant earnings, increased dividend payments, and increased depreciation at replacement costs.

The BEA definition of the national saving rate, which excludes government net capital formation from national saving, is compared in figure 11.5 for the two countries. It reveals a surprising fact about Japan—though one that is already apparent from a look at Japan's private saving

Table 11.1
Net Saving as Percent of NNP with and without Revaluation

Year	\ Japan (1)	(2)	(3)	(4)	(5)	\ United States (1)	(2)	(3)	(4)	(5)
1970	23.8	25.6	2.1	−.4	51.2	7.8	−3.1	−1.2	1.6	5.2
1971	20.8	28.7	2.0	−.9	50.6	8.6	.4	−2.0	1.3	8.3
1972	21.9	96.5	.1	−.3	118.2	7.7	7.6	−.3	1.3	16.2
1973	21.4	57.8	1.0	−1.0	79.2	9.2	9.4	.6	2.4	21.6
1974	15.6	−89.2	.4	−1.6	−74.2	7.6	4.1	−.4	3.4	14.7
1975	15.2	−13.1	−3.5	−.4	−1.8	8.9	−.2	−4.6	1.8	5.9
1976	17.0	−8.8	−4.7	−.2	3.4	7.7	7.8	−2.4	1.6	14.8
1977	16.1	−.8	−4.8	.2	10.7	7.6	15.2	−1.0	2.1	23.9
1978	18.0	23.5	−7.3	−.2	34.0	7.9	21.1	.0	2.3	31.3
1979	15.5	52.3	−5.4	.4	62.8	7.0	7.3	.7	2.8	17.8
1980	13.8	31.4	−4.9	1.7	42.0	6.1	1.2	−1.3	3.0	8.9
1981	13.7	29.6	−5.5	.5	38.3	6.8	1.8	−1.0	2.1	9.8
1982	12.9	17.4	−4.4	.5	26.3	6.1	−9.0	−4.3	1.5	−5.7
1983	12.4	1.9	−4.9	.5	9.9	6.7	−1.0	−4.6	1.0	2.0
1984	12.5	2.0	−2.6	.6	12.4	8.4	−7.5	−3.8	1.1	−1.8
Average	16.7	17.0	−2.8	−.0	30.8	7.6	3.7	−1.7	1.9	11.5

(1) Private saving.
(2) Net revaluation (adjusted for general inflation) of private tangible and financial assets. The general inflation rate during the year is represented by the rate of change of the deflator for consumption expenditure from the last quarter of the previous year to the last quarter of current year.
(3) Government budget surplus.
(4) Net revaluation of government net financial assets.
(5) Sum of (1), (2), (3), and (4).
NNP is net of service flows from government tangible assets.
Source: Data Appendix.

rate in figure 11.3—that the national saving rate has declined quite sharply since 1970. In the late 1970s there was only a small difference between the national saving rates in the two countries. If one takes the view that private, not national, saving is the relevant saving concept, a good part of the decline in Japan's national saving rate after 1974 is attributable to the large budget deficit shown in figure 11.4. Government saving, the sum of the budget surplus and net government capital formation, has also been negative since 1976, while reported government saving (not shown) has been positive for all years.

The saving rates displayed thus far do not allow for revaluation or capital gains/losses. This leads to an understatement of saving by net

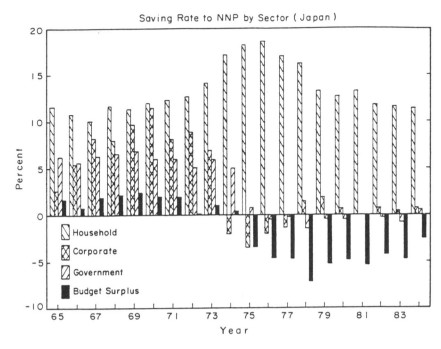

Figure 11.4
Saving rate to NNP by sector (Japan).

debtors in an inflationary environment. Column (2) in table 11.1 reports
net revaluations—that is, changes in nominal values minus changes in
value attributable to changes in the general price level—on private (tangible and financial) assets as a percent of NNP for Japan and the United
States.[10] (To make the Japanese data comparable to the U.S. data, I use the
BEA convention here.) The huge capital gains and losses for Japan come
principally from the value of land, which is over 75 percent of the value
of total private assets. Column (3) in table 11.1 reports the size of the
budget surplus (government saving under the BEA definition). Net revaluation of government net financial assets is in column (4). It shows
the well-known fact that the U.S. government has gained substantially
as a net debtor. Since the ratio of net government financial liabilities to
NNP was low in Japan in the inflationary period of the 1970s (the ratio
was *minus* 6 percent in 1974) and since the inflation rate has been low
in the 1980s when the ratio is rapidly rising (it was 30 percent in 1984),
net revaluation for the Japanese government has been small. The total
national saving rate inclusive of revaluation is reported in column (5).
The number for Japan may be overstated, as it is strongly dependent on

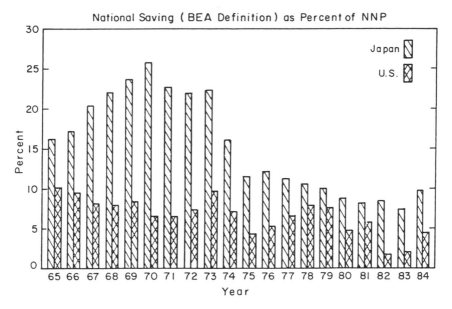

Figure 11.5
National saving (BEA definition) as percent of NNP.

the estimate of land value in the national accounts. The value of land in the private sector (excluding government enterprises) at the end of 1984, according to the Japanese national accounts, is 858 trillion yen. It is substantially higher than the market value of the U.S. private land of $3.3 trillion reported in the Federal Reserve's *Balance Sheets*.

11.2.4 Measurement of Depreciation

Coming back to the saving rates without revaluation, the impact of capital consumption adjustments for Japan is most dramatically shown in figure 11.6 where the ratio of national saving to NNP (with government capital) is shown with and without capital consumption adjustments. In 1984 the difference was over 6 percentage points, about 60 percent of which came from capital consumption adjustments on private assets. Its sheer size makes us wonder if our capital consumption adjustments may have been carried too far. The capital accounts in the Japanese national accounts provide estimates of the value of the nation's depreciable assets for five asset types: housing, nonresidential buildings, other structures, transportation equipment, and machinery and other equipment. (The decomposition of depreciable assets by type is available only for the nation as a

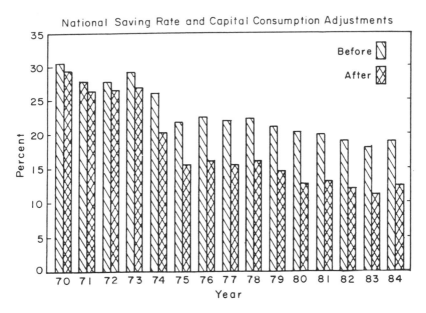

Figure 11.6
National saving rate and capital consumption adjustments.

whole.) The implicit rate of physical depreciation can be calculated for each year and for each asset type as a ratio of depreciation to the year-beginning value of the asset. If the reported value of depreciation is used, the implicit depreciation rate shows a marked downward trend for each of the five asset types, a clear indication that depreciation at historical costs is inappropriate. The overall (asset-weighted) depreciation rate is reported for selected years in column (6) of table 11.2. It clearly shows the impact of the 1973–74 inflation.

If our procedure for capital consumption adjustments, briefly described above, is applied to the five asset types to obtain depreciation at *replacement cost*, we obtain the implicit depreciation rates reported in columns (1)–(5) of table 11.2 along with the asset shares in parentheses and asset price indexes in brackets. The depreciation rate for other structures still shows a downward trend, but it may be attributable to the practice in the Japanese national accounts of not depreciating government assets other than buildings, which also distorts the asset shares in table 11.2 in favor of structures. (The depreciation for transportation equipment shows a steep downward trend for the first three or four years after 1970. We suspect that the 1970 value of the stock of transportation equipment is understated.) The average depreciation rates in the last rows of columns

Table 11.2
Implicit Physical Depreciation Rates

Year	(1)	(2)	(3)	(4)	(5)	(6)	(7)
1970	9.8	6.8	7.8	54.6	22.8	12.5	13.9
	(20.6)	(24.9)	(29.8)	(4.2)	(20.6)		
	[39.5]	[40.0]	[36.5]	[69.4]	[64.6]		
1975	8.8	6.4	6.3	31.2	20.5	7.3	11.0
	(23.5)	(22.7)	(30.0)	(4.7)	(19.1)		
	[70.1]	[70.3]	[67.4]	[91.0]	[93.7]		
1980	9.1	6.8	6.3	31.8	21.9	6.5	10.6
	(26.1)	(21.9)	(34.6)	(3.4)	(14.0)		
	[95.7]	[94.0]	[93.3]	[96.6]	[95.7]		
1984	8.5	6.4	5.7	30.6	21.4	6.6	9.9
	(23.5)	(22.7)	(37.1)	(3.0)	(13.6)		
	[103.0]	[106.3]	[107.3]	[99.0]	[95.5]		
Average	9.0	6.5	6.6	33.5	21.6		

The first row for each year is the depreciation rate, the second row in parentheses is the value share in the nation's stock of depreciable assets, and the third row in brackets is the deflator for the asset at the beginning of the year. Depreciation rates and shares are in percents. Columns (1)–(5) represent the five asset types: (1) housing, (2) nonresidential buildings, (3) other structures, (4) transportation equipments, and (5) machines and other equipment. The depreciation rates reported in these five columns are net of our capital consumption adjustments. Column (6) shows the overall depreciation rate as reported in the Japanese national accounts. Column (7) is the overall depreciation at replacement costs and government depreciable assets.

Source: Columns (1)–(6) from the *1985 Annual Report on National Accounts* (with our capital consumption adjustment procedure applied to columns (1)–(5)). Column (7) from the data appendix.

(1)–(5) do not seem totally out of line with, for example, the average implicit BEA rates reported in Hulten and Wykoff (1981, table 2).[11] Column (7) reports the overall depreciation rate implied by our capital consumption adjustment procedure and implicit in all the saving rates displayed so far. It is not strictly the asset-weighted average of columns (1)–(5) because it is based on our estimate of government capital where the depreciation rate is constrained to be 6.5 percent. It still shows a clear but mild downward trend. This downward trend, which is not apparent in asset-specific depreciation rates in columns (1)–(5), is attributable to the shift in asset value shares in favor of longer-lived assets. This shift in turn is due mainly to the large-scale change in relative asset prices that has continued since at least 1970, shown in brackets. It appear that our capital consumption adjustments are of reasonable magnitude.

We conclude that Japan's aggregate saving rate—however defined—is indeed higher than the comparable U.S. saving rate, but not by as much as is commonly thought. Not only is the level different, but the pattern over time of Japan's saving rate with large peaks and well-defined trends is in sharp contrast to the stationary U.S. pattern. We now turn to the question of how one might explain the difference.

11.3   A Catalogue of Explanations

That Japan's personal saving rate is one of the highest in the world was recognized in Japan as early as 1960. A concise survey of the early literature can be found in Komiya (1966). The most recent and most exhaustive survey is Horioka (1985b) which lists over thirty possible factors that might contribute to Japan's high personal saving rate. A striking feature of the Japanese literature is its lack of a neoclassical perspective: the personal saving rate as a fraction of personal disposable income is the center of attention. Also, no attention has been given to the measurement of depreciation which, as we have seen, is very important. This section is a catalogue of explanations of Japan's high saving rate that have been offered in the literature and still enjoy some currency. They will be examined later.

High Income Growth
An association of the income growth rate and the saving rate is consistent with several alternative hypotheses of saving. Both the life-cycle hypothesis (with finite lives) and the permanent income hypothesis (with infinite horizon) imply that a temporary rise in the growth rate raises the saving rate. For a permanent increase in the growth rate, the permanent income hypothesis would predict a lower saving rate (if the real interest rate is unchanged). In the life-cycle hypothesis, the initial impact of a permanent increase in the growth rate on the saving rate is probably to lower it, but the long-run impact is a higher saving rate, because older and dissaving generations are, in the long run, outweighed by younger and wealthier generations. The habit persistence hypothesis predicts a positive response of the saving rate to either a permanent or a temporary increase in productivity growth. For Japan the relation between the growth rate and the saving rate is far from clear-cut. Figure 11.7 contains the graph of the GNP growth rate and the personal saving rate. They tend to move in opposite directions, especially during and shortly after the first oil crisis. This is inconsistent with the habit persistence hypothesis. Comparing figure 11.7 with figures 11.3, 11.5, and 11.6, we see that the private and

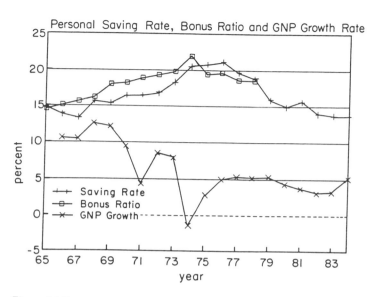

Figure 11.7
Personal saving rate, bonus ratio and GNP growth rate.

the national saving rates are more closely related to GNP growth than the personal rate.

The correlation of the saving rate with the growth rate is actually difficult to interpret because there can be a reverse causation running from saving to growth through capital accumulation. However, the clear prediction by the life-cycle hypothesis that a secularly high growth rate should be associated with a high saving rate could explain Japan's higher saving rate. This will be examined in the next section where we perform a saving rate simulation based on the life-cycle hypothesis.

Demographics
The proportion of the aged has historically been small in Japan. Also, the life expectancy of the Japanese is now the longest in the world. According to the life-cycle hypothesis, these demographic factors should raise the aggregate saving rate. This, too, will be taken up in the next section.

Underdeveloped Social Security System
The reasoning is that because Japan's social security system is underdeveloped people have strong needs to provide for old age by themselves. Japan's social security system has expanded rapidly since 1973. If

the household sector is the relevant boundary, this explanation is inconsistent with the data because the personal saving rate actually increased after 1973. The decline in the private saving rate could be explained by the enlarged social security system. The role of social security will be taken up in section 11.7.

Bonus System
In postwar Japan, workers receive large lump-sum payments twice a year. The bonus system originated in large firms and has spread to smaller ones. The amount depends on the profitability of the firm and the industry, although less so in recent years. The evidence that appears to support this bonus hypothesis is that the ratio of bonuses to regular employee compensation is closely related to the personal saving rate, as shown in figure 11.7. (The data on the bonus ratio is from Ishikawa and Ueda (1984)). The bonus hypothesis was advanced very early and gained popularity when both the bonus ratio and the personal saving rate rose after 1973 and then slowly started to decline. This fact can, however, be explained straightforwardly by a neoclassical perspective that households can see through the corporate veil. Bonuses are a transfer of corporate saving to personal saving. If it is private saving that matters, the bonus ratio should raise personal saving. The bonus hypothesis cannot be an explanation of a high private saving rate.[12]

Tax Incentives
The Japanese tax system encourages saving because income from capital is very lightly taxed at the personal level. This issue will be examined in section 11.8.

High Housing/Land Prices
As Horioka (1985a) reports: "The annual Public Opinion Survey on Saving ... has consistently found that the five most important motives for household saving in Japan are those relating to illness/unexpected disaster, education and marriage, old age, land/housing purchases, and peace of mind. Moreover, a comparison of the Japanese findings and those of a similar U.S. survey shows that the biggest differences are that the motives relating to education and marriage and land/housing purchases are far more important in Japan, while the old age motive is far more important in the United States." As documented in Hayashi, Ito and Slemrod (1985, incomplete), the Japanese had to accumulate probably as much as 40 percent of the purchase price of a house while borrowing the

remaining fraction from government loans (subsidized and therefore rationed) and from private financial institutions. The high down-payment ratio and the nondeductibility of interest expense for mortgage borrowing may contribute to high savings by younger generations. Like the first three explanations above, this explanation has life-cycle considerations in mind. Some evidence will be presented in section 11.5 to gauge the relevance of high housing prices.

Bequests

This is probably the least popular explanation in Japan. There is a casual discussion in Shinohara (1983) to the effect that perhaps the Japanese may like to leave large bequests. Horioka (1984), after rejecting the standard life-cycle hypothesis on the basis of household survey data and various opinion surveys, also notes at the end the importance of bequests and their connection to the prevalence of the extended family in Japan. To anticipate, my conclusion is that bequests are probably the most important factor.

Cultural Factors

If all else fails, there is a cultural explanation. The Japanese are simply *different*. They are more risk-averse and more patient. If this is true, the long-run implication is that Japan will absorb all the wealth in the world. I refuse to comment on this explanation. Horioka (1985b), after examining various studies that address the cultural issue, concludes that the available evidence is mixed.

11.4   Explanation by the Life-Cycle Hypothesis

The life-cycle hypothesis of saving (Modigliani and Brumberg (1954), Ando and Modigliani (1963)) asserts that people's saving behavior is strongly dependent on their age. Aggregate saving can be explained by such demographic factors as age distribution and life expectancy, and such economic factors as the age profile of earnings. The hypothesis is attractive because it generates very specific empirical predictions about aggregate saving if data are available on demographics, the age profile of earnings, and asset holdings. This section performs a standard "steady-state" simulation of aggregate saving under the life-cycle hypothesis. The steady-state assumption allows us to impute rather than observe the age profile of asset holdings. The profile of asset holdings by the age of a person (rather than by the age of a head of household) is difficult to observe for the case of Japan because of the prevalence of the extended family.

Before getting into the actual simulation, however, a precise definition of the life-cycle hypothesis is in order. Its essential feature, eloquently expounded by Modigliani (1980), is that people are selfish and do not plan to leave bequests. It is this feature which, coupled with the single-peaked age-earnings profile, leads to the prediction that people save to prepare for their retirement. An equally important, but often implicit, assumption is that people can purchase annuities and life insurance at actuarially fair prices. This means (see Barro and Friedman (1977)) there is only one constraint, the lifetime budget constraint, faced by the consumer:

$$\sum_{i=0}^{\infty} q(t, v, i)(1 + r)^{-i}c(t + i, v + i)$$

$$= \sum_{i=0}^{\infty} q(t, v, i)(1 + r)^{-i}w(t + i, v + i) + A(t, v), \tag{1}$$

where $c(t, v)$, $w(t, v)$, and $A(t, v)$ are, respectively, consumption, earnings and initial assets of a consumer aged v at time t. $q(t, v, i)$ is the probability at time t that the consumer of age v survives into period $t + i$. r is the real rate of return. This version will be referred to as the strict life-cycle model.

In the absence of complete annuity markets, perfect insurance, as represented by equation (1), against living "too long" is not available. Involuntary bequests are the price to be paid to self-insure against longevity risk. But, as Kotlikoff and Spivak (1981) point out, longevity risk can be partially insured against if selfish parents "purchase," in exchange for bequests, a promise by children to provide assistance in old age. This class of models may be called the selfish life-cycle model with imperfect insurance.

Other models of saving include the strategic bequest model recently proposed by Burnheim, Shleifer, and Summers (1985) and the model of dynastic altruism of Barro (1974) and Becker (1981). In the latter model parents care about the welfare of their children and thus behave as if their planning horizon is infinite. In the former model, parents are not necessarily altruistic toward their children but use bequests to influence their children's action. I do not here intend to confront all these models with the Japanese data in a formal fashion. Since most of the explanations surveyed in the previous section have the strict life-cycle model in mind,

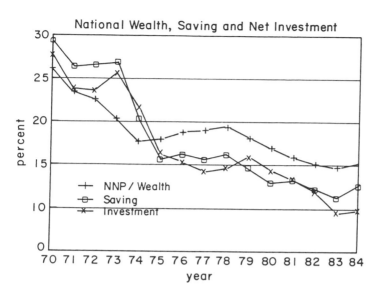

Figure 11.8
NNP—Wealth ratio and saving and investment rates.

the first order of business is to test it on Japanese data by a simulation technique.

If the strict life-cycle model is applicable to Japan, it should for realistic values of relevant parameter values generate the aggregate saving rate and the wealth-income ratio as observed in Japan. If we take seriously the numbers in the capital accounts of the Japanese national accounts, the ratio of national wealth (including land) to (capital consumption-adjusted) NNP was about 4 in 1970 and about 6 in 1980 (see figure 11.8, where the inverse of the wealth-NNP ratio is plotted). The inputs to the simulation are: (i) the actual age-earnings profile ($w(t, v)$), (ii) the actual age distribution of the population, (iii) survival probabilities (q), and (iv) a constant annual real rate of return of 4 percent.[13] There are two parameters: the longitudinal consumption growth rate (h) implicit in the age-consumption profile and the secular productivity growth rate (g). Thus the longitudinal consumption profile is assumed to be

$$c(t + i, v + i) = c(t, v)(1 + h)^i, \tag{2}$$

and the prospective earnings profile is

$$w(t + i, v + i) = w(t, v)(1 + g)^i. \tag{3}$$

Table 11.3
Age Distribution of Earning and Population

	Earnings						
	20–29	30–39	40–49	50–59	60–69	70–79	80–89
Japan, 1970	0.12	0.22	0.26	0.28	0.13	0.0	0.0
Japan, 1980	0.09	0.22	0.28	0.29	0.13	0.0	0.0
United States, 1972–73	0.17	0.24	0.26	0.22	0.11	0.0	0.0
	Population (Fraction of total population)						
	20–29	30–39	40–49	50–59	60–69	70–79	80–89
Japan, 1970	0.19	0.16	0.11	0.09	0.06	0.03	0.01
Japan, 1980	0.14	0.17	0.14	0.11	0.07	0.04	0.01

See note 13 for the source of the Japanese data. The U.S. earnings profile is obtained from the *Consumer Expenditure Survey, 1972–73*, Bureau of Labor Statistics Bulletins 1992 and 1997, Table 3.

The potential lifespan is represented by seven ten-year periods. The first period corresponds to ages 20–29 and the last to 80–89. Under the steady-state assumption that earnings and assets of a consumer of given age v grow at a constant rate g over time, we can calculate for each combination of h and g the aggregate saving rate and wealth-NNP ratio.[14]

Table 11.3 displays the actual age profile of earnings for 1970 and 1980 with the sum normalized to unity, along with the U.S. earnings profile.[15] For lack of data, earnings for those aged 70 and over are set at zero. The share of earnings for ages 20–29 has declined in Japan, mainly due to a decline in the labor force participation rate brought about by the increase in college enrollment. Earnings in Japan peak in the 50–59 age group because of lump-sum retirement payments. It may be argued that the high earnings by those aged 50–59 do not reflect productivity; rather the earnings are a return from implicit saving whose amount equals the excess of true productivity over actual earnings at younger ages. Without the retirement payment adjustment, earnings for groups 40–49 and 50–59 are nearly the same, but the steady-state calculations do not change significantly.[16] Table 11.3 also shows the actual age distribution of the population over the seven age groups. The postwar baby boom generation is now approaching the prime earning ages. There are now more 40–59-year-olds, which should increase the aggregate saving rate.

The steady-state values of the aggregate saving rate and wealth-income ratio expressed at annual rates are shown in table 11.4. The table suggests

Table 11.4
Steady-State Simulation Results

Panel A. Japanese Earnings Profile, Japanese Age Distribution of Population

1970	Saving rate (%)			Wealth-income ratio		
Annual consumption growth (h)	Annual productivity growth			Annual productivity growth		
	0%	5%	10%	0%	5%	10%
$h = 0\%$	3	−81	−680	−0.5	−7.8	−30.4
5%	32	28	−87	6.6	1.2	−4.1
10%	52	66	53	10.0	5.0	1.9

1980	Saving rate (%)			Wealth-income ratio		
Annual consumption growth (h)	Annual productivity growth			Annual productivity growth		
	0%	5%	10%	0%	5%	10%
$h = 0\%$	8	−64	−596	−0.9	−8.9	−35.1
5%	33	27	57	7.0	1.5	−3.9
10%	52	68	60	10.5	5.5	2.3

Panel B. U.S. Earnings Profile, Japanese Age Distribution of Population

1970	Saving rate (%)			Wealth-income ratio		
Annual consumption growth (h)	Annual productivity growth			Annual productivity growth		
	0%	5%	10%	0%	5%	10%
$h = 0\%$	7	−50	−400	1.1	−5.0	−17.9
5%	34	30	−47	7.5	2.2	−2.3
10%	54	70	61	10.6	5.4	2.3

1980	Saving rate (%)			Wealth-income ratio		
Annual consumption growth (h)	Annual productivity growth			Annual productivity growth		
	0%	5%	10%	0%	5%	10%
$h = 0\%$	10	−35	−330	1.6	−5.2	−19.7
5%	34	36	−23	8.5	2.2	−1.9
10%	53	72	67	11.6	6.1	2.8

In Panel B, the actual 1970 Japanese age distribution of population is used for 1970, and the actual 1980 Japanese age distribution of population is used for 1980.

several conclusions: Consumption must rise very rapidly through life for the selfish life-cycle model to be consistent with the observed values of the aggregate saving and wealth-income ratios, because the Japanese age-earnings profile is much steeper. To isolate the effect of the earnings profile, Panel B of table 11.4 displays the simulation result which uses the 1972–73 U.S. earnings profile for both the 1970 and 1980 simulations, but still uses the same actual Japanese age distribution of population. Comparing the saving rates in Panel B with those in Panel A for the same year for each combination of the consumption growth rate and the productivity growth rate, we can see that with the age structure fixed the difference in the earnings profile between the United States and Japan should make the U.S. saving rate *higher*. Looking at Panel B for 1970 and 1980 and thus holding the age profile of earnings fixed, we see that the Japanese demographics also work against the life-cycle hypothesis: it predicts a rising aggregate Japanese saving rate.

Another surprising conclusion is that the saving rate generally *declines* with the productivity growth rate under the Japanese age-earnings profile and demographics. This has a clear and simple explanation. Since earnings are highly skewed toward older ages, quite contrary to the usual textbook picture of hump saving, saving is done primarily by older generations. As the secular productivity growth rate goes up, aggregate saving becomes dominated by a younger and wealthier generation whose saving rate is lower than the saving rate for older generations. It is still true that the *very* old are dissaving, but their weight in the actual age distribution is tiny.

Since a primary source of the failure of the life-cycle model to mimic the observed saving and wealth-income ratios is dissaving by younger generations, the introduction of liquidity constraints may alter the conclusion. The result (not shown) of a simulation in which consumption is constrained not to exceed the sum of income and initial assets indicates that the saving and wealth-income ratios are now higher because the negative saving by the young is constrained from below, but that the demographics still works clearly against the model and the inverse relation of the aggregate saving rate with the productivity growth rate remains.

11.5 Evidence from Household Survey Data

11.5.1 Household Surveys

The failure of the steady-state life-cycle simulation to mimic the aggregate saving rate and wealth-income ratio means that the actual Japanese age profiles of consumption and asset holdings differ greatly from the life-cycle predictions. We now examine them in order to locate possible deviations of the Japanese saving behavior from the life-cycle models. To this end, survey data on households grouped by age of head of household are essential. Several household surveys in tabulated form are publicly available in Japan. The *Family Income and Expenditure Survey* (FIES) is a monthly diary survey of about 8,000 households. It has no information on assets and imputed rents and no information on income for households other than the so-called *worker household* (namely, households whose head is on a payroll). The *Family Saving Survey* annually collects data on balances and changes in financial assets and liabilities and pretax annual income. It has no information on expenditures and physical assets. The sample size is less than six thousand, insufficient to give reliable tabulations by age. These two surveys do not cover one-person households. The *National Survey of Family Income and Expenditure* (hereafter National Survey), conducted every five years since 1959, is a very large sample (over 50,000) and covers most types of households (the exceptions are agriculture and fishing). It obtains information through biweekly collection of diaries on expenditures on various items, imputed rent, income, taxes, and financial assets. The shortcoming of this survey is that it covers only three months (September, October, and November) and that except for the pretax income for the twelve-month period ending in November no information is available on monthly income and taxes for nonworker households, which are about 30 percent of the sample. The 1974 and 1979 tapes on individual households have been extensively analyzed by Ando (1985). Our present study uses only the published tabulations in the National Survey Reports.

Table 11.5A displays some cross-section information for the United States, taken from the *1972–73 Consumer Expenditure Survey*. Table 11.5B contains similar information for Japan taken from the 1974 National Survey Report. One-person households are counted as a half household in the tabulation for Japan. Since average monthly income and taxes are not available for nonworker households, we show disposable income, consumption expenditure and the saving rate separately for worker households. Income and expenditure variables are at annual rates.[17] The value of owned homes (which includes the value of land) is obtained from data on imputed rent assuming that the annual real rate of return is 4 percent and the depreciation rate 1 percent. The definition of disposable income and consumption expenditure is brought closer to the national income definition by using the following formulas:

Table 11.5A
Selected Family Characteristics, Income and Expenditure by Age of Family Head, U.S.,
1972–73

	<24	25–34	35–44	45–54	55–64	65+	Implied average	NIPA average
Households in the universe (millions)	6.3	14.2	12.0	13.0	11.5	14.3	71.3 (total)	
Family size	1.8	3.2	4.3	3.5	2.3	1.7	2.9	
Persons 65 and over	.0	.0	.0	.1	.1	1.3	.3	
Percent homeowners	9	40	68	73	74	66	59	
Disposable income (thousands)	$5.6	$9.9	$12.2	$13.3	$10.6	$6.3	$9.9	$12.4
Consumption expenditure (thousands)	$6.5	$9.4	$11.0	$11.1	$8.5	$5.4	$8.8	$10.9
Saving rate (%)	−15	5	10	17	20	13	12	8
Market value of owned home (thousands)	$2.2	$11.3	$18.7	$19.4	$17.1	$12.1	$14.3	$11.1

The NIPA averages are the averages implied by the National Income and Product Accounts and the U.S. Balance Sheets for the total number of households of 71.3 million. They are averaged over 1972 and 1973.
Source: Consumer Expenditure Survey, 1972–73, Bureau of Labor Statistics, Bulletins 1992 and 1997, Table 8. *1985 Economic Report of the President. Balance Sheets for the U.S. Economy, 1945–84* (Board of Governors of the Federal Reserve System).

$$\text{consumption expenditure} = \text{total consumption expenditure}$$
$$+ \text{ income in kind (including imputed rent),} \quad (4)$$

$$\text{disposable income} = \text{total income (including social security}$$
$$\text{benefits and pensions)}$$
$$+ \text{ income in kind (including imputed rent)}$$
$$- \text{ depreciation on owned home (20 percent}$$
$$\text{of imputed rent)}$$
$$- \text{ interest part of loan repayments (6 percent times}$$
$$\text{financial liabilities outstanding).} \quad (5)$$

Unless otherwise stated, this is the definition of disposable income and consumption that we employ throughout the article. Although the remaining conceptual differences make the comparison with the national accounts data more or less meaningless (see Ando (1985) for detailed discussion) it appears from the last two columns of table 11.5B that the National Survey severely underreports asset values.

From the viewpoint that the private sector or the nation is the relevant boundary, the definition of income should include anticipated capital

Table 11.5B
Selected Family Characteristics, Income and Expenditures by Age of Family Head, Japan, 1974

	<24	25–34	35–44	45–54	55–64	65+	Implied NIPA average	NIPA average
Households in the universe (millions)	1.0	5.4	6.7	4.9	2.5	1.1	21.6 (total)	
Family size	2.2	3.5	4.3	3.9	3.6	3.5	3.8	
No. of older parents	.06	.17	.25	.27	.32	.27	.24	
Percent homeowners	8	37	62	75	81	85	60	
1974 pretax income (millions)	¥2.1	¥2.2	¥2.6	¥3.2	¥3.1	¥2.5	¥2.7	¥3.1
Consumption expenditure (millions)	¥1.6	¥1.7	¥2.0	¥2.2	¥2.0	¥1.7	¥2.0	¥2.3
Net financial assets (millions)	¥.7	¥.9	¥1.3	¥2.2	¥2.3	¥3.6	¥1.7	¥3.3
Market value of owned home (millions)	¥.4	¥1.9	¥3.1	¥3.6	¥3.8	¥3.8	¥2.9	¥9.8
For worker households:								
Disposable income (millions)	¥2.2	¥2.3	¥2.5	¥3.0	¥2.7	¥2.2	¥2.5	
Consumption expenditure (millions)	¥1.6	¥1.8	¥2.0	¥2.3	¥2.1	¥1.7	¥2.0	
Saving rate (%)	25	21	21	21	21	21	21	

As the National Survey does not cover households in agriculture and fishing, the number of households in the universe is 21.6 million (where singles are counted as a half). It is used to calculate the NIPA averages. The 1974 pretax income is for the period for December 1973 to November 1974. The number of older parents living with the head is for worker households. *Source: 1974 National Survey*, vol. 1, part 1, Table 6. *1986 Annual Report on National Accounts.*

gains on stocks. We should bear in mind that the saving rate displayed in the tabulations is the personal saving rate, exclusive of revaluations. We know from table 11.1 that there were large capital losses on private assets in 1974 and large capital gains in 1979. To the extent that some components of revaluation were anticipated, the saving rate for 1974 in table 11.5B is overstated.

Several differences between the United States and Japan are clearly noticeable from tables 11.5A and 11.5B. First, the share in the total universe of households headed by persons 65 and over is very small in Japan. Second, the average number of old people living with younger households is much higher. Third, home-ownership does not decline after the household head retires. These are just different aspects of the same important fact about Japan, emphasized in Ando (1985), that elderly parents often invite one of their children (usually the eldest son) and his family to move into their house or, less frequently, the parents move into the younger household. According to the *Basic Surveys for Welfare Administration*, over 80 percent in 1960 and 67 percent in 1983 of persons 65 or over lived with their children. For persons 80 years or over, the proportion was 90 percent in 1983. Thus data such as those given in table 5B organized by age of head of household give only a mixture of the saving behavior by the young and the old. This certainly makes the interpretation of the data less straightforward. We will come back to this issue of household merging shortly.

11.5.2 High Housing/Land Prices?

The fourth difference is that the saving rate does not depend very much on age.[18] This could be explained by the saving behavior of the elderly living with younger families, but, as we will see (in table 11.9, Panel A), the pattern is clearly observed for nuclear families as well. This is why the life-cycle models fail to explain the Japanese saving rate. Fifth, unlike the United States, there is no indication of dissaving by very young households. This can be explained by a combination of liquidity constraints, the extremely high Japanese housing prices, and the high down-payment required to purchase a house.

This brings us to the explanation mentioned in section 11.3 that the Japanese saving rate is high because the Japanese have to save a great deal to purchase a house whose price is several times their annual income. The National Survey Reports since 1974 have separate tabulations for the three largest metropolitan areas. We can therefore calculate the saving rate separately for urban and rural areas. Since housing prices are much higher in urban areas, the saving rate must be higher as well. We can actually get more information from the National Survey Reports because since 1979 the tabulations are further broken down to three household types: homeowners; renters *without* a plan to purchase a house within the next five years; and renters *with* such a plan.

Table 11.6 displays the saving rate by region and household type for 1979 and 1984. (As disposable income is not available for nonworker households, the saving rate is calculated for worker households only.) As predicted by the housing price hypothesis, the saving rate for renters with purchase plans is several percent over that for other types of households

Table 11.6
Saving Rates by Age, Type and Region, Worker Households

	1979		1984	
	Urban	Rural	Urban	Rural
1. Homeowners	18	19	18	20
2. Renters without purchase plans	19	19	18	20
3. Renters with purchase plans	25	24	19	21
Average	19	19	18	20

Source: *1979 National Survey Report*, vol. 1, part 1, Table 26, and vol. 1, part 2, Table 18. *1984 National Survey Report*.

in 1979. However, the saving rate for those who plan to purchase a house in urban areas is about the same as that in rural areas, which suggests that the elasticity of substitution between housing and other forms of consumption may be close to unity. It is not the price of houses per se that is driving the saving rate up. More important are the unavailability of housing loans and the tendency of the Japanese to own, rather than rent, houses despite no tax advantages on mortgage payments. Another piece of evidence in the table unfavorable to the housing-price hypothesis is that the saving rate averaged over household types is, if anything, higher for rural areas, where houses are much cheaper. This underscores the general principle that a high saving rate for the young population by itself does not translate into a high aggregate saving rate. If for some reason or other the young are forced to save more than they otherwise would, the life-cycle hypothesis implies that the involuntary saving will be spent in the later stages of life and thus reduce the saving rate for older generations. The high housing price does not seem to have any relevance in very recent years, because the table shows that for 1984 saving rates are not at all affected by the intent to purchase a house.

11.5.3 Asset Holdings by the Aged

The prevalence of children living with parents creates two problems that must be borne in mind in analyzing Japanese household survey data. First, as already mentioned, tabulation by age of the household head does not fully reveal the life cycle of a typical person, because of the presence of the elderly in the extended family. Second, since the household survey defines the head of a household to be the main income earner, there is a sample selection bias, in that heads of extended families in older age

Table 11.7
Age Profile of Asset Holdings by Older Two-or-more-Person Households, 1974 and 1979

	Age of head in 1974			
1974	56–60	61–65	66–70	71–75
Sample size	1572	1418	927	553
Mean	1946	1936	1815	1813
First quantile	1185	1153	1095	1107
Second quantile (median)	1760	1755	1662	1660
Third quantile	2455	2456	2293	2323

	Age of head in 1979			
1979	61–65	66–70	71–75	76–80
Sample size	1623	1187	615	245
Mean	1971	1839	1865	1847
First quantile	1160	1038	1080	965
Second quantile (median)	1785	1565	1636	1515
Third quantile	2512	2351	2398	2291

In ten thousands of 1979 yen.
Source: Ando (1985).

groups are high-income people whose earnings are greater than the earnings of their adult offspring in their prime earning ages.

This sample selection bias is particularly relevant when we examine the issue of asset decumulation by the aged, a popular test of the selfish life-cycle models. Table 11.7 combines two of the tabulations given in Ando's (1985) study. The table is arranged to make it easy to trace over the five-year period of 1974–79 the asset holdings by cohorts defined by five-year age groups. The tabulation is for two-or-more-person households whose head was over 56 in 1974, so both nuclear and extended families are included. Assets here consist of financial assets (excluding the present value of social security benefits), the market value of any owned home (whose main component, of course, is the value of land), and consumer durables. They are stated in 1979 prices. The mean asset holdings do not decline as cohorts age. The essential aspect of the life-cycle models does not seem to hold. This, however, is a premature conclusion, for three reasons. The first is probably familiar to American researchers, while the other two are specific to the prevalence of the extended family. First, poor people at the lower end of the 1974 asset distribution are more likely to die and thus disappear from the asset distribution for 1979. Second, of old nuclear families, poor ones may be more likely to disappear as they are merged into younger households. Third, by the very design of the survey, old household heads of extended families are the ones who still dominate their sons in terms of income. This is the sample selection bias mentioned above.

For these reasons the lower end in the 1974 asset distributions becomes tapered as time goes on. However, it should still be the case that if the old are decumulating, the upper ends of the asset distribution shift to the left. For those who were 56–60 years old in 1974, there is no attrition in the first place because the sample sizes for 1974 and 1979 are about the same. Thus simply comparing the mean is enough to conclude that there is no asset decumulation. For the 61–65-year-olds in 1974, there is a slight reduction in the sample size (from 1,418 to 1,187), and the whole upper end seems to have shifted to the left between 1974 and 1979. But the shift is very small—averaging across quartiles less than 10 percent over five years. For the 66–70-year-olds the sample size declines by a third over the five-year period. If assets were neither accumulated nor decumu-lated, the 1979 second quantile should be somewhere between the 1974 second and third quantiles. But in the table the 1979 second quantile is actually less than the 1974 quantile, indicating that asset decumulation may have occurred. We get the same conclusion for the 71–75-year-olds. Thus, there is some evidence of slight asset decumulation by the old. We hasten to add, however, that the conclusion is based on the assumption of no attrition for the upper end of the asset distribution. Also, the sample size for the very old may not be large enough to deem the quantile esti-mates reliable.

11.5.4   Importance of Bequests

Thus, the evidence on old persons maintaining independent households with or without their children is not very favorable to the selfish life-cycle models. Does the same conclusion apply to the elderly living with younger generations—the majority of the older population in Japan? Ando (1985) claims that there is strong evidence that they decumulate assets. He drew this conclusion from an equation explaining asset hold-ings for preretirement households. The equation shows a positive effect on household assets of the presence of the elderly in the household. This by itself is not surprising because when older parents retire they bring previously accumulated assets to younger households. What is significant is that the positive effect rapidly declines as the age of the older person increases. However, it seems that Ando's conclusion is premature because it ignores the role of bequests.

The saving behavior of the elderly living with younger generations can be inferred from a comparison of the nuclear family with the extended family. Table 11.8 displays the age profile of pretax income, expenditure, and financial asset holdings for 1979 and 1984. Because the tabulation in the 1979 and 1984 National Survey Reports by family type (nuclear and extended) do not show income in kind and imputed rent by age, consumption expenditure and income in the table are not adjusted for it. The market value of owned homes cannot be estimated, either. Taxes also are not shown because the National Surveys have no data on taxes for non-worker households. The profiles for nuclear families are in Panel A, and the profiles for extended families (households with adults of more than one generation) are in Panel B. One-person households are counted as half a nuclear household.[19] If entries in Panel A are subtracted from the corresponding entries in Panel B, we obtain Panel C. It therefore contains the difference in income, expenditure, and assets brought about by the presence of older parents. Consistent with Ando's conclusion, financial assets attributable to the elderly start to decline as we move to the right across age groups in Panel C.[20] This pattern of asset *decumulation* by the elderly, however, is inconsistent with the low expenditure relative to income shown in Panel C. Although table 8 shows pretax income, similar tabulations (not shown) based on disposable income for worker households indicate that the average tax rate is somewhere between 13 percent and 17 percent depending on age and family type and is somewhat higher for nuclear families. Thus if the pretax income is multiplied by 0.85 it serves as a lower bound for the difference in personal disposable income (though not adjusted for income in kind). Comparison of this estimate of disposable income and consumption expenditure in Panel C indicates that the elderly in younger extended households are *accumulating*. Put differently, then, how is it that nuclear families are accumulating assets so rapidly without the help of parents?

Our answer is that nuclear families do receive help from their parents —in the form of *bequests*. As we move to the right across age groups in Panel C, both parents and children (heads of household) get older. More and more parents die as they get older. If parents in an extended family leave bequests, the extended family turns into a nuclear family with additional assets. Furthermore, as the head of a nuclear family gets older, more and more parents who maintain independent households die and leave bequests, not to extended families, but to the nuclear family. In short, for

Table 11.8
Age Profile of Income, Expenditure, and Asset Holdings by Family Type, All Households, 1979 and 1984

1979, Panel A (nuclear)	20–29	30–39	40–49	50–59	60+
Households in the universe (millions)	1.7	6.1	5.3	3.1	1.1
Family size	3.0	3.8	3.9	3.2	2.5
Pretax income	3545	4278	5356	6243	4917
Consumption expenditure	2614	2917	3515	3863	2865
Net financial assets	2086	1247	3052	6512	8604
Panel B (extended)					
Households in the universe	0.1	1.3	1.5	0.8	0.4
Family size	4.6	5.4	5.3	4.5	5.5
Pretax income	4792	5188	5999	6728	7179
Consumption expenditure	3016	3314	3954	4005	3794
Net financial assets	1851	3148	4753	7326	8860
Panel C (Panel B–Panel A)					
Family size	1.6	1.6	1.4	1.4	2.9
Pretax income	1247	911	643	485	2262
Consumption expenditure	401	397	439	142	929
Net financial assets	765	1901	1701	814	256
1984, Panel A (nuclear)	20–29	30–39	40–49	50–59	60+
Households in the universe	1.3	6.2	6.0	4.2	1.5
Family size	2.9	3.8	3.9	3.1	2.5
Pretax income	3650	4555	5740	6446	5550
Consumption expenditure	2625	2955	3565	3843	3148
Net financial assets	1088	829	1967	6177	10174
Panel B (extended)					
Households in the universe	0.1	1.4	1.9	1.4	0.6
Family size	4.6	5.4	5.4	4.6	5.3
Pretax income	4842	5662	6452	6960	6915
Consumption expenditure	3249	3348	3887	4085	3447
Net financial assets	1304	3224	4489	7124	7841
Panel C (Panel B–Panel A)					
Family size	1.7	1.7	1.5	1.5	2.8
Pretax income	1191	1108	712	513	1365
Consumption expenditure	624	393	321	243	309
Net financial assets	215	2395	2522	947	−2334

Income, expenditure and assets in thousands of 1984 yen. Income and expenditure are not adjusted for income in kind. Pretax income is for the period from December of the previous year to November of the current year.
Source: 1979 *National Survey Report*, vol. 1, part 1, Table 23. 1984 *National Survey Report*.

middle-aged and older families, being an extended family is more like a signal of not yet having received bequests. The next section formalizes this argument to arrive at the flow of intergenerational transfers.

11.6 Calculation of Intergenerational Transfers

The sharp contrast between positive saving and declining assets shown in Panel C suggests a substantial amount of intergenerational transfers. We digress in this section to evaluate the quantitative importance of bequests. Since saving and asset holdings by age in 1979 are given in table 11.8, we can calculate asset holdings by age in 1984 that would have been obtained through saving accumulated over the five-year period 1979–84 in addition to the 1979 asset were it not for intergenerational transfers. (This calculation becomes rather complicated because within each age group there are inflows and outflows of households between the nuclear and extended families.) The difference between the actual and predicted 1984 asset holdings is then attributable to transfers. Aggregating transfers over age groups of recipients, we arrive at an estimate of the aggregate flow of transfers over the 1979–84 period. Clearly, this procedure captures only *intergenerational* rather than *intragenerational* transfers. It is the former that we are most interested in. And the captured flow of transfers would include bequests as well as gifts *inter vivos*.

This simple idea cannot be implemented for the 1979–84 period, though. For one thing, table 11.8 presents data by ten-year age groups, whereas we need tabulations organized by five-year groups. Second, the table gives no information on real assets. The value of owned homes is by far the most important household wealth in Japan. Fortunately, the 1969 and 1974 National Survey Reports do give such needed information, albeit only for worker households.[21] The age profiles of disposable income, consumption expenditures, and the sum of financial assets and the market value of owned homes are displayed in table 11.9 for 1969 and 1974. As in table 11.7, the tabulation for the second year in table 11.9 is shifted to the left by five years for tracking cohorts. For example, the saving rate for a typical nuclear family whose head was 25 to 29 years old in 1969 is 17 percent. Moving down vertically in the same column across panels, we see that five years later its saving rate is 21 percent. To eliminate the sample selection bias that parents (who are also the household heads) in older extended families are rich while parents (who are not the household heads) in younger extended families are relatively poor, extended families in the 55–59 group are put into the 25–29 groups, the

Table 11.9
Age Profile of Income, Expenditure, and Asset Holdings by Family Type, Worker Households, 1969 and 1974

1969, Panel A (nuclear)	25–29	30–34	35–39	40–44	45–49	50–54
Households in the universe	1.4	1.6	1.7	1.4	0.9	0.7
Family size	2.7	3.4	3.8	3.9	3.8	3.6
Percent homeowners	15	29	41	51	56	63
Disposable income	1765	1729	1913	2133	2302	2432
Consumption expenditure	1460	1460	1606	1786	1945	2039
Saving rate (%)	17	16	16	16	16	16
Total assets	1640	2574	3124	3805	4027	4894
Panel B (extended)						
Households in the universe	0.2	0.3	0.4	0.4	0.2	0.1
Family size	4.6	5.1	5.3	5.3	5.2	5.1
Percent homeowners	79	76	79	78	78	80
Disposable income	2033	2100	2158	2348	2570	2695
Consumption expenditure	1791	1899	1867	2016	2271	2319
Saving rate (%)	12	10	13	14	12	14
Total assets	4921	4844	4866	5209	6073	5799
Panel C (Panel B–Panel A)						
Family size	1.9	1.7	1.5	1.5	1.4	1.4
Disposable income	268	371	244	215	269	262
Consumption expenditure	331	439	261	230	326	280
Saving rate (%)	−24	−18	−7	−7	−21	−7
Total assets	3282	2270	1742	1404	2046	905

1974, Panel A (nuclear)	25–29	30–34	35–39	40–44	45–49	50–54
Households in the universe	2.2	2.1	1.8	1.5	0.9	—
Family size	3.6	3.9	3.9	3.7	3.3	—
Percent homeowners	33	46	56	67	70	—
Disposable income	2218	2393	2641	2916	2954	—
Consumption expenditure	1746	1887	2064	2320	2291	—
Saving rate (%)	21	21	22	20	22	—
Total assets	2480	3048	3770	4732	5237	—
Panel B (extended)						
Households in the universe	0.5	0.5	0.5	0.4	0.3	—
Family size	5.2	5.5	5.4	5.1	4.8	—
Percent homeowners	88	89	90	91	89	—
Disposable income	2854	2759	2888	3205	3209	—
Consumption expenditure	2206	2260	2324	2554	2528	—
Saving rate (%)	23	18	20	20	21	—
Total assets	6473	6226	6528	6750	7018	—

Table 11.9 (cont.)

Panel C (Panel B–Panel A)						
Family size	1.6	1.6	1.5	1.4	1.4	—
Disposable income	636	366	248	289	255	—
Consumption expenditure	459	373	260	234	237	—
Saving rate (%)	28	−2	−5	19	7	—
Total assets	3993	3178	2757	2019	1782	—

Income, expenditure and assets in thousands of 1974 yen. The number of households in millions. Income and expenditure are adjusted for income in kind and imputed rent. Total assets are the sum of net financial assets and the market value of owned homes. Data for the 50–54 age bracket for the 50–54 age bracket for 1974 are not given, because they are added to the 25–29 bracket.
Source: 1969 National Survey Report, vol. 1, Table 17. 1974 National Survey Report, vol. 1, Tables 6 and 21.

60–64 group into the 30–34 group, and the 65-and-over group into the 35–39 group. This is why data for 1974 for cohorts in the 50–54 age group in 1969 get lost and are not shown in table 11.9. This means that we cannot calculate transfers going to the households in the 1969 50–54 group.

A somewhat detailed description of the calculation of the flow of intergenerational transfers is as follows. Households are classified into three categories:

(a) young nuclear, whose head was under 55 in 1969 (and under 60 in 1974),

(b) young extended, whose younger generation was under 55 in 1969 (and hence under 60 in 1974),

(c) old independent, whose head was 55 or over in 1969 (and 60 or over in 1974, or may have disappeared due to death or household merging by 1974).

As one-person households are counted as a half of (a), all households except for single-parent households (whose number is small and which are ignored in our calculation) fall into one of the three categories. Households in (a) and (b) are further classified by five-year age groups according to the age in 1969. Thus table 11.9 contains the income, consumption and asset information for (a) and (b). Let $W(i, j, t)$ and $S(i, j, t)$ be the average total wealth and saving (at 1974 prices) of households of type i ($i = a, b$) in age group j ($j = 1$ for the 25–29 group, $j = 2$ for the 30–34, and so forth) in year t. Let $N(i, j, t)$ be the number of such households. If $p(i, k; j)$ is the fraction of households in the (i, j) cell in year t ($= 1969$) moving into the $(k, j + 1)$ cell in $t + 1$ ($= 1974$), we have, for each age band j,

$$N(a, j + 1, t + 1) = N(a, j, t)p(a, a; j) + N(b, j, t)p(b, a; j), \tag{6}$$

where we assume that young households never disappear. We assume that the flow of saving in real terms is constant over the five-year period for each type of household. If $L(i, j, t)$ is the predicted wealth (stated at 1974 prices) of a typical household in the (i, j) cell in year t that can be accounted for by accumulated saving on top of initial assets in year t, it can be written as[22]

$$L(i, j, t) = 5.0^*S(i, j, t) + W(i, j, t). \tag{7}$$

Thus the aggregate flow of intergenerational transfers is

$$TR = \sum_j N(a, j + 1, 1974)W(a, j + 1, 1974)$$

$$- \sum_j N(a, j, 1969)p(a, a; j)L(a, j, 1969)$$

$$- \sum_j N(b, j, 1969)p(b, a; j)L(b, j, 1969), \tag{8}$$

where all the wealth variables $W(a, j + 1, 1974)$, $L(a, j, 1969)$ and $L(b, j, 1969)$ are stated in 1974 prices. The first sum is actual aggregate wealth held in year $t + 1$ ($= 1974$) by all households of type (a). The second sum is the wealth accumulated through saving by households that stayed in (a), and the third sum represents the wealth of households which moved from (b) to (a) during the 1969–74 period. Here $S(b, j, t)$ and $W(b, j, t)$ are those that are attributable to the younger generation in the extended family. Note that intergenerational transfers occur only from (c) to (a) or from (b) to (a).

Table 11.9 gives data on: $N(i, j, t)$ ($i = a, b; t = 1969, 1974$), $S(a, j, 1969)$ and $W(a, j, t)$ ($t = 1969, 1974$) for each j. To estimate $S(b, j, 1969)$ and $W(b, j, 1969)$, we have to divide the saving and wealth of the extended family between the younger generation and the older generation. We assume the elderly neither accumulate nor decumulate. Thus their saving is zero (so that $S(b, j, 1969) = S(a, j, 1969)$ for all j). For the 25–29 age group $W(b, j, 1969)$ equals $W(a, j, 1969)$, so that from Panel C for 1969 we see the asset holdings by the elderly in the 25–29 group to be 3,282 thousand yen (in 1974 prices). Assuming a productivity growth rate of 5 percent, asset holdings by the elderly in the 30–34 group are then this 3,282 thousand multiplied by $(1 - .05)^{**}5$, which enables us to calculate $W(b, j, t)$ for this age group, and so forth. Finally, the values for S and W

are blown up to agree with the implied aggregate averages to account for the underreporting noted in table 11.5B. Data on $p(b, a; j)$ can be obtained from the 1969 mortality table assuming that parents are thirty years older than their children. (If there are two parents in the extended family, $p(b, a, j)$ should be the probability that *both* parents die within five years.) We are thus assuming that an extended family becomes a nuclear family only when the dependent elderly die. Using equation (6), $p(a, a; j)$ can be calculated from $p(b, a; j)$. This completes the description of the calculation procedure.

There is one problem of head counting: the number of nuclear families in the 30–39 age group in 1974 is too large to be accounted for by the number of extended and nuclear families in the 25–34 group in 1969. (We see from table 11.8 that the same phenomenon happened between 1979 and 1984.) Without further information, it is impossible to resolve the question of where those extra nuclear families came from. We decided to ignore this 1969 25–34 group in the summation in equation (8). We have already discarded the 1969 50–54 age group. This leaves only three age groups for 1969: 35–39, 40–44 and 45–49. Thus our aggregation captures only a part of aggregate flow of transfers.

The result is that aggregate wealth held by worker nuclear households in 1974 in the 40–54 age group stood at 78.0 trillion yen.[23] Of that, the amount that was accumulated by saving by those households since 1969 in addition to their 1969 wealth holdings was 70.0 trillion yen. The flow of transfers was thus 8 trillion yen. If this is adjusted by the fraction of worker households in the universe, we arrive at an annual flow of 11.5 trillion. Compared with the 1974 year-end aggregate private wealth of 598 trillion, it looks small. Our calculation thus captures only a part of the total flow of intergenerational transfers. Moreover, looking at the tabulation for 1969 in table 11.9, we note from Panel C negative savings and not-so-rapidly declining total assets. Thus the year 1969 might have been a poor (though inevitable) choice. Our calculations also rely on the average total asset holdings for the 25–29 age group in 1969. But that average may be unreliable, since the estimated number of households in that cell is small. Thus, our estimate should be taken as a very loose lower bound for the true aggregate flow of intergenerational transfers.

11.7   Intergenerational Transfers

The evidence already presented points to the importance of intergenerational transfers. Their implication for the aggregate saving rate, however, depends critically on whether or not they are based on intergenerational altruism. Even if parents are not altruistic toward their children, they still leave bequests if they die prematurely (accidental bequests); bequests are used as payments to children for their service rendered to care for older parents; or parents hold wealth in bequeathable form to influence their children's action. In any of the three models the implications of the standard life-cycle model for the saving rate would still hold. Although it is difficult to draw a firm conclusion from the data at our disposal about the nature of bequests, the following pieces of evidence seem largely consistent with intergenerational altruism.

Saving by Retirees
Japan's social security system was greatly expanded in 1973. It is now essentially a pay-as-you-go system. Quite likely, this large-scale transfer of resources from the young to the old engineered by the government was not anticipated. The average annual old age benefit per person covered by the annuity benefit program for those employed in the private sector (*Kosei Nenkin*, the largest public annuity program) is 538 thousand yen in 1974 and 1,360 thousand in 1983, an increase in real terms of 53 percent. The model of dynastic altruism predicts that this increase will be entirely saved by the old to offset the government-engineered transfer. It is supported by the fact observable from a comparison of income and consumption in Panel C of table 11.9 with Panel C of table 11.8 that the saving attributable to the elderly in extended families appears to have increased in several recent years. This is inconsistent with the selfish life-cycle models, which predict that the increase in annuities will be consumed.

Does this conclusion favorable to dynastic altruism also apply to older persons maintaining independent households? Since 1969 the National Survey Reports have data on pretax annual income, consumption expenditure, and assets of retired couples where the husband is 65 or over and the wife is 60 or over. They are shown in table 11.10. The personal saving rate shows no tendency to increase, which appears inconsistent with dynastic altruism. But for older households revaluation of assets may be an important component of income. For 1974 and 1979, there is a great deal of uncertainty in estimating net revaluation (revaluation excluding change in value attributable to general inflation) that might have been perceived by the households over the three-month period of September through November, because as reported in the table (and also in table 11.2) price changes were so large. The real price of housing was more or less constant in 1969 and 1984, so that net revaluation of an owned

Table 11.10
Saving Behavior of Retired Older Couples

	1969	1974	1979	1984
Sample size	242	407	653	951
Percent homeowners	80	81	81	86
Percent of pension recipients	n.a.	n.a.	n.a.	94
Pretax income	1494	1907	2278	2457
Consumption expenditure	1082	1468	1872	1899
Income in kind (incl. imputed rent)	285	302	n.a.	n.a.
Value of owned home	4581	5059	n.a.	n.a.
Net financial assets	4934	5566	6934	8684
General inflation rate (%)	5.1	22.9	4.7	2.4
Rate of change of deflator for the stock of houses	n.a.	7.7	13.7	2.2
Rate of change of deflator for housing investment	4.1	19.8	12.8	2.3
Saving rate (%)	28	23	18	23
Saving rate with revaluation	13	?	?	16

Income, expenditure and assets in thousands of 1984 yen. Income and expenditure are not adjusted for income in kind. Pension recipients are defined as couples whose main source of income is a public or private pension. The saving rate does not take taxes into account. The saving rate with revaluation includes in income net revaluation of net financial assets. It is not calculated for 1974 and 1979 because of the uncertainty about the size of net revaluation of owned homes.
Source: 1969 National Survey Report, vol. 1, Table 24. 1974 National Survey Report, vol. 1, Table 27. 1979 National Survey Report, vol. 7, Table 16. 1984 National Survey Report. 1986 Report on National Accounts.

home can be ignored. If only the net revaluation of financial assets is taken into account, the saving rate is 13 percent in 1969 and 16 percent in 1984. Still, the sharp increase in saving predicted by dynastic altruism is absent.

It may be that, as conjectured in Ando (1985), the saving behavior of older persons who maintain independent households is different from that of older persons living with their children. This is perhaps not surprising. It is hard to imagine that social security has any big impact on the consumption behavior of the elderly in the extended family, because there must be some in-house sense of proportion regarding consumption within the extended family. If social security benefits for older parents are raised with a simultaneous increase in the social security tax on their children living under the same roof, older parents, even without a strong sense of altruism toward their children, would find it morally hard to raise their spending at their children's expense.

Euler Equation

There is another way to examine the impact of social security on the consumption behavior by the aged. Every five years since 1959 the National Survey Reports have tabulations by age where the age groups are also five years. As we did in table 11.9, we can track from year t to $t+1$ a cohort in the jth 5-year age group in year t by looking at the $(j+1)$th age group in year $t+1$. For example, a cohort in the 20–24 age group in 1969 was in the 25–29 age group in 1974. If $C(j, t)$ and $Y(j, t)$ are consumption and disposable income of a representative cohort in age group j in year t, we can get from the National Survey Reports data on $C(j, t)$ and $Y(j, t)$ for $j = 1$ (20–24-year-olds), 2 (25–29-year-olds), . . . , 9 (60–64-year-olds) (nine age groups) and for $t = 1959$, . . . , 1984 (six time points). Thus the synthetic cohort analysis as done by Browning, Deaton and Irish (1985) is feasible here. For each cohort, we assume that the Euler equation applies:

$$\ln C(j + 1, t + 1) = \ln C(j, t) = a + br_t + e(j, t). \tag{9}$$

Here, the left-hand side is the growth rate of consumption from year t to $t+1$. When interest rates are high, it pays to reduce consumption now relative to future consumption. Thus the consumption growth rate should increase with the expected real rate r_t. This r_t is the expectation as of year t to $\ln[(1 + R_t)P_t/P_{t+1}]$, where R_t is the nominal rate on a 5-year bond and P is the price index. The sum of the first two terms on the right-hand side, $a + br_t$, is the planned rate of consumption growth. But actual growth can differ from the planned rate, perhaps because the interest rate forecast proved to be wrong, or because earnings change unexpectedly over the period t through $t+1$. The last term $e(j, t)$ represents those unexpected developments happening to cohort j. As the 1973 expansion of Japan's social security system was an unexpected development that transferred resources from younger generations to older generations, the selfish lifecycle hypothesis predicts that consumption growth from year 1969 to 1974 for older cohorts should be greater than $a + br_t$ and their $e(j, t)$ positive.

As we have data on $C(j, t)$ for six time points (1959, 1964, 1969, 1974, 1979, and 1984), the consumption growth rate can be calculated for five consecutive periods. Thus the sample size for estimating equation (9) is 45 (five times nine age groups). Growth rates and interest rates are stated at annual rates. Because the Euler equation presupposes that expenditure is perishable, we use food expenditure for consumption. Table 11.11 reports

Table 11.11
Estimation of Euler Equation on Synthetic Cohort Data

Regression #	Real rate of interest	Social security dummy	Log of real disposable income	R^2	Other included variables
1	−0.14 (1.8)	—	—	0.55	AGE, AGE²
2	−0.29 (3.0)	−0.024 (2.4)	—	0.61	AGE, AGE²
3	−0.027 (0.5)	—	−0.043 (6.8)	0.79	AGE, AGE²
4	−0.098 (1.3)	−0.011 (1.4)	−0.041 (6.2)	0.80	AGE, AGE²
5	—	−0.013 (1.9)	—	0.84	AGE, AGE², time dummies
6	—	—	−0.13 (4.9)	0.89	AGE, AGE², time dummies
7	—	−0.010 (1.8)	−0.12 (4.7)	0.90	AGE, AGE², time dummies

All variables are stated at annual rates. The dependent variable is the growth rate of real food expenditure over five-year periods. Real disposable income is the ratio of nominal disposable income to the food component of the CPI. The nominal rate used to construct the real rate is the rate on 5-year discount bonds issued by financial institutions. The price index used to calculate the real interest rate is the food component of the CPI. See the text for the definition of the social security dummy. Numbers in parentheses are the t values. The data source is the National Survey Reports.

various regression results. In all regressions, AGE (1 for 20–24-year-olds, 2 for 25–29-year-olds, and so forth) and AGE squared are included to account for possible age differences in the intercept term a in equation (9). Equation (9) is estimated in Regression 1. The actual real rate is used in place of r_t. It picked a wrong sign. In Regression 2, to examine the impact of the unexpected 1973 expansion of the social security system, a dummy variable which takes a value of unity for cohorts over 44 years of age for the 1969–74 period is added to the equation. It also has a negative coefficient, which means, contrary to the life-cycle prediction, that the 1973 change *reduced* consumption by older generations.

In Regressions 3 and 4, the log of disposable income, $\ln Y(j, t)$, is included to test for liquidity constraints with or without the social security dummy. If people wish to borrow to finance current consumption but are prevented from doing so, a higher level of disposable income leads to an increase in current consumption, thereby reducing the consumption growth over the following five years. Thus if there are liquidity constraints, the disposable income variable should pick up a negative coefficient, which is what is happening in Regressions 3 and 4. The social security dummy still picks up negative coefficients.

For the expected real rate r_t, we have used the actual real rate. This amounts to conferring on consumers perfect foresight about future prices and thus may be unrealistic. Regressions 5–7 use time dummies in place of the actual real rate. Thus the $a + br_t$ term in equation (9) can change its value over the five periods, reflecting changes in the expected real rate and possible economywide shocks that affect all generations uniformly. Again, the disposable income coefficients are significantly negative and the social security dummy picks up the "wrong" sign.

The Extended Family and Bequests
Finally, the fact that most older parents invite their children to move in has two further implications for theories of bequests. First, because if older parents get sick or incapacitated children would feel obliged to take care of them, accidental bequests are clearly less important. Second, the merging of older and younger households means that long before older parents' death there is a de facto transfer from older parents to the children of housing—by far the most important component of wealth.[24] The strategic aspect of bequests looks less significant for Japan.

11.8   The Role of Taxes

To examine the only remaining major issue, the effect of taxes on saving, we need to address two issues. One is the effective marginal tax rate on income from saving, and the other is the so-called (after-tax) interest elasticity of saving. A good deal of work has been done on the first issue. A comprehensive official description of Japan's tax system can be found in *An Outline of Japanese Taxes* (various years) by the Ministry of Finance. A good economist's description is in Horioka (1985b, section 4), Shoven and Tachibanaki (1985) and Makin (1985). The treatment of personal interest and dividend income in the Japanese tax system differs considerably from that in the United States. The notorious *Maruyu* system implies that interest income from a principal of up to 6 million yen (about $30 thousand) for "nonsalaried" workers and 12 million yen for "salaried" workers is nontaxable. Because abuse of this system is so common, it is difficult to estimate the marginal tax rate on interest income. Capital gains on stocks are not taxed if the gain is less than a certain amount and if the number of transactions is not large (less than fifty transactions a year). But this provision, too, can be avoided by trading stocks through several different brokers. The tax rate on dividend income is at most 35 percent, as high-income taxpayers can elect to have interest and dividends taxed separately at that rate, and for many middle- and low-income earners it is substantially less. Since the return from Japanese stocks has been mainly in the form of capital gains, the average tax rate on income from equity capital is very low. These facts led Shoven and Tachibanaki (1985) to assume very low marginal personal tax rates on interest income and income from equity (9.6 percent and 18.1 percent respectively). The very generous tax treatment of income from capital at the personal level is in sharp contrast to taxes on labor income whose top combined national and local statutory marginal rate is close to 80 percent.

At the corporate level, it appears that income is more heavily taxed in Japan than in the United States.[25] Although there is not much difference in the statutory corporate tax rate, the U.S. treatment of depreciation allowances and investment tax credits is more generous, at least in the 1980s. So the marginal tax rate on income from new capital at the corporate level in Japan is higher. The generous tax treatment at the personal level coupled with a relatively heavy tax burden at the corporate level must at least in part be responsible for the recent capital outflow from Japan to the United States.

The present Japanese tax system is thus geared to encourage saving. The other issue is whether it has been effective in promoting saving. The conventional approach to analyzing the response of saving to changes in the after-tax rate of return to saving is the saving function, which relates aggregate saving to the after-tax interest rate. Because of many serious problems, including the Lucas critique, the saving function approach seems to have been discredited by now. The modern approach that replaces it is the Euler equation approach, discussed in the previous section, which looks at the relation between consumption growth and the real interest rate. If saving is elastic to the interest rate, it should show up as a positive relation of the real interest rate with the growth rate of consumption from one period to the next, because increased current saving makes the level of current consumption relative to future consumption lower. The evidence presented in table 11.11, however, shows no such relation; in fact the sign of the real rate coefficient is the opposite of the theoretical prediction. Saving does not seem sensitive to the interest rate.

To check the robustness of this conclusion, the same form of the Euler equation (9) is estimated on monthly aggregate data on food expenditure.

Table 11.12
Estimation of Euler Equation on Monthly Aggregate Data

Equation #	Real rate of interest	Log of real disposable income	Estimation technique	Durbin-Watson statistic
1a	0.10 (1.1)	—	forward filtering	—
1b	0.11 (4.3)	—	OLS	1.3
2a	0.08 (0.96)	−0.003 (1.3)	forward filtering	—
2b	0.12 (4.5)	−0.014 (3.6)	OLS	1.4

The dependent variable is the growth rate of real food expenditure from the month to the month one year ahead, namely, $\ell n(c_{t+12}) - \ell n(c_t)$. The nominal rate used for constructing the real rate is the rate on one-year time deposits. The food component of the CPI is used to calculate the real rate. The log of real disposable income is $\ell n(y_t)$ where y_t is disposable income of month t divided by the food component of the CPI. Because the consumption growth rate is over one-year periods while the sampling interval is a month, the error term will be a moving average of order 11. The forward filtering technique proposed in Hayashi and Sims (1983) is used for equations 1a and 2a. Because the ex-post real rate is potentially correlated with the error term, it is instrumented in equations 1a and 2a by the current one-year nominal rate, current and 12 lags of the monthly food inflation rate, and current and 12 lags of the log of monthly disposable income. They explain about 39 percent of monthly variations in the real rate. The data period is from January 1963 through October 1985. Numbers in parentheses are the t values. The data on monthly food expenditure and disposable income for worker households are taken from the *Annual Reports of the Family Income and Expenditure Survey*.

The *Annual Reports of the Family Income and Expenditure Survey* contain data since 1963 on average monthly expenditure and disposable income for worker households. For reasons explained in the previous section, food expenditure is used for the estimation. (For details of the estimation see the note to table 11.12.) The real rate coefficient is now positive (the right sign), but still insignificantly different from zero. The negative effect of disposable income suggests the presence of liquidity constraints, but it too is insignificant. The wrong sign of the real rate coefficient found in table 11.11 may be explainable by the correlation between the ex-post real rate (used for the expected real rate) and the error term that represents unexpected developments (over the five-year periods). On the other hand, the real rate coefficients in table 11.12, while corrected for the correlation with the error term, suffer from the possible aggregation bias. The Euler equation holds for each individual. Since each year the oldest generations are replaced by new younger generations, it is not necessarily true that the Euler equation holds for aggregate consumption. On the whole, then, there is no strong evidence for a high interest elasticity of saving or for the effectiveness of the tax incentives for saving.

11.9 Concluding Comments

If one subscribes to the dynastic view of Barro (1974) and Becker (1981), it seems that all the evidence presented in this chapter—the insensitivity of the aggregate saving rate to demographics, saving rates that are independent of age, the possibly significant flow of intergenerational transfers, the insignificance of the social security dummy, and certainly the prevalence of the extended family—are parsimoniously explainable, although we must hasten to add that no direct and formal test of the dynastic model against other theories of bequests was given in the article.[26] A large flow of bequests by itself does not lead to high saving rates. One can easily construct a stationary economy with a zero saving rate in which assets are passed on from one generation to the next and in which each generation consumes all of its income. The existence of a significant flow of bequests does, however, imply that the infinite horizon assumption may be a good approximation. Add to this the fact that Japan had to start with a low level of wealth. The infinite horizon optimal growth model implies that the economy's response to the low initial wealth is a high saving rate that gradually stabilizes to a lower level as wealth approaches its steady-state value. Japan's saving rate has been high because the Japanese desire to accumulate wealth in order for their children to lives as well as Americans do.

That this simplistic view is consistent with Japan's experience in the last fifteen years (though not in the 1960s, which are not included in the figure) can be seen from figure 11.8, which includes a plot of the national saving rate and the (reciprocal of) the national wealth-NNP ratio. (If private saving and private wealth are used one gets a similar picture.) Japan has come a long way toward the steady state. She still has some room to accumulate faster than the United States because her per capita income at a current yen/dollar exchange rate is about 85 percent of the U.S. level. Given Japan's track record, it will not take long to fill the gap. If the infinite horizon view is correct, the rise in the national saving rate that occurred in 1984 is not likely to persist. The plot in the figure of net national investment in tangible assets indicates that Japan's large trade surplus in the 1980s is due more to slumping investment than to saving, which is not high by historical standards.

Data Appendix

This appendix describes and presents the Japanese aggregate time-series data used in the text. All the raw data come from the *1986 Annual Report on National Accounts* and the *Report on Revised National Accounts on the Basis of 1980*. The former includes the most recent (1985) benchmark revision with the base year of 1980. The latter is a companion volume that extends the benchmark revision back to either 1965 or 1970 depending on the series. The series in the capital transactions (saving/investment) accounts and the capital accounts (balance sheets and reconciliations) currently starts in 1970. The variable labels and their values are displayed in tables 11.A1 through 11.A5. They are stated in trillions of current yen. As a general rule, variable labels with "_H" are for the household sector (including private nonprofit institutions serving households), "_C" for the corporate sector (nonfinancial corporations and financial institutions), and "_G" for government. The value of the stock of assets is at the beginning of the year. Revaluations are gross (that is, without adjustments for general inflation). As mentioned in the text, the Japanese national accounts report depreciation in the capital transactions accounts at historical costs, do not adjust after-tax income for capital transfers (wealth taxes and lump-sum transfers), and do not depreciate government depreciable assets either in the capital transactions accounts or in the capital accounts (except for buildings). Data necessary for correcting these are available only for the period after 1969. The data presented in this appendix for 1970–84 are all corrected values unless otherwise noted. The variables listed in the tables can therefore be grouped into four categories: (1) those that are directly available from the National Accounts Reports, (2) those that require capital consumption adjustments, (3) those that also require adjustments for capital transfers, and (4) those that are influenced by our estimate of government depreciable tangible assets.

(1) The following variables are available directly from the Reports after consolidating five sectors into the three sectors (household, corporate and government.)

GNP = gross national product.

CON = personal consumption expenditure.

PCON = deflator for CON.

Table 11.A1
Output, Expenditure and Prices

Year	GNP	GNP_A	NNP_A	GNP_BEA	NNP_BEA	CON	PCON
1965	32.71	32.71	28.35	31.70	27.86	19.17	32.8
1966	37.99	37.99	32.97	36.82	32.40	22.06	34.1
1967	44.53	44.52	38.64	43.15	37.98	25.30	35.6
1968	52.77	52.77	45.83	51.15	45.05	28.92	37.6
1969	62.10	62.10	53.82	60.19	52.90	33.33	39.5
1970	73.19	74.06	63.23	71.78	62.15	38.33	41.5
1971	80.59	81.65	69.34	78.94	68.05	43.23	45.0
1972	92.40	93.65	79.56	90.47	78.05	49.90	47.8
1973	112.52	114.14	95.87	110.10	93.92	60.31	50.5
1974	134.00	136.43	110.00	130.77	107.32	72.91	57.7
1975	148.17	151.33	122.63	144.28	119.40	84.76	70.9
1976	166.42	169.81	137.84	162.08	134.31	95.78	76.3
1977	185.53	189.44	153.97	180.56	149.95	107.08	83.2
1978	204.47	208.84	170.34	198.82	165.84	117.92	87.8
1979	221.82	226.81	183.93	215.32	178.75	130.08	91.3
1980	240.10	245.93	196.69	232.44	190.60	141.32	95.6
1981	256.82	263.41	211.25	248.00	204.26	149.38	102.3
1982	269.70	276.76	221.77	259.97	214.11	159.61	105.9
1983	280.57	287.92	230.32	270.15	222.19	167.81	107.9
1984	298.59	306.17	245.81	287.59	237.32	176.14	109.9
1985	n.a.	n.a.	n.a.	n.a.	n.a.	n.a.	112.5

GNP = gross national product,
GNP_A = gross national product with our estimate of government depreciable tangible assets,
NNP_A = net national product with our estimate of government depreciable tangible assets,
GNP_BEA = gross national product without government tangible assets,
NNP_BEA = net national product without government tangible assets,
CON = personal consumption expenditure,
$PCON$ = price index for CON at the 4th quarter of previous year.
In trillion yen except for PCON. For 1965–69 the numbers do not incorporate capital consumption adjustments.

Table 11.A2
Depreciation and Net Saving

Year	DEPH_H	CCAJ_H	DEPH_C	CCAJ_C	DEPH_G	CCAJ_G	SVG_H	SVG_C	SVG_G	SVG_BEA
1965	n.a.	n.a.	n.a.	n.a.	n.a.	n.a.	3.34	.83	1.79	.47
1966	n.a.	n.a.	n.a.	n.a.	n.a.	n.a.	3.54	1.81	1.85	.25
1967	n.a.	n.a.	n.a.	n.a.	n.a.	n.a.	3.87	3.17	2.42	.73
1968	n.a.	n.a.	n.a.	n.a.	n.a.	n.a.	5.34	3.65	2.99	.97
1969	n.a.	n.a.	n.a.	n.a.	n.a.	n.a.	6.08	5.20	3.68	1.30
1970	2.36	.47	7.05	-.24	.33	.87	7.57	7.24	3.78	1.29
1971	2.71	.56	7.83	-.22	.37	1.06	8.56	5.59	4.16	1.36
1972	3.19	.66	9.22	-.65	.42	1.25	10.10	7.01	4.06	.07
1973	3.87	1.58	10.96	-.23	.47	1.63	13.54	6.60	5.68	.93
1974	4.79	2.79	12.42	3.45	.55	2.42	18.88	-2.11	5.52	.46
1975	5.77	2.48	12.59	4.05	.67	3.15	22.31	-4.19	1.00	-4.13
1976	6.80	3.00	13.12	4.86	.79	3.42	25.62	-2.76	-.63	-6.28
1977	7.79	3.21	14.33	5.29	.90	3.96	26.14	-1.98	-.22	-7.16
1978	8.77	3.33	15.18	5.71	1.05	4.45	27.48	2.39	-2.40	-12.12
1979	9.68	4.27	16.77	5.85	1.20	5.12	24.33	3.40	-.83	-9.63
1980	10.63	5.38	18.71	7.11	1.39	6.01	25.02	1.30	-.92	-9.41
1981	11.46	5.07	21.02	6.20	1.60	6.83	27.86	.03	-.07	-11.26
1982	12.11	5.05	22.34	6.36	1.75	7.38	25.98	1.58	-.54	-9.43
1983	12.67	5.24	23.83	6.21	1.89	7.75	26.61	.91	-1.81	-10.78
1984	13.28	4.99	25.44	6.56	2.02	8.07	27.91	1.65	1.31	-6.27

$DEPH\_x$ = depreciation at historical costs as reported in the Japanese national accounts ($x = H$ for household, C for corporate, and G for government), $CCAJ\_xx$ = excess of depreciaton at replacement costs over depreciation at historical costs ($x = H, C, G$).
SVG_x = net saving in sector x after capital consumption adjustments,
SVG_BEA = government saving in net financial assets, i.e., budget surplus. The difference between SVG_G and SVG_BEA is net government capital formation.
In trillion yen. The data on saving for 1965–69 incorporate neither capital consumption adjustments nor adjustments on capital transfers.

Table 11.A3
Household Capital Accounts

Year	TA_H	KD_H	FA_H	DTA_H	DKD_H	DFA_H	RTA_H	RKD_H	RFA_H	GCD	CD	RCD
1970	119.15	20.61	40.03	1.93	3.97	5.39	24.29	1.29	−1.12	2.35	8.74	.35
1971	145.37	25.86	44.31	.95	4.11	7.08	27.88	.82	1.36	2.69	9.76	.16
1972	174.20	30.79	52.75	1.02	5.37	10.52	69.65	6.40	12.48	3.34	10.70	.20
1973	244.88	42.56	75.74	.66	6.95	8.80	71.57	9.89	4.00	4.15	12.09	2.29
1974	317.10	59.40	88.55	3.49	6.61	13.28	10.54	6.43	−4.28	4.55	15.90	3.47
1975	331.14	72.44	97.54	4.92	7.22	14.09	20.30	1.81	−3.47	5.02	20.46	.17
1976	356.35	81.47	108.16	6.58	8.39	17.12	28.43	7.61	4.78	5.87	21.99	.49
1977	391.37	97.47	130.06	6.45	7.83	18.47	26.70	2.58	−.40	6.34	24.17	.49
1978	424.52	107.87	148.13	8.41	8.38	19.89	49.11	4.62	6.21	7.38	26.64	.56
1979	482.04	120.88	174.23	6.42	8.62	18.94	88.27	14.92	3.84	8.23	29.34	.84
1980	576.73	144.42	197.01	3.50	7.07	16.93	88.44	7.32	−.55	8.10	32.82	.96
1981	668.67	158.80	213.39	2.20	6.09	25.13	79.07	2.74	1.65	8.60	36.20	.44
1982	749.94	167.64	240.16	2.11	5.34	25.63	43.65	2.06	−3.23	9.27	38.87	−.30
1983	795.70	175.04	262.57	.64	3.93	25.84	25.19	.19	7.56	10.07	41.15	−.18
1984	821.53	179.16	295.97	.54	3.56	26.45	26.56	3.56	8.21	10.44	43.91	.00
1985	848.63	186.29	330.29	n.a.	n.a.	n.a.	n.a.	n.a.	n.a.	n.a.	46.96	n.a.

TA = stock at year beginning of tangible assets,
KD = stock of depreciable tangible assets,
FA = stock of net financial assets,
DTA = net investment in tangible assets,
DKD = net investment in depreciable tangible assets,
DFA = net investment in net financial assets,
RTA = gross revaluation (without adjustment for general inflation) of tangible assets,
RKD = gross revaluation of depreciable tangible assets,
RFA = gross revaluation of net financial assets,
GCD = durables expenditure,
CD = stock of consumer durables,
RCD = gross revaluation of consumer durables.
In trillion yen.

Table 11.A4
Corporate Capital Accounts

Year	TA_C	KD_C	FA_C	DTA_C	DKD_C	DFA_C	RTA_C	RKD_C	RFA_C
1970	94.78	30.85	-42.86	13.35	9.17	-5.97	9.16	2.24	1.40
1971	117.30	50.26	-47.43	12.36	8.58	-6.44	8.19	1.12	-1.74
1972	137.85	59.96	-55.61	13.52	8.68	-8.59	23.93	5.31	-13.30
1973	175.31	73.95	-77.50	18.81	11.45	-9.76	42.52	18.11	-4.14
1974	236.64	103.51	-91.40	15.13	9.62	-15.07	19.58	17.38	4.47
1975	271.35	130.51	-102.01	9.88	8.19	-10.17	10.08	2.12	3.06
1976	291.30	140.82	-109.12	8.97	7.20	-9.76	18.57	9.58	-5.06
1977	318.84	157.60	-123.94	8.50	7.27	-8.47	10.83	4.47	1.20
1978	338.17	169.34	-131.21	7.45	8.25	-4.28	21.97	5.35	-7.25
1979	367.59	182.94	-142.74	12.99	10.96	-11.29	46.88	13.29	-4.09
1980	427.47	207.19	-158.11	15.02	12.24	-10.09	45.99	12.81	-.91
1981	488.48	232.24	-169.12	16.18	13.47	-12.72	25.02	2.86	-2.93
1982	529.68	248.56	-184.77	14.89	13.10	-14.42	17.13	2.05	4.86
1983	561.70	263.72	-194.33	12.75	13.10	-10.10	7.30	-.28	-9.43
1984	581.75	275.29	-213.85	15.68	13.99	-11.83	12.94	3.95	-7.87
1985	610.37	293.24	-233.55	n.a.	n.a.	n.a.	n.a.	n.a.	n.a.

See note to table A3.

Table 11.A5
Government Capital Accounts

Year	TA_G	KD_G	FA_G	DTA_G	DKD_G	DFA_G	RTA_G	RKD_G	RFA_G	KD_B_G
1970	27.01	18.40	3.47	2.51	2.08	1.29	2.52	1.45	.05	18.40
1971	32.12	22.01	4.81	3.23	2.63	1.36	2.25	1.04	-.29	21.97
1972	37.66	25.74	5.88	4.18	3.38	.07	6.59	2.99	.09	25.84
1973	48.62	32.30	6.03	5.09	4.27	.93	12.74	8.57	-.10	32.51
1974	67.04	45.73	6.87	5.04	4.03	.46	8.36	8.55	-.11	45.49
1975	80.83	58.71	7.22	5.11	4.02	-4.13	2.16	1.85	.03	58.34
1976	88.16	64.65	3.12	5.52	4.39	-6.28	6.59	5.55	-.01	65.18
1977	100.45	74.77	-3.17	6.85	5.41	-7.16	5.22	4.33	.17	76.07
1978	112.68	84.67	-10.16	8.82	7.02	-12.12	7.64	5.31	-.74	86.93
1979	129.36	97.22	-23.02	9.68	7.71	-9.63	12.72	8.67	-.33	100.53
1980	152.11	113.95	-32.97	9.67	7.28	-9.41	12.60	8.17	.90	118.60
1981	174.65	129.65	-41.48	9.80	7.22	-11.26	6.92	3.46	-.37	135.55
1982	191.47	140.43	-53.10	9.18	6.55	-9.43	1.51	1.40	.04	148.24
1983	203.20	148.41	-62.49	8.44	5.83	-10.78	0.65	1.02	-.01	158.36
1984	212.31	155.28	-73.29	7.74	5.05	-6.27	2.82	3.03	-.35	167.46
1985	222.91	163.41	-79.91	n.a.	n.a.	n.a.	n.a.	n.a.	n.a.	178.03

KD_B_G = stock of government depreciable tangible assets as reported in the National Accounts. For definition of other variables, see note to table A3.

SVG_BEA = government budget surplus, or net investment in government net financial assets. "_BEA" is placed in the label because if we take the U.S. Bureau of Economic Analysis (BEA) convention of ignoring government tangible assets it should equal government net saving. This is available directly from the government capital transactions accounts after 1969. For 1965–69 it is defined as: government net saving + depreciation − gross government capital formation. This should equal net investment in financial assets up to statistical discrepancy.

DEPH_x = reported depreciation in the capital transactions accounts of sector x (x = H, C, G).

DFA_x = net investment in financial assets in the capital accounts of sector x (x = H, C, G). After 1969 DFA_G equals SVG_BEA.

FA_x = stock (at the beginning of the year) of net financial assets for sector x (x = H, C, G).

RFA_x = gross revaluation of net financial assets (x = H, C, G).

GCD = expenditure on consumer durables.

CD − stock of consumer durables at the beginning of the year.

KD_B_G = reported value of government depreciable tangible assets.

As the Japanese national accounts has data on the stock of depreciable tangible assets at replacement costs in the capital accounts of the corporate and household sector (but not for the government sector), the following stock variables are also directly available from the Reports:

TA_x = stock of tangible assets (depreciable tangible assets, nonreproducible tangible assets, and inventories) for sector x (x = H, C).

KD_x = stock of depreciable tangible assets (x = H, C).

(2) As assets are valued at replacement cost in the capital accounts, depreciation at replacement cost implicit in the Japanese National Accounts can be estimated as follows. Because depreciation in the capital transactions accounts are at historical cost, reconciliations in the capital accounts consist of: revaluation, capital consumption adjustments (i.e., the excess of depreciation at replacement cost over depreciation at historical cost), and some other minor items (e.g., accidental loss/gain of assets). If $KD(t)$ is the nominal stock of depreciable assets at the beginning of the year, $P(t)$ its associated deflator, and $N(t)$ nominal net investment, then revaluation in

the National Accounts is calculated as:

$$\text{revaluation} = \frac{P(t+1) - P(t)}{P(t)} KD(t) + \frac{P(t+1) - PA(t)}{PA(t)} N(t), \tag{A1}$$

where $PA(t)$ is an average of the deflator over the year (see *A Guide to the Use of the National Economic Accounting*, p. 233, Economic Planning Agency, 1978). Thus capital gains/losses are conferred on assets acquired during the year. In our calculation $PA(t)$ is taken to be the simple average of $P(t)$ and $P(t+1)$. It is unclear whether nominal net investment $N(t)$ is before or after capital consumption adjustments. We use reported net investment (before capital consumption adjustments) for $N(t)$.

$CCAJ\_x$, our estimate of capital consumption adjustments for the household and the corporate sector $(x = H, C)$, is calculated from the relationship that should hold if the other minor items in reconciliation are ignored:

$CCAJ\_x = (A1)$ for sector x – reconciliation on depreciable assets for sector x.

For 1965–69, $CCAJ\_x$ is set at zero (for lack of data on the capital accounts). With this estimate of capital consumption adjustments, the following variables can be calculated for the household and the corporate sector $(x = H, C)$.

$DTA\_x =$ net investment in tangible assets, equals the reported value less $CCAJ\_x$.

$DKD\_x =$ net investment in depreciable tangible assets similarly calculated.

$RTA\_x =$ gross revaluation of tangible assets, equals the reported value of reconciliation plus $CCAJ\_x$.

$RKD\_x =$ gross revaluation of depreciable tangible assets similarly calculated.

For consumer durables, a different procedure is used because depreciation is not reported at all. We first calculate using data on the nominal stock (CD) and nominal gross investment (GCD), the depreciation rate $\delta(t)$ for each year implicit in the perpetual inventory method:

$$(P(t)/P(t+1))^* CD(t+1) = CD(t) + GCD(t) - \delta(t)^* CD(t), \tag{A2}$$

where $P(t)$ here is the deflator for the stock of consumer durables available from the Reports. The implicit depreciation rate for 1970–84 turned out to be stable over years with a mean of 19.0 percent. Depreciation at replacement costs on consumer durables is thus calculated as 0.19 times CD. Gross revaluation of consumer durables is:

$RCD = $ (A1) with KD replaced by CD, N by $GCD - 0.19^*CD$, and P by the deflator for CD.

(3) To arrive at net saving, we have to subtract from reported net saving capital consumption adjustments and then add capital transfers. The variables

$SVG_x = $ net saving by the household sector $(x = H)$ and by the corporate sector $(x = C)$

are thus calculated. Capital transfers are positive for the corporate sector and negative for the household sector for all years since 1970.

(4) As shown in table 2, the average physical rate of depreciation implicit in the capital accounts for buildings is 6.5 percent. Using the beginning of 1970 value of government depreciable assets as the benchmark and using reported government gross investment series and the reported value of deflator for the stock of government depreciable tangible assets, we generate the stock of depreciable assets by the perpetual inventory method (A2). Namely,

$KD_G = $ government depreciable tangible assets generated by perpetual inventory with a depreciation rate of 6.5 percent.

The benchmark 1970 value in the National Accounts is based on the *1970 National Wealth Survey* which is a sampling survey on the replacement value of assets by type, industry and institutional sector.

The remaining variables for the government sector are now easy to calculate:

$TA_G = $ stock of government tangible assets, equals KD_G plus reported value of the stock of inventories and nonreproducible assets.

$CCAJ_G = $ capital consumption adjustments, equals 0.065^* KD_G minus reported depreciation.

$DKD_G = $ net investment in depreciable tangible assets as reported in the capital accounts of the government minus $CCAJ\_G$.

$DTA\_G =$ net investment in tangible assets, equals DKD_G plus reported net investment in inventories and nonreproducible assets.

$RKD\_G =$ gross revaluation of depreciable assets calculated by (A1) with KD replaced by KD_G, N by DKD_G and P by reported deflator for government depreciable tangible assets.

$RTA\_G =$ gross revaluation of government tangible assets, equals RKD_G plus reported reconciliation on inventories and nonreproducible assets.

$SVG\_G =$ government net saving, equals reported net saving minus $CCAJ\_G$ minus capital transfers to other sectors.

This leaves GNP_A, NNP_A, GNP_BEA and NNP_BEA. Since in the National Accounts the value of government output is taken to be equal to the costs of producing it, GNP must be adjusted for the discrepancy between the reported value (KD_B_G above) and our estimate of the government depreciable assets (KD_G) and depreciation. NNP (net national product) then is this adjusted GNP less national depreciation at replacement costs. We use a rate of return of 4 percent to impute net service flows from government tangible assets. Thus:

$$GNP\_A = \text{reported GNP} + 0.04^*(KD\_G - KD\_B\_G) + CCAJ\_G.$$

$$NNP\_A = GNP\_A - (DEPH\_H + DEPH\_C + DEPH\_G) \\ - (CCAJ\_H + CCAJ\_C + CCAJ\_G).$$

Neither $CCAJ$ nor KD_G is available for 1965–69. Thus for this period GNP_A and NNP_A are equal to respective reported values. The definition of GNP and NNP should be altered if government tangible assets are to be ignored. The BEA definition of Japan's NNP would be:

$$GNP\_BEA = GNP\_A - 0.04^* TA\_G - DEPH\_G - CCAJ\_G.$$

$$NNP\_BEA = NNP\_A - 0.04^* TA\_G.$$

For 1965–69 data on TA_G and $CCAJ\_G$ are not available. We use the 1970 ratio of GNP_A to GNP_BEA to extrapolate GNP_BEA for 1965–69. The same extrapolation method is used for NNP.

Notes

The author is grateful to Tsuneo Ishikawa, Takatoshi Ito, Paul Romer, and other conference participants for discussions and comments on earlier drafts, and especially to Albert Ando, whose detailed written comments helped to improve the final version of the chapter.

1. George Shultz's speech at Princeton University attracted widespread attention in the Japanese press.

2. Kurosaka and Hamada (1984).

3. The top combined national and local personal tax rate is currently 88 percent in Japan. (However, we are told, there is a footnote in the personal tax code that reduces the top marginal rate to 75 percent.) People in high-income tax brackets can spread their income over their spouses and relatives by setting up a token corporation. By paying them high wages and by taking advantage of the more generous tax deductibility provisions in the corporate tax codes, they can understate corporate income and thus avoid double taxation at the corporate and personal levels. In 1983 there were about 1.8 million corporations in Japan. The largest 1.2 percent paid close to 70 percent of the total corporation tax. About 60 percent of all corporations reported negative taxable income.

4. The Japanese national accounts also divide the nation into private and public sectors. Government enterprises are included in the public sector. In retrospect, the focus on private sector might have been more appropriate. Fortunately, as we shall see later, the difference between the national and the private saving rates is small compared to the difference of the personal rate from the private and the national saving rates.

5. A good example is dental services. It is classified as services in the national accounts but in essence it is a purchase of a durable good of good teeth. Hayashi (1985a) reports using Japanese data that food is almost the only commodity that exhibits no durability. Recreational expenditures are found to be more durable than consumer durables.

6. Inventory valuation adjustments are incorporated in the Japanese national accounting.

7. Investment goods prices more than doubled in the 1970s.

8. The estimates of government capital in Boskin, Robinson, and Roberts (1985) are for the federal government only.

9. If the principal is reduced as a consumer repays loans, that reduction in principal is part of saving.

10. The household and corporate sectors are already consolidated in table 11.1, because the data on the market value of equity in the Japanese national accounts seem wholly unreliable. The value of Tobin's q (the ratio of the value of tangible assets at replacement cost to the market value of net financial liabilities) for the corporate sector at the end of 1984 is 0.38 (see table 11.A4). The reported market value of net financial liabilities is less than the reported value of inventory. This low estimate is due to the fact that stocks that are not publicly traded are valued in the Japanese national accounts at their "par" value (a mere 50 yen). By consolidating the household and corporate balance sheets, the problem of a correct valuation of equity can be avoided. This amounts to valuing corporate capital at replacement cost rather than at the market value observed in the financial markets.

11. The average depreciation rates obtained in table 11.2 are close to the asset life reported in the *1970 National Wealth Survey*. Almost all the available estimates of the capital stock in Japan are based on this periodic official sampling survey of the net capital stock of the nation. The survey has not been conducted since 1970.

12. Those who receive bonuses and those who own the company's stock are often different. The neoclassical reasoning is that they are linked with operative bequest and gift motives.

13. The age-earnings profile is constructed as follows. Earnings by age are taken from the *Basic Survey of Wage Structure* (the Ministry of Labor). They are multiplied by the labor force

participation rate taken from the Labor Ministry's *Labor Force Survey*. The earnings for 50–59-year-olds are then multiplied by a factor of 1.18 to accommodate the retirement payments. This factor is calculated from the age-earnings profile displayed in Table 3-24 of the *1985 White Paper on Japanese Economy* (Economic Planning Agency). The survival probability for a cohort in year t in a ten-year age group is calculated as the ratio of the number of the cohort in year $t + 10$ to year t. For 1980, the survival probability is assumed to be the same as in 1970, except for cohorts over 60. For the 60–69-year-olds it is set at $(1 - 0.01483)^{**}10$, where the number 0.01483 is the death probability for 60–69-year-olds reported in a Ministry of Health and Welfare publication. Similarly for the 70–79-year-olds the survival probability is set at $(1 - 0.046045)^{**}10$.

14. Our "steady-state" simulation is a mere replication of the analysis in the second half of Tobin's (1967) paper but using Japanese data on the age-earnings profile and the age distribution. To be more concrete, equations (1)–(3) are sufficient to give the prospective consumption and asset holdings profile $(c(t + i, v + i)$ and $A(t + i, v + i)$ for all $i)$ for those aged $v = 0$ in period t because for $v = 0$ we have $A(t, 0) = 0$ under the selfish lifecycle hypothesis. The steady-state assumption implies that assets held by v-year-olds in period $t + i$ are $(1 + g)^{**}i$ times as large as assets held by v-year-olds in period t. That is, $A(t + i, v)^{*}((1 + g)^{**}(-i)) = A(t, v)$. This allows us to calculate prospective consumption and asset holdings profile for those who are v years old in period t because their initial assets $A(t, v)$ can be set at $A(t + v, v)^{*}((1 + g)^{**}(-v))$. The simulation is partial equilibrium in nature, because what is generated is the supply of saving, that is not guaranteed to equal changes in the capital stock. Also note that the aggregate output growth rate depends on the age distribution as well as on the productivity growth rate g. Our simulation does not take taxes and transfers into account. Proportional income taxes will not affect the saving and wealth-income *ratios*. We also do not consider social security, because assumptions about future expected benefits are inevitably arbitrary. If social security is actuarially fair, then it is clear that the size of the social security system does not affect our steady-state calculations of the national saving rate.

15. The U.S. earnings profile is taken from the 1972–73 Consumer Expenditure Survey. It would have been preferable to obtain it from labor market data.

16. This is because what is crucial in the simulation turns out to be the steepness of the Japanese age-earnings profile. See Hashimoto and Raisian (1985) for a full documentation on the effect of tenure on earnings in Japan and the United States.

17. Monthly figures averaged over the three-month period of September through November are converted to annual rates by using the seasonality factors reported in the *Annual Reports of the Family Income and Expenditure Survey*.

18. This pattern shows up consistently in almost any household survey in Japan for every year. We must, however be careful about the saving rate for the old. The saving rate is for worker households, which automatically excludes retirees. But table 5B indicates that, for all households whose head is 65 or over, average annual income is 2.5 million yen and average expenditure 1.7 million yen. For those households the average tax rate would be at most 15 percent. Thus their personal saving rate must be over 20 percent.

19. At the time of writing, the 1984 National Survey Report was not yet published, but I was given access to the 1984 tabulations in computer printout form. The tabulation for 1984 in table 8 does not take single-person households into account. It would make little difference to the results.

20. The difference in financial assets for the 20–29 age group in Panel C is small for the sample selection bias I have mentioned. Because the survey defines the household head to be

the main income earner, older persons in a young extended family where the household head is the son tend to be low-income people, unable to earn more than 20–29-year-olds do. Their contribution to household assets is therefore small. Because table 8 is a cross-sectional tabulation of assets, we must also be aware of the cohort effect due to economic growth that asset holdings by v-year-olds in year $t+i$ are $(1+g)^{**i}$ times as large as asset holdings by v-year-olds in year t, where g is the long-term growth rate. The cross-sectional decline in asset holdings reported in Panel C of the table is too steep to be accounted for by the growth factor, however.

21. The tabulations by age and family type (nuclear and extended) in the 1969 and 1974 National Survey Reports have no separate listing of imputed rent, although income in kind is listed. The tabulation by age alone does list imputed rent, which shows a more or less stable proportion to food expenditure across age. This proportion is used to separate out imputed rent from income in kind. Disposable income and consumption expenditure are then calculated by the formulas (4) and (5) in section 11.5.

22. In equation (7) it is not necessary to multiply $S(i, j, t)$ or $W(i, j, t)$ by $(1 + r)$, where r is the real rate of return, because $S(i, j, t)$ already incorporates the return from assets as it is defined as disposable income less consumption. If $S(i, j, t)$ were defined as after-tax labor income less consumption, then the interest rate adjustment would have been necessary. During the early 1970s revaluation of assets was substantial (see table 1). In the actual calculation of $L(i, j, t)$, we multiplied $S(i, j, t)$ by a factor of 2.13. This factor translates net saving to saving inclusive of net revaluation. To calculate this factor, we first calculate annual personal net saving and net revaluation at 1974 prices, and then take the averages over the 1970–74 period. The factor is the ratio of the sum of average real net saving (14.5 trillion in 1974 yen) and average real net revaluation (16.4 trillion) to the average real net saving.

23. From Panel A for 1974 in table 11.9 the stock of aggregate total assets for the 1974 40–54 age group (i.e., the 1969 35–49 group) is: $1.8*3.770 + 1.5*4.732 + 0.9*5.237 = 18.6$. If this is multiplied by a factor of 3.55, we arrive at 66 trillion yen. The factor of 3.55 is to adjust for the underreporting already mentioned. If we compare this factor with the information given in the last two columns of table 5B, the factor seems a bit too large. The factor one can calculate from table 5B for financial assets is $3.3/1.7 = 1.9$ and for houses it is $9.8/2.9 = 3.4$. But table 5B is for all households. If the similar calculation is done for worker households and the asset-weighted average over financial assets and houses is taken, one comes out with the factor of 3.55.

24. The actual transfer of ownership does not usually occur until the death of the parents. In 1983 taxable bequests were valued at 5.0 trillion yen, while taxable gifts were 0.6 trillion (see *Annual Statistical Report of the Tax Bureau*, the only official source of data on taxes in Japan). A standard guidebook on Japanese bequest and gift taxes indicates that bequests are taxed slightly less heavily. The effective bequests tax rate is much lower on houses than on financial assets, because the assessed value of real estate is often less than half the market value. This may explain why the Japanese prefer owning a house to renting.

25. See Adno and Auerbach (1985) for a comparison of the cost of capital in Japan and the United States.

26. The existence of liquidity constraints is not inconsistent with the dynastic model. Suppose that people do not come to realize the linearity of the family until they reach middle age. Until then the only limits on their consumption are liquidity constraints. Their parents *do* think about the family. Because of liquidity constraints they can determine their impatient son's consumption through transfers. Thus family consumption is effectively controlled by the parents. Also, liquidity constraints do not necessarily invalidate the Ricardian doctrine of the equivalence of taxes and deficits. See Hayashi (1985b).

References

Ando, A. 1985. The savings of Japanese households: A micro study based on data from the National Survey of Family Income and Expenditure. University of Pennsylvania. Mimeo.

Ando, A., and A. Auerbach. 1985. The corporate cost of capital in Japan and the U.S.: A comparison. NBER Working Paper 1762.

Ando, A., and F. Modigliani. 1963. The life cycle hypothesis of saving: Aggregate implications and tests. *American Economic Review* 53:55–84.

Barro, R. 1974. Are government bonds net wealth? *Journal of Political Economy* 82:1095–1117.

Barro, R., and J. Friedman. 1977. On uncertain lifetimes. *Journal of Political Economy* 85:843–49.

Becker, G. 1981. *A treatise on the family.* Cambridge: Harvard University Press.

Boskin, M., M. Robinson, and J. Roberts. 1985. New estimates of federal government tangible capital and net investment. NBER Working Paper 1774.

Browning, M., A. Deaton, and M. Irish. 1985. A profitable approach to labor supply and commodity demands over the life-cycle. *Econometrica* 53:503–44.

Burnheim, D., A. Shleifer, and L. Summers. 1985. The strategic bequest motive. *Journal of Political Economy* 93:1045–76.

Eisner, R. 1985. The total incomes system of accounts. *Survey of Current Business* 55:24–48.

Hashimoto, M., and J. Raisian. 1985. Employment tenure and earnings profiles in Japan and the United States. *American Economic Review* 75:721–35.

Hayashi, F. 1985a. The permanent income hypothesis and consumption durability: Analysis based on Japanese panel data. *Quarterly Journal of Economics* 100:1083–1113.

―――. 1985b. Tests for liquidity constraints: A critical survey. NBER Working Paper 1720.

Hayashi, F., and C. Sims. 1983. Efficient estimation of time-series models with predetermined, but not exogenous, instruments. *Econometrica* 51:783–98.

Hayashi, F., T. Ito, and J. Slemrod. 1985. Housing finance imperfection: A simulation analysis for a comparison of the U.S. and Japan. University of Minnesota. Incomplete mimeo.

Horioka, C. 1984. The applicability of the life-cycle hypothesis to Japan. *Kyoto University Economic Review* 54(2):31–56.

―――. 1985a. Household saving in Japan: The importance of target saving for education and housing. Kyoto University. Mimeo.

―――. 1985b. A survey of the literature on household saving in Japan: Why is the household saving rate so high in Japan? Kyoto University. Mimeo.

Hulten, C., and F. Wykoff. 1981. The measurement of economic depreciation. In *Depreciation, inflation and the taxation of income from capital,* ed. C. Hulten, 81–125. Washington, D.C.: Urban Institute.

Ishikawa, T., and K. Ueda. 1984. The bonus payment system and Japanese personal savings. In *The economic analysis of the Japanese firm*, ed. M. Aoki, 133–92. (Contributions to Economic Analysis Series no. 151). Amsterdam: North-Holland.

Komiya, R. 1966. The supply of personal savings. In *Postwar economic growth in Japan*, ed. R. Komiya, 157–86. (trans. Robert Ozaki). Berkeley: University of California Press.

Kotlikoff, L., and A. Spivak. 1981. The family as an incomplete annuities market. *Journal of Political Economy* 89:372–91.

Kurosaka, Y., and K. Hamada. 1984. Why is the personal saving rate so high? In *Macro Keizaigaku to Nihon Keizai* [Macroeconomics and the Japanese economy]. Tokyo: *Nihon Hyoronsha*.

Makin, J. 1985. Saving rates in Japan and the United States: The roles of tax policy and other factors. Washington, D.C.: American Enterprise Institute. Mimeo.

Modigliani, F. 1980. The life cycle hypothesis of saving twenty years later. In *Contemporary Issues in Economics*, ed. M. Parkin, 2–36. Manchester: Manchester University Press.

Modigliani, F., and R. Brumberg. 1954. Utility analysis and the consumption function: An interpretation of cross-section data. In *Post-Keynesian economics*, ed. K. Kurihara, 388–436. New Brunswick, N.J.: Rutgers University Press.

Ruggles, R., and N. Ruggles. 1982. Integrated economic accounts for the United States, 1947–80. *Survey of Current Business* 52(5):1–53.

Shinohara, M. 1983. The determinants of post-war savings behaviour in Japan. In *The Determinants of National Saving and Wealth*, ed. F. Modigliani and R. Hemming, 143–80. London: Macmillan.

Shoven, J., and T. Tachibanaki. 1985. The taxation of income from capital in Japan. Stanford University. Mimeo.

Tobin, J. 1967. Life cycle saving and balanced growth. In *Ten economic studies in the tradition of Irving Fisher*, ed. W. Fellner, 231–56. New York: Wiley.

Addendum to Chapter 11:
An Update of Data
Appendix

Since the paper forming this chapter was published nearly ten years ago, there have been several developments that call for a revision of my procedure for calculating the Japanese aggregate saving rate series and other time series reported in the data appendix to this chapter. First, the Economic Planning Agency (EPA) of the Japanese government extended most tables of the National Income Accounts (NIA) back to 1955 (EPA 1988). They include the capital transactions (use-of-saving) accounts (the "capital finance accounts" in the NIA) by sector in the flow section of the NIA and the balance sheets and the reconciliation accounts by sector in the stock section, accounts that are crucial in our procedure for backing out from the NIA the replacement cost depreciation implicit in the NIA. It is now possible to extend all the time series presented in the data appendix back to 1955 from 1965 or 1970, with much less splicing. Second, my procedure has gone through scrutinies by several researchers.[1] The only criticism to date that I think is valid and worth incorporating into my procedure is Iwamoto's (1994) point that there is a simpler and more accurate procedure for backing out replacement cost depreciation from the stock section of the NIA. As will be discussed below, the effect of this refinement is to raise net national saving by about 1 percent of NNP. Still, the effect of using replacement cost rather than historical cost depreciation to calculate net saving is very substantial: the national saving rate gets lower by as much as 4 percent for years around 1980. Third, I now realize that the EPA's estimates of the government capital stock in the stock section of the NIA, like the capital stocks of other sectors, incorporate replacement cost depreciation, contrary to my presumption in the data appendix that the NIA does not depreciate government capital. It is true that, for most government depreciable assets, their depreciation is not included in the line called depreciation in the flow section, so government net capital formation in the flow section is severely overstated. But, depreciation at replacement costs is included in the government's reconciliation account of the stock section, which means that the government capital stock in the balance sheet of the stock section incorporates replacement cost depreciation. Therefore, it is not necessary to provide a separate and independent perpetual inventory estimate of government capital, as I did in the data appendix to this chapter.

All these changes contribute to a substantial simplification of my estimation procedure. Below I describe in great detail a modified procedure for calculating all the time series presented in the data appendix tables. The rule for naming the time series is the same as in the data appendix. Thus, series labels with "_H" are for the household sector (including nonprofit institutions, which have a separate account in the NIA for the years since 1970), those with "_C" are for corporations (consisting of nonfinancial and financial corporate sectors, which have separate accounts in the NIA), and those with "_G" are for the government. Series names starting with "D" are net changes and those with "R" are revaluations (nominal capital gains or losses without adjustments for general inflation). Thus, for example, DTA_H is net investment in tangible assets for the household sector. Tangible assets consist of depreciable tangible assets (or depreciable assets or capital), inventories, and nonreproducible tangible assets (such as land and forests).

11A.1 The Two Identities Related to Saving and Investment

The capital transactions account of the flow section of the NIA for each sector x $(= H, C, G)$ is the use-of-saving identity

$$GK\_x + DLAND\_x + DINV\_x + DFA\_x$$

$$= SVGH\_x + DEPH\_x + CTR\_x, \tag{1}$$

where GK_x is gross investment in depreciable tangible assets, $DLAND\_x$ is net land purchases, $DINV\_x$ is net inventory investment, DFA_x is net increase in financial assets (referred to in the NIA as the "saving-investment gap"), $SVGH\_x$ is net saving (in the NIA definition), $DEPH\_x$ is historical cost depreciation, and CTR_x is capital transfers received. Capital transfers are positive for the corporate sector because of various capital grants from the government. They are negative for the household sector due to gift and inheritance taxes. Each of the terms in (1) is available directly from the NIA.

Three features about this identity are relevant for our purposes. First, as is emphasized in the chapter text, $DEPH\_x$ is valued at historical costs.

Second, also mentioned in the text, any reasonable definition of saving should include capital transfers. For example, for the household sector, we wouldn't think of inheritance taxes paid to the government as part of saving; we should deduct them from income, so that they do not show up as a debit item in CTR_H. Doing so amounts to defining gross saving as SVGH_x + DEPH_x + CTR_x and net saving at historical costs as SVGH_x + CTR_x. And this is consistent with the BEA (U.S. Bureau of Economic Analysis) definition of saving. Third, as was pointed out by Iwamoto (1994), investment in nonreproducible tangible assets other than net land purchases, which I denote by E_x, is included in GK_x. It includes investment in land improvement and plantation and orchard development. Using this E_x, the use-of-saving identity can be rearranged as

$$(GK\_x - E\_x) + (DLAND\_x + E\_x) + DINV\_x + DFA\_x$$

$$= (SVGH\_x + CTR\_x) + DEPH\_x. \qquad (1')$$

Here, (GK_x − E_x) is gross investment in depreciable tangible assets and (DLAND_x + E_x) is net (= gross) investment in nonreproducible tangible assets.[2] As noted in Iwamoto (1994), the term E_x becomes relevant when replacement cost depreciation is to be backed out from the stock section of the NIA. Although data on the total of E_x over sectors, E_H + E_C + E_G, is available from a supplementary table in the stock section of the NIA, its sector breakdown is not available.

The accumulation identity for depreciable tangible assets linking the capital transaction account, the balance sheet, and the reconciliation account of sector x (= H, C, G) is

$$KD\_x(t + 1) = KD\_x(t) + GK\_x(t) - DEPH\_x(t) + RECKD\_x(t), \qquad (2)$$

where KD_$x(t + 1)$ is the capital stock of sector x at the beginning of year $t + 1$ (i.e., at the end of year t), GK_x is gross fixed investment (*including* investment on nonreproducible tangible assets other than net land purchases) for year t, DEPH_x is historical cost depreciation for year t, and RECKD_x is the value in the reconciliation account for year t. Each of these terms is available directly from the NIA: KD_x and RECKD_x are available by sector from the stock section and, as already mentioned, GK_x and DEPH_x are from the capital transactions accounts.

Since in (2) depreciation is at historical costs whereas KD_x is at replacement costs, the reconciliation account should include capital consumption adjustments (the gap between replacement cost and historical cost depreciation) as well as revaluation. Furthermore, the inclusion in GK_x of E_x (investment in nonreproducible tangible assets besides net land purchases) has to be undone. Indeed, an EPA publication (1978, 233) states that the reconciliation $RECKD\_x$ consists of the following four items:

$$RECKD\_x = RKD\_x - E\_x - CCAJ\_x + UKD\_x. \tag{3}$$

Here, RKD_x is revaluation and $CCAJ\_x$ is capital consumption adjustments defined by

$$CCAJ\_x = DEPR\_x - DEPH\_x, \tag{4}$$

where $DEPR\_x$ is replacement cost depreciation. The term UKD_x accounts for the incorporation of the capital stock of Okinawa's sector x in 1972:

$$UKD\_x(t) = \begin{cases} \text{capital stock of Okinawa's sector } x \\ \text{at the beginning of 1972} \quad \text{if } t = 1972, \\ 0 \quad \text{otherwise.} \end{cases} \tag{5}$$

Substituting (3) and (4) into (2), we obtain

$$KD\_x(t+1) = KD\_x(t) + [(GK\_x(t) - E\_x(t)) - DEPR\_x(t)]$$
$$+ RKD\_x(t) + UKD\_x(t). \tag{6}$$

Here, $GK\_x - E\_x$ is gross investment in depreciable tangible assets and so $GK\_x - E\_x - DEPR\_x$ is net investment at replacement costs. This equation (6) makes it clear why E_x enters the reconciliation account as a debit item, as in (3): it offsets the inclusion of GK_x of investments in nonreproducible assets other than net land purchases.

The EPA does not provide the breakdown of $RECKD\_x$, so RKD_x, E_x, $CCAJ\_x$, UKD_x, and $DEPR\_x$ are unavailable to outside researchers. However, the same EPA publication EPA (1978, 233) states that revaluation is calculated as

$$RKD\_x(t) = \frac{PKD\_x(t+1) - PKD\_x(t)}{PKD\_x(t)} [KD\_x(t) + UKD\_x(t)]$$

$$+ \frac{PKD\_x(t+1) - APKD\_x(t)}{APKD\_x(t)}$$

$$\times [GK\_x(t) - E\_x(t) - DEPR\_x(t)], \tag{7}$$

where PKD_$x(t)$ is the deflator for the capital stock at the beginning of year t (i.e., at the end of year $t - 1$) and APKD_$x(t)$ is some average deflator value for year t. The deflator PKD_$x(t)$ for years since $t = 1970$ is available from the NIA. It is not clear from the EPA (1978) how the average deflator is calculated.

The central question is how to calculate replacement cost depreciation (DEPR_x) for each sector x, under suitable assumptions for E_x, UKD_x, and APKD_x, from KD_x, GK_x, DEPH_x, RECKD_x, PKD_x, and E ($\equiv$ E_H + E_C + E_G), which are available directly from the NIA tables.

11A.2   Estimating Net Investment and Revaluation for Depreciable Assets

My original procedure for backing out replacement cost depreciation from the NIA, presented in the chapter text, is to first use (7) with DEPR_x replaced by DEPH_x to calculate RKD_x and then use (3) to solve for CCAJ_x. It ignores the term UKD_$x(t)$ (which equals zero except for $t = 1972$) and, as pointed out by Iwamoto (1994), the term E_x. Iwamoto (1994) also observes that (6) and (7) can be used to solve for DEPR_x, without the replacement of DEPR_x by DEPH_x in (7), as

$$\text{DEPR}\_x(t) = \text{GK}\_x(t) - \text{E}\_x(t) - \text{APKD}\_x(t)$$

$$\cdot \left[\frac{\text{KD}\_x(t+1)}{\text{PKD}\_x(t+1)} - \frac{\text{KD}\_x(t) + \text{UKD}\_x(t)}{\text{PKD}\_x(t)} \right]. \tag{8}$$

This makes intuitive sense: net investment in depreciable tangible assets, GK_x − E_x − DEPR_x, converted into real terms by APKD_x, should equal the increase in the real capital stock.

To calculate DEPR_x using (8), I need to estimate E_x, UKD_x, and APKD_x under some assumptions. I follow Iwamoto (1994) and estimate E_x from the economywide E ($\equiv$ E_H + E_C + E_G) by

$$\text{E}\_x = \left[\frac{\text{GK}\_x}{\text{GK}\_\text{H} + \text{GK}\_\text{C} + \text{GK}\_\text{G}} \right] \cdot \text{E}. \tag{9}$$

For UKD_$x(t)$, which equals the capital stock of Okinawa's sector x at the beginning of year 1972 (i.e., at the end of year 1971) for $t = 1972$ and 0 otherwise, I assume that Okinawa's capital stock is 0.0691215 percent of the mainland's capital stock for each sector:

$$\text{UKD}\_x(1972) = 0.0691215\% \text{ of KD}\_x(1972). \tag{10}$$

This factor 0.0691215 percent is Okinawa's share of Japan's GNP in 1972.[3] For APKD_x, I maintain the same assumption as in the data appendix:

$$APKD\_x(t) = (PKD\_x(t+1) + PKD\_x(t))/2. \tag{11}$$

To implement the calculation described above for the earlier period of 1955–69, I need to estimate asset deflators PKD_x, which are available only for the years since 1970. For this purpose I use the flow deflator for gross investment available from the flow section of the NIA. More specifically,

PI _ H(t) = average over fourth quarter of year $t - 1$ and the first
       quarter of t of the deflator for the housing component
       of gross private investment expenditure,

PI _ C(t) = average over fourth quarter of year $t - 1$ and the first
       quarter of t of the deflator for the firm structure and
       equipment component of gross private investment
       expenditure,

PI _ G(t) = average over fourth quarter of year $t - 1$ and the first
       quarter of t of the deflator for the general government
       component of gross public investment expenditure.   (12)

For $t = 1955$, PI_x(1955) refers to the average over the fourth quarter of 1954 and the first quarter of 1955. Since PI_x is available only from the first quarter of 1955, the value for the first quarter of 1955 is assigned to PI_x(1955). For each sector x, the series for $t = 1955, \ldots, 1970$ is multiplied by PKD_x(1970)/PI_x(1970) so that the two series PI_x and PKD_x agree at $t = 1970$. This is the only splicing in our procedure.

Given DEPR_x, we can easily calculate capital consumption adjustments (CCAJ_x), net investment (DKD_x), and revaluation (RKD_x) on depreciable tangible assets. CCAJ_x can be calculated from (4). RKD_x (revaluation) can be calculated by solving (3) for RKD_x:

$$RKD\_x = RECKD\_x + E\_x + CCAJ\_x - UKD\_x. \tag{13}$$

By construction, the RKD_x thus calculated equals the RKD_x given by (7). DKD_x (net investment) is

$$DKD\_x = \text{gross investment} - \text{replacement cost depreciation}$$

$$= (GK\_x - E\_x) - DEPR\_x. \tag{14}$$

11A.3   Net Investment and Revaluation for Other Assets

Obtaining net investment and revaluation for nonreproducible tangible assets, inventories, and net financial assets is much easier because depreciation for those assets is zero. We have identified gross investments in those assets in the use-of-saving equation (1′). Since tangible assets consist of depreciable assets, nonreproducible tangible assets, and inventories, we have

$$DTA\_x = (GK\_x - E\_x) + (DLAND\_x + E\_x) + DINV\_x - DEPR\_x$$

$$= GK\_x - DEPR\_x + DLAND\_x + DINV\_x. \qquad (15)$$

Net investment in financial assets, DFA_x, is as in the NIA's use-of-saving identity.

To obtain revaluation on tangible assets, turn to the reconciliation accounts of the stock section for components of tangible assets. By aggregating over the three components of tangible assets, we obtain

$$\text{reconciliation on tangible assets} = RTA\_x - CCAJ\_x + UTA\_x, \qquad (16)$$

where RTA_x is revaluation on tangible assets of sector x and UTA_x accounts for inclusion in 1972 of tangible assets of Okinawa's sector x. Unlike the reconciliation for depreciable assets in (3), E_x does not enter (16) because the reclassification that called for E_x to enter in (3) as a debit item is internal to tangible assets. The method for estimating $UTA\_x(1972)$ is analogous to that for depreciable tangible assets:

$$UTA\_x(1972) = 0.0691215\% \text{ of } TA\_x(1972). \qquad (17)$$

Reconciliation on tangible assets and TA_x is available directly from the stock section of the NIA.

The relationship between revaluation and reconciliation for net financial assets is even simpler:

$$\text{reconciliation on net financial assets of sector } x$$
$$= RFA\_x + UFA\_x, \qquad (18)$$

where RFA_x is revaluation on net financial assets of sector x. UFA_x is estimated as

$$UFA\_x(1972) = 0.06912125\% \text{ of } FA\_x(1972). \qquad (19)$$

FA_x is available from the NIA. Reconciliation on net financial assets can be read off from the reconciliation accounts of the NIA as follows:

reconciliation on net financial assets of sector x
  = reconciliation on gross financial assets of sector x
    − reconciliation on liabilities other than equity of sector x
    − reconciliation on equity of sector x.   (20)

For households and government, reconciliation on equity is zero.

11A.4   Net Saving

Net saving for each sector x, SVG_x, is the sum of net investments in tangible and net financial assets. Because of the use-of-saving identity (1), SVG_x can be written in several equivalent forms:

$$SVG\_x = DTA\_x + DFA\_x$$

$$= GK\_x - DEPR\_x + DLAND\_x + DINV\_x$$

$$+ DFA\_x \quad (by \ (15))$$

$$= SVGH\_x + CTR\_x + DEPH\_x - DEPR\_x \quad (by \ (1))$$

$$(x = H, C, G). \quad (21)$$

The formula makes it clear that, unlike Iwamoto (1994), I treat E_x, investment in nondepreciable assets other than net land purchases, as part of saving.[4]

Government saving, SVG_G, thus calculated includes government net capital formation. The BEA definition of government saving, which does not recognize government capital, is

$$SVB\_BEA = DFA\_G,   \quad (22)$$

which is simply the government's budget surplus.

11A.5   Consumer Durables

The stock section of the NIA also has the balance sheet, the reconciliation account, and gross expenditure on consumer durables, broken down to five consumer durable categories, for the period since 1970. The accumulation identity for consumer durable category g ($g = 1, 2, \ldots, 5$) is

$$CD\_g(t+1) = CD\_g(t) + GCD\_g(t) + RECCD\_g(t),   \quad (23)$$

where $CD_{-}g(t+1)$ is the stock of consumer durable of category g at the beginning of year $t+1$ (i.e., at the end of year t), $GCD_{-}g$ is gross expenditure on consumer durable g, and $RECCD_{-}g$ is reconciliation. These items are available from the stock section of the NIA. EPA (1978, 234–36) states that the reconciliation has three components:

$$RECCD_{-}g = RCD_{-}g - DEPCD_{-}g + UCD_{-}x, \tag{24}$$

where $RCD_{-}g$ is revaluation, $DEPCD_{-}g$ is replacement cost depreciation, and $UCD_{-}g$ accounts for the incorporation of Okinawa in 1972. The breakdown of the reconciliation is not available from the NIA. However, EPA (1978, 234–36) states that revaluation is calculated as

$$RCD_{-}g(t) = \frac{PCD_{-}g(t+1) - PCD_{-}g(t)}{PCD_{-}g(t)} [CD_{-}g(t) + UCD_{-}g(t)]$$

$$+ \frac{PCD_{-}g(t+1) - APCD_{-}g(t)}{APCD_{-}g(t)} [GCD_{-}g(t) - DEPCD_{-}g(t)], \tag{25}$$

where $PCD_{-}g(t)$ is the deflator at the beginning of year t (end of year $t-1$), available from the stock section as the ratio of the nominal value of the stock of consumer durable g to its real value.

To estimate replacement cost depreciation for consumer durables, I use the same methodology I used for depreciable tangible assets. Equations (23)–(25) can be solved for $DEPCD_{-}g$ as

$$DEPCD_{-}g(t) = GCD_{-}g(t) - APCD_{-}g(t)$$

$$\cdot \left[\frac{CD_{-}g(t+1)}{PCD_{-}g(t+1)} - \frac{CD_{-}g(t) + UCD_{-}g(t)}{PCD_{-}g(t)} \right], \tag{26}$$

where $APCD_{-}g(t)$ is some average deflator value for year t. I assume that it is given by

$$APCD_{-}g(t) = [PCD_{-}g(t+1) + PCD_{-}g(t)]/2. \tag{27}$$

Regarding, $UCD_{-}g$, the adjustment for Okinawa's stock of consumer durable g, I apply the same factor used for depreciable tangible assets:

$$UCD_{-}g(1972) = 0.0691215\% \text{ of } CD_{-}g(1972). \tag{28}$$

Given $DEPCD_{-}g$ and $UCD_{-}g$ thus estimated, revaluation on consumer durable g, $RCD_{-}g$, can be calculated by solving (24) for $RCD_{-}g$.

11A.6   Net National Product

We have considered all the series displayed in tables 11.A2–A5 of the data appendix. This leaves the output measures in table 11.A1. Since government assets are not recognized in the BEA definition, gross profits for the government sector should be deducted from the NIA definition of GNP to obtain the BEA definition of GNP. As pointed out by Iwamoto (1994), net profits for the government in the NIA appear to be set to zero, so gross profits equal historical cost depreciation in the NIA. Therefore, to arrive at GNP under the BEA definition, one only has to deduct *historical cost* depreciation from the GNP in the NIA:

$$GNP\_BEA = GNP - DEPH\_G. \qquad (29)$$

Thus it is not necessary to make the distinction between GNP in the NIA and GNP_A of the data appendix. The BEA definition of NNP is

$$NNP\_BEA = GNP\_BEA - (DEPR\_H + DEPR\_C). \qquad (30)$$

11A.7   Relevant Tables of the NIA

Of all the items considered above, addendum table 1 lists the source NIA tables for items available directly from the NIA, in the order considered above.

11A.8   Results

Results of my calculation for the period 1955–94 are contained in addendum tables 2 and 3. All data incorporate the March 1996 benchmark revision of the National Accounts (EPA (1996)). Addendum table 2 displays depreciation at historical costs and replacement costs by sector and NNP under the BEA definition. I report depreciation on government capital even though it does not go into the calculation of net saving and NNP. The large discrepancy between historical and replacement cost depreciation for government implies that net government capital formation in the NIA is severely overstated. The net saving rates reported in addendum table 3 reflect the depreciation adjustment and the adjustment for capital transfers described above. Since the sum of capital transfers over sectors is very small, amounting to net transfer receipts from foreigners, the capital transfer adjustment has very little effect on national saving, although it affects the allocation of national saving between sectors.

Addendum Table 1
Relevant NIA Tables

Series	Source NIA table or equation	Available since
GK_x, DLAND_x, DINV_x, DFA_x, SVGH_x, DEPH_x, CTR_x	1-[2]-III, tables for "real transactions" for various sectors	1955
E	2-III-1, column called "capital transactions for nonreproducible assets"	1955
KD_x	2-II, balance sheets for various sectors	1955
RECKD_x	2-II, reconciliation accounts for various sectors	1955
PKD_x	2-IV-1, table of deflators for various sectors	1970 (end of 1969)
PI_x	3-[1]-III-1, table of deflators for components of gross investment, line 3-(1)-a-(a) for private housing, line 3-(1)-a-(b) for private firm equipments, line 3-(1)-b-(c) for government	1955
Reconciliation on tangible assets	2-II, reconciliation accounts for various sectors	1955
TA_x, FA_x	2-II, balance sheets for various sectors	1955
Reconciliation on gross financial assets, liabilities excluding equity, and equity	2-II, reconciliation accounts for various sectors	1955
CD_g, GCD_g, RECCD_g	2-IV-2	1970
PCD_g	2-IV-2, ratio of nominal to real values	1970
GNP	1-[2]-I-1, last line	1955

Addendum Table 2
Depreciation and NNP (BEA Definition) in Trillion Yen

Year	DEPH_H	CCAJ_H	DEPH_C	CCAJ_C	DEPH_G	CCAJ_G	NNP_BEA
55	0.304	0.259	0.576	0.358	0.044	0.246	6.859
56	0.358	0.332	0.678	0.510	0.049	0.279	7.520
57	0.367	0.300	0.766	0.625	0.054	0.313	8.763
58	0.393	0.179	0.831	0.512	0.060	0.218	9.570
59	0.424	0.098	0.971	0.411	0.066	0.136	11.219
60	0.483	0.133	1.197	0.646	0.071	0.260	13.468
61	0.536	−0.073	1.588	0.315	0.081	0.005	16.860
62	0.619	0.270	1.874	0.599	0.098	0.202	18.441
63	0.716	0.020	2.227	0.589	0.109	0.121	21.394
64	0.845	0.159	2.858	0.317	0.124	0.067	25.142
65	0.992	0.314	3.226	0.753	0.144	0.299	27.344
66	1.145	0.249	3.699	0.371	0.178	0.115	32.431
67	1.396	0.192	4.271	0.235	0.217	−0.179	38.314
68	1.673	0.625	5.021	0.807	0.250	0.240	44.449
69	1.985	0.455	6.006	−0.750	0.284	−0.454	54.086
70	2.355	0.220	7.048	−0.412	0.327	2.727	63.651
71	2.708	0.363	7.834	−0.590	0.369	0.368	69.907
72	3.194	0.432	9.215	−0.800	0.416	0.633	79.944
73	3.865	1.051	10.960	−1.009	0.471	1.723	97.182
74	4.789	2.138	12.425	2.070	0.553	1.512	112.023
75	5.772	1.796	12.586	2.834	0.668	−0.751	124.515
76	6.799	2.034	13.120	3.703	0.786	1.976	139.975
77	7.786	2.564	14.327	3.933	0.900	2.233	156.020
78	8.769	2.584	15.177	4.348	1.053	2.712	172.543
79	9.679	3.312	16.768	4.381	1.197	3.657	186.487
80	10.626	4.547	18.683	5.584	1.393	5.293	199.267
81	11.489	4.201	20.970	4.613	1.599	4.117	214.544
82	12.184	4.399	22.280	4.962	1.752	4.030	225.092
83	12.788	4.223	23.745	5.001	1.892	4.220	234.429
84	13.464	4.505	25.301	5.576	2.012	4.595	250.190
85	14.071	4.377	27.467	5.813	2.078	1.697	267.751
86	14.571	4.059	29.490	4.814	2.144	5.253	281.608
87	15.211	3.813	31.475	5.083	2.245	5.109	293.987
88	16.107	4.068	33.966	4.680	2.325	5.454	315.129
89	17.314	4.412	38.309	3.391	2.458	5.918	336.965
90	18.556	4.930	41.923	3.910	2.508	6.128	361.145
91	19.848	5.441	46.168	4.773	2.525	6.858	383.407
92	20.882	5.026	49.317	6.271	2.624	7.394	391.945
93	21.645	5.792	49.971	6.860	2.767	7.303	392.785
94	22.168	4.489	50.438	8.514	2.974	7.413	394.433

Addendum Table 3
Saving Rates as Percents of NNP (BEA Definition)

Year	SVG_H/ NNP_BEA	SVG_C/ NNP_BEA	SVG_BEA/ NNP_BEA	National saving rate
55	7.23	−3.17	−0.93	3.13
56	7.58	−4.60	0.95	3.93
57	7.77	−2.08	1.76	7.45
58	9.02	−1.74	0.13	7.41
59	10.78	0.56	0.95	12.30
60	10.79	3.01	2.08	15.87
61	12.68	5.74	2.80	21.22
62	10.94	2.77	1.68	15.39
63	11.70	3.08	1.20	15.98
64	11.46	4.28	0.95	16.68
65	11.63	1.59	0.54	13.76
66	10.87	5.30	−0.38	15.79
67	9.98	8.72	0.88	19.59
68	11.39	7.66	0.99	20.05
69	11.41	11.58	1.37	24.37
70	12.11	11.90	1.90	25.92
71	12.52	8.53	1.33	22.38
72	12.93	8.96	−0.15	21.74
73	14.48	7.59	0.61	22.69
74	17.43	−0.64	0.43	17.22
75	18.46	−2.39	−3.30	12.78
76	18.99	−1.15	−4.39	13.46
77	17.17	−0.40	−4.54	12.23
78	16.36	2.17	−6.51	12.03
79	13.56	2.61	−5.63	10.54
80	12.97	1.43	−5.32	9.09
81	13.56	1.11	−4.60	10.07
82	12.08	1.33	−4.32	9.09
83	11.70	1.25	−4.38	8.57
84	11.22	1.60	−2.49	10.32
85	10.94	1.97	−0.97	11.94
86	10.92	2.67	−1.11	12.48
87	9.29	2.77	0.55	12.60
88	8.35	3.63	1.77	13.76
89	8.38	2.55	2.96	13.89
90	7.65	2.37	3.42	13.44
91	8.47	1.76	3.44	13.67
92	8.52	1.34	1.74	11.61
93	8.73	1.85	−1.94	8.63
94	8.78	0.71	−2.53	6.96

Comparison of addendum table 2 with table 11.A2 shows that replacement cost depreciation estimates are somewhat lower under the modified
procedure than under my original procedure in this chapter. For example,
for 1984, my original estimates of DEPR_H and DEPR_C are 4.99
and 6.56 trillion yen, respectively, as seen from table 11.A2. Under the
same original procedure but with the current revised NIA data, they are
5.397 and 7.378 trillion yen, respectively, for 1984. Under the modified
procedure, as seen from addendum table 2, they become 4.505 and
5.576 trillion yen. The difference the new procedure makes for the sum of
DRPR_H and DEPR_C is 2.695 trillion yen, which is 1.08 percent of
NNP. Thus, my original procedure understated the net national saving
rate by about 1 percent for 1984.[5] The capital consumption adjustment is
still very substantial under the modified procedure: (CCAJ_H + CCAJ_C)/
NNP_BEA exceeds 4 percent for the years 1976–82.

Notes

This is an expanded version of Hayashi (1994).

1. See Dekle and Summers (1991), Iwamoto (1994), and Horioka (1995). Dekle and Summers
(1991) questioned the validity of my procedure for estimating replacement cost depreciation on the ground that the implied depreciation rate was implausibly high. As my reply
(Hayashi 1991) makes clear, their criticism, based on serious misunderstandings of the Japanese National Income Accounts and depreciation in general, provides no reason for altering
my procedure. The procedure employed by Horioka (1995) to calculate the household
saving rate is very similar to the method to be presented here.

2. It is not necessary to distinguish between gross and net for investments in nonreproducible tangible assets.

3. EPA (1982) states that Okinawa's gross national expenditure in 1972 is 487.492 billion
yen, whereas the nation's gross national expenditure (including Okinawa's) is 71014.234
billion yen.

4. This treatment of E_x is consistent with the BEA definition, which includes land improvement and plantation and orchard development as part of saving and investment. I
am grateful to C. Horioka for this piece of information.

5. Iwamoto's (1994) saving rate estimates are *lower* than my original estimates because he
excludes investment in nonreproducible assets (E_H + E_C) from saving.

References

Dekle, R., and L. Summers. 1991. Japan's high saving rate reaffirmed. *Bank of Japan Monetary and Economic Studies* 9 (September): 63–78.

EPA. 1978. *How to read and use national accounts* (in Japanese). Tokyo, Japan: Ministry of Finance Printing Bureau.

————. 1982. *Prefectural income accounts, 1982 edition* (in Japanese). Tokyo, Japan: Ministry of Finance Printing Bureau.

————. 1988. *Report on national accounts from 1955 to 1969* (in Japanese). Tokyo, Japan: Ministry of Finance Printing Bureau.

————. 1996. *Annual report on national accounts, 1996 edition* (in Japanese). Tokyo, Japan: Ministry of Finance Printing Bureau.

Hayashi, F. 1991. Reply to Dekle and Summers. *Bank of Japan Monetary and Economic Studies* 9 (September): 79–89.

————. 1994. Japan's saving rate: An update. Center for Japanese Economy and Business Discussion Paper no. 89, Columbia Business School.

Horioka, Charles. 1995. Is Japan's household saving rate really high? *Review of Income and Wealth* 41, no. 4 (December): 373–99.

Iwamoto, Y. 1994. Japan's saving rate is indeed lower than Professor Hayashi revealed. *Japan and the World Economy* 8:35–41.

12

Life Cycle and Bequest Savings: Evidence from a Large Cross-Section of Japanese Households

12.1 Introduction

There has been intense interest in the savings and capital accumulation behavior of the Japanese and U.S. economies among economists and policy planners of both countries. In the United States, it is stimulated by the pervasive impression that the saving rate is much higher in Japan than in the U.S. and that this higher savings rate has led to faster accumulation of capital and the faster rate of growth of productivity of labor. In Japan, there is a widespread concern that the country's saving pattern may change dramatically with the rapid aging of its population.

During the past year, we have gained access to two fairly important new data sets containing detailed information on savings behavior by Japanese and American households. First we were granted the permission by the Statistics Bureau of the Japanese Government to access data generated by the 1979 and 1984 rounds of the National Survey of Family Income and Expenditure (hereafter referred to as the NSFIE). Second, the Survey of Consumer Finances for 1983, hereafter referred to as the SCF83 conducted for the Board of Governors of the Federal Reserve System and painstakingly edited by the Board's staff, has become available. While they are two radically different sets of data, they appear to let us ask parallel questions on savings behavior of households in Japan and the United States, and this chapter reports preliminary results of our attempt to do so.

In an ideal world, we would like to have constructed a basic, structural model of the savings behavior which, when supplemented by institutional

Originally published as sections I–III of "Life Cycle and Bequest Savings: A Study of Japanese and U.S. Households Based on Data from the 1984 NSFIE and the 1983 Survey of Consumer Finances," and without appendixes, in *Journal of the Japanese and International Economies* 2 (December 1988): 450–91, with A. Ando and R. Ferris. Reprinted with the permission of Academic Press.

details and parameter values specific to each country, explain the savings pattern of both countries. The data, however, did not permit us to undertake such an ambitious task. In the Japanese case, where the relative price of land is extraordinarily high and continues to increase at a very rapid rate, the role of land and real capital gains associated with its ownership in the savings behavior of households seems exceptionally difficult to model. In this chapter, therefore, we concentrate on two specific, narrow, and almost purely empirical issues, namely, (1) whether older, retired persons save or dissave in Japan and in the United States, and (2) whether the elasticity of savings with respect to some measure of the life-time earnings is unitary or not. The first is a critical test in determining the validity of the life-cycle theory, while the second is an important ingredient of both the life-cycle theory and the permanent income hypothesis, at least as formulated by their originators.

In the case of the SCF83, we have apparently good information on income and the balance sheet items for households in the survey. We also have some information on the history of earnings by both husbands and wives, and hence we can construct direct estimates of life-time earnings patterns for families in the survey, even for retired persons, although our estimates leave a good deal of uncertainties. On the other hand, the SCF83 did not collect information on expenditure by families, so that we cannot estimate flow of savings for these families. One important feature of this sample is that a serious attempt was made to bring sufficient number of very wealthy families into the sample while making sure that observed cell means can be interpreted as a sampling value of the corresponding population cell means through the adjustment of sampling weights.

On the basis of information generated by this survey, a number of features concerning the asset accumulation behavior of households emerge, of which three most important ones from the perspective of the study reported in this chapter are:

1. Virtually all families accumulate wealth through their working lives, reaching the peak value just after their retirement.

2. After retirement, these families dissave, but certainly not all of their wealth. Taking into account that individuals die at different ages and they do not know in advance the timing of their death, on average, these families appear to dissave about one-third of their peak wealth by the time of their death, leaving two-thirds of the peak wealth as bequests. A very large fraction of wealth left as bequests appears to be their homes.

3. In this sample, the ratio of net worth to the life-time earnings is more or less constant over the distribution of life-time earnings for very young households; however, as families age, this ratio becomes more and more positively related to the size of life-time earnings of the family. The conclusion appears to be quite clear that the elasticity of savings with respect to the relative position of the life-time earnings in its distribution within each age cohort is considerably greater than unity.

These conclusions are somewhat weakened by the fact that the SCF83 is a relatively small sample, containing only some 4,000 families. In 1986, the Federal Reserve Board conducted reinterviews of most of the families in this sample, and we expect that such a reinterview survey will greatly increase the value of this sample.

The NSFIE, on the other hand, is based on a very large sample, containing over 50,000 households. It collects information not only on flows of income and expenditure and hence of savings, but also on financial assets and liabilities, although underestimates of balance sheet items appear to be quite severe. It does not directly collect information on the value of houses and stocks of consumer durables, but we have estimated their values based on information in the sample and an information for prices gathered from outside this sample. Major items missing in our estimates of net worth in this sample, therefore, are the value of unincorporated businesses and the value of real estate other than the principal residence owned by these households. At this time, we have completed a preliminary analysis of the 1984 survey.

Our findings may be summarized as follows:

1. As in the case of the United States, virtually all households save and accumulate wealth until the age of their head is about 60.

2. In the NSFIE, it appears that even those households whose heads are older than 60 continue to save and to accumulate wealth, so that virtually no one dissaves except for very poor, single-person families, mostly older women.

3. However, this direct observation may be considered suspect, because many Japanese workers retire just before 60 and they tend to merge with younger households, presumably their children. Those who are remaining independent over the age of 60, and therefore enter the NSFIE sample, tend to be those who are wealthy or remain active in their income earning activities, or both. Therefore, there exists a serious possibility of sample selection biases being present in our estimates. We therefore distinguish

between nuclear families (singles and those families consisting of a husband and his wife and their children) and extended families (those families which include, in addition to nuclear members, one or more parents of the husband and/or of his wife) and analyze them separately, attempting to extract as much information as possible on the behavior of older persons living with younger families.

4. We find that, in the case of young nuclear families, their rate of accumulation of wealth is greater than what can be accounted for by their rate of saving. In the case of older independent families, the rate of accumulation of wealth is smaller than that implied by their rate of saving. These observations are consistent with the existence of significant intergenerational transfers of wealth. Evidence on dependent older families (members of extended families) is harder to interpret because only income, not expenditure and balance sheets, can be allocated to members of extended families. We observe that their saving is somewhat larger than the saving of corresponding young nuclear families and that their total net worth (whose level is, of course, much larger than that of corresponding young nuclear families) increases less than the net worth of corresponding young nuclear families. We believe these patterns are strong evidence that wealth is being transferred within extended families, and they are also consistent with the possibility that there may be additional intergenerational transfers from dependent old families to young nuclear families.

12.2   The NSFIE Data

12.2.1   The National Survey of Family Income and Expenditure

Of the two data sets we will utilize in this chapter, the U.S. data set, the Survey of Consumer Finances of 1983 (SCF83), is better known and has been well documented.[1] We therefore describe the Japanese data set, the National Survey of Family Income and Expenditure (NSFIE), in some detail. The NSFIE has been conducted since 1959. The design of the sample, the sampling procedure, definitions of terms, and other details of the sample along with numerous summary statistics are presented (both in Japanese and in English) in volumes published for each survey by the Statistics Bureau, Management and Coordination Agency (formerly the Prime Minister's Office) of the Japanese government. Such information for the 1984 survey is contained in the *Report on the 1984 National Survey of Family Income and Expenditure Survey* (hereafter the *1984 National Survey*

Report), which consists of nine volumes. The total sample size of the NSFIE is about 50,000, making it one of the largest surveys of this type in the world. The sample is a stratified random sample based on geographical locations with different sampling ratios, similar to the procedure used by the Bureau of Labor Statistics in the United States for its Surveys of Consumer Expenditures in 1950 and 1960 (but not in 1972–73). Because of the differences in residential arrangements for single-person families on the one hand and two-or-more person families on the other, the Statistics Bureau has chosen to carry out two separate surveys, one for two-or-more-person families and another one for singles, with the overall sampling ratio for singles being considerably less than that for two-or-more-person families. The sampling ratios that differ across regions and between the types of family (two-or-more-person or single-person) will be taken into account when we calculate the estimate of population aggregates (see table 12.1 below). In the tabulations of cell means in table 12.3, we will not take the regional variability in the sampling ratio into account, because occasionally we will be interested in distributional statistics like standard error and median.[2]

Several features of the survey are pertinent for understanding the quality and content of the NSFIE data. For two-or-more-person families, the information come in three parts. First, respondents are required to keep a diary recording receipts and expenditures on hundreds of items throughout the three-month period of the survey (September, October, and November). The diary is collected twice a month. This set of information is recorded in the tape as three-month average receipts and expenditures. Receipts include average monthly income. Second, in the first month (September), the household characteristics (e.g., age, occupation, sex, relation of the family members, and physical characteristics of the dwelling) are filled out in a form by the respondent. Third, in the last month of the survey (November), respondents report information on financial assets, consumer durables, and annual income for the twelve-month period ending in November. This information was collected by the interviewers. It is not clear from the description of the survey in the *1984 National Survey Report* whether respondents were encouraged to consult financial records in an effort to obtain complete and accurate responses. One valuable piece of information included is a breakdown of annual income by income component (employment, agriculture, business, work at home, pension, receipts from others, rental income, interests plus dividends, other, and income in kind), each of which (except for income in kind) is further broken down among family members (head, spouse, and "other members"). This will prove useful when we examine the saving behavior of extended families (multigeneration families).

Information collected for singles is roughly the same as that obtained for two-or-more-person households, except that some information, such as characteristics of the dwelling, is abbreviated, and the diary was kept for only one month (for the 1984 survey) rather than for three months.

12.2.2 Imputation of Variables (Summary of Appendix 12.1)

The framework of our analysis dictates specific definitions of critical variables to be used in our analysis, and since they are not necessarily the same as definitions of variables for which the survey collected information, we must fill them as best as we can using information from other sources. For our purposes, we have carried out several imputations as follows.

1. *Consumer durables.* The survey supplies information on purchases of durables, and on the number of durable goods of various types owned at the time of the survey. We must estimate the current value of the stock of durables and flows of gross and net rent associated with these stocks.

2. *Houses and residential land.* The survey contains information on fairly detailed characteristics of houses in which the household resides, and the general location of the house. From this information, we must first estimate the market value of the house, the size of the land associated with the house and its market value, and the flow of gross and net rent associated with these properties. In this study, by utilizing the relation between floor space and site size and information on housing prices and construction materials costs from outside sources, we have made a major effort to estimate the market value of residential houses and land.

3. *Personal income tax.* Diary records of the survey register two types of taxes, namely, income tax on wages and salaries withheld by employers, and "other taxes." "Other taxes" is defined to be all taxes other than withheld tax and tax collected as a part of the purchase price (presumably most sales taxes). The latter specifically includes real estate taxes, residence tax, inheritance tax, registration tax, and automobile tax. Unfortunately, we cannot rely on this information to estimate taxes paid by families in general, for two main reasons. First, this information is not recorded for nonworker households. Second, because the diary records refer to the three months of September, October, and November, if some tax is

paid once a year in some other month, it will simply not be recorded. We have therefore imputed income taxes to each household based on their income and the information on effective tax rates by income classes extracted from the *1984 Annual Report* of the National Tax Bureau and the *1987 Annual Report on National Accounts*.

4. *Social security contributions.* As in the case of taxes, we are unable to rely on the contribution to the social security programs reported in the diary. We are therefore forced to impute to each household some estimated social security contribution amounts. We have done these imputations separately for annuity programs and for health programs, and have tried to take into account specific features of these programs as much as possible. However, as we found that information provided by the survey is not enough to apply provisions of the law to each family accurately, especially in the case of health insurance, the best we could do is to employ some proportional scheme on pretax income.

For each of four cases above, a more detailed description of our procedure is given in appendix 12.1 at the end of this chapter.

12.2.3   Comparison to the National Income Numbers

Before embarking on any kind of analysis of the data, it is very important to know to what extent the sample is an unbiased representation of the population of Japanese households. Since we know the sampling ratio for each region for this stratified sample, we can blow up the numbers in the data to arrive at the *implied aggregates* that should match the corresponding figures in aggregate statistics. The annual income and expenditure data in the Japanese National Income Accounts (NIA) are based on the commodity flow method and are most likely to be more accurate than the implied aggregates obtainable from survey data.

Comparing the implied aggregates calculated from the NSFIE with the NIA numbers is not straightforward, however, because the NIA involves many stages of imputations and transformations while the survey data concern cash items (except for purchases on installment credits), which results in several conceptual differences between the two sets of numbers. The differences concern the treatment of (i) employment income, (ii) business income, (iii) interest payments, (iv) medical expenditure, (v) social security benefits, and (vi) depreciation. We must "undo" these NIA imputations and transformations on the NIA numbers to arrive at accounts that can also be derived from the NSFIE. Such accounts are displayed in table

Table 12.1a
Comparing Implied Aggregates to NIA Numbers, 1984

Balance sheet

Item	(1) NIA	(2) NSFIE	(3) $\frac{(1)-(2)}{(1)}$
1. housing	756.0	873.0	−0.15
2. stock of consumer durables	47.1	36.0	0.24
3. financial assets	507.5	225.3	0.56
4. currency	19.1	0.0	1.00
5. demand deposits	32.7	17.3	0.47
6. savings accounts	274.2	108.4	0.60
7. bonds	48.4	31.3	0.35
8. stocks	56.6	17.6	0.69
9. life insurance	66.8	40.5	0.39
10. other	9.8	10.2	−0.05
11. financial liabilities	181.6	85.6	0.53

Income/expenditure account

Item	(1) NIA	(2) NSFIE	(3) $\frac{(1)-(2)}{(1)}$
12. consumption expenditure	161.1	142.4	0.12
13. cash expenditure	136.8	117.4	0.14
14. food and tobacco	39.7	32.0	0.19
15. cloth	11.2	8.8	0.22
16. rent and utililities	8.2	10.8	−0.31
17. furniture	9.5	5.0	0.47
18. medical expenditure	5.3	2.6	0.51
19. transportation	17.0	12.0	0.29
20. recreation and education	16.3	15.2	0.07
21. other	29.5	31.1	−0.05
22. imputed rent	24.3	25.0	−0.03
23. (durables expenditure)	10.4	11.0	−0.06
24. income tax	19.2	14.8	0.23
25. social security contribution	11.0	10.8	0.02
26. pension	5.8	6.6	−0.14
27. health insurance	5.3	4.2	0.20
28. net saving	27.7	25.2	0.09
29. total disbursements	219.1	193.1	0.12

Table 12.1a (cont.)

Income/expenditure account

Item	(1) NIA	(2) NSFIE	(3) $\frac{(1)-(2)}{(1)}$
30. category (i)	196.3	177.9	0.09
31. employment income	152.7	134.2	0.12
32. bus. income + rental income	16.9	29.8	−0.77
33. pension	12.7	11.0	0.14
34. other income	14.0	2.9	0.80
35. category (ii)	11.5	4.3	0.62
36. gross interest income	24.4	11.6	0.53
37. (−) interest payment	−17.1	−7.4	0.57
38. dividends	4.2	0.2	0.96
39. category (iii)	11.3	10.9	0.03
40. net imputed rent	11.3	10.9	0.03
41. total income	219.1	193.1	0.12
42. disposable income	188.8	167.5	0.11
43. net savings rate (%)	15	15	

Note: Except for rates, in trillion yen.

12.1a. Details of the derivation of the accounts from the NIA and from the NSFIE are in appendix 12.2. Briefly, "medical expenditure" in table 12.1a does not include transfers from the government, and employer contribution to social security is included neither in "employment income" nor in "social security contribution."

Barring the remaining conceptual differences and possible errors in the NIA numbers, the two sets of numbers displayed in table 12.1a for 1984—one derived from the NIA (column (1)) and the other from the NSFIE (column (2))—should agree if the data were ideal.[3] There are two sources of discrepancy. The first is *reporting errors*: respondents may under- or overreport many of the income, expenditure, and asset items. Second, the survey may not be a representative sample of the population. If rich households are missed by the survey, the implied aggregates are necessarily less than the corresponding national aggregates.

Looking at the balance sheet in table 12.1a, we see that both financial assets and liabilities are severely underestimated by more than 50 percent. On the other hand, the values of physical assets (housing and consumer durables), which we recall are constructed by us from the NSFIE on quantities using extraneous information on market prices, are closer to the NIA values. For housing, however, our imputation ended up overestimating by 15 percent.

Turning to the income/expenditure account in table 12.1a, the extent of underestimation is fairly uniform across expenditure components (except for imputed rent, which is calculated from the estimated value of houses). The difference may be attributable to the remaining definitional differences in the expenditure components. Overall, consumption expenditure is underestimated by 12 percent. The income components in table 12.1a can be grouped into three categories: (i) those that are directly available from the NSFIE ("employment," "business" (the sum of "income from agriculture," "income from business other than agriculture," and "work at home"), plus "income from rental properties," "pension," and "other"), (ii) those that are calculated from the NSFIE data on the stock of financial assets ("gross interest income," "interest payment" and "dividends"), and (iii) those that are calculated from physical assets ("imputed rent"). The latter two categories therefore inherit the underestimation for balance sheet items.[4] The combined effect is an underestimation of disposable income by 11 percent. Since income and expenditure are equally underestimated, the savings rate calculated from the NSFIE is virtually the same as the NIA savings rate.

Is the gap between the NIA aggregates and the implied aggregates due to reporting errors or misrepresentation of the population? We expect both are present in our sample. All survey results are subject to reporting errors. We are under no illusion that our data set is free from measurement errors. Since participating in this survey is far from a trivial task, as respondents are required to keep diaries on hundreds of expenditure items, nonresponse errors are most likely to be present in this diary survey. Although the *1984 National Survey Report* does not discuss the refusal rate, we would expect it to be substantial, making this survey data not a true representation of the population.

The issue of reporting errors versus underrepresentation can be decided if we have a good estimate of the income and asset distribution for the population. Fortunately, the Japanese Ministry of Health and Welfare has conducted a unique survey where *every* household in randomly chosen regions are sampled. The survey that is comparable to the 1984 NSFIE survey is the 1985 Basic Survey on the Life of the People (*Kokumin Seikatsu Kiso Chousa no Gaikyo*), which in 1985 randomly selected 940 regions and surveyed about 40,000 households.[5] Figure 12.1 displays the income distribution obtained from this survey. This should be compared with the income distribution obtained from the 1984 NSFIE for the com-

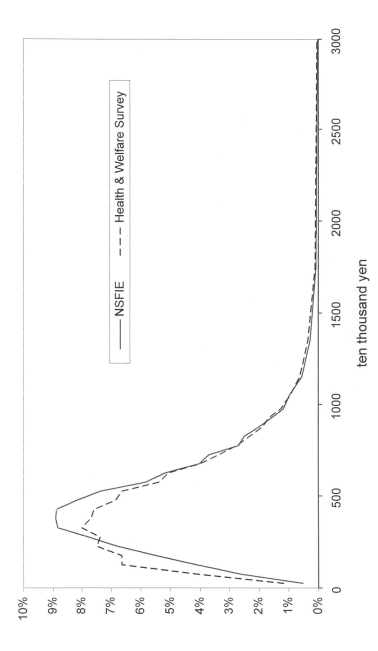

Figure 12.1
Income distribution (mean = 495 [NSFIE], 493 [Health & Welfare Survey]).

parable income concept (pretax annual income). (Since per capita nominal income grew by about 4 percent from 1984 to 1985, the 1985 income distribution from the Ministry of Health and Welfare survey should be shifted to the left proportionately by about 4 percent.) Clearly, NSFIE misses a significant fraction of low-income households. The mean for the two surveys came out close (493 vs. 495) because NSFIE also misses a small fraction of high-income households, meaning that aggregate values implied by this Ministry of Health and Welfare data would be an underestimate of equal magnitudes of national aggregates. It follows that the discrepancies with the NIA numbers reported in table 12.1a are almost entirely due to reporting errors.

This last conclusion is consistent with the pattern of the underestimation in table 12.1a. Our estimate of the value of housing is greater than the NIA number because we imputed the housing value using the housing characteristics and data on land value and construction material costs. The same observation applies to the stock of durables. The reason that the underestimation is especially severe for stocks is probably that some respondents report par values or purchase prices rather than market values of shares. Expenditures are less severely underestimated than incomes partly because income data are not collected through diaries.

That the overall mean income for the NSFIE is close to an estimate of the true population mean is reassuring, but that is not enough to warrant our analysis below, because we will be looking at means *by age*. If most of the rich people missed by the NSFIE are concentrated in higher age brackets, the age profile of mean wealth calculated from the NSFIE is biased downward. To see to what extent this is a problem, we compare income distribution by age in the two surveys. Panel A of table 12.1b shows the income distribution by the age of the household head in the Health and Welfare survey. We calculated in panel B the income distribution by age from the NSFIE using the same income and age brackets. Looking at the age distribution (column sums) first, we see that the NSFIE misses a significant fraction of the old, rich, or poor. To double-check this, we looked at another Ministry of Health and Welfare survey, the 1984 Basic Survey for Welfare Administration, which sampled about 88,000 households randomly to collect information about people's health conditions. Panel C of table 12.1b displays the age distribution from this 1984 survey. It appears that the 1985 Ministry of Health and Welfare survey, whose results are displayed in panel A, underrepresents young cohorts. Even so, it still is true that the NSFIE oversamples the young and under-

Table 12.1b
Income Distribution by Age

Panel A: Income Distribution, Health and Welfare, 1985

Income range	Income midpoint	<30	30–39	40–49	50–59	60–69	70+	row sum (%)
				(cell fraction, %)				
<250	154.0	3.2	3.5	3.6	4.4	5.2	5.2	25.0
250–418	333.5	2.6	7.5	5.3	4.5	3.5	1.7	25.0
418–628	515.5	0.9	7.1	7.5	5.4	2.9	1.3	25.0
628+	970.1	0.2	3.3	7.0	8.9	3.7	1.9	25.0
Column sum (%)		6.9	21.3	23.3	23.2	15.3	10.1	100.0
Mean income		292.5	463.2	555.8	586.3	461.7	381.2	493.2

Panel B: Income Distribution, NSFIE (farmers included)

Income range	Income midpoint	<30	30–39	40–49	50–59	60–69	70+	row sum (%)
				(cell fraction, %)				
< 250	154.0	5.4	2.5	1.9	2.9	4.2	2.7	19.5
250–418	333.5	5.0	9.7	5.0	3.5	2.7	1.0	27.0
418–628	515.5	1.2	9.6	9.7	5.5	2.3	0.5	28.8
628+	970.1	0.3	4.0	8.5	8.7	2.6	0.7	24.7
Column sum (%)		12.0	25.8	25.1	20.5	11.7	4.9	100.0
Mean income		286.4	462.6	579.4	617.6	455.2	331.6	495.3
Difference in mean income (H&W − NSFIE)		6.1	0.6	−23.6	−31.3	6.5	49.6	−2.1

Panel C: Age Distribution, Health and Welfare, 1984

		Age brackets			
<30	30–39	40–49	50–59	60–69	70+
		(cell fraction, %)			
13.3	21.3	23.4	21.2	12.5	8.2

Note: Income in ten thousand yen. Cell fractions are in percents. Source of panel A is *Kokumin Seikatsu Kiso Chousa no Gaiyo, 1985*, a Ministry of Health and Welfare publication. Source of panel C is the 1984 Basic Survey for Welfare Administration.

samples the old. This would not be a problem if for each age bracket the NSFIE is an unbiased representation of the income distribution within the cohort. This, however, is not the case. At both ends of the age distribution, the NSFIE underrepresents the rich, making the mean age-income profile more hump shaped in the NSFIE than in the Ministry of Health and Welfare survey. For our purposes, this is not a serious problem, because as explained in the next section, we correct the age profile of wealth by the age profile of income when we look at the slope of the age-wealth profile. We will mention this cohort misrepresentation in the analysis below whenever necessary.

12.2.4 Adjustment for Reporting Error

Since we have no national income data by cohorts, the adjustment for under- and overreporting as shown in table 12.1a must be done uniformly for all cohorts, if at all. One obvious choice is to normalize all the items to the NIA figures. This adjustment raises the savings rate for older cohorts by more than it does for younger cohorts because the degree of under-reporting is more for capital income than for labor income. However, this adjustment turned out to be small enough not to overturn any of the results reported in the chapter. In particular, our analysis in section 12.3, which looks at the slopes of age profiles, gets affected very little. For this reason the discussion in the text uses exclusively unadjusted data. Relevant tables (table 12.3a and 12.3c) adjusted for reporting error are discussed in appendix 12.3.

12.3   Wealth Decumulation by the Aged?

12.3.1   Basic Issue and Methodology

The basic question we wish to address is embarrassingly simple: Do the aged dissave? The standard life-cycle hypothesis implies that wealth should decline with age. If the old continue to save after retirement, it would be very difficult to explain it by the life-cycle hypothesis. This is the case even if we explicitly recognize the role of pension wealth: It is true that it is the sum of bequeathable wealth (net financial assets plus the value of housing, which is the wealth definition we will use in this chapter) and pension wealth, which should decline with age under the life-cycle hypothesis. But the prediction of the life-cycle hypothesis with uncertain lifetime is that bequeathable wealth should be zero after retirement if there are private annuity markets (Yaari (1965)) and should decline with age otherwise (Bernheim (1986)).[6]

There is a large empirical literature on this issue of whether wealth declines with age. An exhaustive survey can be found in Kennickell (1984). More recent studies using panel data on wealth include Bernheim (1986) and Hurd (1986a,b). A fair summary of the literature is that it is surprisingly difficult to document the declining age-wealth profile. It is therefore important to address the same old issue using new data sets.[7] That is, we wish to test whether a *typical* person after retirement decumulates wealth as the age advances.

Given our data sets, we cannot directly observe the *longitudinal* age profile of wealth, that is, the profile of wealth as a person ages, which is what the prediction of the life-cycle hypothesis is about. What we can observe is the *cross-section* profile. Thus we have to somehow translate a cross-section profile into a longitudinal profile. Let $w(a, t)$ be the *log* of wealth held by a typical person in the cohort of age a at the end of year t. The longitudinal profile refers to the trajectory of $w(t - s, a - s)$ over s for a fixed combination of (a, t). The cross-section profile in year t is the trajectory of $w(a, t)$ over a. We have the following obvious identity:

longitudinal growth rate

$$= w(a, t) - w(a - 1, t - 1)$$

$$= [w(a, t) - w(a - 1, t)] + [w(a - 1, t) - w(a - 1, t - 1)]. \qquad (3.1)$$

The left-hand side is the growth rate (change in logs) of the longitudinal profile for cohort (a, t) at age a (the *longitudinal growth rate*), and the first bracketed term on the right hand side is the *cross-section growth rate* of the cross-section age profile, and the second bracketed term is the *cohort effect*, which refers to how much wealthier is cohort $(a - 1, t)$ relative to the cohort one year older (which is cohort (a, t)). If the economy is in a steady state, this cohort effect should be the productivity growth rate. With an estimate of the cohort effect, we can calculate the value of the left-hand side from the cross-section profile of wealth. In other words, we have to tilt the cross-section profile to arrive at the longitudinal profile of the cohort in question. A downward-sloping cross-section age-wealth profile for the aged is not sufficient to prove wealth decumulation; one has to show that the slope is negative even after "tilting." We will repeatedly refer to this estimate by formula (3.1) supplemented by an estimate of the cohort effect as the *stock-based estimate* of the longitudinal growth rate.

If we have data on the *flow* of saving, which we do for the Japanese data, then there is an alternative and obvious way to calculate the longitudinal growth rate for cohort (a, t). If we ignore for a moment capital gains, then the rate of change of wealth must equal the savings rate (as usually defined in the national accounts) divided by the wealth-income ratio:

$$\text{longitudinal growth rate} = s(a, t)/[W(a, t)/Y(a, t)], \tag{3.2}$$

where $s(a, t)$ is the savings rate during year t, $W(a, t)$ is the *level* of wealth, and $Y(a, t)$ is disposable income for cohort (a, t).[8] We will refer to this estimate by (3.2) as the *flow-based* estimate of the longitudinal growth rate.

How do we modify the estimate if there are net capital gains, that is, changes in real asset prices? Suppose that capital gains are totally unanticipated. Capital gains would shift the whole cross-section profile by, say, 5 percentage points, so the first bracketed term of the right-hand side of the identity (3.1) will not be affected by net capital gains. The second bracketed term of (3.1), however, is now 5 percentage points higher than the value of the cohort effect had there been no capital gains. The longitudinal growth rate $w(a, t) - w(a - 1, t - 1)$ now equals (3.2) plus the same 5 percentage points. That is, if we just ignored unexpected net capital gains, we would not include the 5 percentage points either in the cohort effect or in savings. Thus the stock-based estimate (3.1) and the flow-based estimate (3.2) still agree as they estimate the same object of the longitudinal growth rate less the rate of unexpected net capital gains.

If, on the other hand, capital gains are anticipated, then we have to add them to saving precisely because anticipated capital gains do not influence the cohort effect. Thus, the flow-based estimate (3.2) becomes

$$\text{longitudinal growth rate} = s(a, t)/[W(a, t)/Y(a, t)]$$

$$+ (\text{expected capital gains})/W(a, t) \tag{3.3}$$

For the Japanese data, we can directly measure the savings rate and the wealth-income ratio. For capital gains, most of them must be in the value of land and the value of stocks. Estimating expected capital gains necessarily involves some arbitrariness. We assume that the amount of expected nominal capital gains is about 8 percent of the value of land and stocks. More precisely, expected capital gains = 0.08 × (value of land + value of stocks)

− (inflation rate during 1984)

× (value of wealth).   (3.4)

See appendix 12.1 for more details on disposable income, consumption, and wealth. Of course, this figure of 8 percent is arbitrary. For the most part, therefore, we will perform the growth rate analysis ignoring (expected) capital gains. The role of expected capital gains will be mentioned whenever they are deemed important. (For the record, the actual rate of change of the real value of land during 1984 was virtually 0 percent.[9])

Another issue is how to measure the cohort effect (the second bracketed term in the stock-based estimate (3.1)). As mentioned above, in a steady state, the productivity growth rate is a good estimate. If we have a good measure of *permanent income*, then there is an alternative estimate of the cohort effect, which is the negative of the cross section growth rate of permanent income:

estimate of the cohort effect = −[log PI(a, t) − log PI($a − 1$, t)],   (3.5)

where PI(a, t) is permanent income for a typical person in cohort (a, t), and use has been made of the fact that PI($a − 1$, $t − 1$) = PI(a, t). This estimate is good even if the economy is not in a steady state.[10]

12.3.2   The U.S. Age-Wealth Profile

For the U.S. data, the 1983 Survey of Consumer Finances, we do not have information on the flow of saving. We therefore present only the stock-based estimate of the longitudinal wealth growth rate. Panel A of table 12.2 reports the cross-section age profile of wealth. For each five-year age bracket, both mean and median are reported because they differ from each other greatly due to the high skewness of the U.S. wealth distribution. To arrive at the longitudinal profile, we have to tilt the age profile in panel A by the cohort effect. For the United States, where the productivity growth has been relatively stable compared to other countries, the steady state assumption is a reasonable one to make, and we take the productivity growth rate to be 1 percent. In panel B, the age profile of panel A is tilted by 1 percent around the 55–59 age bracket, to arrive at the longitudinal age profile of a typical person who happened to be between 55 and 59 years of age. It shows quite clearly that wealth declines with age after age 65 or so.

Table 12.2
Age Profile of Wealth: United States

Panel A: Before the Cohort Adjustment

					Age of the head								
	<25	25–29	30–34	35–39	40–44	45–49	50–54	55–59	60–64	65–69	70–74	75–79	80+
# households	295	439	423	398	379	339	341	332	341	298	229	161	128
Mean of wealth	9	24	48	80	97	233	157	199	205	281	164	133	107
Standard deviation	20	56	186	387	2201	1497	859	569	1126	1769	502	660	530
Median	2	6	20	40	56	61	79	93	98	106	63	58	33

Panel B: After the Cohort Adjustment

					Age of the head								
	<25	25–29	30–34	35–39	40–44	45–49	50–54	55–59	60–64	65–69	70–74	75–79	80+
Mean of wealth	6	17	38	66	83	211	150	199	216	310	190	163	138
Median	2	5	16	33	48	56	75	93	102	117	73	71	43

Note: In thousand dollars. Wealth is the sum of net financial assets and the value of housing. The data source is the Survey of Consumer Finances 1983. Details of the derivation are in Scott Hoyt, "Life Cycle Hypothesis of Saving and the Elasticity of Household Wealth with Respect to their Permanent Income", Univ. of Penn., 1988. The cohort adjustment assumes a 1 percent per year growth rate. The point of tilting is the 50–54 age bracket. Figures for open-ended age classes at both ends are adjusted as though the mean age in 24-or-less is five years less than the 25–29 age class and the mean of the 80-and-over class is five years greater than the mean of the 75–79 class.

This is probably the strongest evidence to date for wealth decumulation by the aged. Kennickell (1984) and Ando and Kennickell (1987) examined available evidence up to and not including this SCF83, and concluded that there appears to be very little dissaving after retirement. Based on comparisons with aggregate data and other evidences, there seems to be a reasonable ground for believing that the 1983 Survey of Consumer Finances provides more reliable information on wealth holdings of households than earlier data.

12.3.3 Special Issues Concerning Japan

We now turn to the Japanese data, the NSFIE. Since the NSFIE has flow information as well as stock information, we can calculate the longitudinal growth rate both ways (see (3.1) and (3.2)). For Japan, however, application of the growth rate analysis is not straightforward, because of the prevalence of the *extended family*. Of all people 60 years or older in Japan, more than half of them live with their children; about 20 to 25 percent of all the households in Japan are extended families. The existence of extended families implies that there are *two* categories of older people: those still maintaining an independent household (the independent old) and those living with children (the dependent old). For our purposes, this creates three problems. The first is a *mixing of the young and the old*: obviously, wealth and the flow of saving for the dependent old cannot be observed, because for wealth and consumption the NSFIE has no breakdown among family members.[11] Thus we cannot directly observe the savings behavior of the majority of the aged. However, there is an indirect way to infer it, which involves a comparison of nuclear families and extended families whose younger generation is similarly aged. This will be done in section 12.3.5 below.

Second, because the definition of the "head" of the household in the NSFIE is the main income earner (i.e., the person normally earning the highest income), there is a *sample selection by design* that extended families in older age brackets are a combination of rich parents and poor children while those in younger age brackets are poor parents and rich children. We can easily fix this problem by redefining the *head* for the extended family to be the younger generation.

The third problem, which we refer to as *self-selection*, is less obvious. As it turned out, the economic status of the independent old is substantially better than that of the dependent old, and the proportion of the independent old in the cohort declines with age because more and more older people get merged with younger households as the age advances. We have to make adjustments for this self-selection bias when we estimate the cohort effect for the independent and the dependent old separately. To see this more clearly, imagine distributions of permanent income, one for the 70-year-old cohort, and the other for the 80-year-old cohort in 1984. Because of productivity growth, the whole distribution for 80-year-olds is lower than that for 70-year-olds. Suppose that 70-year-old individuals in the top 40 percentile and 80-year-old individuals in the top 20 percentile in their respective permanent income distributions are the independent old. Then the mean of permanent income for the independent 70-year-old can be *lower* than the mean permanent income for the independent 80-year-old, even though the unconditional mean of permanent income (unconditional on the living arrangement) is higher for 70-year-olds. In other words, the pool of the independent old gets overrepresented by "winners" and the dependent old overrepresented by "losers," as the age advances. This self-selection bias implies that the standard cohort adjustment of using productivity growth rate is no longer valid. If, however, we have a good estimate of permanent income, then the other cohort adjustment (3.5) is still valid as it automatically adjusts for the overrepresentation of "winners."[12]

With the second problem being fixed by redefining the household head, our analysis of the NSFIE data set must deal with the first and the third problems. The first step of our analysis is to define what we mean by a nuclear family and an extended family. We define a *generation* to be an adult 25 years or older with or without a spouse. If a generation is a couple, its *age* is the age of the husband. We define a nuclear family to be a household containing just one generation with or without children. Thus nuclear families include adult singles as well as couples with or without children. The definition of an extended family is then a household containing two generations. Whether children (people under 25) are present or not does not influence the definition. The following household types are neither nuclear nor extended: three adult generation families, families living with relatives or living with unrelated adults, and families with more than two parents. An old couple living with an unmarried adult child is an extended family according to our definition. The *head* of a nuclear family is the husband if the generation is a couple (if the generation consists of just one adult, then the definition of the head is obvious). The head of an extended family is the *younger generation*. If the younger generation is a couple, then the husband is the head.

The reason for this particular definition is threefold. First, we include singles in the pool of nuclear families because otherwise the definition of a generation is not symmetric. The older generation in an extended family is either an old couple or a father or a mother. Thus the size of an older generation is either two or one, just like the size of the younger generation, under our definition. Second, we want the only difference between an extended family and a nuclear family to be an older generation. The motivation will become clear as we proceed. The third reason is purely data related. In the NSFIE the breakdown of an income component is only three-way: "head" (in the sense of main income earner), its spouse, and "other family members." If there are more than three generations or if there are unrelated adults in the household, "other family members" include them, making the separate identification of income for the younger and the older generations impossible.

Under this definition of the household type, 29,465 families qualified as nuclear and 8,717 extended.

12.3.4 Wealth Accumulation by Younger Nuclear Families

With all these preliminaries, we are now ready to look at the Japanese data and apply the growth rate analysis. The easiest object for application is younger nuclear families. There is no apparent difference in income between the younger generation in extended families and the generation in nuclear families similarly aged.[13] So, for younger cohorts, there is no self-selection bias that would complicate the cohort adjustment. Panel A of table 12.3a displays the cross-section profiles of income, consumption, and wealth. The row labeled "cross-section growth rate" reports the first term on the right-hand side of (3.1). More precisely, the cross-section growth rate in percents per year for age bracket a is calculated as

$$100 \times [\log(W(a, 1984)) - \log(W(a - 1, 1984))]/5, \tag{3.6}$$

where the cohort index a now stands for the age bracket. We divide the log difference by five because the width of age brackets is five years. For example, the cross section growth rate for the cohort between 35 and 39 years of age is 9.6 percent per year. To obtain the *stock-based* estimate of the longitudinal growth rate (i.e., the estimate using (3.1)) for the cohort in age bracket a, a cohort adjustment is needed. Since there is no selection bias for the young, we use the standard cohort adjustment of productivity growth rate. Thus, one *adds* something like 5 percent to the cross-section

Table 12.3a
Age Profile of Income, Expenditure, and Asset Holdings by Family Type

Panel A: Nuclear (includes singles)

	25–29	30–34	35–39	40–44	45–49	50–54	55–59	60–64	65–69	70–74	75–79	80–84	85+	All
Number of households	3676	5061	5909	5538	4880	3667	2571	2013	1570	1144	599	159	37	36823
Family size	1.9	3.2	3.7	3.8	3.6	3.0	2.2	1.7	1.6	1.6	1.5	1.5	1.5	3.0
Disposable income	272	345	404	466	523	540	484	368	295	255	215	189	163	411
Consumption expenditure	249	319	364	405	444	428	391	312	258	232	206	194	180	356
Saving rate (%)	9	8	10	13	15	21	19	15	13	9	4	-3	-10	13
Net financial assets	112	103	70	129	269	448	700	810	751	668	597	700	413	295
Wealth	402	1003	1623	2253	2773	3033	3399	3438	3364	3064	2829	2584	2056	2170
Cross section growth rate (%)		18.3	9.6	6.6	4.2	1.8	2.3	0.2	-0.4	-1.9	-1.6	-1.8	-4.6	
Wealth growth rate (%)	5.8	2.7	2.4	2.7	2.9	3.7	2.7	1.6	1.1	0.8	0.3	-0.2	-0.8	

Panel B: Extended

	25–29	30–34	35–39	40–44	45–49	50–54	55–59	60–64	65–69	70–74	75–79	80–84	85+	All
Number of households	933	1309	1867	1703	1385	900	416	159	40	5	0	0	0	8717
Family size	4.0	5.2	5.5	5.4	5.1	4.4	3.6	3.1	2.9	3.0	n.a.	n.a.	n.a.	4.9
Number of parents	1.8	1.6	1.5	1.3	1.3	1.2	1.1	1.1	1.0	1.2	n.a.	n.a.	n.a.	1.4
Age of parents	57	63	67	71	74	78	81	85	87	88	n.a.	n.a.	n.a.	69
Disposable income	603	560	570	591	627	648	639	534	420	362	n.a.	n.a.	n.a.	595
Consumption expenditure	484	459	478	508	523	533	489	455	399	312	n.a.	n.a.	n.a.	494
Saving rate (%)	20	18	16	14	17	18	23	15	5	14	n.a.	n.a.	n.a.	17
Net financial assets	544	427	474	455	551	666	114	1188	859	952	n.a.	n.a.	n.a.	501
Wealth	3845	3630	4166	4277	4520	4653	4898	5217	4276	4544	n.a.	n.a.	n.a.	4234

	25–29	30–34	35–39	40–44	45–49	50–54	55–59	60–64	65–69	70–74	75–79	80–84	85+	All
Cross section growth rate (%)		−1.1	2.8	0.5	1.1	0.6	1.0	1.3	−4.0	1.2	n.a.	n.a.	n.a.	n.a.
Wealth growth rate (%)	3.1	2.8	2.2	2.0	2.3	2.5	3.1	1.5	0.5	1.1	n.a.	n.a.	n.a.	n.a.
Yparpen + yparbus	134	116	94	65	56	48	38	39	27	6	n.a.	n.a.	n.a.	69
Cross section growth rate (%)		−2.3	−5.3	−8.4	−4.8	−4.1	−7.8	1.3	−20.6	−103.0	n.a.	n.a.	n.a.	n.a.

Panel C: extended minus Nuclear

	25–29	30–34	35–39	40–44	45–49	50–54	55–59	60–64	65–69	70–74	75–79	80–84	85+	All
Disposable income	331	214	166	125	103	108	156	166	125	107	n.a.	n.a.	n.a.	184
Consumption expenditure	235	140	113	103	79	105	99	143	141	80	n.a.	n.a.	n.a.	138
Saving rate (%)	29	35	32	18	24	3	37	14	−13	25	n.a.	n.a.	n.a.	25
Net financial assets	433	324	404	326	282	217	−586	379	108	283	n.a.	n.a.	n.a.	205
Wealth	3443	2627	2544	2024	1747	1620	1499	1780	912	1481	n.a.	n.a.	n.a.	2065
Cross section growth rate (%)		−4.4	−0.8	−5.2	−4.3	−2.1	−2.5	4.7	−29.9	39.6	n.a.	n.a.	n.a.	
Wealth growth rate (%)	2.8	2.8	2.1	1.1	1.4	0.2	3.8	1.3	−1.8	1.8	n.a.	n.a.	n.a.	

Note: Income, expenditure and assets in ten thousand yen. Disposable income excludes transfers from outside the household, and consumption excludes regular remittance. Wealth is net financial assets plus the value of housing and rental properties. Rows labeled "cross section growth rate" report the growth rate per year of the cross section profile (change in logs) right above them. "Wealth growth rate" is the ratio of the savings rate to the wealth-disposable income ratio. "yparpen" is the parents' pension income and "yparbus" is the parents' business income. The age of parents is the age of the parent if there is only one parent, and the age of the father if both father and mother are alive. The cross section growth rate of wealth is converted to an annual rate using the ages of parents of the adjoining intervals (see section 12.3.6 for more precise details).

growth rate to arrive at the longitudinal growth rate. For the 35–39 cohort, for example, the stock-based longitudinal growth rate is about 14 percent. That is, the steep cross-section profile gets even steeper after the cohort adjustment.

Because the NSFIE has the flow of savings, we can calculate the *flow-based* estimate of the longitudinal growth rate (i.e., the estimate based on (3.2)), which is reported in the row labeled "wealth growth rate." For example, for the 35–39 cohort, the estimate is 2.4 percent. Thus we have a quite apparent puzzle that the flow-based estimate is much lower than the stock-based estimate of the same object:

flow-based estimate (given by 3.2)

< stock-based estimate (given by 3.1). (3.7)

In other words, the cross-section age-wealth profile for young nuclear families is far too steep to be accounted for by their own saving. This gap is only slightly narrowed if we include our estimate of expected capital gains as part of saving. The flow-based estimate with capital gains is given by the left-hand side of (3.3). If we take the formula (3.4) for capital gains, then for younger nuclear families the wealth growth rate goes up by about 3 percentage points. For example for the 35–39 bracket, it goes up from 2.4 percent to 5.8 percent, still nowhere near the stock-based estimate of 14 percent.[14]

12.3.5 Wealth Accumulation by Extended Families

Although there is a fairly obvious resolution of the apparent puzzle, we leave the puzzle as is for awhile and turn to extended families. Panel B of table 12.3a displays the cross section age profiles. It is important to keep in mind that income, consumption, and wealth for extended families are for the two generations combined (the problem of mixing the young and the old we mentioned earlier). We get around this mixing problem by assuming (for a moment) that the income, consumption, and wealth attributable to the younger generation in extended families are the same as what is observed for nuclear families similarly aged. Then the difference in income, consumption, and wealth between extended and nuclear families in the same age bracket (remember that the age of the head for extended families is the age of the *younger* generation) is the addition brought about by the presence of the older generation. Such differences are displayed in panel C of table 12.3a. There the age profile of this incremental wealth is fairly steeply declining. Now the cohort adjustment needed to convert cross-section into longitudinal profiles is not simple, because the dependent old in the pool of extended families are not typical individuals of older cohorts. We need a measure of permanent income for the dependent old to adjust for this selection bias. Fortunately, there is such a measure because we can observe for extended families the income of the older generation. The sum of their pension income and business income is as good a measure of permanent income as one can possibly get because the NSFIE has no information on past history of income. This sum is reported in panel B in the row labeled "yparpen + yparbus." The last row of panel B reports the cross-section growth rate in percents per year of this measure of permanent income for the dependent old. It is calculated as

$$100 \times [\log(\text{PI}(a, 1984)) - \log(\text{PI}(a - 1, 1984))]/[pa(a) - pa(a - 1)],$$

$$(3.8)$$

where a here refers to the age bracket for the younger generation, $\text{PI}(a, 1984)$ is the sum of pension and business income for parents whose children are in the age bracket a, and $pa(a)$ is the age of the parents (reported in panel B). In other words we use the parents' age to convert growth rate into an annual rate, which is what one should do. This replaces our estimate (3.5) of the cohort effect.

The cross-section growth rate of incremental wealth is also reported in panel C. Since this incremental wealth is for the older generation, we use the parents' age to calculate the growth rate per year:

$$100 \times [\log(V(a, 1984)) - \log(V(a - 1, 1984)]/[pa(a) - pa(a - 1)],$$

$$(3.9)$$

where $V(a, 1984)$ is incremental wealth. To arrive at the longitudinal growth rate of wealth, we *subtract* the cross-section growth rate of permanent income from the cross-section growth rate of incremental wealth. For example for the 35–39 age bracket, the stock-based estimate of the longitudinal wealth growth rate is $4.5 = -0.8 + 5.3$ percent. The stock-based longitudinal growth rate is positive except for the 30–34 bracket. One cannot conclude from the fairly steeply declining cross-section age profile of incremental wealth that the dependent old decumulate.

What about the flow-based estimate of longitudinal wealth growth? The wealth growth rate by (3.2) using incremental income, consumption, and wealth is also reported in panel C, which consistently report positive growth uniformly for all age brackets (except for the 65–69 age bracket where the parents' age (reported in panel B) is 87). The flow-based evidence is that except for those really old the dependent old save. The flow-based estimate and the stock-based estimate do not always agree. If for the flow-based estimate capital gains are included as (3.4), then the flow-based estimate tends to be higher than the stock-based estimate. So, here is another and much weaker puzzle: we have a discrepancy between the stock-based estimate and the flow-based estimate of the same object, but this time (for some age brackets) the direction of inequality is reversed:

flow-based estimate (given by (3.2))

> stock-based estimate (given by (3.1) with (3.5)).   (3.10)

It should now be apparent that the two puzzles (3.7) and (3.10) are intimately related. Let us take up the first puzzle that nuclear families accumulate too fast to be justified by their own savings. This is due to a missing item in the formula for the flow estimate (3.2). Apart from capital gains, saving is not the only source of wealth increase, if there are *transfers* from outside the household. Furthermore, since transfers between younger nuclear families net out, average wealth growth for a typical younger nuclear family over and above its own saving must be due to *intergenerational transfers*. The large gap in (3.7) must be due to transfers flowing *into* the pool of nuclear families. Since the size of the gap in (3.7) (which is 14 percent for the 35–39 age bracket) is far greater than the wealth growth rate warranted by saving (2.4 percent for the same age bracket, and 5.8 percent if expected capital gains are included), we conclude that the flow of intergenerational transfers are in the same magnitude as the flow of saving or even larger.[15]

As an (important) aside, we note that with transfers, wealth accumulation/decumulation and positive/negative saving are two separate things. A person who is dissaving in that his income (excluding transfers) is less than expenditure (again excluding transfers to others) could be accumulating wealth if he receives a large amount of transfers. In this case, whether the wealth profile is downward sloping (even after cohort adjustments) is a *nonissue*. A steeply declining age-wealth profile (like the one shown in table 12.2 for the United States) is consistent with the standard life-cycle hypothesis; it is also consistent with other theories of saving. One cannot infer anything about the flow of saving from an age profile of wealth holdings, unless one has a theory linking savings with transfers.[16]

If we recognize transfers as another source of wealth growth, then the assumption we made earlier for the younger generation in extended families—that their wealth holding is similar to the wealth holdings by nuclear families similarly aged—is unwarranted, because for extended families intergenerational transfers are just internal transactions if transfers are an inter vivos gift (except for gifts that go to relatives living outside the household). If transfers take the form of bequests, then the younger generation receiving transfers cannot be in an extended family. It follows from this that the incremental wealth reported in panel C is contribution by the dependent old *less* the amount of transfers received by their children's contemporaries in the nuclear family pool. The incremental wealth growth in panel C thus severely underestimates the contribution in wealth by the dependent old. It is then not surprising at all that the reverse inequality (3.10) holds more often than not for the younger age brackets. What is surprising is that it does not hold for all younger age brackets. However, we do not wish to put too much emphasis on this reverse inequality for extended families, since in panel C we are looking at differences in the flow level of saving which itself is a difference between income and consumption which in turn are measured with error. What does come out of this analysis, however, is that the dependent old are most likely to save, as both the stock-based evidence and the flow-based evidence point to that direction.

12.3.6 More on Wealth Accumulation by the Dependent Old

There is another way to infer wealth accumulation by the aged. Table 12.3b displays wealth for extended families cross-tabulated by the age of the younger generation and by the age of the older generation. For each cell defined by the two ages, both the mean and the median are reported. It is somewhat surprising to those who are used to looking at the U.S. wealth distribution that they are so close to each other. Part of it is because the NSFIE misses rich people. But there is no denying that the Japanese wealth distribution is much less skewed.

The main point, however, is the virtually flat wealth profile against the age of the older generation. If the head's age is the same, extended families with older parents hold roughly as much wealth as those with relatively younger parents. Since permanent income is lower for older parents than for relatively younger parents, the virtually flat cross-section age-wealth profile reported in rows of table 12.3b gets translated into an upward-sloping longitudinal wealth profile for the dependent old. Here, then, is a piece of stock-based evidence that the dependent old do save. We argued in the previous subsection that one cannot infer from the age

Table 12.3b
Total Wealth by the Age of Parent—Extended Families

Age of younger generation	Age of older generation in the extended family							
	50–54	55–59	60–64	65–69	70–74	75–79	80–84	85+
25–29								
Cell mean	3887	4041	3630	3680	3251	2735	3657	—
Maximum	27363	29927	24441	20320	7994	5320	3657	—
(Cell size)	(302)	(370)	(154)	(43)	(17)	(5)	(1)	(0)
30–34								
Cell mean	3540	4043	3720	3199	2992	3465	5142	3130
Maximum	21492	30344	39222	11253	13278	17429	10479	4305
(Cell size)	(66)	(380)	(434)	(244)	(127)	(48)	(5)	(3)
35–39								
Cell mean	5662	4308	4371	4316	3905	3577	3025	2829
Maximum	25881	23356	112969	26609	41110	26881	8702	7911
(Cell size)	(15)	(177)	(549)	(553)	(381)	(141)	(41)	(10)
40–44								
Cell mean	3816	4960	4320	4280	4082	4646	4003	4272
Maximum	5653	19582	33255	38131	30758	64992	20529	11920
(Cell size)	(4)	(24)	(180)	(484)	(574)	(312)	(100)	(25)
45–49								
Cell mean	—	4955	3987	4635	4652	4508	4000	4652
Maximum	—	5946	15701	35024	42769	36436	27114	16472
(Cell size)	(0)	(2)	(23)	(213)	(532)	(390)	(166)	(59)
50–54								
Cell mean	—	—	4196	3867	5035	4825	4494	3985
Maximum	—	—	6609	9340	65051	37194	20273	12620
(Cell size)	(0)	(0)	(9)	(28)	(187)	(333)	(249)	(94)
55–59								
Cell mean	—	—	—	4011	5716	5595	4606	4414
Maximum	—	—	—	6279	24369	50917	69859	17773
(Cell size)	(0)	(0)	(0)	(5)	(31)	(109)	(178)	(93)

Note: Wealth in ten thousand yen. Wealth is net financial assets plus housing plus the value of rental properties owned.

profile of wealth whether the flow of saving is positive or negative. But this criticism does not apply here in full force, since intergenerational transfers are internal to an extended family except for "leakages," namely gifts that go to family members outside the extended family. Of course, "leakages" only strengthen our claim that the dependent old save.

12.3.7 Wealth Accumulation by the Independent Old

Let us now look at the independent old. The upper half of panel A of table 12.3c is just a replication of the older end of panel A of table 12.3a, with a few new items added. The lower half of panel A displays a breakdown of pretax income by components. Panel B, which now tabulates extended families *by the age of the older generation*, carries similar income information for the dependent old in extended families. As we might have expected, transfer income[17] for extended families is very low. If one tracks the number of the old in panel A and in panel B across age brackets, one can see the process of older people getting merged with their children as they age. If one compares the sum of pension income and business income, which is our measure of permanent income for the old, between the two panels across age brackets, one can see *self-selection* process where older independent people are overrepresented by "winners."

Panel C of table 12.3c combines panel A and panel B. The means reported in panel C therefore are an unconditional means over all individual, winners or losers, belonging to the same age cohort. It is not surprising, then, that the cross section growth rate of permanent income (pension plus business income) in panel C is more or less uniform across the age brackets.[18] The standard cohort adjustment of using the long-run productivity growth rate is a good one as long as the cohort is well represented. An argument is often made that the long-run productivity growth rate overstates the cohort effect for the aged because wealthier people tend to live longer. In the case of Japan, this does not seem important.[19]

We are now ready to do the growth-rate analysis for the independent old. Going back to panel A of the same table 12.3c, we see that the cross-section age profile of permanent income is substantially flatter than the profile we have just seen in panel C. This of course is due to the self selection bias. Combining this profile with the wealth profile and using (3.1) and (3.5), we arrive at the stock-based estimate of the longitudinal wealth growth rate. The estimate is negative except for the 80–84 bracket. The flow-based estimate by (3.2) is in the row labeled "wealth

Table 12.3c
Age Profile of Income for the Aged by Family Type

Panel A: Nuclear (includes singles)

	60–64	65–69	70–74	75–79	80–84	85+	All
Number of households	2013	1570	1144	599	159	37	5521
Number of the old	3281	2524	1764	879	237	55	8739
Fraction of females (%)	59	59	60	60	51	52	59
Family size	1.7	1.6	1.6	1.5	1.5	1.5	1.6
Disposable income	368	295	255	215	189	163	301
Consumption expenditure	312	258	232	206	194	180	264
Saving rate (%)	15	13	9	4	−3	−10	12
Net financial assets	810	751	668	597	700	413	735
Wealth	3438	3364	3064	2829	2584	2056	3239
Cross-section growth rate (%)		−0.4	−1.9	−1.6	−1.8	−4.6	
Wealth growth rate (%)	1.6	1.1	0.8	0.3	−0.2	−0.8	
Employment income	140	59	39	22	6	12	79
Business income	55	39	31	17	12	8	40
Capital income	33	34	31	27	36	19	32
Pension	114	136	131	129	110	101	125
Cross-section growth rate (%)		3.5	−0.7	−0.4	−3.1	−1.8	
Pension + business income	169	175	162	145	123	109	165
Cross-section growth rate (%)		0.7	−1.6	−2.2	−3.4	−2.4	
Pension + business + capital	203	209	193	172	158	129	197
Cross-section growth rate (%)		0.6	−1.7	−2.3	−1.7	−4.2	
Other income	10	9	7	6	13	12	5
Regular transfer income	3	5	6	8	11	10	5

Panel B: Extended by Age of Parents

	60–64	65–69	70–74	75–79	80–84	85+	All
Number of households	1351	1572	1852	1352	816	394	7337
Number of the old	1986	2248	2482	1812	1012	457	9996
Number of parents	1.5	1.4	1.3	1.3	1.2	1.2	1.4
Number of mothers	1.0	0.9	0.9	0.9	0.9	0.8	0.9
Fraction of females (%)	65	66	68	66	69	70	67
Employment income	64	35	31	30	31	22	37
Business income	58	38	25	15	12	2	29
Capital income	14	10	8	8	6	2	9
Pension	53	55	46	38	35	32	46
Cross-section growth rate (%)		0.9	−3.8	−3.5	−1.7	−1.9	
Pension + business income	111	93	71	54	47	34	75
Cross section growth rate (%)		−3.5	−5.3	−5.6	−2.5	−6.5	
Other income	5	1	1	1	1	2	2
Regular transfer income	1	1	1	1	1	1	1

Table 12.3c (cont.)

Panel C: All the old

	60–64	65–69	70–74	75–79	80–84	85+	All
Number of households	3364	3142	2996	1951	975	431	12858
Number of the old	5267	4772	4245	2690	1249	512	18735
Fraction of females (%)	61	62	65	64	66	68	63
Employment income	110	47	34	28	27	21	55
Business income	56	38	27	16	12	3	34
Capital income	25	22	17	14	11	4	19
Pension income	89	96	78	66	48	38	80
Cross-section growth rate (%)		1.3	−4.0	−3.4	−6.6	−4.5	
Business + pension income	146	134	106	82	60	41	114
Cross-section growth rate (%)		−1.7	−4.7	−5.1	−6.3	−7.7	
Other income	8	5	3	3	3	3	5
Regular transfer income	2	3	3	3	2	2	3

Panel D: Singles (Component of Panel A)

	60–64	65–69	70–74	75–79	80–84	85+	All
Number of households	276	228	194	118	30	7	853
Fraction of females (%)	89	87	84	79	53	57	84
Disposable income	168	148	133	116	122	90	146
Consumption expenditure	190	162	159	151	152	117	168
Saving rate (%)	−13	−9	−19	−30	−24	−31	−16
Net financial assets	407	351	344	295	684	100	369
Wealth	1905	1902	1849	1737	2037	996	1866
Cross-section growth rate (%)		−0.0	−0.6	−1.2	3.2	−14.3	
Wealth growth rate (%)	−1.1	−0.7	−1.4	−2.0	−1.4	−2.8	
Employment income	53	17	11	1	1	0	24
Business income	10	11	10	6	2	0	9
Capital income	14	14	13	9	33	4	14
Pension	71	85	82	82	68	71	79
Cross-section growth rate (%)	3.9	−0.9	0.1	−3.6	0.9		
Pension + business income	81	96	91	88	70	71	88
Cross-section growth rate (%)	3.6	−1.0	−0.7	−4.5	0.3		
Other income	8	8	6	6	15	17	8
Regular transfer income	6	6	10	11	10	13	8

Note: The incomes in Panel B are for the older generations. Regular transfer income does not include public transfer payments.

growth rate." It is positive except for those who are really old. Thus again we obtain the same reverse inequality (3.10). If capital gains are included, the flow-based estimate is about 2 to 3 percentage points higher. The reverse inequality (3.10) we observed for some extended families, we recall, was an artifact of transfers flowing into the pool of nuclear families. The reverse inequality (3.10) that holds for almost all the independent old here indicates the part of the transfers going to nuclear families that are inter vivos gifts. The amount of inter vivos gifts suggested by the reverse inequality for the independent old, however, is nowhere near the huge gap in the inequality (3.7) for young nuclear families. We therefore conclude that the bulk of intergenerational transfers is in the form of bequests.[20]

The last panel of the table, panel D, is to show that our characterization of the independent old as "winners" is a bit oversimplified, although this does not invalidate any of the analysis so far. The independent old can be divided between old nuclear families and old singles. Even after taking account of the fact that the sample means for singles are per person while the sample means in panel A are per "generation" whose size is either one or two persons, the economic status of an independent single person is considerably worse than an old person in an old nuclear family. Put differently, if one picks a single old male and a single old female randomly from the pool of old singles and forces them to marry to form an old nuclear family, it looks less wealthy than a typical genuine nuclear family. This is also the finding by Hurd (1986a,b) for the United States, that older couples are wealthier than old singles. This creates a sample selection process within the independent old: relatively younger singles in the independent old tend to be over-represented by "losers." This explains the relatively flat cross section profile of permanent income for older singles.

Since cell sizes are small, we cannot place too much significance on the stock-based and the flow-based estimates of the longitudinal growth rates for old singles, but the fact that the savings rate is uniformly negative for all age brackets should be taken seriously. If there is any household that follows the life-cycle hypothesis, it must be those old singles. It is reassuring to find that they decumulate assets as predicted by the life-cycle hypothesis. But this finding has another implication. It has been argued in the literature that uncertain lifetime and fear of catastrophic illness justify the lack of wealth decumulation by the aged. If that were the case, the old singles in the NSFIE should have been saving. Our finding that old singles actually dissave while other types of the aged who are most likely to have children do not implies that bequest motive is an important reason for the lack of wealth decumulation.

12.4 Concluding Remarks

In this study, we combined the stock-based and the flow-based information available from the NSFIE to document a significant flow of intergenerational transfers flowing into the pool of younger nuclear families. One source of those transfers is the independent old, most of whom appear to not only save toward the end of their life but also give wealth to their children. These inter vivos gifts, however, are a minor source of transfers. The bulk of transfers take place in the form of bequests. Bequests come not only from the independent old, who appear to hold onto their wealth until death, but also from the pool of extended families that seem to keep accumulating wealth no matter what the age of the parents is. When the parents in an extended family die, the extended family becomes nuclear, bringing with it the wealth that has been nurtured while the parents were alive. The obvious agenda for future research is to construct a theory capable of explaining these findings.

Appendix 12.1: Data Appendix

1 Consumer Durables

We recognize stock of durable goods, which depreciates over time while yielding imputed income to its owners. In symbols, we have

$$\text{DVALTOT} = \sum_{i=1}^{75} \text{DP}_i \times \text{DQ}_i \times (1 - d_i)^{a(i)}$$

$$\text{DDEPRTOT} = \sum_{i=1}^{75} d_i \times \text{DP}_i \times \text{DQ}_i \times (1 - d_i)^{a(i)-1}$$

$$\text{YMDUR} = rcd \times \text{DVALTOT} + \text{DDEPRTOT}$$

where

$\text{DP}_i =$ price of i-th durable good in 1984 or 1979,

$d_i =$ the rate of depreciation (the declining balance procedure at a constant rate),

$\text{DQ}_i =$ number of durable goods, available from the survey,

$a(i) =$ the age of the durable good in question in 1984,

$rcd =$ real, net rate of return (taken to be 4%).

Information on DQ_i ($i = 1, 2, \ldots, 75$) was collected in the Durable Goods, Yearly Income, and Savings Schedule of the National Survey of Family Income and Expenditure Survey (hereafter the NSFIE), and reported in the tape provided by the Statistics Bureau. For most items, DP was published in *the Annual Report on the Retail Price Survey*, Table 1, Statistics Bureau, Prime Minister's Office. In a few cases in which DP was not explicitly reported in this reference, we have obtained a typical price of the item by visiting department stores. For d_i, we obtained a table showing the schedule of useful lives for groups of durable goods from the National Tax Bureau, Ministry of Finance, and converted information contained therein into equivalent rates of depreciation assuming the declining balance procedure. The specific rates used were reported as Table III-14, in an earlier paper by Ando (1985). Finally, the age of the durable goods, $a(i)$, was explicitly reported for each item in the 1979 survey, but not in the 1984 survey. Under the circumstances, we have computed the mean age for each of the durable goods for 1979, and assumed that the age of the corresponding type of durable goods in 1984 was equal to the mean age for 1979. We assume that $rcd = 4$ percent.

2   Value of Residential Property and Its Service Flows

The NSFIE does not directly report the value of residential properties, but through a series of questions in the Household Schedule it does provide fairly detailed characteristics of the house itself. Unfortunately, the size of the land associated with the house is not reported.

In view of the overwhelming importance of the value of the residential property in the balance sheet of Japanese households, we have devoted a major effort to estimating the value of residential properties, including the value of land. We describe our procedure below.

A   Value of Housing Structure (HSTRCVAL)

Among housing characteristics reported in the NSFIE are house material (HHOUSMAT), physical type of the house (HHOUSTYP), and floor space in square meters (HFLRSP). (See Household Schedule, for example, Report of the NSFIE, 1984, vol. 2, pt. 1, p. 42). The Ministry of Construction publishes the Annual Report on Construction Statistics, in which they report, for each prefecture in Japan, total new space of residential structure created and their total costs classified by specific material of construction. (See, for example, Ministry of Construction, *Annual Report on Construction Statistics*, 1986 edition, Table 27, pp. 78–101). From this information, for each prefecture and for each of the materials used, we can infer the average cost of construction per square meter in 1984. This information, combined with HHOUSMAT and HFLRSP, enable us to estimate the reproduction cost of residential structure for each household in 1984. Since we also know the approximate age of the structure as of November 1984, we can estimate the value of the structure net of depreciation once the rate of depreciation is given. More specifically, from the age of the structure as of November 1984, we calculate the age of the structure at the beginning of 1984, and then calculate the value of housing structure *net of* depreciation. We then depreciate the value to arrive at the value of the structure at the end of 1984. We have adapted the depreciation rate of 9 percent for this purpose, and applied the declining balance method at the constant rate of 9 percent. This estimate of 9 percent is taken from Hayashi (1986, Table 2).

B   The Size of the Land Associated with House (HLANDSIZ)
We have obtained from the published report of the Housing Survey of 1983, Table 15,[21] the joint distribution of the site size and the floor space, conditional on the physical type of the house (HHOUSETYP) for each prefecture in Japan. We imputed the mean value of the site size to each household owning a house, given their location, the type of the house and the floor space, all reported in the NSFIE.

The exception is the case of housing units located in multifloor apartment buildings. For these units, in the absence of better information, we have imputed to each apartment the site size equal to the one normally estimated for a detached house divided by the number of floors in the apartment building in question.

C   Market Value of Land (HLANDVAL)
In a set of information called *Chika-Koji* (Land Price Survey) assembled by the Bureau of Land Management, the market value per square meter of typical land as of January 1 of each year is reported for a sample of over sixteen thousand locations. The location code in the NSFIE is a five-digit code (the first two digits are designation of prefecture; the last three refer to more specific locations). Each five-digit location contains several data points sampled by *Chika Koji*, which have to be averaged for each location. This task is facilitated by a separate publication by a private publisher, which reports the average for each five-digit location.[22] After

matching these codes, we can estimate the market value of land as of January 1, 1984, and the market value as of January 1, 1985, for each household, by multiplying HLANDSIZ by this average land price for the location.

The only complication arises because some locations that appear in the NSFIE do not appear in *Chika-Koji*. In these cases, we attempted to identify locations that do appear in *Chika-Koji* and are reasonably similar to those in the NSFIE. In the end, we were able to estimate site values for all but a few hundred multi-person and a few dozen single-person households in the NSFIE. These exceptional households are all located in isolated areas like remote islands.

D   Flow of Services from Owner-Occupied Housing (YMHOUS)

The after-tax net rental-price ratio (denoted r) on housing of 1.4947 percent is obtained as follows. From p. 344 of Supporting Table 1 of the Stock section of the *1987 Annual Report on National Accounts*, we get the value of housing structure (for the whole nation) at the end of 1983 (beginning of 1984) estimated at 149.178 trillion yen, and the value of residential land at 720.965 trillion at the end of 1983. So the total housing value is 870.143 trillion. From pp. 187–88 of Supporting Table 2 of the Flow section, we get the following numbers for the real estate industry of which owner-occupied housing is a part:

gross domestic output at factor prices	29.204 trillion
minus depreciation	8.172
minus indirect tax	1.700
minus labor input	1.072
equals: net profit	18.260

Since depreciation in the Japanese National Account is at book value, a capital consumption adjustment must be applied. Since we assume the depreciation rate is 9.0 percent, the implied depreciation at market value is 0.09×149.178 trillion $= 13.426$ trillion. Thus the capital consumption adjustment is $13.426 - 8.172 = 5.254$ trillion. So net profit after capital consumption adjustment is $18.260 - 5.254 = 13.006$ trillion. The after-tax net rental-price ratio is then 1.4947 percent ($=13.006/870.143$).

For real estate owners, we treat the property tax as an indirect tax on the imputed service flow from the asset. The indirect rate (t) is calculated as follows. On p. 187 of Supporting Table 2 of the Flow section of the *1987 Annual Report on National Accounts*, the amount of indirect tax on the real estate industry is given at 1.700 trillion yen. This is divided by the value of the property of 870.143 to get $t = 0.1954$ percent.

The depreciation rate (d) is assumed to be 9 percent as previously discussed.

Gross imputed rent from owner occupied housing (YMHOUS) is then defined as

$$\text{YMHOUS} = (r + t + d) \times (\text{HSTRCVAL, beginning of 1984}) + (r + t)$$
$$\times (\text{HLANDVAL, beginning of 1984}).$$

It should be noted that, given this last formula, the real capital gain (or loss) is not included as a part of imputed income from owner-occupied housing.

3 Value of Rental Property (ARENTAL)

The income from rental properties is reported in Durables, Yearly Income, and Savings Schedule of the NSFIE. We assume that this income is gross of depreciation and property taxes. We can then trace back to the estimated value of rental properties if we know the appropriate rental-price ratio, depreciation rate, tax rate, etc. The formula for this purpose is

$$\text{ARENTAL1} = \text{YMRENT}/z,$$

$$\text{ARENTAL} = \{(1 + \text{INFLSTRC}) \times (1 - L) \times (1 - d)$$
$$+ (1 + \text{INFLLAND}) \times L\} \times \text{ARENTAL1},$$
where

$\text{ARENTAL1} = $ estimated value of rental property, beginning of 1984,

$\text{ARENTAL} = $ estimated value of rental property, end of 1984,

$\text{YMRENT} = $ gross rental income,

$z = L \times (r + t) + (1 - L) \times (r + t + d),$

$\text{INFLSTRC} = $ rate of change of the construction price index,

$\text{INFLLAND} = $ rate of change of the price of land,

$L = $ land fraction of the rental property.

Variables r, t, and d are defined above. As discussed in the previous section of this appendix, at the end of 1983 the value of housing for the nation as a whole is 870.143 trillion yen. Of that, the value of land is 720.965 trillion. So L equals 0.8286 (=720.965/870.143). For INFLSTRC, we use the GNP deflator for housing in the last quarter of 1983 and in the last quarter of 1984. They are reported on pp. 446 and 447 of Table [1]-III-1 of part 3 of the *1987 Annual Report*. For INFLLAND, we use the land price discussed in section 2.C above. Thus, INFLLAND varies across the five-digit locations, while INFLSTRC is common to the sample.

4 Personal Income Tax

For worker families, NSFIE reports earned income taxes in a daily account book and other direct taxes as a part of an item called "other taxes." But this information is difficult to use for several reasons. First, most non-worker families (and this category includes many managers and officers of corporations) do not report any information on taxes. Second, "other taxes" cannot be split among income tax on income other than earned income, real estate taxes, inheritance taxes, and others, so that we cannot construct the total income tax from the data even for those reporting taxes. Third, taxes reported are for the months of September, October, and November. While this is not likely to cause major problems for with-held earned income tax, for most other taxes the amount paid during this period is unlikely to be the full amount of the tax.

Given this situation, we have estimated approximate income tax liabilities for families by using the family's total reported income as the basic information. We have adopted this simplified procedure rather than applying the detailed tax code to individual families in estimating their income taxes partly because we do not have enough detailed information for each family to follow such a procedure, and partly because, in Japan, withheld taxes and taxes paid with returns are not integrated and it is difficult to define the effective rate of taxation applicable to a family with a given level of total income if the family has income from employment as well as from other sources.

We begin by estimating the ratio of total direct taxes reported in national income and product account to the concept of income that is available in both national income accounts and in NSFIE, and can serve as a good indicator of the tax base for individual households (in the sense of adjusted gross income; taxable income cannot be estimated from data in NSFIE because we cannot estimate exemptions and deductions applicable to each family). The concept of income used is the following:

	1984	1979
Employment Income (table 12.1a, line 31)	152.7	112.0
plus: Social Security Pension (table 12.1a, line 33)	12.7	6.9
plus: Business Income and Other Income (table 12.1a, lines 32 and 34)	43.4	36.2
plus: Gross Interest Income (table 12.1a, line 36)	24.4	13.4
plus: Dividends (table 12.1a, line 38)	4.2	2.9
minus: S.S. Contributions (table 12.1a, line 25)	11.0	7.3
equals: Tax base	226.4	164.1

Using the result of the above computation as the tax base, the overall average rate of the direct taxes paid by the household sector is given by

	1984	1979
(a) Tax Base	226.4	164.1
(b) Total Direct Taxes[23]	20.3	12.5
(c) (b)/(a)	.090	.076

We wish to have a set of approximate average rates of income tax applicable to income classes by size of income. For this purpose, we must relate our estimates to statistical information reported in the *Annual Statistical Report* of the National Tax Office.[24] From this report for 1984 and 1979, we have the following:

	1984	1979
(a) Total Personal Income Tax Withheld (p. 57, Table 3-1-(1))	11.6[25]	7.1
(b) Total Personal Income Tax Collected with Returns (p. 22, Table 2-1-(1))	2.7	2.2
(c) Total Personal Income Tax Collected (a) + (b)	14.3	9.3
(d) Tax Base (see above)	226.4	164.1
(e) (c)/(d)	.063	.057

These figures for tax collected are considerably smaller than the figures for the total direct taxes reported in national accounts, cited above. The difference is mainly due to the fact that total direct taxes include income taxes, taxes on residents, and other general income type taxes imposed by local governments on citizens. We believe that these latter types of taxes are very close to a proportional income tax in their characteristics. The only information on effective tax rates by income classes given in the *Annual Report of the National Tax Bureau* is one given in Table 3-2-(3), p. 65, and it refers to employment income of those who were employed throughout the year. Since this is the only information on effective average rates by income classes, we have no option but to assume that the pattern of average effective rates given in this table is applicable to all income of all tax payers. We therefore compute the average effective rate for each income class from this table, and then adjust them proportionately so that the overall effective rate is the one given above, namely, 6.3 percent for 1984 and 5.7 percent for 1979. We then assume that the difference between these effective rates and the effective rates of total direct taxes computed from national accounts, that is, 2.7 percent for 1984 and 1.9 percent for 1979, is due to proportional taxes imposed by localities, as argued above. The results of these manipulations are the effective tax rates shown in the schedule below; to compute income taxes we multiply these rates by taxable income, which is defined as the sum of employment income, social security pension benefits, business income, other income, gross interest income, dividends, less social security contributions (see table 12.1).

Income Class (in ten thousand yen)	Effective Average Tax Rates 1984	1979
$0 < Y \leqslant 100$	(.0072 + .027)	(.0100 + .019)
$100 < Y \leqslant 150$	(.0218 + .027)	(.0283 + .019)
$150 < Y \leqslant 200$	(.0333 + .027)	(.0361 + .019)
$200 < Y \leqslant 300$	(.0389 + .027)	(.0376 + .019)
$300 < Y \leqslant 400$	(.0403 + .027)	(.0370 + .019)
$400 < Y \leqslant 500$	(.0427 + .027)	(.0422 + .019)
$500 < Y \leqslant 800$	(.0503 + .027)	(.0569 + .019)
$800 < Y \leqslant 1000$	(.0714 + .027)	(.0583 + .019)
$1000 < Y \leqslant 2000$	(.1152 + .027)	(.1327 + .019)
$2000 < Y \leqslant 3000$	(.1632 + .027)	(.1898 + .019)
$3000 < Y \leqslant 5000$	(.2553 + .027)	(.2832 + .019)
$5000 < Y$	(.3638 + .027)	(.3858 + .019)
All	(.063 + .027)	(.057 + .019)

Comparing effective tax rates for 1979 and 1984, it is interesting to note that, before the flat rate is added, the effective average rate is higher for 1979 than for 1984 for every income bracket, but the overall effective rate turns out to be higher for 1984 than for 1979 because the distribution of nominal income shifted up between these two years.

5 Social Security Contributions: Annuity Programs

Social security programs have been undergoing major revisions during the past several years, and it is possible that the system will be further revised in response to the heavier demand resulting from the increasing proportion of retired persons in the population. This situation makes it rather difficult to judge exactly which individuals are or should be anticipating their future contributions and benefits to be. In this appendix, we confine ourselves to the estimation of the current cash flows of contributions to and benefits from the social security programs.

A Benefits

Cash flows of benefits from social security programs for the twelve-month period ending in November of the survey year are reported in the Durables, Yearly Income, and Savings Schedule of the NSFIE. We will simply accept the reported figures, since the implied aggregate seems to be more or less in line with figures detailed in National Income Account, as detailed in the next section. It should be remembered, however, that noncash benefits, especially medical services, are not recorded in the NSFIE. Since we do not have any information about health and other factors determining the size of the medical services needed by each family, we have done nothing to estimate the value of these in-kind services.

B Contributions: Annuity Programs

1984 Under the revised social security program, the annuity program for employees of private enterprise (Kosei-Nenkin) and the one for government employees (Kyosai-Nenkin) are in the process of being unified, and in 1984, contributions of employees belonging to these two types of programs have become essentially the same, although it will take some time before the benefits also become uniform. In discussing contributions, therefore, it is convenient to refer to employees belonging to the old Kosei-Nenkin and the old Kyosai-Nenkin as a single group, so we shall refer to the program covering both of them as the "employee annuity" program.

All government employees and their spouses, and employees of virtually all private enterprises and public agencies and other organizations are covered by the employees' annuity program, except those working in private enterprises employing fewer than five persons. Owners of these exempt, small private enterprises can petition to be included in the program provided that they do so with the consent of at least half or more of their employees.[26] Since we cannot identify employers with fewer than five employees in the NSFIE (the class of enterprises with the smallest number of employees identified in the NSFIE is the category of employers with 30 or fewer employees), we have no choice but to assume that all employees (including managers) are covered by the employees' annuity program. This procedure will lead to an overestimate of social security contributions.

The remaining annuity program under the old system, called *Kokumin Nenkin* (here translated as the Citizen's Annuity Program) covered all those who were not covered by the other two programs. Under the new system, the statutory principle is that everyone belongs to the citizen's annuity program, and that the employees' annuity program provides supplementary coverage for employees and their spouses. From the point of view of employees and their spouses, however, their contributions to both programs are calculated together as a percentage of their monthly wage and are deducted by employers as a single deduction, and thus it is more natural for them to view themselves as belonging to a single program, at least until they become eligible to receive benefits from these programs.[27]

Since the formula that determines the amount of contribution an individual is required to make to the social security pension program differs depending on the program to which the person belongs, the most critical issue in estimating the contribution by families in the NSFIE is the determination, for each member of the family, to which program he or she belongs. We follow the following rule for making this determination:

1. If the head of a family is employed, and between ages 20 and 60, we assume that the head and his/her spouse belong to the employees' program.

2. If the head of a family is not employed but between ages 20 and 60, then we assume that he/she and his/her spouse belong to the citizens' program.

3. All persons in the family other than the head and his/her spouse who are between ages 20 and 60 and are employed are assumed to be covered by employees' program, and to pay the standard contribution to the program.

4. If the head of the family is employed, we assume that any female in the family other than the spouse of the head, who is between ages 20 and 60 and who is not employed, is covered under the program to which the head belongs, and she does not pay independent premium.

5. If there is a second male between ages 20 and 60 in the family besides the head, and if this second male is not employed, then he pays the premium for the citizens' annuity program.

6. If the head of the family is not employed and between ages 20 and 60, then other members of the family who are between ages 20 and 60 and who are not employed all belong to the citizens' annuity program and each pays the standard contribution to the program.

This set of rules of thumb appear to leave four (and maybe more) possible cases of misclassification, but given limited information available in the NSFIE, these misclassifications cannot be eliminated. First, it may be possible that some members of the family whom we have classified as belonging to either the employees' program or the citizens' annuity program on their own may be covered under the program to which the head belongs, and hence he/she may not be paying independent premium. Second, it is possible that those who are between ages 60 and 65 and who have not completed the required number of years of contributing may be continuing to make contributions in order to bring their eventual benefits up as close as possible to the full amount. Since we do not know which individuals between ages 60 and 65 are making such contributions in the NSFIE sample, we have no option but to ignore this possibility. Third, if an individual in a household other than its head is an employee or a manager, both that person and his/her spouse should also be classified as belonging to the employees' annuity program rather than to the citizen's annuity program. However, in the NSFIE sample, except for the head of a household, we have no way of identifying precisely who is married to whom among members of the family, and hence, we have ignored this problem. Finally, as we have already discussed, there is the uncertainty associated with employees and managers of establishments with fewer than five employees.

Once an individual is identified as belonging to the citizen's annuity program, then his/her contribution is simply a fixed amount per year, and for 1984, it was ¥ = 74,000 per year. If an individual is in the employees' annuity program, his/her contribution was, in 1984, 5.3 percent of their compensation, with the minimum compensation being ¥ = 540,000 per year and the maximum ¥ = 4,920,000 per year.[28,29]

1979 For 1979, we follow the following procedure:

1. For persons employed by nongovernment employers and their spouses, we follow the same procedure as in 1984 (at that time, spouses who were not employed had a choice between being included in their employed spouse's program and belonging to the citizens' program on their own. Since we do not know which choice was made by spouses in our sample, we are assuming that they chose to be covered by their employed spouse's program. In 1979, the minimum and the maximum tax base was $Y = 360,000$ and $Y = 3,840,000$, and the contribution rate applicable to employees was 4.55 percent.[30]

2. For persons employed by governments (both national and local) and their spouses, we do not have a sufficiently detailed description of the system as it existed in 1979 to write out an approximate formula, although we know that the details varied from one local agency to another and the whole system was extremely complex.[31] Under the circumstances, we will estimate their contribution to the social insurance program as twelve times the monthly contribution to Social Security (SS) reported in the journal for these families. Note that Social Security (SS) includes medical and other social security contributions, and it covers the entire family, not any individual member.

3. For persons between ages 20 and 60 who are not students, and who are not employed except those who are spouses of employed heads of families and those who are members of families headed by government employees, we must assume that they belong to the Citizens' Annuity program. The required contribution for those belonging to the Citizens' Annuity program in 1979 was approximately $Y = 4,300$ per month, or $Y = 51,600$. This figure was estimated as follows: we know that the contribution amount for 1985 was $Y = 6,740$ per month (*Hoken to Nenkin no Doko*, 1985, vol. 32, no. 13, p. 181). We also know that it was increased by $Y = 350$ per month for four times prior to 1985 and after 1980, and adjusted for the cost of living index. Thus, $6740 - 1400$ $(= Y = 350 \times 4) = 5340$. The CPI was 92.6 for 1979 and 114.4 in 1985 (Bank of Japan, *Economic Statistics Annual*, 1985, p. 319). Thus, we have $5,340 \times 92.6/114.4 = 4,300$.

6 Social Security Program: Health Insurance

Public health insurance programs in Japan are fairly comprehensive. Their structure is quite complex, involving many alternative programs whose administrators have considerable discretion over the details of programs. For our purposes, it is impossible to estimate the value of benefits received by any household in the NSFIE sample since there is no information in the survey about either the nature of benefits provided during the period in question or any other basis for estimating the benefits. Hence, we have not made any attempt to estimate benefits from the public health insurance program, and we have let the underestimation of medical expenses in the data generated by NSFIE remain unadjusted.

Contributions, too, are impossible to estimate in any detail for individual households in the sample, and we have in the end adopted a very simple approximate rule to impute contributions by those households to the health insurance portion of the social security program. Before we come to the description of the simple rule of approximation, however, we will outline briefly the structure of health insurance programs and explain why it is not possible to do imputations taking its structure more explicitly into account.

There are two basic health insurance programs that closely parallel the two annuity programs, the employees' annuity program and the citizens' annuity program, and we will refer to them as the employees' health program and the citizens' health program.[32]

The employees' health program can be administered either by the national government, or by a cooperative. A cooperative can be established by a single employer with more than three hundred employees (in practice by an employer with more than 1,000 employees) or as a joint venture by two or more employers whose combined number of employees is three thousand or more. For those who are covered by the government administered programs, the contribution rate can be set by the Minister of Welfare within the range of 6.6 percent and 9.1 percent (these rates are the combined rate for employer and employee contributions, which are normally split equally between the two). For those who are covered by cooperative administered programs, the contribution rates can be determined by each cooperative within the range of 3 percent to 9.5 percent, with the provision that the contribution rate of the employees cannot exceed 4.5 percent. Furthermore, those cooperatives that used to belong to the Kyosai Hoken program have even greater discretion in determining the contribution rate. Thus, even within this program, it is difficult to determine the correct contribution rate for each individual in the NSFIE sample without knowing much more detailed information on their employment conditions.

For the citizens' health insurance program, the structure of an individual's contributions is even more complex. First of all, the program can be administered by the government, but this time by local governments rather than by national government, or by a cooperative of individuals linked, for example, with trade associations. Each local government has the option of financing the program by a "citizen's health insurance tax," or through the citizen's insurance fees. Substantively, two methods have very similar effects, but the former is much more rigidly controlled by legislation while the latter is only loosely regulated. The tax or contribution rate of these cases is determined by the requirement of the projected medical expenses of insured, and hence there is no simple way to relate the contribution amount or the tax payment of an individual to his or her resources.

In the case of cooperatives, the administrator of a cooperative has substantial discretion on the exact contribution rate, again depending on the projected medical expenses of the insured, and in this case the contribution is especially uncertain because each cooperative is free to define the coverage within broad limits.[33]

The above description makes it clear that it is impossible to write down any reasonable imputation formula that takes account of the detailed statutory provisions, using only the information provided in the NSFIE sample. Consequently, we have adopted a simple rule designed to approximate family contributions while insuring that the implied aggregate it generates would be more or less consistent with corresponding figures in national income and product accounts. For this purpose, we first note the following:

	1979	1984
(1) Total Employment Income (table 12.1a)	112.0	152.7
(2) Employee Contribution to Health Insurance, Employee Programs[34]	2.39	3.47
(3) = (2)/(1)	2.13%	2.27%

(3) is an underestimate of the contribution rate because the denominator of the ratio, (1), is the total compensation for all employees, while the correct ratio should include only the compensation of "covered" employees. This means that employees of enterprises with fewer than five

employees who did not apply to be covered by the system voluntarily should have been excluded. The problem is that, at least among sources to which we have access at the moment, we cannot locate information on the proportion of compensation earned by employees of firms with fewer than five employees in the total compensation.

We have supposed, as a trial figure, that the compensation of non-covered workers is roughly 15 percent of the total. This makes the employer contribution rate approximately 2.61 percent in 1984 and 2.45 percent in 1979. We do this for three reasons. (1) The employees working for firms with fewer than five employees appear to be 20 percent of the total number of workers in nonagricultural industries (Mainly Working Total under Nonagricultural Industries, *Employment Status Survey, Whole Japan*, p. 51, Statistics Bureau, Government of Japan, 1979); (2) the compensation rate of workers in smaller firms is known to be lower than the compensation rate in larger firms in Japan; (3) some workers in firms with fewer than five employees belong to the employees' health insurance program through joint application of the owner-manager and the employees. For these reasons, we have supposed, as a trial figure, that the compensation of noncovered workers is roughly 15 percent of the total. This makes the employer contribution rate approximately 2.61 percent in 1984 and 2.45 percent in 1979.

For those who are covered by the citizens' health insurance program, the contribution rate varies from one individual to another depending on the group to which the individual belongs. Since we have little information to take account of this variation, we again compute a crude approximation based on the effective rate on aggregate data. We use, as the base, the part of employee compensation that we did not include in the base of contribution to the employees' health insurance program, and add to it operating surplus (business income) of the household sector. Thus, we have

	1979	**1984**
(1) 15% × Employment Income (Table 12.1a, line 31)	16.8	22.9
(2) Business and Other Income (Table 12.1a, the sum of lines 32 and 34)	36.3	43.4
(3) =(1)+(2)	53.1	66.3
(4) Contribution to Citizen's Health Insurance Program[35]	1.17	1.78
(5) (4)/(3)	2.2%	2.7%

We thus take 2.7 percent of the sum of the four components of yearly income reported, income from employment, income from agriculture, income from business other than agriculture, and income from homework, as our estimate of contribution to the citizens' health insurance program for 1984. The same procedure, with the contribution rate of 2.2 percent, is applied to 1979 data. In the case of citizens' health insurance, the contribution is computed for each member of the household separately for all members of the household except those who are younger than 20 or older than 59, and students.

It should be noted that, for 1979, we have followed a procedure in which the total contribution to the social insurance, including contribution to health insurance, of a household whose head is employed by government is directly taken from diary data. Therefore, for 1979, for households headed by a government worker, these imputation formulas do not apply.

It turns out that the implied aggregate total contribution to all medical insurance programs comes quite close to the figure reported in the national account.

7   Converting Monthly Averages into Annual Rates

The National Survey collects expenditure data through diaries and monthly average expenditures. We convert monthly averages into annual rates using the seasonality factors reported in the *1984 Annual Report on the Family Income and Expenditure Survey*. This is done for each of the expenditure components 16 through 23, and 25, displayed in table 12.1a of this chapter.

8   Calculation of Imputed Interest and Dividend Income

The November segment of the survey collects information on annual income components. One of the components is the sum of interest income and dividend income. As a proportion of total reported income, the sum is very small compared to the proportion reported in the NIA. Also, quite a few households report zero interest plus dividend income even though they hold interest-bearing assets and stocks. Because of this severe underreporting, we decided to impute interest and dividend income separately for the family as a whole from the data on its portfolio, in the following fashion.

Interest Receipts
refer to estimated family *gross* interest income that can be inferred from the raw data on assets in the savings schedule. In ten thousand yen. The formula is

0.0575 × ATDPO (2+-year postal time deposits rate 1/18/82–1/4/84)
+ 0.0288 × ADDPO (postal demand deposits rate since 1/4/84)
+ 0.0575 × ATDBANK (1-year time deposits rate 1/18/82–1/4/84)
+ 0.015 × ADDBANK (demand deposits rate since 1/4/84)
+ 0.062 × ALIFINS (2-year loan trust rate 1/21/82–1/6/84)
+ 0.062 × ASECTRST (same)
+ 0.062 × ASECBOND (same)
+ 0.0575 × AOTHFIN (same for ATDBANK).

(Source: Bank of Japan, *Economic Statistics Monthly*, December 1984, pp. 109–10.)

Here,

ATDPO is time deposits at the postal savings system,
ADDPO is demand deposits at the postal savings system,
ATDBANK is time deposits at banks,
ADDBANK is demand deposits at banks,
ALIFINS is actuarial value of life insurance,
ASECTRST is the value of investment in trust funds,
ASECBOND is (the face value of) bonds, and
AOTHFIN is other financial assets that includes deposits with the employer.

Interest Payments
refer to estimated family interest *payments* that can be inferred from the raw data on assets in the savings schedule. In ten thousand yen. The formula is

0.0792 × LLH (housing loan rate, 4/23/84)
+ (0.0792 + 0.06) × (LOTHLH + LOUTBAL) (the 6% is the estimated gap between mortgage rate and consumer credit rate)

(Source: Bank of Japan, *Economic Statistics Monthly*, December 1984, pp. 109–10.)

Here,

LLH is liabilities for purchasing houses (mortgage loan balance),
LOTHLH is other liabilities, and
LOUTBAL is installment debts.

Dividend Income
imputed family dividend income that can be inferred from the raw data on
assets in the savings schedule. In ten thousand yen. The formula is
$0.0102 \times$ ASECSTCK, where ASECSTCK is the market value of stocks
held, and 0.0102 is the dividend-price ratio in November 1984 (Source:
Bank of Japan, *Economic Statistics Monthly*, December 1984, p. 123).

9 Disposable Income, Consumption, and Wealth

Disposable income is defined by the following steps. Unless otherwise
indicated in square brackets, all components are directly available from
the survey tape.

pretax gross annual income (YGROSS)

= employment income
+ business income (income from agriculture, nonagriculture
   business, and homework)
+ pension income
+ income from rental properties
+ other income
+ income in kind (e.g., home-grown food, gift in goods)
+ imputed interest receipts [see section 8]
+ imputed interest payments [see section 8]
+ imputed dividend income [see section 8]
+ gross imputed rent from owner-occupied housing [YMHOUS
   in section 2.D]

disposable income (YDINIA)

= YGROSS
− income tax [see section 3]
− social security contribution: annuity programs [see section 5]
− social security contribution: health insurance [see section 6]
− depreciation on owner-occupied housing and rental properties
   [$d \times$ {HSTRCVAL at the beginning of $1984 + (1 - L) \times$ ARENTAL1}
   in sections 2 and 3]

- estimated property tax on owner-occupied housing and rental
  properties [t × {HLANDVAL at the beginning of 1984
  + HSTRCVAL at the beginning of 1984 + ARENTAL1}
  in sections 2 and 3]

consumption (CONSNIA)

= annualized flow of cash monthly expenditure (which includes
  income in kind but excludes repairs and additions to owner-
  occupied housing *and* excludes regular remittance to outside the
  household) [see section 7]
+ gross imputed rent from owner-occupied housing [YMHOUS
  in section 2.C]

economic disposable income (YDIEC)

= YDINIA
+ net service flow from consumer durables [rcd × DVALTOT in
  section 1]

It should be emphasized here that we do not include remittance from outside the household as part of income.

economic consumption (CONSEC)

= CONSNIA
- annualized flow of monthly expenditure on durables [see section 7]
+ net service flow from consumer durables [rcd × DVALTOT in
  section 2.C]
+ depreciation on consumer durables [DDEPRTOT in section 1]

Since we obviously cannot attribute to each individual household either
the medical transfers from the government or the employer contribution
to social security, our consumption measure still does not include the
government medical transfer and our pretax gross disposable income still
does not include the employer contribution.

There is one sticking point concerning capital gains. The nominal rate
of increase of the residential land price between January 1, 1984 and
January 1, 1985 is about 2.2 percent on average. The inflation rate from
the last quarter of 1983 to the last quarter of 1984 as measured by the
price deflator for consumption expenditure is 2.374 percent (see the *1987
Annual Report on National Accounts*). Thus, during 1984, there was no net
capital gains on land, which means that the real net rate of return on land

during 1984 was not much different from the extremely low rental-price ratio of 1.4947 percent. During 1984 land prices did not go up by as much as expected. To the extent people expect capital gains on land and base their savings decision on it, our measure of disposable income that does not incorporate capital gains is inappropriate. This is more so for dividend income, which we estimate as the dividend-price ratio times the value of the stock. Since the return on Japanese stocks is almost all in the form of capital gains, the expected capital gains on stocks should be included in income as they influence people's savings behavior. Therefore, we create another version of disposable income that does include expected capital gains on land and stocks:

disposable income with capital gains (YDINIA2)

= YDINIA

+ 0.08 × (HLANDVAL at the end of 1984)

+ 0.08 × (value of stocks reported in the survey)

− 0.02374 × (value of total wealth, the sum of net financial assets
   and the value of housing and the value of rental properties).

In this definition, we take the expected nominal rate of capital gains for land and stocks ⸙ be 8 percent. The last line in the definition is to account for the capital losses due to inflation. As mentioned above, the inflation rate for 1984 was 2.374 percent. This amounts to assuming that the expected real rate of total return is 8 percent + 1.4947 percent − 2.374 percent per year for land and 8 percent + 1.02 percent − 2.374 percent for stocks (where 1.4947% is the rent-land price ratio and 1.02% is the dividend-stock price ratio). The reason we do not use beginning of the year values as the base for the rate of return is that we do not have such information for stocks (recall that the values of financial assets and liabilities are as of November 1984).

Finally, the definition of wealth is displayed below.

wealth (AALLWOCD)

= net financial assets (ADDBANK + ADDPO + ATDBANK + ATDPO
+ ALIFINS + ASECTRST + ASECBOND + AOTHFIN − LLH
− LOTHLH − LOUTBAL)

+ value of housing (HLANDVAL + HSTRCVAL at the end of 1984)

+ value of rental properties owned (ARENTAL).

10 Sample Selection: Elimination of "Bad" Data

For all of the analysis performed, we have used a subset of the original NSFIE data. We have eliminated a number of observations because of missing or bad data. Below we review the methods we used to decide which were "good" observations.

Flags
The NSFIE data contained a number of "special flag" variables. These flags were created by the Statistics Bureau to inform users of the data that some part of the observations were missing. We used only those observations for which all of the flags indicated complete data.

Data Consistency
In a number of cases we noticed that some data seemed inconsistent. For example, one variable that was supposed to be the sum of a set of component variables didn't equal that sum. Most of these cases were caught using the flag checks above. For completeness, however, we only used observations that passed these consistency checks.

Land Value
Because of the importance of housing value in total assets we wanted to use only those observations where, if the household owned their home, we had been able to successfully estimate the value of their house, as explained above. For a few cases we were unable to do this and we did not use those observations.

Number of Observations (1984 data)

	MULTI	SIMUL	BOTH
TOTAL	50864	4086	54950
After flag check	47407	3868	51275
After consist check	47407	3868	51275
After Land Value check	46609	3835	50444
After eliminating farmers	42201	3784	45985

Appendix 12.2: Derivation of the Comparison Accounts

Introduction

To match up the implied aggregates and the numbers in the National Accounts we must make sure they have the same definition. It is, however, impossible to start from the items in the National Survey of Family Income and Expenditure data (hereafter the NSFIE) to construct variables having the same definition employed in the National Income Accounting. For example, EMPLOYMENT INCOME in the National Accounts includes EMPLOYER CONTRIBUTION TO SOCIAL SECURITY. Since the NSFIE does not record that item, it is impossible to construct from the NSFIE employment income as defined in the National Accounts. Since this item is also counted in SOCIAL SECURITY CONTRIBUTION in the National Accounts, calculated disposable income is not affected by the inclusion/exclusion of this item. As another example, GOVERNMENT MEDICAL TRANSFERS are included in both DISPOSABLE INCOME and CONSUMPTION EXPENDITURE. Failure to take government medical transfers (which is about 6% of disposable income) into account therefore leads to overestimation of saving.

On the other hand, it is also impossible to construct the NSFIE items from the National Accounts. This is because for some income and asset components the NSFIE employs a finer classification. Therefore, we set up comparison accounts that can be constructed from both the NSFIE or the National Accounts. The transition from the National Accounts to the Comparison Accounts is more involved than the transition from the NSFIE.

The Comparison Account: Balance Sheet

entry #	assets	entry #	liabilities
1.	housing	11.	total liabilities
2.	consumer durables		
3.	financial assets		
4.	currency		
5.	demand deposits		
6.	other deposits		
7.	bonds		
8.	stocks		
9.	life insurance		
10.	other assets		

The Comparison Account: Income and Expenditure

entry #	expenditure	entry #	income
12.	cons. expenditure (sum of 13 and 22)	30.	income category (i)
		31.	employment income
13.	cash expenditure (sum of 16–23)	32.	business income + rental income
14.	food and tobacco	33.	pension income
15.	clothes and footware	34.	other income
16.	rent and utilities	35.	income category (ii)
17.	furniture	36.	gross interest income
18.	medical	37.	(−) interest payment
19.	transportation and communication	38.	dividends
		39.	income category (iii)
20.	recreation and education	40.	net imputed rent
21.	other		
22.	grossimputed rent		
23.	(durables expenditure)		
24.	income tax		
25.	social security cont.		
26.	pension		
27.	medical insurance		
28.	net saving		
29.	total disbursements (sum of 12, 24, 25, 28)	41.	total income (sum of 30, 35, 39)
		42.	disposable income (41 minus 24 minus 25)
		43.	savings rate (ratio of 28 to 42)

Derivation from the National Accounts: Balance Sheet Items

Derivation of the Balance Sheet items from the National Income Accounts is relatively straightforward. All the tables in the National Accounts refer to those in the *1987 Annual Report on National Accounts*.

entry #	derivation from the National Accounts
1.	VALUE OF LAND OF HOUSEHOLDS: Part 2, Table II-5, line 3(1).
	plus $x1 \times (x2/x3)$, where
	$x1 =$ VALUE OF HOUSING STRUCTURE OF THE ENTIRE NATION: Part 2, Table III-1, line $1(2)\langle 1\rangle$,
	$x2 =$ VALUE OF LAND OF HOUSEHOLDS: Part 2, Table II-5, line 3(1),
	$x3 =$ RESIDENTIAL LAND OF THE ENTIRE NATION: Part 2, Table III-1, line $1(3)\langle 1\rangle$(a).
2.	TOTAL CONSUMER DURABLES: Part 2, Table IV-2, line below line 5.
4.	CURRENCY: Part 2, Table II-5, line 4(1).
5.	DEMAND DEPOSITS: Part 2, Table II-5, line 4(2).
6.	OTHER DEPOSITS: Part 2, Table II-5, line 4(3).
7.	BONDS: Part 2, Table II-5, line 4(4).
8.	STOCKS: Part 2, Table II-5, line 4(5).
9.	LIFE INSURANCE: Part 2, Table II-5, line 4(6).
10.	OTHER FINANCIAL ASSETS: Part 2, Table II-5, line 4(7).
11.	TOTAL LIABILITIES: Part 2, Table II-5, line 5.

Derivation from the National Accounts: Income and Expenditure

For the income and expenditure items, the derivation from the National Accounts is more involved for the following reasons:

i. EMPLOYMENT INCOME in the Income and Expenditure Account in the National Accounts includes *employer contribution to social security (pension and national health insurance)*, which is included in SOCIAL SECURITY CONTRIBUTION by the household sector.

ii. BUSINESS INCOME includes *imputed rent from owner occupied housing* while *interest payments for housing loans* are deducted. It is not possible from the *Annual Report* to distinguish imputed rent from owner-occupied housing from rent from rental properties. Therefore imputed rent (see *y2* below) includes rent from rental properties as well.

iii. INTEREST PAYMENTS therefore do not include *interest payments for housing loans*.

iv. MEDICAL EXPENDITURE and DISPOSABLE INCOME include *transfer payments from the national health insurance*.

v. SOCIAL SECURITY BENEFITS includes many items (e.g., unemployment insurance) that are neither pension benefits nor transfer payments from the national health insurance. SOCIAL SECURITY CONTRIBUTION also includes payments other than for pension and health insurance.

vi. DEPRECIATION in the Japanese National Accounts is at historical values. Since depreciation on owner occupied housing we imputed for the micro data set is at replacement costs, we need a corresponding figure for the National Accounts. To be consistent with this treatment of imputed rent, we perform capital consumption adjustment on BUSINESS INCOME in the National Accounts, and assume that business income reported in the NSFIE is net of depreciation at replacement costs. Of course this requires an estimate of replacement cost depreciation for the household sector and its breakdown between housing and other assets, which are available from Hayashi (1986). See $y8$, $y9$, $y10$ and $y11$ below.

We must "undo" these transformations in the National Accounts to arrive at the Comparison Accounts. To facilitate the explanation of the derivation, we first define the following items that are involved in the above transformation:

$y1$ = EMPLOYER CONTRIBUTION TO SOCIAL SECURITY
PENSION AND NATIONAL HEALTH: Part 1-[3], Table 10, line below line 6(2).

$y2$ = IMPUTED RENT FROM OWNER OCCUPIED HOUSING
(including cash rents from rental properties):
$(r + t) \times$ {VALUE OF LAND OF HOUSEHOLDS: Part 2, Table II-5, line 3(1)}
plus $(r + d + t) \times \{x1 \times (x2/x3)\}$,
where
$r =$ after-tax net rental-price ratio on real estate,
$d =$ depreciation rate,
$t =$ indirect tax rate on real estate.
(For the values of r, d, and t, see section 2 of appendix 12.1. For $x1$, $x2$ and $x3$, see item 1 above.)

$y3$ = INTEREST PAYMENT FOR HOUSING LOANS:
$i \times$ HOUSING LOANS FOR THE HOUSEHOLD SECTOR,
where $i =$ nominal interest rate on housing loans (obtained from Bank of Japan, *Economic Statistics Monthly*, see section 8 of appendix 12.1 for the exact source and the value for the interest rate),

HOUSING LOANS FOR THE HOUSEHOLD SECTOR is obtainable from Part 2, Table IV-4(2), below line 5, total of housing loans (this is 73.992 trillion for 1984).

$y4$ = TRANSFER PAYMENTS FROM NATIONAL HEALTH INSURANCE:

        Part 1-[3], Table 9, line 1(1)$\langle 1 \rangle a$

plus Part 1-[3], Table 9, line 1(1)$\langle 4 \rangle a$

plus Part 1-[3], Table 9, line 1(2)

plus Part 1-[3], Table 9, line 1(3)

plus Part 1-[3], Table 9, line 1(4)$\langle 1 \rangle a$

plus Part 1-[3], Table 9, line 1(4)$\langle 2 \rangle a$

plus Part 1-[3], Table 9, line 1(4)$\langle 3 \rangle a$

plus Part 1-[3], Table 9, line 1(4)$\langle 4 \rangle a$

plus Part 1-[3], Table 9, line 1(5).

$y5$ = PENSION BENEFITS:

        Part 1-[3], Table 9, line 1(1)$\langle 1 \rangle b$

plus Part 1-[3], Table 9, line 1(1)$\langle 2 \rangle$

plus Part 1-[3], Table 9, line 1(1)$\langle 4 \rangle b$

plus Part 1-[3], Table 9, line 1(4)$\langle 1 \rangle b$

plus Part 1-[3], Table 9, line 1(4)$\langle 2 \rangle b$

plus Part 1-[3], Table 9, line 1(4)$\langle 3 \rangle b$

plus Part 1-[3], Table 9, line 1(4)$\langle 4 \rangle b$

plus Part 1-[3], Table 9, line 2, veterans's annuity.

$y6$ = NONPENSION, NONHEALTH INSURANCE PREMIUM PART OF THE SOCIAL SECURITY CONTRIBUTION PAID BY THE EMPLOYEE:

        Part 1-[3], Table 10, line 1(3), employees

plus Part 1-[3], Table 10, line 1(4)c, employees

plus Part 1-[3], Table 10, line 1(4)d, employees

plus Part 1-[3], Table 10, line 5, employees

plus Part 1-[3], Table 10, line 6, employees

plus Part 1-[2], Table II-5, line 6, employees

minus Part 1-[3], Table 10, total for social security contribution.

$y7$ = PENSION COMPONENT OF SOCIAL SECURITY CONTRIBUTION BY THE EMPLOYEE, equals:

        Part 1-[3], Table 10, line 1(1)a, employees

plus Part 1-[3], Table 10, line 1(4)a, employees

plus Part 1-[3], Table 10, line 2, employees,

plus   Part 1-[3], Table 10, line 3(1)b, employees,
plus   Part 1-[3], Table 10, line 3(2)b, employees,
plus   Part 1-[3], Table 10, line 3(3)b, employees,
plus   Part 1-[3], Table 10, line 3(4)b, employees,
plus   Part 1-[3], Table 10, line 4.

$y8$ = DEPRECIATION: Part 1-[2], Table III-5, line 6.

$y9$ = DEPRECIATION ON PRIVATE HOUSING: Part 1-[3], Table 17, line 1(1).

$y10$ = DEPRECIATION FOR THE HOUSEHOLD SECTOR AT REPLACEMENT COSTS (source: Hayashi (1986, Table A2)).

$y11$ = DEPRECIATION ON STRUCTURES, equals:
value of housing structure ($x1 \times x2/x3$ in the definition of item 1 above) times d (depreciation rate). (See section 2 of appendix 12.1 for the calculation of d.)

Using this notation, the derivation of the Comparison Income/Expenditure items from the National Accounts is as follows.

entry #	derivation from the National Accounts
12.	sum of 13 and 22, should equal: TOTAL CONSUMPTION EXPENDITURE: Part 1-[2], Table II-5, line 1
minus	**y4**.
14.	FOOD, BEVERAGE, AND TOBACCO: Part 1-[3], Table 13, line 1.
15.	CLOTHES AND FOOTWARES: Part 1-[3], Table 13, line 2.
16.	RENT AND UTILITIES: Part 1-[3], Table 13, line 3.
minus	**y2**.
17.	FURNITURE, HOUSEHOLD APPLIANCES: Part 1-[3], Table 13, line 4.
18.	MEDICAL: Part 1-[3], Table 13, line 5
minus	**y4**.
19.	TRANSPORTATION & COMMUNICATION: Part 1-[3], Table 13, line 6.
20.	RECREATION: Part 1-[3], Table 13, line 7.
21.	OTHER: Part 1-[3], Table 13, line 8.
plus	TOTAL CONSUMPTION EXPENDITURE: Part 1-[2], Table II-5, line 1

	minus	TOTAL CONSUMPTION EXPENDITURE: Part 1-[3], Table 13, line below line 8
22.		**y2**
23.		DURABLES: Part 1-[3], Table 12, line 1.
24.		INCOME TAX: Part 1-[2], Table II-5, line 4(1).
25.		SOCIAL SECURITY CONTRIBUTION: Part 1-[2], Table II-5, line 6
	minus	**y1**
	minus	**y6**.
26.		25–27.
27.		**y7**.
28.		NET SAVING: Part 1-[2], Table II-5, line 10
	plus	**y8**
	minus	**y10**.
31.		EMPLOYMENT INCOME: Part 1-[2], Table II-5, line 11
	minus	**y1**.
32.		BUSINESS INCOME: Part 1-[2], Table II-5, line 12
	minus	**y2**
	plus	**y3**
	plus	**(y8−y9)**
	minus	**(y10−y11)**.
	plus	RENTAL INCOME: Part 1-[2], Table II-5, line 13(3)
	minus	RENTAL PAYMENTS: Part 1-[2], Table II-5, line 2(3).
33.		**y5**.
34.		residual, should equal: LIABILITY INSURANCE PAYMENTS: Part 1-[2], Table II-5, line 14
	plus	SOCIAL SECURITY BENEFITS: Part 1-[2], Table II-5, line 15
	plus	"SOCIAL HELP MONEY": Part 1-[2], Table II-5, line 16
	plus	"UNFUNDED EMPLOYMENT WELFARE": Part 1-[2], Table II-5, line 17
	plus	OTHER TRANSFERS RECEIPTS: Part 1-[2], Table II-5, line 18
	minus	LIABILITY INSURANCE PREMIUMS: Part 1-[2], Table II-5, line 3
	minus	OTHER TAXES: Part 1-[2], Table II-5, line 4(2)

	minus	PENALTIES AND FEES: Part 1-[2], Table II-5, line 5

minus PENALTIES AND FEES: Part 1-[2], Table II-5, line 5
minus TRANSFERS TO PRIVATE NONPROFIT
       INSTITUTIONS: Part 1-[2], Table II-5, line 7
minus CONTRIBUTIONS TO "UNFUNDED EMPLOY-
       MENT WELFARE": Part 1-[2], Table II-5, line 8
minus OTHER TRANSFER PAYMENTS: Part 1-[2],
       Table II-5, line 9
minus **y4**
minus **y5**
minus **y6**
plus   **y9**
plus $[t/(r + t)] \times ($**y2**−**y11**$)$.

36.   INTEREST INCOME: Part 1-[2], Table II-5, line 13(1).
37.   INTEREST PAYMENT ON CONSUMER LOANS:
      Part 1-[2], Table II-5, line 2(1)
plus INTEREST PAYMENT ON OTHER LOANS:
      Part 1-[2], Table II-5, line 2(2)
plus **y3**.
38.   DIVIDEND INCOME: Part 1-[2], Table II-5, line
      13(2).
40. $[r/(r + t)] \times ($**y2**−**y11**$)$.

Derivation from the NSFIE

The derivation is straightforward, but the way the balance sheet and income and expenditure items in the NSFIE are distributed in the comparison accounts involves some degree of arbitrariness which cannot be avoided. Below, the NSFIE items in capital letters are defined and described in appendix 12.1. Other NSFIE items, which are not in capital letters, are directly available from the tape.

To arrive at implied aggregates from the NSFIE, we take the sample means weighted by the regional sampling ratios for two-or-more-person households and for singles, multiply them by an estimate of the number of households for each of the two household types, and then add the two. For the population estimate of the number of households, we use the ones in the *Basic Survey for Welfare Administration, 1984* (Ministry of Health and Welfare). The estimated number of two-or-more person households is 30.095 million and that for singles is 7.243 million.

entry #		derivation from the NSFIE
1.		MARKET VALUE OF LAND (for homeowners)
	plus	VALUE OF HOUSING STRUCTURE (for homeowners)
	plus	VALUE OF RENTAL PROPERTY.
2.		TOTAL MARKET VALUE OF THE STOCK OF DURABLE GOODS IN EXISTENCE AT THE END OF 1984.
4.		not available in the NSFIE.
5.		demand deposits at banks and at the postal savings system.
6.		time deposits at banks and at the postal savings system.
7.		bonds and bond mutual funds
	plus	loan trust and money trust.
8.		stocks
9.		life insurance
10.		deposits with the employer and other deposits.
11.		liabilities for purchasing houses and land
	plus	liabilities other than for housing and land purchases
	plus	outstanding value of monthly and yearly installments.
14.		food expenditure
	minus	restaurant expenditure
	plus	expenditure on tobacco.
15.		clothes and footware.
16.		rent for structure and land
	plus	utilities.
17.		furniture.
18.		medical.
19.		transportation and communications.
20.		education
	plus	reading and recreation.
21.		other living expenditure
	minus	tobacco
	plus	restaurant expenditures
	minus	regular remittance to others.
22.		FLOW OF SERVICES FROM OWNER OCCUPIED HOUSING.
23.		expenditures on durables.

24.		PERSONAL TAXES.
26.		SOCIAL SECURITY CONTRIBUTIONS: ANNUITY PROGRAM.
27.		SOCIAL SECURITY CONTRIBUTIONS: HEALTH INSURANCE.
28.		(This is the residual item.)
31.		employment income.
32.		income from agriculture and fishery
	plus	income from business other than agriculture and fishery
	plus	income from homework.
	plus	income from rental properties
	minus	DEPRECIATION ON RENTAL PROPERTIES
	minus	ESTIMATED PROPERTY TAX ON RENTAL PROPERTIES.
33.		pension income.
34.		other income
	plus	family income in kind.
36.		INTEREST RECEIPTS.
37.		INTEREST PAYMENTS.
38.		DIVIDEND INCOME.
40.		IMPUTED RENT FROM OWNER OCCUPIED HOUSING
	minus	DEPRECIATION ON OWNER OCCUPIED HOUSING
	minus	ESTIMATED PROPERTY TAX ON OWNER OCCUPIED HOUSING.

Appendix 12.3: Table 12.3 with Data Adjusted for Under/ Over-Reporting

In this appendix we report the results for table 12.3 when assets/liabilities, imputed income tax, imputed social security, and asset income imputed from assets/liabilities are all adjusted to match the underestimate ratio of 86 percent for cash income and expenditure. A description of this adjustment process is in section 12.2.4. Of the items reported in table 12.3 of the text, only the cross-section growth rate of wealth and the wealth growth rate along with disposable income and consumption expenditure are reported here, because those are the variables that form the basis of the

Table 12.A1
Age Profile of Income, Expenditure, and Asset Holdings by Family Type

Panel A: Nuclear (includes singles)

	25–29	30–34	35–39	40–44	45–49	50–54	55–59	60–64	65–69	70–74	75–79	80–84	85+	All
# households	3676	5061	5909	5538	4880	3667	2571	2013	1570	1144	599	159	37	36823
Family size	1.9	3.2	3.7	3.8	3.6	3.0	2.2	1.7	1.6	1.6	1.5	1.5	1.5	3.0
Disposable income	273	341	391	453	515	542	499	389	319	277	235	208	176	410
Consumption expenditure	246	310	350	387	424	408	372	294	242	216	191	180	167	341
Saving rate (%)	10	9	11	15	18	25	25	25	24	22	19	14	5	17
Net financial assets	190	176	120	237	507	848	1312	1511	1438	1280	1180	1328	811	551
Wealth	410	860	1304	1876	2445	2857	3450	3601	3547	3211	2943	2789	2089	2010
Cross-section growth rate (%)		14.8	8.3	7.3	5.3	3.1	3.8	0.9	−0.3	−2.0	−1.7	−1.1	−5.8	
Wealth growth rate (%)	6.7	3.6	3.2	3.5	3.7	4.7	3.7	2.7	2.2	1.9	1.5	1.0	0.4	

Panel B: Extended

	25–29	30–34	35–39	40–44	45–49	50–54	55–59	60–64	65–69	70–74	75–79	80–84	85+	All
# households	933	1309	1867	1703	1385	900	416	159	40	5	0	0	0	8717
Family size	4.0	5.2	5.5	5.4	5.1	4.4	3.6	3.1	2.9	3.0	n.a.	n.a.	n.a.	4.9
Disposable income	606	560	572	589	629	658	666	565	445	390	n.a.	n.a.	n.a.	599
Consumption expenditure	458	432	449	479	495	504	634	499	479	287	n.a.	n.a.	n.a.	476
Saving rate (%)	25	23	21	19	21	23	5	12	−8	26	n.a.	n.a.	n.a.	21
Net financial assets	1024	808	914	876	1088	1270	2142	2189	1607	1777	n.a.	n.a.	n.a.	1052
Wealth	3585	3267	3796	3851	4200	4434	5177	5349	4277	4479	n.a.	n.a.	n.a.	3932
Cross-section growth rate (%)		−1.9	3.0	0.3	1.7	1.1	3.1	0.7	−4.5	0.9	n.a.	n.a.	n.a.	
Wealth growth rate (%)	4.1	3.9	3.2	2.9	3.2	3.5	0.6	1.2	−0.8	2.3	n.a.	n.a.	n.a.	

Panel C: Extended Minus Nuclear

	25–29	30–34	35–39	40–44	45–49	50–54	55–59	60–64	65–69	70–74	75–79	80–84	85+	All
Disposable income	333	220	181	137	114	116	167	175	126	113	n.a.	n.a.	n.a.	188
Consumption expenditure	212	122	99	92	71	96	262	206	237	71	n.a.	n.a.	n.a.	135
Saving rate (%)	36	44	45	33	38	17	−57	−17	−89	37	n.a.	n.a.	n.a.	29
Net financial assets	834	632	795	639	581	421	830	678	168	497	n.a.	n.a.	n.a.	502
Wealth	3175	2407	2492	1975	1755	1577	1726	1748	730	1268	n.a.	n.a.	n.a.	1922
Cross-section growth rate (%)		−4.6	0.9	−5.4	−3.5	−3.0	2.9	0.3	−46.4	38.0	n.a.	n.a.	n.a.	
Wealth growth rate (%)	3.8	4.0	3.3	2.3	2.4	1.3	−5.5	−1.7	−15.3	3.3	n.a.	n.a.	n.a.	

Table 12A.2
Age Profile of Income for the Aged by Family Type

Panel A: Nuclear

	60–64	65–69	70–74	75–79	80–84	85+	All
# households	2013	1570	1144	599	159	37	5521
Disposable income	389	319	277	235	208	176	323
Consumption expenditure	294	242	216	191	180	167	247
Saving rate (%)	25	24	22	19	14	5	23
Net financial assets	1511	1438	1280	1180	1328	811	1397
Wealth	3601	3547	3211	2943	2789	2089	3400
Cross-section growth rate (%)		−0.3	−2.0	−1.7	−1.1	−5.8	
Wealth growth rate (%)	2.7	2.2	1.9	1.5	1.0	0.4	

Panel B: Extended by Age of Parents

	60–64	65–69	70–74	75–79	80–84	85+	All
# households	1351	1572	1852	1352	816	394	7337
Disposable income	589	586	597	614	604	580	596
Consumption expenditure	443	461	476	480	464	463	465
Saving rate (%)	25	21	20	22	23	20	22
Net financial assets	924	940	1014	1092	1370	1553	1064
Wealth	3710	3788	3926	4270	4216	4327	3974
Cross-section growth rate (5)		0.4	0.7	1.7	−0.3	0.5	
Wealth growth rate (%)							

Panel D: Singles

	60–64	65–69	70–74	75–79	80–84	85+	All
# households	276	228	194	118	30	7	853
Disposable income	180	160	145	125	138	92	157
Consumption expenditure	177	149	146	138	139	108	155
Saving rate (%)	2	7	−1	−11	−1	−18	1
Net financial assets	796	690	667	565	1266	209	718
Wealth	1956	1919	1860	1678	2288	876	1889
Cross-section growth rate (%)		−0.4	−0.6	−2.1	6.2	−19.2	
Wealth growth rate (%)	0.2	0.6	−0.1	−0.8	−0.0	−1.9	

discussion in section 12.3. Hence adjusted numbers for the items shown in panel C of Table 12.3c are not shown here.

Notes

This is an expanded version of sections 1–3 of Hayashi, Ando, and Ferris (1988).

1. For a concise summary of results from the survey, see "Survey of Consumer Finances, 1983," *Federal Reserve Bulletin* (September 1984): 679–92, and "Financial Characteristics of High-Income Families", *Federal Reserve Bulletin* (March 1986): 163–77.

2. In the NSFIE, singles are sampled about 2.7 times less often than two-or-more-person families. When we integrate singles into nuclear families in the next section, we will give a weight of 2.7 to singles observations.

3. In the calculation for table 12.1a, we decided to drop farmers from the NSFIE sample. This is because we do not have any information on the market value of farmland detailed enough to be matched with the five-digit location code in the NSFIE. When we used the residential land price, the implied aggregate value of farmland turned out to be about thirty times the value reported in the Japanese National Income Accounts. To the extend that income, expenditure, and assets for farmers do not differ from those for the rest of the population, the numbers reported in column (2) of table 12.1a should agree with those in column (1). Before the 1984 survey, the NSFIE did not cover farmers.

4. The reason item 40 (net imputed rent) is less severely overestimated relative to item 1 is that rental income from rental properties in the NSFIE, being directly observable, is included in item 32, while the imputed rent in column (1) for the NIA includes cash rental income from rental properties owned. (The NIA has no separate listing of imputed rent proper). This also explains the overestimate by the NSFIE of item 16, and partly explains why item 32 (business income plus rental income) is overestimated, but probably more important is the fact that the division of income between employment income and business income may differ between the NIA and the NSFIE.

5. This survey also has data on asset and liabilities, but the information was based on completed questionnaires that were mailed to the respondents in advance, which caused a number of nonresponses. The income data was collected by having interviewers actually visit the households. Results of the 1986 survey are contained in *Kokumin Seikatsu Kiso Chousa no Gaikyo*, a Ministry of Health and Welfare publication.

6. If there are no private annuities market, then the consumer under lieftime uncertainty values the stream of prearranged annuity (e.g., social security benefits and fixed labor income) using simple discounting. Thus the value of annuity wealth for a retired consumer does not decline with age if the flow value of annuities conditional on the consumer being alive does not depend on age. See Bernheim (1986) for a formal argument.

7. To anticipate, we will argue that whether wealth declines with age may not have any direct relation with the question of whether older families dissave when there are significant intergenerational transfers.

8. Disposable income includes net imputed rent from owner-occupied housing and consumption includes gross imputed rent from owner-occupied housing. Service flows from consumer durables are not included in income or consumption. Wealth therefore excludes the stock of consumer durables. Thus, except for our failure to include government medical transfers in

income and consumption, our income and expenditure measures are strictly comparable to those in the national accounts. Since government medical transfers are included neither in expenditure nor in disposable income, our savings measure is strictly comparable to that in the national accounts. A receptive reader may anticipate that this formula will be modified later on. The modification is independent of the treatment of capital gains. See section 12.3.5.

9. See, for example, the Bank of Japan's *Economic Statistics Annual 1987*, p. 331.

10. This estimate implicitly assumes the unitary elasticity of wealth holding with respect to permanent income in that the percentage difference in average wealth between *cohorts* equals the percentage difference in average permanent income between the same cohorts. This is consistent with the situation where the wealth–permanent income ratio differs across persons *within the same cohort.*

11. As mentioned in section 12.2, income can be broken down between generations in the extended family.

12. Here, the cohort adjustment (adjustment for differences in wealth) by permanent income does assume that the wealth–permanent income ratio is constant *across individuals in the same cohort* (which consists of "winners" in the pool of the independent old and "losers" in the pool of the dependent old). This assumption of unitary elasticity of wealth with respect to permanent income within the cohort for older cohorts must be true if people have no bequest motives. If the elasticity is different from unity, then the correct cohort adjustment in (3.5) times the elasticity of wealth holdings with respect to permanent income.

13. The younger generation's income (as defined by the sum of employment income and business income) in extended families is lower than that for the nuclear families in the same age brackets. For example, for the 35–39 age bracket, employment income is 382 ten thousand yen for nuclear and 365 for extended, and business income is 63 versus 68. Thus income (employment plus business) is 445 versus 433. This income differential can be explained as follows. Households whose main source of income is business tend to be extended. If the father and the son share a family business and hence form an extended family, the father tends to retain a substantial share of family business income well after his retirement age. In fact, for extended families, if the reported breakdown of family business income between the two generations is changed to fully reflect the breakdown of family employment income, then the head's income becomes *higher* for extended. Probably this adjustment of the breakdown of business income between the two generations is overdone. There is thus no apparent evidence that a child living with his/her old parent is less wealthy than his/her contemporaries in the pool of nuclear families. Anyway, if the heads in extended families are poorer than their contemporaries in the pool of nuclear families, then the flow-based evidence (to be presented below) that the dependent old save would be stronger.

14. As mentioned in section 12.2.3, the NSFIE tends to overstate the slope of the age-wealth profile because relatively younger cohorts of young families are overrepresented by relatively low income families (see table 12.1b). However, the upward bias for the slope as inferred from table 12.1b is at most 1 percent, a negligible magnitude.

15. And, transfers take place largely in the form of housing. This follows because the age profile of net financial asset for young nuclear families is much less steep than the age profile of wealth (net financial assets plus housing). The same conclusion can be obtained from the National Tax Bureau's *1984 Annual Report*: about 68 percent of bequests is land. Since the value of land assessed by the tax authority is about a third or a quarter of the market value, the land share of bequests at market prices is nearly 90 percent.

16. In our analysis, we are careful not to include transfers in income or consumption. The NSFIE reports only "regular" transfers to and from the household. Lump sum (one-time) transfers are not captured by the survey data.

17. The NSFIE data on transfer income do not include public transfers. Presumably, public transfers, if any, are in "other income."

18. The cross-section growth rate is smaller in absolute value for the 60–65 bracket, because the starting age for social security benefits is 65. Almost all pension income is social security benefits. Private pension for those currently old in Japan is not important. They received a large sum of lump sum severance pay on their retirement.

19. This statement, however, must be qualified somewhat, because as discussed in section 12.2.3 the NSFIE tends to underrepresent high-income families for older cohorts.

20. This whole growth-rate analysis applied to different segments of the population can be used to calculate the flow of intergenerational transfers and its breakdown between gifts and bequests. This is left for future research.

21. 1983 Housing Survey of Japan, Statistical Table for Prefecture, Table 15, Detached and Tenement Houses by Kind of Dwelling, Site Area, and Area of Floor Space, pp. 36–37.

22. *Movement and Analysis of Land Prices* (Tokyo: Diamond Publishing Co.) The 1986 edition has data both for January 1, 1984 and January 1, 1985.

23. Economic Planning Agency, *Annual Report on National Accounts*, 1987, p. 91, line 4.

24. National Tax Bureau, Government of Japan, *Annual Statistical Report* (in Japanese), 1979 and 1984.

25. Note that these figures include all withheld taxes on employee compensation, dividends, interest income, pensions, etc.

26. *Kosei-Nenkin Code*, chap. 2, section 1, paragraph 6.

27. Ministry of Welfare, Bureau of Annuity, and Social Security Administration, Division of Annuity, *Explanation of Revisions of Annuity System* (Tokyo: Research Institute for Social Insurance, 1986) (in Japanese). The proposition given above is outlined on pp. 39–40 of this document.

28. *Ibid.*, pp. 39–41. Figures given in this citation, however, refer largely to 1985 and subsequent years. Specific figures for 1984 were reported to us by Mrs. M. Yamashita in her letter of July 12, 1987.

29. The contribution of employees and managers described above represents only the worker contribution. Employers also contribute an equal amount on behalf of their employees. Anyone earning less than the minimum contributes as though he is earning the minimum amount. Similarly, anyone earning more than the maximum contributes as though he is earning the maximum amount. Actually, contributions are based on the "standardized" compensation amount, but the proportional scheme described above seems to be a good approximation.

30. See Health and Welfare Statistics Association, *Hoken to Nenkin no Doko* (Direction of Health Insurance and Annuity Programs), vol. 32, no. 13 (Tokyo: Health and Welfare Statistics Association, 1985), p. 173, Tables 2 and 4.

31. *Ibid.*, pp. 186 and 44, for example.

32. *Ibid.*, especially chaps. 2 and 3. The employee's health insurance program includes *Kenko Hoken*, which literally means "health insurance" and covers those who belong to the *Kosei Nenkin* system of annuity programs, and the *Kyosai Kumiai* system which covers those who belong to the *Kyosai Nenkin* system of annuity programs. Under the reformed system, they are virtually identical in structure and coverage. Citizen's health program (*Kokumin Kenko Hoken*) covers those who belong to the citizen's annuity program (*Kokumin Nenkin*). In addition, there is a special health and annuity program for mariners, but in terms of budget amount, it is relatively small and hence it is ignored in this discussion. Finally, there is the *Rojin Kenko Hoken*, or the health insurance program for the elderly. This program provides comprehensive health for the elderly, but elderly persons do not contribute to this program; it is financed by contributions from the National Treasury, contributions from provincial governments, and contributions from health insurance programs covering younger persons listed above. In other words, the health insurance program for the elderly may be thought of as a joint venture among all other health insurance programs, provincial governments, and the national government to provide the health care for the elderly free of charge.

33. *Ibid.*, pp. 94–160.

34. *Annual Report on National Accounts*, 1987 edition, pp. 238–39, the sum of rows 1(1)a, 3(1)b, 3(2)b, 3(3)b, and 3(4)b, and 4.

35. *Ibid.*, row 2.

References

Ando, Albert 1985. The savings of Japanese households: A micro study based on data from the National Survey of Family Income and Expenditure, 1974 and 1979. Economic Planning Agency, Government of Japan.

Ando, Albert, and Arthur Kennickell. 1987. How much (or little) life cycle is there in micro data? The cases of the United States and Japan. In *Macroeconomics and Finance, Essays in Honor of Franco Modigliani*, ed. R. Dornbusch, S. Fischer, and John Bossons, 159–223. Cambridge, MA: MIT Press.

Bernheim, B. Douglas. 1986. The economic effects of social security: Toward a reconciliation of theory and measurement. Mimeo., Stanford University.

Hayashi, Fumio. 1986. Why is Japan's saving rate so apparently high? In *NBER Macroeconomics Annual 1986*, ed. S. Fischer, 147–210, Cambridge, MA: MIT Press.

Hayashi, F., A. Ando, and R. Ferris. 1988. Life cycle and bequest savings: A study of Japanese and U.S. households based on data from the 1984 NSFIE and the 1983 Survey of Consumer Finances. *Journal of the Japanese and International Economies* 2, 450–91.

Hurd, Michael D. 1986a. Mortality risk and bequests. Mimeo., SUNY.

————. 1986b. Savings of the elderly and desired bequests. Mimeo., SUNY.

Kennickell, Arthur. 1984. *An investigation of life cycle savings behavior in the United States*, Ph.D. diss., University of Pennsylvania.

Yaari, M. 1965. Uncertain lifetime, life insurance, and the theory of the consumer. *Review of Economic Studies* 32 (April): 137–50.

13

Housing Finance Imperfections and Private Saving: A Simulation Analysis

13.1 Introduction

It is widely noted that one of the major differences between the U.S. and Japanese economies is found in the institutions and regulations of financial markets. In addition, the tax incentives for saving and borrowing in the two countries are quite different. Most of the interest income from consumer savings is tax exempt and interest payments of consumer mortgages and debts are not tax deductible in Japan, while the opposite is true in the United States.[1] Institutional arrangements concerning housing, one of the major expenditure items in a lifetime for most consumers, are also quite different in the two countries. Many economists have suggested that differences in housing financing between the two countries may be partially responsible for the large gap in the personal saving rate between the two countries. (See Hayashi (1986) for a survey of the literature.) In a world with perfect capital markets where a consumer can borrow and lend over his life cycle, whether a consumer decides to rent housing or purchase a house would not have any effect on the lifetime consumption–saving pattern. However, in the presence of a liquidity constraint (i.e., a down-payment requirement) purchasing a house may create a distortion in the lifetime consumption–saving decision. A higher down-payment requirement may induce households to postpone consumption early in the life cycle in order to build up enough assets to qualify for buying a house.

The goal of this paper is to investigate the effect of tax incentives and down-payment requirements on households' tenure choice (own or rent)

Originally published as "Housing Finance Imperfections, Taxation, and Private Saving: A Comparative Simulation Analysis of the United States and Japan" in *Journal of the Japanese and International Economies* 2 (September 1988): 215–38, with T. Ito and J. Slemrod. Reprinted with the permission of Academic Press.

concerning housing and on consumption–saving patterns, with a comparison of the United States and Japan in mind. In particular, a life-cycle simulation model will be constructed to quantify the effect of these policies on the personal saving rate. The methodology is based on that of Slemrod (1982), who constructed a life-cycle model with endogenous homeownership decisions.[2] He showed that although the favorable tax treatment of owner-occupied housing in the United States encourages an early purchase of housing, the down-payment constraint induces the consumer to delay the purchase to avoid distortion in the consumption–saving pattern. Thus, an optimal lifetime pattern of tenure choice of housing is determined as a trade-off between the tax incentives and the required distortions in the lifetime consumption stream.

In this paper, we apply an expanded version of the Slemrod model to a comparative study of the U.S. and Japanese housing markets. The model predicts that due to the imperfect capital market, transaction costs, and the relatively higher housing price, the Japanese are induced to save more toward the down payment and to acquire a home later in their life cycle.

Reasonable values are substituted from the stylized facts of the two countries. Most parameter values in the simulation model are based on observed data of the U.S. and Japanese economies. Some parameter values are chosen so that the tenure pattern and saving rates that our model predicts are matched with the observed tenure pattern in each country.

Exercises with the simulation model are developed to show how much the difference in tax incentives contributes to the savings rate gap between the two countries. It is particularly interesting to investigate how tax reform would affect the aggregate saving rate and housing tenure choice, since reforms have been implemented or proposed recently in both countries. On April 1, 1988, Japan abolished most of the tax exemption for saving and replaced it with a uniform low tax rate. Furthermore, a tax break for the purchase of owner-occupied housing, in one form or another, has been proposed in Japan. In the United States, incentives for saving have been introduced in the form of the all-savers' certificate and individual retirement accounts, although these programs have been cut back recently. In addition, some recent tax reform proposals, in particular flat tax proposals, feature the elimination of the tax deductibility of home mortgage interest payments.

In the discussion of tax reform in either country, no one has presented quantitative estimates showing how much the house tenure pattern and the saving rate would change due to the proposed reform. This paper will take up this task using a simulation model.

In Section 13.2, we describe a life-cycle model with endogenous housing tenure choice which is a special case of Slemrod's (1982) model. Sections 13.3 and 13.4, respectively, summarize the stylized facts of the U.S. and Japanese housing markets. Section 13.5 presents the results of various exercises using the simulation model to investigate the effect of changes in the economic environment in both countries. Section 13.6 offers some concluding remarks.

13.2   A Life-Cycle Model with Housing Tenure Choice

In this section, we describe a six-period life-cycle model which will be used for the simulation analyses to be discussed later. Each period is meant to represent 10 years of a person's adult lifetime. The household, which lives six periods, chooses the consumption of a composite commodity and housing services for each period over the lifetime. Housing services may be obtained either by purchasing a house or by renting housing. Imperfect capital markets are assumed in that the household cannot borrow to finance nonhousing consumption. The household can, however, obtain a mortgage toward purchase of a house, provided it can come up with a down payment which is some fraction of the house value. The liquidity constraint may be binding for two reasons. First, when income early in the life cycle is less than income later, as will be assumed, consumption smoothing may become impossible. Second, if owner-occupying as opposed to renting is preferred, the household has to save in order to accumulate enough wealth for the down payment. Even if the liquidity constraint for consumption smoothing is binding, there may be positive saving in order to build up the down payment.

The desirability of owning a house comes from two sources. First, it is assumed that a house owned would yield services with higher utility than the identical house if rented. This assumption is meant to represent the advantage of eliminating the principal–agent relationship if one rents from oneself; i.e., a renter cannot alter, paint, and improve a house as desired, and a renter is subject to a risk of termination of lease or rent increase in the future. Second, in the United States, the imputed income from owner-occupied housing is untaxed, while interest payments are tax deductible and interest income from saving is taxable. This feature makes owing a house more attractive than renting one, unless there are offsetting tax advantages offered to landlords. This argument does not apply identically to Japan, where interest payments are not tax deductible and most of personal interest income is (until recently) practically tax exempt. To the extent that rental income is taxed, however, there is a tax-related advantage to owning housing as opposed to renting in Japan as well as in the United States.

It is assumed that in the first period the household cannot purchase a house because of the liquidity and down-payment constraints. Likewise, by the beginning of the last period, the household must sell any owned housing and move into a rental unit, consuming all the proceeds of the house sale in the last period. (We abstract from the bequest motive until later.) Thus the household has a choice of owing a house during any of the second, third, fourth, and fifth periods, but can buy only once. For each own/rent lifetime pattern, the household can calculate the optimal consumption/saving pattern by maximizing the discounted sum of lifetime utility subject to the lifetime budget constraint and the liquidity and down-payment constraints. By comparing the maximized levels of lifetime utility for different patterns of tenure choice, the household picks the own/rent pattern that yields the highest utility. (For simplicity, depreciation on a house is ignored.)

We assume housing purchases and sales take place at the end of a period. When a house is purchased with a down payment d of the house value, the down-payment expenditure is deducted from income of the period of house purchase. The mortgage debt $(1 - d)$ becomes $(1 + R)$ $(1 - d)$ at the beginning of the next period, where R is the (before tax) interest rate. An equal payment of V for m periods amortizes the mortgage debt. (Later, $m = 2$ for Japan and $m = 3$ for the United States will be chosen.) The interest portion of the mortgage repayment is tax deductible in the United States. Thus the "net" mortgage repayment $V(m)$ in the United States is the mortgage payment less the (deductible) interest portion of the repayment for the mth installment. When a house is sold, the value of the house, less remaining mortgage, is used for consumption after the period of the sale.

The instantaneous utility function is assumed to be log linear in consumption and housing services (with weight α), and lifetime utility is assumed to be additively separable over time. For example, suppose that household purchases a house at period $t(b)$ and sells at period $t(s)$. The household has to solve the following problem: Maximize with respect to $t(b), t(s), \{c(t), t = 1, \ldots, 6\}, \{h(t), t = 1, \ldots, t(b), t(s) + 1, \ldots, 6\}$, H,

$$\sum_{t=1}^{t(b)} \beta^{t-1}\{\log c(t) + \alpha \log h(t)\} + \sum_{t=t(b)+1}^{t(s)} \beta^{t-1}\{\log c(t) + \alpha \log \gamma H)\}$$

$$+ \sum_{t=t(s)+1}^{6} \beta^{t-1}\{\log c(t) + \alpha \log h(t)\}$$

subject to $A(0) = 0$,

$$A(t) = (1 + R(1 - \tau))A(t - 1) + y(t) - c(t) - P_r P_h h(t),$$
$$t = 1, \ldots, t(b) - 1$$

$$A(t) = (1 + R(1 - \tau))A(t - 1) + y(t) - c(t) - P_r P_h h(t) - dP_h H,$$
$$t = t(b)$$

$$A(t) = (1 + R(1 - \tau))A(t - 1) + y(t) - c(t) - V(m)(1 - d)P_h H,$$
$$t = t(b) + 1, \ldots, t(s) - 1$$

$$A(t) = (1 + R(1 - \tau))A(t - 1) + y(t) - c(t) - V(m)(1 - d)P_h H + P_h H,$$
$$t = t(s)$$

$$A(t) = (1 + R(1 - \tau))A(t - 1) + y(t) - c(t) - P_r P_h h(t),$$
$$t = t(s) + 1, \ldots, 6$$

$$A(t) \geq \max[0, dP_h H + \sum_{m-1}^{t-t(b)} \{V - (V - V(m))/\tau\}]$$

[liquidity constraint], $t = 1, \ldots, 5$

$A(6) = 0$ [no bequest condition],

where $y(t)$ and $c(t)$ are labor income and consumption in period t, respectively; $A(t)$ is the end-of-the-period financial asset value; h is the size of a rental unit (which could vary every period); H is the size of an owner-occupied unit (which remains constant once purchased); R is the interest rate on financial assets and liabilities; P_r is the price per period of a rental unit; P_h is the price of the owner-occupied house; γ, τ, d are parameters representing the pride-of-ownership coefficient, the tax rate on income from saving and financial assets, and the required down-payment ratio, respectively. We define the unit of H such that P_h can be normalized to one. Under the assumption of a Cobb–Douglas utility function, H has a unit price elasticity. Therefore, the normalization does not affect the qualitative results in this chapter.

There is an implicit arbitrage condition assumed between rental property investment and financial asset investment. P_r equals R due to arbitrage between the financial asset and real asset if both incomes are taxable, as in the United States. P_r equals $R(1 - \tau^r)$ if interest income on financial assets is not taxed but rental income is taxed, as in Japan, where τ^r is the tax rate on rental income. Saving in this model is defined as the change in total wealth.

The liquidity constraint implies that total borrowing must be less than or equal to the value of owned housing. The calculation of $V(m)$ needs some explanation. For Japan, where there is no tax deductibility for interest payments, $V(m) = V$, and the equal installment is calculated from a condition that the mortgage be just paid up after the maturity of the mortgage. For the United States, $V(m)$ represents the equal payments of mortgage less the tax rebate resulting from tax deductibility of the mortgage interest payment.[3]

Due to the time separability and log linearity of the utility function, backward induction yields an explicit solution for optimal consumption, (rent/own) housing service for all periods.

One extension of the model that we will consider is to include a bequest motive. In particular, we require that housing of value q be left as a bequest. Assuming that the heirs are 30 years younger than the parents, the bequest is equally divided among the heirs who are at the end of their third period of life. Because population is larger and the lifetime income is higher for later generations, the size of the house per heir has to be adjusted accordingly, so that

$$q_h = q/\{((1 + n)(1 + g))^3\},$$

where q is the benefactor's house size, q_h is the heir's house size obtained at the end of the third period, n is the population growth rate, and g is the (generational) income growth rate.

13.3   Characteristics of the U.S. Housing Market

Data for mortgage financing with a government guarantee are available from the U.S. Department of Housing and Urban Development (HUD). In 1979, the average ratio of mortgage value to the value of a new one-family, house whose finance was government guaranteed was 0.921. This ratio seems very high, partly due to a sample bias of government guarantees. The average loan-to-value ratio, $1 - d$, of conventional mortgage financing, according to the Federal Home Loan Bank Board (1982), for a new home was 0.731 in 1980 and 0.748 in 1981. Based on these data, our first stylized fact is that the down-payment ratio is about 25 to 30% for conventional mortgages and only about 10% for housing with government loan guarantees. We select 25% as a benchmark of the U.S. down-payment ratio.

Second, the average age of mortgagor was about 30 for an owner-occupant transaction in 1980, according to the "FHA Trends of Home Mortgage Characteristics." Another source, the "Annual Housing Survey," confirms that among the cohort of household heads, 25–30 years old, more than 50% own a house rather than rent.

Third, the average maturity of a mortgage is about 30 years, according to HUD (1979, p. 295). Fourth, the house-value/annual-income ratio, $P_h H/y(b)$, is 1.97 for a typical transaction of one-family housing, according to HUD (1979, p. 134). Last, the life-cycle income pattern of the U.S. household is calculated by multiplying the average income for an age bracket by the labor participation rate in 1980. (Source: U.S. Department of Commerce, 1981; Department of Labor, 1985.) As a proportion of the average income of those 20–30 years old, the incomes of the six age brackets we are interested in are calculated as follows, after normalizing so that $y(1) + y(2) + \cdots + y(6) = 1$:

$$y_t(1) = 0.169; \quad y_t(2) = 0.248; \quad y_t(3) = 0.257;$$

$$y_t(4) = 0.218; \quad y_t(5) = 0.108; \quad y_t(6) = 0.000.$$

Since this income pattern with respect to age bracket is an observation at a point of time t, the lifetime pattern of a generation must be estimated in order to be used in the life-cycle maximization problem of one particular generation. In the steady state, this can be done by multiplying by the growth rate of (real) lifetime income over a generation. We assume that members of a generation receive $(1 + g)$ as much income in every age bracket as members of a generation earlier so that

$$y_{t+s}(k) = (1 + g)^s y_t(k), \qquad k = 1, 2, \ldots, 6.$$

The decade population (of those 15 years old and over) growth rate, n, is calculated as 20.04%, the rate observed from 1970 to 1980. The decade income growth rate over one generation (10 years apart), g, is fixed at 10%.[4]

13.4   Stylized Facts in the Housing Markets in Japan

13.4.1   Loans vs. Self-Financing[5]

The ratio of down payment (literally translated as a ratio of self-financing) is defined as the ratio of the average amount the owner of a new home raised to the average cost of construction or purchase of the home. In the 1980s, the ratio of down payment has been about 40% for both custom-made homes and homes purchased from developers. The rest, about 60% of purchase costs, comes from subsidized and privately financed loans.

However, there are two problems with using these figures. First, "down payment" in the Japanese survey is literally defined as "the portion of self-financing," including the owner's savings, gifts to the owner, and sales of other real assets. "Loans" in the survey refer to funds other than the owner's. If a new owner borrows without collateral some amount of money from his parents and applies it toward the "down payment" to the developer, the amount of money would still be counted as "loans" instead of "down payment." The ratio of "down payment" may therefore be biased downward. Although the exact division between "self-finance" and "loans" may not be comparable to the division into "down payment" and "mortgages" in the United States, this is the closest approximation possible and the direction of possible bias would not weaken our argument.

Second, the ratio of 40% is inclusive of second-time buyers who have trade-ins. If we take the down-payment ratio of the first-time buyers only, the down-payment ratio is about 35%. In light of these facts, a plausible average for the down-payment ratio for the first-time buyer is about 35%. This is our *first stylized fact* for the Japanese hosing market.

13.4.2   Average Age of New Owners

The average age of the heads of households who built custom-made houses in 1985 is about 43.9. However, if only first-time buyers are surveyed, the average age is about 40.

This evidence is not quite sufficient for the purpose of our study of an own/rent tenure choice in the life-cycle context. Although it shows a distribution of ages of purchasers, it does not show in the cross section how many of the cohorts have previously owned houses. In order to overcome the difficulty, we consulted a source of representative cross-sectional data in Japan, the "Family Saving Survey" collected by the Statistics Bureau of the Prime Minister's Office. The survey shows that the house ownership ratio (among the cohort) increases monotonically up to the age of 65. At the age of 65, 86.7% of heads of households own housing. It is between the ages of 35 and 39 when the majority of the cohort become home-owners. The ownership rate increases rapidly between the ages of 30 and 40. From this we derive only the *second stylized fact*: In Japan, the average age of initial home purchase is about 40.

However, looking at the percentage of households holding liabilities for purchase of houses and/or land, we note that less than 40% of house-holds hold such liabilities. Investigating other statistics, we can conclude that more than one-third of house owners have no liabilities connected to housing. This is supporting evidence that liabilities due to home/land purchases are rather quickly paid up.

13.4.3 Japanese Idiosyncrasies: Extended Families

Care must be taken in comparing the Japanese housing market with its U.S. counterpart, in light of the prevalence of extended families. It is still common in Japan for young adults between the age of 18 and the time of marriage to live with their parents, if they live in the same town. The prevalence of this arrangement is partly due to the high relative cost of housing, both rental and owner-occupied, and partly due to social customs.

Even after their marriage, it is not uncommon for children to continue to live with their parents. This phenomenon appears in the above-mentioned survey concerning the question of what kind of housing the new owner had before. About 13% of owner construction and 6% of buyers used to "live together (with family)." This is a significant proportion, because as mentioned earlier the survey includes replacement and improvement demand for homes.

It is common in Japan that when parents become very old, or especially when one of them dies, the surviving parents are "looked after" by one of the children. A parent (or parents) might move into a house of one of the children, usually the eldest son; or the family of a child might move into the parents' house. In the former case, they lose the "head of household" status and become dependents in the household survey, thus dropping out of statistics using a classification by the age of head of households. In the latter case, in "return" for taking care of parents, it is usual, though not legally required, that the child who looks after the parents inherits the parent's home. (This is an extreme form of "strategic bequests," as advo-cated by Bernheim et al. (1985).) The parent(s) usually remains as the legal owner of the house. One reason for this arrangement is that for real estate, as opposed to financial securities, the inheritance tax is reduced since the assessed value for the inheritance tax is usually significantly less than the market value. In either case, it is rare that the elderly sell the home in order to move into a rental unit. These social and economic aspects of Japan partly explain why the ratio of homeowners among those 65 years old and over, among "heads of households," does not (seem to) decline.

To repeat, the second case implies that a typical Japanese family keeps an owner-occupied house, or even buys a new, larger home, after retirement. This is very much in contrast to the typical U.S. household that sells a big house after the children become adults. This aspect might not be adequately dealt with in a model based on the standard life-cycle theory, in particular Slemrod's life-cycle model of tenure choice.

Careful consideration of the bias caused by extended families in our study must be given. As for the effect of the living-in arrangement after the parents become old, there are two conflicting effects on the validity of our study. If the first case (parents moving into their children's home) is dominant, we do not have to worry about the comparability of the two countries, since an apparently high ownership ratio among the retired household heads is caused by selection bias (upward). In other words, in reality as opposed to the data, many sell their houses and live with a son's family or a daughter's family. Thus, the life-cycle framework of own/rent tenure choice still applies. However, if the second case (a son's or daughter's family moving into the parents' home) is dominant, then a bequest motive should be seriously modeled, and it may be the case that we have to argue that the difference in saving and houseownership between the United States and Japan is due to the extended family practice and a peculiar bequest motive in Japan. (See Hayashi (1986) for the extended family explanation of why the Japanese saving rate is so high.) Since we will not analyze the bequest motive in depth, we are implicitly assuming the second aspect of extended family relationship to be relatively insignificant. Further theoretical and empirical analysis is required to investigate how much the Japanese extended family relationship would affect housing tenure choice and saving decisions.

13.4.4   Life-Cycle Labor Income Pattern and Price of Housing

We need the life-cycle labor income pattern for the typical Japanese household for our simulation model. The method of calculation is the same as that used for the United States., The result is given in Hayashi (1986, Table 3):

$y_t(1) = 0.09;$ $y_t(2) = 0.22;$ $y_t(3) = 0.28;$

$y_t(4) = 0.29;$ $y_t(5) = 0.13;$ $y_t(6) = 0.00.$

The above number is the cross-section observation at time t of the income pattern with respect to age brackets. As was discussed in the preceding section, the income pattern of a particular generation also depends on the growth rate of labor income over generations. The decade income growth rate, g, is approximated at 40%.[6] The population (age 15 and over) growth rate, n, is approximated at 13.05%.

Last, in Japan, about a third of the price of housing services can be traced to land, which is scarce and expensive. The average housing-value/annual-income ratio, $P_h H/y(b)$, for buyers of a house with land (excluding those who rent land and who are given land by family and relatives), constructed from a survey done by Ministry of Construction (1982, p. 82), was 5.29.

13.5   Simulations

13.5.1   Benchmark

In this section, the model presented in Section 13.2 is used as a simulation model with relevant parameter values derived from the observed facts summarized in Sections 13.3 and 13.4. Those parameters for a typical resident in each country are summarized in Table 13.1.

First, we calculate the optimum housing tenure choice predicted by our simulation model. Given a rent–own pattern of housing for six periods, maximum lifetime utility is calculated by solving a dynamic problem of consumption (size of housing and consumption goods) and saving. The model then compares the maximized values of lifetime utility to decide the optimal pattern of tenure choice.

The model, as summarized for the benchmark case in Table 13.2, predicts that the representative Japanese resident rents in periods 1, 2, and 6 of his life, and that the representative U.S. resident rents in periods 1 and 6 only. That is, the typical Japanese purchases a house when he is 40 years old with a 20-year mortgage and the typical American purchases a house when he is 30 years old with a 30-year mortgage. These predicted patterns match the stylized facts summarized in previous sections.

Table 13.1
Benchmark Parameters

		Stylized facts[a]						
	$P_h H/y(b)$	R	τ^r	τ	d	Mortgage maturity (years)	Aggregate saving rate (%)	Tenure choice[b]
U.S.	0.195	0.5	0.3	0.3	0.25	30	8.0	ROOOO?
Japan	0.529	0.5	0.3	0.0	0.35	20	18.29	RROOO?

Stylized facts: Cross-section income pattern at period t

	$y_t(1)$	$y_t(2)$	$y_t(3)$	$y_t(4)$	$y_t(5)$	$y_t(6)$	g	n
U.S.	0.169	0.248	0.257	0.218	0.108	0.000	0.10	0.20
Japan	0.090	0.220	0.280	0.290	0.130	0.000	0.40	0.13

Benchmark parameter values: Assumptions

	α	β	P_r	γ
U.S.	0.15	0.75	R	1.4
Japan	0.15	0.75	$R(1 - \tau^r)$	1.4

[a] τ^r is the tax rate on rental income; τ is the tax rate on savings on financial assets; R is the interest rate; d is the down-payment ratio.
[b] R = rent; O = own.

The saving rate predicted by the model is 8.81% for the United States and 10.49% for Japan. Hayashi (1986) calculates private saving rates for the two countries after correcting for the difference in statistical definitions. According to Hayashi's estimates, the average private saving rates for the United States and Japan during the 1970s were 8.0 and 18.3%, respectively. Thus the prediction for the United States is quite reflective of the stylized fact but the prediction for Japan falls short of the actual rate by 8 percentage points.

The model also shows that the housing stock share in national wealth is much lower in Japan than in the United States despite the high saving rate. We will investigate factors that contribute to the low housing stock in Japan by simulation experiments later.

The model overpredicts the housing size for the United States, while it underpredicts the housing size for Japan. The discrepancy might be a signal that our utility function is misspecified. However, without the Cobb–Douglas assumption, the explicit form of solution is hard to obtain.

In the rest of this section, simulations with respect to the bequest motive, down-payment ratio, and the income growth rate will be con-

Table 13.2
Benchmark U.S.–Japan Comparison

	Benchmark theoretical prediction						Facts[a]
U.S., no bequest ($q = 0$)							
Tenure pattern	R	O	O	O	O	R	ROOOO?
Labor income profile[a]	0.169	0.273	0.311	0.290	0.158	0.000	
Aggregate saving rate (%)			8.81				8.0
Wealth/income[b]			2.70				
Housing/wealth[c]			0.74				
House size			0.078				0.053
Japan, no bequest ($q = 0$)							
Tenure pattern	R	R	O	O	O	R	RROOO?
Labor income profile	0.090	0.380	0.549	0.796	0.499	0.000	
Aggregate saving rate (%)			10.49				18.29
Wealth/income			2.85				
Housing/wealth			0.61				
House size			0.11				0.29
Japan, with bequest ($q = 0.11$)							
Tenure pattern	R	R	O	O	O	O	RROOO?
Labor income profile	0.090	0.308	0.549	0.796	0.499	0.000	
Aggregate saving rate (%)			11.26				18.29
Wealth/income			3.06				
Housing/wealth			0.52				
House size (purchased)			0.08				0.29
House size (inherited)			0.03				

[a] The labor income and saving rate profile is a lifetime labor income stream of a typical agent in the model. The profiles are calculated as longitudinal predictions, while the aggregate saving rate is a cross-section prediction.

[b] Wealth is the sum of financial assets and housing equity (value minus outstanding mortgage). Income is measured on an annual basis.

[c] The value of land is not included in either housing or wealth. The observed ratio of the value of the housing/wealth ratio is indeed higher in the United States than in Japan, as suggested by this simulation table. However, the value of land is much higher in Japan than in the United States. See also footnote 2 in the next.

ducted to evaluate the impact of changes in the financial institutions and economic environment on the housing market.[7]

13.5.2 Bequest Motive in Japan

One reason that the benchmark simulation underpredicts the Japanese saving rate is its failure to consider the bequest motive.[8] If the oldest generation does not consume all its wealth, especially the proceeds from the house sale which becomes available at the beginning of the last period of the life cycle, then the aggregate saving rate would increase.

Without a bequest motive, the assumption that the individual sells the house at the beginning of the sixth period is not critical. However, with a bequest motive, the assumption becomes problematic. In Japan houses are often used as a vehicle for making a bequest, partly because of the tax advantage of bequeathing housing relative to financial assets.[9]

How large a bequest motive is required to generate a saving rate comparable to the actual rate? Table 13.2 (the third panel) shows the saving rate that results when the representative individual is required to bequeath housing of 0.2, the house size which would be owned without a bequest motive (i.e., the benchmark case). The experiment is conducted on the assumption that the household may purchase additional housing (add rooms) to supplement the bequest, and that the housing is held through the last period of life. In addition, the house is assumed to be bequeathed without debt against it.

The calculated saving rate with the bequest assumption of house size 0.2 is 11.18%. Hence, the bequest motive increases the aggregate saving rate by 0.7 percentage point. Modeling this type of bequest does increase the aggregate saving rate, but the magnitude of the increase is small compared to the U.S.–Japan gap. This is because adding the bequest motive has two offsetting effects on saving. On the one hand, the person is not presumed to consume the proceeds of the house sale at the end of the fifth period. This increases the aggregate saving rate. On the other hand, when a housing bequest is expected in the third period, less saving is the first and second periods for the down payment is required.

In order to assess the sensitivity of the saving rate to the housing bequest, experiments with different size of housing bequest were conducted. A bequest house size of 0.054 yields an aggregate saving rate of 9.88%, while a bequest house size of 0.163 yields an aggregate saving rate of 12.60%. These simulation exercises suggest that the saving rate is somewhat sensitive with respect to this form of bequest motive, but cannot generate large changes in saving.

13.5.3 Non-Steady State

One of the key assumptions in the benchmark case is that the economy is in a steady state. The growth rates of population and real income and a (normalized) labor—income profile were assumed to have stayed the same for all generations. This assumption is particularly troublesome in the case of Japan. Economic growth in Japan from 1950 to 1973 averaged around 10% a year, about twice as much as the growth rate assumed for the Japanese benchmark in the preceding section. It is well known that in a standard life-cycle model where the young are savers, a higher growth rate implies a higher saving rate. This is because the older generation of dissavers has a much smaller "economic weight" than the younger generation of savers. Even if the rate of trend growth is halved as it was in Japan after the first oil crisis, the economic weight of older generations is very small due to rapid economic growth in the past. Hence, it is not surprising that the benchmark model underpredicted the actual saving rate.

We then simulate the life-cycle saving—consumption pattern for each generation using the actual (time-varying) economic growth rates in the past and the benchmark rate for the future. The income pattern for each generation is calculated using the actual 10-year economic growth rate and the cross-section age—income profile at 1980. The interest rate is assumed to be constant over time. For example, a generation born in 1920 is assumed to have had perfect foresight, and to have known the life-cycle income path from 1920 to 1980. (We, however, are assuming the house-tenure decision to be RROOOR in this exercise.) The same procedure is applied to other generations. The aggregate saving rates at year t, $t = 1980, \ldots, 2030$, are calculated by aggregating the income and saving for different generations, who are at the different stages of the life cycle with time-varying income growth rates. We use the actual population weights of different generations for the past and the projected population weights for the future.

Table 13.3 shows the simulated Japanese saving rate from 1980 to 2030. In 1980, the rate is 16.12, significantly higher than that of the (steady-state) benchmark case and approaching the actual saving rate of 18.29. This is as expected due to rapid economic growth in the 1950s and 1960s, which implies that those who are dissaving have a small weight in the

Table 13.3
Simulated Japanese Saving Rate, 1980–2030, in Non-steady State

	1980	1990	2000	2010	2020	2030
Actual saving rate	18.29	na	na	na	na	na
Projected saving rate	16.29	14.97	15.03	12.96	8.09	5.27
Wealth/income	2.3	2.8	3.3	3.7	3.7	4.3
Housing/wealth	0.73	0.67	0.53	0.45	0.47	0.41

Assumed parameters: Economic growth rates (%) for each decade

1900–1910: 27.03	1940–1950: −29.23
1910–1920: 44.44	1950–1960: 130.67
1920–1930: 22.94	1960–1970: 170.99
1930–1940: 64.20	1980–1990 and on: 41.90

Population weights

	20–29	30–39	40–49	50–59	60–69	70–79
1960	.212	.252	.206	.161	.106	.063
1970	.286	.241	.192	.134	.097	.049
1980	.298	.245	.178	.142	.092	.045
1990	.194	.194	.225	.181	.133	.072
2000	.195	.181	.177	.201	.153	.093
2010	.177	.192	.175	.167	.178	.112
2020	.177	.178	.189	.169	.152	.134

Source: Various years of Census and "Projection of the Japanese Population" by Jinkou Mondai Kenkyuukai.

Japanese economy of 1980. The assumption of steady economic growth from 1980 on assures that the aggregate saving rate converges to the steady-state benchmark in the future. Our simulation shows that the saving rate will drop by 1 (percentage) point in 10 years, 3 points in 30 years, and 8 points in 40 years. The simulated Japanese saving rate will become very much like the American one in a half-century.

We conclude this section with three observations. First, with a non-steady-state assumption, the simulated saving rate is much higher than the benchmark. However, the model still underpredicts the actual saving rate. Second, the saving rate is projected to decline in the future as the lower growth rate persists. These results are consistent with the theoretical prediction that the saving rate is very sensitive to the economic growth rate.

Table 13.4
Effects of Changes in Down-Payment Ratio

	Down-payment ratio				
	15%	25%	30%	35%	40%
United States, no bequest					
T	ROOOOR	ROOOOR	ROOOOR	ROOOOR	ROOOOR
$S(\%)$	8.29	8.81	9.03	9.22	8.21
W/I	3.4	2.7	2.7	2.8	2.8
H/W	0.91	0.74	0.70	0.66	0.84
Japan, no bequest					
T	RROOOR	RROOOR	RROOOR	RROOOR	RROOOR
$S(\%)$	9.37	9.98	10.25	10.49	10.71
W/I	2.5	2.7	2.8	2.9	2.9
H/W	0.76	0.67	0.64	0.61	0.58
Japan, no bequest, non-steady state, 1980					
T	RROOOR	RROOOR	RROOOR	RROOOR	RROOOR
$S(\%)$	14.30	15.03	15.44	16.12	16.44
W/I	2.1	2.2	2.3	2.3	2.3
H/W	0.84	0.79	0.75	0.73	0.72

Note: Cases highlighted in boxes represent the stylized values of the down-payment ratio in each country.

13.5.4 Simulations with Respect to Down-Payment Ratios

We next investigate how much difference the down-payment constraint makes in the housing tenure choice and the saving rate. Of course, the higher the down-payment ratio, the more distortion in the lifetime consumption pattern required to finance the same amount of owned housing.

Table 13.4 shows how sensitive the housing tenure pattern is with respect to changes in the down-payment ratio. The U.S. housing tenure pattern would look like Japan's (housing purchase postponed until the third period) if the down-payment requirement were raised to 40%. In Japan, the tenure pattern currently observed in the United States would not emerge even at a down-payment ratio of 15%. Therefore, although a change in the down-payment ratio could alter the tenure choice pattern, the change would have to be very large. The observed tenure pattern in each country is predicted for a wide range of the down-payment ratios around the respective benchmark cases.

Table 13.4 also shows that the aggregate saving rate is positively related to the down-payment ratio. An increase of 10% in the down-payment ratio increases the saving rate by less than 1 percentage point in each country, given that the tenure choice pattern is not altered. The magnitude of the down-payment ratio effect is not as large as one might think, because there are two offsetting impacts from a higher down-payment ratio. First, higher saving is required for a given size of house. Second, a higher down-payment ratio causes a smaller house to be purchased given the tenure choice pattern. The simulation results show that the first effect is only barely dominant.

Table 13.4 also shows how the relative share of housing in national wealth would be affected if the down-payment ratio were changed. When the down-payment ratio in Japan becomes as low as 15% the housing share in national wealth becomes comparable to that in the United States.

In sum, this model suggests that the difference in the required down-payment ratios in the United States and Japan is not a major source of the difference in the saving rate. However, a large enough decline in the required down-payment ratio in Japan would induce a saving rate and life-cycle tenure pattern similar to those of the United States. In Japan, casual evidence suggests that the down-payment ratio was higher in the 1950s and 1960s, so that it could have been a stronger factor for a high saving rate in the past.

13.5.5 Simulations with Respect to the Income Growth Rate

First, note that the benchmark model is constructed in such a way that the slope of the earning profile for one generation is positively related to the expected income growth over generations. This feature comes from the fact that the observed cross-section data must be converted into a steady-state lifetime earning profile. Thus, in the following experiments using the steady state, faster growth implies a steeper earning profile.

Results of the sensitivity analysis with respect to the income growth rate are summarized as follows. It is well known that the aggregate saving rate increases, if the steady-state growth rate of labor income over generations increases so long as the younger generations are the savers. This is confirmed in our simulation model.[10] In fact, if the Japanese growth rate is only 10%, the growth rate of the United States, then the predicted steady-state Japanese saving rate (without a bequest motive) would be 6.62%, which is even below the current U.S. saving rate simulated in the model. The tenure choice of the Japanese case is not affected by the change in the income growth rate.

However, in the United States the renting period is extended by 10 more years if income grows at the Japanese rate, i.e., the age earning profile becomes steeper. The steeper earning profile implies that the utility penalty imposed by the distortion caused by saving toward down payments becomes more burdensome. The saving rate is increased to 8.67%, which is far short of the actual and less even than the simulated Japanese saving rate.

13.5.6 Simulations of Tax Reforms

Our final simulation experiments concern changes in the tax laws which determine incentives for saving and borrowing. As was discussed in the Introduction, the tax incentives affecting saving and borrowing in the two countries are quite different.

The United States and Japan (prior to the change on April 1, 1988) differ in two aspects: the tax exemption of the interest income from saving in Japan only and the tax deductibility of mortgage interest payments in the United States only. For each aspect, the simulation will be conducted for hypothetical situations given all other parameters.

Our model gives simulation results, shown in Table 13.5, for a full range of interesting policy questions both in the United States and in Japan: How much would the U.S. low saving rate be stimulated if interest income becomes tax exempt? How would tenure choice and average housing size be affected if mortgage payments become nondeductible? What are the combined effects of tax-exempt saving and the nondeductible interest payments? The last question can be paraphrased as follows. If the United States switched to the Japanese tax system, what would happen to the saving rate and housing tenure pattern?

The effect of allowing tax-exempt saving in the United States is shown in the (Yes–Yes) column in Table 13.5. The simulated aggregate saving rate increases by 1.5%, without changing the tenure choice pattern. The increase is not insignificant, if one is interested in raising the saving rate. However, even with an increase of 1.5%, the gap in the saving rates of the two countries would remain large.[11]

Suppose next that mortgage interest payments become not tax deductible in the United States. This is the case indicated by (No–No) in Table

Table 13.5
Effects of Tax Reforms on the Saving Rate

U.S.: Using U.S. parameters and income profiles

	Tax treatment			
	No. 1	No. 2 (Japan[a])	No. 3 (U.S. status quo)	No. 4
Interest income tax exempt?	Yes	Yes	No	No
Interest payments tax deductible?	Yes	No	Yes	No
Tenure choice	ROOOOR	ROOOOR	ROOOOR	ROOOOR
Aggregate saving (%)	10.27	9.94	8.81	8.43

Japan: No bequest, steady state, using Japan parameters and income profiles

	No. 1	No. 2 (Japan status quo[a])	No. 3 (U.S.)	No. 4
Interest income tax exempt?	Yes	Yes	No	No
Interest payments tax deductible?	Yes	No	Yes	No
Tenure choice	RROOOR	RROOOR	RRROOR	RRROOR
Aggregate saving (%)	10.83	10.49	7.01	6.98

Japan: No bequest, non-steady state, 1980, using Japanese parameters and income profiles

	No. 1	No. 2 (Japan status quo[a])	No. 3 (U.S.)	No. 4
Interest income tax exempt?	Yes	Yes	No	No
Interest payments tax deductible?	Yes	No	Yes	No
Tenure choice	RROOOR	RROOOR	RRROOR	RRROOR
Aggregate saving (%)	16.51	16.12	9.86	9.84

[a] Prior to April 1, 1988.

13.5. The model predicts that the saving rate would be reduced by a small amount, less than 0.5%. This result contrasts with the usual presumption that the tax deductibility of interest payments reduces the saving rate because it makes the cost of borrowing less. However, since buying a house does not represent dissaving (rather a change in portfolio) the aggregate saving rate in fact decreases when the cost of borrowing to buy a house rises, due to the decreased saving required to purchase the now-optimal smaller house.[12]

Suppose that the United States switched to the (former) Japanese tax system so that interest income is tax exempt and mortgage interest payments are not tax deductible. In this case the model predicts that the saving rate would increase by 1 percentage point.

Simulation experiments are then conducted for the Japanese case in order to answer questions symmetric to the U.S. experiments: How much would the high Japanese saving rate be reduced if the tax-exempt saving system is abolished? Would the typical Japanese tenure choice pattern be affected by the favorable tax treatment on mortgage payments, as in the United States? What would be the combined effect, i.e., if Japan switched to the U.S. tax system?

The first question is quite relevant since the Japanese government has just abolished the tax-exempt status of the "maru-yu" accounts. The second question is also relevant, since adopting a more favorable tax treatment of mortgage payments is always proposed when housing problems are discussed in Japan. The presumption is that the housing stock is one area where Japan lags behind the United States.

The model predicts that abolition of the "maru-yu" accounts in Japan causes a drop in the steady-state saving rate by 3 to 4 percentage points. The housing tenure pattern would also change, so that the Japanese would rent 10 more years before purchasing a house. The large change in the saving rate comes from the change in tenure pattern. Since a house is not owned until the beginning of the fourth period, the distortion in saving for the down-payment in the first half of the working life becomes much less.

If Japan were to introduce tax deductibility of mortgage interest payments, then the model predicts a very slight increase in the aggregate saving rate, without changing the tenure choice pattern. If Japan adopts the U.S. tax system with respect to interest income and interest payments, then the model predicts a drop in the saving rate of 3.5 percentage points.

The third panel of Table 13.5 shows what the non-steady-state aggregate saving rate would be if the hypothetical tax regime had been in place during the postwar period. In 1980, the saving rate would have been lower by 6 percentage points had the "maru-yu" not been available.

The tax-exempt status of interest income has a stronger impact on the saving rate than the tax deductibility of mortgage interest payments in both countries. The latter does not change the aggregate saving rate more than 50 basis points in any case in either country. Simulation results indicate that differences in the tax incentives between the two countries explain only 3 to 4 percentage points of the gap 10 percentage points between the saving rates of the two countries.

13.6   Concluding Remarks

We constructed a simulation model in order to evaluate the effects of changes in housing finance institutions and tax policy on housing tenure patterns and the aggregate private saving rate. Simulation results suggest that the factors do not offer a complete explanation of the large gap between the saving rates of the two countries. There are two reasons behind this conclusion. First, although the typical down-payment ratio varies across the two countries, the variation is not sufficient to affect the aggregate saving rate by a significant amount. Second, tax reform experiments indicate that only 1 to 4 percentage points of the 10-point gap are attributable to the difference in the tax incentives.

The model, in particular the one with non-steady-state assumptions, suggests that the difference in the income growth rate over generations can explain a greater amount of the saving rate gap. Given the difference in the income growth rates, we suspect also that the Japanese have a stronger bequest motive, perhaps due to their extended family relationships. Finally, our simulations suggest that the Japanese saving rate will drop significantly in the long run, as the economy moves to a new low-growth steady state that subjects interest income to taxation.

As is true for all numerical simulation analyses, the quantitative results presented here depend on our choices concerning the specification of the model. Several aspects of this specification are especially worthy of note. The use of a log-linear utility function implies an intertemporal and intratemporal elasticity of substitution equal to one. This is likely to overstate the actual degree of substitutability, and thus understate the welfare cost of a given distortion in saving/consumption patterns. For example, with less intertemporal substitutability, an increase in the required down-payment ratio is more likely to cause a household to postpone and reduce the size of a housing purchase, rather than have to reduce consumption early in the life cycle.

The six-period formulation is also rather arbitrary and allows the consideration of only large discrete changes in the lifetime tenure pattern. A model with more peirods would be able to treat the more continuous adjustment of tenure patterns in response to a change in the economic environment. The cost of implementing such a model is, of course, the increased computational expense.

Finally, an improved model would more carefully treat the bequest motive and, in general, transactions between generations. Differences in these transactions between the United States and Japan potentially play a large role in the determination of housing decisions and saving decisions as well as in the effect of tax policy and other institutional arrangements on these decisions.

In spite of these qualifications, we believe that this analysis represents a valuable contribution to the quantitative analysis of the interaction of housing market institutions, tax policy, and saving behavior in the United States and Japan. It has demonstrated the importance of treating demand for housing and saving behavior simultaneously within the context of a dynamic model.

Notes

Financial support from a Sloan Foundation grant on transactions costs administered by the University of Minnesota is gratefully acknowledged. This work was initiated when Fumio Hayashi was visiting at the Department of Economics, University of Minnesota. We thank the Ministry of Construction, Japan, for supplying us with data. Comments on previous versions by Patric Hendershott, Tsuneo Ishikawa, Joyce Manchester, David Wise, Naoyuki Yoshino participants of a seminar at the Ministry of Finance, Japan, and anonymous referees were very very helpful.

1. In Japan, interest income from the following savings (with a ceiling on principal amounts) was tax exempt prior to April 1, 1988: (i) regular postal saving up to 3 million yen; (ii) postal saving earmarked for housing purchase up to 0.5 million yen; (iii) "Maru-yu," that is, any deposits in bank securities and mutual funds, up to 3 million yen; (iv) "special maru-yu," that is, government and municipal bonds, new issues and secondary, up to 5 years after issue, up to 3 million yen; and (v) only for employees of age 54 or younger, for the purpose of accumulating assets for housing and retirement funds, up to 5 million yen. Thus a young employee who wants to save for a housing purchase can receive tax-free interest up to 14.5 million yen ($90,625, if 1 = 160 yen). Even beyond the tax exempt ceiling, there are financial instruments (discount bonds issued by investment banks and governments) which are subject to a low tax rate (16%) regardless of the income tax bracket of the bondholder. About 58% of personal savings is in one of the above forms of tax-exempt savings (Bank of Japan, 1986; p. 158). As of April 1, 1988, tax exemptions for types (i) and (iii) are replaced by a 20% interest income tax. Tax-exempt "new maru-yu" accounts can be held by the elderly (65 years or older), the handicapped, or single mothers.

2. As in Slemrod's model, land, a nonreproducible asset, is not explicitly introduced in our model. The value of land relative to total household wealth is much higher in Japan than in the United States. Morever, land has presumably appreciated more than financial wealth. The potentially important role of land in the saving process and its implications for the differential performances of the United States and Japan are not explored in this paper. One simplification adopted in the paper is that the model considers only the demand side of the asset. The supply of housing is not modeled and the general equilibrium response of prices to changes in policies is not included in the analysis.

3. For Japan, suppose that the mortgage matures in two periods (20 years). The condition of equal payments is $(1 + R)\{(1 - d)(1 + R) - V\} - V = 0$. Solving this, we have

$$V(m) = V = (1 - d)(1 + R)^2/(2 + R), \quad m = 1, 2;$$

$$V(m) = 0, \qquad\qquad\qquad m = 3, \ldots.$$

In addition, interest income from saving is tax exempt, i.e., $\tau = 0$. For the United States, suppose that the mortgage matures in three periods (30 years). The condition of equal payments is $(1 + R)[(1 + R)\{(1 - d)(1 + R) - V\} - V = 0$. Solving this, we have $V = (1 - d)(1 + R)^3 / \{1 + (1 + R) + (1 + R)^2\}$. In the period of first installment, the interest portion of the mortgage payment is $(1 - d)R$. Therefore multiplying the tax rate τ, we obtain the amount of tax saving, $\tau(1 - d)R$. The "net" mortgage payment is defined as $V(1) = V - (1 - d)R\tau$. Since the principal balance is shrinking as the installment continues, the interest portion of the installment changes. Accordingly the net mortgage payment in the mth installment is calculated as

$$V(2) = V - \{(1 - d)(1 + R) - V\}R\tau$$

$$V(3) = V - [(1 + R)\{(1 - d)(1 + R) - V\} - V]R\tau.$$

4. There are various ways to approximate the decade income growth, depending on which income measures and which deflator is used. For example, the per capita real GNP growth over the past 10 years less the population growth rate is about 10% of that of the United States.

5. The facts are summarized from the survey study of the Ministry of Construction in Japan, conducted annually since 1974. (See Ministry of Construction, 1986.) The survey of 1985 covered about 10,000 individuals who ordered custom-made homes or bought homes from developers.

6. Again, the income growth rate can be approximated in several ways. For example, the growth rate of household disposable income less the CPI growth rate less the population (age 15 and over) growth rate from 1970 and 1980 would yield about 41%, while the per capita real GNP growth rate is about 40%.

7. We also investigated how robust the benchmark result is with respect to the pride-of-ownership parameter, about which we do not have strong confidence. The tenure choice pattern and the saving rate predicted by the model were found to be not sensitive with respect to this parameter for either country.

8. One of the reasons that the bequest motive is more important in Japan is the popularity of the extended family relationship. If parents expect to live with (and/or to be taken care of by) children, they might leave bequests in return.

9. It is well known in Japan that the assessed value of real estate for inheritance is about one-half or one-third of the market value, while financial assets are assessed at the full market value. Therefore, a rational agent who plans to bequeath should do so in the form of real assets, ceteris paribus. This tax treatment works against dissaving of housing among the elderly in Japan.

10. However, Hayashi (1986) obtained an opposite result in a model where there is no liquidity or down-payment constraint. This is due to the fact that the steep labor income profile causes the very young to be borrowers.

11. Note that the model is not general equilibrium in nature, so that the interest rate is held constant when tax policy and the capital stock are changed. Introducing general equilibrium considerations would presumably dampen the predicted changes in the saving rate.

12. Remember that a liquidity constraint equivalent to a ban on borrowing in excess of housing capital is imposed in the model. Therefore, tax incentives for borrowing will not increase the demand for the composite consumption good during the first period, when the liquidity constraint is binding. If our focus is shifted from the down-payment constraint to

borrowing constraints for consumption, we would investigate the effect of eliminating the tax deductibility of interest payments on consumer loans. In this case elimination could raise the saving rate.

References

Bank of Japan (1986). "Annual Economic Statistics."

Bernheim, B. D., Shleifer, A., and Summers, L. (1985). The strategic bequest motive, *J. Polit. Econo.* 93, 1045–1076.

Federal Home Loan Bank Board (1982). "Savings and Home Finance Source Book."

Hayashi, F. (1986). Why is Japan's saving rate so apparently high? *in* "NBER Macroeconomic Annual, 1986," MIT Press, Cambridge, MA.

Office of Prime Minister (1982). "Family Saving Survey."

Ministry of Construction (various years). "Results of Survey on Financing Private Housing."

Slemrod, J. (1982). Down-payment constraints: Tax policy effects in a growing economy with rental and owner-occupied housing, *Public Finance Quart.* 10, 193–217.

U.S. Department of Commerce (1981). "Money Income of Households, Families, and Persons in the United States: 1980."

U.S. Department of Labor (1985). "Handbook of Labor Statistics."

U.S. Department of Housing and Urban Development (1979). "Statistical Yearbook."

Index